the **contexts** reader

american sociological association

the **contexts** reader

edited by JEFF GOODWIN, New York University

and JAMES M. JASPER

Graduate Center, City University of New York

 W. W. NORTON & COMPANY • NEW YORK LONDON

W. W. Norton & Company has been independent since its founding in 1923, when William Warder Norton and Mary D. Herter Norton first published lectures delivered at the People's Institute, the adult education division of New York City's Cooper Union. The Nortons soon expanded their program beyond the Institute, publishing books by celebrated academics from America and abroad. By mid-century, the two major pillars of Norton's publishing program—trade books and college texts—were firmly established. In the 1950s, the Norton family transferred control of the company to its employees, and today—with a staff of four hundred and a comparable number of trade, college, and professional titles published each year—W. W. Norton & Company stands as the largest and oldest publishing house owned wholly by its employees.

Every effort has been made to contact the copyright holders
of each of the selections. Rights holders of any selections not credited
should contact W. W. Norton & Company, Inc. for a correction
to be made in the next printing of our work.

The text of this book is composed in Sabon
with the display set in Futura.
Editor: Karl Bakeman
Production manager: Jane Searle
Project editor: Lory A. Frenkel
Editorial assistant: Rebecca Arata

Library of Congress Cataloging-in-Publication Data

The contexts reader / Jeff Goodwin and James M. Jasper, editors.—1st ed.
    p. cm.
  "Co-published with the American Sociological Association."
  Includes bibliographical references.
  ISBN 978-0-393-92989-8 (pbk.)
  1. Social problems. I. Goodwin, Jeff. II. Jasper, James M., 1957–
III. American Sociological Association.
  HN16.C674 2008
  361.10973—dc22
                                                    2007013478

W. W. Norton & Company, Inc., 500 Fifth Avenue,
New York, N.Y. 10110
www.wwnorton.com

W. W. Norton & Company Ltd., Castle House,
75/76 Wells Street, London W1T 3QT

1 2 3 4 5 6 7 8 9 0

contents

preface

The Contexts Reader brings together some of the best articles to appear in *Contexts* magazine during its first five years of publication (2002–2006). *Contexts* was established by the American Sociological Association to introduce sociological research and perspectives to non-specialists. Claude Fischer, of the University of California at Berkeley, made an abstract proposal into a reality, first creating and then editing the magazine for its first three years. We became the editors at the beginning of 2005. The articles that appear in *Contexts* are not technical; even when they summarize complex research they are written (we hope) in a clear and accessible style.

Contexts has proved popular for classroom use, as its articles are more lively and pointed than textbook summaries but more readable and less technical than scholarly journal articles. For this reason we have designed the *Reader* with undergraduate courses in mind. But we think the *Reader* will prove useful to anyone who wants to learn about a wide range of current sociological thinking. The *Reader* includes up-to-date articles on fourteen areas of sociology, including education, work, gender and sexuality, race and ethnicity, crime, politics, and sociological methods.

This *Reader* would not have been possible without the efforts of many people, not least the extraordinary authors whose work is included. We would also like to thank Claude Fischer, who set high standards for all of us. At the American Sociological Association, Sally Hillsman and Karen Edwards have energetically championed the magazine, as have successive ASA Councils and Publications Committees. The Journals Division of the University of California Press has provided enormous technical and marketing help. We also thank *Contexts'* first image editor, the indefatigable Jon Wagner, who is responsible for most of the photos in this volume. The magazine has flourished thanks to the hard work of its first three managing editors, Scott Savitt, David Linker, and Darren Ressler. Jonathan Wynn drafted the study and discussion questions for the *Reader*. We also appreciate the work of the *Contexts Reader* advisory panel, which provided us with invaluable ideas about what to include in, and how to organize, the *Reader*. The panel, ably chaired by Caroline Persell, also included Rebecca Adams, Tina Martinez, Jodi O'Brien, Richard Schaefer, and Patricia Warren. Finally, we thank Karl Bakeman of W. W. Norton, a *Contexts* fan himself, who encouraged and facilitated this project with exemplary energy and enthusiasm.

If you would like to learn more about *Contexts*, including how to subscribe, please visit our Web site at www.contextsmagazine.org.

Jeff Goodwin
James M. Jasper

the **contexts** reader

part 1

Self and Community

robert zussman

keyword: the self

spring 2005

For years I have asked the students in my large, introductory sociology classes to complete the sentence, "I can really be myself when . . ." Virtually none seem to have had any problem understanding the task. They all seem to have some idea of a "self" and even some idea of a "real self." Very occasionally, I am surprised by an answer, but of the roughly 2,000 students who have responded to my request, all but perhaps 20 have completed the sentence in either of two ways. Roughly one-third answer that they can be themselves when they are alone. Another two-thirds answer that they can be themselves in small circles of intimates ("with close friends," "with my family"). The answers suggest that what the students mean by the *self* differs from *personality*: Whereas *personality* refers to a repertoire of behaviors performed in public, *self* seems to refer to something more permanent, independent of behavior, apart from performance, and fundamentally private. The answers lack both a sense of the long, sometimes complex, history of the term and a feeling for the deeply moral meanings embedded in it.

As a reflexive pronoun (*myself, yourself,* and so on), *self* is virtually as old as the English language. But as a noun, it is of recent vintage. The *Oxford English Dictionary* helpfully defines the self, in this sense, as "that which in a person is really and intrinsically *he* (in contradistinction to what is adventitious); the ego (often identified with the soul or mind as opposed to the body); a permanent subject of successive and varying states of consciousness." The *OED* identifies one of the first uses of *self* in this sense by the British philosopher John Locke, in the following formulation in his 1690 *Essay Concerning Human Understanding*: "Self is that conscious thinking thing, whatever Substance, made up of Spiritual, or Material, Simple, or Compounded, it matters not, which is sensible, or conscious of Pleasure and Pain."

> The self is a language in which various parties articulate visions of what is good and right.

As implied in the *OED* definition, the self is deeply implicated in claims about morality. Although the idea of the self as that which is intrinsic or essential to the person is a scant three centuries old, the roots of the concept can be found in the older notion of the "soul." The self is a secularized version of an originally religious concept. The self, to be sure, is not identical to the soul. Unlike *soul, self* implies no particular relationship to God and no set of distinctively religious obligations. But in other respects the religious roots of the term are deeply revealing: Like *soul, self* is a term laden with ethical implications. By claiming to identify that which is intrinsic to the person—indeed by claiming that there is anything at all intrinsic to the person—*self* implies absolute standards. The *self* is a language in which various parties articulate visions of what is good and right. Because these visions are based on what is imagined to be some essential characteristic of personhood—rather than the merely "adventitious"—they appear to be prior to and independent of any particular social arrangements. As a result, these visions may be turned against society, made into critical tools to condemn a society for preventing self-realization. But they may also be turned against individuals, made into critical tools by which a person may be judged to have failed timeless standards of self-realization. Claims about the self are both tools of social criticism and tools of social control.

The meaning of the term *self* is neither fixed nor uncontested. In the three centuries since Locke's early formulation, the use of the term has evolved in a variety of directions. In contrast to Locke's seemingly cavalier formulation of what constitutes the self ("Spiritual or Material, Simple, or Compounded, it matters not"), various movements in both philosophy and popular usage have attempted to fill in what Locke left unspecified. In these we can read much of the history of moral life. From the long reach of Protestantism came a sanctification of everyday life. The self was not only to be found in higher activities. It could also, and especially, be found in work, in a "calling." It could be found in marriage and in the family, in a blending of love and responsibility. By the nineteenth century, the term was turning in a different direction. From the Romantic movements of that long century (in the writings of Rousseau, Whitman, and many others) came an exaltation of the self in relation to nature, an emphasis on emotions rather than reason, on an inner voice rather than social convention. These Romantic strands continued—and intensified—in the twentieth century, particularly in the rise of the psychoanalytic movement and the various movements that have splintered from it. The Protestant version of the self, even in its secularized forms, emphasized *character*, a term more in favor one hundred years ago than today, suggesting notions of rectitude and probity, innate but cultivated, exercised in self-discipline. In contrast, according to Freud and others, the self is something that must be discovered in hidden feelings; it is a set of impulses repressed but never lost. In the long march of modernity, the term has come, with increasing frequency and intensity, to refer to something deeply inward, which stands as an alternative to and in opposition to the social. Yet, the term has never entirely lost its moral meanings.

> . . . it is precisely the ambiguity of the term *self* that gives it vitality in the world beyond academic disciplines and even in some remote corners of sociology itself.

To many social critics, the inward turn of the self signals a danger, particularly as the ideas of theology, art, and the human sciences make their way into popular culture in what seems to them a debased form. To some, the inward turn in the language of selfhood seems to express *and* encourage solipsism, narcissism, self-indulgence, excessive individualism, and a host of other woes. What Robert Bellah has called "the nervous search for the true self"—a self detached from social and cultural contexts—he and others criticize as a turn away from the larger moral meanings that can be found only in participation in communities.

There is some truth to these charges, particularly as they point to the loss of community membership, which is a central dimension of our conception of the self. But it is also easy to exaggerate. Karen Cerulo, in her analysis of movies, television, popular music, and public opinion polls, has shown that the "cultural scripts" of *individualism*, a term fundamental to contemporary meanings of the self, are cyclical, reaching their peak in the "me generation" of the 1970s but declining since then.

The language of the self continues to essentialize and moralize, even in popular culture. As Donal Carbaugh has shown in his study of *Donahue*, conducted not long after the height of the "me generation," a strong moral sense remains deeply embedded in a "code of the self," even in the context of a popular television talk show that we might expect would be most given over to self-indulgence. Donahue, his guests, and his audience use *self* to express an independence from and even opposition to "traditional social roles." But they do not stop there. The self, according to those who appear on *Donahue*, requires awareness not only of one's own self but also of the selves of others. And to be fully realized, the self must also be worked out in constant relation to others. While the concept of the self may be used to criticize one set of moral standards ("traditional social roles"), it may simultaneously be used to express new moral commitments to one's self and to others. Similar uses of the term can be found in any number of unlikely places—in prisons as part of an effort to rehabilitate prisoners, in self-help groups like Codependents Anonymous, where participants use the language of the self to search for moral grounding in the wake of broken marriages and broken relations with children, among groups of preoperative transsexuals who use the language of the "true self" to justify their anticipated operations.

The most sustained attack on the notion of the self as an entity, as that which a person "really and intrinsically" is, has come not from popular culture or usage but from the human sciences. From the moment that Locke offered his formulation of the self as "a conscious thinking thing," others have stressed not the identity of the self but the multiplicity of selves—and, by implication, the *inessentiality* of any particular self. While traces of this idea appear throughout the eighteenth and nineteenth centuries (particularly in distinctions between better and worse selves or present and former selves), the sustained development of this alternative notion of selfhood appears fully only in the twentieth century in the works of the psychologist William James, the social psychologist George Herbert Mead, and, most familiarly, the sociologist Erving Goffman.

Goffman is explicit: "The self . . . as a performed character, is not an organic thing that has a specific location, whose fundamental fate is to be born, to mature, and to die; it is a dramatic effect arising diffusely from a scene that is presented. [The] self does not derive from its possessor . . . [but] is a *product* of a scene that comes off, and is not a *cause* of it." Here, there would seem to be no intrinsic self at all. But even Goffman cannot escape the self altogether. Even while denying an essential self, Goffman insistently calls on a strategic actor constantly maneuvering to make effective presentations. This shadow self is remarkably similar to Locke's "conscious thinking thing." And no less than in Locke, the shadow self in Goffman's account becomes a moralizing tool, a standard against which social arrangements are evaluated for their potential to honor or degrade, and individuals are evaluated for the authenticity of their performances.

Today, the term *self* enjoys, at best, an uncomfortable position within sociology, avoided for its ambiguities and imprecision, abandoned by many for terms like *identity* or even *self-concept*, which are presumed to be more precise because they make no pretense to speak beyond social and psychological processes to that which is real and intrinsic. Fair enough. But it is precisely the ambiguity of the term *self* that gives it vitality in the world beyond academic disciplines and even in some remote corners of sociology itself. It seems to me unlikely that we, as sociologists, can say whether there are human essences, let alone what those essences are. And it is probably dangerous even to try. Still, to ignore how the term is deployed in high culture, in popular culture, and in everyday speech is to miss centuries of efforts to think and talk about what is good and right. In *The Brothers Karamazov*, Dostoevsky's Grand inquisitor announces, "If there is no God, then everything is permitted." Today, we might say the same of the self.

RECOMMENDED RESOURCES

Robert Bellah, Richard Madsen, William Sullivan, Ann Swidler, and Steven Tipton. *Habits of the Heart* (University of California Press, 1985).

> Bellah and his colleagues argue that contemporary languages of the self are insufficient to express the depths of Americans' moral commitments.

Donal Carbaugh. *Talking American: Cultural Discourse on Donahue* (Ablex, 1988).

> One of the few empirical studies that looks specifically at how the term *self* is used, concentrating on its use on a once highly popular talk show.

Karen Cerulo. "Individualism . . . *Pro Tem*: Reconsidering U.S. Social Relations." In *Culture in Mind: Toward a Sociology of Culture and Cognition*, ed. Karen Cerulo (Routledge, 2002).

> Cerulo uses multiple measures drawn from public opinion polls, movies, television, and popular music to show cycles of emphasis on individualism in American cultural scripts.

Erving Goffman. *The Presentation of Self in Everyday Life* (Doubleday Anchor, 1959).

> This is the most influential discussion of a "dramaturgical" approach to the self.

REVIEW QUESTIONS

1. Before you read this essay, how might you have defined "the self"? How would you define it now?
2. Complete the sentence, "I am . . ." as many times as you can, up to twenty.
3. Zussman shows how the sociological definition of the "self" differs from the way we use it in everyday life. Goffman, for example, suggests that who we are depends on the situations (scenes) in which we participate. Think about two situations in which you act, feel, or think differently. Do the people in these settings have different ideas about who you are? If so, why? If not, why not?

jack barbalet

keyword: emotion

spring 2006

2

I magine a world without emotion, and you have a world devoid of human beings—and a good deal of animal life as well. Humans without emotions could not choose among alternatives, could not act because they would lack a sense of involvement, would be without commitment or conviction, without purpose or direction. All of these things require emotions. People without emotions, could they exist, would not simply be bored or depressed, for these conditions have significant emotional content. Indeed, people without emotions cannot exist. If someone suffers a neurological disease, for instance, that robs her of emotional faculties and capacities, she also loses the qualities normally associated with being a person.

Emotions are not optional extras. They are implicated in all human action, including thought. As the early twentieth-century philosopher and psychologist William James observed, emotions underwrite the values, interests, and meanings that make social life possible. Once we recognize this—and it is now supported by the most advanced psychological and neurological research—it follows that emotions underlie not only irrational action (such as gratuitous cruelty, self-destructive behavior, unnecessary inefficiency), and nonrational action (in pursuit of, say, aesthetic or erotic concerns), but also rational action (which uses means appropriate to the end, enhances our well-being, and broadens our understanding). This is a remarkable con-

clusion because it contravenes the notion, characteristic of Western thought for more than a thousand years, that emotions and rationality are necessarily opposed. In fact, the reverse is true: rational action requires the engagement of the appropriate emotions.

The most common understanding of emotion, and the oldest, emphasizes the bodily sensations and excited feelings that characterize our experience of emotions such as anger, fear, and love. By focusing on such emotions to form a conception of emotion in general, commentators support the view that emotions are involuntary, disordering processes that distract people from their proper concerns and activities. This view appears in ancient Greek philosophy, as when Plato, in his critique of dramatic poetry in *The Republic*, supposes that emotion is either pleasure or pain, dissociated from thought or knowledge. From this perspective, emotion belongs to the body and its sensations, as opposed to thought and mind (what today we call cognition).

A student of Plato's, Aristotle, took note of his teacher's account of emotion but developed an alternative to it. In his treatment of anger in *Rhetoric*, Aristotle agrees that emotion has a biological component, namely the physical sensation of pain. But he goes on to show that it also contains a complex cognitive element. In addition to bodily feelings, anger includes a perception of an undeserved slight and also an intention, namely, desire for revenge. Without these additional cognitive parts, according to Aristotle, there is no emotional experience of anger, only a physical sensation, which by itself is not sufficient for the emotion as such.

Since the time of the ancient Greeks we have enormously expanded our knowledge of the physical structures and processes underlying emotions, as well as of the cognitive and cultural aspects of emotions, yet we still use the different approaches to emotion articulated by Plato and Aristotle to summarize the alternative perspectives on emotion.

The advance of knowledge concerning emotion may even have increased the distance between these approaches and paradoxically generated commonly held misunderstandings about emotions. The application of laboratory techniques and experimentation to the study of emotions during the nineteenth and twentieth centuries profoundly affected every aspect of knowledge about emotions, especially in the fields of physiology and neurology. In the concept of the "cognitive appraisal process," for example, the type and intensity of an emotion depends on the subject's interpretation and evaluation of its circumstances. This is an extremely complex process requiring both a rapid and automatic response from the central nervous system as well as more controlled and conscious activities, sociologically described as the "interpretation and definition of the situation."

Unfortunately, the physiological and cultural aspects of the cognitive appraisal process have become disconnected in research and theory about emotions. The first gave rise to a neurological revolution in emotions research, reported, for example, in the work of Antonio Damasio (*Descarte's Error*, 1994) and Joseph LeDoux (*The Emotional Brain*, 1998). The second aspect of the cognitive appraisal process corresponds to what is known as the constructionist theory of emotions.

Many sociologists who have written on emotions over the last two decades hold that emotions are constructed by cultural factors. This position, called social or cultural constructionism, claims that emotional experiences depend on cultural cues and interpretations. It follows that values, norms, linguistic practices, belief patterns, and so on, form the basis of emotional experience. From this perspective, biological and even social structural factors are irrelevant to both the formation and understanding of emotions. One aspect of the constructionist approach is that emotions are more or less voluntarily managed in terms of the culturally defined requirements of a situation. We are sad at a funeral, for instance, because we cognitively understand the cultural organization of death and, by applying this knowledge, we align our emotions with our circumstances.

Emotions do attract cultural tags or names. They also become integrated into the broader conceptual repertoire of cultures, and the values and beliefs implicit in a prevailing culture become infused into the commonly understood meanings of those emotions. This is one reason that translating the words for some emotions from one language to another is often difficult. But there is a problem in this view: by treating emotions as strategic evaluations derived from local meaning systems, the constructionist approach reveals itself to be a captive of cultural preferences. Some emotions escape cultural tagging, but it does not follow that we do not experience such emotions or that they have no significance. Additionally, we frequently experience some socially important emotions unconsciously and therefore cannot account for them in strictly cultural terms, as Thomas Scheff has demonstrated for the emotion of shame.

Emotions are always physical, involving the hormonal, muscular, and neural systems, and they are always social-structural, resulting from being in a position of power over others, for instance, or subjected to the power of others. They are also always cultural: the objects of a person's emotions are necessarily determined by the values and expectations of the surrounding culture. Thus fear makes us sweat and feel weak in the knees and results from our powerlessness; and what we fear—be it traffic, communists, or terrorist outrage—comes from the culture in which we live. This broader approach to emotions has a place in the history of sociology predating the constructionist account.

Although the "sociology of emotions," as a focus of sociological research and identity, began in the 1980s, sociologists have been interested in emotions since the beginning of the discipline. The founder of modern economics, the eighteenth-century Scotsman Adam Smith, initiated cultural sociology as well, with his book *The Theory of Moral Sentiments* (1759), in which emotions play a key explanatory role. Less known but equally important as a pioneer sociologist, Smith's compatriot and contemporary, Adam Ferguson, also developed a theory of society that involved categories of emotions. Their general perspective, that emotions are the ultimate bases of social behavior and action, influenced the first generation of American and European sociologists.

Pioneer American sociologists, such as Lester F. Ward (1841–1913) and Edward A. Ross (1866–1951), for example, argued that the dynamic forces in society are desires and feelings, and that institutions result from sentiments or emotions. In Europe also, in the early decades of the twentieth century, social processes and institutions were treated in terms of emotions, as in the work of Vilfredo Pareto (1848–1923), Ferdinand Tönnies (1855–1936), Emile Durkheim (1858–1917), Georg Simmel (1858–1918), Edvard Westermarck (1862–1939), and Max Weber (1864–1920). Each of them saw emotion as an evolutionary basis for social relations and institutions. While they agreed that emotions provided

the historical foundation of social institutions, they disagreed about whether rational purpose displaced emotion as history developed.

Tension has existed in social thought since the nineteenth century concerning the question of human conduct. The usual position assumed that people normally act rationally, but acknowledged a potential decline to nonrational, even bestial behavior. This tension was institutionally resolved with the civic incorporation through enfranchisement of new segments of the adult population. Such developments did not reflect a theoretical solution to the tension between emotion and rationality, however. Nevertheless, after two world wars, political states regulated their economies and populations in ways that reinforced the constitutionalism and therefore the political rationalism that had been developing during the nineteenth century, and the industrial heartland could by this time be regarded as largely pacified. With the consolidation of the industrial order, the working classes were no longer seen as a threat to "civilization," and economic organizations had become sufficiently large and impersonal to be regarded, in that sense at least, as rational.

Out of these developments, a new model of social action arose in accordance with the new social and civic experience, and became prominent in sociological thinking. Beginning in the middle of the twentieth century, then, emotion disappears as an explanatory variable in sociology. Perhaps more than anyone else, Max Weber inspired this new turn in sociology.

Weber distinguishes four ideal types of social action, one of which is "affectual," or emotional, action. Such action is usually associated with his concept of charismatic leadership, although his treatment of the latter does not rely on a serious discussion of affective action. Weber's leading American interpreter, Talcott Parsons, complained that its definition is inadequate, and that affective action is only a "residual category" in Weber's work. Not only does Weber consign affective action to a marginal place in his sociology, he sees emotion as having a diminishing role in historical societies. In his discussion of bureaucracy, for example, Weber argues that a "peculiarity of modern culture" is the demand for calculability. It follows, he continues, that bureaucracy "succeeds in eliminating from official business love, hatred, and all purely personal, irrational, and emotional elements that defy calculation." For Weber, then, and many of his followers, emotion is not only irrational but also premodern.

And yet not all sociologists of the mid-twentieth century accepted the idea that emotions were irrelevant. In this context we usually hear about Erving Goffman and his study of social organization in terms of embarrassment, published in 1956, and C. Wright Mills' introductory comments in *White Collar* (1951), noting that when "white-collar people get jobs, they sell not only their time and energy but their personalities, . . . their smiles, and their kindly gestures, and they must practice the prompt repression of resentment and aggression." Alvin Gouldner is another author who, though seldom mentioned in this context, has a firm grasp on the continuing relevance of emotion in society and in sociology. In an early paper, "Metaphysical Pathos and the Theory of Bureaucracy" (1955), he argues that social theories "evoke through their associations and through a sort of empathy which they engender, a congenial mood or tone of feelings," which means that "[social] theory reinforces or induces in the adherent a subtle alteration in the structure of sentiments through which [the sociologist] views the world" and that "commitment to a theory may be made because the theory is congruent with the mood or deep-lying sentiments of its adherents, rather than merely because it has been cerebrally inspected and found valid."

Gouldner's commitment to the fundamental role of emotion in social thought and practice does not lead him to assume that antirational impulses are necessarily at work.

Gouldner expanded the idea that developments in or changes of a social theory must be explained in terms of emotion in a later book, *The Coming Crisis of Western Sociology* (1970), which explains the relation between emotion and rationality quite differently than does Weber. In particular Gouldner shows that "[w]hen . . . new sentiments begin to find or create their own appropriate language, the possibilities of larger solidarities and of rational public discussion are extended." Appropriate sentiments are the basis of rationality, not its obverse. This is an extremely important point.

Emotions are clearly not a new or even recent interest in sociology. From the beginning, sociologists regarded emotions not as private experiences outside of social processes but as integral to social action and social organization. Sociological theories about emotions are not unitary or singular, but represent several different perspectives. Finally, while we cannot assert that emotions are rational, we can no longer insist that emotion is necessarily opposed to rationality. Sociologists should keep this point in mind because it means that we can effectively understand the normal processes of social interaction and change in terms of the underlying emotions that are implicit in them. We should not use emotions only to make sense of social outbursts and other pathological episodes, but to understand all the routine and core elements of social life.

RECOMMENDED RESOURCES

Jack Barbalet. *Emotion, Social Theory, and Social Structure: A Macrosociological Approach* (Cambridge University Press, 2001).

A major statement of the sociological perspective on emotions that treats leading themes in the discipline in terms of emotions.

Jack Barbalet, ed. *Emotions and Sociology* (Blackwell, 2002).

An international collection in which authors discuss different subfields of sociology (political sociology, economic sociology, sociology of science, and so on) from the perspective of emotions.

Robert H. Frank. *Passions Within Reason: The Strategic Role of the Emotions* (W. W. Norton, 1988).

An important statement by an economics professor concerning the emotional basis not only of ethical and social behavior but also of market behavior.

Jeff Goodwin, James M. Jasper, and Francesca Polletta, eds. *Passionate Politics: Emotions and Social Movements* (University of Chicago Press, 2001).

A leading analysis of social movements and politics that explores the dynamics of interaction and conflict through attention to the emotions involved.

REVIEW QUESTIONS

1. Before reading this essay, how might you have defined *emotion*? How would you define *anger*, *fear*, or *love*?
2. Explain the apparent tension between rational action and emotion. How does sociology offer another way to understand the relation between the two?
3. How have social and cultural "constructivists" rendered "biological and even social structural factors . . . irrelevant to both the formation and understanding of emotions"?
4. Write a long paragraph summarizing the formations of emotions presented in this reading. What are the differences between Weber's and Parsons' explanation of the term emotion and that of Mills and Gouldner? Take a concrete example of an emotion, and relate it to one of these explanations. What does this perspective illuminate? How does it change your everyday understanding of emotions?

bonnie erickson

social networks: the value of variety

3

winter 2003

people are healthier and happier when they have intimates who care about and for them. but they also do better when they know many different people casually.

Having close kin and intimate friends helps with many things, from coping with every-day problems to living longer. But what about the hundreds of more casual connections individuals have? What of acquaintances, work-mates, and neighbors? We tend to make such fast friends easily and lose them without notic-ing. Nonetheless, these seemingly thin social bonds are quite valuable when they are diverse.

Variety is the key. Knowing many kinds of people in many social contexts improves one's chances of getting a good job, developing a range of cultural interests, feeling in control of one's life, and being healthy. Some-times knowing many kinds of people is helpful because it improves the chances of having the right contact for some purpose: hear-ing of an attractive job opening, borrowing a lawnmower, getting the home cleaned.

Network variety can also be useful in itself, for example in jobs that call for diverse con-tacts. Either way, the critical matter is the vari-ety of acquaintances and not the mere number.

understanding acquaintanceship

Sociologists have measured acquaintance net-works by focusing on occupations. People in dif-ferent occupations differ from each other in many important ways. The work we do re-flects much of our pasts, such as schooling and family background, and shapes the ways we live, such as tastes and lifestyles. Generally, someone who knows people in diverse kinds of jobs will thereby know people who are diverse in many respects. The standard strategy is to present a respondent with a list of occupations that range from very high to very low in pres-tige, and ask whether the respondent knows anyone in each. The greater the number of oc-cupations within which a respondent has a con-tact, the more the vari-ety in the respondent's social network.

Researchers using this measure have found interesting dif-ferences between respondents in different na-tions. For example, a study in Albany, New York, and a study in East Germany before the fall of the Communist regime each asked re-spondents about the same 10 occupations: Did they know anyone who was a lawyer, small busi-ness owner, teacher, engineer, motor mechanic, secretary, bookkeeper/office clerk, salesperson, porter/janitor, or waiter?

The average respondent in Albany knew some-one in 4.5 of these occupations, compared to an average of 3.8 for East Germans, so the American networks were about 20 percent more diverse.

> Knowing many kinds of people in many social contexts improves one's chances of getting a good job, developing a range of cultural interests, feeling in control of one's life, and being healthy.

One resource for keeping track of diverse acquaintances. (Photo by Jon Wagner)

This is not surprising given that East Germans were wary of strangers in a totalitarian society in which about one in ten people in every work group was an informant for the secret police.

Such acquaintances are a more diverse set than are the few people to whom we feel really close—both because weak ties greatly outnumber strong ones, and because our close ties are usually limited to people very much like ourselves. For example, when I studied the private security industry in Toronto I asked whether people knew close friends, relatives, or anyone at all in each of 19 occupations. My respondents knew relatives, on average, in about two of these occupations, close friends in about half a dozen and anyone at all in about a dozen.

In every country that has been studied in this way, being of higher status goes with having a wider variety of acquaintances. In the Toronto

security industry, business owners had contacts in 15 occupations, managers in 13, supervisors 10, and mere employees 9. In Hungary, before and even more so after the end of Communism, wealthier people had more diverse networks than the less wealthy. In Taiwan, more highly educated people have more diverse acquaintances than the less educated, and men have more diverse acquaintances than women do. In general, every kind of social advantage tends to generate a network advantage, which in turn helps the socially advantaged to stay ahead.

networks and jobs

Diverse networks can help people to get good jobs. Having a variety of acquaintances improves a jobseeker's chances of having one really useful contact, and variety itself is a qualification for some upper-end jobs.

People in North America find their jobs with the help of a contact roughly half the time. We might assume that such helpers must be close friends and relatives willing to work hard for the job hunter. But this is not the usual story in Western nations. Close friends and kin want to help, but often cannot do very much because they are too much alike: they move in the same social circles and share information and influence, so they can do little for the candidate beyond what he or she can do alone. But acquaintances are more varied, less like each other, more likely to have new information and more likely to include people highly placed enough to influence hiring. Thus family and close friends provide fewer jobs (and often worse jobs) than do people outside the intimate circle. This is the surprising finding that Mark Granovetter called "the strength of weak ties" (the title of one of the most frequently cited articles in social science).

The strength of strong ties applies best to the few people at the top, because they have highly placed kin and friends who collect a lot of information and can exert a lot of influence. In general, more highly placed people can connect a jobseeker to more highly placed jobs, and one big advantage of having a diverse network is the improved chance of knowing such a useful contact. The Albany study found that people with more diversified acquaintances were more likely to get help from contacts holding more prestigious jobs, which led in turn to getting a job with higher prestige. On the other hand, for most people, using a friend or relative as a contact meant using someone with a lower-ranking job, and hence getting a worse job. For the few who came from privileged backgrounds, all kinds of helpers—friends, relatives, or acquaintances—were in high-status positions on average, and all those kinds of contacts helped them get good jobs.

Having a diverse set of acquaintances matters where there is a fairly free market in jobs and a fairly rich supply of jobs. If jobs are scarce, those in the know will hoard access to good ones for people they care about the most, so strong ties are more valuable in these circumstances. In non-market systems run by the state, the private use of personal contacts to get jobs may be risky: networking subverts state power and policy, and influential people may not want to be responsible for the occupational or political errors of acquaintances whom they help. Well-placed people still provide personal help, but mainly to jobseekers or intermediaries whom they know well and can trust. Thus studies show that both the Chinese and the East Germans (before the change of regime) used strong ties the most, far more often than in the West.

Diversified acquaintances are valuable as an ensemble when employers want to recruit both a person and the person's contacts, to make his or her network work for the organization. This is especially true for higher-level jobs because it is only higher-level jobs that include consequen-

Diverse acquaintance networks help individuals locate health services and assistance. (Photo by Jon Wagner)

tial responsibility for the "foreign affairs" of the organization. For example, in my study of the private security industry in Toronto, I asked employers how they hired for jobs from security guard up to manager and asked whether the employer required "good contacts" for these positions. For lower-level jobs, they did not. But for upper-level jobs, employers often did want people with contacts they could use to monitor the industry and its environment, to get information, to recruit new customers, and to maintain good relationships with powerful outsiders such as the police.

When employers think of good contacts, what do they mean? In a word, variety. Employers named desirable contacts of many kinds (in their own industry, government, the police, senior management, etc.) and sometimes explicitly wanted variety as such ("all available"). The more varied a person's network, the more that network can do for the organization.

Employees with more network variety got jobs with higher rank and higher income. This was true whether or not people got those jobs through someone they knew. Again, a network of acquaintances is more useful than one of intimates, because acquaintances have the diversity employers seek.

Does all this add up to "it's not what you know, but who you know?" Not really. Sometimes what you know is critical. Even in the security industry, which has no formal certifications, employers often want to hire people with contacts and skills, not contacts instead of skills. Because employers look for both, using personal connections helps most to get a job at the top or bottom of the ladder, not in the middle. At the bottom, skill requirements are modest. Employers just want a reliable employee and jobseekers just want an adequate job. Using contacts is one cheap way to make this match.

> People with wider networks are better informed about most things, but they may not realize how many of their good health practices go back to a thousand tiny nudges from casual conversations.

At the top, skill requirements are important but also hard to measure (how do you know whether someone will be a dynamic manager with current knowledge of the market, for example?) so employers look for prospects they know or candidates recommended by people they trust. In the middle, skill requirements are serious and fairly easy to measure through credentials (like a recent computer programming degree from a good school) or experience (like a strong track record in sales), so who the candidate knows matters less.

networks and health

Knowing people is important in getting a job, but it also matters for other areas of our lives that are less obvious, such as good health. Research has long shown that having close friends and family is good for a person's health. People who say they have someone they can count on feel less depressed, get less physically ill and live longer than those who do not. The newer news is that having a variety of acquain-tances also improves health. In a study of a Toronto social movement, I asked people about both the diversity of their contacts outside the group and the diversity of their contacts within the group. I found that people with more diversified general networks were less depressed, and people with more diverse contacts in the group more often felt that participation had improved their health. Such findings may seem odd, because our intimates play a more obvious role in our health. We discuss our health concerns with those we trust and get care from those who care about us.

Acquaintances make more subtle contributions in small, invisible increments over the long run. One such contribution is a sense of control over one's life, a well-documented source of good health. People who feel more in control are less depressed just because of that, since feeling pushed around is a miserable and unwelcome experience. Moreover, having a sense of control encourages people to tackle problems they encounter, so they cope better with stress. This valuable sense of control grows with the diversity of acquaintances.

People with diverse contacts consciously adapt to different situations and manage conflicting obligations. They have to decide whom to see, how to act appropriately with others differing in their expectations, how to balance sometimes conflicting demands. As they navigate their intricate options, they develop a well-grounded sense of control over their lives. Thus I found that members with more diversified acquaintances outside the Toronto movement felt more in control of their lives overall, and members with more diversified acquaintances within the group more often felt that participation had empowered them.

Acquaintance diversity also contributes to being better informed about health. People with wider networks are better informed about most things, but they may not realize how many of their good health practices go back to a thousand tiny nudges from casual conversations. They may know that they are committed to pushing down the broccoli and getting some exercise, while forgetting how many acquaintances mentioned the importance of such healthy habits. My study of the security industry shows a clear link between diversity and information flow, not only about health, but on a variety of topics. People with more varied connections knew more about each of several different kinds of things: the arts (books and artists), popular culture (sports stars), and business culture (business magazines and restaurants suited to power dining).

Feeling in control and being well-informed both flow from the diversity of the whole ensemble of acquaintances. But health, like work, sometimes benefits from a varied network because varied connections are more likely to include particular useful ones. For example, people who knew many kinds of people in the social movement group were much more likely to get some help with health (from organic vegetables to massage) from associates in the group. They knew what to look for and whom to trust to provide it.

Diverse networks also improve people's health indirectly, by helping them get ahead economically, and wealthier people tend to be healthier people. But the connection between wealth and health might suggest that all these benefits of having a variety of acquaintances might really just reflect the advantages of high social position. People with more network variety, better jobs, more feelings of control and better health may be that way because they come from more privileged circumstances. It is important to note, therefore, that all the studies that I have described have taken into account other characteristics of individuals, such as educational attainment and gender. Nonetheless, the diversity of acquaintanceship itself improves health and happiness.

what next?

Other possible benefits of network variety are yet to be studied. Students of politics have speculated that interacting with a range of people expands one's sources of political information and activity, and increases tolerance for others different from oneself—but this is only speculation at present because political research has focused exclusively on close relationships such as the handful of people with whom a person discusses important matters.

Another critical avenue for future work is the way in which we think about and measure network diversity. At present, almost all studies focus on the variety of occupations within which a respondent knows someone. This works very well, because occupation goes with so many important differences of resources, views, lifestyles and so on. But occupation is not the only way in which the social world is carved up into different kinds of people—gender and ethnicity also shape networks.

For instance, men occupy more powerful positions in organizations, so knowing a variety of men may help one's job search more than knowing a wide variety of women. But women take more responsibility for health, including the health of others, so knowing a good range of women may be better for one's health than knowing many kinds of men. In countries like the United States or Canada, ethnic groups have distinctive cultures and, sometimes, even labor markets. Knowing a variety of people in an ethnic group may lead to better jobs within the ethnic economy, to richer knowledge of the ethnic culture, to better access to alternative medicines, and to feeling better about the group. At the same time, having acquaintances exclusively in an ethnic group may cut one off from broader social benefits.

Indeed, there are many kinds of network variety: variety of occupation, gender, ethnicity, and much more. Each probably goes with a somewhat different menu of benefits. Future research should elaborate on the finding that, not only is knowing people good for you, but knowing many different kinds of people is especially good for you.

RECOMMENDED RESOURCES

Rose Laub Coser. "The Complexity of Roles as a Seedbed of Individual Autonomy." In Louis A. Coser (ed.), *The Idea of Social Structure: Papers in Honor of Robert K. Merton* (Harcourt Brace Jovanovich, 1975).

> Explains why acquaintance variety should lead to a greater sense of control over one's life and to more sophisticated language and more abstract thinking as well.

Bonnie H. Erickson. "Culture, Class, and Connections." *American Journal of Sociology* 102 (1996): 217–51.

> Shows that knowing many kinds of people goes with knowing a lot about many kinds of culture—and how knowing about culture matters at work.

Claude S. Fischer. *To Dwell Among Friends* (University of California Press, 1982).

> Strong ties matter too. This book describes their benefits and the kinds of people who benefit more or less.

Mark Granovetter. "The Strength of Weak Ties." *American Journal of Sociology* 78 (1973): 1360–80.

> Enormously influential, this essay concerns the advantages of acquaintances both for individuals and for communities.

Nan Lin. "Social Networks and Status Attainment." *Annual Review of Sociology* 25 (1999): 467–87.

> Authoritative review of research on networks and getting a job. It includes references to the Albany, East Germany, and China studies discussed in this article.

Nan Lin, Karen Cook, and Ronald S. Burt (eds.). *Social Capital: Theory and Research* (Aldine de Gruyter, 2001).

> Includes a number of recent, high quality theoretical discussions and research reports concerning the benefits of social networks, including a chapter on the Toronto security industry study.

Barry Wellman (ed.). *Networks in the Global Village* (Westview, 1999).

> A wide-ranging collection of studies on strong ties and weak ties, around the world and on the Internet.

REVIEW QUESTIONS

1. Sociologists have found that having diverse social connections is important for finding out about job opportunities. Once someone applies for a job, however, do you think knowing someone influential is enough to get the person hired? Why or why not? What other factors might be involved?
2. Erickson adds interesting elements to the discussion of mental health. What two things does she think healthy people develop in order to have a varied network?
3. Besides occupational diversity, what other forms of diversity exist in your own social networks? Do you think other forms of diversity might have effects similar to occupational diversity? Why or why not?
4. Activity: Use your cell phone or address book as the basis for a chart of your own social network. What are the broad categories that define your interactions with them? What are the overlapping social spheres? How are your acquaintances connected to each other?

barry wellman

connecting communities: on and offline   **4**
fall 2004

the internet is no longer a separate world for the techno-savvy. tens of millions of people around the world now go online daily. rather than isolating users in a virtual world, the internet extends communities in the real world. people use it to connect in individualized and flexible social networks rather than in fixed and grounded groups.

The 2004 documentary film *Almost Real* tells true-life Internet stories. For some characters, the Internet provides an escape from human interaction. A recluse living alone on an abandoned North Sea oil rig runs a data storage haven supposedly free of government interference. An antisocial eight-year-old boy hides from his schoolmates through home schooling and the Web. Meanwhile, the Internet brings other people together. A man and woman in a bondage and domination relationship communicate daily over Webcams thousands of miles apart. And teenagers socialize by incessantly playing a cooperative online game.

These stories are fascinating but misleading because they describe people whose social lives are wholly online. Few people dedicate most of their waking lives to the Internet. The Internet usually supplants solitary activities, like watching television, rather than other forms of social life. Most uses of the Internet are not "almost real," but are actual, quite normal interactions. The Internet has become an ordinary part of life.

Consider my own use. I have received several e-mail messages in the past hour. Friends confirm dinner for tonight. Even though it is the weekend, a student sends a question and expects a quick answer. So does a graduate student from Europe, with an urgent request for a letter of recommendation. Cousin Larry shares some political thoughts from Los Angeles.

I arrange to meet friends at a local pub later in the week. My teenage niece avoids e-mail as "for adults," so I send her an instant message. And one of my most frequent correspondents writes twice: Ms. Miriam Abacha from Nigeria, wanting yet again to share her millions with me.

In addition to communication, the Internet has become an important source of information. To check facts for this article, I use Google to search the Web. It is too rainy to go out and buy a newspaper, so I skim my personalized Yahoo! News instead. My friend Joe is driving to my house for the first time and gets his directions online from MapQuest.

The Internet has burrowed into my life, but is not separate from the rest of it. I integrate offline and online activities. I e-mail, chat, Web search, and instant message—but I also walk, drive, bike, bus, fly, phone, and send an occasional greeting card. I am not unique. Both the exotic aura of the Internet in the 1990s and the fear that it would undermine "community" have faded. The reality is that using the Internet both expands community and changes it in subtle ways.

digital divides

Between 1997 and 2001, the number of Americans using computers increased by 27 percent—from 137 million to 174 million—

An 18-year-old girl uses her laptop and an Internet connection to create a personalized music CD for a close friend. She and her acquaintances tie their Internet shopping and browsing to local friendships through online messaging, phone calls, and meeting in person. (Photo by Jon Wagner)

while the online population rose by 152 percent. Nielsen NetRatings reported in March 2004 that three-quarters of Americans over the age of two had accessed the Internet. Many used the Internet both at home and at work, and about half went online daily. Instant messaging (IM) has spread from teenagers to adults in growing popularity, with more than one-third of all American adults now IM-ing.

A decade ago, the Internet was mainly North American, and largely the domain of young, educated, urban, white men. It has since become widely used. About one-third of users live in North America, one-third in Europe and Japan, and one-third elsewhere. India and China host many users, although the percentages of their population who are online remain small. China now has the second largest number of Internet users, growing from half a million in 1997 to 80 million in January 2004. Although the proliferation of computers is no longer headline news, 41 million PCs were shipped to retailers

and customers worldwide in the first quarter of 2004.

As more people go online, the digital divide recedes. Yet even as the overall percentage of people online rises, differences in usage rates persist: between affluent and poor, young and old, men and women, more and less educated, urban and rural, and English and non-English readers. Moreover, there are substantial international differences, even among developed countries. For instance, the digital divide between high-income households and low-income households ranges from a gap of more than 60 percentage points in the United Kingdom to less than 20 percentage points in Denmark. In the United States, 79 percent of relatively affluent people (family income of $75,000 or more) were Internet users in September 2001, when just 25 percent of poor people (family income of less than $15,000) were online. And while the gender gap is shrinking in many developed countries, it is increasing in Italy and Germany as men get connected at a higher rate than women. Moreover, the digital divide cuts several ways. For instance, even among affluent Americans, there was a 31 percentage point gap in Internet access between those with a university education (82 percent) and those with less than a high school education (51 percent).

Digital divides are particularly wide in developing countries, where users tend to be wealthy, students, employees of large corporations, or people with easy access to cybercafes. The risk of a "digital penalty" grows as Internet use among organizations and individuals becomes routine. Those without access to the Internet will increasingly miss out on information and communication about jobs, social and political news, and community events.

The many who are using the Internet and the many more who will eventually use it face the question of how the experience might affect their lives. Fast messages, quick shopping, and instant reference works aside, widespread concerns focus on the deeper social and psychological implications of a brave new computer-mediated world.

hopes, fears, and possibilities

Just a few years ago, hope for the Internet was utopian. Entrepreneurs saw it as a way to get rich, policy makers thought it could remake society, and business people hoped that online sales would make stock prices soar. Pundits preached the gospel of the new Internet millennium. For example, in 1995, John Perry Barlow, co-leader of the Electronic Frontier Foundation, said, "We are in the midst of the most transforming technological event since the capture of fire. I used to think that it was just the biggest thing since Gutenberg, but now I think you have to go back farther."

The media generally saw the Internet as a weird, wonderful, and sometimes scary thing. The cover of the December 1999 issue of *Wired* depicted a lithesome cyber-angel leaping off a cliff into the glorious unknown. Major newspapers unveiled special Internet sections, and new computer magazines became fat with ads, advice, and influence. The meltdown of the dot-com boom in March 2000 snuffed out many dreams of a radiant Internet future. The pages of *Wired* magazine shrank by 25 percent from September 1996 to September 2001 and another 22 percent by September 2003. Revenue and subscription rates also plummeted. The editors ruefully noted in February 2004 that their magazine "used to be as thick as a phone book."

The advent of the Internet also provoked fears of personal danger and the loss of community. News media warned of men posing as women online, cyber-stalking, identity theft, and dangerous cyber-addiction. As recently as March 2004, computer scientist John Messerly warned that "computer and video games . . . ruin the social and scholastic lives of many students."

Much of the hype and fear about the Internet has been both *presentist*—thinking that the world started anew with its advent—and *parochial*—thinking that only things that happened on the Internet were relevant to understanding it. Yet, sociologists have long known that technology by itself does not determine anything. Rather, people take technology and use it (or discard it) in ways its developers never dreamed. For example, the early telephone industry marketed its technology simply as a tool for practical business and spurned the notion that it could be a device for sociability. Indeed, telephones, airplanes, and automobiles enabled far-flung communities to flourish well before the coming of the Internet.

Technologies themselves neither make nor break communities. Rather, they create possibilities, opportunities, challenges, and constraints for what people and organizations can do. For example, automobiles and expressways make it possible for people to live in sprawling suburbs, but they do not determine that people will do so. Compare the sprawl of American cities with the more compact suburbs of neighboring Canada. The Internet's low cost, widespread use, asynchronicity (people do not have to be connected simultaneously), global connectivity, and attachments (pictures, music, text) make it possible to communicate quickly and cheaply across continents and oceans. For example, emigrants use e-mail to chat with family and friends back home and visit Web sites to learn home news. *Yahoo! India Matrimonial* links brides and grooms in India, Europe, and North America. In countries with official censorship, emigrants use e-mail to gather news from back home and post it on Web sites for information hungry readers. Thus, the Internet allows mobile people to maintain community ties to distant places and also supports face-to-face ties closer to home.

community online and offline

Online communication—e-mail, instant messaging, and chat rooms—does not replace more traditional offline forms of contact—face-to-face and telephone. Instead, it complements them, increasing the overall volume of contact. Where some had feared that involvement in the Internet would detract from "real life" ties with friends and relatives, intensive users of e-mail contact others in person or by phone at least as frequently as those who rarely or never use the Internet. People who frequently use the Internet to contact others also tend to be in frequent contact with people in other ways (even after taking into account differences of age, gender, and education). Extroverts especially benefit from its use, simply adding another means of communication to their contact repertoire. For example, a 2001 National Geographic survey reports that North Americans who use e-mail to discuss important matters do so an average of 41 times per month, in addition to having an average of 84 face-to-face discussions and 58 phone discussions. Those who do not use e-mail to discuss important matters have about the same number of monthly face-to-face discussions, 83, but only 36 phone discussions. Thus, those who use e-mail report 183 significant discussions per month, 54 percent more than for those who do not use e-mail. The result: the more e-mail, the more overall communication.

This is not surprising, because the Internet is not a separate world. When we talk to people about what they do on the Internet, we find out that the great majority of the people they e-mail are people they know already. They are keeping in touch between visits, often by exchanging jokes, sharing gossip, or arranging to get together. If they e-mail someone they have not already met in person, they are frequently arranging a face-to-face meeting. Telephone calls also get intermixed with e-mails, because phone chats

better convey nuances, provide more intrinsic enjoyment, and better accommodate complex discussions. Andrea Baker's book *Double-Click* reports that few cyber-dates stay online; they either proceed to in-person meetings or fade away. People also bring to their online interactions such offline baggage as their gender, age, family situation, lifestyle, ethnicity, jobs, wealth, and education.

E-mail is not inherently better or worse than other modes of communication. It is just different. E-mails are less intrusive than visits or phone calls and often come with useful attachments, be they baby pictures or maps to someone's home. The spread of high-speed ("broadband") Internet access makes it easier for people to integrate the Internet into the rest of their lives without long waits. By April 2004, 39 percent of U.S. Internet users had broadband at home and 55 percent either at work or home. Broadband means that people can always leave their Internet connection on so that they can spontaneously send e-mails and search Web sites. Broadband connections also make it easier to surf the Web and download large image, music, and video files.

This neighborhood protest against the United States' military campaign in Iraq was one of many organized by both word-of-mouth and Internet communication. (Photo by Jon Wagner)

The longer people have been on the Internet, the more they use it. Most Americans—and many in the developed world—have online experience. According to the Pew Internet and American Life study, by February 2004 the average American had been using the Internet for six years. Internet use is becoming even more widespread as home users get access to broadband networks and as access proliferates from desk-bound computers to small portable devices such as "third-generation" mobile phones and personal digital assistants (Palm, Pocket PC). Yet, these small-screen, small-keyboard, lower-speed instruments are used differently than computers: to contact a small number of close friends or relatives or to coordinate in-person meetings. Far from homogenizing people's communications, Internet technology is used in different ways by different people.

the internet globally and locally

A decade ago analysts believed that as the rest of the world caught up to the United States in Internet use, they would use it in similar ways. Experience shows that this is not always so. For example, in Scandinavia and Japan, people frequently use advanced mobile phones to exchange e-mail and short text messages. Their Internet use is much less desktop-bound than that of Americans. Teens and young adults are especially heavy users of e-mail on their Internet-connected mobile telephones. Time will tell whether young people continue their heavy mobile use as they get older. Manuel Castells and his associates have shown that people in Catalonia, Spain, use the Internet more for information and services than for communication. They extensively search the Web to answer questions and book tickets, but they are much less likely to exchange e-mails. This may be because many Catalans live near each other and prefer to meet in cafés at night. Mobile phones sit beside them,

ready to incorporate other close friends and relatives into conversations via short text messages. Many developing countries exhibit a different mode of use. Even if people can afford to connect to the Internet from their homes, they often do not have reliable electrical, telephone, or broadband service. In such situations, they often use public access points such as Internet cafés or schools. They are connecting to the Internet while their neighbors sit next to them in person.

Such complexities illuminate the role the Internet can play in specifically local communities. The issue is whether the Internet has fostered a "global village," to use Marshall McLuhan's phrase, and thereby weakened local community. Some intensive and engrossing online communities do exist, such as the "BlueSky" group of young male friends who appear to live online, as described by Lori Kendall in her book *Hanging Out in the Virtual Pub*. Yet, they are a small minority. Despite the Internet's ability to connect continents at a single bound, it does not appear to be destroying local community.

For example, in the late 1990s Keith Hampton and I studied "Netville" near Toronto, a suburban housing tract of middle-priced single-family homes. The teachers, social workers, police officers, and technicians who lived there were typical people buying homes to raise young families. The community was exceptional in one important way: As part of an experiment by the telephone company, many residents were given free, high-speed Internet access and became members of a neighborhood e-mail discussion group.

When we compared those who were given this Internet access with those who did not receive it, we found that those on the Internet knew the names of three times as many neighbors as those without Internet access. The "wired" residents had been invited into the homes of an average of 4 neighbors, compared to 2.5 for the unwired, and they regularly talked with twice as many neighbors. The Internet gave wired residents opportunities to identify others in the neighborhood whom they might want to know better. E-mail and the discussion group made it easier for them to meet fellow residents who were not their immediate neighbors: the wired residents' local friends were more widely dispersed throughout Netville than those of the unwired. The e-mail discussion group was frequently used to discuss common concerns. These included household matters such as plumbing and yardwork, advice on setting up home computer networks, finding a local doctor, and skills for hire such as those of a tax accountant or carpenter. As one resident commented on the discussion group: "I have walked around the neighborhood a lot lately and I have noticed a few things. I have noticed neighbors talking to each other like they have been friends for a long time. I have noticed a closeness that you don't see in many communities."

Not only did these wired residents talk to and meet one another more, they did most of Netville's civic organizing online, for example, by warning neighbors about suspicious cars in the development and inviting neighbors to social events such as barbeques and block parties. One typical message read: "For anybody interested there is a Sunday night bowling league looking for new people to join. It's lots of fun with prizes, playoffs, and more. For both ladies and gents. If interested e-mail me back or give me a call."

These community activities built bonds for political action. When irate Netville residents protested at City Hall against the developer's plans to build more houses, it was the wired Internet members who organized the protest and showed up to make their voices heard. Others grumbled, just like new residents of housing developments have often grumbled, but the Internet supplied the social bonds and tools for organiz-

ing, for telling residents what the issues were, who the key players were, and when the protest would be.

The Netville experience suggests that when people are offered an easier way of networking with the Internet, the scope and amount of neighborly contact can increase. Evidence from other studies also shows that the Internet supports nearby relationships. For example, the National Geographic Society asked visitors to its Web site about their communication with friends and relatives living within a distance of 30 miles. Daily Internet users contacted nearby friends and relatives 73 percent more often per year than they contacted those living further away.

At the same time, the Internet helped Netville's wired residents to maintain good ties with, and get help from, friends and relatives who lived in their former neighborhoods. The evidence shows that Internet users are becoming "glocalized," heavily involved in both local and long-distance relationships. They make neighborly contacts—on- and offline—and they connect with far-flung friends and relatives—mostly online.

"networked individualism"

As the Internet has been incorporated into everyday life, it has fostered subtle changes in community. In the old days, before the 1990s, places were largely connected—by telephone, cars, planes, and railroads. Now with the Internet (and mobile phones), people are connected. Where before each household had a telephone number, now each person has a unique e-mail address. Many have several, in order to keep different parts of their lives separate online. This change from place-based community to person-based community had started before the Internet, but the developing personalization, portability and ubiquitous connectivity of the Internet are facilitating the change. By April 2004, 17 percent of American users could access the Internet wirelessly from their laptop computers and the percentage is growing rapidly. As wireless portability develops from desktops to laptops and handheld devices, an individual's whereabouts become less important for contact with friends and relatives.

The Internet and other new communication technologies are facilitating a basic change in the nature of community—from physically fixed and bounded groups to social networks, which I call "networked individualism." These technologies are helping people to personalize their own communities. Instead of being rooted in homes, cafés, and workplaces, people are becoming connected as individuals, available for contact anywhere and at any time. Instead of being bound up in a neighborhood community where all know all, each person is becoming an individualized switchboard, linking a unique set of ties and networks. In a society where people rarely know friends of friends, there is more uncertainty about who will be supportive under what circumstances, more need to navigate among partial social networks, and more opportunity to access a variety of resources. The Internet provides communication and information resources to keep in closer touch with loved ones—from new friends to family members left behind in international migrations.

RECOMMENDED RESOURCES

Manuel Castells. *The Rise of the Network Society* (Blackwell, 2000).

An insightful account of the transformation of societies into social networks.

Steve Jones and Philip Howard, eds. *Society Online: The Internet in Context* (Sage Publications, 2003).

An important compendium of research, with much representation from the authoritative Pew Internet in American Life studies.

Howard Rheingold. *The Virtual Community: Homesteading on the Electronic Frontier* (MIT Press, 2000).

A popular and sound account of life online.

Barry Wellman and Caroline Haythornthwaite, eds. *The Internet in Everyday Life* (Blackwell, 2000).

A score of original research articles documenting many of the ideas presented in this article.

http://www.pewinternet.org.

The Pew Internet in American Life studies have carried out a large number of surveys on Internet use in American life.

http://virtualsociety.sbs.ox.ac.uk.

A British scholarly network doing a variety of mostly qualitative analyses of Internet and society.

http://www.webuse.umd.edu.

An interactive statistical database that makes it relatively easy to analyze a variety of surveys about the Internet and American life.

http://www.worldinternetproject.net.

Contains the reports of survey researchers in many nations on the nature of the Internet and society.

REVIEW QUESTIONS

1. Explain the "digital divide." What are three of the factors Wellman uses to describe it? Who is on either side of it?
2. Debate the "presentist" and "parochial" ways of thinking about the Internet. How does sociological thinking differ from those beliefs?
3. Using the example of Netville, wherein technology and geographic proximity combined to develop stronger ties between neighbors as compared to those who did not have Internet access, what do you hypothesize are the unseen consequences of these linkages? Can you think of any negative effects?

4. Activity: Keep an Internet journal for three days, recording how long you were online, what Web sites you visited (you can use the history function to make it easier), and what sorts of interactions you had with others online (how many times you instant messaged, how many e-mails you sent, how many e-mails you received, what you purchased online, etc.). Then estimate the time you spent face-to-face with people in those three days. Are there any friends you interact with solely on the Internet? If so, how do your Internet-only relationships differ from those that involve face-to-face contact? Prepare a synopsis of your activities to discuss in class.

mitch berbrier

why are there so many "minorities"?   **5**

winter 2004

lesbians and gays, appalachians, women, the disabled, fat people, even white supremacists are claiming to be "minorities," and demanding to be treated just like other minorities, especially african americans. these struggles for the right to be a minority are struggles for much more than a label.

The term "hearing-impaired" is offensive to deaf people. Can you imagine calling a black person "white-impaired" or a woman "male-impaired"? Most of us who are culturally Deaf don't want or need to become hearing in order to consider ourselves as normal. We are a minority group with our own language, culture and heritage.
> —Doug Bahl, college teacher and president
>   of the Minnesota Association
>   of Deaf Citizens, Minneapolis
>   Star Tribune, Sept. 23, 1992

Much of American political conflict for the past generation has concerned who qualifies as a "minority." Many would say minorities are groups lacking power and experiencing discrimination, who therefore merit redress. But to whom this definition applies is hotly debated. African Americans typically represent the prime example of a minority, but that has engendered further controversy over who, if anyone, can claim to be like them. Labels matter. Legally, being a minority opens up some avenues for concrete benefits; culturally, it gives groups a claim for attention in the media and public debates; psychologically, it helps develop a sense of pride and self-acceptance. That is why the fight over a word is so serious.

Sociologist Louis Wirth usually gets the credit (or blame) for the current definition of "minority." In 1945, he described it this way: "A group of people who, because of their physical or cultural characteristics, are singled out from the others in the society in which they live for differential and unequal treatment, and who therefore regard themselves as objects of collective discrimination."

This definition has had lasting effect. For example, scholars for decades have asserted that minority status is never about a group's size (i.e., it does not mean less than half of the population), but rather about proportions of power. Groups lacking power are vulnerable to discrimination and exploitation.

In the United States, specific groups get recognized as minorities in two ways: some groups are assigned minority status by others and some assert it in the hopes of getting their group recognized. Either way, comparison with African Americans is at the heart of the matter. Groups that want to be recognized as minorities must reckon with the fact that the more a group is seen as similar to African Americans, the more of a minority it becomes. This is a legacy of the Civil Rights Movement, which made it possible for activists to claim minority status, and policy makers to confer it.

assigning minority status

To see how this happens, consider a policy document—a Department of Labor "Affirmative Action Plan"—that I found posted on the Internet. The document defines affirmative action as "procedures . . . for the identification, positive recruitment, training, and motivation of . . . minority and female (minority and non-minority) apprentices including the establishment of goals and timetables . . . so as to allow full utilization of the work potential of minorities and women." The term minorities (usually paired with women) is repeated at least 23 times in this three-page document, but it is never defined there.

Who are these official minorities and how did they achieve that status? John Skrentny documents a "minority rights revolution"—in a book of that name—that took place from 1965 to 1975. It arose in part from a growing, worldwide emphasis on human rights following World War II, but mostly from the Civil Rights Movement (see "How Social Movements Matter," *Contexts*, Fall 2003.) Skrentny shows how legislation created in response to that activism (for the first time since Reconstruction) legitimated government policies (as well as business and school practices) in support of specific social groups. He also shows how laws and policies designed initially to redress wrongs specifically perpetrated against African Americans were extended to other newly defined "minorities." While policy makers were usually silent about how exactly they determined which groups merited minority status, it was clear that groups had to be seen as disadvantaged. He also found that policy makers routinely used African Americans as a comparative benchmark. That is, to the extent that elites and policy makers sensed that a group was disadvantaged in a way similar to blacks, they were more likely to see the group— and officially designate it—as a minority. Latinos and Native Americans were most likely to be seen in this way; Asian Americans less frequently so. This minority status was often assigned by officials without serious lobbying by members of the groups themselves, most notably in the cases of Latinos and Native Americans.

Native Americans enact an alternative "Thanksgiving" celebration in this sunrise ceremony on Alcatraz Island, Thanksgiving Day, 2002. Government officials granted minority status to Native Americans for affirmative action purposes though they did not lobby to be categorized as a minority. (Photo by Jon Wagner)

beyond official minorities

Government officials are not the only ones who confer minority status. The media, for example, has helped confer minority status on several groups. Hundreds of recent articles tout Latinos as the "largest minority" in the United States, overtaking African Americans, according to the 2000 census. In our schools and in our ordinary conversations, as well as in the media, we continually hear, read about, or use the phrase "racial and ethnic minorities." While the exact meaning of this phrase may differ among people, at the very least it implies that racial or ethnic distinction is a qualification for minority status. But while "whites" are usually thought of as one of the American "racial" groups, they are all but defined out of the minority concept. Certain white individuals may be considered minorities—for example if they are also Latino, lesbian, or Appalachian, but the key difference between racial or ethnic groups and racial or ethnic *minorities* is the exclusion from the dominant group—the "whites."

"White ethnics" (e.g., Poles, Italians, Slavs) are therefore a particularly interesting, and messy, case. Officials rarely if ever define them as minorities for the purpose of public policy—in part because policy makers believe that they are neither sufficiently disadvantaged nor sufficiently similar to blacks. Still, many of these groups are customarily referred to as "ethnic minorities." Having a recognized "ethnic" status—which usually means having a territorial, linguistic, or cultural heritage rather than physical distinction like skin color—qualifies groups as minorities. On the other hand, many if not most of these white ethnics are fully assimilated into American life (as simply whites), and are unlikely to see themselves as minorities—or even ethnics for that matter.

Following in Louis Wirth's footsteps, social scientists have also tried to confer minority status on one group or another. One early example of this was the 1951 article "Women as a Minority Group" by Helen Hacker. She methodically identified ways that the position and experiences of women matched those of groups understood to be minorities, such as blacks and Jews. This kind of research may have helped galvanize some of the minority status claims made by activist women over the years. Many have held that women are systematically victimized as a group, and disadvantaged to a sufficient degree to be considered a minority. Some have gone further, claiming that women have a unique culture or way of being, conferring upon them certain ethnic-like qualities that might further qualify them as a minority. Of the many groups discussed in this article that are not racial or ethnic, women have been most consistently identified as worthy of being treated as a minority, even if they have not been literally labeled as a minority group (as in the phrase "women and minorities are encouraged to apply").

"just like blacks"

Since the 1950s, a variety of other groups have tried to get recognized as minorities. There are certain themes to which they repeatedly return in asserting their claims. One has been to contend that their group fits Wirth's criteria of oppressed victims of discrimination. Disability rights activists often describe discrimination in employment, lack of access to public facilities, and social stigmatization. In 1995, Congress agreed and passed the Americans with Disabilities Act, in which the disabled were defined as "a discrete and insular minority . . . subjected to a history of purposeful unequal treatment, and . . . political powerlessness . . . resulting from stereotypical assumptions."

Many groups also take a second, "ethnic" approach to minority status, emphasizing group characteristics such as culture, history, and language. This particular combination has been used by activists for the self-defined Deaf, as in the passage quoted at the beginning of this article. Their appeal draws on Americans' support for pluralism, the ideology that diverse cultures and heritages merit preservation. Deaf activists emphasize not only that the Deaf have a unique culture, but also that they share a scientifically recognized language (American Sign Language). Some even exclude from their minority the small "d" deaf people who do not sign.

The third and most widespread theme involves comparing one's group to established minorities, claiming to be "just like them," particularly in terms of prejudice or discrimination (while remaining culturally distinct). The most prominent comparisons, by far, are to African Americans. What policy makers did in Skrentny's study—comparing groups to African Americans to determine whether they are minorities—is mirrored in the claims of activists of all sorts (who are themselves predominantly white). Deaf Culture activists talk about Deaf Power

Much of "fat activism" tries to improve obese people's self-image, and to critique popular attitudes toward obesity, as well as male idealizations of women's bodies. As part of this effort, some activists have claimed minority status.

1. One of the biggest issues that we have to deal with is legitimizing the movement, or establishing ourselves as an oppressed group. . . .
2. Fat people know they are discriminated against, but we have to first establish this issue as a valid one before people's minds and attitudes can be changed. . . . Fat people are just as legitimate a minority group as blacks or gays or the physically challenged or women. . . .
3. We need the same type of protection. We need federal legislation, and if we can't get federal legislation, we need local and state legislation to protect us.
4. But the main hurdle, I believe, is fat people themselves—too many of them are still buying into what society says about them. NAAFA needs to . . . bring them in and give them some positive reinforcement for who they are.
—Sally Smith, 1989, in her role as President of the National Association for the Advancement of Fat Acceptance (NAAFA). Source: *Radiance Magazine*.

This example shows four elements of the assertion of minority status: 1. the emphasis on discrimination; 2. the comparison to more recognized minorities; 3. the pursuit of "instrumental goals," in this case, government protection from discrimination; and 4. the pursuit of "expressive goals," in this case, positive psychological self-image.

(echoing Black Power), Deaf is Dandy (Black is Beautiful), Deaf pride, Deaf studies, a Deaf-centric curriculum, and a concern about audists (versus racists). Gay rights activists stress gay pride, and in the 1960s proclaimed: "Gay is Good." The signal text of fat activism is *Fat Power*, and advocates complain about a "sizist" society. Disability rights activists, too, routinely borrow black symbols and imagery. In one example cited by Sharon Groch, disability rights activist Robert Mauro, conveying outrage and offense at labels applied to the disabled, wrote that " 'Disabled' is like 'Black,' 'Handicapped' is like 'Colored' . . . [and] 'cripple' is like 'nigger.' "

This third strategy reflects an unanticipated result of the Civil Rights Movement, placing African Americans at the center of, what I call, "minority cultural space." That is, if you use the term "minority" and do not specify who you are talking about, people assume you are referring to African Americans. Scholars of social movements repeatedly describe how the Civil Rights Movement is notable not only for its effects on blacks, but as a cultural innovation that provided other activists with a resonant rhetoric of "rights" for the disenfranchised, "power" for the powerless, and "pride" for the stigmatized. "Minorities" have come to be seen as "groups like blacks"—people who are not only victims of discrimination, but who also deserve rights, find power in collective action, and have a moral obligation to be proud of and preserve their lifestyle, culture, and heritage.

African Americans, while serving as the most common point of reference, are not the only benchmarks. Many activists point to other groups, such as Jews, women, Latinos, or Mexican Americans. Such claims testify to the success the groups have had in becoming "minorities," whether they sought to or not.

minority status gains benefits, establishes legitimacy, and curtails stigma

Achieving minority status helps activists realize two main types of social movement goals identified by sociologists: instrumental goals and expressive goals. Instrumental goals are tangible benefits, including protection from attack or discrimination. Social scientists have long known that when power or resources are divided along group lines, those kinds of groups become more important to people. Thus, when the federal government creates policies that benefit officially defined minorities, it not only bestows formal minority status on some groups, it also encourages others to try to get recognized in this manner. The same holds true for policies adopted by other institutions, such as when major corporations and universities establish outreach programs.

Activists claiming minority status are also pursuing expressive goals—less tangible benefits, such as collective awareness and cultural legitimacy. As my research on activism among gays, the Deaf, and white supremacists illustrates, a common objective is to be considered normal rather than deviant and to develop an identity that is a source of pride rather than shame. Since the 1950s, for example, a central goal of gay activist claims to minority status has been to rid people of the notion that homosexuality is a disease, and to provide an alternative interpretation of it. The activism has had notable success. In 1973, for example, activists convinced the American Psychological Association

to drop homosexuality from its list of mental disorders. The Deaf have similarly charged that the "hearing" world has sought repeatedly to medicalize their condition. Many reject the "hearing-impaired" label as demeaning and a way that a dominant group imposes a sense of inferiority upon a subordinate one. Emphasizing their positions as a minority (like African Americans) legitimates their group, as well as themselves, as normal and worthy. Those who feel stigmatized often see minority status as a way out. Kenneth Jernigan, then-president of the National Federation of the Blind, remarked in 1975: "In the past we have tended to see ourselves as others have seen us. We have accepted the public view of our limitations . . . but no more! That day is at an end. Our problem is that we have not been perceived as a minority. Yet that is what we are—a minority, with all that the term implies."

Claims to minority status often reflect this quest for both personal affirmation (self-image) and cultural legitimacy (image and treatment of the group by society at large). So powerful is the perceived legitimacy of being recognized as a minority that a wing of the white supremacist movement, following the lead of people like David Duke, Wilmot Robertson, and, more recently, Jared Taylor, is making similar claims: encouraging whites to love their own people, preserve and take pride in their heritage, and overcome the oppression they suffer from, for example, Hollywood and affirmative action programs.

"minority" as a cultural tool

Not all claims to be a minority are equally successful. While the disabled and gays and lesbians have been somewhat successful, recognition of fat people as minorities or even deaf people—whose arguments are more well-known—is still uncommon. And of course, white supremacist claims to being a minority are barely noticed, overshadowed by the less-tactful rhetoric and the violence of their ideological compatriots. Attaining minority status takes more than the right rhetoric. Many factors—such as the size of groups, wider cultural trends, political clout, organizational skills, time and money, the degree to which a group is despised or pitied—help determine which aspirants to the label of minority win it. Ultimately, the wider public—with elites in government, business, and academia having much influence—decides which group is "really" a minority and can use that label for instrumental ends.

Some critics argue that, because it evokes the notion of numbers rather than power, the term minority is misleading or nonsensical, and better terms might be, for example, "oppressed" or "subordinate." However, the term minority actually connotes much more than oppression or disadvantage: It connotes social legitimacy, profound injustice, and the right to redress past wrongs. The word has become an important cultural tool wielded by politicians and activists alike in pursuit of widely varying ends. Like many other products of scientific research, the term "minority" is being used by people in ways that the man who coined the phrase, Louis Wirth, probably never imagined. Like other critical words, such as *nation, individual, freedom,* and *family,* the definition of *minority* is the result of evolving social usage. And however arbitrary it may seem, that meaning becomes part of the reality people must face. Once a group is or is not recognized as a "minority," both its members and outsiders must deal with the implications of the label.

the uncertain future of minorities

Given its social construction, it is difficult to predict the future of the term "minorities." The history of another socially created concept—"race"—provides a cautionary tale. Decades after anthropologists began questioning this curious idea, and with numerous studies across the disciplines debunking genetic conceptions of it, "race" remains a prominent social marker. Moreover, while originally used to help justify slavery, "race" has been fiercely asserted by those it initially helped subordinate. For example, during the 1990s, among the most active opponents of a multiracial category in the U.S. census were African-American activists, who were concerned that such a step would decrease their numbers and result in losing hard-won rights.

The definition of minority is probably following a similarly complex path. It has been attacked from several standpoints. First, given the uniquely wretched history of Africans in America, the ubiquitous comparisons often raise the ire of black activists who argue that no other group was enslaved nor experienced the institutionalized discrimination of the Jim Crow era, and that blacks remain the group most frequently victimized by prejudice. One public example of this frustration came during the controversy in 1992 over President Clinton's desire to allow gays and lesbians to serve openly in the military. Several African-American opponents expressed particular outrage at the comparisons that were repeatedly being made to the racial integration of the military some 45 years earlier.

Second, some people in all of the groups described in this article have expressed discomfort with the minority label, and for a variety of reasons. For example, Peter Skerry reports in his book, *Mexican Americans: The Ambivalent Minority,* that for many "minority" implies a powerlessness that they reject. Minority may also connote marginality (i.e., the feeling of being outside of society), or a leftist preference for big government that these groups reject.

Third, the concept has been attacked across the political spectrum. Those on the right assail it for promoting a victim culture, in which people make demands for "minority set-asides," and for promoting "identity politics," part of the multiculturalism that they feel threatens to break up the United States. Some on the left also criticize identity politics because it divides groups of the poor rather than uniting them to fight for economic justice.

If any of these attacks gathered steam, there would be fewer "minorities." Yet, claims for minority status will continue precisely because they are so tied to multiculturalism. Some sociologists have recently noted how "diversity" has taken on almost universal value in the United States. (*We Are All Multiculturalists Now* is the title of a well-known 1997 book by Nathan Glazer.) In the 2003 University of Michigan admissions cases, the U.S. Supreme Court legitimated the goal of attaining diversity, rather than the goal of redressing discrimination, as a constitutional basis for affirmative-action programs. This emphasis on cultural identities and self-esteem means a very different type of minority status than one based on historical oppression; it is broader and aimed less at reducing long-standing inequalities.

In the short term, however, "minorities" will continue to be part of our culture. As long as people keep using the concept, as long as policy makers include the term in their laws, and as long as organizations continue to act on it (as when "Minority Affairs" departments are established in businesses or universities), then some social activists for groups who are stigmatized or experience discrimination (or think they do) will continue to assert that their group is a *minority*.

RECOMMENDED RESOURCES

Mitch Berbrier. "Making Minorities: Cultural Space. Stigma Transformation Frames, and the Categorical Status Claims of Deaf, Gay, and White Supremacist Activists in Late Twentieth Century America. "*Sociological Forum* 17 (2002): 553–91.

In this study, I show how minority claims are a part of social movement strategies and tie in to the cultural status of African Americans.

Philip Gleasop. "Minorities (Almost) All: The Minority Concept in American Social Thought." *American Quarterly* 43 (1991): 392–424.

A historian documents and interprets the intellectual and academic history of the minority concept.

Earl Lewis. "Constructing African Americans as Minorities." In *The Construction of Minorities*, eds. Andre Burguiere and Raymond Grew (University of Michigan Press, 2000).

An account of how African Americans came to be seen as the prototypical minority group.

Daniel D. Martin. "From Appearance Tales to Oppression Tales: Frame Alignment and Organizational Identity." *Journal of Contemporary Ethnography* 31 (2002): 158–206.

Describes stigma management in three organizations—Weight Watchers, Overeaters Anonymous, and the National Association to Advance Fat Acceptance.

David Nibert. "Minority Group as a Sociological Euphemism: A Note on the Concept of 'Privileged/Oppressed Groups.'" *Race, Gender & Class* 3 (1996): 129–36.

This short article critiques the choice of the term "minority" by sociologists.

Edward Sagarin. ed. *The Other Minorities: Nonethnic Collectivities Conceptualized as Minority Groups* (Ginn and Company, 1971).

This series of articles by activists and social scientists explores possible variations among minority groups, many relying on Louis Wirth's definition.

John D. Skrentny. *The Minority Rights Revolution* (Harvard University Press, 2002).

Documents how "official minorities" came to be recognized from 1965 to 1975, showing the importance of extending laws and practices initially intended for African Americans to other groups.

Louis Wirth. "The Problem of Minority Groups." In *The Science of Man in the World Crisis,* ed. Ralph Linton (Columbia University Press, 1945).

Defines, explains, and endorses the classic sociological concept of minorities.

REVIEW QUESTIONS

1. Identify and describe two "social movement goals" mentioned in this essay. Can you think of an example of a social group that has fought for these goals? What were they fighting for? What were their tactics? What were the results?

2. Berbrier writes that claims of minority status are for self-affirmation and cultural legitimacy. Thinking sociologically, what social institutions might minority group seek legitimacy from and why?

3. Because the term *minority* has moved from its original foundation of race to class, gender, religion, and beyond, it leads the reader to wonder where we are headed as a society. Thinking about the tensions between minority-group solidarity and larger notions of community (like "city" or "nation"), and a few of the issues from the final section of this essay, write a paragraph on what you believe the ramifications of these trends might be.

lee clarke

panic: myth or reality?

6

fall 2002

images of group panic and collective chaos are ubiquitous in hollywood movies, mainstream media and the rhetoric of politicians. but, contrary to these popular portrayals, group panic is relatively rare. in disasters people are often models of civility and cooperation.

It was like a disaster movie, only more unreal. The smoke and debris chased would-be survivors of the World Trade Center disaster through the glass and steel canyons of New York City. It was "chaos," the media told us. The description seemed viscerally correct, for how could such an unforeseen disaster generate anything but panic? A construction worker who was on the 34th floor of the North Tower recounted, "The whole building shook. We saw debris flying and then there was an explosion. We hit the stairwell; it was a mass panic."

Such a story represents a common tale about panic, which the Oxford English Dictionary defines as an "excessive feeling of alarm or fear . . . leading to extravagant or injudicious efforts to secure safety." We often see self-interest added to the common tale, the idea that people react so strongly that they will sacrifice others to save themselves. In other words, people become overly frightened and then overreact in ways that hurt themselves or others. However, this image of panic makes a necessary link between fear and reckless action, sometimes with a measure of selfishness thrown in. In fact, such behavior doesn't happen as often as one might think.

Nonetheless, Hollywood producers tell tales of panic-stricken chaos in movie and television depictions of catastrophes. The media are quick to report panic after building fires or mass transit crashes. Leaders seem to believe that the general population is prone to irrational panic, as witnessed by Washington's reluctance to fully inform the public about anthrax.

However, we have nearly 50 years of evidence on panic, and the conclusion is clear: people rarely panic, at least in the usual sense that word is used. Even when people feel "excessive fear"— a sense of overwhelming doom—they usually avoid "injudicious efforts" and "chaos." In particular, they are unlikely to cause harm to others as they reach for safety and may even put their own lives at risk to help others.

> After five decades studying scores of disasters such as floods, earthquakes, and tornadoes, one of the strongest findings is that people rarely lose control.

panic myths

Movies fuel the idea that people are quick to panic. *Independence Day, Armageddon,* and *Earthquake in New York* are typical: people climb over friends, family, and strangers to save themselves. The films suggest a tipping point beyond which people are so overcome with fear that they put self-interest over regard for others. After all, the reason we think it's wrong to yell "fire" in a crowded theater—even if the theater is on fire—is our assumption that the ensuing panic would cause more death than the fire itself. In Hollywood's depictions, panic strips away people's veneer of social responsibility to reveal raw selfishness.

Officials also perpetuate such images. Before the Y2K rollover, for example, politicians and business managers urged people not to overreact, not to panic, if there were software failures. Alan Greenspan, chair of the Federal Reserve Board, worried that people would rush to take their money out of banks. As the critical moment approached, John Koskinen, chair of the President's Commission on Year 2000 Conversion, became concerned less about failing machines than about panic: "As it becomes clear our national infrastructure will hold, overreaction becomes one of the biggest remaining problems."

Decision makers sometimes withhold information because they believe that panic will ensue. For example, during the nuclear incident at Three Mile Island, utility representatives failed to tell people and even government officials how serious the situation was because they were trying to "ease the level of panic and concern."

The general public probably holds this notion of panic, too. It is not unusual to read quotes from survivors of catastrophes—recall the World Trade Center survivor—in which people interpret the behavior of others, or even themselves, in terms of panic. What they are usually reporting, though, are feelings of fear and not panic-stricken behavior.

panic facts

Panicky behavior is rare. It was rare even among residents of German and Japanese cities that were bombed during World War II. The U.S. Strategic Bombing Survey, established in 1944 to study the effects of aerial attacks, chronicled the unspeakable horrors, terror, and anguish of people in cities devastated by firestorms and nuclear attacks. Researchers found that, excepting some

uncontrolled flight from the Tokyo firestorm, little chaos occurred.

An enormous amount of research on how people respond to extreme events has been done by the Disaster Research Center, now at the University of Delaware. After five decades studying scores of disasters such as floods, earthquakes, and tornadoes, one of the strongest findings is that people rarely lose control. When the ground shakes, sometimes dwellings crumble, fires rage, and people are crushed. Yet people do not run screaming through the streets in a wild attempt to escape the terror, even though they are undoubtedly feeling terror. Earthquakes and tornadoes wreak havoc on entire communities. Yet people do not usually turn against their neighbors or suddenly forget personal ties and moral commitments. Instead the more consistent pattern is that people bind together in the aftermath of disasters, working together to restore their physical environment and their culture to recognizable shapes.

Consider a few cases where we might have expected people to panic. The first, investigated by Norris Johnson, happened during Memorial Day weekend in 1977, when 165 people perished trying to escape a fire at the Beverly Hills Supper Club in Southgate, Kentucky. The supper club case recalls the fire-in-the-theater concept in which panic supposedly causes more deaths than the failure to escape in time.

Roughly 1,200 people were in the club's Cabaret Room, which had three exits. Two exits were to the side and led outdoors, and one was in the front and led to another part of the club. When the club's personnel, having discovered fire in the building, started telling customers to leave, a handful of people went to the front entrance while the others started filing calmly out of the other exits. However, the people who tried to get out of the front entrance soon ran into smoke and fire, so they returned to the Cabaret Room.

Survivors reported feeling frightened, but few acted out their fear. People were initially calm as they lined up at the two side exits, near which all of the deaths occurred. When smoke and fire started pouring into the Cabaret Room, some began screaming and others began pushing. As fire entered the room, some people jumped over tables and chairs to get out.

Notice what they did not do. They did not pick up those chairs and use them to strike people queued up in front of them. They did not grab their hair and shove them aside in a desperate rush to get out. They did not overpower those more helpless than themselves. They did not act blindly in their own self-interest. In Kentucky, few people acted out of panic. Indeed, had people developed a sense of urgency sooner, more would have gotten out and fewer would have died. Panic was probably not the cause of any of the deaths. It is more accurate to say that the building layout was inadequate for emergencies. The second case, also researched by Johnson, happened in December 1979 at the Riverfront Coliseum (as it was then called) in Cincinnati, where 11 people were killed at a rock concert by The Who. The concertgoers were killed in a crush that was popularly perceived as a panic. The reality was far different. Approximately 8,000 people were waiting for the concert, but the building was not built to accommodate that many people waiting at once. After the doors opened, about 25 people fell. Witnesses say there was little panic. In fact, people tried to protect those who had fallen by creating a human cordon around them. But the push of the people behind was too strong. The crowd trampled the 25 people out of ignorance rather than panic. Like the Beverly Hills club, Cincinnati's Riverfront Coliseum was not de-

People die the same way they live, with friends, loved ones, and colleagues—in communities. When danger arises, the rule—as in normal situations—is for people to help those next to them before they help themselves.

signed to fail gracefully. Users would be safe as long as they arrived in anticipated numbers and behaved in ways designers had anticipated.

Consider, also, the tragic flight of American Airlines 1420. In Little Rock, Arkansas, on June 1, 1999, Flight 1420 tried to land in a severe thunderstorm. As the pilots approached, they couldn't line the plane up with the runway and by the time they righted the craft they were coming in too fast and too hard. Seconds after the plane touched down, it started sliding and didn't stop until after lights at the end of the runway tore it open. The plane burst into flames, and 11 of the 145 aboard were killed.

The National Transportation Safety Board's "Survival Factors Factual Report" has more than 30 pages of survivor testimony. Most survivors who were asked about panic said there was none. Instead there were stories of people helping their spouses, flight attendants helping passengers, and strangers saving each other's lives. One fellow said that after the plane came to rest "panic set in." But his description of subsequent events doesn't look much like panic. Having discovered the back exit blocked, he found a hole in the fuselage. Then, "he and several men," says the report, "tried to pull the exit open further." He then allowed a flight attendant and "six to eight people" to get out before he did. Another passenger said that people panicked somewhat. But in his telling, too, people worked together to push an exit door open. He himself helped pick up a row of seats that had fallen atop a woman. As "smoke completely filled the cabin from floor to ceiling," people could barely see or breathe; yet they "were in a single file line [and] there was no pushing and shoving." We would not expect that much order if everyone was panicking.

The same message rises from the rubble of the World Trade Center. Television showed images of people running away from the falling towers, apparently panic-stricken. But surely no one would describe their flight as evincing "excessive fear" or "injudicious effort." Some survivors told of people being trampled in the mass exodus, but those reports are unusual. More common are stories such as the one from an information architect whose subway was arriving underneath the Trade Center just as the first plane crashed. He found himself on the north side of the complex, toward the Hudson River: "I'm looking around and studying the people watching. I would say that 95 percent are completely calm. A few are grieving heavily and a few are running, but the rest were very calm. Walking. No shoving and no panic." We now know that almost everyone in the Trade Center Towers survived if they were below the floors where the airplanes struck. That is in large measure because people did not become hysterical but instead created a successful evacuation.

Absent a full survey of disasters, we do not have statistical evidence that chaotic panic is rare, but consider the views of E. L. Quarantelli, cofounder of the Disaster Research Center and a don of disaster research. He recently concluded (in correspondence to me) that "I no longer believe the term 'panic' should be treated as a social science concept. It is a label taken from popular discourse. . . . During the whole history of [our] research involving nearly 700 different field studies, I would be hard pressed to cite . . . but a very few marginal instances of anything that could be called panic behavior."

panic rules

That people in great peril usually help others, even strangers, seems to contradict common sense. It also contradicts the idea that people are naturally self-interested. If people are so self-regarding, why do they act altruistically when their very lives are at stake? One answer is that people sometimes act irrationally by going against what is in their best interests. From this view, the men on American Airlines Flight 1420 were not exercising sound judgment when they helped free the woman whose legs were pinned. They could have used the time to save themselves.

If cases like this were rare, it might be reasonable to call such behavior irrational. But they're not rare, and there is a better explanation of them than irrationality. When the World Trade Center started to burn, the standards of civility that people carried around with them every day did not suddenly dissipate. The rules of behavior in extreme situations are not much different from rules of ordinary life. People die the same way they live, with friends, loved ones, and colleagues—in communities. When danger arises, the rule—as in normal situations—is for people to help those next to them before they help themselves. At the Supper Club fire and The Who concert, people first helped their friends and family. As we have seen, people help strangers. That's one of the big lessons from the World Trade Center. Such behavior seems odd only if we're all naturally selfish. Instead, an external threat can create a sense of 'weness' among those who are similarly threatened.

Disasters, like other social situations, have rules, and people generally follow them. They are not special rules, even though disasters are special situations. The rules are the same ones at work when the theater is not on fire. Human nature is social, not individually egoistic. People are naturally social, and calamities often strengthen social bonds.

failing gracefully

All of this is not to say that the stereotypic panic reactions never happen. Individuals do experience feelings of uncontrollable dread. The American Psychological Association says 1 out of every 75 people might suffer a "panic attack," an overwhelming sense of fear that's out of proportion to a perceived threat or to no threat at all. We've all heard the post–September 11 stories about powdered milk being mistaken for anthrax. There are also occasional soccer stampedes and bona fide cases of uncontrolled flight. It would be folly to say that people are always sensible. There are overreactions to scares about witches, drugs, and sex. Scholars dub such phenomena "moral panics," or overreactions that are governed by people's moral sensibilities rather than actual threat. Nonetheless, the panic of popular imagery is rare.

The myth of panic endures because it provides an easy explanation for complex things. For example, attributing the deaths at The Who concert to panic detracts attention from an engineering failure (the building could not accommodate so many people waiting at once), a management failure (not forecasting the demand for entry into the concert), and an organizational failure (once the disaster began it could not be stopped). Or consider a soccer "stampede" in Ghana in 2001 in which 130 people were killed. Calling that event a panic would deflect attention away from the police who fired tear gas into a crowd of about 30,000 and from the fact that the exits were locked. The idea of panic works to blame the victims of a disaster, deflecting attention from the larger contexts of people's behavior.

An alternative to panic as an explanation of how people respond to disasters is the idea of failing ungracefully. In software engineering a system that fails "gracefully" can take discrete breakdowns without crashing the whole computer program. In the present context social relationships and artifacts (walls, machines, exits, etc.) no longer function as they were designed. Such conditions make collective panic more likely. U.S. air traffic control fails gracefully. A new procedure begun in 2000 tracks data so that

if one component fails, another is immediately available; controllers do not panic because their monitoring systems are highly reliable. Modern elevator systems are designed to fail with grace. In January 2000, a cable on one of the Empire State Building's elevators broke, sending its occupant on a quick 40-story drop; but other safety systems kicked in to control the elevator's stop. An example of ungracefulness was the system of building football rally bonfires at Texas A&M University. When, in November 1999, that system started to fail, there was little to prevent loss of life and 12 were killed.

not panicking about panic

Dispelling the myth of public panic highlights the sociality rather than the individuality of human nature. It leads to optimism about people. If people generally act well under the most trying of circumstances—precisely when it would be easiest to turn their backs on others—it gives us reason to look for the good and the sensible in them at other times as well. Jettisoning the myth of public panic could also increase elites' trust of people. Politicians and corporate managers have a litany of responses after some mishap:

"There was never any danger to the public."

"Everything is under control."

"There is no reason for concern."

Behind such public pacifiers is the presumption that people cannot be trusted with bad news.

Communications based on that presumption generate distrust and suspicion. The U.S. Army is headed down that road. The Army is destroying America's stockpile of chemical weapons. Army representatives have asserted that none of the chemicals could be released into the environment. The Army has been wrong. There have been releases of mustard gas and of Sarin gas. After the accidents Army representatives assured everyone that "there was no danger to the surrounding communities or to the environment."

University of Arizona researchers found that a lot of people do not trust the U.S. Army's promises. The Army's attitude is one of public pacification; it assumes that people are prone to irrational panic. The problem is that in the event of a real hazardous mustard gas release, people may not trust what Army personnel have to say.

Before, during, and after disasters, the "general public" warrants trust and respect. Panic is often used as a justification by high-level decision makers to deny knowledge and access to the public, on the presumption that people cannot handle bad news. Research on how people respond to life-threatening disasters and the stories from the World Trade Center show that people handle even the most terrifying news civilly and cooperatively. Our leaders would do well to see us as partners in recovery rather than as a "constituency" to be handled.

RECOMMENDED RESOURCES

Lee Clarke. *Mission Improbable: Using Fantasy Documents to Tame Disaster* (University of Chicago Press, 2000).

> Shows how and why leaders, claiming to fear public panic, sometimes overpromise safety.

Kai Erikson. *A New Species of Trouble: Explorations in Disaster, Trauma, and Community* (W. W. Norton, 1995).

> Masterful collection of stories about how people respond to catastrophe; community and trust rather than panic are the key issues.

William F. Freudenburg. "Risk and Recreancy: Weber, the Division of Labor, and the Rationality of Risk Perceptions." *Social Forces* 71 (1993): 900–32.

> People worry about risk not because they are panicky but because our leaders often don't warrant trust.

John Hersey. *Hiroshima* (Bantam Books [1946] 1986).

> Best existing account of what it was like to be at a nuclear ground zero. Resignation and depression were more prevalent than panic.

Irving Leste Janis. *Air War and Emotional Stress* (McGraw-Hill, 1951).

> The Japanese response to atomic attacks: little panic.

Norris R. Johnson. "Panic and the Breakdown of Social Order: Popular Myth, Social Theory, Empirical Evidence." *Sociological Focus* 20 (1987): 171–83.

> Close investigation of some modern disasters, in search of the elusive panic.

E. L. Quarantelli. "Sociology of Panic." In *International Encyclopedia of the Social and Behavioral Sciences* (Pergamon Press, 2001).

> A don of disaster research revisits a conclusion he reached many years before: "panic" isn't a useful scientific concept.

REVIEW QUESTIONS

1. How can you use Barbalet's earlier discussion to better understand the emotional component to panic?
2. The essay explains how, during disasters, people tend to follow "normal rules" rather than "special" ones. Can you think of a personal experience of a high-tension situation where "normal rules" applied? Can you recall any evidence to the contrary?
3. Authorities like the police, the government, and the military often promote the element of panic when faced with explaining a disaster. What would their reasons be for doing this, and why do you feel the public accepts such an explanation?

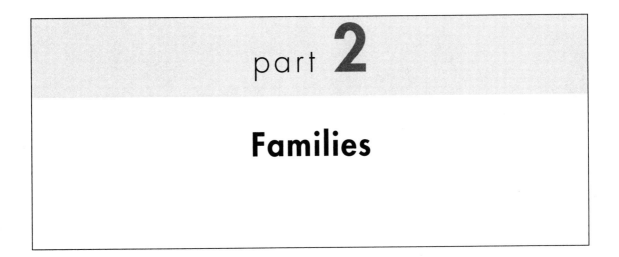

part **2**

Families

tey meadow and judith stacey

keyword: families

7

fall 2006

According to the town of Black Jack, Missouri, Fondray Loving, Olivia Shelltrack, and their three children are not a family. The couple has lived together for 13 years and are raising their own two children as well as at-home-mom Olivia's daughter from a previous relationship. They eat meals together, display vacation photos on their refrigerator, and attend PTA meetings. However, when they went to City Hall to secure a certificate of occupancy for the house they purchased in this St. Louis suburb, they learned that their new town prohibits more than three people from sharing a residence if they are not related by blood, marriage, or adoption. Because Shelltrack and Loving have chosen not to marry, they do not qualify as a family under their local housing laws.

Most people can identify the members of their family, but what defines "the family" depends on who is doing the defining. From policy makers who regard families as units for administrative purposes like distributing health care and determining ownership of property, to cultural critics who bemoan or celebrate what they view as the decline of the nuclear family to entertainment executives who capitalize on our seemingly limitless fascination with diverse domestic relationships, the question of what counts as a family today is hotly contested across a range of political issues. Though many of these issues appear to have ancient pedigrees, it turns out that "the family" is a fairly recent historical innovation.

The *Oxford English Dictionary* locates the entry of the word family into the English language as late as the fifteenth century, when it was used to denote the servants of a household. It has since been used to designate a wide range of collectives: the retinue of a nobleman, the staff of a high-ranking military officer or state official, groups of individuals or nations bound together by religious or political ties, even members of local units of the Mafia. Only during the Victorian era did our present common meaning of family—an intimate set of people related by blood, law, and sentiment, and particularly a married woman and man and their children—come to dominate. Ask the average person, and you might also hear that families are sites of love and care, or sometimes of violence, abuse, and deprivation. Feminist anthropologists Jane Collier and Sylvia Yanagisako make a point of identifying the family as an ideology rather than an institution, one that prescribes norms for domestic arrangements that change over time, but more slowly than the economic and social conditions that undergird them.

As the word family has evolved in its usage, so too have domestic arrangements shifted in the course of the long historical transformations often referred to as "modernization." The "modern family" in the West, comprising a male breadwinner, female homemaker, and their children, evolved from a patriarchal, premodern economy in which work and family life were thoroughly integrated. In the United States during the nineteenth century, industrialization turned most men into breadwinners outside the home and women into homemakers by separating paid employment from domestic work. Originating within the white middle class, this family structure came to represent modernity and normality. Yet it was not until the mid-twentieth century that significant percentages of male workers could earn enough to sustain such a family, and it has always exceeded the reach of most African Americans and new immigrants. Slaves were not allowed to marry and had no parental rights. Since Emancipation, many African-American and new immigrant mothers have tended the modern family homes and children of relatively privileged whites instead of being able to tend to their own. As working-class families seldom have been able to support full-time homemakers, the 1950s model of domesticity has remained a ubiquitous social ideal, but rarely more than a white, middle-class reality.

Rigidly defined economic roles for men and women developed along with new gender ideologies to sustain them. The nineteenth century brought increasingly romanticized ideals of a voluntary "companionate marriage" as well as the "cult of true womanhood"—a celebration of female domesticity and maternalism—that continue to permeate Western gender and family ideology. Analogous legal doctrines stressed the importance of maternal nurturance during the "tender years" of childhood. Feminist sociologist Deniz Kandiyoti suggests that women's economic dependence on men, prescribed by a supposed complementary and natural division of labor, was but a new version of the premodern, "patriarchal bargain," in which women accept overt subordination in exchange for male protection and secure social status. Other scholars stress how the new, female-only domestic sphere formed the backdrop to women's solidarity and the beginnings of grassroots feminist organizing.

While high mortality rates kept premodern family patterns diverse and unpredictable, notable declines in mortality and fertility made modern family life more linear and homogenous. By the mid-twentieth century, a life-course journey from the cradle through courtship, marriage, procreation, parenting, and grandparenthood to the grave became so common that the family began to appear natural, universal, and self-evident. Social scientists tend to reflect the tacit cultural understandings of their era. Functionalist sociologists working in that period, notably Talcott Parsons and William Goode, tended to assume the naturalness or inevitability of the nuclear family form. During the post-World War II period, they developed a theory rooted in the conviction that U.S. family history would prove to be a global model. Arguing that the modern nuclear family was ideally suited to support an industrial economy, Goode predicted its spread throughout the modernizing world.

This "family modernization thesis" presumed the superiority of Western cultural forms, a presumption often shared by political authorities. In fact, so convinced have Western governments been of the superiority of our gender and family patterns that they have often imposed them on subjugated peoples. The United States, for example, disrupted matrilineal and extended kin systems among several New World cultures by awarding land titles exclusively to male-headed, nuclear household units. Similarly, after the Civil War, the Freedman's Bureau vigorously promoted monogamous marriage and the morality of the nuclear family among former slaves. Because slaves frequently were sold to other plantations, many entered several de facto marriages without any rituals terminating their previous unions. Others engaged in serial cohabitations, multiple sexual partnerships, and plural marriages. Legal scholar Katherine Franke and historian Deborah Gray White maintain that the right to civil marriage carried great symbolic value for emancipated slaves, but within the larger Reconstruction project of "civilizing" them, marriage also provided an opportunity to impose European norms of morality on African Americans.

In numerous other instances, legal disruption of the family and kinship relationships practiced by cultural minorities and indigenous peoples has been justified in the name of its civilizing effects. For example, polygyny (the marriage of men to multiple wives) is a common practice in preindustrial societies throughout the world, frequently for economic and procreative ends. Although polygyny is a patriarchal kinship form, some women have favored it for the companionship and shared workload it can provide. Women in Botswana, for example, revise our familiar aphorism, "A woman's work is never done," to claim that "Without cowives, a woman's work is never done."

Polygyny was also widely practiced among Mormons in the Utah territories after Joseph Smith's Celestial Revelation in 1843. Smith's followers, women as well as men, considered what they called "patriarchal marriage" to be a biblical prerequisite to higher levels of salvation. In horrified response, the Republican Party platform of 1856 paired polygamy with slavery and pledged itself to eliminate these "twin relics of barbarism." Over the next several decades, the U.S. government employed increasingly coercive tactics against Mormon plural marriage, from curtailing the property or voting rights of polygynists (a precursor to the contemporary plight of the Loving-Shelltrack family), to direct legislation against bigamy and refusing Utah's application to the union until the Latter Day Saints church finally capitulated and renounced the practice in 1890.

Diverse critical traditions in sociology have been less enamored than mid-twentieth century modernization theorists with the ruling ideas, policies, and practices of the industrializing and globalizing West. Most critical sociologists regard family patterns and relationships as products of their social and historical contexts, no more inevitable than any other feature of social life. Marxists since Friedrich Engels have stressed the ways that struggles between capitalists and workers have shaped and challenged modern family forms, including the very concepts of privacy and intimacy. Inspired by the spirit of second-wave feminism, scholars such as Heidi Hartmann, Nancy Chodorow, and Arlie Hochschild have analyzed how male domination and privilege work within the changing (and unchanging) gender division of family, emotions, and labor; how women comply with the coercive features of male-dominated families; and the moments of resistance in which they refuse to do so. Work by feminist sociologists of color, including Bonnie Thornton Dill, Patricia Hill Collins, Pierrette Hondagneu-Sotelo, and Evelyn Nakano Glenn, in turn, has challenged the unwitting ways in which these feminist scholars validated the white, middle-class, nuclear family form even as they criticized it.

European postindustrial theorists such as Anthony Giddens, Zygmunt Bauman, and Ulrich Beck have explored the implications of the dramatic "transformation of intimacy" that became evident late in the twentieth century. Family scholars continue to debate who gained and who lost ground when sexuality was freed from reproduction and the romantic nineteenth century ideals of voluntary companionate marriage gave way to a more individualized, and destabilizing, pursuit of what Giddens termed the "pure relationship." Clearly prominent among the beneficiaries and innovations are new forms of intimacy and kinship among self-identified lesbians, gays, and queers. Upending the long-held presumption of most family scholars and citizens that family life is inevitably a heterosexual product, gays and lesbians began composing what queer scholars Kath Weston and Jeffrey Weeks call "families of choice."

The new millennium provides family scholars, regardless of their intellectual orientation, with resounding evidence that family diversity is ubiquitous and family change unceasing. Postindustrial labor conditions and the spread of a global marketplace underwrite continually shifting occupational and personal opportunities and crises. Women now participate fully in an increasingly unstable and competitive worldwide labor force, with profound implications for gender identity, procreation, and parenting. Throughout advanced industrial societies, rising numbers of men and women alike are deferring or foregoing marriage and parenthood. When they do marry, their divorce rates are high, and remarriages are frequent, rendering family constellations increasingly complex. Single individuals now reside alone in a full quarter of U.S. households, while far fewer families conform to the 1950s ideal of a married male breadwinner, at-home mom, and their children. Most of us know single parents, step-families, cohabiting couples (many of whom have children), interracial families, and children adopted from abroad. More and more of us know parents who have used assisted reproductive technologies (ART), including gay and lesbian couples and individuals. Despite such changes in the family, however, tenacious patterns of historical disadvantage and discrimination continue to maintain sharp racial and class disparities in family forms and fortunes.

Anyone who reads a newspaper or watches television knows that these changes provoke considerable fear and anxiety. This "postmodern family condition" has fueled culture wars over "family values" and political contests over

issues such as no-fault divorce, abortion, welfare, "father-lessness," sex education, faith-based marriage-promotion initiatives, same-sex marriage, and lesbian and gay adoption and custody rights. Family sociology itself plays a part in these conflicts as politicians and advocates frequently draw upon research on the causes and effects of divorce, single parenthood, sex education, gay parenting, and the like to buttress their claims. At the core of these controversies lies a fundamental ideological divide over whether it is better to promote a "one size fits all" model for American family life or to give broader acceptance and support to family diversity.

Should the Loving-Shelltrack household count as a family entitled to occupy their new home in Missouri or not? Whatever our personal and political viewpoints may be on the risks, opportunities, and social legitimacy of contemporary family patterns, one prediction seems certain. In the foreseeable future, family sociologists face no threat of running out of new research material.

RECOMMENDED RESOURCES

Nancy F. Cott. *Public Vows: A History of Marriage and the Nation* (Harvard University Press, 2000).

> This engaging political history of marriage in the United States as a pivotal public institution demonstrates how the state has used it to impose Christian standards of morality on diverse communities of Native Americans, slaves, and new immigrants.

Anthony Giddens. *The Transformation of Intimacy: Sexuality, Love and Eroticism in Modern Societies* (Stanford University Press, 1993).

> An optimistic, interpretive essay on the development of the individual pursuit of love and sexuality for their own sake as an intrinsic part of the transition to late modernity in the West.

William J. Goode. *World Revolution and Family Patterns* (The Free Press, 1963).

This classic example of the "family modernization thesis" remains one of the most cited works in family sociology. Goode studies post–World War II changes in gender and family patterns in five major regions of the world.

Judith Stacey. *Brave New Families: Stories of Domestic Upheaval in Late 20th Century America,* 2nd ed. (University of California Press, 1998).

This ethnographic study of the impact of postindustrial society, feminism, and fundamentalism on working-class families in the Silicon Valley depicts the emergence of the postmodern family condition of diversity, fluidity, and political conflict.

Kath Weston. *Families We Choose: Lesbians, Gays, Kinship* (Columbia University Press, 1991).

This path-breaking urban ethnography examines how lesbians and gay men in San Francisco actively drew upon ties rooted in friendship and love, as well as biology, to construct their own forms of family and kinship.

REVIEW QUESTIONS

1. Before reading this essay, how might you have defined *family?*
2. What is the "family modernization thesis" and how does it explain declines in mortality and fertility rates in modern times?
3. Provide an example of how Western governments have imposed their gender and family patterns onto subjugated peoples.
4. How have the majority of critical sociologists viewed family patterns and relationships as compared to mid-twentieth-century modernization theorists?
5. Describe the fundamental ideological divide that the authors locate at the core of the controversies over "family values."

dan clawson and naomi gerstel

caring for our young: child care in europe and the united states

8

fall/winter 2002

parents in the united states struggle to find and afford even mediocre private child care. most european countries provide quality publicly-funded programs. should child care emphasize education or play? parents or peers? organized care or parental involvement?

When a delegation of American child care experts visited France, they were amazed by the full-day, free *écoles maternelles* that enroll almost 100 percent of French three-, four-, and five-year-olds:

> Libraries better stocked than those in many U.S. elementary schools. Three-year-olds serving one another radicchio salad, then using cloth napkins, knives, forks, and real glasses of milk to wash down their bread and chicken. Young children asked whether dragons exist [as] a lesson in developing vocabulary and creative thinking.

In the United States, by contrast, working parents struggle to arrange and pay for private care. Publicly funded child care programs are restricted to the poor. Although most U.S. parents believe (or want to believe) that their children receive quality care, standardized ratings find most of the care mediocre and much of it seriously inadequate.

Looking at child care in comparative perspective offers us an opportunity—almost requires us—to think about our goals and hopes for children, parents, education, and levels of social inequality. Any child care program or funding system has social and political assumptions with far-reaching consequences. National systems vary in their emphasis on education; for three- to five-year-olds, some stress child care as preparation for school, while others take a more playful view of childhood. Systems vary in the extent to which they stress that children's early development depends on interaction with peers or some version of intensive mothering. They also vary in the extent to which they support policies promoting center-based care as opposed to time for parents to stay at home with their very young children. Each of these emphases entails different national assumptions, if only implicit, about children and parents, education, teachers, peers, and societies as a whole.

What do we want, why and what are the implications? Rethinking these questions is timely because with changing welfare, employment, and family patterns, more U.S. parents have come to believe they want and need a place for their children in child care centers. Even parents who are not in the labor force want their children to spend time in preschool. In the United States almost half of children less than one year old now spend a good portion of their day in some form of non-parental care. Experts increasingly emphasize the potential benefits of child care. A recent National Academy of Sciences report summarizes the views of experts: "Higher quality care is associated with outcomes that all parents want to see in their children." The word in Congress these days, especially in discussions of welfare reform, is that child care is good—it saves money later on by helping kids through school (which keeps them out of jail), and it helps keep mothers on the job and families together. A generation ago, by contrast, Nixon vetoed a child care bill as a "radical piece of social legislation" designed to deliver children to "communal approaches to child rearing over and against the family-centered approach." While today's vision is clearly different, most attempts to improve U.S. child care are incremental, efforts to get a little more money here or there, with little consideration for what kind of system is being created.

The U.S. and French systems offer sharp contrasts. Although many hold up the French system as a model for children three or older, it is only one alternative. Other European countries provide thought-provoking alternatives, but the U.S.-French contrast is a good place to begin.

france and the united states: private versus public care

Until their children start school, most U.S. parents struggle to find child care, endure long waiting lists, and frequently change locations. They must weave a complex, often unreliable patchwork in which their children move among relatives, informal settings and formal center care, sometimes all in one day. Among three- to four-year-old children with employed mothers, more than one out of eight are in three or more child care arrangements, and almost half are in two or more arrangements. A very small number of the wealthy hire nannies, often immigrants; more parents place their youngest children with relatives, especially grandmothers, or work alternate shifts so fathers can share child care with mothers (these alternating shifters now include almost one-third of families with infants and toddlers). Many pay kin to provide child care—sometimes not because they prefer it, but because they cannot afford other care, and it is a way to provide jobs and income to struggling family members. For children three and older, however, the fastest-growing setting in the United States is child care centers—almost half of three-year-olds (46 percent) and almost two-thirds of four-year-olds (64 percent) now spend much of their time there.

In France, participation in the *école maternelle* system is voluntary, but a place is guaranteed to every child three to six years old. Almost 100 percent of parents enroll their three-year-olds. Even nonemployed parents enroll their children, because they believe it is best for the children. Schools are open from 8:30 a.m. to 4:30 p.m. with an extended lunch break, but care is available at modest cost before and after school and during the lunch break.

Integrated with the school system, French child care is intended primarily as early education. All children, rich and poor, immigrant or not, are part of the same national system, with the same curriculum, staffed by teachers paid good wages by the same national ministry. No major political party or group opposes the system.

When extra assistance is offered, rather than targeting poor children (or families), additional resources are provided to geographic areas. Schools in some zones, mostly in urban areas, receive extra funding to reduce class size, give teachers extra training and a bonus, provide extra materials and employ special teachers. By

> French child care is intended primarily as early education. All children, rich and poor, immigrant or not, are part of the same national system, with the same curriculum, staffed by teachers paid good wages by the same national ministry.

targeting an entire area, poor children are not singled out (as they are in U.S. free lunch programs).

Staff in the French *écoles maternelles* have master's degrees and are paid teachers' wages; in 1998, U.S. preschool teachers earned an average of $8.32 an hour, and child care workers earned $6.61, not only considerably less than (underpaid) teachers but also less than parking lot attendants. As a consequence employee turnover averages 30 percent a year, with predictably harmful effects on children.

What are the costs of these two very different systems? In almost every community across the United States, a year of child care costs more than a year at a public university—in some cases twice as much. Subsidy systems favor the poor, but subsidies (unlike tax breaks) depend on the level of appropriations. Congress does not appropriate enough money and, therefore, most of the children who qualify for subsidies do not receive them. In 1999, under federal rules 15 million children were eligible to receive benefits, but only 1.8 million actually received them. Middle- and working-class families can receive neither kind of subsidy. An Urban Institute study suggests that some parents place their children in care they consider unsatisfactory because other arrangements are just too expensive. The quality of care thus differs drastically depending on the parents' income, geographic location, diligence in searching out alternatives, and luck.

The French system is not cheap. According to French government figures, the cost for a child in Paris was about $5,500 per year in 1999. That is only slightly more than the average U.S. parent paid for the care of a four-year-old in a center ($5,242 in 2000). But in France child care is a social responsibility, and thus free to parents, while in the United States parents pay the cost. Put another way, France spends about 1 percent of its Gross Domestic Product (GDP) on government-funded early education and care programs. If the United States devoted the same share of its GDP to preschools, the government would spend about $100 billion a year. Current U.S. government spending is less than $20 billion a year ($15 billion federal, $4 billion state).

The 11 European nations included in a recent study all have significantly better child care and paid leave than the United States. These models challenge us to think even more broadly about childhood, parenting, and the kind of society we value.

other european alternatives

When the American child care community thinks about European models, the French model is often what they have in mind. With its emphasis on education, the French system has an obvious appeal to U.S. politicians, educators and child care advocates. Politicians' central concern in the United States appears to be raising children's test scores; in popular and academic literature, this standard is often cited as the major indicator of program success. But such an educational model is by no means the only alternative. Indeed, the U.S. focus on the French system may itself be a telling indicator of U.S. experts' values as well as their assessments of political realities. Many advocates insist that a substantial expansion of the U.S. system will be possible only if the system is presented as improving children's education. These advocates are no longer willing to use the term "child care," insisting on "early education" instead. The French model fits these priorities: it begins quasi-school about three years earlier than in the United States. Although the French obviously assist employed parents and children's center activities are said to be fun, the system is primarily touted and understood as educational—intended to treat children as pupils, to prepare them to do better in school.

The 11 European nations included in a recent Organization for Economic Cooperation and Development study (while quite different from one another) all have significantly better child care and paid leave than the United States. Each also differs significantly from France. Offering alternatives, these models challenge us to think even more broadly about childhood, parenting, and the kind of society we value.

nonschool model: denmark

From birth to age six most Danish children go to child care, but most find that care in non-school settings. Overseen by the Ministry of Social Affairs (rather than the Ministry of Education), the Danish system stresses "relatively unstructured curricula" that give children time to "hang out." Lead staff are pedagogues, not teachers. Although pedagogues have college degrees and are paid teachers' wages, their role is "equally important but different" from that of the school-based teacher. "Listening to children" is one of the government's five principles, and centers emphasize "looking at everything from the child's perspective."

The Danish model differs from the French system in two additional ways that clarify its nonschool character. First, in the Danish system, pedagogues care for very young children (from birth to age three as well as older children ages three to six). The French preschool (*école maternelle*) model applies only to children three and older. Before that, children of working parents can attend *crèches*. *Crèche* staff, however, have only high school educations and are paid substantially less than the (master's degree-trained) *écoles maternelles* teachers. Second, while the *écoles maternelles* are available to all children, the Danish system (like the French *crèches*) is only available to children with work-

ing parents because it is intended to aid working parents, not to educate children.

The Danish system is decentralized, with each individual center required to have a management board with a parent majority. But the system receives most of its money from public funding, and parents contribute only about one-fifth of total costs.

Given its nonschool emphasis, age integration, and the importance it assigns to local autonomy, the Danish system might be appealing to U.S. parents, especially some people of color. To be sure, many U.S. parents—across race and class—are ambivalent about child care for their youngest children. Especially given the growing emphasis on testing, they believe that preschool might give them an edge, but they also want their children to have fun and play—to have, in short, what most Americans still consider a childhood. Some research suggests that Latina mothers are especially likely to feel that center-based care, with its emphasis on academic learning, does not provide the warmth and moral guidance they seek. They are, therefore, less likely to select center-based care than either white or African-American parents, relying instead on kin or family child care providers whom they know and trust. U.S. experts' emphasis on the French model may speak not only to political realities but also to the particular class and even more clearly race preferences framing those realities.

mothers or peers

The United States, if only implicitly, operates on a mother-substitute model of child care. Because of a widespread assumption in the United States that all women naturally have maternal feelings and capacities, child care staff, who are almost all women (about 98 percent), are not required to have special training (and do not need to be well paid). Even for regulated providers, 41 out of 50 states require no preservice training beyond orientation. Consequently, in the United States the child-staff ratio is one of the most prominent measures used to assess quality and is central to most state licensing systems. The assumption, based on the mother-substitute model, is that emotional support can be given and learning can take place only with such low ratios.

Considering the high quality and ample funding of many European systems, it comes as a surprise that most have much higher child-staff ratios than the United States. In the French *écoles maternelles*, for example, there is one teacher and one half-time aide for every 25 children. In Italy, in a center with one adult for every eight children (ages one to three years) the early childhood workers see no need for additional adults and think the existing ratios are appropriate. Leading researchers Sheila Kamerman and Alfred Kahn report that in Denmark, "what is particularly impressive is that children are pretty much on their own in playing with their peers. An adult is present all the time but does not lead or play with the children." In a similar vein, a cross-national study of academic literature found substantial focus on adult-child ratios in the United States, but very little literature on the topic in German-, French- or Spanish-language publications. Why not? These systems have a different view of children and learning. Outside the United States systems often center around the peer group. In Denmark the role of staff is to work "alongside children, rather than [to be] experts or leaders who teach children." Similarly, the first director of the early childhood services in Reggio, Italy, argues that children learn through conflict and that placing children in groups facilitates learning through "attractive," "advantageous,"

and "constructive" conflict "because among children there are not strong relationships of authority and dependence." In a non-European example, Joseph Tobin, David Wu, and Dana Davidson argue that in Japan the aim is ratios that "keep teachers from being too mother-like in their interactions with students . . . Large class sizes and large ratios have become increasingly important strategies for promoting the Japanese values of groupism and selflessness." Such practices contrast with the individuallistic focus in U.S. child care.

The child care system in the United States is a fragmentary patchwork, both at the level of the individual child and at the level of the overall system. Recent research suggests that the quality of care for young children is poor or fair in well over half of child care setting.

family leaves and work time

When we ask how to care for children, especially those younger than three, one answer is for parents to stay home. Policy that promotes such leaves is what one would expect from a society such as the United States, which emphasizes a mothering model of child care. It is, however, European countries that provide extensive paid family leave, usually universal, with not only job protection but also substantial income replacement. In Sweden, for example, parents receive a full year and a half of paid parental leave (with 12 months at 80 percent of prior earnings) for each child. Because so many parents (mostly mothers) use family leave, fewer than 200 children under one year old in the entire country are in public care. Generous programs are common throughout Europe (although the length, flexibility, and level of payment they provide vary).

The United States provides far less in the way of family leaves. Since its passage in 1993, the Family and Medical Leave Act (FMLA) has guaranteed a 12-week job-protected leave to workers of covered employers. Most employers (95 percent) and many workers (45 percent), however, are not covered. And all federally mandated leaves are unpaid.

The unpaid leaves provided by the FMLA, like the private system of child care, accentuate the inequality between those who can afford them and those who can't. Although the FMLA was touted as a "gender neutral" piece of legislation, men (especially white men) are unlikely to take leaves; it is overwhelmingly women (especially those who are married) who take them. As a result, such women pay a wage penalty when they interrupt their careers. To address such inequities, Sweden and Norway have introduced a "use it or lose it" policy. For each child, parents may divide up to a year of paid leave (say nine months for the mother, three for the father), *except* that the mother may not use more than eleven months total. One month is reserved for the father; if he does not use the leave, the family loses the month.

Finally, although not usually discussed as child care policy in the United States, policy makers in many European countries now emphasize that the number of hours parents work clearly shapes the ways young children are cared for and by whom. Workers in the United States, on average, put in 300 hours more per year than workers in France (and 400 more than those in Sweden).

conclusion

The child care system in the United States is a fragmentary patchwork, both at the level of the individual child and at the level of the overall system. Recent research suggests that the quality of care for young children is poor or fair in well over half of child care settings. This low quality of care, in concert with a model of intensive mothering, means that many anxious mothers privately hunt for high-quality substitutes while trying to ensure they are not being really replaced. System administrators need to patch together a variety of funding streams, each with its own regulations and paperwork. Because the current system was fashioned primarily for the affluent at one end and those being pushed off welfare at the other, it poorly serves most of the working class and much of the middle class.

Most efforts at reform are equally piecemeal, seeking a little extra money here or there in ways that reinforce the existing fragmentation. Although increasing numbers of advocates are pushing for a better system of child care in the United States, they rarely step back to think about the characteristics of the system as a whole. If they did, what lessons could be learned from Europe?

The features that are common to our peer nations in Europe would presumably be a part of a new U.S. system. The programs would be publicly funded and universal, available to all, either at no cost or at a modest cost with subsidies for low-income participants. The staff would be paid about the same as public school teachers. The core programs would cover at least as many hours as the school day, and "wrap-around" care would be available before and after this time. Participation in the programs would be voluntary, but the programs would be of such a high quality that a majority of children would enroll. Because the quality of the programs would be high, parents would feel much less ambivalence about their children's participation, and the system would enjoy strong public support. In addition to child care centers, parents would be universally offered a significant period of paid parental leave. Of course, this system is expensive. But as the National Academy of Science Report makes clear, not caring for our children is in the long term, and probably even in the short term, even more expensive.

Centers in all nations emphasize education, peer group dynamics, and emotional support to some extent. But the balance varies. The varieties of European experience pose a set of issues to be considered if and when reform of the U.S. system is on the agenda:

- To what degree should organized care approximate school and at what age, and to what extent is the purpose of such systems primarily educational?
- To what extent should we focus on adult-child interactions that sustain or substitute for mother care as opposed to fostering child-child interactions and the development of peer groups?
- To what extent should policies promote parental time with children versus high-quality organized care, and what are the implications for gender equity of either choice?

These are fundamental questions because they address issues of social equality and force us to rethink deep-seated images of children and parents.

RECOMMENDED RESOURCES

Candy J Cooper. *Ready to Learn: The French System of Early Education and Care Offers Lessons for the United States* (French American Foundation, 1999).

Janet Gornick and Marcia Meyers. "Support for Working Families: What the United States Can Learn from Europe." *The American Prospect* (January 1–15, 2001): 3–7.

Suzanne W. Helburn and Barbara R. Bergmann. *America's Childcare Problem: The Way Out* (Palgrave/St. Martin's, 2002).

Sheila B. Kamerman and Alfred J. Kahn. *Starting Right: How America Neglects Its Youngest Children and What We Can Do About It* (Oxford University Press, 1995).

Peter Moss. "Workforce Issues in Early Childhood Education and Care Staff."

Paper prepared for consultative meeting on International Developments in Early Childhood Education and Care, The Institute for Child and Family Policy, Columbia University, May 11–12, 2000.

Organization for Economic Co-operation and Development. *Starting Strong—Early Education and Care: Report on an OECD Thematic Review.* Online. www.oecd.org.

Jack P. Shonkoff and Deborah Phillips, eds. *From Neurons to Neighborhoods: The Science of Early Childhood Development* (National Academy of Sciences, 2000).

REVIEW QUESTIONS

1. If the importance of a particular role were measured by salary, how do U.S. child care employees fare compared to those in European countries?
2. Clawson and Gerstel mention the "more individualistic" focus of U.S. child care facilities, but there is also a focus on how families are often left to raise children alone (i.e., to depend upon one's extended family for child care rather than government programs). What do you feel are the positive and negative consequences of this emphasis? How does this affect the careers of parents and the education of their children?
3. The authors conclude with three "fundamental" questions. Pick one of them and write a two-paragraph essay on your own perspective on this issue. Reflect on your personal experiences, and how they relate to the larger issues addressed in this essay. Are they different? Why, or why not?

andrew j. cherlin

should the government promote marriage? 9

fall 2003

the bush administration's recent proposal to set aside federal welfare funds for marriage promotion programs renews a long-standing controversy about what makes a model family. but much more than symbolism is at stake in the debate over whether public policies should encourage marriage, and whether such policies are likely to be effective.

Is getting parents to marry the answer to the difficulties that children in single-parent families face? This question became a focus of debate when the Bush administration proposed in 2002 to include funds for promoting marriage in legislation extending the welfare reform act. As of this writing, it appears that the proposal will succeed. Although the marriage promotion fund (about $300 million per year) is relatively modest compared to the total cost of welfare, the proposal generated more controversy per dollar than any other part of the bill. The strong opinions on both sides reveal the high stakes of the debate.

On one side is the "marriage movement"—a loose group of conservative and centrist activists, religious leaders, and social scientists who want to strengthen the institution of marriage. Some of them advocate marriage because they are morally certain that it provides the best kind of family. Others, including most of the social scientists in this camp, favor it because they believe children's well-being would improve if more of their parents were married.

On the other side are "diversity defenders"— liberal activists, feminists, and sympathetic social scientists who argue that single-parent families can be just as good for children if they receive the support they need. The marriage movement favors public policies that encourage marriage. The diversity defenders favor policies that provide services and economic opportunities to low-income parents, whether married or not, and their children. In the end, the evidence suggests that the benefits of marriage promotion would be marginal. But the real debate may be far more about symbols than substance.

the decline of marriage

Most observers on both sides agree that the social institution of marriage is substantially weaker than it was 50 years ago. In mid-twentieth-century America, marriage was the only acceptable context for having a sexual relationship and for bearing and raising children. In 1950, just 4 percent of children were born to unmarried women. (Fifty years later, the figure was 33 percent.) Most women, and many men, abstained from sexual intercourse until they were engaged to be married. When an unmarried woman became pregnant, relatives pressured her and her partner to agree to a "shotgun wedding." Once married, couples were less likely to divorce—approximately one in three marriages begun in the 1950s ended in divorce, compared to one in two today. Consequently, even among the poor, most families had two parents.

In the ensuing decades, however, the likelihood that a child would spend a substantial portion of time in a single-parent family grew. More adults had children outside of marriage, choosing either to remain single or live with their partners without marrying. Divorce became more common. As a result, about half of all children are projected to spend some time in a single-parent family while growing up. Although these trends cut across class, racial, and ethnic lines, poor children and black children are more likely to be raised in single-parent families than are middle-class children and white children, respectively.

statistics and politics

Although the marriage movement and the diversity defenders tend to agree that the institution of marriage is weaker, they disagree about the consequences that has for society. Their debates have two levels, the statistical and the political. The statistical debate concerns whether the findings of social scientific research, most of it analyses of survey data, show marriage to be beneficial, and divorce and childbearing outside of marriage detrimental to children. While such research shapes the debates by providing facts for policy makers, those who dispute the numbers often skate on the surface of the subject. A deeper, political dispute lies beneath the statistical arguments, reflecting basic disagreement about whether the government should favor one model of family life above all others.

the statistical debate

Most social scientists would agree that, on average, children who grow up in a one-parent family are more disadvantaged than children who grow up with two parents. As Sara McLanahan wrote in the spring 2002 issue of *Contexts*:

> They are more likely to drop out of high school, less likely to attend college, and less likely to graduate from college than children raised by both biological parents. Girls from father-absent families are more likely to become sexually active at a younger age and to have a child outside of marriage. Boys who grow up without their fathers are more likely to have trouble finding (and keeping) a job in young adulthood. Young adult men and women from one-parent families tend to work at low-paying jobs.

But we cannot conclude from these differences that growing up in a single-parent family causes these unwanted outcomes. Both conditions—the number of parents in the home while growing up and problems in adulthood—could be caused by other factors. For example, poverty could cause parents to divorce and also prevent their children from attending college. Research by McLanahan and Gary Sandefur suggests that as much as half of the apparent disadvantage of growing up in a single-parent family is due to the lower incomes these families typically have.

In addition, some families have pre-existing problems, such as genetic predispositions to depression, that raise the probability that parents will divorce and the probability that their children will have mental health problems. In these cases, the divorce would not be the reason for the children's misfortunes. Several colleagues and I examined an extensive British study that followed individuals from birth to adulthood. As

> Some families have pre-existing problems, such as genetic predispositions to depression, that raise the probability that parents will divorce and the probability that their children will have mental health problems. In these cases, the divorce would not be the reason for the children's misfortunes.

expected, we found that people whose parents had been divorced had poorer mental health as adults. But by looking at records of their childhood, we found that some portion, although not all, of their difficulties could be accounted for by behavior problems and psychological distress that were visible early in their lives, before their parents had divorced. Our study and others like it suggest that being short a parent in the home is not responsible for all the ills these children show. Therefore, a policy aimed at reducing single-parent families and increasing two-parent families would most likely not eliminate such problems.

Nevertheless, family structure has something to do with the difficulties children experience. Our study and others do find some differences that could be due to divorce or birth outside of marriage. Only a minority of children in single-parent families actually experience problems later, but divorce and childbearing outside of marriage are so common that this minority still represents a large number of children. Taken together, all of these findings suggest that while the number of parents matters, it matters less than most people think; and it matters less than many other factors for how children fare.

the political debate

If the debate ended with social scientific studies and statistics, marriage promotion policies would not be so contentious. But there is a deeper level to the controversy. The politics of single parenting involve not simply disagreements about data, but about how Americans view the autonomy of women, the authority of men, and the imposition of a particular moral

> The politics of single parenting involve not simply disagreements about data, but about how Americans view the autonomy of women, the authority of men, and the imposition of a particular moral view of family life on those who choose other lifestyles.

view of family life on those who choose other lifestyles. Until the mid-twentieth century, marriage was taken for granted as the central institution of family life. Men held considerable power in marriages because of social norms and because they typically earned more money. In the stereotypical mid-twentieth-century marriage, women restricted themselves to home and family. As recently as 1977, two-thirds of those interviewed in the General Social Survey—a national sample of adults repeated every year or two—agreed that "It is much better for everyone involved if the man is the achiever outside the home and the woman takes care of the home and family." By 1998, just one-third agreed with the same statement.

Since mid-century, new options have made it possible for women to live full lives outside of marriage. New job opportunities provide independent income and welfare provides an income floor (although the recent welfare reform now limits reliance on that floor to five years). The birth control pill allows for sexual activity without unwanted pregnancies, and the greater acceptability of raising a child outside of marriage allows single women to have children if they want. At the same time, the economic fortunes of men without college educations have diminished, reducing the attractiveness of marriage for many women. All told, alternative paths to parenthood other than long-term marriage are more feasible and more attractive.

Feminists fought for these gains in women's autonomy, and many of them see the pro-marriage movement as an attempt to reassert men's control over women's lives. Being a single parent may not be easy, but it is a more viable alternative than it used to be and many feminists defend women's freedom to follow this path. Other liberals argue that gay and lesbian parents, whether single or partnered, should receive the same acceptance and support as heterosexual parents. These diversity defenders argue for public policies that would provide more income support, child care options, and flexible work arrangements for single-parent families to minimize any remaining disadvantages of these nonmarital choices.

But it can be difficult to disentangle the political debate from the statistical debate. Often the political debate constitutes the unspoken subtext of a seemingly statistical argument. In an influential 1972 book, *The Future of Marriage*, Jessie Bernard argued that men get most of the rewards in marriage because women do most of the work in the home while being denied (at least in the 1950s and 1960s) the opportunity to work outside the home. Bernard claimed, for example, that married women are more depressed than single women, whereas married men are less depressed than single men. The subtext is that marriage, at least in its current form, oppresses women, and that policies that promote marriage should be resisted by feminists. More recently, Linda J. Waite and journalist Maggie Gallagher argued in their book, *The Case for Marriage: Why Married People Are Happier, Healthier, and Better Off Financially*, that marriage is just as beneficial for women as it is for men. The subtext here is that because marriage is not an oppressive institution, opposition to pro-marriage policies is misguided. Although Waite and Gallagher persuasively demonstrate that marriage is not all bad for women, their attempt to show that it benefits women as much as men is less convincing.

Marriage, it would seem, is valued as long as it is consistent with the expressive individualism that Americans hold most dear. That is why pro-marriage policies that seem to interfere with individual decisions and self-expression are not broadly popular.

marriage and morality

In some writing on marriage, the political and moral claims are in plain view. Consider *The Marriage Problem: How Our Culture Has Weakened Families*, a recent book by political scientist James Q. Wilson. He endorses an evolutionary model in which men are by nature promiscuous and women are by nature more interested in raising children. Marriage, he argues, is the cultural invention that restrains men and provides mothers and children with support and protection. Wilson concludes that more women need to emphasize marriage over career, even though this may limit their autonomy. He offers sympathy, but little more, for the difficulty of this choice. Postponing marriage, Wilson writes, is risky: "Older women lose out in the marriage race much faster than do men. It may be unfair, but that is the way the world works" (p. 12). Women's lot in life, the book implies, is to make the selfless choice to marry for the good of their children.

Even if one agreed with Wilson's view of the need for marriage, his exhortations are increasingly out of step with Americans' moral views. Although most Americans still value marriage, they hesitate to impose their preferences on others. Rather, the American philosophy, Alan Wolfe argues, is "moral freedom": Each person should be free to decide what is a good and virtuous life. Each is free, in other words, to choose his or her own morality. For example, Americans view divorce as a serious and unwelcome step. But they tend to believe that each person should be allowed to decide when a marriage no longer works. As Grace Floro, a Dayton housewife and one of Wolfe's interview subjects said: "How loyal can you be if somebody's wronged you? When is loyalty appropriate and when isn't it? You can be loyal to a fault just like you can be honest to a fault. That's what makes life so difficult. Nothing is black and white and every circumstance merits its own judgment" (p. 55).

Americans' view of marriage was also apparent in a 1999 *New York Times* national survey. Respondents were presented with a list of values and asked how important each was to them. After the replies were tallied, the values were ranked by the percentage of people who said each was "very important." The top-ranking values largely reflected self-reliance ("Being responsible for your own actions," "Being able to stand up for yourself") and self-expression ("Being able to communicate your feelings"). "Having children" came in sixth. "Being married" ranked tenth—below "Being a good neighbor." Marriage, it would seem, is valued as long as it is consistent with the expressive individualism that Americans hold most dear. That is why pro-marriage policies that seem to interfere with individual decisions and self-expression are not broadly popular.

but do they work?

In addition, the effectiveness of pro-marriage policies is an open question. The best case for such programs has been made by Theodora Ooms of the Center for Law and Social Policy, who advocates support for "healthy marriages" (those that are relatively conflict-free and provide good parenting to their children), but not to the exclusion of helping single parents. Ooms argues for programs that provide young adults

who wish to marry with "soft services" such as communication and conflict resolution skills, along with more traditionally liberal programs such as greater income support for the working poor. But soft-service interventions such as teaching relationship skills are based on programs developed for middleclass couples; whether they can be adapted to help the poor and near-poor has yet to be determined. Before trying to institute them nationwide, some small-scale pilot projects ought to be attempted.

Even the Bush administration acknowledges that not all marriages are equally good for children. Its officials state that they, too, are only interested in promoting healthy marriages . . . The problem is that it is hard to support healthy marriages without concurrently supporting unhealthy marriages.

It is also questionable whether all unmarried mothers should be encouraged to marry. Consider a study several collaborators and I conducted with more than 2,000 low-income children and their mothers in Boston, Chicago and San Antonio. We followed the families over a one-and-a-half-year period and found that more of the mothers were married by the end than had been at the beginning. But very few of the new wives' marriages involved the fathers of their children. Unfortunately, the research literature shows that children in stepfamilies fare no better than children in single-parent families. The addition of a stepfather to the household usually brings an increase in income, but it also complicates the family situation. The role of the stepfather is often unclear, and teenagers may reject his presence as they cope with the typical issues of adolescence. Moreover, the marriages of the mothers in our sample broke up at a faster rate than the already high national rates would predict, thus exposing their children to much family change—a father moved out, for example, or a stepfather moved in. Studies suggest that experiencing several such family changes may in itself harm children's well-being. We concluded that encouraging poor, single mothers to marry may not benefit as many children as pro-marriage boosters would think.

Even the Bush administration acknowledges that not all marriages are equally good for children. Its officials state that they, too, are only interested in promoting healthy marriages, although that phrase is never defined. The problem is that it is hard to support healthy marriages without concurrently supporting unhealthy marriages. Consider West Virginia, which now gives women who are receiving welfare a bonus of $100 per month if they marry. There may be good reasons why some mothers have not married the fathers of their children (e.g., violence, drug addiction), but they may be tempted to do so by the promise of an additional $100 per month. It is not clear that, on balance, children benefit from the marriages this policy encourages.

symbols and practices

Despite the attention paid to social science research, the debate over marriage promotion is, at heart, a debate over symbolism more than statistics. Should our government state symbolically that marriage is preferred over other family forms, as the marriage movement urges, or should it make the symbolic statement that individuals should be free to choose any form, as the diversity defenders desire? The marriage-promotion provision in the welfare reauthorization bill may be more important as a statement of how our government thinks family life should be lived than as a source of funds for particular programs. Such statements may influence the way people view marriage and family life, even if they never participate in a federally funded marriage enrichment course. Interested groups are fighting hard to have their symbolic perspective prevail. The likely inclusion of marriage-promotion funds signals the renewed strength

of the pro-marriage view; their rejection would have signaled the continued strength of the family pluralists.

But symbolism does not justify major new legislation. A new initiative should have the promise of efficiently meeting its goals, and the proposed marriage promotion policy fails this test. If low-income single mothers are urged to marry, the kinds of families that would be formed often would not match the healthy, two-biological parent, steady-breadwinner model that policymakers envision. Effective programs for promoting marriage among the poor do not yet exist. Even if they could be developed, fewer children would benefit from them than their supporters suggest. And if overdone, they could hurt some of the children they intend to help.

RECOMMENDED RESOURCES

Jesse Bernard. *The Future of Marriage* (Bantam, 1972).

> An influential book that argues marriage is good for men but bad for women.

Andrew J. Cherlin, P. Lindsay Chase-Lansdale, and Christine McRae. "Effects of Parental Divorce on Mental Health throughout the Life Course." *American Sociological Review* 63 (1998): 239–49.

> Suggests some of the apparent effects of parental divorce on mental health were visible before the parents divorced.

Andrew J. Cherlin and Paula Fomby. "A Closer Look at Children's Living Arrangements in Low-Income Families." Policy Brief 02-03, Welfare, Children, and Families Study, 2002. Online. http://www.jhu.edu/~welfare/19837BriefLivingArrang.pdf.

> A report on changes in family structure among a sample of low-income, urban families. It finds an increase in families composed of a mother, her children, and a man other than the father of the children.

Theodora Ooms. "Marriage and Government: Strange Bedfellows?" 2002. Washington D.C.: Center for Law and Social Policy. Online. http://www.clasp.org/DMS/Documents/1028563059.86/MarriageBrief1.pdf.

A policy brief that argues for marriage promotion programs from a liberal perspective.

Linda J. Waite and Maggie Gallagher. *The Case for Marriage: Why Married People are Happier, Healthier, and Better Off Financially* (Doubleday, 2000).

Waite and Gallagher argue that marriage benefits both women and men equally.

James Q. Wilson. *The Marriage Problem: How Our Culture Has Weakened Families* (HarperCollins, 2002).

Contends that the decline in marriage has been detrimental to society and suggests that women should place a higher priority on marriage and child-rearing.

Alan Wolfe. *Moral Freedom: The Search for Virtue in a World of Choice* (W. W. Norton, 2001).

Maintains that the American philosophy is "moral freedom," in which each person is free to decide what is a good and virtuous life.

REVIEW QUESTIONS

1. Compare the positions of the "marriage movement" and the "diversity defenders." Which do you find more compelling?
2. According to this essay, why can you *not* make the following assumption: As compared to a child who is raised by both biological parents, being raised in a single-parent home increases the chances of that child dropping out of college and decreases the chances of enrollment?
3. The debate surrounding marriage is a difficult one, with multiple dynamics at play. Do you think the same factors that affect marriage between heterosexuals affect gay marriages? Discuss those issues, and consider how they might differ.

kathryn edin and maria kefalas

unmarried with children

spring 2005

10

have poor, unmarried mothers given up on marriage, as middle-class observers often conclude? to the contrary, most of the time they are simply waiting for the right partner and situation to make it work.

Jen Burke, a white tenth-grade dropout who is 17 years old, lives with her stepmother, her sister, and her 16-month-old son in a cramped but tidy row home in Philadelphia's beleaguered Kensington neighborhood. She is broke, on welfare, and struggling to complete her GED. Wouldn't she and her son have been better off if she had finished high school, found a job, and married her son's father first?

In 1950, when Jen's grandmother came of age, only 1 in 20 American children was born to an unmarried mother. Today, that rate is 1 in 3—and they are usually born to those least likely to be able to support a child on their own. In our book, *Promises I Can Keep: Why Poor Women Put Motherhood Before Marriage*, we discuss the lives of 162 white, African-American, and Puerto Rican low-income single mothers living in eight destitute neighborhoods across Philadelphia and its poorest industrial suburb, Camden. We spent five years chatting over kitchen tables and on front stoops, giving mothers like Jen the opportunity to speak to the question so many affluent Americans ask about them: Why do they have children while still young and unmarried when they will face such an uphill struggle to support them?

romance at lightning speed

Jen started having sex with her 20-year-old boyfriend Rick just before her 15th birthday. A month and a half later, she was pregnant. "I didn't want to get pregnant," she claims. *"He wanted me to get pregnant."* "As soon as he met me, he wanted to have a kid with me," she explains. Though Jen's college-bound suburban peers would be appalled by such a declaration, on the streets of Jen's neighborhood, it is something of a badge of honor. "All those other girls he was with, he didn't want to have a baby with any of them," Jen boasts. "I asked him, 'Why did you choose me to have a kid when you could have a kid with any one of them?' He was like, 'I want to have a kid with *you*.'" Looking back, Jen says she now believes that the reason "he wanted me to have a kid that early is so that I didn't leave him."

In inner-city neighborhoods like Kensington, where child-bearing within marriage has become rare, romantic relationships like Jen and Rick's proceed at lightning speed. A young man's avowal, "I want to have a baby by you," is often part of the courtship ritual from the beginning. This is more than idle talk, as their first child is typically conceived within a year from the time a couple begins "kicking it." Yet while poor couples' pillow talk often revolves around dreams of shared children, the news of a pregnancy—the first indelible sign of the huge changes to come—puts these still-new relationships into overdrive. Suddenly, the would-be mother begins to scrutinize her mate as never before, wondering whether he can "get himself together"—find a job, settle down, and become a family man—in time. Jen began pestering Rick to get a real job instead of picking up day-labor jobs at nearby construction sites. She also wanted him to stop hanging out with his ne'er-do-well friends, who had been getting him into serious trouble for more than a decade. Most of all, she wanted Rick to shed what she calls his "kiddie mentality"—his habit of spending money on alcohol and drugs rather than recognizing his growing financial obligations at home.

Rick did not try to deny paternity, as many would-be fathers do. Nor did he abandon or mistreat Jen, at least intentionally. But Rick, who had been in and out of juvenile detention since he was eight years old for everything from stealing cars to selling drugs, proved unable to stay away from his unsavory friends. At the beginning of her seventh month of pregnancy, an escapade that began as a drunken lark landed Rick in jail on a carjacking charge. Jen moved back home with her stepmother, applied for welfare, and spent the last two-and-a-half months of her pregnancy without Rick.

Rick sent penitent letters from jail. "I thought he changed by the letters he wrote me. I thought he changed a lot," she says. "He used to tell me that he loved me when he was in jail. . . . It was always gonna be me and him and the baby when he got out." Thus, when Rick's alleged victim failed to appear to testify and he was released just days before Colin's birth, the couple's reunion was a happy one. Often, the magic moment of childbirth calms the troubled waters of such relationships. New parents typically make amends and resolve to stay together for the sake of their child. When surveyed just after a child's birth, eight in ten unmarried parents say they are still together, and most plan to stay together and raise the child.

Promoting marriage among the poor has become the new war on poverty, Bush style. And it is true that the correlation between marital status and child poverty is strong. But poor single mothers already believe in marriage. Jen insists that she will walk down the aisle one day, though she admits it might not be with Rick. And demographers still project that more than seven in ten women who had a child outside of marriage will eventually wed someone. First, though, Jen wants to get a good job, finish school, and get her son out of Kensington.

> . . . more than seven in ten women who had a child outside of marriage will eventually wed someone.

Most poor, unmarried mothers and fathers readily admit that bearing children while poor and unmarried is not the ideal way to do things. Jen believes the best time to become a mother is "after you're out of school and you got a job, at least, when you're like 21. . . . When you're ready to have kids, you should have everything ready, have your house, have a job, so when that baby comes, the baby can have its own room." Yet given their already limited economic prospects, the poor have little motivation to time their births as precisely as their middleclass counterparts do. The dreams of young people like Jen and Rick center on children at a time of life when their more affluent peers plan for college and careers. Poor girls coming of age in the inner city value children highly, anticipate them eagerly, and believe strongly that they are up to the job of mothering—even in difficult circumstances. Jen, for example, tells us, "People outside the neighborhood, they're like, 'You're 15! You're pregnant?' I'm like, it's not none of their business. I'm gonna be able to take care of my kid. They have nothing to worry about." Jen says she has concluded that "some people . . . are better at having kids at a younger age. . . . I think it's better for some people to have kids younger."

when i became a mom

When we asked mothers like Jen what their lives would be like if they had not had children, we expected them to express regret over foregone opportunities for school and careers. Instead, most believe their children "saved" them. They describe their lives as spinning out of control before becoming pregnant—struggles with parents and peers, "wild," risky behavior, depression, and school failure. Jen speaks to this poignantly. "I was just real bad. I hung with a real bad crowd. I was doing pills. I was really depressed. . . . I was drinking. That was before I was pregnant." "I think," she reflects, "if I never had a baby or anything, . . . I would still be doing the things I was doing. I would probably still be doing drugs. I'd probably still be drinking." Jen admits that when she first became pregnant, she was angry that she "couldn't be out no more. Couldn't be out with my friends. Couldn't do nothing." Now, though, she says, "I'm glad I have a son . . . because I would still be doing all that stuff."

Children offer poor youth like Jen a compelling sense of purpose. Jen paints a before-and-after picture of her life that was common among the mothers we interviewed. "Before, I didn't have nobody to take care of. I didn't have nothing left to go home for. . . . Now I have my son to take care of. I have him to go home for. . . . I don't have to go buy weed or drugs with my money. I could buy my son stuff with my money! . . . I have something to look up to now." Children also are a crucial source of relational intimacy, a self-made community of care. After a nasty fight with Rick, Jen recalls, "I was crying. My son came in the room. He was hugging me. He's 16 months and he was hugging me with his little arms. He was really cute and happy, so I got happy. That's one of the good things. When you're sad, the baby's always gonna be there for you no matter what." Lately she has been thinking a lot about what her life was like back then, before the baby. "I thought about the stuff before I became a mom, what my life was like back then. I used to see pictures of me, and I would hide in every picture. This baby did so much for me. My son did a lot for me. He helped me a lot. I'm thankful that I had my baby."

Around the time of the birth, most unmarried parents claim they plan to get married eventually. Rick did not propose marriage when Jen's first child was born, but when she conceived a second time, at 17, Rick informed his dad, "It's time for me to get married. It's time for me to straighten up. This is the one I wanna be with. I had a baby with her, I'm gonna have another baby with her." Yet despite their intentions, few of these couples actually marry. Indeed, most break up well before their child enters preschool.

i'd like to get married, but . . .

The sharp decline in marriage in impoverished urban areas has led some to charge that the poor have abandoned the marriage norm. Yet we found few who had given up on the idea of marriage. But like their elite counterparts, disadvantaged women set a high financial bar for marriage. For the poor, marriage has become an elusive goal—one they feel ought to be reserved for those who can support a "white picket fence" lifestyle: a mortgage on a modest row home, a car and some furniture, some savings in the bank, and enough money left over to pay for a "decent" wedding. Jen's views on marriage provide a perfect case in point. "If I was gonna get married, I would want to be married like my Aunt Nancy and my Uncle Pat. They live in the mountains. She has a job. My Uncle Pat is a state trooper; he has lots of money. They live in the [Poconos]. It's real nice out there. Her kids go to Catholic school. . . .

That's the kind of life I would want to have. If I get married, I would have a life like [theirs]." She adds, "And I would wanna have a big wedding, a real nice wedding."

Unlike the women of their mothers' and grandmothers' generations, young women like Jen are not merely content to rely on a man's earnings. Instead, they insist on being economically "set" in their own right before taking marriage vows. This is partly because they want a partnership of equals, and they believe money buys say-so in a relationship. Jen explains, "I'm not gonna just get into marrying him and not have my own house! Not have a job! I still wanna do a lot of things before I get married. He [already] tells me I can't do nothing. I can't go out. What's gonna happen when I marry him? He's gonna say he owns me!"

Economic independence is also insurance against a marriage gone bad. Jen explains, "I want to have everything ready, in case something goes wrong. . . . If we got a divorce, that would be my house. I bought that house, he can't kick me out or he can't take my kids from me." "That's what I want in case that ever happens. I know a lot of people that happened to. I don't want it to happen to me." These statements reveal that despite her desire to marry, Rick's role in the family's future is provisional at best. "We get along, but we fight a lot. If he's there, he's there, but if he's not, that's why I want a job . . . a job with computers . . . so I could afford my kids, could afford the house. . . . I don't want to be living off him. I want my kids to be living off me."

Why is Jen, who describes Rick as "the love of my life," so insistent on planning an exit strategy before she is willing to take the vows she firmly believes ought to last "forever?" If love is so sure, why does mistrust seem so pal-pable and strong? In relationships among poor couples like Jen and Rick, mistrust is often spawned by chronic violence and infidelity, drug and alcohol abuse, criminal activity, and the threat of imprisonment. In these tarnished corners of urban America, the stigma of a failed marriage is far worse than an out-of-wedlock birth. New mothers like Jen feel they must test the relationship over three, four, even five years' time. This is the only way, they believe, to insure that their marriages will last.

Trust has been an enormous issue in Jen's relationship with Rick. "My son was born December 23rd, and [Rick] started cheating on me again . . . in March. He started cheating on me with some girl—Amanda. . . . Then it was another girl, another girl, another girl after. I didn't wanna believe it. My friends would come up to me and be like, 'Oh yeah, your boyfriend's cheating on you with this person.' I wouldn't believe it. . . . I would see him with them. He used to have hickies. He used to make up some excuse that he was drunk—that was always his excuse for everything." Things finally came to a head when Rick got another girl pregnant. "For a while, I forgave him for everything. Now, I don't forgive him for nothing." Now we begin to understand the source of Jen's hesitancy. "He wants me to marry him, [but] I'm not really sure. . . . If I can't trust him, I can't marry him, 'cause we would get a divorce. If you're gonna get married, you're supposed to be faithful!" she insists. To Jen and her peers, the worst thing that could happen is "to get married just to get divorced."

Given the economic challenges and often perilously low quality of the romantic relationships among unmarried parents, poor women may be right to be cautious about marriage. Five years after we first spoke with her, we met with Jen

> . . . children, far from being liabilities, provide crucial social-psychological resources—a strong sense of purpose and a profound source of intimacy.

again. We learned that Jen's second pregnancy ended in a miscarriage. We also learned that Rick was out of the picture—apparently for good. "You know that bar [down the street?] It happened in that bar. . . . They were in the bar, and this guy was like badmouthing [Rick's friend] Mikey, talking stuff to him or whatever. So Rick had to go get involved in it and start with this guy. . . . Then he goes outside and fights the guy [and] the guy dies of head trauma. They were all on drugs, they were all drinking, and things just got out of control, and that's what happened. He got fourteen to thirty years."

these are cards i dealt myself

Jen stuck with Rick for the first two and a half years of his prison sentence, but when another girl's name replaced her own on the visitors' list, Jen decided she was finished with him once and for all. Readers might be asking what Jen ever saw in a man like Rick. But Jen and Rick operate in a partner market where the better-off men go to the better-off women. The only way for someone like Jen to forge a satisfying relationship with a man is to find a diamond in the rough or improve her own economic position so that she can realistically compete for more upwardly mobile partners, which is what Jen is trying to do now. "There's this kid, Donny, he works at my job. He works on C shift. He's supervisor! He's funny, three years older, and he's not a geek or anything, but he's not a real preppy good boy either. But he's not [a player like Rick] and them. He has a job, you know, so that's good. He doesn't do drugs or anything. And he asked my dad if he could take me out!"

These days, there is a new air of determination, even pride, about Jen. The aimless high school dropout pulls ten-hour shifts entering data at a warehouse distribution center Monday through Thursday. She has held the job for three years, and her aptitude and hard work have earned her a series of raises. Her current salary is higher than anyone in her household commands—$10.25 per hour, and she now gets two weeks of paid vacation, four personal days, 60 hours of sick time, and medical benefits. She has saved up the necessary $400 in tuition for a high school completion program that offers evening and weekend classes. Now all that stands between her and a diploma is a passing grade in mathematics, her least favorite subject. "My plan is to start college in January. [This month] I take my math test . . . so I can get my diploma," she confides.

Jen clearly sees how her life has improved since Rick's dramatic exit from the scene. "That's when I really started [to get better] because I didn't have to worry about what *he* was doing, didn't have to worry about him cheating on me, all this stuff. [It was] then I realized that I had to do what I had to do to take care of my son. . . . When he was there, I think that my whole life revolved around him, you know, so I always messed up somehow because I was so busy worrying about what *he* was doing. Like I would leave the [GED] programs I was in just to go home and see what he was doing. My mind was never concentrating." Now, she says, "a lot of people in my family look up to me now, because all my sisters dropped out from school, you know, nobody went back to school. I went back to school, you know? . . . I went back to school, and I plan to go to college, and a lot of people look up to me for that, you know? So that makes me happy . . . because five years ago nobody looked up to me. I was just like everybody else."

Yet the journey has not been easy. "Being a young mom, being 15, it's hard, hard, hard, you know." She says, "I have no life. . . . I work from 6:30 in the morning until 5:00 at night. I leave here at 5:30 in the morning. I don't get home until about 6:00 at night." Yet she measures her worth as a mother by the fact that she has managed to provide for her son largely on her own. "I don't depend on nobody. I might live with my dad and them, but I don't depend on them, you know." She continues, "There [used to] be days when I'd be so stressed out, like, 'I can't do this!' And I would just cry and cry and cry. . . . Then I look at Colin, and he'll be sleeping, and I'll just look at him and think I don't have no [reason to feel sorry for myself]. The cards I have I've dealt myself so I have to deal with it now. I'm older. I can't change anything. He's my responsibility—he's nobody else's but mine—so I have to deal with that."

Becoming a mother transformed Jen's point of view on just about everything. She says, "I thought hanging on the corner drinking, getting high—I thought that was a good life, and I thought I could live that way for eternity, like sitting out with my friends. But it's not as fun once you have your own kid. . . . I think it changes [you]. I think, 'Would I want Colin to do that? Would I want my son to be like that . . . ?' It was fun to me but it's not fun anymore. Half the people I hung with are either . . . Some have died from drug overdoses, some are in jail, and some people are just out there living the same life that they always lived, and they don't look really good. They look really bad." In the end, Jen believes, Colin's birth has brought far more good into her life than bad. "I know I could have waited [to have a child], but in a way I think Colin's the best thing that could have happened to me. . . . So I think I had my son for a purpose because I think Colin changed my life. He saved my life, really. My whole life revolves around Colin!"

> Given the economic challenges and often perilously low quality of the romantic relationships among unmarried parents poor women may be right to be cautious about marriage.

promises i can keep

There are unique themes in Jen's story—most fathers are only one or two, not five years older than the mothers of their children, and few fathers have as many glaring problems as Rick—but we heard most of these themes repeatedly in the stories of the 161 other poor, single mothers we came to know. Notably, poor women do not reject marriage; they revere it. Indeed, it is the conviction that marriage is forever that makes them think that divorce is worse than having a baby outside of marriage. Their children, far from being liabilities, provide crucial social-psychological resources—a strong sense of purpose and a profound source of intimacy. Jen and the other mothers we came to know are coming of age in an America that is profoundly unequal—where the gap between rich and poor continues to grow. This economic reality has convinced them that they have little to lose and, perhaps, something to gain by a seemingly "ill-timed" birth.

The lesson one draws from stories like Jen's is quite simple: Until poor young women have more access to jobs that lead to financial independence—until there is reason to hope for the rewarding life pathways that their privileged peers pursue—the poor will continue to have children far sooner than most Americans think they should, while still deferring marriage. Marital standards have risen for all Americans, and the poor want the same things that everyone now wants out of marriage. The poor want to marry too, but they insist on marrying well. This, in their view, is the only way to avoid an almost certain divorce. Like Jen, they are simply not willing to make promises they are not sure they can keep.

RECOMMENDED RESOURCES

Kathryn Edin and Maria Kefalas. *Promises I Can Keep: Why Poor Women Put Motherhood Before Marriage* (University of California Press, 2005).

How low-income women make sense of their choices about marriage and motherhood.

Christina Gibson, Kathryn Edin, and Sara McLanahan. "High Hopes but Even Higher Expectations: A Qualitative and Quantitative Analysis of the Marriage Plans of Unmarried Couples Who Are New Parents." Working Paper 03-06-FF, Center for Research on Child Wellbeing, Princeton University, 2004. Online at http://crcw.princeton.edu/workingpapers/WP03-06-FF-Gibson.pdf.

The authors examine the rising expectations for marriage among unmarried parents.

Sharon Hays. *Flat Broke with Children: Women in the Age of Welfare Reform* (Oxford University Press, 2003).

How welfare reform has affected the lives of poor moms.

Annette Lareau. *Unequal Childhoods: Class, Race, and Family Life* (University of California Press, 2003).

A fascinating discussion of different childrearing strategies among low-income, working-class, and middle-class parents.

Timothy J. Nelson, Susan Clampet-Lundquist, and Kathryn Edin. "Fragile Fatherhood: How Low-Income, Non-Custodial Fathers in Philadelphia Talk About Their Families." In *The Handbook of Father Involvement: Multidisciplinary Perspectives*, eds. Catherine Tamis-LeMonda and Natasha Cabrera (Lawrence Earlbaum Associates, 2002).

What poor, single men think about fatherhood.

REVIEW QUESTIONS

1. What does *family* mean? Discuss the prevailing myths surrounding this term, and whether or not we commonly use an adequate definition. Then, discuss how social scientists make a distinction between *family* and *household*.
2. Edin and Kefalas reject the notion that impoverished mothers have "abandoned the marriage norm." Why? Can you identify the factors that hamstring these mothers as compared to their richer counterparts?
3. The authors use the story of Jen as a window through which we can see the broader issues that confront the other 161 poor mothers in their study. What do you think are the advantages and disadvantages of this form of representing research?
4. This essay does not mention the increase in cohabitation in American society. Can you think of how this might challenge some of the authors' findings? Why or why not?

zhenchao qian

breaking the last taboo: interracial marriage in america

11

fall 2005

interracial marriages are becoming more common, but skin color still matters in america. as minorities—especially asian and hispanic americans—move up the ladder and integrate neighborhoods, they increasingly marry whites. still, strong racial identities and lingering prejudice, particularly toward african americans, limit this most intimate form of integration.

Guess Who's Coming to Dinner, a movie about a white couple's reaction when their daughter falls in love with a black man, caused a public stir in 1967. That the African-American character was a successful doctor did little to lower the anxieties of white audiences. Now, almost four decades later, the public hardly reacts at all to interracial relationships. Both Hollywood movies and TV shows, including Die Another Day, Made in America, ER, The West Wing, and Friends, regularly portray interracial romance.

What has changed? In the same year that Sidney Poitier startled Spencer Tracy and Katherine Hepburn, the Supreme Court ruled, in Loving v. Virginia, that laws forbidding people of different races to marry were unconstitutional. The civil rights movement helped remove other blatant legal barriers to the integration of racial minorities and fostered the growth of minority middle classes. As racial minorities advanced, public opinion against interracial marriage declined, and rates of interracial marriage grew rapidly.

Between 1970 and 2000, black-white marriages grew more than fivefold from 65 to 363 thousand, and marriages between whites and members of other races grew almost fivefold

from 233 thousand to 1.1 million. Proportionately, interracial marriages remain rare, but their rates increased from less than 1 percent of all marriages in 1970 to nearly 3 percent in 2000. This trend shows that the "social distance" between racial groups has narrowed significantly, although not nearly as much as the social distance between religious groups. Interfaith marriages have become common in recent generations. That marriages across racial boundaries remain much rarer than cross-religion marriages reflects the greater prominence of race in America. While the interracial marriage taboo seems to be gradually breaking down, at least for certain groups, intermarriage in the United States will not soon match the level of intermarriage that European immigrant groups have achieved over the past century.

public attitudes

Americans have become generally more accepting of other races in recent decades, probably as a result of receiving more education and meeting more people of other races. Americans increasingly work and go to school with people from many groups. As racial gaps in income narrow, more members of racial minorities can afford to live in neighborhoods that had previously been white. Neighbors have opportunities to reduce stereotypes and establish friendships. Tolerance also grows as generations pass; elderly people with racist attitudes die and are replaced by younger, more tolerant people. The general softening of racial antagonisms has also improved attitudes toward interracial marriage.

In 1958, a national survey asked Americans for the first time about their opinions of interracial marriage. Only 4 percent of whites approved of intermarriage with blacks. Almost 40 years later, in 1997, 67 percent of whites approved of such intermarriages. Blacks have been much more accepting; by 1997, 83 percent approved of intermarriage. Whites' support for interracial marriage—which may to some extent only reflect respondents' sense of what they should tell interviewers—lags far behind their support of interracial schools (96 percent), housing (86 percent), and jobs (97 percent). Many white Americans apparently remain uneasy about interracial intimacy generally, and most disapprove of interracial relationships in their own families. Still, such relationships are on the increase.

interracial dating

According to a recent survey reported by George Yancey, more than one-half of African-, Hispanic-, and Asian-American adults have dated someone from a different racial group, and even more of those who have lived in integrated neighborhoods or attended integrated schools have done so. Most dates, of course, are casual and do not lead to serious commitments, and this is especially true for interracial dating. Analyzing data from the National Longitudinal Study of Adolescent Health, Kara Joyner and Grace Kao find that 71 percent of white adolescents with white boyfriends or girlfriends have introduced them to their families, but only 57 percent of those with nonwhite friends have done so. Similarly, 63 percent of black adolescents with black boyfriends or girlfriends have introduced them to their families, but only 52 percent of those with nonblack friends have done so. Data from another national survey show similar patterns for young adults aged 18 to 29 (61 percent versus 51 percent introducing for whites, and 70 percent versus 47 percent for blacks).

> White wives get more than their "share" of well-educated black husbands.

While resistance to interracial relationships in principle has generally declined, opposition remains high among the families of those so involved. Interracial couples express concern about potential crises when their families become aware of such relationships. Their parents, especially white parents, worry about what those outside the family might think and fear that their reputations in the community will suffer. Maria Root notes that parents actively discourage interracial romance, often pointing to other peoples' prejudice—not their own—and expressing concern for their child's well being: "Marriage is hard enough; why make it more difficult?"

The dating and the parental reservations reveal a generation gap: Young men and women today are more open to interracial relationships than their parents are. This gap may be due simply to youthful experimentation; youngsters tend to push boundaries. As people age, they gradually learn to conform. Kara Joyner and Grace Kao find that interracial dating is most common among teenagers but becomes infrequent for people approaching 30. They attribute this shift to the increasing importance of family and friends—and their possible disapproval—as we age. When people are ready to be "serious," they tend to fall in love with people who are just like themselves.

interracial cohabitation and marriage

Who pairs up with whom depends partly on the size of the different racial groups in the United States. The larger the group, the more likely members are to find marriageable partners of their own race. The U.S. Census Bureau classifies race into four major categories: whites, African Americans, Asian Americans and American Indians. Hispanics can belong to any of the four racial groups. (On racial classification, see Jennifer Lee and Frank D. Bean, "Beyond Black and White: Remaking Race in America," *Contexts*, Summer 2003.) Whites form the largest group, about 70 percent of the population, and just 4 percent of married whites aged 20 to 34 in 2000 had nonwhite spouses. The interracial marriage rates are much higher for American-born racial minorities: 9 percent for African Americans, about 39 percent for Hispanics, 56 percent for American Indians, and 59 percent for Asian Americans (who account for less than 4 percent of the total population). Mathematically, one marriage between an Asian American and a white raises the intermarriage rate for Asian Americans much more than for whites, because whites are so much more numerous. Because of their numbers as well, although just 4 percent of whites are involved in interracial marriages, 92 percent of all interracial marriages include a white partner. About half of the

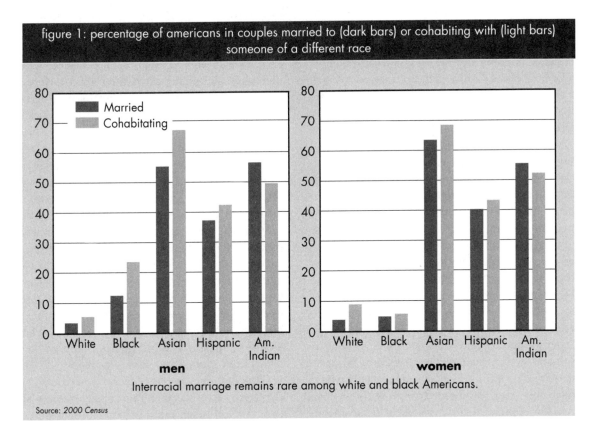

figure 1: percentage of americans in couples married to (dark bars) or cohabiting with (light bars) someone of a different race

Interracial marriage remains rare among white and black Americans.

Source: 2000 Census

remaining 8 percent are black-Hispanic couples. Racial minorities have more opportunities to meet whites in schools, workplaces, and neighborhoods than to meet members of other minority groups.

Some interracial couples contemplating marriage avoid family complications by just living together. In 2000, 4 percent of married white women had nonwhite husbands, but 9 percent of white women who were cohabiting had nonwhite partners [see Figure 1]. Similarly, 13 percent of married black men had nonblack spouses, but 24 percent of cohabiting black men lived with nonblack partners. Hispanics and Asian Americans showed the same tendency; only American Indians showed the opposite pattern. Black-white combinations are particularly notable. Black-white pairings accounted for 26 percent of all cohabiting couples but only 14 percent of all interracial marriages. They are more likely to cohabit than other minority-white couples, but they are also less likely to marry. The long history of the ban on interracial marriage in the United States, especially black-white marriage, apparently still affects black-white relationships today.

Given differences in population size, comparing rates of intermarriage across groups can be difficult. Nevertheless, statistical models used by social scientists can account for group size, determine whether members of any group are marrying out more or less often than one would expect given their numbers, and then discover what else affects intermarriage. Results show that the lighter the skin color, the higher the rate of intermarriage with white Americans. Hispanics who label themselves as racially "white" are most likely to marry non-Hispanic whites. Asian Americans and American Indians are next in their levels of marriage with whites. Hispanics who do not consider themselves racially white have low rates of intermarriage with whites. African Americans are least likely of all racial minorities to marry whites. Darker skin in America is associated with discrimination, lower educational attainment, lower income, and segregation. Even among African Americans, those of lighter tone tend to experience less discrimination.

race and education

Most married couples have similar levels of education, which typically indicates that they are also somewhat similar in social position, background, and values. Most interracial couples also have relatively equal educational attainments. However, when interracial couples do differ in their education, a hierarchy of color is apparent. The darker the skin color of racial minorities, the more likely they are to have married whites "below" them, that is, with less education than themselves. Six of ten African Americans who marry whites with different levels of education marry whites less educated than themselves. Hispanics also tend to marry whites less educated than themselves, but Asian Americans marry whites at about the same educational level.

Highly educated minority members often attend integrated colleges, and their workplaces and neighborhoods are integrated. Although they often develop a strong sense of their group identity in such environments, they also find substantial opportunities for interracial contact, friendship, romance, and marriage. College-educated men and women are more likely to marry interracially than those with less education. The fact that Asian Americans attend college at unusually high rates helps explain their high level of intermarriage with whites. The major exceptions to the interracial influence of higher education are African Americans.

Although middle-class African Americans increasingly live in integrated neighborhoods, they are still much more segregated than other minorities. Well-educated African Americans are less likely to live next to whites than are well-educated Hispanics and Asian Americans. One reason is that middle-class black Americans are so numerous that they can form their own middle-class black neighborhoods, while middle-class Hispanic and Asian-American communities are smaller and often fractured by differences in national origin and language. In addition, studies show clearly that whites resist having black neighbors much more than they resist having Hispanic or Asian American neighbors. (On residential segregation, see "Fences and Neighbors: Segregation in Twenty-First-Century America" on page 456.)

Residential and school segregation on top of a long and relentless history of racial discrimination and inequality reduce African Americans' opportunities for interracial contact and marriage. The geographic distance between blacks and whites is in many ways rooted in the historical separation between the two groups. In contrast, the distance of Hispanics and Asian Americans from whites has more to do with their current economic circumstances; as those improve, they come nearer to whites geographically, socially, and matrimonially.

a man and a woman

Black-white couples show a definite pattern: 74 percent involve a black husband and a white wife. Asian American-white couples lean the other way; 58 percent involve an Asian-American wife. Sex balances are roughly even for couples that include a white and a Hispanic (53 percent involve a Hispanic husband) or a white and an American Indian (49 percent involve Indian husbands).

I mentioned before that most black-white couples have similar educations; nonetheless, white women who marry black men "marry up" more often than those who marry white men.

This is especially striking because the pool of highly educated white men greatly outnumbers the pool of highly educated black men. More than half of black husbands of white women have at least some college education, but only two-fifths of black husbands of black women do. In that sense, white wives get more than their "share" of well-educated black husbands. This further reduces the chances that black women, especially highly educated black women, will marry, because they often face shortages of marriageable men. African-American women often resent this. Interviewed by Maria Root, one black man in such a relationship reported being accused of "selling out" and "dissing his black sisters."

Half a century ago, Robert Merton proposed a "status exchange" theory to explain the high proportion of marriages between black men and white women. He suggested that men with high economic or professional status who carry the stigma of being black in a racial caste society "trade" their social position for whiteness by marriage. On the other hand, some social scientists argue that racialized sexual images also encourage marriages between white women and black men. Throughout Europe and the West, people have long seen fair skin tone as a desirable feminine characteristic, and African Americans share those perceptions. For example, Mark Hill found that black interviewers participating in a national survey of African Americans rated black women interviewees with lighter skin as more attractive than those with darker skin. But they did not consider male interviewees with light skin any more attractive than darker-skinned men.

Asian Americans show a different pattern; in most of their marriages with whites, the husband is white. Although Asian-American men are typically more educated than white men, in the mixed couples, white husbands usually have more education than their Asian-American wives. As with white wives of black men, the wives have "married up" educationally. Some speculate that Asian-American women tend to marry white men because they perceive Asian-American men to be rigidly traditional on sex roles and white men as more nurturing and expressive. The emphasis in Asian cultures on the male line of descent may pressure Asian-American men to carry on the lineage by marrying "one of their own." But what attracts white men to Asian-American women? Some scholars suggest that it is the widespread image of Asian women as submissive and hyper-feminine (the "Madame Butterfly" icon).

the future of interracial marriage

Rates of interracial marriage in the future will respond to some conflicting forces: the weakening of barriers between groups; increasing numbers of Hispanics and Asians in the nation; and possible rising ethnic consciousness. The continued progress of racial minorities in residential integration and economic achievement promotes contact between members of different races as equals. The color line, however, probably will not disappear. Marriage between African Americans and whites is likely to remain rare. Stubborn economic differences may be part of the reason for the persistence of this barrier, but cultural experiences also play a role. In recent years, the middle-class African-American population has grown, yet the persistence of residential segregation reduces the opportunities for contact between blacks and whites. African Americans also maintain a strong racial identity compared to that of other minorities. In the 1990 census, for example, less than 25 percent of children born to a black-white couple were identified by their parents as white—a much lower percentage than for other biracial chil-dren. In the 2000 census, blacks identified themselves or their children as multiracial much less often than did other racial minorities. The stronger racial identities of African Americans, forged by persistent inequality, discrimination, and residential isolation, along with continued white resistance, will hold down the increase in marriages across the black-white divide.

Increases in the relatively high marriage rates of Hispanics and Asian Americans with whites may slow as new immigrants keep arriving from their homelands. Immigration expands the marriage pools for the native-born, who are more able to find spouses in their own racial or ethnic groups. These pools are expanded further by the way the wider society categorizes Hispanics and Asian Americans. They distinguish among themselves by national origin (Cuban versus Mexican or Thai versus Chinese), but whites tend to lump them into two large groups. Common experiences of being identified as the same, along with anti-Latino and anti-Asian prejudice and discrimination, help create a sense of pan-ethnic identity. This in turn inhibits marriage with whites, fosters solidarity within the larger group, and increases marriage rates between varieties of Hispanics and Asian Americans. Interethnic marriage is frequent among American-born Asians despite small group sizes and limited opportunities for contact. For example, in 1990, 18 percent of Chinese-Americans and 15 percent of Japanese-Americans aged 20 to 34 married spouses of other Asian ethnic groups (compared to 39 percent and 47 percent who married whites).

Many people view the increasing number of interracial marriages as a sign that racial taboos are crumbling and that the distances between racial groups in American society are shrinking. However, marriages across racial boundaries remain rarer than those that cross religious, educational, or age lines. The puzzle is whether interracial marriages will develop as marriages between people of different nationalities did among European immigrants and their descendants in the early twentieth century. Diverse in many ways when they entered the country, these twentieth-century European Americans, such as Italians, Poles, and Greeks, reached the economic level of earlier immigrants within a couple generations. Their success blurred ethnic boundaries and increased the rate of interethnic marriage. Many of their descendants now define themselves simply as white despite their diverse national origins. For most white Americans, ethnic identities have become largely symbolic.

Similar trends for interracial marriages are unlikely in the near future. The experiences of European Americans show the importance of equal economic achievement in dissolving barriers, so what happens economically to recent immigrants and African Americans will be important. Even then, the low levels of interracial marriage for middle-class African Americans suggest that this particular color line will persist as a barrier to marriage. And the continuing influx of Asian and Latino immigrants may reinforce those groups' barriers to intermarriage.

RECOMMENDED RESOURCES

Zhenchao Qian. "Breaking the Racial Barriers: Variations in Interracial Marriage between 1980 and 1990." *Demography* 34 (1997): 478–500.

An overview of changes in interracial marriage by sex and educational attainment for native-born whites, African Americans, Hispanics, and Asian Americans.

Zhenchao Qian and Daniel T. Lichter. "Measuring Marital Assimilation: Intermarriage among Natives and Immigrants." *Social Science Research* 30 (2001): 289–312.

A comparison of interracial marriages between natives and immigrants, showing how immigration may slow down the increases in interracial marriage.

Maria P. P. Root. *Love's Revolution: Interracial Marriage* (Temple University Press, 2001).

Presents in-depth interviews with interracial couples.

Howard Schuman, Charlotte Steeh, Lawrence Bobo, and Maria Krysan. *Racial Attitudes in America: Trends and Interpretation* (Harvard University Press, 1997).

Using national poll data since 1942, the authors paint a changing picture of racial attitudes for whites and blacks.

George Yancey. "Who Dates Interracially: An Examination of the Characteristics of Those Who Have Dated Interracially." *Journal of Comparative Family Studies* 33 (2002): 179–90.

A report on the dating practices of different racial groups.

REVIEW QUESTIONS

1. As one factor among many, in what ways does skin color affect interracial marriage?
2. Why does Qian find differences between rates of interracial dating and interracial marriage?
3. As of June 2006, there are four states wherein ethnic "minorities" are the majority of the population, and eight states that have more than 40 percent minority population. According to the U.S. Census Bureau, more than 90 percent of future U.S. population growth will be from "minority" communities, and it appears that interracial marriage rates will only increase over time. Based on Qian's essay, what sociological factors might inhibit such growth?

4. Writer Richard Rodriguez points out that, unlike other cultures that have developed terms like *mulatto, mestizo,* and *creole,* the United States has never had a diverse and positive way of explaining multiple heritages. Instead, we have recently adopted hyphenated terms such as *African-American* and *Asian-American.* What are the positive and negative consequences of such designations? Discuss the ramifications of interracial marriage for these definitions. How might they change over time?

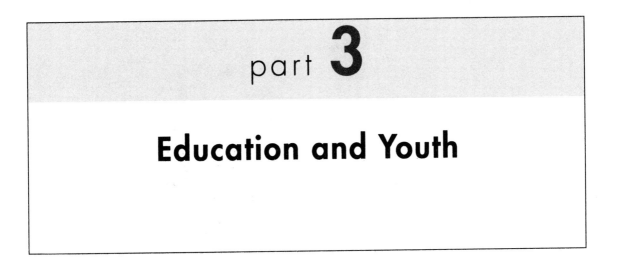

part **3**

Education and Youth

alejandro portes

english-only triumphs, but the costs are high **12**

spring 2002

the long war between english-only and bilingual education appears to have been settled, with english-only education winning. but its costs are high for immigrant families, the communities where they reside, and society as a whole.

The surge of immigration into the United States during the past 30 years has brought a proliferation of foreign languages, and with it fears that the English language may lose its predominance and cultural unity may be undermined. Several conservative national organizations, including the powerful U.S. English, have been established to combat this trend. U.S. English describes the cultural threat in somber tones:

"Where linguistic unity has broken down, our energies and resources flow into tensions, hostilities, prejudices, and resentments. These develop and persist. Within a few years, if the breakdown persists, there will be no retreat. It becomes irrevocable, irreversible. Society as we know it can fade into noisy Babel and then chaos."

What is the likelihood of such a catastrophe? Every period of high immigration has given rise to nativist movements warning of cultural disintegration, and thus calling for the immediate linguistic assimilation of foreigners. Almost a century before the emergence of the U.S. English organization, President Theodore Roosevelt wrote: "We have room for one language here and that is the English language; for we intend to see that the crucible turns our people out as Americans, and not as dwellers in a polyglot boarding house."

These fears are proving unfounded.

> Immigrant children today are rapidly embracing English over their native languages. The threat is less of a Babel-like society than of a society without cultural memory—at a cost to both immigrant children and the nation.

new "threats" to english

German, Polish, and Italian immigrants were targeted as threats to cultural unity in the past, as migrants from Mexico, Russia, and China are today. The agents vary, but the perceived threat is the same. In the past, these fears have proven unfounded. In no other country, among 35 nations compared in a detailed study by sociologist Stanley Lieberson and his colleagues, did foreign languages fade as swiftly as in the United States. Linguists such as Joshua Fishman and Calvin Veltman have documented how this process takes place. First-generation immigrants learn as much English as they can, but continue to speak their mother tongue at home. The second generation grows up speaking the mother tongue at home, but English in school and at work. By the third generation, English becomes the home language and the transition to monolingualism is completed.

Illustrative of this trend, the 1990 census found that 92 percent of the U.S. population spoke only English. The remaining 8 percent were almost exclusively first-generation immigrants undergoing the initial stages of linguistic assimilation. Immigration accelerated during the 1990s, raising the question of whether language assimilation continues to be as swift today as it was in the past. In part to address this question, Rubén G. Rumbaut and I surveyed a large sample of children of immigrants—the new second generation—attending public and private schools in Miami/Fort Lauderdale and San Diego, two of the metropolitan areas most affected by contemporary immigration. The resulting Children of Immigrants Longitudinal Study (CILS) collected data on over 5,200 students from 77 different nationalities attending eighth and ninth grades in 1992–93. We followed the sample and reinterviewed 82 percent of them three years later, when most were about to graduate from high school.

Miami is the main entry and settlement area for immigrants from Cuba, Nicaragua, Haiti, and other Caribbean and South American countries. San Diego is a primary destination for migrants from Mexico, El Salvador, the Philippines, and Southeast Asia. Despite this diversity, the patterns of language assimilation were uniform. At the time of the first survey, 94 percent of respondents spoke English fluently by the age of 14, and the figure rose to 98 percent three years later. The overwhelming majority not only knew but preferred English, with 72 percent preferring English over their native tongue in middle school and 88 percent preferring it by senior high school. Remarkably, more than 95 percent of Cuban-American children attending private bilingual schools in the heart of the Cuban enclave in Miami preferred English.

losing mother tongues

Relatively few retained their parental tongues. If one defines fluency as the ability to speak, understand, read, and write well, no second-generation group was fluent in its mother tongue by age 17. Less than one-third of the

Chinese and Italian specialty food stores in San Francisco, California. (Photo by Jon Wagner)

sample (29 percent) were able to communicate easily in both English and a foreign tongue. English-Spanish bilingualism was the most common, but most Latin-American children (65 percent) had lost fluency in their parental language. Among other nationalities, more than 90 percent of the children lacked native language fluency. Languages that literally disappeared in this second-generation sample included Chinese, French, Haitian Creole, Korean, Portuguese, Philippine Tagalog, and Vietnamese. By age 17 on the average, the majority of these youths had become exclusively English-speaking.

is complete language assimilation desirable?

These trends raise the question of whether complete language assimilation—acquisition of fluent English and abandonment of native languages—is desirable. There are good reasons for this concern.

Seventy years ago, the case for exclusive English speaking was buttressed by the scholarship of the time that considered migrant children's retention of their native language as a sign of intellectual inferiority. Madorah Smith, a prominent

Students collecting writing boards in a Spanish–English bilingual kindergarten. (Photo by Jon Wagner)

psychologist in the 1930s, declared bilingualism to be a hardship devoid of any advantage. In her view, echoed by most of her colleagues, "An important factor in the retardation of speech is the attempt to make use of two languages." The studies that supported this conclusion commonly paired poor immigrant children with middle-class native-born Americans. The studies also did not distinguish between fluent bilinguals and limited bilinguals whose command of one language or the other was poor.

bilingual students better?

This perception started to change in the 1960s, with a study of French-Canadian children conducted by psychologists Elizabeth Peal and Wallace E. Lambert. They compared a sample of monolingual 10-year-old children with a group of fluent bilinguals matched by sex, age, and family status. Contrary to the common wisdom of the time, this study found that bilinguals outperformed their monolingual counterparts in almost all cognitive tests. Similar results were subsequently obtained by other psychologists with any number of language combinations, including English-French, English-Chinese, German-French,

and English-Spanish. The association of bilingualism with better cognitive development raised the question of cause and effect. Did brighter children perform better in school and retain their parental languages better, or did bilingualism itself produce enhanced cognitive performance?

In an attempt to shed light on this relationship, psychologists Kenji Hakuta and Rafael Diaz examined Puerto Rican students in New Haven, Connecticut. They discovered that bilingualism at an early age influenced subsequent cognitive development. Linguists contributed a series of studies that sought to clarify the nature of this relationship. According to Werner Leopold, bilinguals' enhanced cognitive performance is explained by their having more than one conception for a concrete thing, thus liberating them from the "tyranny of words." For another linguist, Jim Cummins, bilinguals are able "to look at language, rather than through it, to the intended meaning."

Although all of these studies were based on small samples, sociologists working with larger samples have reinforced these findings. For example, Rumbaut and Cornelius compared fluent bilingual students with limited bilinguals of the same national origin and with English monolinguals in the entire San Diego school system in the late 1980s. Without exception, fluent bilinguals outperformed limited bilinguals and English-only students in standardized tests and grade point averages, even after statistically controlling for parental status and other variables.

greater self-esteem

More recently, our CILS study in south Florida and southern California confirmed the positive association between bilingualism and better academic performance. We also found that children who were fluent bilinguals in the early high school years had significantly higher educational aspirations and self-esteem three years later.

There are positive social aspects of bilingualism as well. Retaining the parental tongue allows children to better understand their cultural origins. This, in turn, reinforces their sense of self-worth. Bilingualism also increases communication between immigrant youths and their parents, reducing the generational conflicts commonly found in families in which parents remain foreign monolinguals and the children have shifted entirely to English. Family cohesion and open communication enable parents to better guide their children.

Family cohesion is also important for immigrant communities. Immigrant children—now numbering 13.8 million—already make up one-fifth of the American population under age 18. Their presence is even greater in those metropolitan areas where immigrants concentrate. Due to low average incomes, immigrants cluster in central city areas and their children attend neglected public schools. There they are exposed to behavior and role models that are not conducive to school achievement. Parental guidance and control are often the only counterweights to the lure of youth gangs and drugs. How many in this growing population will assimilate "downward" into the urban underclass or move upward into the middleclass mainstream largely depends on how much solidarity, guidance, and support their families can provide.

The importance of bilingualism is underlined by statistical analyses Lingxin Hao and I conducted on the CILS survey. Fluent bilinguals are more likely than English-only speakers who are similar to them in age, sex, national origin, time in the United States, and other factors to have greater solidarity and less conflict with their parents, as well as higher levels of self-esteem and ambition.

english-plus

There is a final argument for an "English-plus" approach. Economic globalization and the expansion of the immigrant population in the United States have resulted in a growing labor market for skilled bilingual workers. This demand ranges from multinational corporations to government agencies to retail outlets. As Saskia Sassen has noted, New York, and to a lesser extent other American metropolitan areas, have become "global cities" with a primary economic function of coordinating and managing financial and information flows worldwide. The pressure of linguistic assimilation results in a growing shortage of bilingual and multilingual personnel, often in the very cities experiencing accelerated immigration. As a Miami business leader recently tellingly observed, "There are 600,000 Hispanics in this area and my firm has difficulty finding a bilingual person capable of writing a proper business letter in Spanish."

The individual and family advantages of fluent bilingualism combine with the growing requirements of the American labor market to make it preferable to either form of monolingualism. The question is whether school programs can be put in place to bring about this outcome or whether forces of assimilation will continue to prevail.

the bilingual education debate

In 1998, California voters approved by an overwhelming margin Proposition 227, the so-called English for the Children initiative. Its primary proponent, millionaire Ronald Unz, made this argument: "Inspired in part by the example of my own mother, who was born in Los Angeles into a Yiddish-speaking immigrant home but had quickly and easily learned English as a young child, I never understood why children were being kept for years in native-language classes, or why such programs continued to exist."

Unz was motivated to action by the spectacle of immigrant children confined, year after year, to inferior foreign language classes and unable to learn English. He proposed instead to shift them to English-immersion classes following the model of his erstwhile Yiddish-speaking mother. In public school bureaucracies, bilingual education had come to mean remedial education in foreign languages that led to both inferior schooling and delayed learning of English. Not surprisingly, many immigrant parents lobbied in favor of Proposition 227 as a means to obtain proper education for their children.

The system against which Unz and his supporters rallied is not bilingual education at all, but a well-intentioned albeit misguided security blanket thrown at immigrant children. The terminological confusion of calling this "bilingual education" has clouded the issue in the public mind. True bilingual education for immigrant students involves vigorous instruction in English, along with deliberate efforts to preserve the parental tongue through teaching of selected topics in that language. For native English speakers, true bilingual instruction starts early, in grammar school if possible, and is followed by regular teaching of certain subjects in the chosen foreign language.

True bilingual education is currently practiced in only a handful of "dual language" schools, either private or public "magnet" units. These schools obtain remarkable results, both sustaining fluency in two languages among foreign students and creating it among native English speakers. Moreover, maintaining bilingual fluency in high school requires only one or two hours per day rather than half the total class time. In the CILS sample, the only group in which fluent bilinguals predominated were Cuban-American students attending private bilingual schools in Miami. These schools combine regular teaching of most subjects in English with one or two hours of daily instruction in Spanish.

In part as a result of the success of these schools, the U.S. Department of Education has called for a significant expansion of magnet language programs in public school systems across the country. In defense of this position, former secretary of education Richard W. Riley noted the sharp difference between American students, most of whom end up as English monolinguals, and European students, who commonly speak two or more languages fluently. Riley saw no reason why American children could not equal the linguistic accomplishments of their European peers. There is indeed no psychological reason why Riley's vision cannot be realized. The obstacles are rather social and political.

The strong assimilationist bent of American society, supported by the militant advocacy of nativist organizations, has rendered the preservation of foreign languages a near impossibility. Only in large ethnic enclaves, such as that of Cubans in Miami or in a few elite schools, have such efforts proven successful. Linguist Joshua Fishman has noted that Americans generally approve of foreign languages learned in Paris or in elite universities, but disapprove of immigrants' efforts to pass their languages on to their offspring. The implementation of this ideology by school systems across America has led to the present situation in which activists treat acquisition of English and preservation of foreign languages as a zero-sum game. Fluent bilingualism is a casualty. The result is a massive loss of a cultural resource that should be the birthright of immigrant children. Additional costs are added burdens in the upbringing of these children and unnecessary shortages of fluent multilingual workers. English-only is winning, but its costs are high for immigrant families, the communities where they settle, and society as a whole.

RECOMMENDED RESOURCES

Joshua A. Fishman. *Language Loyalty in the United States* (Mouton, 1966).

Kenji Hakuta. *Mirror of Language: The Debate on Bilingualism* (Basic Books, 1986).

Werner F. Leopold. *Speech Development of a Bilingual Child: A Linguist's Record* (AMS Press, 1970).

Stanley Lieberson, Guy Dalto, and Mary Ellen Johnston. "The Course of Mother Tongue Diversity in Nations." *American Journal of Sociology* 81 (1975): 34–61.

Ted Mouw and Yu Xie. "Bilingualism and the Academic Achievement of First- and Second-Generation Asian-Americans." *American Sociological Review* 64 (1999): 232–52.

Elizabeth Peal and Wallace E. Lambert. *The Relation of Bilingualism to Intelligence* (American Psychological Association, 1962).

Alejandro Portes and Lingxin Hao. "E Pluribus Unum: Bilingualism and Loss of Language in the Second Generation." *Sociology of Education* 71 (1998): 269–94.

Rubén G. Rumbaut and Wayne A. Cornelius. *California's Immigrant Children: Theory, Research, and Implications for Educational Policy* (Center for U.S.-Mexican Studies, University of California, San Diego, 1995).

REVIEW QUESTIONS

1. Summarize the results of the Children of Immigrants Longitudinal Study. What did this study discover about bilingualism and academic performance?
2. Portes claims that second-generation Americans speak their "mother tongue" at home and English at school, but by the third generation the "transition to monolingualism is completed." Are you able to track your family's language transition? Can you use your family's experience to reflect upon whether or not you feel that complete language assimilation is desirable?
3. Many Americans have long believed, as Hector St. John de Crevecoeur observed in 1782, that in America, "individuals of all nations are melted into a new race," which partly explains why the issue of language in schooling is hotly contested: fidelity to one's "parent tongue" stands out as an affront to the expectation of assimilation in American society. Yet, there are identifiable positive effects of full bilingualism. What are they, and how does this conflict with the "melting pot"?
4. Activity: Go to the World Bank's education data Web site, http://devdata.worldbank.org/edstats/cd.asp, and select the United States. What percentage of the GDP was devoted to public expenditure on education in 1990, 2000, and 2004? Now, match those numbers with those of Norway and a third country of your choice. What do you find? What are other points of comparison?

george farkas

the black-white test score gap

13

spring 2004

the supreme court's 2003 decision to uphold affirmative action in college admissions suggests that special treatment may be unnecessary in 25 years. but achieving equality without affirmative action will require overcoming a black-white test score gap that appears as early as preschool and is rooted in child-rearing practices.

When Supreme Court Justice Sandra Day O'Connor cast the deciding vote upholding affirmative action at the University of Michigan in 2003, she also suggested an expiration date for this policy. "We expect that 25 years from now the use of racial preferences will no longer be necessary" for racial balance, she wrote in her 5-4 majority opinion. Many consider this 25-year time-span to be overly optimistic because the black-white gap in standardized test scores of the sort used to decide college admissions is very large and has not changed since 1990. The average score for African-American 12th graders on the National Assessment of Educational Progress (NAEP) reading test matches the average score for white eighth graders. In a Washington, D.C., school district with mostly black students, 7 in 10 of all fourth graders recently scored below "basic" in mathematics and 6 in 10 scored below basic in reading.

Some commentators attribute the black-white test score gap to culturally biased tests rather than cognitive skills. In fact, black children perform at lower levels than white children due to experiences early in life. It may take longer than a quarter century before black students applying for college have the same average skills and test scores as white applicants.

is the gap real?

Research shows that when blacks and whites attend school together, black students typically get lower grades. For example, a recent study of the upper-middle-class community of Shaker Heights, Ohio, found that almost 80 percent of white students but fewer than 3 percent of black students graduated with honors (which required a grade-point average of at least 3.0). Grades may be poor indicators of ability because grading standards vary across classes, schools, and districts. Teachers may also be biased. Nationally standardized, computer-graded tests provide more reliable and comparable measures of academic performance. Over the past 10 years, research projects employing a variety of such tests have found the black-white gap in every age group.

Questions on these examinations are not esoteric. Tests for preschool and elementary school-age children ask students to name and write down letters of the alphabet, test oral vocabulary, assess the ability to read simple words and sentences, and test knowledge of numbers, counting, shapes, and simple mathematical operations. Tests for older elementary-school children include grade-appropriate problem solving and mathematical operations (e.g., the multiplication table up to 10×10), vocabulary, and reading and writing about passages on social studies and science. For middle and high school students, the tests focus on vocabulary, grammar, reading comprehension, writing simple essays, and solving basic geometry and algebra problems. These skills are required for high school graduation, college attendance, and military service. They are needed for most jobs, particularly those paying above the minimum wage. Thus, being able to perform these tasks and demonstrate these skills on tests is important. In this sense, the black-white test score gap is very real, with substantial consequences for the life chances of African-American students.

As large as the black-white test-score gap is, it used to be larger. It decreased by about 40 percent from 1970 to 1990, but has held steady since then. Researchers are unsure why the gap stopped narrowing at that time. Each of the following explanations has its proponents: biased testing, discrimination by teachers, test anxiety among black students, disparities between blacks and whites in income or family structure, and genetic and cultural differences between blacks and whites. Before evaluating these explanations, consider recent research.

recent evidence

Much of the latest research focuses on "culture," broadly defined as the skills, knowledge, habits, and behaviors parents, caretakers, and peers teach students. Child-rearing cultures vary strongly by class and race because residential segregation keeps these groups separate. The story of Eliza Doolittle in *My Fair Lady*, whose distinctively working-class vocabulary and dialect are remade by Professor Higgins, illustrates class differences. It is not just that poor children learn to speak with a different accent than middle-class children. Rather, parents with lower education and income tend to talk less and use a smaller vocabulary with their chil-

dren than do middle-class parents. Lower-class parents typically teach their children fewer of the skills and behaviors that schools and teachers expect and that test scores measure.

Developmental psychologists Betty Hart and Todd Risley had their research team spend one hour every month in the homes of 42 families, as the child in the family grew from one to three years old. The families ranged across three economic levels—professionals, middle- and working-class, and low-income—and were both black and white. During each hour, the researchers recorded every word spoken between parent and child. The researchers found striking differences across the three groups in the amount of verbal interaction and the number of different words parents used (see figure 1). By the age of three, the professional parents had spoken 35 million words to their children, the middle- and working-class parents had spoken 20 million words to their children, and the lower-class parents had spoken only 10 million words to their children.

Due to these parents' verbal styles, the children of professionals added words to their vocabulary at a much higher rate than did the middle- and working-class children, and these in turn had much higher vocabulary growth rates than did the poorer children (see figure 2). By 18 to 20 months, the professional-class children's vocabulary growth trajectories accelerated away from those of the other children, and by two years, the middle- and working-class children's vocabulary had separated from that of the lower-class children. By 36 months of age, the professional-class children had a vocabulary more than double that of the poorest children. Hart and Risley concluded that by three years of age children have internalized the "conversational culture" of their family. And because these cultures vary by the educational and income levels of the parents, the children learn to understand the world and to interact with

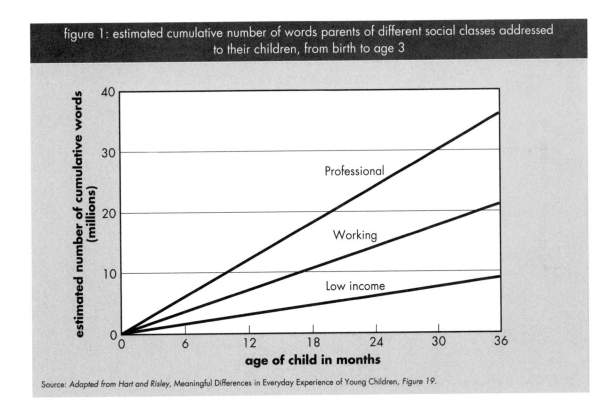

figure 1: estimated cumulative number of words parents of different social classes addressed to their children, from birth to age 3

Source: *Adapted from Hart and Risley,* Meaningful Differences in Everyday Experience of Young Children, *Figure 19.*

others using the linguistic tools characteristic of those class levels. Consequently, children from high, middle, and low social class families begin school with very different bases upon which to build success in reading and mathematics.

Christopher Jencks and Meredith Phillips pursued the question of preschoolers' vocabularies into the arena of race, using a large national survey that measured the spoken vocabularies of thousands of children. (In the Peabody Picture Vocabulary Test used in this survey, interviewers read words to children, who then choose one of four pictures that best represents their meaning.) Jencks and Phillips found that among children aged three to six, the vocabulary knowledge of black children lags behind that of white children by about a

year. Although the educational and income levels of the parents also strongly affect vocabulary knowledge, taking these into account still leaves a significant portion of the black-white vocabulary gap unexplained. That is, black children from the same class backgrounds as white children typically have smaller vocabularies than their white counterparts. Kurt Beron and I have further analyzed these data, extending them to 13 years of age. Our findings are illustrated in figure 3. Again, race and class separately influence children's oral vocabulary, with white children from lower-class families having about the same vocabulary knowledge as black children from upper-class families. These differences already exist by 36 months of age, and the class and race gaps persist into adolescence.

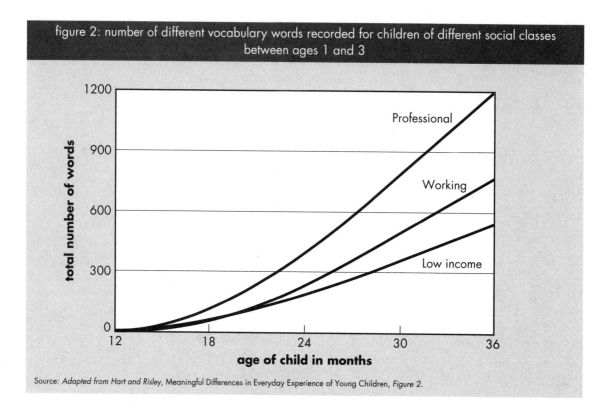

figure 2: number of different vocabulary words recorded for children of different social classes between ages 1 and 3

Source: *Adapted from Hart and Risley,* Meaningful Differences in Everyday Experience of Young Children, *Figure 2.*

The newest research from the Early Childhood Longitudinal Study of Kindergarten (ECLS-K) also supports these findings. Researchers measured pre-reading and pre-mathematics knowledge and skills for a national sample of approximately 20,000 students when they entered kindergarten in 1998, and have continued to follow these students as they progress up the grades. These data show large black-white gaps in pre-reading and pre-mathematics skills at kindergarten entry. They also show these gaps widening over the school years.

The ECLS-K interviewers also asked teachers how engaged their students were in class instruction. Typically, teachers believed that black students were less likely than white students to persist at tasks, be eager to learn, or pay atten-

tion, and more likely to argue, fight, or get angry with others. These patterns were found even when the black children came from similar social class backgrounds as the white children, and when the teacher doing the rating was black. Persistence, paying attention, and other forms of school engagement help determine how much each student learns. Further, since they often start with weaker skills and are less engaged in school, black students are less likely than white students to be placed in higher ability groups or classes where more material is taught and learning proceeds faster. Taken together, the initial disadvantage, the weaker school engagement, and the lower track placement explains most of the widening in the black-white test score gap that occurs as students grow up.

which explanations are best supported?

The most popular explanation for the black-white test score gap is bias. Indeed, all standardized tests *are* biased, as are all textbooks, if "bias" means that they focus on skills involving Standard English vocabulary and grammar, abstract thought and argument, and mathematics concepts more commonly taught and learned in white than in black families. But since these skills are required to succeed in K-12 schooling, to attend college, and to get jobs paying middle-class wages, test makers and school personnel can hardly be accused of bias for requiring them. The issue is not so-called "intelligence," but the skills demanded by the job market.

Discrimination by teachers no doubt exists, but it is unlikely to account for much of the test score gap. A large portion of the gap is already present before schooling begins. Furthermore, about one in three African-American kindergarten and first-grade students have an African-American teacher, and studies show that black students do not achieve higher test scores when their teachers are black.

Experiments by social psychologist Claude Steele have found that black students suffer from race-related test anxiety—sensitivity that their performance will be weighed as a measure of inherent black ability—and that this distraction lowers their performance (see "From Summer Camps to Glass Ceilings" on page 481). Related experiments by Michael Lovaglia find that black students not only worry about doing badly on standardized tests, but also worry about doing too well and thus being accused of "acting

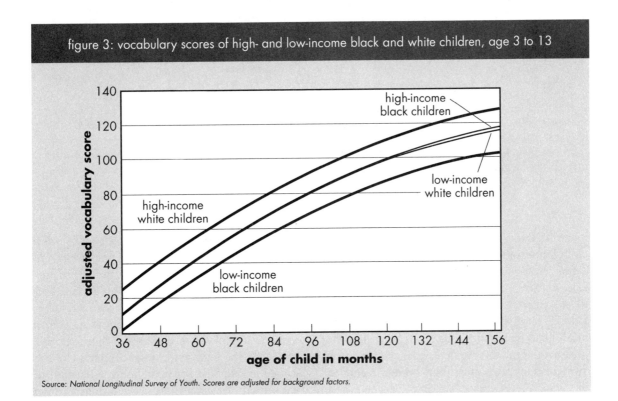

figure 3: vocabulary scores of high- and low-income black and white children, age 3 to 13

Source: National Longitudinal Survey of Youth. Scores are adjusted for background factors.

The Zoo

I like to go the zoo with my family.
We all like to see the hippos, tigers, and monkeys.
When I go to the zoo, I like to eat cotton candy and corndogs and peanuts.
I like to ride the train that goes around the zoo.
I like to go to the zoo with my class. We ride the bus.
We have so much fun.

Teacher: Mrs. Clowers   Tutor: Pat Rigdon
Student: DeVron Snead   1st grade

John Everett's Family

I live in a house with my mother and father. My room is decorated with Star Wars.
Sometimes I go out to my sister's house, and I play with my niece and we go to the beach too.
I have a dog. He is a puppy and he is messy. He likes to dig and tear up paper.
My family enjoys fishing. My family also enjoys going to church.
I have many friends like Bryan and Mrs. Pat.
At school I learn reading, writing and spelling.

Mrs. Pat

John Everett
fourth Grade   Ms Davis
Tutor: Pat Rigdon

Illustrated essays produced by black students working with individual reading tutors. The work of a first-grade student is on the left, that of a fourth-grade student on the right. In supplementing the efforts of parents and teachers, college students and paraprofessional tutors can help children regain the academic ground they lost from starting school without adequate pre-reading and pre-mathematics skills. The black-white test score gap used to be larger than it is now, and without continuing intervention, it could increase yet again. Both illustrations courtesy of the author and the Reading One-to-One Program, Duval County Public Schools, Florida.

white." However, these findings apply in special circumstances: small groups of older students sensitive to racial issues who are taking tests within a manipulated experiment. Again, the fact that the test score gap is found even among very young children, including those in all-black neighborhoods, casts doubt on the likelihood that test anxiety arising from race awareness explains more than a modest portion of the gap.

Research supports the idea that black-white differences in social class, family structures, and child-rearing behaviors explain much of the test score gap. Despite economic progress, black parents still lag behind white ones in employment and income. Black families therefore have fewer resources, a situation that is exacerbated by the high percentage of black children raised in single-parent households. Financial and parenting resources improve children's school engagement, course grades and test scores. Significant portions—but usually not all—of the black-white test score gap disappear once social class differences between the groups are adjusted for. When one compares black and white children who come from similar economic and family circumstances, their test scores are typically closer than when one compares all black and white children. The percentage of the overall test score gap that can be explained by background varies greatly across studies depending on the study design, the year, and the test used. Most show that differences in children's class and family backgrounds explain about half of the black-white test score gap; fewer studies find that these background differences explain most or even all the gap. The latter studies suggest that, so long as blacks continue to close the economic gap with whites, successive generations of black students will narrow and eventually eliminate the test-score gap with whites.

However, there is also reason to be less optimistic. The black-white gaps in education and income (among adults) have narrowed significantly since 1990, yet the test score gap has remained unchanged. Further, SAT scores show a significant black-white gap within every family income level. This gap is so large that, in 2002, the average SAT score for blacks from families earning $80,000 to $100,000 per year was substantially lower than the average for whites from families earning $20,000 to $30,000 per year. Clearly, more than class background is involved.

What about a genetic basis for the test score gap? This suggestion, made by Richard Herrnstein and Charles Murray in their 1994 book, *The Bell Curve,* created a storm of controversy. Psychologist Richard Nisbett recently reviewed the research on this question and concluded that there is no evidence for the genetic superiority of individuals with either African or European ancestry. Instead, there is strong evidence for a significant effect of the mother's child-raising practices on the black-white test score gap. For example, he points to the fact that mixed-race children with a white mother show significantly higher IQ test scores than those with a black mother, even though the race mixture of their genetic inheritance is similar. By contrast, mixed-race children fathered by black GIs in Germany (with German women) had identical IQ scores to those fathered by white GIs with German women. (And this despite the fact that the black-white test score gap among GIs is similar to that in the population as a whole.)

This brings us back to differences in home environment. Much of these differences originate in the distinct child-rearing resources and styles of white and black mothers and caregivers even within the same class. Nisbett draws on an ethnographic study by Shirley Brice Heath of class and race differences in child-rearing to conclude that "systematic differences between the socialization of black and white children begin in the cradle." Such differences probably affect later cognitive skills. For example, parents of poor black children tend not to read to them, or train them in abstractions such as the form and color of objects, or teach them how to take information learned in one area and apply it to another. Other researchers, such as Hart and Risley, document both class and race differences in the verbal responses parents give to young children, with middle-class and white parents more likely to be encouraging and positive, and lower-income and black parents more likely to be discouraging and punitive. The large differences in skills and habits that appear by school age set the stage for continuing racial differences in cognitive performance and learning styles. Thus, culture and child-rearing, differing by class and by race, and operating from birth to adulthood, complete the explanation for the black-white test score gap.

how can the gap be closed?

The national trend toward smaller class sizes in school may help close the gap because smaller classes have been shown to disproportionately benefit African-American students. So will the current emphasis on phonics instruction for beginning readers, since this too particularly helps African-American students. However, the black-white school achievement gap will never be closed as long as African-American students continue to have lower pre-reading and pre-mathematics skills when they enter kindergarten and first grade.

We must work to increase the oral vocabulary and early alphabetic and phonemic (letter-sound linkage) awareness of African-American children during their preschool years. Research has shown that these skills best predict success in learning to read by first grade. We must also strive to increase preschool instruction in numbers, counting, shapes, and other prerequisites of elementary school mathematics because the kindergarten pre-mathematics gap is as large as the pre-reading gap.

We must also insure that most African-American children attend preschool, and we must strive to improve the quality and quantity of instruction provided by Head Start and similar preschool programs. Despite more than 30 years of existence, Head Start has no national instructional curriculum in pre-reading and pre-mathematics skills. Instead, the program tends to focus on social skills, based on the mistaken belief that young children are not "developmentally ready" to learn letters, shapes, and advanced vocabulary. Meanwhile, white middle-class mothers continue teaching these skills and knowledge to their children, who enter kindergarten better prepared to succeed than black and poor children. In low-income neighborhoods, Head Start teachers often have only a high school diploma, and often learned their own skills at the same

low-performing schools that the children will soon be entering. The recent *No Child Left Behind* initiative of the U.S. Department of Education emphasizes training preschool and day care providers to offer better instruction to low-income children. Unfortunately, this initiative has been caught up in ideological struggles, and success is uncertain.

More generally, African-American parents (particularly those with limited schooling) must interact more with their children in ways that will better prepare them for school. Some intervention programs seek to help them do so. However, these have shown at best mixed success in reaching those low-income households that are most in need.

Potentially more promising is a new program, Early Head Start, which attempts to work with children prior to the usual Head Start ages. Low-income parents bring children as young as 12 months of age to a preschool center, where trained caregivers provide the stimulation the children may not otherwise receive at home. This and related initiatives offer some hope of progress in increasing the school readiness levels of black children by the time they reach first grade. However, even if these programs are successful, follow-up will be necessary to insure that these children do not fall behind later. My own contribution has been to develop a one-to-one tutoring program in reading, using low-cost college students and other paraprofessionals. This has been implemented in a large number of locations, and shows promise of helping children who have fallen behind during early elementary school.

the clock is ticking

The black-white test score gap is both real and consequential for the life chances of African-American students. Recent research has clearly demonstrated that this gap begins in the home at very early ages, and increases further during the school years. The nation is beginning to confront this issue, but it is difficult to improve the skills and knowledge that so many children bring to kindergarten, particularly when these are strongly determined by parenting styles, which in turn are rooted in class- and race-based experience. Nor will it be possible to substantially improve the middle and high school performance of African-American students if, as is now the case, they start school with reading and mathematics skills substantially below grade-level.

Justice O'Connor suggested a 25-year delay before ending affirmative action in college admissions. To ensure continuing equality of opportunity, the 18-year-old African Americans taking the SAT that year will have to be better prepared than the 18-year-olds of today. We have seven years before those children will be born. We had better get busy.

RECOMMENDED RESOURCES

Jonathan Crane., ed. *Social Programs That Work* (Russell Sage Foundation Press, 1998).

This anthology evaluates successful intervention programs for low-income children.

George Farkas. *Human Capital or Cultural Capital? Ethnicity and Poverty Groups in an Urban School District* (Aldine de Gruyter, 1996).

In this book I explain how early skills and student behavior gaps lead to ethnic achievement gaps in urban school districts.

George Farkas. "Racial Disparities and Discrimination in Education: What Do We Know, How Do We Know It, and What Do We Need to Know?" *Teachers College Record* 105 (2003): 1157–88.

Reviews the research literature on racial gaps in education.

Ronald Ferguson. "A Diagnostic Analysis of Black-White GPA Disparities in Shaker Heights, Ohio."

Brookings Papers on Education Policy 2001. (The Brookings Institution, 2001).

Investigates the black-white achievement gap in one affluent suburban school district.

Betty Hart and Todd Risley. *Meaningful Differences in Everyday Experience of Young Children* (Paul Brookes Publishing Co., 1995).

Includes detailed evidence on how social class determines parents' conversations with preschool children, leading to differences in the children's vocabulary.

Christopher Jencks and Meredith Phillips, eds. *The Black-White Test Score Gap* (Brookings, 1998).

One of the best collections of research papers on the nature, history, and causes of the test score gap; it includes Richard Nisbett's review of the evidence on racial differences in IQ scores.

Catherine Snow, M. Susan Burns, and Peg Griffin, eds. *Preventing Reading Difficulties in Young Children* (National Academy Press, 1998).

Explains what research has taught us about effective reading instruction, particularly at young ages and for at-risk students.

REVIEW QUESTIONS

1. Farkas mentions several possible explanations for why the test gap between blacks and whites has held steady since 1990. Identify them.
2. Restate the author's explanation for how race and class affect differently the oral vocabulary of black and white children.
3. Because Farkas states that a "large portion of the gap is already present before schooling begins," there is a danger in misreading this as "blaming the victim." What would you identify as the larger structural reasons that could explain preschooling differences rather than "individualistic" reasons? Defend your position.

4. Activity: The author mentions that there are other aspects to a broad definition of "culture" that can be examined in relation to educational achievement. Write a short essay on other life skills that differentiate white and black child rearing (e.g., artistic expression, nurturing one's siblings, being encouraged to lead a group), and hypothesize why some skill sets are highly valued in school while others are not.

frank f. furstenberg, jr., sheela kennedy, vonnie c. mcloyd, rubén g. rumbaut, and richard a. settersten, jr.

growing up is harder to do
14

summer 2004

in the past several decades, a new life stage has emerged: early adulthood. no longer adolescents, but not yet ready to assume the full responsibilities of an adult, many young people are caught between needing to learn advanced job skills and depending on their family to support them during the transition.

In the years after World War II, Americans typically assumed the full responsibilities of adulthood by their late teens or early 20s. Most young men had completed school and were working full-time, and most young women were married and raising children. People who grew up in this era of growing affluence—many of today's grandparents—were economically self-sufficient and able to care for others by the time they had weathered adolescence. Today, adulthood no longer begins when adolescence ends. Ask someone in their early 20s whether they consider themselves to be an adult, and you might get a laugh, a quizzical look, a shrug of the shoulders, or a response like that of a 24-year-old Californian: "Maybe next year. When I'm 25."

Social scientists are beginning to recognize a new phase of life: early adulthood. Some features of this stage resemble coming of age during the late nineteenth and early twentieth centuries, when youth lingered in a state of semi-autonomy, waiting until they were sufficiently well-off to marry, have children, and establish an independent household. However, there are important differences in how young people today define and achieve adulthood from those of both the recent and the more distant past.

This new stage is not merely an extension of adolescence, as has been maintained in the mass media. Young adults are physically mature and often possess impressive intellectual, social, and psychological skills. Nor are young people today reluctant to accept adult responsibilities. Instead, they are busy building up their educational credentials and practical skills in an ever more demanding labor market. Most are working or studying or both, and are developing romantic relationships. Yet, many have not become fully adult—traditionally defined as finishing school, landing a job with benefits, marrying and parenting—because they are not ready, or perhaps not permitted, to do so. For a growing number, this will not happen until their late 20s or even early 30s. In response, American society will have to revise upward the "normal" age of full adulthood, and develop ways to assist young people through the ever-lengthening transition.

Among the most privileged young adults—those who receive ample support from their parents—this is a time of unparalleled freedom from family responsibilities and an opportunity for self-exploration and development. For the less advantaged, early adulthood is a time of struggle to gain the skills and credentials required for a job that can support the family they wish to start (or perhaps have already started), and a struggle to feel in control of their lives. A 30-year-old single mother from Iowa laughed when asked whether she considered herself an adult: "I don't know if I'm an adult yet. I still don't feel quite grown up. Being an adult kind of sounds like having things, everything is kind of in a routine and on track, and I don't feel like I'm quite on track."

changing notions of adulthood

Traditionally, the transition to adulthood involves establishing emotional and economic independence from parents or, as historian John Modell described it, "coming into one's own." The life events that make up the transition to adulthood are accompanied by a sense of commitment, purpose, and identity. Although we lack systematic evidence on how adulthood was defined in the past, it appears that marriage and parenthood represented important benchmarks. Nineteenth-century American popular fiction, journalism, sermons, and self-help guides rarely referred to finishing school or getting a job, and only occasionally to leaving home or starting one's own household as the critical turning point. On the other hand, they often referred to marriage, suggesting that marriage was considered, at least by middle-class writers, as the critical touchstone of reaching adulthood.

By the 1950s and 1960s, most Americans viewed family roles and adult responsibilities as nearly synonymous. In that era, most women married before they were 21 and had at least one child before they were 23. For men, having the means to marry and support a family was the defining characteristic of adulthood, while for women, merely getting married and becoming a mother conferred adult status. As Alice Rossi explained in 1968: "On the level of cultural values, men have no freedom of choice where work is concerned: they must work to secure their status as adult men. The equivalent for women has been maternity. There is considerable pressure upon the growing girl and young woman to consider maternity necessary

for a woman's fulfillment as an individual and to secure her status as an adult."

Research conducted during the late 1950s and early 1960s demonstrated widespread antipathy in America toward people who remained unmarried and toward couples who were childless by choice. However, these views began to shift in the late 1960s, rendering the transition to adulthood more ambiguous. Psychologists Joseph Veroff, Elizabeth Douvan, and Richard Kulka found that more than half of Americans interviewed in 1957 viewed someone who did not want to get married as selfish, immature, peculiar, or morally flawed. By 1976, fewer than one-third of a similar sample held such views. A 1962 study found that 85 percent of mothers believed that married couples should have children. Nearly 20 years later, just 40 percent of those women still agreed, and in 1993 only 1 in 5 of their daughters agreed. Arland Thornton and Linda Young-Demarco, who have studied attitudes toward family roles during the latter half of the twentieth century, conclude that "Americans increasingly value freedom and equality in their personal and family lives while at the same time maintaining their commitment to the ideals of marriage, family, and children." While still personally committed to family, Americans increasingly tolerate alternative life choices.

To understand how Americans today define adulthood, we developed a set of questions for the 2002 General Social Survey (GSS), an opinion poll administered to a nationally representative sample of Americans every two years by the National Opinion Research Center. The survey asked nearly 1,400 Americans aged 18 and older how important each of the following traditional benchmarks was to being an adult: leaving home, finishing school, getting a full-time job, becoming financially independent from one's parents, being able to support a family, marrying, and becoming a parent.

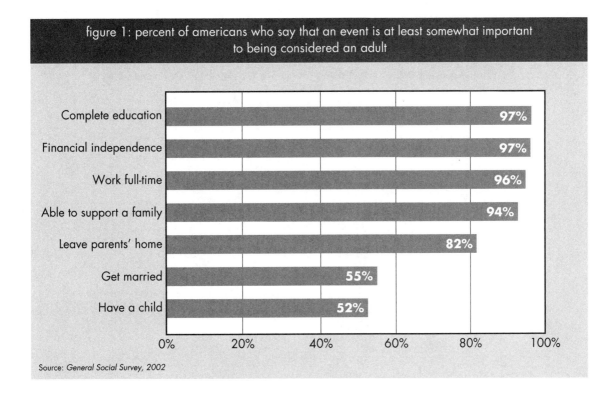

figure 1: percent of americans who say that an event is at least somewhat important to being considered an adult

Complete education — 97%
Financial independence — 97%
Work full-time — 96%
Able to support a family — 94%
Leave parents' home — 82%
Get married — 55%
Have a child — 52%

0%   20%   40%   60%   80%   100%

Source: *General Social Survey, 2002*

The definition of adulthood that emerges today does not necessarily include marriage and parenthood. As shown in figure 1, the most important milestones are completing school, establishing an independent household, and being employed full-time—concrete steps associated with the ability to support a family. Ninety-five percent of Americans surveyed consider education, employment, financial independence, and the ability to support a family to be key steps on the path to adulthood. Nonetheless, almost half of GSS respondents do not believe that it is necessary to actually marry or to have children to be considered an adult. As a young mother from San Diego explained, having a child did not make her an adult; instead she began to feel like an adult when she realized that "all of us make mistakes, but you can fix them and if you keep yourself on track . . .

everything will come out fine." Compared with their parents and grandparents, for whom marriage and parenthood were virtually a prerequisite for becoming an adult, young people today more often view these as life choices, not requirements.

the lengthening road to adulthood

Not only are the defining characteristics of adulthood changing, so is the time it takes to achieve them. To map the changing transitions to adulthood, we also examined several national surveys that contain information on young adults both in this country and abroad. Using U.S. Census data collected as far back as 1900, we compared the lives of young adults over time. We also conducted about 500 in-depth interviews with young adults living in different

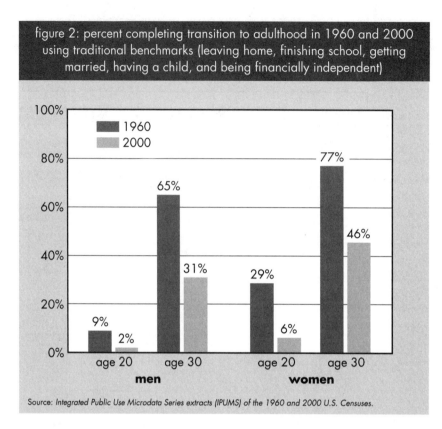

figure 2: percent completing transition to adulthood in 1960 and 2000 using traditional benchmarks (leaving home, finishing school, getting married, having a child, and being financially independent)

Source: *Integrated Public Use Microdata Series extracts (IPUMS) of the 1960 and 2000 U.S. Censuses.*

parts of the United States, including many in recent immigrant groups.

Our findings, as well as the work of other scholars, confirm that it takes much longer to make the transition to adulthood today than decades ago, and arguably longer than it has at any time in America's history. Figure 2, based on the 1960 and 2000 U.S. censuses, illustrates the large decline in the percentage of young adults who, by age 20 or 30, have completed all of the traditionally defined major adult transitions (leaving home, finishing school, becoming financially independent, getting married, and having a child). We define financial independence for both men and women as being in the labor force; however, because women in 1960 rarely combined work and motherhood, married

full-time mothers are also counted as financially independent in both years. In 2000, just 46 percent of women and 31 percent of men aged 30 had completed all five transitions, compared with 77 percent of women and 65 percent of men at the same age in 1960.

Women—who have traditionally formed families at ages younger than men—show the most dramatic changes at early ages. Although almost 30 percent of 20-year-old women in 1960 had completed these transitions, just 6 percent had done so in 2000. Among 25-year-olds (not shown), the decrease is even more dramatic: 70 percent of 25-year-old women in 1960 had attained traditional adult status, in 2000 just 25 percent had done so. Yet, in 2000, even as they delayed traditional adulthood, 25-year-old women greatly increased their participation in the labor force to levels approaching those of 25-year-old men. The corresponding declines for men in the attainment of traditional adult status are less striking but nonetheless significant. For both men and women, these changes can largely be explained by the increasing proportion who go to college and graduate school, and also by the postponement of marriage and childbearing.

If we use the more contemporary definition of adulthood suggested in figure 1—one that excludes marriage and parenthood—then the contrasts are not as dramatic. In 2000, 70 percent of men aged 30 had left home, were financially independent, and had completed their schooling, just 12 points lower than was true of 30-year-old men in 1960. Nearly 75 percent of 30-year-old women in 2000 met this standard, compared to nearly 85 percent of women in 1960. Nonetheless, even these changes are historically substantial, and we are not even taking into account how many of these independent, working, highly educated young people still feel that they are not yet capable of supporting a family.

The reasons for this lengthening path to adulthood, John Modell has shown, range from shifting social policies to changing economic forces. The swift transition to adulthood typical after World War II was substantially assisted by the government. The GI Bill helped veterans return to school and subsidized the expansion of education. Similarly, government subsidies for affordable housing encouraged starting families earlier. At the same time, because Social Security was extended to cover more of the elderly, young people were no longer compelled to support their parents. The disappearance or reduction of such subsidies during the past few decades may help to explain the prolongation of adult transitions for some Americans. The growing cost of college and housing forces many youth into a state of semi-autonomy, accepting some support from their parents while they establish themselves economically. When a job ends or they need additional schooling or a relationship dissolves, they increasingly turn to their family for assistance. Thus, the sequencing of adult transitions has become increasingly complicated and more reversible.

However, the primary reason for a prolonged early adulthood is that it now takes much longer to secure a full-time job that pays enough to support a family. Economists Timothy Smeeding and Katherin Ross Phillips found in the mid-1990s that just 70 percent of American men aged 24 to 28 earned enough to support themselves, while fewer than half earned enough to support a family of three. Attaining a decent standard of living today usually requires a college education, if not a professional degree. To enter or remain in the middle class, it is almost imperative to make an educational commitment that spans at least the early 20s. Not only are more Americans attending college than ever before, it takes longer to complete a degree than in years past. Census data reveal that from 1960 to 2000, the percentage of Americans aged 20, 25, and 30 who were enrolled in school more than doubled. Unlike during the 1960s, these educational and work investments are now required of women as well as men. It is little wonder then that many young people linger in early adulthood, delaying marriage and parenthood until their late 20s and early 30s.

Those who do not linger are likely those who cannot afford to and, perhaps as a result, views on how long it takes to achieve adulthood differ markedly by social class. Less-educated and less-affluent respondents—those who did not attend college and those at the bottom one-third of the income ladder—have an earlier expected timetable for leaving home, completing school, obtaining full-time employment, marriage, and

A faculty mentor helps a PhD student adjust her graduation hood. To earn credentials required for many middle-class jobs, students must invest in schooling throughout their 20s or even beyond. (Photo by Jon Wagner)

parenthood. Around 40 percent of the less well-off in the GSS sample said that young adults should marry before they turn 25, and one-third said they should have children by this age. Far fewer of the better-off respondents pointed to the early 20s, and about one-third of them said that these events could be delayed until the 30s. These social class differences probably stem from the reality that young people with more limited means do not have the luxury of investing in school or experimenting with complex career paths.

new demands on families, schools, and government

The growing demands on young Americans to invest in the future have come at a time of curtailed government support, placing heavy demands on families. Growing inequality shapes very different futures for young Americans with more and less privileged parents.

Early adulthood is when people figure out what they want to do and how best to realize their goals. If they are lucky enough to have a family that can help out, they may proceed directly through college, travel or work for a few years, or perhaps participate in community service, and then enter graduate or professional school. However, relatively few Americans have this good fortune. Youth from less well-off families must shuttle back and forth between work and school or combine both while they gradually gain their credentials. In the meantime, they feel unprepared for marriage or parenting. If they do marry or parent during these years, they often find themselves trying to juggle too many responsibilities and unable to adequately invest in their future. Like the mother from Iowa, they do not feel "on track" or in control of their lives.

More than at any time in recent history, parents are being called on to provide financial assistance (either college tuition, living expenses, or other assistance) to their young adult children. Robert Schoeni and Karen Ross conservatively estimate that nearly one-quarter of the entire cost of raising children is incurred after they reach 17. Nearly two-thirds of young adults in their early 20s receive economic support from parents, while about 40 percent still receive some assistance in their late 20s.

A century ago, it was the other way around: young adults typically helped their parents when they first went to work, if (as was common) they still lived with their parents. Now, many young adults continue to receive support from their parents even after they begin working. The exceptions seem to be in immigrant families; there, young people more often help support their parents. A 27-year-old Chinese American from New York explained why he continued to live with his parents despite wanting to move out, saying that his parents "want me [to stay] and they need me. Financially, they need me to take care of them, pay the bills, stuff like that, which is fine."

As young people and their families struggle with the new reality that it takes longer to attain adulthood, Americans must recognize weaknesses in the primary institutions that facilitate this transition—schools and the military. For the fortunate few who achieve bachelor's degrees and perhaps go on to professional or graduate training, residential colleges and universities seem well designed. They offer everything from housing to health care while training young adults. Likewise, the military provides a similar milieu for those from less-privileged families. However, only about one in four young adults attend primarily residential colleges or join the military after high school. The other three-quarters look to their families for room and board while they attend school and enter the job market. Many of these youth enter community colleges or local universities that provide much less in the way of services and support.

The least privileged come from families that cannot offer much assistance. This vulnerable population—consisting of 10 to 15 percent of young adults—may come out of the foster care system, graduate from special education programs, or exit jails and prisons. These youth typically lack job skills and need help to secure a foothold in society. Efforts to increase educational opportunities, establish school-to-career paths, and help students who cannot afford post-secondary education must be given higher priority, even in a time of budget constraints. The United States, once a world leader in providing higher education to its citizens, now lags behind several other nations in the proportion of the population that completes college.

Expanding military and alternative national service programs also can help provide a bridge from secondary school to higher education or the labor force by providing financial credit to those who serve their country. Such programs also offer health insurance to young adults, who are often cut off from insurance by arbitrary age limits. Finally, programs for the vulnerable populations of youth coming out of foster care, special education, and mental health services must not assume that young people are fully able to become economically independent at age 18 or even 21. The timetable of the 1950s is no longer applicable. It is high time for policy makers and legislators to address the realities of the longer and more demanding transition to adulthood.

RECOMMENDED RESOURCES

Frank F. Furstenberg, Jr., Thomas D. Cook, Robert Sampson, and Gail Slap, eds. *Early Adulthood in Cross-National Perspective* (Sage Publications, 2002).

> The contributors describe the emergence of this life stage across countries and the wide variation between them in the patterns of adult transitions.

Reed W. Larson, Bradford B. Brown, and Jeylan T. Mortimer, eds. *Adolescents' Preparation for the Future: Perils and Promises* (The Society for Research on Adolescence, 2002).

> The articles in this interdisciplinary book consider how well adolescents in different societies are being prepared for adulthood in a rapidly changing and increasingly global world.

John Modell. *Into One's Own: From Youth to Adulthood in the United States 1920–1975* (University of California Press, 1989).

> Documents dramatic twentieth-century changes in the transition to adulthood and places these shifts within the context of larger economic, political, and technological changes.

Alejandro Portes and Rubén G. Rumbaut. *Legacies: The Story of the Immigrant Second Generation* (University of California Press, 2001).

> Includes findings from the Children of Immigrants Longitudinal Study on the adaptation of second-generation immigrants during adolescence.

Robert Schoeni and Karen Ross. "Material Assistance Received from Families during the Transition to Adulthood." In *On the Frontier of Adulthood: Theory, Research, and Public Policy*, eds. Richard Settersten, Jr., Frank Furstenberg, Jr., and Rubén Rumbaut (University of Chicago Press, 2004).

Estimates the amount of financial assistance given to young adults by their families at different points during early adulthood.

Richard A. Settersten, Jr., Frank F. Furstenberg, Jr., and Rubén G. Rumbaut, eds. *On the Frontier of Adulthood: Theory, Research, and Public Policy* (University of Chicago Press, 2004).

Describes prolonged and complex patterns of school, work, and family transitions for young adults in America and Western Europe.

Timothy Smeeding and Katherin Ross Phillips. "Cross-National Differences in Employment and Economic Sufficiency." *Annals of the American Academy of Political and Social Science* 580 (2002): 103–33.

Examines the economic independence of young adults in seven industrialized countries.

Arland Thornton and Linda Young-DeMarco. "Four Decades of Trends in Attitudes Toward Family Issues in the United States: The 1960s Through the 1990s." *Journal of Marriage and the Family* 63 (2001): 1009–37.

The authors review survey data showing changes in Americans' attitudes toward the family.

REVIEW QUESTIONS

1. How do the authors define "early adulthood"? How do they explain the incidence of prolonged early adulthood in the United States?
2. Examine figure 2. How are the lives of young people in 2000 different from those in 1960? What do you think accounts for these differences?
3. Discuss positive and negative effects of postponing adulthood on parenting. How do you suspect this changes childrearing practices? How does having children change the careers of middle-aged workers?
4. Activity: C. Wright Mills describes the "sociological imagination" as the ability to connect "private troubles" with "public issues." Write a paragraph using your sociological imagination to examine how something you previously thought of as a private trouble in your own childhood education is connected to larger social issues.

jay gabler and jason kaufman

chess, cheerleading, chopin: what gets you into college?

15

spring 2006

do extracurricular activities increase students' likelihood of attending college, including prestigious institutions? yes, but grades, test scores, and family background still matter more.

Emma Daugherty, a promising student at a Catholic high school in Saint Paul, Minnesota, had not even finished tenth grade when colleges and universities began contacting her. Her mailbox filled with brochures, key chains, and pens; her phone rang with calls from college students encouraging her to apply to their schools. The attention was flattering, but she remained nervous about her prospects of admission. It was not clear what selective institutions like Georgetown and Notre Dame were looking for. "It was very difficult to decide exactly what mattered to schools," says Emma, now a sophomore at Notre Dame. "When I visited schools, they all mentioned the same handful of things that mattered for admissions, but they rarely ranked them."

The college admissions process is increasingly stressful and mysterious for students, parents, and guidance counselors alike. State schools and regional universities, once seen as fallback options, now draw from a widening pool of applicants and are increasingly selective, while the most prestigious universities have become even more desirable—and much more difficult to get into. Top colleges attract so many highly qualified applicants that it is hard to predict which ones they will admit. In this competitive environment, what makes the difference? What distinguishes applicants in admissions officers' eyes? Unsure of the answer, students often sign up for numerous extracurricular *activities*. While she enjoyed her active schedule, Emma admits that she had an eye toward college admissions when she signed up for her school's student council, French Club, National Honor Society, newspaper staff, and varsity volleyball team.

Of course, only a fraction of high school students aim to attend selective schools like Georgetown or Notre Dame. Many high school graduates do not attend college at all, and in disadvantaged neighborhoods, high school dropout rates remain high. Annette Lareau has documented the contrasting lifestyles of economically advantaged children (whose parents shuttle them from soccer to piano lessons) and economically disadvantaged children (whose parents lack the time or resources to involve their children in such activities). For the latter, the question is not what will gain students admission to Berkeley or Stanford but what activities help kids get to college, period.

For both groups, what matters—if anything? Will participating in 4-H make Whitney more attractive to Harvard? Will playing varsity football make Ken more likely to get into North Dakota State? What about intramural sports? Field trips to museums? Dance lessons? Math Club?

ten thousand teenagers can't be wrong

In 1988, researchers at the United States Department of Education sat down with thousands of eighth-graders nationwide to ask them hundreds of questions about their activities and achievements at home and at school and to gather information about their families and communities. The National Educational Longitudinal Survey (NELS), as it was called, has followed these students to the present day. We recently looked at the results of this survey and made some interesting discoveries about which activities matter when it comes to college matriculation—and which do not. Because much research has demonstrated that students of different races face distinct challenges and opportunities in school, we decided to make the several thousand white students followed by NELS the focus of our initial study. We used a statistical technique that allowed us to correct for the fact that one of our outcomes (matriculation at an elite college) is a subset of another (matriculation at college). Thus, we are able to ask two questions: (a) What activities and attributes increase a given student's chances to matriculate at college? (b) What activities make it more likely that, given college matriculation, a particular student will matriculate at a highly competitive school? (Note that our research focuses upon matriculation. That is, we are not yet certain whether a given activity changes a student's likelihood of applying versus being admitted to college—we only know whether or not it makes someone more likely to get in the door.)

Grades and standardized test scores, of course, matter a great deal, as do parents' income and education. Even when we consider these, however, we find that participation in some extracurricular activities in high school makes it much more likely that a student will go on to college. The accompanying table summarizes the results for these extracurricular activities.

extracurricular activities in the college attainment process		
Does participation make students more likely to...		
Outside of school	Pursue a B.A.?	Pursue a B.A. at an "elite" college or university?
Art classes	No	No
Dance classes	Yes	No
Music classes	Yes	No
Parent uses public library	No	No
Child uses public library	No	No
Parent visits art museums	No	Yes
Child visits art museums	No	No
In school		
School play	No	No
School music group	Yes	No
Interscholastic team sport	Yes	No
Interscholastic individual sport	No	No
Intramural team sport	No	No
Intramural individual sport	No	No
Cheerleading	No	No
School government	Yes	No
Academic honor society	No	No
Yearbook or school newspaper	No	Yes
Public service club	No	No
Academic club	No	No
Hobby club	No	Yes

Source: *Selected results from Kaufman and Gabler, "Cultural Capital and the Extracurricular Activities of Girls and Boys in the College Attainment Process. These results differ slightly from the result in the paper; they reflect the correction of a minor methodological error.*

basketball or bruegel?

Participation in varsity team sports makes college matriculation much more likely; participation in student government does also. Among activities pursued outside of school, taking dance or music classes also makes a difference. To understand the importance of these activities, consider some of the seemingly fundamental attributes that do not matter much: whether English is a student's first language, whether a student lives in a rural or urban area, and even whether parents limit TV or check whether homework is done. None of these, independently, makes a student more likely to attend college.

We were interested, however, not only in whether extracurricular participation mattered for college entrance in general, but in whether it mattered for admission to highly selective colleges in particular. To answer this question, we looked at which students attended one of the colleges most highly ranked overall (or just most selective) according to *U.S. News* in the year the NELS respondents were college-shopping. The list included both prestigious research universities such as UCLA and Penn, and selective teaching colleges like Carleton and Vassar. Only a small percentage of high school seniors went on to attend one of these nationally known institutions.

What activities make a college-bound student more likely to attend a highly selective institution? Some of the obvious choices turn out to make little difference. When it comes to these elite schools, sports do not matter—nor, surprisingly, do student council or French Club. Working on the school yearbook or newspaper makes a difference—but music, dance, and art lessons do not seem to matter. Surprisingly, participation in a school hobby club makes a student much more likely to attend one of these selective institutions—though the survey question wording prevents us from knowing whether participation in the carpentry club or photography club matters as much as, say, chess club.

Perhaps our most interesting finding, however, concerned not what the students themselves did—but what their parents did. Students whose parents visited art museums regularly were much

more likely to attend an elite college than students whose parents did not. It does not even seem to matter whether students themselves visit museums—so long as their parents do. This is true across the spectrum, even when we take parents' income and education into account.

polishing apples

So what does this all mean? Are there any lessons here for social scientists—or for students aspiring to college? Though our study is unique in considering all these activities together and in looking at highly selective institutions in particular, sociologists have long been asking related questions, and their insights may help us make sense of our results.

Several authors have pointed to the "résumé factor"—most notably Randall Collins, author of *The Credential Society*. It makes sense to think that activities or achievements should make students more likely to gain admission to college (whether or not they actually gained any skills or knowledge from the activity), just because admissions officers are impressed by lists of activities.

An impressive list of activities on an application cannot hurt, but the histories of the NELS participants suggest that more is going on. Although some activities, like student council or school band, make a student more likely to attend college, the advantage they confer is not always clear. For example, why does student government participation make a student more likely to go to college but no more likely to attend a particularly selective institution? Why does photography club make a difference but not membership in the National Honor Society? Why do activities like dance lessons taken outside of school—activities that are less likely to be listed or mentioned on a college application—make such a significant difference? All these pad a résumé equally well.

One answer may lie in the work of French

sociologist Pierre Bourdieu, who coined the term *cultural capital*. According to Bourdieu, knowledge about elite culture (for example, fine art) is an asset just as surely as money or social connections are assets. Someone who can show familiarity with classical music or modern art probably has a privileged background: the person knows about and has developed a taste for art forms (for example, ballet or abstract art) and for activities (for example, foreign travel or squash) that are not widely experienced outside elite circles. Teachers, employers, and others in gatekeeping positions detect this sophistication and reward those who display it.

Critics have argued that Bourdieu's theory of cultural capital, based upon research in France decades ago, is less relevant to contemporary life in the United States. This is a fair criticism, but elite knowledge can take many forms. In the United States today, children of highly educated, well-to-do parents may share a taste for popular music or movies with their less privileged peers, but they are also more likely than those peers to be familiar with more diverse art forms and pastimes, from ballet to golf and world music. Even on a college application, these differences in students' experiences are likely to be apparent. Elite colleges are especially likely to pay attention to these differences. Admissions officers at these schools must choose a few students from a large number of highly qualified applicants; with competition so intense, even relatively subtle clues might make an applicant seem more like "college material." These schools often conduct applicant interviews and place great weight on applicants' personal statements, and a chance mention of the new Bertolucci film or the Ruscha show at the Whitney may tip an applicant from one pile to the other.

Besides making admission to college more likely among students who apply, cultural tastes may also increase the likelihood of applying to college in the first place: teachers and guidance counselors may be more likely to encourage such students to apply to college.

If Bourdieu is correct—and much research suggests he is—this might help explain why dance lessons make more of a difference for college admission than cheerleading. Cultural sophistication also seems the best explanation for our finding that parents' patronage of art museums makes students more likely to enter elite schools. Students from such families are likely to be surrounded by information about elite culture, from coffee-table art books to DVDs of foreign films. Professional educators—who tend themselves to be well educated and conversant in this culture—are likely to favor such students. Family life, argued Bourdieu, is the crucible of cultural capital—occasional school field trips are not enough to change a child's fundamental outlook on life. The children of the wealthy have a valuable leg up in today's educational rat race.

full-court press

While cultural awareness may impress an admissions officer at Amherst, most high school students do not even get to that interview. Among the seniors in our nationwide sample, barely half applied to bachelor's degree programs. The great majority of those who did apply ended up attending four-year programs, though not always at their first-choice school. Might some extracurricular activities help motivate students to seek higher education? Can playing for the school's basketball team increase students' interest in school itself?

Willard Waller, a pioneering sociologist of education in the 1930s, thought this was the primary justification for extracurricular activities. School-based extracurriculars, he argued, serve to win students' hearts and minds. Cheering for the Central High hockey team is equivalent to cheering for Central High and all it stands for. If this is true, cheering for Central High may encourage investment in the educational process more generally, thus promoting college attendance.

This might help explain why we found that students who played varsity team sports were more likely to attend college. Athletic recruiting and scholarships probably play a role as well. If we extend Waller's logic to nonathletic extracurriculars, this might also explain why students who participate in activities like student council are more likely to attend college but not more likely to attend so-called elite colleges. Cultural sophistication matters more for the latter; social "investment" in school matters more for the former.

Interestingly, participation in varsity sports based on individual competition (for example, swimming or track as opposed to hockey or football) does not seem to make a difference in predicting college matriculation. This could be for any number of reasons. Colleges' demand for players of these sports may be less intense, with fewer recruiting slots for golf stars versus basketball stars.

Or Waller might be on to something, and the school solidarity fostered at a football game or a basketball game might do more to invest students in school life, thus making them more likely to apply to college. Star football players are more likely to be heroes for their fellow students and teachers than star swimmers. Sociologists since Emile Durkheim have emphasized the importance of collective rituals in shaping individual beliefs and motivations—and interscholastic competitions are certainly collective rituals. (From this perspective, it is not surprising that intramural sports do not increase participants' likelihood of achieving higher education, since they are not as tightly intertwined with school life as are varsity sports.)

These explanations are not mutually exclusive. Cultural awareness seems to explain why

experiences and background outside of school can make students more likely to attend selective institutions, and the credential value and socializing effects of activities like student council and varsity sports help explain why students who participate in them are more likely to attend college than those who do not. Further, it seems reasonable to think that something more straightforward is happening: many of these activities increase students' technical skills and social competence, making them more attractive candidates for colleges in any number of ways. Such skills would also be evident to the counselors and teachers who steer students toward college—and write their recommendation letters. These processes are not mutually exclusive—music lessons may well improve students' study skills, cognitive skills, and cultural capital.

sociology homework

Many questions remain. Our results for white students may not hold among African-American, Hispanic, or Asian-American students. There are also important differences between boys and girls: for example, prior research shows that cultural awareness is especially important for college-bound girls. Our look at the NELS students supports this: regular visits to the library, for example, appear to improve girls' (but not boys') chances of attending selective colleges.

The bottom line? Extracurricular activities matter. Some activities significantly increase students' likelihood of attending college and may even make them more likely to attend a prestigious institution. That said, there are no magic bullets. Grades and test scores still trump the effect of any extracurricular activity. Further, several seemingly desirable activities ranging from library use to honor-society participation had no mentionable effect on college attendance.

Many extracurricular activities may accomplish precisely what they are intended to do:

build students' skills and self-confidence while raising their aspirations. Yet our research shows that it is harder to bootstrap one's way into an elite college than previously thought. Only a few activities matter, and the most important predictors in our data have to do with family background rather than extracurricular activities. Meaningful participation in extracurricular activities of real interest to students may be beneficial in many ways, but a wall full of participation ribbons will not by itself open college gates.

RECOMMENDED RESOURCES

Pierre Bourdieu. *Distinction: A Social Critique of the Judgment of Taste* (Harvard University Press, 1984).

> A dense, encyclopedic treatment of the role of cultural capital at work, home, and school in twentieth century France.

Randall Collins. *The Credential Society: An Historical Sociology of Education and Stratification* (Academic Press, 1979).

> The book perhaps most closely associated with the argument that much social stratification is built on formal educational credentials—or the lack thereof.

Jason Kaufman and Jay Gabler. "Cultural Capital and the Extracurricular Activities of Girls and Boys in the College Attainment Process." *Poetics* 32 (2004): 145–68.

> A more detailed report on our research.

Annette Lareau. *Unequal Childhoods: Class, Race, and Family Life* (University of Chicago Press, 2003).

> An acclaimed report detailing some dramatic differences in family life among the economically privileged and the less privileged.

Jacques Steinberg. *The Gatekeepers: Inside the Admissions Process of a Premier College* (Viking, 2002).

> A fascinating, readable, behind-the-scenes look at the college admissions process.

Willard Waller. *The Sociology of Teaching* (Wiley, 1932).

> A classic text in the sociology of education, describing the school as a functional system that works first and foremost to perpetuate itself.

REVIEW QUESTIONS

1. You may be quite familiar with the college application process. What do you make of Gabler and Kaufman's finding that a student's activities appear to be less important than his or her parents' activities? In order to better position yourself for a college application, can you identify any activities that you participated in on this list? Reflect on your experiences in relation to these findings.
2. Do you think that Pierre Bourdieu's theory of "cultural capital" explains who gets admitted to state schools as well as it explains who gets admitted to private schools? Why or why not?
3. The essay mentions gender briefly (e.g., that how much parents visit the library improves girls' chances of attending an elite school), but doesn't mention two other major forces in society: race and class. Write two paragraphs on how you think these affect college admissions. In particular, the article mentions how privileging a few activities benefits some more than others, but can you see the valuation of particular activities as a way to exclude other groups? How? Discuss your opinion.

part **4**

Culture and Media

joseph r. gusfield

keyword: culture

winter 2006

16

We understand words by examining their contexts and by comparing them with other, related words. In both its history and its present uses, *culture* has displayed a rich diversity of meanings; some clear and others ambiguous, some popular and others academic.

The origins of the word lie in the concept of cultivation, distinguishing that which is grown under human control, as in farming, from the products of nature. This meaning is still found in the idea of "cultured pearls" or in medical phrases such as "culturing bacteria." This contrast between nature and culture still pervades the variety of the word's meanings.

Varied uses of the word also point to differences of method and perspective in history, sociology, and anthropology. A "cultural approach" is distinct from other perspectives such as biological, genetic, or social-structural. British usage in the mid-nineteenth century contrasted primitive societies as uncivilized and uncultured with contemporary Western societies as civilized and cultured. Culture was a state of being to be attained, synonymous with *civilization*. We still use this developmental meaning, referring to people as *cultured* or *uncultured*. This is not surprising since the word is almost always used to describe groups or societies or parts of a group, as with *subcultures*. In more common usages *culture* has a collective reference, as in the "culture of the State department" or the "culture of French Canadians."

Close to this usage of *culture* to mean *civilization* is its use to refer to specific institutions of knowledge and creativity such as art, language, science, religion, film, and literature, which the sociology of culture has taken as its subject matter. Here the focus is on ideas rather than their associated material practices. Forms of thought, knowledge, language, and art that are often associated with the concept of civilization are distinguished from technological practices and institutions.

How this use of *culture* relates to wider concepts of culture has been an abiding issue in the humanities as well as in sociology. The question of whether art and religion reflect a society's culture or whether they influence the development of that society is relevant to the role of intellectuals and artists in modern societies—as T. S. Eliot realized in 1949.

The word is perhaps most frequently used to refer to the practices and patterns that distinguish one society or group from others. In 1874 the anthropologist E. B. Tyler defined culture as "that complex whole which includes knowledge, belief, art, morals, custom, and any other capabilities and habits acquired by man as a member of society." The definition includes two elements—that which differentiates one group or society from others and the concept of acquired or learned behavior.

Cultural diversity contrasts with the idea of a universal human nature implied in biological explanations of human behavior. Anthropology has argued that human behavior is produced by discrete human cultures rather than determined by biological or genetic nature. Margaret Mead and Ruth Benedict made this view a part of the college education of several generations of American students. The word *culture* not only points to substance but embodies a perspective on societies—a way of explaining differences, often called "cultural determinism." Though anthropologists themselves have criticized the perspective in recent years, it remains associated with their discipline. Against this emphasis on culture is a more universal view of human nature, in examples such as the nuclear family or taboos against incest or eating human flesh.

Tylor's definition, however, is a loose collection of practices and ideas that differ in their significance and constraining character. In Spain the evening meal usually occurs at 10 p.m. or later, in the United States, it occurs at 6 p.m. or shortly after. Neither society supports this practice with a sense of moral certitude. These are habits. They differ from intensely held beliefs or preferences that are perceived as morally binding because they reflect "human nature." Stoning to death has been the prescribed punishment for adultery in some societies, in contrast to a much milder treatment in others.

Tyler saw cultures as collections of rules and beliefs with different levels of significance. Other anthropologists have used culture to refer to a pervasive quality of a society. In this sense cultures are integrated and manifested in a variety of actions. Ruth Benedict in *Patterns of Culture* (1934) distinguished two types of primitive society: The Dionysian, which values psychological states of excess, contrasted with the Apollonian, with its measured values for sticking to the middle of the road. Pervasiveness and constraint are the salient dimensions of culture in much social research. Its pervasiveness suggests that a culture is shared by a group and, as in Benedict's work, permeates much of its activity.

Culture constrains through its exclusiveness. Actions are bounded by the categories and rules that exclude alternatives. Members of a society may be unaware that their actions and beliefs are unique to their society. Louis Dumont, in *Homo Hierarchicus,* asserts that "the concept of the self in Western societies differs from the concept of the self as a part of a group in India. The principle of equality permeates Western society, while that of hierarchy permeates Indian culture." We might even reasonably assert that culture "has" us more than we have it, as Bennett Berger put it.

The constraining quality of culture is perhaps its most vital aspect in social research. Here it contrasts with social structure. Karl Mannhem's conception of ideology, for instance, explains knowledge, including political doctrines, by reference to the social and economic position of adherents and spokespersons. In a similar vein, "bourgeois culture" is often thought to reflect the capitalist middle class.

The conflict between cultural and structural perspectives fuels one of the most common debates in the human sciences. Karl Marx stated the structural approach succinctly in *The German Ideology.* "It is not the consciousness of man that determines existence but the existence that determines consciousness." This assertion of social structure as source and explanation of ideas has often been contrasted with cultural approaches such as Max Weber's in his famed *The Protestant Ethic and the Spirit of Capitalism.*

Weber related Protestant ideals to the moral and ethical elements of the character that prized capitalistic behavior. The human meaning of the economic behavior of capitalism could not be understood without seeing its cultural framework of ethical and cognitive ideas. The cultural roots of economic behavior were independent or quasi-independent of economic interests.

What was prized was the character of capitalists presented through their economic behavior. The meaning of economic behavior could not be assumed; it had to be studied.

Over the past three decades the narrower use of culture to refer to the meanings of objects and events has gained favor, in what has been called "the cultural turn." This is also part of the general intellectual movement toward emphasis on the subject rather than on objective conditions as the sources of action. Studies of social problems have focused on how conditions come to be interpreted as public problems. Studies of social movements have examined the process of framing—which involves the categories of language and belief by which situations are defined. Even scientific knowledge has been found to use cognitive paradigms that lead and limit theory and experience. Bruno Latour and Steve Woolgar capture much of this perspective in the title of their seminal work, *Laboratory Life: The Social Construction of Scientific Facts*.

Clifford Geertz, a major figure in the cultural turn, reconceptualized the term *ideology* in contrast to its traditional utilitarian usage. "The function of ideology," he wrote in *The Interpretation of Cultures*, "is to make an autonomous politics possible by providing the authoritative concepts that render it meaningful, the suasive images by means of which it can be sensibly grasped." This perspective leads the analyst to examine the discourses we use to interpret events and objects and give them meaning. It recognizes that meanings may be multiple and may differ across and within groups. The ways in which symbol systems enable people to interpret their experience, even to construct their experience in a shared way, has become the central focus of a cultural perspective.

The cultural turn has resulted in a more searching assessment of the limits and utility of the concept of culture. Cultures characterize modern societies at different levels of uniformity or conflict; they have diverse relations to social structure; and they are more or less pervasive and constraining. The problem of the relationship of culture to practice also remains important. *Culture* remains an indispensable though ambiguous concept in the discourse of the social sciences.

RECOMMENDED RESOURCES

Bennett Berger. *An Essay on Culture: Symbolic Structure and Social Structure* (University of California Press, 1995).

Shows off recent efforts in the sociology of culture.

Victoria E. Bonnell and Lynn Hunt, eds. *Beyond the Cultural Turn: New Directions in the Study of Society and Culture* (University of California Press, 1999).

Historians and sociologists suggest paths of research that follow from the triumph of cultural constructionism.

T. S. Eliot. *Notes Towards the Definition of Culture* (Harcourt, Brace, 1949).

A classic statement of culture as cultivation, including its frequently conservative implications.

Clifford Geertz. *The Interpretation of Cultures* (Basic Books, 1973).

Perhaps the most influential work in the cultural turn of the social sciences.

Joseph R. Gusfield. *The Culture of Public Problems: Drinking, Driving and the Symbolic Order* (University of Chicago Press, 1981).

Explores a number of aspects of meaning in the recognition and punishment of drunk driving.

Marshall Sahlins. *Culture and Practical Reason* (University of Chicago Press, 1976).

Another anthropologist influentially debunks materialist accounts of social life in favor of cultural approaches.

REVIEW QUESTIONS

1. Before reading this essay, how do you think you might have defined *culture?*
2. *Culture* is a tricky word in everyday usage, since it tends to include very different notions of both "ideas" and "practices." In your own words, explain what Bennett Berger means when he says that culture "has" us more than we have it.
3. What are the differences between the Marxist and Weberian positions on culture? How do they relate to theories that maintain culture is a set of beliefs and practices? How has the "cultural turn" affected these two sociological positions?

richard a. peterson

roll over beethoven, there's a new way to be cool

17

summer 2001

for generations, preference for "high" and disdain for "popular" culture was a means the elite used to distinguish themselves from the masses, in sharp contrast, the display of high status today relies on familiarity with the full range of cultural fare. this change in evaluation of status poses a challenge for the future of the fine arts.

At a recent classical music concert, I overheard a well-dressed matron comment: "It is a pity that men don't wear tuxedos any more." Pitiable or not, it is true that few American men wear formal attire these days. Tuxedo wearing is now restricted to men in wedding parties, those attending high school proms, and waiters at ritzy restaurants. The passing of the tux as the obligatory public armor of high status signals more than a style change. Statistics demonstrate a systematic change in the way people display high status, a change from the selective highbrow snob to the cosmopolitan "omnivore."

In the old days, a highbrow showed his or her status by embracing the elevated and rejecting the common—Rothko not Rockwell, Beethoven not The Beatles. Today, the true connoisseur enjoys it all: National Public Radio, Public Enemy, Britney Spears, Ingmar Bergman, Spike Lee, and Lucinda Williams. Valuing so many aesthetics erodes patronage of the fine arts and will profoundly affect their future.

the upscaling of shakespeare

In his study of how cultural distinctions arose in America, historian Lawrence Levine notes that in the first half of the nineteenth century the works of Shakespeare were part of popular culture, widely known by all sectors of society. In the second half of the century, those trying to draw a clear line between the fine arts and popular culture elevated the Bard to being the icon of civilization. Only people with refined cultural experience, the fine arts entrepreneurs argued, could truly understand Shakespeare and his ilk. Only those with a large cranial capacity as signaled by a high brow had the ability to fully understand the fine arts. These cultural elites and the art they espoused came to be called "highbrow," as contrasted with the popular or "lowbrow" culture of the masses.

Levine shows that cultivating the fine arts was not sufficient to ensure highbrow status. Aspirants to high status had not only to patronize the sublime but also to avoid the base. As *Harpers* magazine said in 1883, certain artworks are "Not only tests of taste but even of character. If a man gives himself to Shakespeare and Chaucer, we have a clue to the man. [Likewise] the man who among all operas prefers [the inferior Italian] *Don Giovanni* or the *Barber of Seville*... Involuntarily reveals himself as he makes his preferences known." The caste-like nature of the system was not lost on commentators at the time. They regularly called Boston's cultural elite "Brahmins."

Paul DiMaggio provides a concrete example of how elites fashioned the distinction between highbrow and lowbrow in his study of the founding of the Boston Museum of Fine Arts and the Boston Symphony Orchestra. Until the 1870s, orchestra concerts were a mix of classical music, sentimental songs, theatrical numbers, and martial music. Then a small group of the Boston elite set out to purge orchestral performances of all but fine art music. They invested in concert halls, created and subsidized the orchestra, imported a conductor and key players from Germany, and saw to it that newspaper reviews stressed the differences between highbrow fine art and lowbrow popular culture. A parallel process took place in the formation of the Museum of Fine Arts. Its founders channeled money to Harvard University, using the resources of one bastion of highbrow culture to promote the creation of another. Indeed, the proliferation of American liberal arts colleges in this period can be seen, in part, as a device to sharpen highbrow discrimination in the rising generation of the privileged class.

At the same time, other signs of status became available to an ever-widening public. An exaggerated focus on proper etiquette and the correct placement and use of dinnerware and other status props led, as historian Arthur Schlesinger notes, to the proliferation of books and courses on etiquette in the final decades of the nineteenth century. These learning tools made it easier for anyone with a bit of money to acquire the external signs of refinement, leading, as Levine shows, to an ever-greater reliance on the fine arts as the litmus test of highbrow status. The advantage of arts appreciation as a status marker lay in the fact that it took years to cultivate the eye and ear to be able to distinguish the true gems of literature, painting, and concert halls from inferior works. As important, arts events

Print and frame shop selling fine art reproductions, posters of celebrities, labels from fruit crates, illustrations from children's books, maps, and much more. (Photo by Jon Wagner)

became a prime pretext for social gatherings of the elect, and generous patronage of the arts was the hallmark of the stalwart defender of "all that was best" of civilization. In such a context, a rendering of a work by Shakespeare was the revelation of a sacred mystery.

debasing the coin

In the first third of the twentieth century, a brow level between high and low, the "middlebrow," was identified. Essayist Margaret Widdemer, writing in a 1933 issue of the *Saturday Review of Literature*, identified middlebrow culture as mechanically aping highbrow tastes. Current judgments of taste were being read, she said, directly from the pages of newspaper and magazine reviews. At the same time such symbols of Western civilization could be purchased as "The Complete Works of . . . ," reproductions or superficial knock-offs of the original thing. Busts of Shakespeare and copies of the *Mona Lisa* became widely available. The RCA-Victor record company offered recorded "Treasures of Opera" and a multi-disk "Introduction to Good Music" on its high-priced "Red Seal" imprint, and RCA's newly formed radio network offered excerpts from the masters played by its NBC studio orchestra. Widdemer was shocked at this debasement of the high-art symbols of distinction.

By mid-century distinctions between highbrow and lowbrow were widely used in public discourse, and in 1949 *Life,* the ubiquitous middle-class magazine of the time, ran an article with a series of pictures on how to distinguish each of the three types of culture. The brow levels were identified by their distinctive tastes in consumption, with listings of representative clothes, food, perfume, drink, cars, television programs, and other consumer items. Such tip sheets proliferated, but essayist Russell Lynes cautioned that the status value of any specific symbol of taste cheapened over time. For example, he pointed out that Whistler's *Arrangement in Gray and Black, No. 1* had been highbrow in the era 1870–90. By 1910–20 it had become middlebrow and was called *Portrait of the Artist's Mother.* By 1940–50 the same painting, called *Whistler's Mother,* was considered lowbrow. Lynes recognized an inverse process as well. For example, he noted that *The Crossroads of Life,* a D. W. Griffiths film that was lowbrow in the teens, had been revalorized as highbrow by the 1940s.

Mass culture critics of the 1950s decried what they saw as the eroding effects of commercially disseminated popular culture. As Herbert Gans shows in his book *Popular Culture and High Culture,* they were galvanized by the fear that "bad culture drives out the good," resulting in what essayist and poet T. S. Eliot called a "wasteland." David Riesman took issue with

In the old days, a highbrow showed his or her status by embracing the elevated and rejecting the common—Rothko not Rockwell, Beethoven not The Beatles. Today, the true connoisseur enjoys it all: National Public Radio, Public Enemy, Britney Spears, Ingmar Bergman, Spike Lee, and Lucinda Williams. Valuing so many aesthetics erodes patronage of the fine arts and will profoundly affect their future.

this argument. Presciently, in 1950 he argued in *The Lonely Crowd* that standards were not being debased; rather, a new way of evaluating status was replacing the old. The older way, identified as "inner direction," stood on a set of generalized standards of value and behavior inculcated early in life that acted like a gyroscope, so that the inner-directed person went through life "on the straight and narrow" path. Riesman identified the then-emerging new pattern as "other direction." Rather than being driven by guilt, the other-directed person feels anxiety at the prospect of getting out of step with his fellows. In Riesman's view this person develops a radar that continually scans the social environment to find his or her other-directed way. Riesman became widely known for this work—his likeness appeared on the cover of *Time* magazine—but the work was resolutely ignored by his fellow sociologists. As Gans notes, while some debated whether mass culture had triumphed, most sociologists studied social class apart from culture and were blind to the changing standards of taste.

Unfortunately the 1950s saw no large-scale surveys of cultural taste, but early in the next decade French sociologist Pierre Bourdieu conducted the first such survey. He found a pattern showing highbrow exclusiveness—appreciating the "fine" and disdaining the "coarse"—in the professional class, a less clear pattern of choices among those in business, and lowbrow tastes among the working class. More recently, Michèle Lamont has shown that upper-middle-class Parisians still use highbrow standards of taste in evaluating others, but people of the same class in a French industrial city, as well as Americans in New York and Indianapolis, are much less concerned about taste.

the markers of status are a'changin'

"Highbrow" terminology is archaic, formal attire is seldom worn, and the word *suit* is used as a term of derision even among those who regularly wear suits. Virtually every college graduate (95 percent) polled for the General Social Survey of 1993 agreed with the assertion that "excellence is just as likely to be found in folk culture or popular culture as in traditional high culture."

With a group of associates, I have studied the meaning of these findings that seem so inconsistent with the expectations of earlier times. We use the General Social Survey as well as the Survey of Public Participation in the Arts, which has been collected periodically since 1982 by the Census Bureau for the National Endowment for the Arts. First using just the 1982 survey, we found that while those from the most high-status occupations (professionals and executives) are by far the most likely to attend classical music concerts, opera, ballet, and theater and to visit art museums, they do not restrict themselves solely to such highbrow pursuits. Of all the occupational groups, they were also the most likely to take part in a wide range of more plebeian pursuits, from attending sports events to gardening. What is more, they say they are interested in many types of popular music ranging (in 1982) from blues to rock, only drawing the line at country music. Thus highbrow exclusion is giving way to an enthusiastic embrace of most, if not all, cultural forms. It remains true that well-educated people with high-status occupations are the most likely to take part in fine arts activities of all sorts, but these same people are also more likely than others to engage in a broad range of popular-culture activities. Since they accept such diverse fine art and pop cultural pursuits, we call these new cosmopolitans "omnivores."

Using both 1982 and 1992 data, we show the growth of omnivorousness over time. Americans born since World War II are more likely to be omnivorous than their elders, and each generation has become more omnivorous over time. The evidence suggests that omnivorous taste does not mean that the omnivore consumes everything indiscriminately. Rather, it means being open to appreciating everything. While hostile to snobbishness, omnivorousness does not imply an indifference to distinctions; its emergence suggests new rules about what makes for good or bad taste. The criteria of distinction, of which omnivorousness is an expression, center not on what one consumes but on the way the items are understood. For the omnivore, expressions of all sorts are appreciated in terms of their own aesthetic.

In the case of music, over the years cultural experts have rethought successive "low" forms of music, such as jazz, country, blues, bluegrass, and rock. Expressions first generally viewed as nonmusical and morally corrupting each became a music to be appreciated on its own aesthetic terms. Ken Burns's ten-hour PBS series *Jazz*, for example, shows how a music of lowly origins was reconceived as art. Purged of its derogatory "rap" label, hip-hop music is currently in the early stages of such conversion, as scholarly evaluations are published and courses on hip-hop enter the college curriculum.

beethoven has been rolled

The full ramifications of the shift from highbrow snob to cosmopolitan omnivore in the second half of the twentieth century have yet to be fully explored. Nonetheless, the effect of this change on arts participation is all too clear to managers in the fine arts sector. Public arts participation had expanded rapidly over the third quarter of the twentieth century as numerous new orchestras, dance companies, theaters, and arts museums were formed and old ones expanded their offerings. What is more, the arts seemed slated for even more rapid expansion in the final quarter of the century as the exceptionally large group of people born following World War II reached adulthood. Not only were these baby boomers numerous, but many had the profile of arts appreciators. They were college-educated, urban, and, for their age, both affluent and unencumbered by young children in the home.

The arts boom did not continue. National levels of fine arts participation rose only gradually after 1980, and even this masks another, more fundamental change. The arts audience is aging significantly more rapidly than the general population. Shown in the study we conducted for the National Endowment for the Arts, the average age of people attending ballet and art museums increased seven years between 1982 and 1997, while audiences for theater and classical music aged five and six years, respectively. Only the audience for opera aged more slowly than Americans generally, but opera lovers were the oldest in the first place. The reason for this aging is not hard to find. Relatively fewer high-status middle-class baby boomers follow their elders as patrons of the arts. At the same time, they are much more likely to attend various low-status activities and appreciate more diverse kinds of music than those of lower-class standing. The latter are more likely to take part in a narrow range of activities associated with their ethnicity, occupation, and locality. We call such low-status people "univores." Some univores are devoted to ethnic music, rap, religious music, or heavy metal while shunning the other forms, a pattern that contrasts with the typically more affluent omnivores, who are more likely to be somewhat knowledgeable about most, if not all, these different styles of music and their associated subcultures.

The shift to omnivorousness helps explain the aging of the arts audience: The fine arts have lost

Posters at retail store catering to diverse musical tastes. Above poster features recording by a mountain fiddler, classical music cellist, and jazz bassist. (Photo by Jon Wagner)

their special importance in status display. In the era of the highbrow, participation in and donations to the fine arts were essential to status. Now, the fine arts are only one of many sorts of cultural activity that compete for time, energy, and money in the quest for status. In a recent nod to omnivorous tastes, the British Council, which is the government agency responsible for publicizing the best of Great Britain among people around the world, has changed its representation of what is best about Britain. For generations Shakespeare and the other notable writers and scientists alone were used to illustrate Britain's excellence, but in 2000, the council changed its publicity thrust. It now portrays England as the cradle of the game the world knows as football and the home of some of that sport's great current players. Promotional displays feature young, handsome David Beckham, soccer celebrity and husband of Victoria "Posh Spice" Adams, member of the internationally famous Spice Girls.

Of course, Shakespeare isn't dead yet. In this omnivorous era of mix and match, Will has returned as an all-too-human bumbling young playwright in the film *Shakespeare in Love*. Mozart has also been given humanizing treatment in another hit film, *Amadeus*. It is only a matter of time before a film portrays Ludwig von Beethoven as the Chuck Berry of his day. Arts promoters are finding a variety of ways to enrich the arts by forging closer ties with popular culture.

Moving beyond the realm of culture, there is mounting evidence that omnivores are more socially tolerant, environmentally concerned, and committed to democratic ideas than their highbrow counterparts. Just as there was an affinity between nineteenth-century entrepreneurial capitalism and the highbrow, there seems to be an affinity between omnivorousness and the needs of the world-traveling corporate elite.

RECOMMENDED RESOURCES

Pierre Bourdieu. *Distinction: A Social Critique of the Judgement of Taste* (Harvard University Press, 1984 [1979]).

Explores the ways French taste differs by class; this study has spawned a generation of research.

Herbert J. Gans. *Popular Culture and High Culture: An Analysis and Evaluation of Taste* (Basic Books, 1999).

Updated from a 1970s essay, this edition identifies a range of taste cultures.

Michèle Lamont. *Money, Morals, and Manners: The Culture of the French and the American Upper Middle Class* (University of Chicago Press, 1992).

Lamont asked Frenchmen and Americans how they choose the people with whom they want to associate. Parisians stress manners, New Yorkers money, and the Americans generally stress morals.

Lawrence W. Levine. *Highbrow/Lowbrow: The Emergence of Cultural Hierarchy in America* (Harvard University Press, 1988).

Examines the nineteenth-century creation of the highbrow idea, showing, for example, how the popular Shakespeare became "difficult."

Richard A. Peterson, Pamela C. Hull, and Roger Kern. *Age and Arts Participation: 1982–1997.* National Endowment for the Arts, Research Monograph 34 (Seven Locks Press, 2000).

Shows that American audiences for the fine arts are rapidly aging.

Richard A. Peterson and Roger Kern. "Changing Highbrow Taste: From Snob to Omnivore." *American Sociological Review* 61 (1996): 900–07.

Documents the omnivore-univore pattern and suggests an explanation.

Richard A. Peterson and Albert Simkus. "How Musical Taste Groups Mark Occupational Status Groups." In *Cultivating Differences: Symbolic Boundaries and the Making of Inequality*, eds. Michèle Lamont and Marcel Fournier (University of Chicago Press, 1992).

Omnivorousness as a style of status signaling is introduced here.

REVIEW QUESTIONS

1. Peterson quotes an 1883 article, which states that certain pieces of art are "not only tests of taste, but even of character." Do you feel that this has changed? Write a paragraph on your own consumption of culture, and identify specific instances in which you feel it is closely connected to your character.
2. Peterson makes the interesting claim that "omnivores" have developed a different way of determining what makes for "good" and "bad" taste." What are the criteria?
3. Fancy dress and refined etiquette used to distinguish those who consumed high culture from the masses, but as technology has developed, more people can seemingly acquire more—not just higher—forms of culture. Everyone, for

example, can have a reproduction of Edvard Munch's *The Scream* on his or her dorm wall. Do you feel that this access gives the illusion of a classless society in the United States? Defend your position.

4. Activity: List your top ten favorite music albums/CDs and your top ten favorite movies, and identify both according to genre (hip-hop, romantic comedy, etc.). Now ask one of your parents to do the same. In class, break up in groups and discuss whether or not you feel the diversity of cultural consumption in parents increases the likelihood of "omnivorousness" in your peers.

karen sternheimer

do video games kill?

fall 2006

18

when white, middle-class teens kill, the media and politicians are quick to blame video games. are they right?

As soon as it was released in 1993, a video game called *Doom* became a target for critics. Not the first, but certainly one of the most popular first-person shooter games, *Doom* galvanized fears that such games would teach kids to kill. In the years after its release, *Doom* helped video gaming grow into a multibillion-dollar industry, surpassing Hollywood box-office revenues and further fanning public anxieties.

Then came the school shootings in Paducah, Kentucky; Springfield, Oregon; and Littleton, Colorado. In all three cases, press accounts emphasized that the shooters loved *Doom*, making it appear that the critics' predictions about video games were coming true.

But in the ten years following *Doom*'s release, homicide arrest rates fell by 77 percent among juveniles. School shootings remain extremely rare; even during the 1990s, when fears of school violence were high, students had less than a 7 in 10 million chance of being killed at school. During that time, video games became a major part of many young people's lives, few of whom will ever become violent, let alone kill. So why is the video game explanation so popular?

contemporary folk devils

In 2000 the FBI issued a report on school rampage shootings, finding that their rarity prohibits the construction of a useful profile of a "typical" shooter. In the absence of a simple explanation, the public symbolically linked these rare and complex events to the shooters' alleged interest in video games, finding in them a catchall explanation for what seemed unexplainable—the white, middle-class school shooter. However, the concern about video games is out of proportion to their actual threat.

Politicians and other moral crusaders create "folk devils," individuals or groups defined as evil and immoral. Folk devils allow us to channel our blame and fear, offering a clear course of action to remedy what many believe to be a growing problem. Video games, those who play them, and those who create them have become contemporary folk devils because they seem to pose a threat to children.

Such games have come to represent a variety of social anxieties: about youth violence, new computer technology, and the apparent decline in the ability of adults to control what young people do and what they know. Panics about youth and popular culture have emerged with the appearance of many new technologies. Over the past century, politicians have complained that cars, radio, movies, rock music, and even comic books caused youth immorality and crime, calling for control and sometimes censorship.

Acting on concerns like these, politicians often position themselves as engaged in battles between good and evil on our behalf and claim to offer solutions. The unlikely team of Senators Joseph Lieberman, Sam Brownback, Hillary

Rodham Clinton, and Rick Santorum introduced a bill in March 2005 that called for $90 million to fund studies on media effects. Lieberman commented, "America is a media-rich society, but despite the flood of information, we still lack perhaps the most important piece of information—what effect are media having on our children?" Regardless of whether any legislation passes, the senators position themselves as protecting children and benefit from the moral panic they help to create.

constructing culpability

Politicians are not the only ones who blame video games. Since 1997, 199 newspaper articles have focused on video games as a central explanation for the Paducah, Springfield, and Littleton school shootings. This helped to create a groundswell of fear that schools were no longer safe and that rampage shootings could happen wherever there were video games. The shootings legitimated existing concerns about the new medium and about young people in general. Headlines such as "Virtual Realities Spur School Massacres" (*Denver Post*, July 27, 1999), "Days of Doom" (*Pittsburgh Post-Gazette*, May 14, 1999), "Bloodlust Video Games Put Kids in the Crosshairs" (*Denver Post*, May 30, 1999), and "All Those Who Deny Any Linkage between Violence in Entertainment and Violence in Real Life, Think Again" (*New York Times*, April 26, 1999) insist that video games are the culprit.

These headlines all appeared immediately after the Littleton shooting, which had the highest death toll and inspired most (176) of the news stories alleging a video game connection. Across the country, the press attributed much of the blame to video games specifically and to Hollywood more generally. The *Pittsburgh Post-Gazette* article "Days of Doom" noted that "eighteen people have now died at the hands of avid *Doom* players." The *New York Times* arti-

cle noted above began, "By producing increasingly violent media, the entertainment industry has for decades engaged in a lucrative dance with the devil," evoking imagery of a fight against evil. It went on to construct video games as a central link: "The two boys apparently responsible for the massacre in Littleton, Colo., last week were, among many other things, accomplished players of the ultraviolent video game *Doom*. And Michael Carneal, the 14-year-old boy who opened fire on a prayer group in a Paducah, Ky., school foyer in 1997, was also known to be a video-game expert."

Just as many stories insisted that video games deserved at least partial blame, editorial pages around the country made the connection as well:

President Bill Clinton is right. He said this shooting was no isolated incident, that Kinkel and other teens accused of killing teachers and fellow students reflect a changing culture of violence on television and in movies and video games. (*Cleveland Plain Dealer*, May 30, 1998)

The campaign to make Hollywood more responsible . . . should proceed full speed ahead. (*Boston Herald*, April 9, 2000)

Make no mistake, Hollywood is contributing to a culture that feeds on and breeds violence . . . When entertainment companies craft the most shocking video games and movies they can, peddle their virulent wares to an impressionable audience with abandon, then shrug off responsibility for our culture of violence, they deserve censure. (*St. Louis Post-Dispatch*, April 12, 2000)

The video game connection took precedence in all these news reports. Some stories mentioned other explanations, such as the shooters' social rejection, feelings of alienation at school, and depression, but these were treated mostly as minor factors compared with video games. Reporters gave these other reasons far less attention than violent video games, and frequently discussed them at the end of the articles.

The news reports typically introduce experts early in the stories who support the video game explanation. David Grossman, a former army lieutenant described as a professor of "killology," has claimed that video games are "murder simulators" and serve as an equivalent to military training. Among the 199 newspaper articles published, 17 of them mentioned or quoted Grossman. Additionally, an attorney who has filed several lawsuits against video game producers wrote an article for the *Denver Post* insisting that the games are to blame. By contrast, only 7 articles identified sociologists as experts. Writers routinely presented alternative explanations as rebuttals, but rarely explored them in depth.

> Focusing on extremely rare and perhaps unpredictable outbursts of violence by young people discourages the public from looking closely at more typical forms of violence against young people, which is usually perpetrated by adults.

reporting on research

By focusing so heavily on video games, news reports diminish the broader social contexts. While a handful of articles note the roles that guns, poverty, families, and the organization of schools may play in youth violence in general, when reporters mention research to explain the shooters' behavior, the vast majority of studies cited are studies of media effects, suggesting that video games are a central cause.

Since the early days of radio and movies, investigators have searched for possible effects—typically negative—that different media may have on audiences, especially children. Such research became more intense following the rise in violent crime in the United States between the 1960s and early 1990s, focusing primarily on television. Several hundred studies asked whether exposure to media violence predicts involvement in actual violence.

Although often accepted as true—one scholar has gone so far as to call the findings about the effects of media violence on behavior a "law"—this body of research has been highly controversial. One such study fostered claims that television had led to more than 10,000 murders in the United States and Canada during the twentieth century. This and many other media-effects studies rely on correlation analysis, often finding small but sometimes statistically significant links between exposure to media violence and aggressive behavior.

But such studies do not demonstrate that media violence causes aggressive behavior, only that the two phenomena exist together. Excluding a host of other factors (such as the growing unrest during the civil rights and antiwar movements, and the disappearance of jobs in central cities) may make it seem that a direct link exists between the introduction of television and homicides. In all likelihood any connection is incidental.

It is equally likely that more aggressive people seek out violent entertainment. Aggression includes a broad range of emotions and behaviors, and is not always synonymous with violence. Measures of aggression in media-effects research have varied widely, from observing play between children and inanimate objects to counting the number of speeding tickets a person received. Psychologist Jonathan Freedman reviewed every media-violence study published in English and concluded that "the majority of studies produced evidence that is inconsistent or even contradicts" the claim that exposure to media violence causes real violence.

Recently, video games have become a focus of research. Reviews of this growing literature have also been mixed. A 2001 meta-analysis in *Psychological Science* concluded that video games "will increase aggressive behavior," while a similar review published that same year in a different journal found that "it is not possible to determine whether video game violence affects aggressive behavior." A 2005 review found evidence that playing video games improves spatial skills and reaction times, but did not support the idea that the games increase aggression.

The authors of the *Psychological Science* article advocate the strong-effects hypothesis. Two of their studies were widely reported on in 2000, the year after the Columbine High School shootings, with scant critical analysis. But their research was based on college undergraduates, not troubled teens, and it measured aggression in part by subjects' speed in reading "aggressive" words on a computer screen or blasting opponents with sound after playing a violent video game. These measures do not approximate the conditions the school shooters experienced, nor do they offer much insight as to why they and not the millions of other players decided to acquire actual weapons and shoot real people.

Occasionally reporters include challenges like this in stories containing media-effects claims, but news coverage usually refers to this body of research as clear, consistent, and conclusive. "The evidence, say those who study violence in culture, is unassailable: Hundreds of studies in recent decades have revealed a direct correlation between exposure to media violence—now including video games—and increased aggression," said the *New York Times* (April 26, 1999). The *Boston Herald* quoted a clinical psychologist who said, "Studies have already shown that watching television shows with aggressive or violent content makes children more

aggressive" (July 30, 2000). The psychologist noted that video game research is newer, but predicted that "in a few years, studies will show that video games increase a child's aggression even more than violent TV shows." News reports do not always use academic sources to assess the conclusiveness of media effects research. A *Pittsburgh Post-Gazette* story included a quote by an attorney, who claimed, "Research on this has been well-established" (May 14, 1999).

It is no accident that media-effects research and individual explanations dominate press attempts to explain the behavior of the school shooters. Although many politicians are happy to take up the cause against video games, popular culture itself suggests an apolitical explanation of violence and discourages a broader examination of structural factors. Focusing on extremely rare and perhaps unpredictable outbursts of violence by young people discourages the public from looking closely at more typical forms of violence against young people, which is usually perpetrated by adults.

The biggest problem with media-effects research is that it attempts to decontextualize violence. Poverty, neighborhood instability, unemployment, and even family violence fall by the wayside in most of these studies. Ironically, even mental illness tends to be overlooked in this psychologically oriented research. Young people are seen as passive media consumers, uniquely and uniformly vulnerable to media messages.

missing media studies

News reports of the shootings that focus on video games ignore other research on the meanings that audiences make from media culture. This may be because its qualitative findings are difficult to turn into simple quotations or sound bites. Yet in seeking better understanding of the role of video games in the lives of the shooters and young people more generally, media scholars could have added much to the public debate.

For instance, one study found that British working-class boys boast about how many horror films they have seen as they construct their sense of masculinity by appearing too tough to be scared. Another study examined how younger boys talk about movies and television as a way to manage their anxieties and insecurities regarding their emerging sense of masculinity. Such studies illustrate why violent video games may appeal to many young males.

Media scholars have also examined how and why adults construct concerns about young people and popular culture. One such study concluded that some adults use their condemnation of media as a way to produce cultural distinctions that position them above those who enjoy popular culture. Other researches have found that people who believe their political knowledge is superior to that of others are more likely to presume that media violence would strongly influence others. They have also found that respondents who enjoy television violence are less likely to believe it has a negative effect.

Just as it is too simplistic to assert that video game violence makes players more prone to violence, news coverage alone, however dramatic or repetitive, cannot create consensus among the public that video games cause youth violence. Finger-wagging politicians and other moralizers often alienate as many members of the public as they convert. In an ironic twist, they may even feed the anti-authoritarian appeal that may draw players of all ages to the games.

The lack of consensus does not indicate the absence of a moral panic, but reveals contradictory feelings toward the target group. The intense focus on video games as potential creators of violent killers reflects the hostility that some feel toward popular culture and young people themselves. After, adult rampage shootings in the workplace (which happen more often than school shootings), reporters seldom mention whether the shooters played video games. Nor is an entire generation feared as potential killers.

ambivalence about juvenile justice

The concern in the late 1990s about video games coincided with a growing ambivalence about the juvenile justice system and young offenders. Fears about juvenile "super-predators," fanned by former Florida Representative Bill McCollom's 1996 warning that we should "brace ourselves" against the coming storm of young killers, made the school shootings appear inevitable. McCollom and other politicians characterized young people as a "new breed," uniquely dangerous and amoral.

These fears were produced partially by the rise in crime during the late 1980s and early 1990s, but also by the so-called echo boom that produced a large generation of teens during the late 1990s. Demographic theories of crime led policy makers to fear that the rise in the number of teen males would bring a parallel rise in crime. In response, virtually every state changed its juvenile justice laws during the decade. They increased penalties, imposed mandatory minimum sentences, blended jurisdiction with criminal courts, and made it easier to transfer juvenile cases to adult criminal courts.

So before the first shot was fired in Paducah, politicians warned the public to be on the lookout for killer kids. Rather than being seen as tragic anomalies, these high-profile incidents appeared to support scholarly warnings that all kids posed an increasing threat. Even though juvenile (and adult) crime was in sharp decline, the intense media coverage contributed to the appearance of a new trend.

Blaming video games meant that the shooters were set aside from other violent youth, frequently poor males of color, at whom our get-tough legislation has been targeted. According to the National Center for Juvenile Justice, African-American juveniles are involved in the juvenile justice system more than twice as often as whites. The video game explanation constructs the white, middle-class shooters as victims of the power of video games, rather than fully culpable criminals. When boys from "good" neighborhoods are violent, they seem to be harbingers of a "new breed" of youth, created by video games rather than by their social circumstances. White, middle-class killers retain their status as children easily influenced by a game, victims of an allegedly dangerous product. African-American boys, apparently, are simply dangerous.

While the news media certainly questioned what role the shooters' parents may have played, the press tended to tread lightly on them, particularly the Kinkels of Springfield, Oregon, who were their son's first murder victims. Their middle-class, suburban, or rural environments were given little scrutiny. The white school shooters did more than take the lives of their classmates; their whiteness and middle-class status threatened the idea of the innocence and safety of suburban America.

In an attempt to hold more than just the shooters responsible, the victims' families filed lawsuits against film producers, Internet sites, and video game makers. Around the same time, Congress made it more difficult to sue gun manufacturers for damages. To date, no court has found entertainment producers liable for causing young people to commit acts of violence. In response to a lawsuit filed following the Paducah shootings, a Kentucky circuit judge ruled that "we are loath to hold that ideas and images can constitute the tools for a criminal act," and that product liability law did not apply because the product did not injure its consumer. The lawsuit was dismissed, as were subsequent suits filed after the other high-profile shootings.

game over?

Questions about the power of media and the future of the juvenile justice system persist. In March 2005, the U.S. Supreme Court ruled that juvenile executions were unconstitutional. This ruling represents an about-face in the 25-year trend toward toughening penalties for young offenders. While many human rights and children's advocates praised this decision, it was sharply criticized by those who believe that the juvenile justice system is already too lenient. Likewise, critics continue to target video games, as their graphics and plot capabilities grow more complex and at times more disturbing. Meanwhile, youth crime rates continue to decline. If we want to understand why young people, particularly in middle-class or otherwise stable environments, become homicidal, we need to look beyond the games they play. While all forms of media merit critical analysis, so do the supposedly "good" neighborhoods and families that occasionally produce young killers.

RECOMMENDED RESOURCES

Ronald Burns and Charles Crawford. "School Shootings, the Media, and Public Fear: Ingredients for a Moral Panic." *Crime, Law, and Social Change* 32 (1999): 147–68.

> Examines fears about school shootings in the 1990s, paying special attention to the disproportional nature of the actual threat.

Jonathan L. Freedman. *Media Violence and Its Effect on Aggression: Assessing the Scientific Evidence* (University of Toronto Press, 2002).

A thorough analysis of the body of media-effects research with a critique of methods and interpretation of results.

Erich Goode and Nachman Ben-Yehuda. *Moral Panics: The Social Construction of Deviance* (Blackwell, 1994).

A primer on moral panics, with basic definitions as well as several seminal case studies.

John Springhall. *Youth, Popular Culture and Moral Panics: Penny Gaffs to Gangsta-Rap, 1830–1996* (St. Martin's, 1998).

A history of fears about young people and media.

Franklin E. Zimring. *American Youth Violence* (Oxford University Press, 1998).

A comprehensive look at trends in youth crime and recent changes in juvenile justice, as well as political discourse about youth violence.

REVIEW QUESTIONS

1. What are "folk devils"? What are the functions of these cultural phenomena as they relate to video games?
2. In 2005 a multimillion-dollar lawsuit was filed against a video game company in Alabama, because it was seen as a sort of "murder simulator." Does research show that video games definitely caused this violent behavior?
3. What does Sternheimer identify as the biggest problem with media-effects research?
4. Describe how, by blaming video games, white middle-class shooters are set aside from other violent youth. Discuss the repercussions of this practice.

joshua gamson and pearl latteier

do media monsters devour diversity?   **19**

summer 2004

politicians and critics have long lamented that the rise of huge media conglomerates means the death of diversity in newspapers and on the airwaves. but research suggests that media conglomeration, however distasteful, does not necessarily reduce diversity.

Something odd is going on when Ted Turner, Trent Lott, Al Franken, the National Rifle Association, Jesse Jackson, and Walter Cronkite agree. Opposition to media consolidation has turned these adversaries on most issues into bedfellows. When the Federal Communications Commission (FCC) prepared to further loosen restrictions on media ownership—a move approved by the FCC in June 2003 and then blocked by a circuit court three months later—the decision was met with a motley chorus of criticism. FCC commissioner Jonathan Adelstein called the problem "the McDonaldization of American media." Former Senator Carol Moseley-Braun stated that "we have to ensure that there is a diversity of ownership, a diversity of voice." And Cronkite, the veteran and widely respected news anchor, declared concentration "an impediment to a free and independent press." The new rules would "stifle debate, inhibit new ideas, and shut out smaller businesses trying to compete," said Turner, whose vast holdings include CNN, TBS, and Hanna-Barbera cartoons, and who is a major shareholder in parent company Time Warner AOL. "There are really five companies that control 90 percent of what we read, see and hear. It's not healthy," Turner added.

Critics and policy makers have long been troubled by consolidation among America's mainstream media. Opponents of the Communications Act of 1934—which established the FCC and allocated the majority of the airwaves to commercial broadcasters—warned that commercial, network-dominated radio would squelch, as the ACLU director then put it, the few small stations that "voice critical or radical views." And in 1978, the Supreme Court ruled "it is unrealistic to expect true diversity from a commonly owned station-newspaper combination." Nonetheless, during the past two decades—and with a big boost from the Telecommunications Act of 1996—media ownership has become increasingly concentrated in fewer and fewer hands. Time and Warner Brothers merged into the world's biggest media company in 1989. A decade later, Viacom and CBS set a new record for the largest corporate merger ever. And the 2000 AOL-TimeWarner merger was several times bigger than that.

The critics' logic is this: Citizens need access to diverse sources of news and opinions to make well-informed decisions about how to vote and live. Also, media should address the needs and interests of America's diverse population, and not just those of its elite. When a small group of "gatekeepers" controls how information circulates, the spectrum of available ideas, images, and opinions narrows. Big media companies prefer programming and voices that conform to their own financial interests, and they make it nearly impossible for smaller, independent companies to offer alternatives.

Offices in Berkeley, California, for KPFA, the flagship radio station of the independent Pacifica Broadcasting Network. Consolidated ownership of many local radio stations, most notably by Clear Channel Communications, has dramatically decreased local programming while increasing the number of syndicated shows that air simultaneously in multiple markets. (Photo by Jon Wagner)

This frightening vision is intuitively reasonable. But a close look at decades of scholarship on the relationship between media ownership and content diversity uncovers a surprising story—one much more complicated than the vision of media monsters gobbling up diversity. Scholars have zeroed in on three broadly defined types of diversity in media: format diversity, demographic diversity, and idea diversity.

The research suggests that when it comes to "diversity," media-consolidation critics are, if not barking up the wrong tree, at least in need of a more nuanced, sharper, more carefully directed bark. Indeed, effective opposition to media ownership consolidation may require, ironically, acknowledging the ways media giants sometimes promote diverse content.

format diversity

Suppose you turn on your TV after dinner, and every single channel is broadcasting either an *American Idol* spin-off or a makeover show. That would mean the after-dinner time slot in your area lacks "format diversity"—or variety in programming—turning everything into, as FCC commissioner Adelstein describes it, "Big Mac, fries and a Coke." In particular, observers worry that consolidation undercuts local content. Most experts agree that this has happened to radio since the late 1990s, as Clear Channel Communications has gobbled up stations throughout the country. Programming that was once determined locally is now overseen by Clear Channel programmers headquartered elsewhere, and local disc jockeys have been replaced by a single show that plays simultaneously in multiple markets. Consolidation of radio ownership encourages this centralized, cost-cutting format. The same logic would be expected in newspapers and television; running wire service copy is cheaper than employing staff reporters, and standardized production is less expensive than hiring a team of local broadcasters.

Of course, because different audiences are attracted to different content and format types, it also makes business sense for a conglomerate to maintain different sorts of programming—including locally produced content—just as General Motors produces lines of cars for different types of customers. This can actually promote format diversity. In a market with three competing stations, argues communications law expert Edwin Baker, each station will try to attract the largest possible audience by providing fare that the majority prefers. The stations will wind up sounding pretty similar. In contrast, if all three stations are owned by the same company, ownership has no incentive to compete against itself, and will try to make the stations dissimilar in order to attract different audiences. Similarly, it makes sense for entertainment conglomerates to make their various holdings more rather than less distinct in format, and to build a "diverse portfolio" of media properties. Viacom does not want its UPN (*America's Next Top Model, The Parkers, WWE Smackdown*) to be like its CBS (*CSI, Judging Amy, Late Show with David Letterman*), its Sundance Channel (documentaries on HIV/AIDS, the films of Patrice Chereau) to air the same kind of material as its Spike TV (*Sports Illustrated's 40th Anniversary Swimsuit Special*), or its Downtown Press ("chick-lit" like Alexandra Potter's *Calling Romeo*) to publish what its Atria Press does ("academic" titles like bell hooks' *The Will to Change*). This multiple-brand logic promotes rather than reduces format diversity.

Research suggests that media consolidation does not simply increase or decrease format diversity. Some studies compare the fate of local or public-affairs programming in independent versus conglomerated companies. Others look for shifts in content after a publication is bought by a bigger company. The results are tellingly mixed. Some find big differences between the offerings of independent and corporate-owned outlets, but ambiguous effects on format diversity. Others find little or no difference at all. For example, a 1995 study found that two years after Gannett—owner of *USA Today*, among many other papers—bought the *Louisville Courier-Journal*, the paper devoted almost 30 percent more space to news than it had before, and 7 percent less space to advertising. On the other hand, the average story became shorter, the percentage of hard-news stories smaller, and wire stories came to outnumber staff-written ones. Within the expanded news reporting, the proportions of local, national, and international news changed little. The paper became more like *USA Today*, but simultaneously the "news hole"—the amount of content consisting of news reporting—increased from when it was independently owned. Other studies of Gannett-bought papers—in Arkansas and Florida—found that international and national news decreased after the company took over. Local news, often in the form of crime or disaster stories, actually increased after consolidation.

A recent large-scale, five-year study by the Project for Excellence in Journalism also found mixed results. The researchers asked who produces "higher-quality" local television news, which they defined as news that "covers the whole community," is "significant and informative," demonstrates "enterprise and courage," and is "fair, balanced, and accurate," "authoritative," and "highly local." Although they did not isolate "format diversity" in their study, they nonetheless offer some clues about the relationship between ownership and formats. On the one hand, just as anti-consolidation critics would predict, of 172 newscasts and 23,000 stories, researchers found the "best" programs overall tended to come from smaller station groups or from stations affiliated with but not owned by networks. On the other hand, they also found that "local ownership offered little protection against newscasts being very poor." As an evening's cursory viewing might confirm, local news is weak regardless of whether or not it is part of a conglomerate. Even more to the point, the researchers found that stations whose parent companies owned a newspaper in the same market—exactly the kind of "cross-ownership" that consolidation critics worry about—produced "higher-quality" newscasts, including more locally relevant content. They ran more stories on "important community issues" and fewer celebrity and human-interest stories. Cross-ownership shifted the types of programming provided, but in the direction most critics of cross-ownership seem to favor. Moreover, being owned by a small company, while an advantage when it came to "quality," was certainly no guarantee of a diverse mix of local and nonlocal content.

For a glimpse of how big media corporations—aided by government deregulation—sometimes do reduce format diversity, look at the current state of commercial radio. In a series of scathing articles for Salon, Eric Boehlert exposed Clear Channel as "radio's big bully," known for "allowing animals to be killed live on the air, severing long-standing ties with community and charity events, laying off thousands of workers, homogenizing playlists, and a corporate culture in which dirty tricks are a way of life." Concentrated, conglomerate ownership is certainly a prerequisite for being a big bully, and Clear Channel has used its power to undercut local programming and standardize rather than diversity both music and talk on radio. But radio's striking homogeneity is not just the result of concentrated ownership. As Boehlert wrote in 2001, radio "sucks" (similar-sounding songs, cookie-cutter stars) because record companies, through independent promoters, pay radio stations huge amounts to get their songs on playlists. With or without Clear Channel, material without money behind it—alternative styles of music, music by artists who do not fit the standard celebrity model, innovative and therefore risky formats—does not get airplay. It is not that ownership has no effect on format diversity, only that the impact is neither uniform nor inevitable. It is instead influenced by particular corporate strategies and the inner-workings of particular media industries.

demographic diversity

In everyday conversations, diversity usually refers to demographics: whether a workplace employs or a school enrolls people of various racial, ethnic, gender, and economic categories. How the media represents and addresses the interests of America's diverse populations—who gets seen and heard—is, appropriately, often in question. Studies routinely find that the individuals appearing in mass media are disproportionately white, middle-class men between the ages of 20 and 60. But they have not figured out how, if at all, concentrated corporate ownership affects representation. This should not be surprising. A gap between the diversity of the population and media images of that population existed long before the rise of the media giants. And it clearly cuts across commercial and non-commercial media: studies of public broadcasting's guests show little demographic diversity, while daytime talk shows produced by for-profit conglomerates—however tawdry—offer some of the greatest demographic diversity on television.

Both government agencies and scholars have assumed that the key to ensuring demographically diverse content is demographically diverse ownership. Until recently, the FCC and the courts attempted to promote this kind of diversity by giving licensing preferences to minority-owned (and sometimes female-owned) broadcast stations. The FCC halted the licensing preferences in 1995, and the rapid consolidation of deregulated media companies makes it even less likely that companies and stations will be minority-owned today. Although it might seem reasonable to think that fewer minority-owned companies will mean less demographically diverse content—in surveys, minority owners do report being more likely to produce "minority" programming—studies of content do not back up such claims. Two studies comparing minority-owned (African American and Latino) radio stations to white-owned stations in the 1980s found that owners' ethnic backgrounds did not significantly affect demographic representation in their programming. There are many good reasons to pursue affirmative action in media ownership and employment, but ensuring diversity in media content is not one of them.

If anything has promoted demographic diversity in media content, it is the rise of niche-marketing and narrow-casting, which target previously excluded demographic groups with images of themselves. Although minority owners often typically start that process—gay marketers tapping the gay niche, Latino publishers targeting Latino readers—it proceeds regardless of whether they remain owners. Indeed, niche marketing has become a media-giant staple: Time Warner AOL started the highly successful *People en Español* in 1996, NBC-owned Bravo produced the summer 2003 hit *Queer Eye for the Straight Guy*. Robert Johnson became the first African-American billionaire when he sold Black Entertainment Television to Viacom in 2002, and the largest shareholder of radio's Hispanic Broadcasting Corporation is Clear Channel. Multicultural content and oligopoly media ownership are clearly not incompatible.

idea diversity

Almost everyone pays lip service to the notion that citizenship thrives when people are exposed to a variety of contending viewpoints. As the number of owners decreases, critics of media conglomeration argue, so does the number of voices contributing to the "marketplace of ideas." Media conglomerates with holdings in all kinds of other media and nonmedia industries have the power to censor the news in accordance with their interests. There is plenty of anecdotal evidence that consolidation tips content against ideas critical of the corporate owners. The *Los Angeles Times*, for example, failed in 1980 to cover a taxpayer-funded $2 billion water project that stood to benefit the Times-Mirror Company. Likewise, NBC remained silent on the 1990 boycott of their owner GE. And CBS's *America Tonight* show had a pro-tobacco bias in the mid-1990s, when the Loews Corporation, owner of Lorillard Tobacco, held a controlling interest in CBS. Disney-owned ABC News even cancelled an investigative report about sloppy background checks at Disneyworld. A recent study also found a "synergy bias" among media giants, in which media companies slip unannounced promotions of their other products and services into newscasts—as when ABC devoted two hours of *Good Morning America* to Disneyworld's 25th Anniversary. In short, media corporations act in their own special interests, promote ideas that suit those interests, and sometimes "spike" stories through self-censorship.

Beyond these forms of direct self-interest, though, the connection between ownership concentration and idea diversity is harder to discern. Generally speaking, one might observe that the American media environment has been an inhospitable place for radical, dissenting voices before, during, and after the rise of media giants. More specifically, scholars have found that viewpoint diversity does not line up neatly with particular ownership structures. For example, the recent Project for Excellence in Journalism study of local television measured how many sources were cited in a story and how many points of view were represented in stories involving a dispute or controversy. Locally owned stations presented no more viewpoint diversity than nonlocally owned ones, and small companies no more than big ones. Network-owned-and-operated stations did better than smaller, less well-funded affiliates. The weak connection between viewpoint diversity and monopoly ownership is actually old news. In a classic 1985 study, Robert Entman examined the first page and editorial section of 91 newspapers in three types of markets: competitive local markets with multiple, separately owned papers; monopolistic markets with only one local newspaper; and "quasi-monopolies," where joint-owned or joint-operated papers share a market. He measured diversity as the number of people or organizations mentioned in each story, and the number of stories that presented conflicting opinions. The study found that on no measure did independent papers present more diversity than papers in monopoly or quasi-monopoly situations. In all of the papers, more than half the stories involved fewer than two actors, and less than one-tenth presented conflicting opinions. In other words, regardless of who owned them or how competitive their markets were, the papers were not exactly brimming with lively debate and diverse ideas.

the challenge for media reformers

The radical concentration of global media ownership has spawned at least one excellent, rebellious child: a vibrant, smart, broad-based media reform movement. Groups like Fairness & Accuracy in Reporting, the Media Alliance, the Center for Digital Democracy, Independent Media Centers, the People's Communication Charter, and many others, are growing in strength, alliance, and effectiveness. There are many reasons to object to media oligopolies that research on diversity does not speak to: the concentration of private power over a public resource in a democracy is wrong in principle; standardized media are part of a distasteful, branded, chainstore life of Barnes and Noble, Starbucks, and Disney; corporate, multinational media are increasingly unaccountable to the public; and a corporate press is probably a less adversarial press. But the research on media concentration should challenge this reform move-

ment to relinquish at least one sacrosanct belief. If our goal is vibrant, diverse media content—what the People's Communication Charter, an international activist group, refers to as the "plurality of opinions and the diversity of cultural expressions and languages necessary for democracy"—then research suggests that concentrated ownership is not equivalent to reduced diversity. Sometimes corporate media giants homogenize, and sometimes they do not. Sometimes they shut people up and stifle dissent, and sometimes they open up extra space for new people to be visible and vocal. That they do so not because they are committed to the public good but because diversity sometimes serves their interests does not negate the outcome. And, romantic notions notwithstanding, independently owned and noncommercial media hardly guarantee diverse content.

Just as there are different kinds of diversity, there are also different kinds of ownership concentration. A single corporation might own all the major outlets in a single market, or a chain of newspapers, or a film production company and a theater chain, or music, television, and book companies. These different kinds of concentration promote and inhibit different kinds of content diversity. Researchers, activists, and policy makers must identify the conditions under which concentrated, conglomerated media ownership facilitates diverse media formats, opinions, and demographic representations. A genuine commitment to diverse media content may require an unsettling task: encouraging those conditions even while opposing the corporate domination of media, feeding the giants while trying to topple them.

RECOMMENDED RESOURCES

Ben H. Bagdikian. *The Media Monopoly*, 6th ed. (Beacon Press, 2000).

In this new edition of a now classic book, Bagdikian presents an impassioned argument against media concentration.

C. Edwin Baker. *Media, Markets, and Democracy* (Cambridge University Press, 2002).

Demonstrates that media products are not like other commodities, and he argues that market competition alone fails to give media audiences what they want.

Columbia Journalism Review. "Who Owns What?" Online. http://www.cjr.org/tools/owners.

This informative Web site lists the holdings of approximately 50 major media companies.

Benjamin M. Compaine and Douglas Gomery. *Who Owns the Media? Competition and Concentration in the Mass Media Industry* (Lawrence Erlbaum Associates, 2000).

Provides a detailed look at the current media industry and challenges common assumptions about the dangers of ownership concentration.

David Croteau and William Hoynes. *The Business of Media: Corporate Media and the Public Interest* (Pine Forge Press, 2001).

Contrasts two different views of media conglomeration: the market model, which regards people as consumers, and the public-interest model, which regards people as citizens.

Robert M. Entman. "Newspaper Competition and First Amendment Ideals: Does-Monopoly Matter?" *Journal of Communication* 35 (1985): 147–65.

This study of newspapers in competitive and noncompetitive markets concludes that market competition does not guarantee content diversity.

Robert Horwitz. "On Media Concentration and the Diversity Question," Department of Communication, University of California, San Diego, 2003. Online. http://communication.ucsd.edu/people/ConcentrationpaperICA.htm.

A careful discussion of the media ownership debate, empirical research and the virtues of a "mixed media system."

Philip M. Napoli. "Deconstructing the Diversity Principle." *Journal of Communication* 49 (1999): 7–34.

Argues that the FCC policies on media ownership have long been based on unproven assumptions about the relationship between ownership diversity and content diversity.

REVIEW QUESTIONS

1. This essay describes a "weak connection" between idea diversity and ownership concentration. While this seems counterintuitive, identify the evidence Gamson and Lattleier use to support this idea.
2. "Niche marketing" and "narrowcasting" appear to promote diversity in the cultural industries, but discuss the effects of what might be considered a "ghettoization" or marginalization of representations of particular social groups and ideas.
3. Gamson and Latteier begin by identifying three types of diversity, and end with a puzzle: How does monopolist "corporate domination" foster the very diversity that it seems to hide? How do you see this conundrum affecting each type of diversity? How does media consolidation play a part?
4. Activity: Watchdog groups, like F.A.I.R. (Fairness and Accuracy in Reporting) and Media Matters for America, worry that the control of news programming by corporations is not primarily driven by profits, but that it does lead to censorship of political and social ideas. Drawing from the extensive online reporting of these two watchdog organizations, use examples to write a paragraph on a potential conflict of interest for Viacom or AOL-Time Warner's news operations.

patricia hill collins

black public intellectuals: from du bois to the present

20

fall 2005

black public intellectuals have unprecedented access to the media, but many no longer have daily contact with african-american communities. a few (mostly men) have become academic and media superstars, which helps sustain the illusion that american society is "color blind."

When sociologist W. E. B. Du Bois predicted that the problem of the twentieth century would be the color line, he pointed to a Jim Crow racism whose logic of segregation had permeated American society. Everything under Jim Crow was about color—seeing it, measuring it, finding even one drop of it, and assigning social value to individuals and groups according to their placement in a system of racial apartheid. However, the color line was not just about race. In a country where race and class remain so tightly intertwined, keeping the races segregated also ensured that money would stay in white families and that black Americans would become debtors across generations. This same logic of segregation also shaped ideas about "public" and "private" that were deeply gendered. The public sphere of work and government required a private sphere of gender and sexuality to give it meaning. The color line thus describes one of several strands in the logic of segregation that shaped American society.

When it comes to race, class, gender, and sexuality, we see similar and equally dramatic changes in our own times. In contrast to the turn of the twentieth century, the twenty-first century seems to be characterized by the *absence* of a color line. Legally outlawed in the 1950s and 1960s, the color-line policies of Jim Crow racial

segregation that kept most African Americans from quality education, good jobs, adequate health care, and the best neighborhoods are, for many, a distant memory or a lesson in a high school history text.

Yet when it comes to race, have we really resolved our problems? Formal legal discrimination has been outlawed, yet despite the American public's widespread acceptance of Martin Luther King, Jr.'s dream that we will judge one another by the content of our character and not by the color of our skin, this newfound color blindness seems unable to reverse the social inequalities of the Jim Crow era. By any measure, people of African descent remain disproportionately clustered at the bottom of the social hierarchy. In the United States, housing segregation persists, and when we look at the global context, as Howard Winant reminds us, "the world is a ghetto." Not everyone has enjoyed the border crossings, boundary bending, and marginality-as-a-space-of-radical-subjectivity celebrated within some academic circles. How can this be? How can America be color-blind, color-worshiping, and racially stratified all at the same time? We are left with a curious color blindness that replicates a long-standing color line, a *color-blind racism*, that relies on an apparently new logic of inclusivity.

Many sociologists would like to believe that social conditions do not affect the intellectual work we do and the tools we use to do it. Such beliefs suggest that only black people have the particularity of race, whereas everyone else is simply an individual judged by universalistic criteria. But, like Du Bois, African Americans who do intellectual work in a society that, from one generation to the next, aims to render us servants must continually struggle to create the conditions that make our own intellectual expression possible. Despite his brilliance, Du Bois, for example, found that the injustices of racial segregation profoundly affected his career as a sociologist. His racial touchstone was not an "imagined community"; he knew from experience how the color line affected his everyday life. How could Du Bois ignore the color line when, despite speaking several languages, holding a doctorate from Harvard University, and writing his impressive study, *The Philadelphia Negro*, the University of Pennsylvania refused to offer him a position? They didn't hire black people then, even eminently qualified ones. They were not alone.

As long as the social conditions in which African Americans actually live persist, so will these links between black intellectual expression and the meaning of race in America. Moreover, within these relations of knowledge and power, not all black intellectuals are the same. Du Bois belonged to a privileged class of African-American thinkers. He was part of the elite group of men who had access to literacy, schooling, and jobs that *paid* him to read and think. He was one of the lucky ones whose combination of class and gender enabled him to claim the public limelight. Through his choices to participate or not in these relations of knowledge and power, he leaves a legacy concerning the promises and pitfalls of black intellectual expression that is relevant to the contradictions of our own politics of color-blind racism.

Du Bois's stature as a black intellectual provides an important starting point for sketching out how the placement of African-American intellectuals in the contexts of earlier Jim Crow segregation and current color-blind racism shapes black thought. Du Bois's experiences remain valuable because they differ so dramatically from those of contemporary black intellectuals. During his long and distinguished career, Du Bois moved among academic and activist settings in the context of racial segregation. This movement shaped the questions, themes, and direction of his scholarship. He never attained the comfortable academic positions offered to others with his training and aptitude, yet the challenges of the color line made the intellectual work that he needed to do clear and exceedingly powerful. In contrast, as a class, contemporary black intellectuals have fared far better under the current color-blind color line. Several black intellectual celebrities who claim to be following in the footsteps of Du Bois hold prestigious academic positions at elite colleges and universities. Yet, the direction of their intellectual work on race and racism, as well as the terms of their participation in contemporary racial politics, seem far less clear. How might Du Bois's legacy as a black public intellectual shed light on these contemporary issues?

separating the public and the private

As a sociologist, Du Bois faced the problem of placing himself within what is now the dominant mode of intellectual production associated with Western science. The Western concept of intellectualism was shaped by binary understandings of universalism and particularism and of objectivity and special interests, as well as by public and private distinctions that arose with the new racial formations of the color line. We commonly equate intellectualism with universalism and with values that appear to

DR.W.E.B.DUBOIS

foster the objective, value-free, public science of society.

According to scientific norms, one becomes an intellectual by ceasing to espouse particularistic causes, identities, or special interests. For example, many sociologists see basic research as more important than scholarship that aims at social utility.

Such views of intellectualism put black intellectuals between a rock and a hard place. On the one hand, during Du Bois's career, black intellectuals found it very difficult to be acknowledged as intellectuals, and they certainly were not recognized for their so-called universal scholarship. African Americans were eager to use the tools of science but struggled against widespread perceptions that their essential racial difference—for example, their alleged

biological predisposition for stupidity, uncivilized sexuality, and violence—as well as their personal experiences with racism, made them less suitable for intellectual pursuits. On the other hand, black intellectuals who identified too closely with so-called black special interests by becoming champions of African-American issues risked being accused of an inability to see beyond their own special interests.

There is no way to win against this logic. So how did Du Bois manage to negotiate this dilemma and rise to the status of black public intellectual? Du Bois was a public intellectual, but who was his public? I suggest that living under Jim Crow segregation influenced all aspects of his life and fostered the attention he gave to multiple publics. He had to answer to an African-American public whose fate deeply affected his own. He grappled with the scholarly public that routinely challenged his identity as an intellectual. He also took a broader perspective and understood what was at stake in winning over the minds of both the American public and a global public. Keeping these various audiences in mind grounded his scholarship. Take, for example, Du Bois's description of his African-American students at Atlanta University: "I taught history and economics and something called 'sociology' at Atlanta University. . . . I was fortunate with this teaching in having vivid in the minds of my pupils a concrete social problem of which we all were parts and which we desperately desired to solve. There was little danger, then, of my teaching or of their thinking becoming purely theoretical." Not only did his students keep Du Bois from uncritically embracing universalism—in this case, purely theoretical views on the so-called race problem—but he also saw his work as squarely planted within a tradition of moral social service.

At the same time, the particularity of Du Bois's color-line politics limited his angle of vision. In contrast to his clarity about the way racism elevated the (white) universal over the (black) particular, he was less clear about the need to challenge the public/private binary that framed gender. His treatment of women illustrates this. Du Bois is often touted as a feminist because he wrote and spoke directly on the enfranchisement of women and the need to end discrimination against them. He called for tolerance toward black women and tried to support their interests. He spoke for them and was praised for doing so. Yet his support of the women in his intellectual circle was questionable. In failing to listen to Anna Julia Cooper, Ida B. Wells Barnett, and similar black feminist thinkers of his time, Du Bois missed an opportunity to advance a more complex analysis of race, class, and gender that would have led to a better understanding of the workings of racial segregation and the color line.

The contours of such an analysis were certainly available. For example, Wells Barnett's investigation of lynching gave us a more complex analysis of how race, gender, and sexuality met in constructing the color line. Arguing that lynching was economically motivated, Wells Barnett dared to challenge the common view that lynching was a legitimate punishment for black male rapists. Moreover, she raised the scandalous idea that sexual relations between black men and white women were often consensual. Yet the journalistic forms she chose to communicate her ideas were not associated with "scholarship." Because scholars typically categorized Wells Barnett more as a public *activist* and Du Bois as a public *intellectual*, her ideas remain marginalized, her groundbreaking analysis of the workings of the color line generally dismissed. Foreshadowing the current situation, Du Bois claimed the mantle of black public intellectual, whereas, until recently, black intellectual history largely ignored Wells Barnett.

This leads me to wonder how Du Bois thought of the color line itself. In describing the harm done by the color line, he used the gendered metaphor of the "veil" to challenge racial segregation, yet this same metaphor limited what he was able to see. Just as women can look at men from behind the veil and remain hidden, blacks can look at whites from behind the veil of race with similar results. Du Bois invoked gender, yet could not work within Wells Barnett's framework without seeing how his own achievements depended on the politics of gender. Racism had a profoundly gendered subtext that feminized blackness. (The castration of black lynch victims that Wells Barnett so graphically described points to this.) Feminization in turn creates different, gender-specific issues that go beyond the simple question of how black men and women fared within sociology.

Black cultural critic Hazel Carby suggests that we look beyond Du Bois's obvious accomplishments and pay closer attention to how gender politics frames the very categories of public, private, and intellectual. In discussing Du Bois, Carby suggests that scholars routinely relegate women to the realm of "domestic intellectual labor," whose purpose is to remain invisible and support the accomplishments of male intellectuals. Carby's remarks offer a much-needed gender critique and point out the distinctions between public intellectuals who garner attention in a male-defined "public sphere" and "domestic intellectuals" whose activities support those in the public limelight.

the contradictions of color-blind racism

The 1954 *Brown v. Board of Education* court victory aimed to stamp out color-line policies in the United States. By declaring that "in the field of public education the doctrine of 'separate but equal' has no place," the U.S. Supreme Court decreed that racial segregation violated the Fourteenth Amendment to the U.S. Constitution. Under the *Brown* decision, the solution to racial segregation seemed simple. If the best schools, jobs, and neighborhoods exclude African Americans, then outlaw all exclusionary practices and let black people in. Racial integration, inclusion, and color-blind treatment would fix racism.

At the time of the *Brown* decision, few could have anticipated the challenges to social justice that a new color-blind racism would raise. In numerous ways, American society is just as color-conscious as ever, yet social practices that historically would have been called racist are no longer so called. The tenets of color blindness may have frowned upon the use of racial language, yet the silencing of racial discourse often undermined racial analysis. For example, the early trickle away from public schools by middle-class white parents, who founded private schools to avoid sending their children to integrated public schools, was the beginning of white flight from public institutions of all sorts. Public schools, public health, public transportation, and public libraries are all now devalued in the face of market-based policies that say, "Buy it for yourself if you can." The withdrawal of support for public institutions and the celebration of privatization is seldom labeled racist—the racial etiquette of color-blind racism makes us much too polite for that—yet we can find the roots of privatization in white reactions to the *Brown* decision.

Color-blind racism replicates the long-standing racial hierarchy in ways that disguise the persistence of deeply entrenched, discriminatory policies in housing, education, employment, and the criminal justice system. One characteristic of the new racism is the changing influence of mass media, which now serve as sites where ideas about class, race, gender, and sexuality are reformulated and contested.

Under color-blind racism, blackness, or "color," must be *seen* to demonstrate the alleged color blindness of contemporary economic opportunity. Because a meritocracy requires "color" to prove the absence of racial discrimination, the total absence of black people would signal the failure of color blindness. Yet this visible blackness must be contained and/or stripped of meanings that threaten elites.

Black intellectuals function in this allegedly color-blind context that buys, sells, and rents people and their images for popular consumption. Not only is the phrase "black public intellectual" relatively new, reflecting the social conditions of the late 1990s, but black public intellectuals are also but a small part of a larger group of black domestic intellectuals that is in turn a fraction of African-American civil society. Just as Du Bois was one stellar black public intellectual in a much smaller academic arena, contemporary black public intellectuals are a very small group that has been singled out for disproportionate media attention from a greatly expanded field of American higher education. Here the inclusion of a few token—and hypervisible—African Americans hides the exclusion of the far larger group of African-American children and youth whom the *Brown* decision failed to reach.

Black *public* intellectuals differ from their historical counterparts and from their domestic contemporaries in several ways. First, not only do they have unprecedented access to print media, but broadcast media often seek them out to comment on anything that has to do with race. Black thinkers producing intellectual work for black audiences of black-controlled media are exceedingly rare. Second, unlike Du Bois, many no longer have daily contact with African-American communities or with African Ameri-

> Black thinkers producing intellectual work for black audiences of black-controlled media are exceedingly rare.

cans. Black professors with prestigious university positions have used them to extend their influence beyond the academy. Many link their privileged lifestyles not with the expressed needs of African-American communities but with the demands of mass culture for speakers on the college lecture circuit. Finally, prior to the events of 9/11, black public intellectuals benefited from America's concerns with race, "serving as experts," as Robert Boynton points out, "on everything from the L.A. riots and affirmative action to the nominations of Clarence Thomas and Lani Guinier, and *anything* having to do with Louis Farrakhan."

These criteria produce a short list of black public intellectuals whose mass-media visibility belies their actual numbers and establishes a pecking order among them. Some become academic superstars, like Henry Louis Gates and Cornel West. Consulted less often as a black public intellectual, writer Toni Morrison rounds out the top three. Some are unabashedly self-promoting, like Michael Eric Dyson; others, like Manning Marable, often find themselves in the limelight yet shy away from media attention. The brilliance or the intellectual commitment of this list of academic superstars is less the issue here than the ways in which mass media and institutions of higher education make use of them.

In some respects, many of these new academic superstars resemble African-American musicians who want to "cross over" beyond "race music" by finding a way to broaden their appeal to a mass (white) audience. For artists and intellectuals alike, the real money lies not in black markets but in white ones. Such artists usually begin by appealing to a black market until they feel that they have enough visibility to cross over. Yet they can never become white, and, more important, in the context of an allegedly color-blind society their white audiences do not want them to be white. Rather, black musicians and black public intellectuals alike cross over from the particular-

ism of race into the allegedly universal (and white) space of the public, carrying with them race music and ideas that are valued in a society where color-blind racism rules. They reassure whites that the basic values of a newly color-blind American society are working—in this case, associating intellectuals with racelessness, genderlessness, and objectivity. Describing these marketplace relations, Mark Anthony Neal observes, "The reality is that even in the era of the black public intellectual, black thinkers and artists are rarely allowed a public complexity, but rather are reduced to the smallest possible racial box in order to sell them and their ideas to a mainstream audience, black and nonblack, who have never thought of 'blackness' as being complex at all."

If there is room for only a few black public intellectuals at the top, what happens to the larger number of black intellectuals who never become stars? Colleges, universities, and other American institutions that recruit and train intellectuals remain committed to a universalistic logic. As a result, aspiring intellectuals who enter these institutions often find their concerns with race or ethnicity challenged and undermined by an allegedly universalistic ethos. African-American graduate students, for example, are often advised not to study topics that are "too black," because they will be seen as only being able to do race work and thus limit their careers. Conversely, blacks who can cross over into any category other than "domestic black American" are encouraged to do so. Biracial backgrounds, immigrant status, or anything marketable that upholds beliefs in core American values can "sell."

My discussion of contemporary black intellectuals has so far left out the gender politics of the public/private split that denies black women positions as intellectuals, the racialization and feminization of domestic intellectual work, and the place of contemporary black public intellectuals within these relations. This too is part of Du Bois's legacy as a black public intellectual. Certainly the same public/private binary shapes contemporary black intellectual production, primarily because whites continue to control media sources that anoint a chosen few black men as black public intellectuals. Just as token blacks are included to support the idea that American society is truly color-blind, so token women are included on the list of black public intellectuals.

Moreover, whether they are women or men, white, Latino, Asian, or black, all academics who do the work of counseling students, writing letters of recommendation, sitting on committees, researching papers, and recruiting students occupy the devalued sphere of "domestic" intellectual production. Regardless of their actual race, gender, class, ethnicity, or sexual orientation, these people are feminized and may be stigmatized as socially "black." Black female domestic intellectuals become the template for all those within academia who do this kind of work. In this sense, the public/private split between public and domestic black intellectuals may invoke gender and race, but it is really about power. It reduces most black thinkers to the work of serving institutional agendas, of negotiating the new color-blind racism, and holds them to impossible standards associated with elite black public intellectuals.

These reconfigured public and domestic spheres of academia—as well as those of color-blind racism itself—transcend any notion of conflict between men and women, whites and blacks, or black men and black women. Race, gender, and class all contradict the idea of "inclusion for all," yet they have special meaning for those following Du Bois. Whereas the domestic duties of black intellectuals may resemble those of prior generations, the greatly changed context of American higher education—its embeddedness

in marketplace relations—means that their intellectual labor may yield few benefits to African Americans in general. Doing the domestic intellectual labor of supporting black students and junior faculty, for example, may get a few people through school who then turn around and criticize those who do such labor for not being "scholarly" enough.

black public intellectuals in post-9/11 america

At the end of the twentieth century, race was at the top of the American agenda, and black people starred in public debates about the future of America. Manipulating ideas about black people as the "enemy within" who threatened all that was good about America achieved high art form during this era of color-blind racism. Racial rule relies on fear, and representations of black men as scary rapists and black women as out-of-control, fertile welfare queens masked and justified dramatic changes in social policies from the penal industry to welfare reform. The recognition that race was with us and would not go away created opportunities for black public intellectuals who based success on their rejecting of the social responsibilities of working on behalf of an African-American public. Instead, the Faustian bargain that many in this new group struck forced them to continually renegotiate the tensions linking universalism and particularism.

The events of September 11, 2001, changed all of this. Apparently, shadowy foreign terrorists, imagined as dark-skinned Arabs, can also scare the American public into maintaining racial apartheid. The basic reality of color-blind racism has not changed, but its focus has shifted from domestic to global politics. Black American intellectual efforts that focus exclusively on selling ideas about race to a white public may go out of style when the American public perceives new threats. In a world threatened by a terrorism that can strike anywhere and take any form, why worry about the domestic problem of race and of domestic black people? America knows how to handle them.

Perhaps these new social relations are not inherently bad for black intellectuals. The norms of mainstream thinking suggest that when black intellectuals self-identify as black, they seriously limit themselves by not applying their gifts to loftier questions. Clearly, this puts pressure on black public intellectuals to become critics on behalf of a broader public and not just for a minority African-American public. But how are African-American interests served when they are folded into the concerns of an unsympathetic white American public? What could be more important to African-American intellectuals than contributing to the ongoing struggle for black freedom that has repeatedly enriched American democracy? In this endeavor, we can find a provocative model for today in Du Bois. He earned his reputation as the ultimate black public intellectual not by ignoring color, but by using a particular situation of racial injustice to raise universal questions concerning the very meaning of American democracy. We would do well to heed his legacy.

RECOMMENDED RESOURCES

Michael K. Brown, Martin Carnoy, Elliott Currie, Troy Duster, David B. Oppenheimer, Marjorie M. Schultz, and David Wellman. *White-Washing Race: The Myth of a Color-Blind Society* (University of California Press, 2003).
> An examination of education, crime, poverty, and voting that demonstrates how the myth of color blindness shapes contemporary American society.

Hazel V. Carby. *Race Men* (Harvard University Press, 1998).
> Historical survey of the ideas of W. E. B. Du Bois, Paul Robeson, and other African-American intellectuals.

Harold Cruse. *The Crisis of the Negro Intellectual* (William Morrow, 1967).
> A classic work that analyzes the challenges facing African-American intellectuals and how they respond to them.

Mark A. Neal. *Songs in the Key of Life: A Rhythm and Blues Nation* (Routledge, 2003).
> Points to the contributions and problems of contemporary black popular culture.

Howard Winant. *The World Is a Ghetto: Race and Democracy Since World War II* (Basic Books, 2001).
> A comprehensive, historical analysis that shows the importance of studying race in a global context.

REVIEW QUESTIONS

1. What does Collins mean when she uses the term *color-blind racism*? What would be an example of it?
2. Collins writes about how Du Bois's race prevented his peers from seeing him as an "intellectual" while at the same time framing his work in "a tradition of moral social service." What challenges does Collins see for today's black intellectuals? Can you think of any additional roadblocks?
3. The issue of privatizing public institutions is hotly debated in contemporary culture, but rarely is a claim made that the "withdrawal of support for public institutions and the celebration of privatization" might be racist, as Collins suggests. How does this essay help you think about such trends in terms of race?
4. Activity: Just as in the rest of American society, there are examples and counterexamples of how groups have established their own corners of academia. What do you feel are the

positive effects of African-American and Women's Studies programs at colleges and universities? Are there any negatives you can think of? If your campus has such programs, find out more about them (e.g., When were they established? Is there evidence of "domestic intellectual labor" and "public intellectual labor"? What courses are offered? What groups participate in their classes and activities?).

part **5**

Poverty and Inequality

robert max jackson

keyword: inequalities

21

winter 2007

Just as the reality of pervasive inequality has shaped the organization of modern society, the twin concepts of inequality and equality have continuously informed and challenged social thought. We experience inequality directly when we recognize that some people have fewer opportunities than we do, and others more; some are treated worse, but others better; and some have less desirable lives that we pity, while others we envy. Our thinking about inequality involves powerful ideologies of equal rights and equality that reflect social theorists' repeated efforts to solve the intellectual problem of inequality and address the tensions and adaptations that it produces. Only a society that harbors inequality will generate the idea of equality; others do not need to.

Although inequality has pervaded all societies with recorded histories, the modern concept of social equality emerged only in the seventeenth and eighteenth centuries, as thinkers such as Thomas Hobbes, John Locke, and Jean-Jacques Rousseau produced ideas of natural right and conceptions of a natural order based on equality. Using these Enlightenment ideas, people could blame inequality on specific social institutions and groups, rather than accepting it as God's will or a tragic fact of life, much like disease. This shift in thinking helped inspire the social sciences, as well as motivating numerous utopian efforts to imagine a world without inequality.

Our ideas about inequality and equality derive from our experience of inequality and our efforts to understand it and judge its moral implications. Like those before us, we live and breathe inequality every moment of every day: all our interactions, all our relationships, every aspect of social life involves and responds to inequality. While we all continuously experience inequality, the meaning of that experience differs according to our status. The poor know that the wealthy have more, live better, and work less, but they do not know how it feels to have that freedom, to acquire a sense of privilege, to feel superior in one's identity. Those on top know it is hard and potentially grim to be poor, but they cannot know how it feels to know that the good things in life will never be possible, to feel that your own life can never have the significance that "better" people enjoy, to know that you cannot give your children a chance at a good life.

Building on similar experiences, people of similar status create understandings of the world that congeal into culturally sustained identities and worldviews. People of similar social status have more contact, interact as equals, have analogous experiences and histories, perceive each other as more understandable and accessible, and reinforce each other's perceptions. People of similar economic status share neighborhoods, schools, and colleges, houses of worship, and places of recreation such as parks or bars. People tend to marry those who share their location in the status hierarchies that dominate our lives. Women feel more comfortable with other women, and men with men. Because people generally wish to feel they are just, worthy, and sensible, they develop elaborate justifications for their place in order to confirm their worth. People of similar status comfort each other because they share the same rationales. People of similar status thus come to believe their status privileges are just and their status deficiencies unjust; they acquire a perceptual map of status differences that guides their dealings with others. Inequality divides us into separate nations or communities; we stare at each other across those borders like foreigners, and generally accept them as simple, obvious, and unchangeable.

In social science's formalization of these experiences, *inequality* refers to systematic distinctions that we can rank (more or less, higher or lower) and that concern valued qualities (such as wealth, prestige, education, servitude, and security). We may perceive inequality among individuals and organizations; among segments of a population, such as ethnicities or those in rural versus urban areas; among positions, such as occupations or locations in a hierarchy; and among nations. Inequalities of *positions* differ analytically from inequalities of *individuals*. An organizational chart maps a hierarchy of positions—these remain the same even as different individuals move through them. Other unequal social locations, such as occupations or ranks of wealth, can also be considered positions, although they are more malleable and less clearly defined. The relationships among positions—the structures of inequality—represent the enduring systems through which people move. Whoever occupies a position gets its status, authority, and privileges, and gives them up upon leaving. The resulting *positional inequalities* differ from *status inequalities* that

inhere in personal characteristics such as skin color or sex. The degree of *status* inequality between people reflects the differences in opportunities available to the status groups to which they belong.

Structures of inequality endure when social mechanisms ensure that each new generation adequately replenishes the full range of positions vacated as the older generations die. Mechanisms that sustain systems of positional inequality largely arise from the demands and possibilities of prevailing economic and political structures. For example, inheritance, obstacles to social mobility, and the structure of the economy together sustain wealth inequalities. In contrast, mechanisms of social exclusion, discrimination, and culturally sustained hostilities are more important in the preservation of status inequalities like race.

The varied systems of inequality that social theorists identify are often hard to distinguish clearly in real life because they all are at work at the same time, often mixed together. A person's status is influenced simultaneously by race, gender, parents' status, occupation, wealth, education, and other characteristics, but these are largely inseparable in experience. Similarly, from the perspective of social organization, gender or racial inequality may contribute to or mask economic inequality. Those in privileged positions work hard to defend the existing system, although they must sometimes relax one system of inequality to reinforce another. An economic elite, for instance, may normally use gender and race to reinforce its position, but occasionally it may allow people from these other groups into positions of privilege in order to maintain its own legitimacy.

Indeed, status inequalities are always intermingled with positional inequalities, without which they would disappear. Positional inequalities involve unequal control over resources; without this, the other inequalities would not matter. In a factory, for example, inequality between owners, managers, foremen, and line workers exists even if people's race, sex, and age have no effect on the way they are treated. But if all positions in an organization have the same authority and salary, even if people are prejudiced, they cannot sustain any significant inequality within the organization based on race or sex, as there is nothing for one group to withhold from another. Status inequalities involve differential access to desirable (and undesirable) locations in the systems of positional inequality. For this reason hunting and gathering societies, largely lacking economic or political inequalities, also have little gender inequality.

Removing the implicit and explicit status barriers to positions in economic and political hierarchies is therefore the main way that status groups today fight the status inequalities that disadvantage them. This also means that assimilating previously excluded status groups does not reduce the overall level of economic inequality; indeed, by enhancing the legitimacy of positional inequalities, in theory it could facilitate their capacity to generate inequality.

The particular way that status inequality is embedded in positional inequality is important to its endurance and possible dilution. For example, gender inequality and racial inequality have different relationships to structures of positional inequality. Because economic inequalities are transmitted from one generation to the next via families, and because women are equally distributed in families up and down the economic hierarchy, an end to gender discrimination would mean that women could, in theory, get equal access to the privileges of class in just one generation. But if racial barriers were similarly removed, a group concentrated toward the bottom of the hierarchy, like African Americans in the United States, would still have formidable economic obstacles to overcome. They would be burdened by the weight of class inequality.

The reason is that even when people do not face explicit status barriers, they still tend to end up in the economic hierarchy near the position their parents held. Research shows that parents' income, wealth, education, occupation, and residential location all affect one's eventual place in the economic hierarchy. Privileged positions in these hierarchies offer children not only direct financial support but cultural and interpersonal skills, personal connections, high aspirations, and some insurance against inevitable missteps. Scientific explanations often overlook this last factor, which might include early tutoring, psychological intervention, drug rehabilitation, or legal protection. Privileged children have much more opportunity to garner positive developmental experiences; those without privilege have much more opportunity to accumulate negative experiences.

Yet, we remain surprisingly uncertain about *how much* these factors influence a child's fate. Research from the 1950s to the 1980s found that modern societies were surprisingly meritocratic, with parents' status accounting for well under 20 percent of children's status. On-the-job experiences and sheer luck seemed much more decisive. Improved research techniques in the last two decades, however, suggest a considerably greater influence from family background, perhaps twice what was believed in earlier years. Even these higher figures are, at best, lower bounds because the research techniques being applied only allow us to have confidence about the part of children's outcomes we can attribute to their origins, not about the remainder. Findings about the influence of parental status matter enormously, because less privileged children lack the opportunities to excel—and ideologically, it is difficult to blame these children for their plight. Even in the United States, where "equal opportunity" ideologies dominate policy, it is hard to blame the victims when those victims are kids. Instead, we blind ourselves about class effects by insisting—against the evidence—that the opportunities must be equal.

Such blindness illustrates the critical role that ideologies play in influencing the history of inequality and mediating its effects. How people experience and respond to inequality depends on what they believe causes it, how necessary or avoidable it is, and how fair or unjust it seems. The divergent experiences and interests of those who are advantaged and disadvantaged by inequality induce different interpretations that come into conflict. Karl Marx famously proclaimed in the *Communist Manifesto* that "the ruling ideas of each age have ever been the ideas of its ruling class," suggesting that they can impose views that sustain their dominance. But subordinate groups often develop their own views of things, which can help produce subtle resistance (which is always present) or even outright rebellion (which is rarer). When one of these groups is separated and clearly marked, it is more likely to develop a collective identity that counters the dominant ideology. Categorical distinctions, such as sex, tend to foster this identity better than those of degree, such as income.

Every system of inequality generates tensions between those on top and those below them, tensions expressed in acts of resistance and discipline. Resistance to a system of inequality is inherent in any effort of those who have less to get more or of those under authority who try to evade its rule. It is not that people self-consciously resist the *idea* or *system* of inequality (except perhaps for a small minority); they resist the implications of inequality for their own lives. The disadvantaged mostly resist in quiet ways, by doing a job poorly, violating a rule secretly, or disparaging their "superiors" through jokes and gossip. When noticed, even small acts of resistance or revenge can be punished. For example, workers who do not show

proper respect to a boss can be assigned extra work or even fired. Much of the criminal code in modern capitalist countries is designed to restrain those who would violate systems of inequality, for instance through theft. The disciplining of those who resist has spread with all the efficiency of modern bureaucracy.

What transforms this tension between resistance and discipline from isolated individual actions into organized struggle is one of the great, and as yet not satisfactorily answered, questions regarding inequality. For this to occur, the disadvantaged must have sufficient resources and freedom to organize themselves; they must embrace an ideology that declares inequality unnecessary and unjust, and suggests that overcoming it is a practicable strategy; they must accept a common identity; and they must believe that collective struggle against inequality is a more promising or more noble strategy than pursuing personal advancement. Both common historical circumstances and the willful efforts of dominant groups to avoid or suppress rebellion make these conditions rare. Still, the history of revolutions, rebellions, labor organizations, and social movements that have sought rights for disadvantaged groups shows that the preservation of inequality always requires effort.

Viewing such tensions as inherent to inequality, social scientists have (like utopian novelists) often asked, is inequality necessary? Sociologists Kingsley Davis and Wilbert Moore famously argued that positions in a modern economy carry unequal rewards because higher rewards are needed to attract sufficiently trained and motivated people to fill the jobs important to a society's functioning. In short, inequality is necessary to keep things running. The appeal of this argument is that it reflects widely recognized social practices: firms and communities offer high rewards to fill important positions when adequate personnel are hard to attract, and employers increase salaries to retain people whose contributions they consider exceptional. Scholarly research has also shown that modern nations exhibit surprisingly similar hierarchies of occupational status, as Davis and Moore would predict.

The critical weaknesses of the Davis–Moore argument lies in all that it overlooks: the theory neglects the influence of power on rewards, does not explain how jobs become functionally important, ignores organizations' need to maintain authority relations, and does not identify the mechanisms that would produce functional outcomes. Simply put, the functional causal processes they invoke may indeed produce inequality, but much if not most inequality appears to have different roots. The similarities in patterns of inequality across nations do suggest that similar causal processes are at work, as well as diffusion and borrowing, but they do not offer support for the mechanism that Davis and Moore suggest—the need to offer unequal rewards to allocate people to functional positions. Moreover, the predominance of a social pattern is not, by itself, evidence of its necessity. At one time, for example, across the world, sovereignty was transmitted by kinship, and women were excluded from citizenship; while people believed these conditions were necessary, their elimination in the modern world has shown they are not. Despite their theoretical shortcomings, however, Davis and Moore suggest what could be a useful distinction between functionally necessary inequality and additional inequality due to power—a neglected, potentially progressive kernel of a theory often disparaged as reactionary.

Unavoidable inequality includes not only what a social system needs to work, but also the patterns of inequality that become inevitable in a competitive economy that differentially rewards disparate talents, motivations, luck, and the capacity for exploitation. A feudal system does not produce a warrior class because it needs warriors; to a greater extent, they arise because people in such societies are vulnerable to warriors, some of whom take advantage of that vulnerability. The structure of a modern economy gives varying bargaining power to occupations or jobs, and people generally seek to extract as much reward as their bargaining power allows.

The implications of our many forms of inequality are hard to summarize. Both ordinary people and scholars who study social life, even those who feel that inequality is important, commonly underestimate just how much inequality matters. Inequalities pervade all our relationships, in families, in the workplace, even in anonymous public contexts. The organizations of modern society are hierarchical, and they reflect and respond to the inequalities that surround them. We all react to the promised rewards and the brutal constraints of inequality just as surely, and usually as thoughtlessly, as rats in a maze.

RECOMMENDED RESOURCES

David B. Grusky. *Social Stratification: Class, Race, and Gender in Sociological Perspective* (Westview, 2000).

   The best anthology on inequality, including classical and contemporary pieces.

Robert Max Jackson. *Destined for Equality: The Inevitable Rise of Women's Status* (Harvard University Press, 1998).

   Seeks to explain women's changing status over the past two centuries.

Charles Tilly. *Durable Inequality* (University of California Press, 1999).

   A challenging effort by one of the great living sociologists to render persistent inequalities theoretically understandable.

William Julius Wilson. *The Declining Significance of Race: Blacks and Changing American Institutions* (University of Chicago Press, 1978).

> The most influential study of race in America in the past several decades.

Erik Olin Wright. *Approaches to Class Analysis* (Cambridge University Press, 2005).

> From the premier Marxist sociologist working on class in recent decades, a consideration of alternative approaches to class.

REVIEW QUESTIONS

1. When you hear the word *inequality*, what images or thoughts first come to mind? Why is that so, do you think?
2. Describe the difference between "status inequality" and "positional inequality," and explain why one could "disappear" without the other. Offer a hypothetical person in order to provide a more concrete example of social location based on these two distinctions.
3. Popular media and scholarly research have placed an emphasis on *diversity*. What do you feel the differences are between diversity and the issues raised in this essay? Discuss this issue in two paragraphs using your own opinion, being careful to address contrary evidence.
4. This essay raises the tough question of whether or not inequality within occupational hierarchies is justified. On the one hand, shouldn't skilled practitioners, like neurosurgeons, be compensated proportionate to their expertise? On the other, activists have pointed out that CEO pay has risen from 24 times more than the average worker's pay (in 1965) to 431 times more (in 2004). How do the perspectives offered in Jackson's essay help you understand this issue? What do you think?

david a. snow and leon anderson

street people

22

winter 2003

street people, long visible in the third world, are once again a conspicuous and disturbing feature of most first world cities. studies of street life and the homeless help explain why these people have become more visible, why they are often seen as menacing and what the future holds for them.

Standing in the median of a busy street in a major city, a man in torn clothes peddles the afternoon newspaper to drivers as they roll to a stop at the intersection. It is late on a weekday afternoon and the streets are beginning to fill as rush hour approaches. Employees from nearby businesses scurry through a small park on the way to their cars and bus stops. A disheveled man holding an old McDonald's coffee cup has staked out his favorite spot to hustle spare change from the early evening crowd. Four elderly residents of a nearby cut-rate hotel sit on a park bench chatting. Down the block, behind tables of used books and magazines, men haggle over prices with browsing pedestrians. Across the street, under a drugstore awning, a man strums a guitar slung with a piece of rope around his shoulder. Beside him a sign reads, "Songs on Request. Donations Accepted." Meanwhile, on a terraced ledge, several teenage boys with skateboards practice their moves to the pulsing rap strains of Puff Daddy.

These assorted characters, often called "street people," are presumed to share something that separates them from others using the same public spaces. In the past two decades, the number of street people has risen dramatically in the United States and other affluent nations, but of the various street people, it is particularly the homeless who spark public concern and generate a sense of unease among citizens. Passersby may wonder what new developments have forced these people out into the streets. But street people are an old feature of world cities now reappearing after years of diminished numbers and visibility. They are reappearing because of changes in the economy, the availability of low-income housing, the welfare system, and the physical transformation of cities.

Street people have been a feature of city life dating back to Biblical times. In preindustrial cities, where activities associated with home, work, and leisure were not as neatly separated as in modern cities, the streets were routinely swarming with people. Even there, however, some marginal people—by virtue of their distinct activities—occasioned such vilifying tracts as Martin Luther's *The Book of Beggars*.

who are street people?

Most people use sidewalks for specific purposes: to get from one place to another, for exercise, window-shopping, or a leisurely stroll. Street people, however, use the same spaces for eking out a living and conducting their daily lives. Thus, the boundaries between public and private are blurred, prompting those of us who use these spaces for more conventional purposes to distinguish ourselves from street people. Street

Passersby may look askance at those who use a sidewalk to work, play, eat, or sleep. Downtown, San Francisco, California. (Photo by Jon Wagner)

people engage in at least three types of "out-of-place" public activities: economic, social, and residential.

Their economic activities include quasi-legal and illegal ways to make money such as: hawking newspapers, reselling books and magazines, scavenging and peddling junk and cans, washing windows at stop lights or during traffic jams, panhandling and selling drugs and sex. These activities constitute "shadow work"— work performed outside of the regular world of employment that still depends on standard business enterprise and the commercial traffic associated with it, such as panhandling at a busy intersection or near an ATM machine. Street peoples' social activities include hanging out and conversing on street corners, in building alcoves, and on park benches. Their residential activities include appropriating sidewalks, alcoves, alleys, or parks as places to sleep and store personal belongings.

While some street people engage in only one of these activities, many pursue a couple of them, while others, such as many of the homeless, may engage in all three. Mitchell Duneier observed these differences in his study of 25 poor black men who worked or lived on the sidewalks of Sixth Avenue in New York's Greenwich Village. Duneier's main informant, Hakim,

made his living by selling books on the sidewalk, but rented a small apartment in New Jersey. Most of his street associates—who lived by selling magazines, watching the vendors' tables, or panhandling—either slept on the streets, doubled-up with relatives or friends or alternated between such irregular arrangements. But no matter how they scraped by or where they slept, the Greenwich Village sidewalk was the center of their social life. It is this unconventional use of the streets for working, sleeping, and leisure, combined with their frequently impoverished or disheveled appearance, that makes street people seem like menacing intruders claiming public space.

the "problem" of street people in first world cities

Street people have been a feature of city life dating back to Biblical times. In preindustrial cities, where activities associated with home, work, and leisure were not as neatly separated as in modern cities, the streets were routinely swarming with people. Even there, however, some marginal people—by virtue of their distinct activities—occasioned such vilifying tracts as Martin Luther's *The Book of Beggars*. The social dislocation caused by industrialization and the breakdown of European agrarian economies increased the numbers of such suspect folks, who were targeted by "vagrancy statutes" to control or eliminate them, particularly in England and its colonies.

In time, the problem of vagrancy and street people seemed to disappear in affluent nations, except after major shocks such as wars or economic depressions. The homeless seemed to vanish in part due to economic growth and to welfare systems designed to assist those who could not fit into the industrial economy. At the same time, as Lyn Lofland has described, modern societies changed the way in which they imposed order in cities. Instead of an older "appearential order," in which citizens recognized and handled each other by reading signs of clothing and appearance, the new system employed a "spatial order"—geographic segregation that designated what kinds of people should be found in one place rather than another. These changes did not eliminate street people, but confined them to marginal areas of the city—variously known as "Hobohemia" in Chicago, "Skid Row" in Seattle, the "Tenderloin" in San Francisco, and the "Bowery" in New York. Thus, homeless people's visibility and their interaction with other, more mainstream citizens was minimized.

In the late 1960s and early 1970s, the heady, optimistic days of American urban planning, some planners and sociologists predicted that the marginal residents of skid rows would disappear entirely as urban renewal revived their haunts. However, about a decade later, the numbers of street people started growing—and continued to grow through the last two decades of the twentieth century, not only in U.S. cities but in other major First World cities as well, such as London, Paris, Berlin, and Tokyo.

The homeless street people of the 1980s and 1990s were much more visible than the skid row residents had been, not only because of their increasing numbers, but also because the urban landscape had changed. Beginning in the 1970s in cities throughout the United States, many neighborhoods that housed and provided services for marginal populations became targets for commercial development and financial speculation. From New York's Bowery to Anchorage's Fourth Avenue, developers turned space, once ceded to marginal people, to new uses for business and more affluent people. Urban redevelopment and gentrification thus pushed increasing numbers of homeless street people into prime space for both living and leisure.

City residents have become increasingly uneasy and intolerant of this new presence. Local governments have tried to reestablish a sense of spatial order and security for more affluent residents—forbidding the presence, panhandling, loitering, and movement of homeless street people, particularly in high-visibility spaces. New York City, for instance, has tried to "clean up" Grand Central Station and Washington Square, and has set up shelters and other services for the homeless far from such prime urban space. In the first half of the 1990s, Gwendolyn Dordick studied four groups of homeless street people in four different settings in New York City: a bus station, a public shelter, a makeshift shantytown, and a private shelter. By the mid-1990s, the large number of street people she observed at Penn Station had been dramatically reduced, while the large men's shelter on the northern tip of Manhattan, far away from the city's prime locations, continued to thrive.

Such strategies for segregating destitute street people have a long history in Western societies, harking back at least to what social historians refer to as the era of the Great Confinement (1660 to the end of the nineteenth century) in which authorities made massive efforts to segregate unemployed vagrants, criminals, orphans, and the mentally ill into workhouses. More recently, some cities, such as Las Vegas and Los Angeles, have ceded control of a portion of formerly public downtown space to private interests that strive to ward off undesirables with strategies ranging from erecting architectural barriers to hiring security guards. In some areas, such as the section of Greenwich Village Duneier studied, street people and other citizens have evolved a kind of working accommodation, with both groups contributing to a vibrant street life. But this is more the exception than the rule in American cities. And even where such an order does exist, it is often fragile and subject to recurrent ruptures when street peoples' interactions with business owners and passersby violate expectations for proper social interaction in public space—as when some of the men Duneier studied made lewd comments to passing women.

why have street people [re]appeared?

What else accounts for the apparent growth in the population of street people in American cities, as well as in other major cities in the First World, during the last 20 years? The dearth of affordable low-income housing provides a partial answer. So does the redevelopment of marginal spaces, such as old skid rows. But a shortfall in affordable housing and spatial dislocation explain only part of why the number of street people has increased.

Deindustrialization and economic globalization weakened the demand for unskilled workers throughout much of the developed world. Some of those unable to compete in the new labor markets have turned to making a living on the street. Many of the homeless we observed bartering and panhandling on the streets of Austin, Texas, had originally traveled to Austin in hopes of finding employment in the city's construction boom of the mid 1980s. They pursued jobs through the state employment agency, but with little long-term success. Some then sought work in fast food restaurants, but often were not hired because they lacked a stable address and local work experience. Boxed out of the traditional labor market, many homeless individuals turned to shadow work such as panhandling and collecting aluminum cans from garbage dumpsters, at first as a stopgap measure. As other opportunities failed to materialize, shadow work became their most stable source of income.

> Deindustrialization and economic globalization weakened the demand for unskilled workers throughout much of the developed world. Some of those unable to compete in the new labor markets have turned to making a living on the street.

Also contributing to the increase of street people is the dramatic change in state welfare policies over the past 25 years throughout the developed world. This change, which ended what Gøsta Esping-Andersen dubbed the golden age of welfare states, has progressively reduced and weakened the safety net. For many, survival has become contingent on cobbling together alternative means of subsistence, including street-level shadow work.

In addition, many institutions that used to accommodate the poor, the disabled, and the displaced have weakened or disappeared—cheap residential hotels, single residence occupancy (SRO) housing, workhouses, mental institutions, and neighborhoods such as skid row districts that historically sheltered and served "undesirables." Today much of the SRO stock is gone, as are nearly all of the large mental asylums that were open in the 1950s and early 1960s. The number of shelter beds has grown since the 1980s, but in most cities rarely in sufficient numbers to keep up with the homeless population. And even when shelter space is available many homeless people avoid it, fearing for their safety and resisting the typically demeaning regimentation of shelter life.

Yet another contribution to the growth and the variety of street people is the spread of a youth street culture that embraces hanging out in vibrant public spaces. Often, those hanging out are a mixture of local adolescents with homes and homeless youth, many of whom are transient. Because they idle about, hustle for money, and take over public places for their own amusement, adults often regard them as threatening and speak of them in derogatory terms, as in the case of the "gutter punks" who congregate in a trendy, nightlife area in Tucson, Arizona.

Our conversations with these youth, as well as with some homeless adults, suggest that many choose to be on the streets rather than being forced to avail themselves of institutional alternatives. Certainly the prospect of action and bright lights, opportunities to hustle, the availability of recreational drugs, and freedom from parents and others can make the streets particularly alluring.

But it is difficult to assess the extent of their choice without understanding the options they have and the contexts in which their choices are made. Lacking the money to enter even the low-income housing market, having limited education, few job skills, a dearth of social support off the streets, and in many cases problems with alcohol or drugs, street people often have few real attractive choices. Living with family or friends may not be an option, or may be one that entails conflict, abuse, or a loss of dignity. Fear of physical harm and a lack of freedom frequently make homeless shelters a frightening prospect as well. Thus, to presume that being on the streets is largely a matter of choice is to ignore the unattractive options that confront most people who end up on the streets or who cycle on and off them as many do.

These factors which are increasing the population and visibility of homeless people in the United States, combined with others such as influxes of refugees, are at work on the streets of major cities in other countries as well.

the future of street people

Is the increased number and visibility of street people during the past two decades a historical anomaly, or are street people becoming a permanent feature of the street scene throughout the First World's big cities? The latter is more likely unless there are significant changes in the mismatch between labor markets and people's skills, the withering of the welfare state and the institutions serving the needs of street people, the reconfiguration of urban space resulting from gentrification and the pressure of market forces and refugee and immigration flows into some cities. In other words, unless there are significant changes in the conjunction of conditions that generated the increasing number and visibility of street people, there is little reason to suspect that they will suddenly disappear.

There is an alternative scenario, however: the number of homeless street people may remain the same, or even increase, but become much less visible because of still more vigilant efforts by officials to push them away from high-visibility areas. Short of such drastic exclusionary strategies, or a decrease in the number of street people, middle- and upper-class urbanites will continue to see them as a festering social problem, leading to occasional conflicts and new tactics for controlling them, such as building more antiseptic "pseudo-public environments" like theme parks and malls. But such planning innovations aimed at spatial segregation and "pest control" will likely meet only minimal success. For if anything is certain about street people, it is that they are remarkably creative in their appropriation and use of public space. Thus, the urban street scene will inevitably involve a dance between street people and their advocates and those who favor policies to limit and exclude them.

RECOMMENDED RESOURCES

Martha R. Burt and Laudan Y. Aron. *Helping America's Homeless* (The Urban Institute, 2001).

> Analysis of the demographics and causes of homelessness, and of what has been and what should be done.

Gwendolyn A. Dordick. *Something Left to Lose: Personal Relations and Survival Among New York's Homeless* (Temple University Press, 1997).

An ethnographic study of four groups of homeless people in four different habitats in New York City.

Mitchell Duneier. *Sidewalk* (Farrar, Straus and Giroux, 1999).

Portrait of poor black men who make their livelihood on the sidewalks of Greenwich Village by reselling books and magazines and by panhandling.

John Hagan and Bill McCarthy. *Mean Streets: Youth Crime and Homelessness* (Cambridge University Press, 1998).

Describes homeless youth and their activities in Toronto and Vancouver.

Kim Hopper and Jim Baumohl. "Held in Abeyance: Rethinking Homelessness and Advocacy." *American Behavioral Scientist* 37 (1994): 522–52.

Recasts homelessness as a breakdown of a country's ability to house its surplus populations.

Lyn H. Lofland. *A World of Strangers: Order and Action in Urban Public Space* (Basic Books, 1973).

Outlines the practices and conventions historically used to create social and psychological order in cities.

National Law Center on Homelessness & Poverty. *Out of Sight-Out of Mind? A Report on Anti-Homeless Laws, Litigation and Alternatives in 50 United States Cities* (National Law Center on Homelessness and Poverty, 1999).

An overview of anti-homeless initiatives across major U.S. cities.

David A Snow and Leon Anderson. *Down on Their Luck: A Study of Homeless Street People* (University of California Press, 1993).

A case study of street life and the survival strategies of homeless people in Austin, Texas, in the mid 1980s.

Talmadge Wright. *Out of Place: Homeless Mobilizations, Subcities, and Contested Landscapes* (State University of New York Press, 1997).

Homeless movements fight against redevelopment in Chicago and San Jose.

REVIEW QUESTIONS

1. Describe what Snow and Anderson see as the major changes in urban areas that have caused the "street people" who used to occupy marginal areas to become increasingly visible. Using examples, what do you think of the strategies that municipalities have used to combat this development?

2. Those who believe that being homeless is a matter of personal choice ignore the larger structural issues at hand. Describe the major forces that would lead a homeless person to avoid the few institutional and social network options they might have.

3. In 2006, Hurricane Katrina brought stark images of people in great distress. It raised the issue of how particular groups are relegated to poor parts of urban areas. Discuss the results of spatially segregating not just the homeless, but other socioeconomic groups. What are the civic consequences of this?

4. Activity: Conduct observations of a popular public space in your community, and write about it. A few questions to think of: Is there signage that identifies it as a public space? If there are posted "Rules of Conduct," what are they? Is there a police presence? Are there surveillance cameras that you can map the locations of? Are there public restrooms? Are there places to sit, and how are they designed? How do people use the space? Finally, relate this assignment to the reading.

mark r. rank

as american as apple pie: poverty and welfare

summer 2003

few americans see poverty as a normal state of affairs. yet most will experience poverty and will use welfare at some point in their lives. how can this be, and how does (or should) it change the way we look at poverty in the united states?

For many Americans, the words "poverty" and "welfare" conjure images of people on the fringes of society: unwed mothers raising several children, inner-city black men, high school dropouts, the homeless, and so on. The media, political rhetoric, and often even the research of social scientists depict the poor as alien and often undeserving of help. In short, being poor and using welfare are perceived as outside the American mainstream.

Yet, poverty and welfare use are as American as apple pie. Most of us will experience poverty during our lives. Even more surprising, most Americans will turn to public assistance at least once during adulthood. Rather than poverty and welfare use being an issue of *them*, it is more an issue of *us*.

the risk of poverty and drawing on welfare

Our understanding about the extent of poverty comes mostly from annual surveys conducted by the Census Bureau. Over the past three decades, between 11 and 15 percent of Americans have lived below the poverty line in any given year. Some people are at greater risk than others, depending on age, race, gender, family structure, community of residence, education, work skills, and physical disabilities. (See sidebar, "counting the poor," page 162.)

Studies that follow particular families over time—in particular, the Panel Study of Income Dynamics (PSID), the National Longitudinal Survey (NLS), and the Survey of Income and Program Participation (SIPP)—have given us a further understanding of year-to-year changes in poverty. They show that most people are poor for only a short time. Typically, households are impoverished for one, two, or three years, then manage to get above the poverty line. They may stay above the line for a while, only to fall into poverty again later. Events triggering these spells of poverty frequently involve the loss of a job and its pay, family changes such as divorce, or both.

There is, however, an alternative way to estimate the scope of poverty. Specifically, how many Americans experience poverty at some point

> By the time Americans have reached the age of 75, 59 percent will have spent at least a year below the poverty line during their adulthood, while 68 percent will have faced at least a year in near poverty.

during adulthood? Counting the number of people who are ever touched by poverty, rather than those who are poor in any given year, gives us a better sense of the scope of the problem. Put another way, to what extent is poverty a "normal" part of the life cycle?

My colleague Tom Hirschl and I have constructed a series of "life tables" built from PSID data following families for over 25 years. The life table is a technique for counting how often specific events occur in specific periods of time, and is frequently used by demographers and medical researchers to assess risk, say, the risk of contracting breast cancer after menopause. It allows us to estimate the percentage of the American population that will experience poverty at some point during adulthood. We also calculated the percentage of the population that will use a social safety net program—programs such as food stamps or Aid to Families with Dependent Children (AFDC, now replaced by the Temporary Assistance for Needy Families [TANF] program)—sometime during adulthood. Our results suggest that a serious reconsideration of who experiences poverty is in order.

Figure 1 shows the percentage of Americans spending at least one year living below the official poverty line during adulthood. It also graphs the percentage who have lived between the poverty line and just 25 percent above it—what scholars consider "near poverty."

By the age of 30, 27 percent of Americans will have experienced at least one year in poverty and 34 percent will have fallen below the near-poverty line. By the age of 50, the percentages will have risen to 42 and 50 percent, respectively. And finally by the time Americans have reached the age of 75, 59 percent will have spent at least a year below the poverty line during their adulthood, while 68 percent will have faced at least a year in near poverty.

If we included experiences of poverty in childhood, these percentages would be even

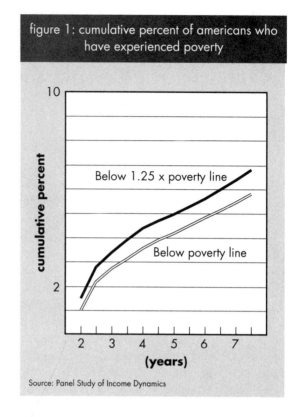

figure 1: cumulative percent of americans who have experienced poverty

Source: Panel Study of Income Dynamics

higher. Rather than an isolated event that occurs only among the so-called "underclass," poverty is a reality that a clear majority of Americans will experience during their lifetimes.

Measuring impoverishment as the use of social safety net programs produces even more startling results. Figure 2 draws on the same PSID survey to show the proportion of people between the ages of 20 and 65 who will use one of the major need-based welfare programs in the United States, including food stamps, Medicaid, AFDC, Supplemental Security Income, and other cash subsidies such as general assistance. By the time Americans reach the age of 65, approximately two-thirds will have, as adults, received assistance for at least a year, while 40 percent will have used a welfare program in at least five separate years. (Again, adding childhood

160   poverty and inequality

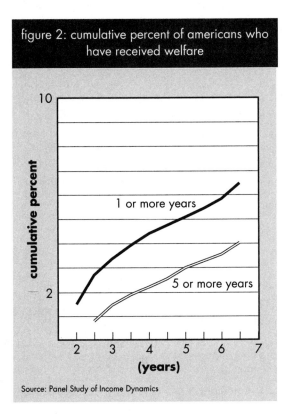

figure 2: cumulative percent of americans who have received welfare

cumulative percent

10

1 or more years

2

5 or more years

(years)

2   3   4   5   6   7

Source: Panel Study of Income Dynamics

across a lifetime, more than 50 years. Over so many years, individuals face many unanticipated events—households split up, workers lose their jobs, family members become sick, and so on—that become financial emergencies. The familiar saying of being "one paycheck away from poverty" is particularly apt. For example, it is estimated that families with average incomes have enough assets to maintain their standards of living for just over one month.

the safety net A second reason poverty rates are so high is that there is little government help to tide households over during financial emergencies. Although most Americans will eventually rely on need-based government aid (as shown in figure 2), that assistance often fails to save them from poverty. Contrary to the rhetoric about vast sums being spent on public assistance, the American welfare system can be more accurately described as minimal. Compared to other Western industrialized countries, the United States devotes far fewer resources to assisting the economically vulnerable.

Most European countries provide a wide range of social and insurance programs that effectively keep families from falling into poverty. These include substantial cash payments to families with children. Unemployment assistance is far more generous in these countries than in the United States, often providing support for more than a year following the loss of a job. Furthermore, universal health coverage is routinely provided along with considerable support for child care.

These social policies substantially reduce the risk of poverty in Europe and Canada, while U.S. social policies—aside from programs specifically directed to aid the elderly—have reduced poverty modestly at best. As economist Rebecca Blank notes in *It Takes a Nation*, "the national choice in the United States to provide relatively less generous transfers to low-income families

experiences would only raise the rates.) Contrary to stereotypes, relying on America's social safety net is widespread and far-reaching.

Of course, people with disadvantages such as single parents or those with fewer skills will have even higher cumulative rates of poverty and welfare use than those shown in figures 1 and 2. Yet to portray poverty as an issue affecting only marginalized groups is clearly a mistake.

why is the risk of poverty so high?

time First, most discussions of poverty look at single years, or five or ten years at a stretch. The life table techniques employed in Figures 1 and 2 are based upon assessing the risk of poverty has meant higher relative poverty rates in the country. While low-income families in the United States work more than in many other countries, they are not able to make up for lower governmental income support relative to their European counterparts" (pp. 141–142).

Scholars who have used the Luxembourg Income Study (LIS), an international collection of economic surveys, have documented the inability of the American safety net to reduce the risk of poverty. For example, Finnish social scientist Veli-Matti Ritakallio has examined the extent to which cash assistance reduces poverty across eight European countries, Canada, and the United States. European and Canadian programs reduce rates of poverty by an average of 79 percent from what they would have been absent the assistance. Finland, for instance, reduced the percentage of its residents who would have been poor from 33 percent down to 4 percent. In contrast, the United States was only able to reduce its percentage in poverty at any

> Contrary to the rhetoric about vast sums being spent on public assistance, the American welfare system can be more accurately described as minimal. Compared to other Western industrialized countries, the United States devotes far fewer resources to assisting the economically vulnerable.

given time from 29 percent to 18 percent. As a result, the current rates of U.S. poverty are among the highest in the industrialized world.

the labor market A third factor elevating the risk of American poverty across the life course is the failure of the labor market to provide enough jobs that pay well enough. During the past 30 years, the U.S. economy has produced increasing numbers of low-paying jobs, part-time jobs, and jobs without benefits. For example, the Census Bureau estimated that the median earnings of workers who were paid hourly wages in 2000 was $9.91. At the same time, approximately 3 million Americans were working part-time because of a shortage of full-time jobs. As journalist Barbara Ehrenreich and others have shown, these jobs simply do not support a family.

A higher percentage of the U.S. workforce falls into this low-wage sector than is true in comparable developed countries. For example, economist Timothy Smeeding and his colleagues have found that 25 percent of all American full-time workers could be classified as being in low-wage work (defined as earning less than 65 percent of the national median for full-time jobs). This was by far the highest percentage of the countries analyzed, with the overall average of non-U.S. countries falling at 12 percent.

In addition, there are simply not enough jobs to go around. Labor economist Timothy Bartik used several different approaches to estimate the number of jobs that would be needed to significantly reduce poverty in the United States. Even in the booming economy of the late 1990s, between 5 and 9 million more jobs were needed in order to meet the needs of the poor and disadvantaged.

To use an analogy, the demand for labor versus the supply of decent paying jobs might be thought of as an ongoing game of musical chairs. That is, the number of workers in the labor market is far greater than the number of jobs that pay a living wage. Using SIPP data for 1999, I estimated this imbalance as ranging between 9 percent and 33 percent, depending upon how poverty and labor market participation were defined. Consequently, between 9 and 33 percent of American household heads were either in nonliving-wage jobs or looking for work. The very structure of the labor market ensures that some families will lose out at this musical chairs game and consequently will run a significant risk of poverty.

Some may point out that U.S. rates of unemployment are fairly low when compared to European levels. Yet Bruce Western and Katherine Beckett demonstrate that these lower rates are largely a result of extremely high rates of incarceration. By removing large numbers of American men from the labor force and placing them into the penal system (thus out of our musical chairs analogy altogether), unemployment rates are kept artificially low. When this factor is taken into account and adjusted for, U.S. unemployment rates fall more into line with those of Europe.

changing the poverty paradigm

A life course perspective shows us that Americans are highly susceptible to experiencing poverty first-hand. Understanding the normality of poverty requires us to rethink several of our most enduring myths. Assuming that most Americans would rather avoid such an experience, it becomes in our enlightened self-interest to ensure that we reduce poverty and establish an effective safety net. This risk-sharing argument has been articulated most notably by the philosopher John Rawls. As well as being charitable, improving the plight of those in poverty is an issue of common concern.

We are also beginning to recognize that, as a nation, we pay a high price for our excessive rates of poverty. Research shows that poverty impairs the nation's health, the quality of its workforce, race relations, and, of course, its future generations. Understanding the commonality of poverty shifts how we choose to think about the issue—from a distant concept of *them*, to an active reality of *us*. In addition, much of the public's resistance to assisting the poor and particularly those on welfare is the perception that the poor are often undeserving of assistance, that their poverty arises from a lack of motivation, questionable morals, and so on. Yet my analysis suggests that, given its pervasiveness, poverty appears systemic to our economic structure. In short, we have met the enemy, and they are us. C. Wright Mills made a similar point about unemployment:

When, in a city of 100,000, only one man is unemployed, that is his personal trouble, and for its relief we properly look to the character of the man, his skills, and his immediate opportunities.

But when in a nation of 50 million employees, 15 million men are unemployed, that is an issue, and we may not hope to find its solution within the range of opportunities open to any one individual. The very structure of opportunities open to any one individual. The very structure of opportunities has collapsed. Both the correct statement of the problem and the range of possible solutions require us to consider the economic and political institutions of the society, and not merely the personal situation and character of a scatter of individuals.

So too with poverty. That America has the highest poverty rates in the Western industrialized world and that most Americans will experience poverty during their lifetimes has little to do with individual motivation or attitudes. Rather, it has much to do with a labor market that fails to produce enough decent paying jobs, and social policies that are unable to pull individuals and families out of poverty when unforeseen events occur. The United States has the means to alleviate poverty, and a range of models from other countries to borrow from. Allowing our policies to be mired in self-righteous moralism while millions of citizens suffer is unconscionable. It is time to shift the debate from one of blame, to one of justice and common concern.

RECOMMENDED RESOURCES

Timothy H. Bartik. "Poverty, Jobs, and Subsidized Employment." *Challenge* 45 (2002): 100–11.

> An argument for the importance of labor demand policies that encourage job growth and improved wages for low-income workers.

Rebecca Blank. *It Takes a Nation: A New Agenda for Fighting Poverty* (Russell Sage Foundation, 1997).

> A review of the characteristics, nature, and current strategies for addressing American poverty.

Barbara Ehrenreich. *Nickel and Dimed: On (Not) Getting By in America* (Henry Holt and Company, 2001).

> A first-hand account of trying to survive on low-wage work in three different settings.

Alice O'Connor. *Poverty Knowledge: Social Science, Social Policy, and the Poor in Twentieth-Century U.S. History* (Princeton University Press, 2001).

> O'Connor critiques the dominant social science emphasis in the past 40 years on analyzing individual attributes as the primary cause of poverty.

James T. Patterson. *America's Struggle Against Poverty in the Twentieth Century* (Harvard University Press, 2000).

> An historical overview of American social policy directed at the alleviation of poverty.

Mark R. Rank. *One Nation Underprivileged: How American Poverty Affects Us All* (Oxford University Press, 2004).

> A new perspective on understanding and addressing U.S. poverty.

Mark R. Rank and Thomas A. Hirschl. "Rags or Riches? Estimating the Probabilities of Poverty and Affluence Across the Adult American Life Span." *Social Science Quarterly* 82 (2001): 651–69.

> An examination of the likelihood that Americans will experience poverty or affluence at some point during their adulthood, which suggests a new conceptualization of social stratification.

Veli-Matti Ritakallio. "Trends of Poverty and Income Inequality in Cross-national Comparison." *Luxembourg Income Study Working Paper*, No. 272 (Maxwell School of Citizenship and Public Affairs, Syracuse University, 2001).

> Uses the Luxembourg Income Study to assess the effectiveness of government policy in reducing poverty among nine developed countries.

Timothy M. Smeeding, Lee Rainwater, and Gary Burtless. "U.S. Poverty in a Cross-national Context."

In *Understanding Poverty*, eds. Sheldon H. Danziger and Robert H. Haveman (Harvard University Press, 2001).

> The authors compare the extent of poverty in the United States and other developed countries.

Bruce Western and Katherine Beckett. "How Unregulated Is the U.S. Market? The Penal System as a Labor Market Institution." *American Journal of Sociology* 104 (1999): 1030–60.

> Shows the role that incarceration plays in lowering overall U.S. unemployment rates.

REVIEW QUESTIONS

1. Identify and describe three factors that make the risk of poverty so high in the United States.
2. Throughout the essay, Rank compares and contrasts the differences between European and U.S. models for combating poverty. Discuss two of those differences, and what they say about our society.
3. Toward the end of the essay, Rank uses a quote from C. Wright Mills to describe the sociological perspective on unemployment. Describe that view in relation to other explanations of poverty (e.g., economic or psychological).
4. Activity: How do you think the U.S. compares to the unemployment and poverty in other countries? First, rank what you feel the order is of the following countries on both variables: Costa Rica, Kenya, Russia, United States, France, and Malaysia. Second, find the C.I.A. World Factbook online (http://www.cia.gov/cia/publications/factbook/), and search the "Economy" sections for each country. What do you find?

*fred block, anna c. korteweg, and kerry woodward,
with zach schiller and imrul mazid*

the compassion gap in american poverty policy

24

spring 2006

why does the world's wealthiest country let so many languish in grinding poverty? and why is the situation getting worse, not better?

Every 30 or 40 years, Americans seem to "discover" that millions of our citizens are living in horrible and degrading poverty. Jacob Riis shocked the nation in 1890 with a book entitled *How the Other Half Lives,* which helped to inspire a change in public opinion and the reforms of the Progressive Era. In the 1930s, the devastation of the Great Depression led FDR to place poverty at the top of the national agenda. In the early 1960s, Michael Harrington's *The Other America* made poverty visible and paved the way for Lyndon Johnson's brief War on Poverty. In 2005, an act of nature became the next muckraker—Hurricane Katrina, which shockingly revealed the human face of poverty among the displaced and helpless victims of the storm's devastation in New Orleans.

But what makes poverty so invisible between such episodes of discovery? The poor are always with us, but why do they repeatedly disappear from public view? Why do we stop seeing the pain that poverty causes?

Our society recognizes a moral obligation to provide a helping hand to those in need, but those in poverty have been getting only the back of the hand. They receive little or no public assistance. Instead, they are scolded and told that they have caused their own misfortunes. This is

our "compassion gap"—a deep divide between our moral commitments and how we actually treat those in poverty.

The compassion gap does not just happen. It results from two key dynamics. First, powerful groups in American society insist that public help for the poor actually hurts them by making them weak and dependent. Every epoch in which poverty is rediscovered and generosity increases is followed by a backlash in which these arguments reemerge and lead to sharp reductions in public assistance. Second, the consequence of reduced help is that the assertions of welfare critics turn into self-fulfilling prophecies. They insist that immorality is the root cause of poverty. But when assistance becomes inadequate, the poor can no longer survive by obeying the rules; they are forced to break them. These infractions, in turn, become the necessary proof that "the poor" are truly intractable and that their desperate situations are rightly ignored.

The results are painfully clear in our official data. In 2004, 37 million people, including 13 million children, lived below the government's official poverty line of $15,219 for a family of three. The number of people in poverty has increased every year for the last four years, rising from 31.6 million in 2000. Moreover, our

children living in poverty (counting all sources of income, including income from government programs)				
	all	women	men	children aged 18 and under	female-headed households
Non-Hispanic whites	8.6	9.5	7.7	10.5	28.2
Blacks	24.7	26.5	22.6	33.6	45.0
Hispanics	21.9	24.0	19.9	28.9	45.1
Asians	9.8	11.3	9.3	10.0	16.3

Source: Income, Poverty, and Health Insurance Coverage in the United States: 2004, Detailed Poverty Tables: 2004. U.S. Census Bureau, Current Population Reports.

government's official poverty line is quite stingy by international standards. If we used the most common international measure, which counts people who live on less than half of a country's median income as poor, then almost 55 million people in the United States, or almost 20 percent of the population, would be counted as poor.

Most distressingly, the number of people living in catastrophic poverty—in households with incomes less than 50 percent of the official U.S. poverty line—has increased every year since 1999. There are now 15.6 million people living in this kind of desperate poverty. This is close to the highest number ever, and it is twice the number of extremely poor people that we had in the mid 1970s, before the cuts in poverty programs of the Reagan administration.

Children, single mothers with children, and people of color—particularly African Americans and Latinos—make up a disproportionate segment of the nation's poorest groups, with women in each group consistently more likely to be poor than men in that group. But poverty is not unusual or rare—as many as 68 percent of all Americans will spend a year or more living in poverty or near-poverty as adults. Nor is poverty always related to not working; there are still 9 million working-poor adults in the United States.

Moreover, poverty has become more devastating over the past generation. Thirty years ago, a family living at the poverty line—earning a living at low-wage work—could still see the American Dream as an achievable goal (see figure 1). With a bit more hard work and some luck, they too could afford a single-family home, comprehensive health insurance, and a college education for their children. Today, for many of the poor, including many of the faces we saw at the New Orleans Superdome and Convention Center, that dream has become a distant and unattainable vision. Even a two-parent family working full-time at the minimum wage earns less than half of what is needed to realize the dream at today's prices. The old expectation that the poor would pull themselves up by their own bootstraps is increasingly unrealistic.

Despite the growing poor population and the increasing difficulty of escaping poverty into economic security through paid work, the government has been doing less and less to help. Aid to

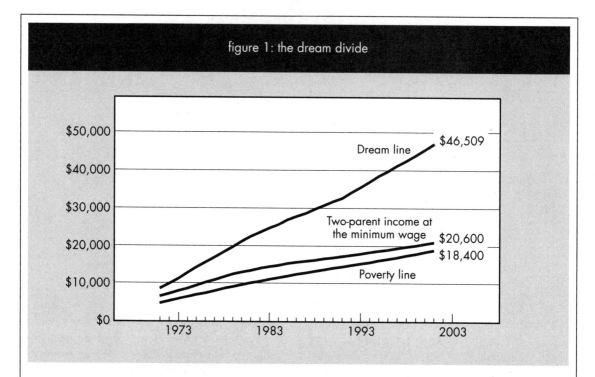

figure 1: the dream divide

Dream line $46,509

Two-parent income at the minimum wage $20,600

$18,400

Poverty line

$50,000

$40,000

$30,000

$20,000

$10,000

$0

1973   1983   1993   2003

The Dream Line is an estimate of the cost for an urban or suburban family of four to enjoy a no-frills version of the American Dream that includes owning a single-family home, full health-insurance coverage, quality child care for a four-year-old, and enough annual savings to assure that both children can attend a public, four-year college or university. The Dream Line is not a wage figure because it includes the full cost of health insurance coverage that is often, but decreasingly, offered as a benefit by employers. The figures are national averages and are lower than what people would pay for these services in the largest and most expensive metropolitan areas on the East and West coasts. The housing figure reflects the cost of mortgage payments on the median-priced existing family home at current interest rates. The Dream Line rises so dramatically because the costs of the four H's—housing, health insurance, high-quality child care, and higher education—have risen so much more rapidly than other consumer prices. Dollar figures have not been adjusted for inflation. More details on the way the Dream Divide was calculated are available at http://www.longviewinstitute.org/research/block/amerdream/view.

Families with Dependent Children (AFDC) used to be our biggest program to help poor people, but federal legislation passed in 1996 ended AFDC and replaced it with Temporary Aid to Needy Families (TANF). TANF's focus on moving recipients from "welfare to work" has led to a major decline in the number of households re-ceiving benefits and a huge drop in cash assistance to the poor. The average monthly TANF benefit was $393 in 2003, compared to $490 in 1997.

Not only are our programs miserly, they reach too few people among those who are eligible, further reducing the chances that those in poverty can achieve the American Dream. Only 60 percent of eligible households receive food stamps. Despite a commitment to provide health insurance to all children under 18, nearly 12 percent of those children remained without such insurance in 2004, and only 27 percent of all poor families received TANF in 2000. Finally, subsidized housing is provided to only 25 percent of those who need it, and current budget proposals would cut this program dramatically.

Against this backdrop of decreasing spending on most antipoverty measures, the Earned Income Tax Credit (EITC) has become our biggest antipoverty program for the working-age population. EITC aids the working poor by providing an income-tax refund to lift the poorest workers above the poverty line. But for families to benefit significantly from the EITC, someone in the household must be earning at least several thousand dollars per year. Each

year, millions of households do not have such an earner because of unemployment, illness, lack of child care, or a mismatch between available skills and job demands. The consequence is a relentless increase in our rate of catastrophic poverty.

Figure 2 shows the combined spending for the two most important cash assistance programs—AFDC/TANF and the EITC. It demonstrates that despite increases in EITC outlays, our total spending on the poor peaked in 1997 and has dropped almost 20 percent since then. Figure 3 takes the further step of adjusting the annual spending for the impact of inflation and the shifting size of the poor population. Spending for each nonelderly poor person peaked at around $1,000 in 1997 and has dropped every year since, with a total decline of close to 30 percent. And if we added food stamps to this chart, the trend would be even stronger, since their real value has also fallen since 1997. There is no

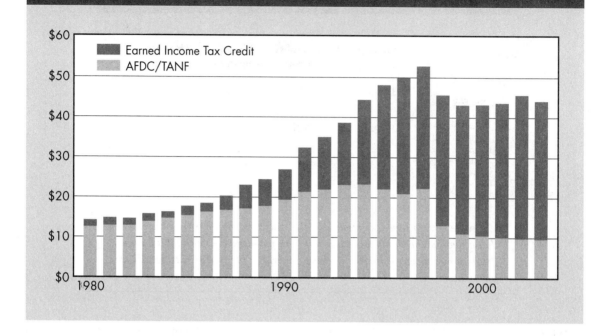

Earned Income Tax Credit
AFDC/TANF

clearer evidence that our compassion gap has deepened poverty.

The compassion gap has been greatly increased by the revival in the 1980s and 1990s of the very old theory that the real source of poverty is bad behavior. Since African-American and Hispanic women and men, as well as single mothers of all ethnicities and races, are disproportionately represented among the poor, this theory defines these people as morally deficient. Its proponents assume that anyone with enough grit and determination can escape poverty. They claim that giving people cash assistance worsens poverty by taking away their drive to improve their circumstances through work. Arguing that poor people bear children irresponsibly and that they lack the work ethic necessary for economic success, they have launched a sustained war on bad behavior that targets those groups most at risk of poverty.

One of the key events in this war was the passage in 1996 of the Personal Responsibility and Work Opportunities Reconciliation Act (PRWORA), which replaced AFDC with TANF. TANF requires single mothers who receive welfare to find paid work, encourages them to marry, and limits their time on aid to a lifetime maximum of five years. Some states have even shorter time limits. Ultimately, this new program treats the inability to work as a personal, moral failing.

can governments solve poverty?

The flip side of the premise that poverty is the result of such moral failings is that government actions cannot solve poverty. Yet our own national experience points to the opposite conclusion. For generations, many of the elderly lived in extreme poverty because they were no longer able

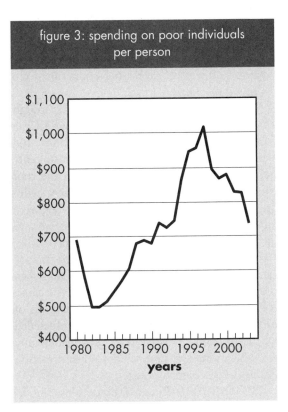

figure 3: spending on poor individuals per person

to work. But the creation of the Social Security system has sharply reduced poverty among seniors by recognizing that most people need government assistance as they age. Yet, rather than celebrating the compassion reflected in this program, the current administration is proposing destructive changes in Social Security that will make it less effective in preventing poverty among this group. And instead of recognizing that most young families also need assistance to survive and thrive, our major antipoverty program, the EITC, leaves out all those families who find themselves squeezed out of the labor market.

Looking abroad also shows that government policies can dramatically reduce poverty levels. The probability of living in poverty is more than twice as high for a child born in the United States than for children in Belgium, Germany, or the Netherlands. Children in single-mother households are four times more likely to be poor in the United States than in Norway. The fact that single-parent households are more common in the United States than in many of these countries where the poor receive greater assistance undermines the claim that more generous policies will encourage more single women to have children out of wedlock. These other countries all take a more comprehensive government approach to combating poverty, and they assume that it is caused by economic and structural factors rather than bad behavior.

understanding the compassion gap: a misguided focus on moral poverty

The miserliness of our public assistance is justified by the claim that poverty is the consequence of personal moral failings. Most of our policies incorrectly assume that people can avoid or overcome poverty through hard work alone. Yet this assumption ignores the realities of our failing urban schools, increasing employment insecurities, and the lack of affordable housing, health care, and child care. It ignores the fact that the American Dream is rapidly becoming unattainable for an increasing number of Americans, whether employed or not.

The preoccupation with the moral failings of the poor disregards the structural problems underlying poverty. Instead, we see increasing numbers of policies that are obsessed with preventing "welfare fraud." This obsession creates barriers to help for those who need it. Welfare offices have always required recipients to "prove" their eligibility. Agency employees are in effect trained to begin with the presumption of guilt; every seemingly needy face they encounter is that of a cheater until the potential client can prove the contrary. With the passage of TANF, the rules have become so complex that even welfare caseworkers do not always understand them, let alone their clients. Some of those who need help choose to forego it rather than face this humiliating eligibility process.

But this system of suspicion also produces the very welfare cheaters that we fear. Adults in poor households are caught in a web of different programs, each with its own complex set of rules and requirements, that together provide less assistance than a family needs. Recipients have no choice but to break the rules—usually by not reporting all their income. A detailed study from ten years ago, conducted by Kathryn Edin and Laura Lein, showed that most welfare mothers worked off the books or took money under the table from relatives because they could not make ends meet with only their welfare checks. Since then we have reduced benefits and added more rules, undoubtedly increasing such "cheating."

Those who lack compassion have made their own predictions come true. They begin by claiming that the poor lack moral character. They use stories of welfare cheaters to increase public concerns about people getting something for nothing. Consequently, our patchwork of poorly funded programs reaches only a fraction of the poor and gives them less than they need. Those who depend on these programs must cut corners and break rules to keep their families together. This "proves" the original proposition that the poor lack moral character, and the "discovery" is used to justify ever more stringent policies. The result is a vicious spiral of diminishing compassion and greater preoccupation with the moral failings of the poor.

the war on bad behavior

The moral focus on poverty shifts our gaze from the social forces that create material poverty to the perceived moral failings of the poor. This shift has led to a war on bad behavior, exemplified by PRWORA, that is not achieving its goals. This war focuses on social problems like teenage pregnancy, high drop-out rates, and drug addiction. But research shows that it has been ineffective. Poverty has risen, and punitive measures have had little effect on the behaviors they were supposed to change.

The reduction of teen pregnancy through abstinence-only sex education was one of the main goals of the Personal Responsibility and Work Opportunity Act. Its drafters mistakenly believed that teen pregnancy is one of the root causes of poverty. In fact, if the teenagers who are having children were to wait until they were adults, their children would be just as likely to be born into poverty. But the drafters' other error was ignoring the fact that teen pregnancy rates had already been declining for years when the new law went into effect, primarily because teenagers were using more effective methods of birth-control. (These gains are now threatened by the dramatic expansion of "abstinence-only sex education," which provides no information on birth-control techniques.)

PRWORA also makes assistance to teen mothers contingent on "good behavior." Teen mothers must stay in school or be enrolled in a training program and live with their parents or under other adult supervision in order to receive aid. While it makes sense to help teens stay in school and learn skills, these coercive efforts are failing the children of teen parents. Teen mothers are just as likely today to drop out of school or live on their own as when the act was passed. The only change is that they are now much less likely to receive government assistance: ill-conceived reforms have ensured that children born to teen mothers experience deeper deprivation.

Neither have PRWORA's efforts to control the behavior of the poor had much impact on illicit drug use. Under TANF, states were required to deny benefits to anyone convicted of a drug crime. This was so obviously counterproductive that Congress amended the law in 1999 to allow states to opt out of this ban. Yet neither policy shift appears to have had much impact. According to Justice Department data, adult drug arrests have been increasing relentlessly, from 1 million per year in the early 1990s to 1.5 million in 2003.

But advocates of the war on bad behavior always have a convenient scapegoat for the failure of their punitive policies: they simply shift the blame to single mothers. TANF requires single mothers to work outside the home regardless of whether work gets them out of poverty. But long hours of work and inadequate child care mean that children are often left with inadequate supervision. When these children get into trouble, the mother gets the blame. Teen pregnancy, drug use, and delinquency are then attributed to the mother's lack of parenting skills. Poor single mothers cannot win; they are failures if they stay home with their kids—providing the full-time mothering that conservatives have long advocated for middle-class children. But they are also failures if they work and leave their children un-

supervised. Viewing poverty as the result of bad behavior produces the conclusion that poor single mothers are bad by definition. Since a disproportionate number of these poor single mothers are African American or Hispanic, this rhetoric also hides the racial history that has excluded people of color from opportunities for generations and the systemic racism that persists today.

This war on bad behavior is a deeply mistaken approach to poverty. It ignores the lived reality of people who face crushing poverty every day. It ignores the fundamental wisdom that we should not judge people until we have walked a mile in their shoes. Most basically, it denies compassion to those who need it most.

what to do? revitalize the american dream

Reversing the compassion gap will not happen overnight. We have to persuade our fellow

percentage of women, men, children, and female-headed households in poverty by racial/ethnic group				
country	year	percent of all children in poverty	percent of all children in single-mother homes in poverty	percent of all children living with single mothers
U.S.	2000	21.9	49.3	19.5
U.K.	1999	15.3	33.8	19.5
Canada	2000	14.9	40.7	13.1
Netherlands	1999	9.8	35.1	8.1
Germany	2000	9.0	37.8	12.5
Belgium	2000	6.7	24.5	10.6
Norway	2000	3.4	11.3	14.5

Note: This table uses the international convention of measuring poverty as income less than 50 percent of the nation's median income.

Source: Luxembourg Income Survey: www.lisproject.org/keyfigures/povertytable.htm.

citizens that the war on bad behavior violates our society's fundamental values. We have to show them how far reality has departed from the American Dream, which holds that a child born in poverty in a ghetto or a barrio has the same chance for success and happiness as a child born in suburban affluence. We have to focus national debate on what policy measures would revitalize the American Dream for all of our citizens.

The reason the American Dream is now beyond reach for so many families is that the price of four critical services has risen much more sharply than wages and the rate of inflation: health care, higher education, high-quality child care, and housing. These are not luxuries, but indispensable ingredients of the dream.

Over the last three decades, our society has relied largely on market solutions to organize delivery of these indispensable services, but these solutions have not increased their supply. Instead, we use the price mechanism to ration their distribution; poor and working-class people are at the end of the line, and they find themselves priced out of the market.

We need new initiatives to expand the supply of these key services while assuring their quality. This requires accelerated movement toward universal health insurance and universal availability of quality child care and preschool programs. We need to move toward universal access to higher education for all students who meet the admissions criteria. (We also need to ensure that all our public schools are preparing students for the higher education and training that most will need in order to succeed in the labor market.) And we need to create new public-private partnerships to expand the supply of affordable housing for poor and working-class families. These efforts would restore the American Dream for millions of working-class and lower middle-class families, while also putting the dream within the reach of the poor.

But we also need new policies that target the poor more directly. This requires restoring the value of the minimum wage. Between 1968 and 2002, the purchasing power of the federal minimum wage fell by a third. We need to reverse this trend and assure that in the future the minimum wage continues to rise with inflation. Most fundamentally, we must do what most other developed nations do—provide a stable income floor for all poor families so that no children grow up in horrible and degrading poverty. We could establish such a floor by transforming our present Earned Income Tax Credit into a program that provided all poor families with sufficient income to cover food and shelter. Households would be eligible for a monthly payment even if they had no earnings. Since such payments would target the poorest individuals and families, this would be a cost-effective way to immediately rescue millions of people from catastrophic poverty. Moreover, since payments would be coordinated through the tax system, a household's income would definitely improve as its labor-force earnings rose.

The key to making these policy initiatives feasible is to remind our fellow citizens what true compassion requires. The war on bad behavior offers us an easy way out. It is easy to believe that those in poverty are responsible for their own problems and that ignoring their needs is the best thing for them. It absolves those of us who are better off from the responsibility of caring for others. However, if we want to live up to our national commitment to compassion, we need to recognize that we have a collective responsibility to ensure that in the wealthiest nation in the world there are not millions of people going hungry, millions without health insurance, and hundreds of thousands without homes. Sure, some of those in poverty have made bad choices, but who has not? It is deeply unfair that those who are not poor get second chances, while the poor do not. Rush Limbaugh pays no price for becoming addicted to painkillers, but millions of poor people go to jail and lose access to public housing and welfare benefits for the same offense.

True compassion requires that we build a society in which every person has a first chance, a second chance, and, if needed, a third and fourth chance, to achieve the American Dream. We are our brother's and our sister's keepers, and we need to use every instrument we have—faith groups, unions, community groups, and most of all government programs—to address the structural problems that reproduce poverty in our affluent society.

Dealing with the inadequacies of our current antipoverty programs is a first step in moving the debate in the right direction. Since the fall of 2002, Congress has been stalemated on reauthorizing the TANF legislation that was first passed in 1996. Action in the immediate future seems unlikely because many governors oppose the more stringent work requirements for TANF recipients proposed by the Bush administration and its conservative allies in the House, because those changes would require the states to pay for new work-experience programs.

A compassionate reauthorization of TANF requires four basic steps. First, we must increase assistance levels to rescue families from the deepest poverty and give them enough income to put them over the poverty line. Second, we must abandon the whole system of mandatory time limits on aid, so that families in poverty no longer find the doors to help closed in their faces. Eliminating time limits is particularly important in ensuring that programs serve the many poor women who are victims of domestic abuse. While TANF is supposed to protect such women, too often they are being forced back into the arms of their abusers. Third, we must recognize basic and postsecondary education and training as a "work activity," so that recipients can prepare for jobs that would get them out of poverty. Finally, we need to improve the child care provisions in TANF. We must do more than provide child care subsidies to only one out of seven children who are federally eligible. Moreover, we must ensure that TANF children get a head start and are not relegated to the lowest-quality child care.

By themselves, these reforms would not close the compassion gap, but they would mark an end to the futile and destructive war on bad behavior. They could represent an initial down payment on restoring the American Dream.

postscript

For more than three years, Congress was unable to agree on a reauthorization of the TANF legislation that was initially passed in 1996. In early 2006, however, the Republican leadership moved the legislation without debate or discussion by including TANF reauthorization in a large deficit-reduction bill that passed both houses by the narrowest of margins. In fact, the legislation might yet be overturned by the courts because the House and the Senate passed slightly different versions of the bill.

If implemented, the new legislation will widen the compassion gap even further because states are required either to place 50 percent of adult recipients in work-related activities or to reduce the number of families receiving benefits. Since many of those currently on the rolls face multiple barriers to employment, these artificial targets are likely to create considerable hardship. Moreover, the allocation for child care is not enough to maintain the current availability of child care, let alone to keep pace with the new participation requirements.

RECOMMENDED RESOURCES

Fred Block and Jeff Manza. "Could We End Poverty in a Postindustrial Society? The Case for a Negative Income Tax." *Politics & Society* 25 (December 1997).

Provides estimates of the cost of a negative income tax to combat poverty.

Kathryn Edin and Laura Lein. *Making Ends Meet: How Single Mothers Survive Welfare and Low-Wage Work* (Russell Sage Foundation, 1997).

> An in-depth look at poor women's income-management strategies that shows that "cheating" is inevitable for welfare-reliant women and that making ends meet on low-wage work is impossible under current conditions.

Martin Gilens. *Why Americans Hate Welfare: Race, Media, and the Politics of Antipoverty Policy* (University of Chicago Press, 1999).

> An analysis of the forces that shape American attitudes toward poverty.

Sharon Hays. *Flat Broke with Children: Women in the Age of Welfare Reform* (Oxford University Press, 2003).

> An ethnography of two welfare offices implementing welfare reform that shows the depth of poor women's poverty and the uphill battle caseworkers face in helping their clients.

Kristin Luker. *Dubious Conceptions: The Politics of Teenage Pregnancy* (Harvard University Press, 1996).

> Argues that teen pregnancy is not the cause of the poverty of single mothers.

Useful Web sites:
Center for Law and Social Policy at www.clasp.org
Longview Institute at www.longviewinstitute.org

U.S. Census at www.census.gov/prod/2005pubs/p60-229.pdf

REVIEW QUESTIONS

1. What is the "Compassion Gap"? What are the two reasons for it? What is the "Dream Line" and the "Dream Divide"?
2. The authors distinguish an individualistic perspective and new sociological perceptions of poverty. Identify a particular example of this distinction as it is presented in the essay, and reflect upon the implications of these different perspectives.
3. As George W. Bush came into office in 2000, he used the term "compassionate conservative" to great effect. This platform, which shifted the responsibility of taking care of the poor to religious institutions and enacted tax cuts designed to promote charitable giving, explains much of the decline in social programs that are evidenced in the article. As Mr. Bush's chief domestic policy adviser, Stephen Goldsmith, described it, this policy aimed to "help in such a way as to stimulate and reinforce self-governance." Building on your answer to the last question, write two paragraphs on what you feel the government's role should be in addressing poverty. Be sure to draw from evidence in this article.

part **6**

Work and the Economy

richard swedberg

keyword: the market

25

spring 2007

The term "market" refers first of all to an area within which exchange takes place. It also refers to a social mechanism for economic growth or what the economists call a mechanism for the efficient allocation of resources. These two meanings are confusing since they differ so greatly. While one emphasizes what goes on *inside* the market, the other puts the emphasis on what happens *outside* the market or, more precisely, the relation of the market to the rest of the economic process.

The term also plays a central ideological role in today's world, adding to the difficulty of assessing the importance of the market for the modern economy and modern society. A quick inspection of today's major ideologies finds references to the market in most of them, from the Right to the Left. Libertarians have one opinion, communists another, and so on. One way to think of the spectrum of political opinions about the market is to imagine a two-by-two table with "efficient/not efficient" on one side, and "positive/negative" on the other. Libertarians, for example, view markets as efficient and good; communists, in contrast, see markets as inefficient and bad. European Social Democrats see markets as efficient but bad, while Keynes and some of his followers favor markets but do not find them efficient. According to Keynesians, markets will eventually self-destruct if the state does not properly intervene. The Keynesians also remind us that our view of the state as

a political actor is often closely related to our view of the market.

Markets have an ideological charge because capitalism has been surrounded by political struggle since its inception. Groups that get their income or resources from "status" as opposed to "contract" (to use the famous terms of the legal historian H. S. Maine) have typically fought capitalism. So have those who rely on "contracts" for their income but get little of it. The ideological battle of capitalism, however, has been waged in terms of the market only since around the time of World War II. For example, this period gave rise to one of the most famous denunciations of capitalism phrased in terms of the market, Karl Polanyi's *The Great Transformation* (1944).

But markets also had their ideological advocates who stepped forward around the same time, such as Friedrich Hayek and Ludwig von Mises, and they eventually got the upper hand. The support of political forces has also been significant for the rise of the market as an ideology, especially with the election of Margaret Thatcher in 1979 and Ronald Reagan in 1980. Reagan, for example, coined the phrase "the magic of the market."

Thatcher's and Reagan's ideology, neoliberalism, claims that the market represents the best solution not only to standard economic problems, but also to many of the problems that have traditionally been handled by the state or local communities. The state, according to this ideology (which has also been called "market fundamentalism"), should first ensure that the market gets to decide. While the state still has a number of noneconomic tasks to perform, its general purpose is to ensure the primacy of market forces. Neoliberalism soon swept the world, providing an ideological justification for the dismantling of the welfare state in the developed countries and for imposing various pro-market reforms via the International Monetary Fund in the developing world (known as the "Washington consensus").

Since the role of any ideology is to support certain actors and not to explain how reality works, neoliberalism has little to say about what a market is and how it operates. Historical research can help us here, especially in gaining a better understanding of the first meaning of "market," namely, an area within which exchange takes place or, to cite one of the definitions in the *Oxford English Dictionary*, "a public space, whether an open space or covered building, in which cattle, provisions, etc. are exposed for sale."

The first markets in history were probably situated on the outskirts of or just outside communities and were intended to serve members of other communities. Eventually these external markets were replaced by internal markets situated inside the community. What we know about early Greece, a few centuries before Christ, illustrates the complexity of early markets.

The *agora* (marketplace) of Athens was situated inside the city in an area set off by boundary stones. Special stands (*stoa*) were constructed where merchants could display their goods. Many social and political activities also took place in the market, where Socrates, for example, harassed wealthy young Athenians for thinking more about their wealth than about their souls. Specially appointed officials kept order in the market, ensured the accuracy of measures and weights, and aimed to prevent the

circulation of forged money. Crimes in the market were punished in special courts.

There was also a special god of the market—Hermes, the god of the merchants as well as of the thieves. This odd pairing is usually explained as the view of the huge land and slave owners in Athens, who considered conquest by force to be the only proper way to procure a fortune. Merchants, with their haggling in the market, were seen as thieves.

The idea of the market as a specially marked off area for exchange was very common during the centuries following the decline of Greece and until the nineteenth century. There were, for example, special market places in the cities during the Middle Ages. There were also the occasional fairs, from Roman times onward, until permanent stock exchanges and other financial markets were created in Amsterdam, Paris, London, and other major cities.

As the money economy expanded, markets also changed. In the nineteenth century, fully integrated national markets appeared for the first time in history, thanks to a combination of economic, political, and technological developments. Political rulers unified nations—and so did the railroad, the telegraph, and other technological innovations. What characterized this new type of market was that buying and selling could take place over a large and diffuse area.

Economic theory reflected this transformation. For Adam Smith and the early economists, the market had been synonymous with the marketplace, but by the 1830s the economist Antoine Cournot could argue that "economists understand by the term *Market*, not any particular marketplace in which things are bought and sold, but the whole region in which buyers and sellers are in such free intercourse that the prices of the same goods tend to equality easily and quickly." In the late nineteenth century, economists developed the "neoclassical" theory of the market. Now, the market was understood primarily as a price mechanism, or a way to determine prices through the interplay of demand and supply. In addition, the idea of the market became excessively abstract. The demand-supply schedule includes no legal system, no state, no people, and no social relations. It is truly a "hypothetical market," as economist John Neville Keynes put it.

Economists used this abstract model of the market without much reflection until the emergence a few decades ago of what has become known as "new institutional economics." According to this brand of thought, the traditional, neoclassical analysis must be complemented by a theory of institutions, including that of the market. This can be done by introducing the idea of transaction cost (or the cost of using the market) into the analysis. The reason today's markets are such complex institutions is that constant attempts are made to lower transaction costs and increase efficiency.

The second major meaning of the term "market" is a social mechanism for economic growth, or what economists refer to as a mechanism for the efficient allocation of resources. This meaning is related to the late-nineteenth-century idea of the market as a price mechanism. The key idea here is that the market—or rather, a full set of interrelated markets—will affect what a country produces in an efficient manner. If the price goes up for Good A, this will eventually be reflected in everything that is needed to produce this good and shift the resources in its direction. Price changes send information to other markets, ensuring efficiency throughout the economy.

As though guided by an invisible hand, this whole process will eventually lead to an increase in the wealth of the nations. By this metaphor, according to modern economists, Adam Smith meant the process of competition. The idea is that consumers will only buy from the bakers, brewers, and butchers who produce the best goods. Other goods will not be produced since they will not be bought. Is this also what happens in reality? Sociologists have difficulty addressing this issue because they have not looked at the role of the market as a growth engine. But this is easy to do with the help of the three well-known concepts that Polanyi used to analyze how economies are organized: redistribution, reciprocity, and exchange. To understand this, we need to start from the common notion that the economic process consists of production, distribution, and consumption. You first produce something, then distribute it, and finally consume it.

Following Polanyi, there should be three major ways to organize whole economies, including the element of distribution. With redistribution, a center in the community, typically the state acts to distribute goods. Whatever is produced goes to the state; state officials then determine who will get what—as in socialism or in the way that Social Security works.

Alternatively, goods can be distributed through reciprocity, or according to norms that obligate members of a family or a community to share what has been produced. Both redistribution and reciprocity have as their primary goal the reproduction of the community or the household. Whatever growth occurs in systems that operate on these principles usually comes simply from having resources left over or not distributed, and it takes the form of slow evolution. If goods are redistributed through exchange, that is, in a market, there will be a very different dynamic. In such a system, all that is produced is not going to consumption or to reproduction, but to profit. This profit is then typically reinvested—and it is this constant reinvestment and search for more profit that makes the market system or capitalism so dynamic, dramatically increasing its potential for growth.

While this Polanyi-inspired model shows why a market-centered economy leads to dynamic growth, it is silent on many issues. It says nothing, for example, about the role of culture in the economic process, or the role of the state in the economic process. It also has nothing to say about the interaction between market-induced growth and society as a whole, including how growth affects stratification or the exploitation of certain groups, for example, ethnic minorities or women. Many issues thus remain to be analyzed before we have a full sociological theory of the market—and before we fully understand the term "market" more generally.

RECOMMENDED RESOURCES

Fernand Braudel. *The Wheels of Commerce* (Fontana Press, 1979).

A great historian provides a fascinating account of the changing role of markets over time.

Karl Polanyi, Conrad Arensberg, and Harry Pearson, eds. *Trade and Markets in the Early Empires: Economies in History and Theory* (Henry Regnery Company, 1957).

This important volume contains many useful concepts for analyzing markets.

Richard Swedberg. "Markets as Social Structures." In *The Handbook of Economic Sociology*, eds. Neil Smelser and Richard Swedberg (Russell Sage Foundation, 1994).

A summary of how economists and sociologists have looked at the market.

Richard Swedberg. "The Economic Sociology of Capitalism: An Introduction and Agenda." In *The Economic Sociology of Capitalism* (Princeton University Press, 2005).

This essay attempts to work out a sociological theory of the market as an engine of economic growth.

REVIEW QUESTIONS

1. Before you read this essay, how might you have defined *markets*?
2. What is *neoliberalism*?
3. How did government intervention in the market exist even in the early days of the Greek agora?
4. According to Polanyi's model of growth, today's embrace of the market remains silent on pivotal issues addressed by sociology. How might "efficiency" in a market economy negatively affect a specific social condition? Select one of the following three situations and discuss it in terms of "market fundamentalism": the employment opportunities of a particularly disadvantaged social group; the mass production of a Balinese cultural artifact to be sold in the United States; the role of state-funded after-school programs in inner-city areas.

cedric herring

is job discrimination dead?

26

summer 2002

political and legal debate in recent years has focused on whether discrimination in favor of african americans is justified. what receives less attention is that employment discrimination against african americans, though illegal, is still alive and well in america.

In November 1996, Texaco settled a case for $176 million with African-American employees who charged that the company systematically denied them promotions. Texaco originally vowed to fight the charges. When irrefutable evidence surfaced, however, Texaco changed its position. The *New York Times* released a tape recording of several Texaco executives referring to black employees as "niggers" and "black jelly beans" who would stay stuck at the bottom of the bag. Texaco also ultimately acknowledged that they used two promotion lists—a public one that included the names of blacks and a secret one that excluded all black employee names. The $176 million settlement was at the time the largest amount ever awarded in a discrimination suit.

Much has changed in American race relations over the past 50 years. In the old days, job discrimination against African Americans was clear, pervasive, and undeniable. There were "white jobs" for which blacks need not apply, and there were "Negro jobs" in which no self-respecting white person would be found. No laws prohibited racial discrimination in employment. Indeed, in several states laws required separation of blacks and whites in virtually every public realm. Not only was racial discrimination the reality of the day, but also many whites supported the idea

that job discrimination against blacks was appropriate. In 1944, 55 percent of whites admitted to interviewers that they thought whites should receive preference over blacks in access to jobs, compared with only 3 percent who offered such opinions in 1972.

Many blatant forms of racism have disappeared. Civil rights laws make overt and covert acts of discrimination illegal. Also, fewer Americans admit to traditional racist beliefs than ever before. Such changes have inspired many scholars and social commentators to herald the "end of racism" and to declare that we have created a color-blind society. They point to declines in prejudice, growth in the proportion of blacks who hold positions of responsibility, a closing of the earnings gap between young blacks and young whites, and other evidence of "racial progress."

However, racial discrimination in employment is still widespread; it has just gone underground and become more sophisticated. Many citizens, especially whites who have never experienced such treatment, find it hard to believe that such discriminatory behavior by employers exists. Indeed, 75 percent of whites in a 1994 survey said that whites were likely to lose a job to a less-qualified black. Nevertheless, clear and convincing evidence of discriminatory patterns against black job seekers exists.

> Racial discrimination in employment is still widespread; It has just gone underground and become more sophisticated.

In addition to the landmark Texaco case, other corporate giants have made the dishonor roll in recent years. In 2000, a court ordered Ford Motor Company to pay $9 million to victims of sexual and racial harassment. Ford also agreed to pay $3.8 million to settle another suit with the U.S. Labor Department involving discrimination in hiring women and minorities at seven of the company's plants. Similarly in 1999, Boeing agreed to pay $82 million to end racially based pay disparities at its plants. In April 2000, Amtrak paid $16 million to settle a race discrimination lawsuit that alleged Amtrak had discriminated against black employees in hiring, promotion, discipline, and training. And in November 2000, the Coca-Cola Company settled a federal lawsuit brought by black employees for more than $190 million. These employees accused Coca-Cola of erecting a corporate hierarchy in which black employees were clustered at the bottom of the pay scale, averaging $26,000 a year less than white workers.

The list of companies engaged in discrimination against black workers is long and includes many pillars of American industry, not just marginal or maverick firms. Yet when incidents of discrimination come into public view, many of us are still mystified and hard-pressed for explanations. This is so, in part, because discrimination has become so illegitimate that companies expend millions of dollars to conceal it. They have managed to discriminate without using the blatant racism of the old days. While still common, job discrimination against blacks has become more elusive and less apparent.

how common?

Most whites think that discriminatory acts are rare and sensationalized by a few high-profile cases and that the nation is well on its way to becoming a color-blind society. According to a 2001 Gallup survey, nearly 7 in 10

whites (69 percent) said that blacks are treated "the same as whites" in their local communities. The numbers, however, tell a different story. Annually, the federal government receives about 80,000 complaints of employment discrimination, and another 60,000 cases are filed with state and local fair employment practices commissions. One recent study found that about 60 percent of blacks reported racial barriers in their workplace in the last year, and a 1997 Gallup survey found that one in five reported workplace discrimination in the previous month.

The results of "social audits" suggest that the actual frequency of job discrimination against blacks is even higher than blacks themselves realize. Audit studies test for discrimination by sending white and minority "job seekers" with comparable résumés and skills to the same hiring firms to apply for the same job. The differential treatment they receive provides a measure of discrimination. These audits consistently find that employers are less likely to interview or offer jobs to minority applicants. For example, studies by the Fair Employment Practices Commission of Washington, D.C., found that blacks face discrimination in one out of every five job interviews and that they are denied job offers 20 percent of the time. A similar study by the Urban Institute matched equally qualified white and black testers who applied for the same jobs in Chicago. About 38 percent of the time, white applicants advanced further in the hiring process than equally qualified blacks. Similarly, a General Accounting Office audit study uncovered significant discrimination against black and Latino testers. In comparison with whites, black and Latino candidates with equal credentials received 25 percent fewer job interviews and 34 percent fewer job offers.

These audit studies suggest that present-day discrimination is more sophisticated than in the old days. For example, discriminating employers do not explicitly deny jobs to blacks; rather, they use the different phases of the hiring process to discriminate in ways that are difficult to detect. In particular, when comparable résumés of black and white testers are sent to firms, discriminatory firms systematically call whites first and repeatedly until they exhaust their list of white applicants before they approach their black prospects. They offer whites jobs on the spot but tell blacks that they will give them a call back in a few weeks. These mechanisms mean that white applicants go through the hiring process before any qualified blacks are even considered.

Discriminatory employers also offer higher salaries and higher-status positions to white applicants. For example, audit studies have documented that discriminatory employment agencies often note race in the files of black applicants and steer them away from desirable and lucrative positions. A Fair Employment Practices Commission study found that these agencies, which control much of the applicant flow into white-collar jobs, discriminate against black applicants more than 60 percent of the time.

Surprisingly, many employers are willing to detail (in confidence to researchers) how they discriminate against black job seekers. Some admit refusing to consider any black applicants. Many others admit to engaging in recruitment practices that artificially reduce the number of black applicants who know about and apply for entry-level jobs in their firms. One effective way is to avoid ads in mainstream newspapers. In one Chicago study, more than 40 percent of the employers from firms within the city did not advertise their entry-level job openings in mainstream newspapers. Instead, they advertised job vacancies in neighborhood or ethnic newspapers that targeted particular groups, mainly Hispanics or white East European immigrants. For the employer who wants to avoid blacks, this strategy can be quite effective when employment ads are written in languages other than English, or when the circulation of such newspapers is

through channels that usually do not reach many blacks.

Employers described recruiting young workers largely from Catholic schools or schools in white areas. Besides avoiding public schools, these employers also avoided recruiting from job-training, welfare, and state employment service programs. Consequently, some job-training programs have had unanticipated negative effects on the incomes and employment prospects of their African-American enrollees. For instance, research on the effect of such training programs on the earnings and employability of black inner-city residents found that those who participated in various job-training programs earned less per month and had higher unemployment rates than their counterparts who had not participated in such programs.

who suffers?

Generally, no black person is immune from discriminatory treatment. A few factors make some even more vulnerable to discrimination than others. In particular, research has shown that African Americans with dark complexions are likelier to report discrimination—one-half do—than those with lighter complexions. Job discrimination is also associated with education in a peculiar fashion: Those blacks with more education report more discrimination. For example, in a Los Angeles study, more than 80 percent of black workers with college degrees and more than 90 percent of those with graduate-level educations reported facing workplace discrimination. Black immigrants are more likely than nonimmigrants to report discrimination experiences, residents of smaller communities report more than those of larger ones, and younger African Americans report more than older ones. Rates of job discrimination are lower among those who are married than among those who are not wed. Research also shows that some employment characteristics also appear to make a difference: African Americans who are hired through personal contacts report discrimination less often, as do those who work in the manufacturing sector and those who work for larger firms.

Discrimination exacts a financial cost. African Americans interviewed in the General Social Survey in 1991 who reported discrimination in the prior year earned $6,200 less than those who reported none. (In addition, blacks earn $3,800 less than whites because of differences in educational attainment, occupation, age, and other factors.) A one-time survey cannot determine whether experiences of discrimination lead to low income or whether low income leads to feeling discriminated against. Multivariate research based on data from the Census Bureau, which controls for education and other wage-related factors, shows that the white-black wage gap (i.e., "the cost of being black") has continued to be more than 10 percent—about the same as in the mid 1970s. Moreover, research looking at the effects of discrimination over the life course suggests a cumulative effect of discrimination on wages such that the earnings gap between young blacks and whites becomes greater as both groups age.

how can there be discrimination?

Many economists who study employment suggest that job discrimination against blacks cannot (long) exist in a rational market economy because jobs are allocated based on ability and earnings maximization. Discrimination, they argue, cannot play a major role in the rational employer's efforts to hire the most productive worker at the lowest price. If employers bypass productive workers to satisfy their racism, competitors will hire these workers at lower-than-market wages and offer their goods and services at lower prices, undercutting discriminatory employers. When presented with evidence that discrimination does occur, many economists point to discriminators' market monopoly: Some firms, they argue, are shielded from competition and that allows them to act on their "taste for discrimination." These economists, however, do not explain why employers would prefer to discriminate in the first place. Other economists suggest that employers may rationally rely on "statistical discrimination." Lacking sufficient information about would-be employees, employers use presumed "average" productivity characteristics of the groups to which the potential employees belong to predict who will make the best workers. In other words, stereotypes about black workers (on average) being worse than whites make it "justifiable" for employers to bypass qualified black individuals. In these ways, those economists who acknowledge racial discrimination explain it as a "rational" response to imperfect information and imperfect markets.

In contrast, most sociologists point to prejudice and group conflict over scarce resources as reasons for job discrimination. For example, racial groups create and preserve their identities and advantages by reserving opportunities for their own members. Racially based labor queues and differential terms of employment allow members to allocate work according to criteria that have little to do with productivity or earnings maximization. Those who discriminate against blacks often use negative stereotypes to rationalize their behavior after the fact, which, in turn, reinforces racism, negative stereotypes, and caricatures of blacks.

In particular, labor market segregation theory suggests that the U.S. labor market is divided into two fundamentally different sectors: (1) the primary sector and (2) the secondary sector. The primary sector is composed of jobs that offer job security, work rules that define job responsibilities and duties, upward mobility, and higher incomes and earnings. These jobs allow incumbents to accumulate skills that lead to progressively more responsibility and higher pay. In contrast, secondary sector jobs tend to be low-paying, dead-end jobs with few benefits, arbitrary work rules, and pay structures that are not related to job tenure. Workers in such jobs have less motivation to develop attachments to their firms or to perform their jobs well. Thus, it is mostly workers who cannot gain employment in the primary sector who work in the secondary sector. Race discrimination—sometimes by employers but at times by restrictive unions and professional associations fearful that the inclusion of blacks may drive down their overall wages or prestige—plays a role in determining who gets access to jobs in the primary sector. As a consequence, African Americans are locked out of jobs in the primary labor market, where they would receive higher pay and better treatment, and they tend to be crowded into the secondary sector. And these disparities compound over time as primary sector workers enhance their skills and advance while secondary sector workers stay mired in dead-end jobs.

An alternative sociological explanation of African-American disadvantage in the U.S. labor market is what can be referred to as "structural discrimination." In this view, African Americans are denied access to good jobs through practices that appear to be race-neutral but that work to the detriment of African Americans. Examples of such seemingly race-neutral practices include seniority rules, employers' plant location decisions, policy makers' public transit decisions, funding of public education, economic recessions, and immigration and trade policies.

In the seniority rules example, if blacks are hired later than whites because they are later in the employers' employment queue (for whatever reason), operating strictly by traditional seniority rules will ensure greater job security and

higher pay to whites than to African Americans. Such rules virtually guarantee that blacks, who were the last hired, will be the "first fired" and the worst paid. The more general point is that employers do not have to be prejudiced in implementing their seniority rules for the rules to have the effects of structural discrimination on African Americans. Unequal outcomes are built into the rules themselves.

These same dynamics apply when (1) companies decide to locate away from urban areas with high concentrations of black residents; (2) policy makers decide to build public transit that provides easy access from the suburbs to central city job sites but not from the inner city to central city job sites or to suburban job sites; (3) public education is funded through local property tax revenues that may be lower in inner-city communities where property values are depressed and higher in suburban areas where property values are higher and where tax revenues are supplemented by corporations that have fled the inner city; (4) policy makers attempt to blunt the effects of inflation and high interest rates by allowing unemployment rates to climb, especially when they climb more rapidly in African-American communities; and (5) policy makers negotiate immigration and trade agreements that may lead to lower employer costs but may also lead to a reduction in the number of jobs available to African Americans in the industries affected by such agreements. Again, in none of these cases do decision makers need to be racially prejudiced for their decisions to have disproportionately negative effects on the job prospects or life chances of African Americans.

what can be done?

Employment discrimination, overt or covert, is against the law, yet it clearly happens. Discrimination still damages the lives of African

Americans. Therefore, policies designed to reduce discrimination should be strengthened and expanded rather than reduced or eliminated, as has recently occurred. Light must be shed on the practice, and heat must be applied to those who engage in it. Some modest steps can be taken to reduce the incidence and costs of racial discrimination:

conduct more social audits of employers in various industries of varying sizes and locations In 2000, the courts upheld the right of testers (working with the Legal Assistance Foundation of Chicago) to sue discriminatory employers. Expanded use of evidence from social audits in lawsuits against discriminatory employers provides more information about discriminatory processes, arms black applicants more effectively, and provides greater deterrence to would-be discriminators who do not want to be exposed. Even when prevention is not successful, documentation from social audits makes it easier to prosecute illegal discrimination. As in the Texaco case, it has often been through exposure and successful litigation that discriminatory employers mended their ways.

restrict government funding to and public contracts with firms that have records of repeated discrimination against black applicants and black employees The government needs to ensure that discriminatory employers do not use taxpayer money to carry out their unfair treatment of African Americans. Firms that continue discriminating against blacks should have their funding and their reputations linked to their performance. Also, as lawsuits over this issue proliferate, defense of such practices becomes an expensive proposition. Again, those found guilty of such activities should have to rely on their own resources and not receive additional allocations from the state. Such monetary deterrence may act as a reminder that racial discrimination is costly.

redouble affirmative action efforts Affirmative action consists of activities undertaken specifically to identify, recruit, promote, or retain qualified members of disadvantaged minority groups to overcome the results of past discrimination and to deter discriminatory practices in the present. It presumes that simply removing existing impediments is not sufficient for changing the relative positions of various groups. In addition, it is based on the premise that to truly affect unequal distribution of life chances, employers must take specific steps to remedy the consequences of discrimination.

speak out when episodes of discrimination occur It is fairly clear that much discrimination against African Americans goes unreported because it occurs behind closed doors and in surreptitious ways. Often, it is only when some (white) insider provides irrefutable evidence that such incidents come to light. It is incumbent upon white Americans to do their part to help stamp out this malignancy.

Now that racial discrimination in employment is illegal, stamping it out should be eminently easier to accomplish. The irony is that because job discrimination against blacks has been driven underground, many people are willing to declare victory and thereby let this scourge continue to flourish in its camouflaged state. If we truly want to move toward a color-blind society, however, we must punish such hurtful discriminatory behaviors when they occur, and we should reward efforts by employers who seek to diversify their workforce by eliminating racial discrimination. This is precisely what happened in the landmark Texaco case, as well as the recent Coca-Cola settlement. In both cases, job discrimination against African Americans was driven above ground, made costly to those who practiced it and offset by policies that attempted to level the playing field.

RECOMMENDED RESOURCES

Katherine P. Dickinson, Terry R. Johnson, and Richard W. West. "An Analysis of the Impact of CETA Programs on Participants' Earnings." *Journal of Human Resources* 21 (1986): 64–91.

Joe Feagin. *Racist America: Roots, Current Realities, and Future Reparations* (Routledge, 2001).

Michael Fix and Raymond J. Struyk. *Clear and Convincing Evidence: Measurement of Discrimination in America* (Urban Institute, 1993).

Peter Gottschall. "Inequality, Income Growth, and Mobility: The Basic Facts." *Journal of Economic Perspectives* 11 (1997): 21–40.

Cedric Herring, ed. *African Americans and the Public Agenda: The Paradoxes of Public Policy* (Sage Publications, 1997).

Joleen Kirschenman and Kathryn M. Neckerman. "'We'd Love to Hire Them, But . . .': The Meaning of Race for Employers." In *The Urban Underclass*, eds. C. Jencks and P. Peterson (Brookings Institution, 1991).

Alice O'Connor, Chris Tilly, and Lawrence Bobo, eds. *Urban Inequality: Evidence from Four Cities* (Russell Sage Foundation, 2001).

Melvin Thomas, Cedric Herring, and Hayward Derrick Horton. "Discrimination over the Life Course: A Synthetic Cohort Analysis of Earnings Differences between Black and White Males, 1940–1990." *Social Problems* 41 (1994): 608–28.

William Julius Wilson. *When Work Disappears: The World of the New Urban Poor* (Vintage Books, 1997).

REVIEW QUESTIONS

1. Herring writes that racism is barely evident for most of us in our everyday experiences, but has headed "underground." Discuss how this covert form of racism has affected popular perceptions of race. Has this approach to understanding racism become a challenge to social scientists? How?
2. How does "labor market theory" relate to issues of racism? What is the "structural discrimination" theory of racism? Which position do you find most compelling?
3. Affirmative action has been debated for years, and Herring claims that such programs are necessary to redress the consequences of discrimination. Discuss both the positive and negative consequences of affirmative action.

gerald f. davis

american cronyism: how executive networks inflated the corporate bubble

summer 2003

"shareholder value" was the sacred mantra of american business in the 1990s. but creating shareholder value can be a fickle undertaking and corporate executives often followed the lead of their colleagues. the result was a contagion of questionable business practices that resulted in the creation of a corporate bubble—and its implosion.

27

The business meltdown of the past three years has undermined faith in the way American corporations are run. For much of the 1990s, scholars and politicians promoted that system as the exemplar of how to organize an economy for growth and adaptability. According to this model, market institutions such as banks and investment firms channel funds to well-run companies and thereby quickly correct business errors. Less efficient economies, such as Japan's, suffered from "crony capitalism," which allowed businessmen's social connections to trump hard-nosed financial decisions.

Now, we have witnessed several of the largest bankruptcies in American corporate history, the disappearance of one of the "Big Five" accounting firms, and a death spiral among numerous telecommunications businesses. While the White House has asserted that Enron and WorldCom officers were just isolated "bad apples," research suggests that the American corporate economy has evolved its own form of crony capitalism. Business leaders are connected by an expansive network that makes their companies receptive to ideas and practices promoted by analysts, consultants, and influential companies. Corporate managers may be motivated by stock prices set on impersonal financial markets, but they pursue high prices in ways that are anything but impersonal. From who serves on boards of directors, to which bank underwrites new securities issues and how financial analysts rate them—personal connections were central to inflating the financial bubble and to its subsequent burst.

American corporations are peculiar because ownership is typically dispersed—neither the company's managers nor anyone else owns dominant stakes. Nonetheless, according to this theory, corporate managers act in the corporation's best interest as long as they base decisions on the gauge of share price.

the american theory of corporate governance

American corporations stand out from businesses in most other large economies in their focus on creating value for shareholders, as defined by increasing share prices on the stock market. The faith in shareholder value follows from the well-established efficient markets hypothesis (EMH) in finance. The EMH states that financial markets are informationally efficient—the price of a company's shares provides the best estimate of that company's future profitability, given all publicly available information. When new information about a company's future prospects becomes public, buyers and sellers respond and the share price adjusts quickly. The accuracy of the share price as an indicator of the company's future earnings is based on the fact that those who are better-informed than others stand to make money. If investors are certain that the market price is too low relative to the company's expected future profitability, they buy shares until the price matches the "true" value. Conversely, if convinced that a company's shares are overpriced, investors will sell. Many buyers and sellers making these calculations means that a company's share price at any given time is the "right" price—and thus an apt proxy for gauging how effectively a company is being managed.

Scholars in what is called the "law and economics" tradition developed from EMH a theory of how corporations are governed, relying heavily on the American experience. American corporations are peculiar because ownership is typically dispersed—neither the company's managers nor anyone else owns dominant stakes. Nonetheless, according to this theory, corporate managers act in the corporation's best interest as long as they base decisions on the gauge of share price. Indeed, the United States has evolved a set of legal and market-based devices that force company management to pursue shareholder value: a market for managers that pays corporate executives according to how much value they create, a market for corporate directors that rewards members of the board for establishing a reputation for integrity, and a market for corporate control that allows outsiders who see a company that is underperforming to take over and oust its managers. Uniting all these markets is the share price prevailing on the stock market which

provides an unbiased assessment of the corporation's value.

According to the theory of shareholder value, these markets are supported by other institutions which ensure that companies play by the rules. Accountants audit a company's financial statements for accuracy and are rewarded for their attentiveness, because the market value of an accounting firm's seal of approval depends on its reputation, which follows from the quality of its audits. Financial analysts working in brokerage firms are like private detectives, rigorously analyzing a corporation's record and future prospects to produce forecasts for clients who reward the analysts when they are accurate. And investment banks that finance stock offerings likewise must maintain their reputation for quality work if they want to receive repeat business. All these devices combine both to guide corporate executives toward shareholder value and to enhance public confidence in the corporate sector. So much for the theory.

the social meaning of shareholder value

As important as share prices are to managers, they provide a curious measure of value. They are based on expectations about the future constructed from present-day information. John Maynard Keynes famously compared playing the stock market to newspaper beauty contests in which the winner is the contestant who accurately picks the beauty chosen by the most other contestants. Thus, market value depends on what others think market value should be. We see this in other markets too, for example when home buyers avoid unusually designed houses not because they dislike them per se, but because they fear that other buyers may dislike them.

Managing for shareholder value means monitoring how players in the market interpret news about the company. This does not mean that managers can focus on image to the exclusion of substance, or that deception goes unpunished. Investors have incentives to uncover falsehoods and can make money by betting against firms that lie. But many managers make decisions calculated to boost perceptions of their firm's value without considering its effects on the company's actual bottom line. For example, when a company buys back some of its own stock, it reduces the supply of shares and it also signals to investors that management believes its shares are underpriced. This move typically leads to increases in share price. Savvy corporate managers in the 1990s found that it was possible to increase value merely by announcing a buy-back program without subsequently following through. Similarly, executive compensation plans explicitly touting their allegiance to shareholder value boost share prices more than the same plans described in more generic terms. And so-called pro forma earnings announcements, which gave more glowing impressions than accountant-certified earnings figures, became rampant in the late 1990s.

> There are many ways firms can and do manipulate analysts. To the extent that these efforts are successful—and to the extent that investors rely on analysts' advice—financial markets are vulnerable to the kind of booms and busts witnessed recently.

Efforts to mold perceptions did not just influence how managers presented corporate decisions, but also what actions they took in the first place. For example, firms that operated in more than one industry found that they were punished by the market—their shares lost value—for being "conglomerates," the corporate equivalent of unusually designed houses, even if they were profitable in every industry. So, Ford spun off its highly profitable Associates First Capital unit with this announcement from its CEO: "We believe the market value of the Associates is neither fully nor consistently reflected in Ford's stock price. Because the market views Ford as an automotive company, it has not fully recognized or rewarded us for our diversification into non-automotive financial services businesses." It was not profitability that was at issue, but the market's evaluation of that profitability.

One of the implications of EMH is uncertainty—future share price changes are a "random walk" that cannot be predicted based on prior price changes or on the company's fundamentals. In a situation such as this, social factors shape business judgments. Thus, studies find that financial analysts, whose job is to uncover information about corporations and render forecasts to their clients, often do little more than mimic the judgments of their peers. In deciding which companies are worth following, analysts commonly choose companies that other analysts have recently added. Analysts who follow the herd are also systematically over-optimistic about the prospects of the companies they follow. Corporate managers often play on this process, for instance, by requiring investment banks they do business with to have their analysts cover the firm.

Analysts also judge corporations by the company they keep. Thus, managers can boost the esteem in which their firm is held by who they choose as partners, underwriters, and who they sign contracts with. Directors are appointed to boards based in part on the contacts they bring with them. Analysts' admiration for companies goes up when well-connected directors are appointed. Biotech firm ImClone gained credibility with analysts and investors from the fact that Dr. John Mendelsohn—noted cancer researcher and president of Houston's M.D. Anderson Cancer Center—served on its board. But this big name did little to help the firm create profitable products. ImClone's CEO later pleaded guilty to insider trading charges after dumping his shares in the company as the FDA was about to announce that ImClone's only significant product, an anti-cancer drug, would not be approved.

There are many ways firms can and do manipulate analysts. To the extent that these efforts are successful—and to the extent that investors rely on analysts' advice—financial markets are vulnerable to the kind of booms and busts witnessed recently.

the pervasive role of social connections

A traditional tenet of shareholder value is that business is transacted through arms-length relationships that prevent personal ties from compromising the operations of the various markets that comprise the system. This presumption stands in stark contrast to the economic systems of most other industrialized nations. Outside the United States, social ties among members of the corporate elite are acknowledged to be widespread and influential. In France, the business elite is predominantly composed of graduates of two exclusive institutions, the Ecole National d'Administration (ENA) and the Ecole Polytechnique. Thus, a network of old school ties pervades the management of large French companies. Japanese *keiretsu* networks, dense social and ownership ties among member companies, the business sector, and government agencies, were by some accounts essential to that nation's robust postwar economic growth. South Korea created a similarly "networked" economic system as a path to rapid industrialization beginning in the 1960s. Chinese economic reformers—building on the successful models of Japan and Korea—encouraged the formation of business groups among companies as part of its program of industrial transformation beginning in the 1980s, and these networks have persisted and spread.

Elsewhere in the world, authorities view network ties among business elites as useful for promoting economic development, and thus to be tolerated or even encouraged. In shareholder capitalism, however, such "cronyism" is seen as a pathology that impedes the proper operation of markets. Social connections can interfere with pragmatic business decisions, which require objectivity and lack of bias. But as economic historian Karl Polanyi argues in *The Great Transformation*, "Man's economy, as a rule, is submerged in his social relationships." Markets detached from social ties are highly artificial and rare, typically requiring exhaustive governmental efforts to sustain. The theory of American shareholder capitalism may describe a world of arms' length, financially driven decision making, but the reality on the ground is quite different.

Consider corporate boards of directors, where the highest-level business decisions are made. While the United States has no institution with the same gate-keeping power as the ENA in France, researchers have found extensive personal networks among the American corporate elite. In particular, there is enormous overlap among corporate boards of directors. Shared directors—individuals serving on two or more boards—have been pervasive on American boards since the early part of the twentieth century, when future Supreme Court Justice Louis Brandeis warned about the undue influence of J. P. Morgan and other New York bankers whose partners served on dozens of corporate boards. More than 80 percent of the 1,000 largest U.S. corporations in 2001 shared at least one director with another large company, and on average any two of the corporations were connected by less than four degrees of separation.

Conseco—considered one of the worst-governed companies—was linked to Colgate Palmolive—one of the best—through this path: Conseco director David Harkins served on the

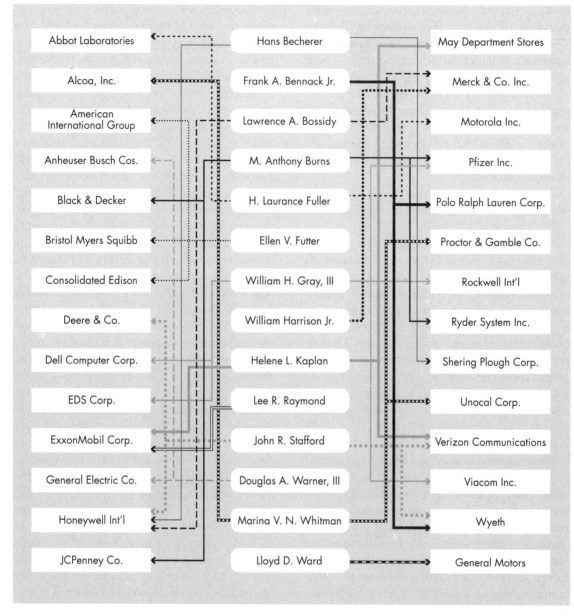

Abbot Laboratories	Hans Becherer	May Department Stores
Alcoa, Inc.	Frank A. Bennack Jr.	Merck & Co. Inc.
American International Group	Lawrence A. Bossidy	Motorola Inc.
Anheuser Busch Cos.	M. Anthony Burns	Pfizer Inc.
Black & Decker	H. Laurance Fuller	Polo Ralph Lauren Corp.
Bristol Myers Squibb	Ellen V. Futter	Proctor & Gamble Co.
Consolidated Edison	William H. Gray, III	Rockwell Int'l
Deere & Co.	William Harrison Jr.	Ryder System Inc.
Dell Computer Corp.	Helene L. Kaplan	Shering Plough Corp.
EDS Corp.	Lee R. Raymond	Unocal Corp.
ExxonMobil Corp.	John R. Stafford	Verizon Communications
General Electric Co.	Douglas A. Warner, III	Viacom Inc.
Honeywell Int'l	Marina V. N. Whitman	Wyeth
JCPenney Co.	Lloyd D. Ward	General Motors

Corporate affiliations of J.P. Morgan Chase & Co.'s Board of Directors, 1999. More than 80 percent of America's 1,000 largest corporations share at least one director with another large company.

Fisher Scientific board with Michael Dingman, who served on the Ford board with Robert Rubin, who served on the Citigroup board with Reuben Mark, CEO of Colgate Palmolive. A flu virus that infected the Enron board in January 2001 could have made its way to 650 of the Fortune 1,000 companies by May through monthly board meetings.

The significance of the small "diameter" of this network was foreseen by C. Wright Mills almost 50 years ago in *The Power Elite*, where he argued that those in powerful positions often seem to know each other or to have acquaintances in common through shared affiliations, which in turn facilitates similar responses to shared problems. As a result, decisions on issues of corporate governance—and by extension shareholder value—were similar among companies due to their closely connected boards of directors. Dozens of studies in recent years document that shared directors spread practices, information, and principles, which accounts for some of the surprising conformity among corporate managers in their approaches to corporate governance.

The adoption of takeover defenses, the creation of investor relations offices, and the development of compensation practices all spread from board to board through shared directors. For example, the controversial "poison pill" defense (fending off a hostile takeover of the company by increasing its cost—for example, by issuing new shares that would have to be redeemed by the new buyer) spread rapidly among large corporations in the mid 1980s when directors of companies that had adopted poison pill approaches touted them to the other boards on which they served. Similarly, companies created investor relations offices after learning about their benefits from directors serving on the boards of other companies that already had them. These networks also proved useful in influencing politicians. The legislatures of states where corporate leaders were closely connected to one another were more likely to adopt anti-takeover legislation protecting local companies than were lawmaking bodies in states with less intertwined corporate entities.

Moreover, to the extent that there is a "culture of the boardroom," it protects its own. Mills wrote of the power elite: "The question is not: are these honorable men? The question is: what are their codes of honor? The answer to that question is that they are the codes of their circles, of those to whose opinions they defer." When Dr. Mendelsohn of the M.D. Anderson Cancer Center came under fire for serving on the boards of two companies implicated in investor fraud—Enron and ImClone—his director colleagues came to his defense. Charles Miller, Chairman of the University of Texas Systems Board of Regents, which oversees the Center, had himself served on a dozen corporate and nonprofit boards. As he put it: "We could all see, 'There but for the grace of God go I.' " The president of Rice University echoed: "All of us at one time or another have been up to our elbows in alligators."

connections outside the executive circle

If analysts and investors are like judges in Keynes's newspaper beauty contest, then corporate managers and boards are in a position analogous to the beauties themselves, adopting the fashions that their judges believe other judges will find appealing. In anticipating market reactions to their actions, some boards had help from the judges themselves. Jack Grubman, the former star telecommunications analyst at Salomon Smith Barney, attended board meetings to advise the directors of a half-dozen firms that he was responsible for analyzing, including WorldCom (subsequently the largest bankruptcy in U.S. history), Global Crossing (also bankrupt), and McLeodUSA (ditto). The intimate relationship between Grubman and the telecom sector he evaluated worked both ways. Salomon Smith Barney set aside shares of firms about to make an initial public offering (IPO) for the personal accounts of telecom executives such as Bernie Ebbers, acquisitive CEO of WorldCom. IPO shares typically shoot up in value on the first day of trading and generally provide an immediate payoff—what one investment banker called "free money." Ebbers, for instance, made $11 million from his IPO shares. Ebbers' firm in turn sent tens of millions of dollars in fees to Salomon for investment banking services (although Salomon insisted there was no *quid pro quo*). Moreover, the value of a firm's IPO depends in part on its affiliations. During the late 1990s, announcing that a newly public firm had a contract or alliance with WorldCom, for instance, generally enhanced its expected profitability and thus the value of its IPO shares. The incentives created through this web of connections among directors, executives, analysts, and investment bankers favored a Potemkin Village approach of building a false facade of value over the hard work of building real value.

Far from being a system characterized by impersonal, calculating relationships, the American corporate system is thick with social connections among the most important decision makers. Corporate directors and the executives they oversee, financial analysts, investment bankers, and state legislators responsible for creating corporate law, are tied together in a dense network that contrasts sharply with the theory of an anonymous market policed by independent analysts, auditors, and legislators. This system is highly susceptible to "contagion" among managers. In the 1990s, the triumph of the ideology of shareholder value prompted the spread of practices thought to create shareholder value—or at least, of ones thought to generate higher share prices. In combination, these helped inflate the financial bubble that eventually, and inevitably, burst.

bottom line

In *The Great Transformation*, Karl Polanyi argued that Adam Smith's theory of how markets create wealth was really a theory of one particular nation—England—and that Smith did not even get that completely right. Self-regulating markets as Smith understood them were quite rare by historical standards and relatively recent even in England. Moreover, efforts to organize society around markets removed from their social contexts were bound to end badly, according to Polanyi—as they did in mid-Victorian England. During the 1970s and 1980s, scholars in the United States evolved a theory of economic institutions guided by the wisdom of impersonal financial markets and their ability to yield prices that provide an unbiased prediction of future value. Markets for managers, directors, financial analysts, accountants, and laws all combined to create a guidance system oriented toward shareholder value—at least in the American experience. Moreover, this system could be distilled and exported to other nations as a blueprint for economic vitality. In the words of Clinton's second Treasury Secretary, Larry Summers: "Financial markets don't just oil the wheels of economic growth—they *are* the wheels." Nations with the "right" set of economic institutions organized around financial markets could attract foreign investment to fuel local economic growth.

But the American theory proved difficult to duplicate internationally and misleading for the United States system itself. As in other nation's economies, the American corporate structure is influenced by crony capitalism. Social networks among key decision makers are rampant and influential, and although the operations of a financial market–oriented system are different in important ways from, say, South Korea, social ties are part of the warp and woof of economic activity even in "shareholder capitalism."

RECOMMENDED RESOURCES

Gerald F. Davis and Michael Useem. "Top Management, Company Directors, and Corporate Control." In *Handbook of Strategy and Management*, eds. Andrew Pettigrew, Howard Thomas, and Richard Whittington (Sage, 2002).

> A critical introduction to the American theory of corporate governance and a review of research on the U.S. and other industrialized economies.

Gerald F. Davis, Mina Yoo, and Wayne E. Baker. "The Small World of the American Corporate Elite, 1982–2001." *Strategic Organization* 1 (2003): 301–26.

> A description of the surprising stability and influence of the networks among U.S. boards of directors over the past 20 years.

Frank H. Easterbrook and Daniel R. Pischel. *The Economic Structure of Corporate Law* (Harvard University Press, 1991).

> An introduction to the law and economics of American corporate governance by influential legal theorists.

Hayagreeva Rao, Henrich R. Greve, and Gerald F. Davis. "Fool's Gold: Social Proof in the Initiation and Abandonment of Coverage by Wall Street Analysts." *Administrative Science Quarterly* 46 (2001): 502–26.

> An examination of the social contagion processes among financial analysts that can promote financial bubbles.

Michael Useem. *Investor Capitalism: How Money Managers Are Changing the Face of Corporate America* (Basic Books, 1996).

> Useem analyzes the rise of "shareholder capitalism" in the United States during the 1980s and 1990s and examines the increasing influence of institutional investors on how corporations were managed during the past decade.

REVIEW QUESTIONS

1. Historian Fernand Braudel quotes an old Italian proverb that says the wise man will "prefer to have friends on the marketplace than money in a chest." How does this phrase make sense in the contemporary marketplace?
2. Reflect on how the emerging "crony capitalism" undermines the ideals of neoliberalism as outlined in Swedberg's keyword essay.
3. C. Wright Mills's *The Power Elite* explained the close connections between the executive branch, the military, and the corporate elite. Some critics of recent U.S. presidents say that they serve as examples of these connections. Do a little research using Mills's framework to trace the connections between these three sectors.

kathleen gerson and jerry a. jacobs

the work-home crunch

28

fall 2004

the decade-long debate over whether americans are working longer hours is misleading. indeed, while well-educated professionals are working more hours than they used to, others with less education are working fewer. and the people under the most pressure are not just overburdened at work. increasingly, these single parents and two-income couples find themselves in a time squeeze between home and work.

More than a decade has passed since the release of *The Overworked American*, a prominent 1991 book about the decline in Americans' leisure time, and the work pace in the United States only seems to have increased. From sleep-deprived parents to professionals who believe they must put in long hours to succeed at the office, the demands of work are colliding with family responsibilities and placing a tremendous time squeeze on many Americans.

Yet beyond the apparent growth in the time that many Americans spend on the job lies a more complex story. While many Americans are working more than ever, many others are working less. What is more, finding a balance between work and other obligations seems increasingly elusive to many workers—whether or not they are actually putting in more time at work than workers in earlier generations. The increase in harried workers and hurried families is a problem that demands solutions. But before we can resolve this increasingly difficult time squeeze we must first understand its root causes.

average working time and beyond

"There aren't enough hours in the day" is an increasingly resonant refrain. To most observers, including many experts, the main culprit appears to be overwork—our jobs just take up too much of our time. Yet it is not clear that the average

American is spending more time on the job. Although it may come as a surprise to those who feel overstressed, the average work week—that is, hours spent working for pay by the average employee—has hardly changed over the past 30 years. Census Bureau interviews show, for example, that the average male worked 43.5 hours a week in 1970 and 43.1 hours a week in 2000, while the average female worked 37.1 hours in 1970 and 37.0 hours in 2000.

Why, then, do more and more Americans feel so pressed for time? The answer is that averages can be misleading. Looking only at the average experience of American workers misses key parts of the story. From the perspective of individual workers, it turns out some Americans are working more than ever, while others are finding it harder to get as much work as they need or would like. To complicate matters further, American families are now more diverse than they were in the middle of the twentieth century, when male-breadwinner households predominated. Many more Americans now live in dual-earner or single-parent families where all the adults work.

These two trends—the growing split of the labor force and the transformation of family life—lie at the heart of the new time dilemmas facing an increasing number of Americans. But they have not affected all workers and all families in the same way. Instead, these changes have divided Americans into those who feel squeezed between

Three businessmen in San Francisco's financial district walk briskly to lunch. More than one-third of male managers and professionals now work 50 hours or more per week, a substantial increase since 1970. (Photo by Jon Wagner)

their work and the rest of their life, and those who have more time away from work than they need or would like. No one trend fits both groups.

So, who are the time-squeezed, and how do they differ from those with fewer time pressures but who may also have less work than they may want or need? To distinguish and describe the two sets of Americans, we need to look at the experiences of both individual workers and whole families. A focus on workers shows that they are increasingly divided between those who put in very long work weeks and who are concentrated in the better-paying jobs, and those who put in comparatively short work weeks, who are more likely to have fewer educational credentials and are more likely to be concentrated in the lower-paying jobs.

But the experiences of individuals does not tell the whole story. When we shift our focus to the family, it becomes clear that time squeezes are linked to the total working hours of family members in households. For this reason, two-job families and single parents face heightened challenges. Moreover, women continue to assume the lion's share of home and child care responsibilities and are thus especially likely to be squeezed for time. Changes in jobs and changes in families are putting overworked Americans and underemployed Americans on distinct paths, are separating the two-earner and single-parent households from the more traditional households, and are creating different futures for parents (especially mothers) than for workers without children at home. (On the issue of which specific schedules people work and the consequences of nonstandard shifts, see "The Economy that Never Sleeps," *Contexts*, Spring 2004.)

a growing divide in individual working time

In 1970, almost half of all employed men and women reported working 40 hours a week. By 2000, just 2 in 5 worked these "average" hours. Instead, workers are now far more likely to put in either very long or fairly short work weeks. The share of working men putting in 50 hours or more rose from 21 percent in 1970 to almost 27 percent in 2000, while the share of working women putting in these long work weeks rose from 5 to 11 percent.

At the other end of the spectrum, more workers are also putting in shorter weeks. In 1970, for example, 5 percent of men were employed for 30 or fewer hours a week, while 9 percent worked these shortened weeks in 2000. The share of employed women spending 30 or fewer hours on the job also climbed from 16 percent to 20 percent (see figure 1). In total, 13 million Americans in 2000 worked either shorter or longer work weeks than they would have if the 1970s pattern had continued.

These changes in working time are not evenly distributed across occupations. Instead, they are

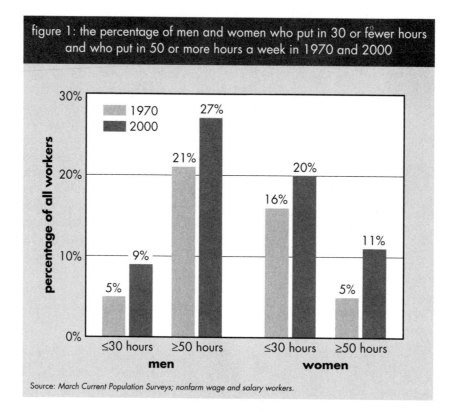

figure 1: the percentage of men and women who put in 30 or fewer hours and who put in 50 or more hours a week in 1970 and 2000

Source: March Current Population Surveys; nonfarm wage and salary workers.

strongly related to the kinds of jobs people hold. Managers and professionals, as one might expect, tend to put in the longest work weeks. More than 1 in 3 men in this category now work 50 hours or more per week, compared to only 1 in 5 for men in other occupations. For women, 1 in 6 professionals and managers work these long weeks, compared to fewer than 1 in 14 for women in all other occupations. And because jobs are closely linked to education, the gap in working time between the college educated and those with fewer educational credentials has also grown since 1970.

Thus, time at work is growing most among those Americans who are most likely to read articles and buy books about overwork in America. They may not be typical, but they are indeed working more than their peers in earlier genera-

tions. If leisure time once signaled an elite lifestyle, that no longer appears to be the case. Working relatively few hours is now more likely to be concentrated among those with less education and less elite jobs.

Workers do not necessarily prefer these new schedules. On the contrary, when workers are asked about their ideal amount of time at work, a very different picture emerges. For example, in a 1997 survey of workers conducted by the Families and Work Institute, 60 percent of both men and women responded that they would like to work less while 19 percent of men and women said that they would like to work more. Most workers—both women and men—aspire to work between 30 and 40 hours per week. Men generally express a desire to work about 38 hours a week while women would like to work about 32 hours. The small difference in the ideal working time of men and women is less significant than the shared preferences among them. However, whether their jobs require very long or comparatively short work weeks, this shared ideal does stand in sharp contrast to their job realities. As some workers are pressured to put in more time at work and others less, finding the right balance between work and the rest of life has become increasingly elusive.

overworked individuals or overworked families?

Fundamental shifts in family life exacerbate this growing division between the over- and under-worked. While most analyses of working time focus on individual workers, time squeezes are typically experienced by families, not isolated individuals. A 60-hour work week for a father means something different depending on whether the mother stays at home or also works a 60-hour week. Even a 40-hour work week can seem too long if both members of a married couple are juggling job demands with family responsibilities. And when a family depends on a single parent, the conflicts between home and work can be even greater. Even if the length of the work week had not changed at all, the rise of families that depend on either two incomes or one parent would suffice to explain why Americans feel so pressed for time.

To understand how families experience time squeezes, we need to look at the combined working time of all family members. For example, how do married couples with two earners compare with those anchored by a sole, typically male, breadwinner? For all married couples, the

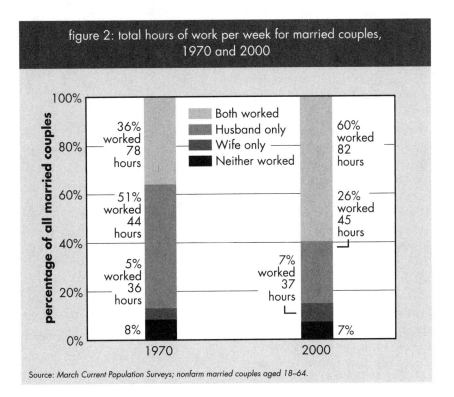

figure 2: total hours of work per week for married couples, 1970 and 2000

Source: *March Current Population Surveys; nonfarm married couples aged 18–64.*

work week has indeed increased from an average of about 53 hours in 1970 to 63 hours in 2000. Given that the average work week for individuals did not change, it may seem strange that the couples' family total grew so markedly. The explanation for this apparent paradox is both straightforward and crucial: married women are now far more likely to work. In 1970, half of all married-couple families had only male breadwinners. By 2000, this group had shrunk to one quarter (see figure 2). In 1970, one-third of all married-couple families had two wage-earners, but three-fifths did in 2000. In fact, two-earner families are more common today than male-breadwinner families were 30 years ago.

Each type of family is also working a little more each week, but this change is relatively modest and certainly not large enough to account for the larger shift in total household working time. Two-earner families put in close to 82 working hours in 2000 compared with 78 hours in 1970. Male-breadwinner couples worked 44 hours on average in 1970 and 45 hours in 2000. The vast majority of the change in working time over the past 30 years can thus be traced to changes in the kinds of families we live in rather than to changes in how much we work. Two-earner couples work about as much today as they did 30 years ago, but there are many more of them because more wives are working.

Single parents, who are overwhelmingly mothers, are another group who are truly caught in a time squeeze. They need to work as much as possible to support their family, and they are less likely to be able to count on a partner's help in meeting their children's daily needs. Although these households are not displayed in figure 2, Census Bureau data show that women headed one-fifth of all families in 2000, twice the share of female-headed households in 1970. Even though their average work week remained unchanged at 39 hours, the lack of child care and other support services leaves them facing time

squeezes at least as sharp. Single fathers remain a much smaller group, but their ranks have also grown rapidly. Single dads work almost as much as single moms—37 hours per week in 2000. Even though this represents a drop of two hours since 1970, single fathers face time dilemmas as great as those facing single mothers. Being a single parent has always posed daunting challenges, and now there are more mothers and fathers than ever in this situation.

At the heart of these shifts is American families' growing reliance on a woman's earnings—whether or not they depend on a man's earnings as well. Women's strengthened commitment to paid employment has provided more economic resources to families and given couples more options for sharing the tasks of breadwinning and caretaking. Yet this revolution in women's work

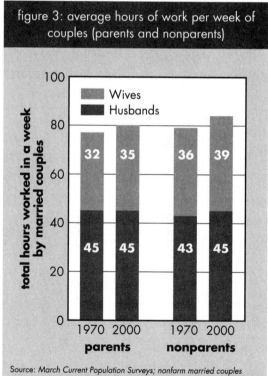

figure 3: average hours of work per week of couples (parents and nonparents)

Source: March Current Population Surveys; nonfarm married couples aged 18–64.

has not been complemented by an equal growth in the amount of time men spend away from the job or in the availability of organized child care. This limited change at the workplace and in men's lives has intensified the time pressures facing women.

dual-earner parents and working time

The expansion of working time is especially important for families with children, where work and family demands are most likely to conflict. Indeed, there is a persisting concern that in their desire for paid work, families with two earners are shortchanging their children in time and attention. A closer look reveals that even though parents face increased time pressure, they cope with these dilemmas by cutting back on their combined joint working time when they have children at home. For example, U.S. Census data show that parents in two-income families worked 3.3 fewer hours per week than spouses in two-income families without children, a slightly wider difference than the 2.6 hours separating them in 1970. Working hours also decline as the number of children increase. Couples with one child under 18 jointly averaged 81 hours per week in 2000, while couples with three or more children averaged 78 hours. Rather than forsaking their children, employed parents are taking steps to adjust their work schedules to make more time for the rest of life.

However, it is mothers, not fathers, who are cutting back. Fathers actually work more hours when they have children at home, and their working hours increase with the number of children. Thus, the drop in joint working time among couples with children reflects less working time among mothers. Figure 3 shows that in 2000, mothers worked almost 4 fewer hours per week than married women without children. This gap is not substantially different than in 1970.

This pattern of mothers reducing their hours while fathers increase them creates a larger gender gap in work participation among couples with children compared to the gender gap for childless couples. However, these differences are much smaller than the once predominant pattern in which many women stopped working for pay altogether when they bore children. While the transition to raising children continues to have different consequences for women and men, the size of this difference is diminishing.

It is also important to remember that the rise in working time among couples is not concentrated among those with children at home. Though Americans continue to worry about the consequences for children when both parents go to work, the move toward more work involvement does not reflect neglect on the part of either mothers or fathers. On the contrary, employed mothers

A school district superintendent works at home. He spends 50 to 60 hours a week at his office, over an hour commuting each day, and like many professionals, another 5 to 10 hours a week working at home. The long hours are easier to manage now that his children have grown up and left home. (Photo by Jon Wagner)

continue to spend less time at the workplace than their childless peers, while employed fathers today do not spend substantially more time at work than men who are not fathers.

solving the time-pressure puzzle

Even though changes in the average working time of American workers are modest, many American families have good reason to feel overworked and time-deprived. The last several decades have witnessed the emergence of a group of workers who face very long work weeks and live in families that depend on either two incomes or one parent. And while parents are putting in less time at work than their peers without children at home, they shoulder domestic responsibilities that leave them facing clashes between work demands and family needs.

The future of family well-being and gender equality will depend on developing policies to help workers resolve the time pressures created by the widespread and deeply rooted social changes discussed above. The first step toward developing effective policy responses requires accepting the social transformations that sent women into the workplace and left Americans wishing for a balance between work and family that is difficult to achieve. Unfortunately, these changes in the lives of women and men continue to evoke ambivalence.

For example, mothers continue to face strong pressures to devote intensive time and attention to child rearing. Indeed, generally they want to, despite the rising economic and social pressure to hold a paid job as well. Even though most contemporary mothers are counted on to help support their families financially, the United States has yet to develop the child care services and flexible jobs that can help workers meet their families' needs. Whether or not mothers work outside the home, they face conflicting expectations that are difficult to meet. These so-

cial contradictions can be seen in the political push to require poor, single mothers to work at a paid job while middle-class mothers continue to be chastised for spending too much time on their jobs and away from home.

To a lesser but still important extent, fathers also face intensifying and competing pressures. Despite American families' increasing reliance on women's earnings, men face significant barriers to family involvement. Resistance from employers and coworkers continues to greet individual fathers who would like to spend less time at work to care for their children. For all the concern and attention focused on employed mothers, social policies that would help bring men more fully into the work of parenting get limited notice or support. New time squeezes can thus be better understood by comparing the large changes in women's lives with the relative lack of changes in the situation for men. The family time bind is an unbalanced one.

Even as family time has become squeezed, workers are also contending with changes in the options and expectations they face at work. Competitive workplaces appear to be creating rising pressures for some workers, especially professionals and managers, to devote an excessive amount of time to their jobs, while not offering enough work to others. In contrast to these bifurcating options, American workers increasingly express a desire to balance the important work of earning a living and caring for a new generation.

Finding solutions to these new time dilemmas will depend on developing large-scale policies that recognize and address the new needs of twenty-first-century workers and their families. As we suggest in our book, *The Time Divide*, these policies need to address the basic organization of American work and community institutions. This includes revising regulations on hours of work and providing benefit protections to more workers, moving toward the norm of a shorter work week, creating more family-supportive workplaces that offer both job flexibility and protections for employed parents, and developing a wider array of high-quality, affordable child care options.

Extending protections, such as proportional benefits and overtime pay, to workers in a wider range of jobs and occupations would reduce the built-in incentives employers have to extract as much work as possible from professionals and managers while offering less work to other employees. If professionals and managers were given overtime pay for overtime work, which wage workers are now guaranteed under the Fair Labor Standards Act, the pressures on these employees to put in endless workdays might lessen. Yet, the Bush administration recently revised these rules to move more employees into the category of those ineligible for overtime pay. Similarly, if part-time workers were offered fringe benefits proportional to the hours they work (such as partial pensions), there would be fewer reasons for employers to create jobs with work weeks so short that they do not provide the economic security all families need.

Reducing the average work week to 35 hours would also reduce the pressures on workers and help them find a better work-family balance. While this goal may seem utopian, it is important to remember that the 40-hour standard also seemed unimaginably idealistic before it was adopted in the early twentieth century. Other countries, most notably France, have adopted this standard without sacrificing economic well-being. A shorter work week still would allow for variation in work styles and commitments, but it would also create a new cultural standard that better reflects the needs and aspirations of most contemporary workers. It would also help single parents meet their dual obligations and allow couples to fashion greater equality in their work and caretaking responsibilities.

Time at work is clearly important, but it is not the whole story. The organization of the workplace and the structure of jobs also matters, especially for those whose jobs and occupations require intensive time at work. Among those putting in very long work weeks, we find that having job flexibility and autonomy help ease the perceived strains and conflicts. The work environment, especially in the form of support from supervisors and coworkers, also makes a difference. In addition, we find that workers with access to such family-friendly options as flexible work schedules are likely to use them, while workers without such benefits would like to have them.

Flexibility and autonomy are only useful if workers feel able to use them. Women and men both express concern that making use of "family-friendly" policies, such as extended parental leaves or nonstandard working hours, may endanger their future work prospects. Social policies need to protect the rights of workers to be involved parents without incurring excessive penalties at the workplace. Most Americans spend a portion of their work lives simultaneously immersed in work for pay and in parenting. Providing greater flexibility at the workplace will help workers develop both short- and longer-term strategies for integrating work and family life. However, even basic changes in the organization of work will not suffice to meet the needs of twenty-first-century families. We also need to join the ranks of virtually all other industrialized nations by creating widely available, high-quality, and affordable child care. In a world where mothers and fathers are at the workplace to stay, we need an expanded network of support to care for the next generation of workers.

These changes will not be easy to achieve. But in one form or another, they have been effectively adopted in other societies throughout the modern world. While no one policy is a cure-all, taken together they offer a comprehensive approach for creating genuine resolutions to the time pressures that confront growing numbers of American workers and their families. Ultimately, these new time dilemmas cannot be resolved by chastising workers (and, most often, mothers) for working too much. Rather, the time has come to create more flexible, family-supportive, and gender-equal workplaces and communities that complement the twenty-first-century forms of work and family life.

RECOMMENDED RESOURCES

James T. Bond. *Highlights of the National Study of the Changing Workforce* (Families and Work Institute, 2003).

Bond reports findings from a major national survey of contemporary American workers, workplace conditions, and work-family conflict.

Janet Gornick and Marcia Meyers. *Families that Work: Policies for Reconciling Parenthood and Employment* (Russell Sage Foundation, 2003).

This important study compares family-supportive policies in Europe and the United States.

Sharon Hays. *The Cultural Contradictions of Motherhood* (Yale University Press, 1997).

Hays examines how American mothers continue to face pressure to practice intensive parenting even as they increase their commitment to paid work.

Jody Heymann. *The Widening Gap: Why America's Working Families Are in Jeopardy and What Can Be Done About It* (Basic Books, 2000).

Drawing from a wide range of data, this study makes a compelling case for more flexible work structures.

Arlie Hochschild. *The Time Bind: When Home Becomes Work and Work Becomes Home* (Metropolitan Books, 1997).

A rich study of how employees in one company try to reconcile the tensions between spending time at work and caring for their families.

Jerry A. Jacobs and Kathleen Gerson. *The Time Divide: Work, Family and Gender Inequality* (Harvard University Press, 2004).

An overview of trends in working time, our book shows why and how time pressures have emerged in America over the past three decades, how they are linked to gender inequality and family change and what we can do to alleviate them.

John P. Robinson and Geoffrey Godbey. *Time for Life: The Surprising Ways Americans Use Their Time* (Pennsylvania State University Press, 1999).

Drawing on time diaries, Robinson and Godbey conclude that Americans' leisure time has increased.

Juliet Schor. *The Overworked American: The Unexpected Decline of Leisure* (Basic Books, 1991).

This early and original analysis of how Americans are overworked sparked a national discussion on and concern for the problem.

REVIEW QUESTIONS

1. While the average working week has shrunk over the last few decades, Gerson and Jacobs note that there have been a number of negative trends obscured by this fact. Summarize at least three significant changes.

2. According to Gerson and Jacobs, "If leisure time once signaled an elite lifestyle, that no longer appears to be the case." There is some sociological research that contradicts this argument. For example, lower-income families might have *more* time to raise their children than the upper classes. What do you think accounts for these shifts? What are the potential consequences?

3. What are the specific policies the authors argue are important for creating a more flexible, family-supportive, and gender-equal workplace and community? Discuss what you think of these recommendations, and whether or not they will be effective.

howard kimeldorf, rachel meyer, monica prasad, and ian robinson

consumers with a conscience: will they pay more?

29

winter 2006

most americans say they will pay more for clothes not made in sweatshops. is this just talk, or will they actually put their money where their mouth is? an in-store test of consumer behavior turns up some surprising results.

Being a consumer—especially in a society as materialistic as ours—comes so naturally to most of us that we hardly give it a second thought. Economists, however, have made it their business to understand what makes consumers tick by carefully dissecting their behavior into its smallest constituent units: the "utilities" that we seek to maximize by consuming the optimum combination of high-quality, low-price goods and services.

This conventional economic model of consumer behavior has come under sharp attack in recent years. Behavioral economists, conducting laboratory experiments and running computer-generated game simulations to test the core assumptions about *Homo economicus*, have found them wanting (see sidebar). Neuropsychologists have repeatedly shown that people experience pleasure when acting against their narrowly defined self-interest, and anthropologists have found that ordinary consumers bear little resemblance to the calculating, self-interested materialists who populate the imagined world of neoclassical economic theory. All three bodies of research support sociologists' long-standing claims that altruistic and ethical considerations are central to the real world of market exchange.

The long history of consumer boycotts in America—from the Boston Tea Party through the union movement of the 1880s to the civil rights movement of the 1960s—demonstrates how ethics influence economic choices. Consumer boycotts have targeted corporations, products, and organizational practices for allegedly violating the rights of their employees, harming the environment, or compromising consumer safety. Monroe Friedman, in one of the few serious studies of the boycott, concludes that it "has been used more than any other organizational technique to promote and protect the rights of the powerless and disenfranchised segments of society."

We hope to outline the limits and possibilities of contemporary consumer activism as a "weapon of the weak." We examine the trend away from the traditional boycott, which relies on consumer abstinence to punish offending firms, to the more proactive "buycott" strategy that urges consumers to increase their support for exemplary firms. This tactic arose in the United States in the late nineteenth century with the emergence of the National Consumers League (NCL), dedicated to improving the working conditions of women and children. Appealing to the conscience of its mostly middle-class constituency, the NCL called upon consumers to resist the temptation of low-priced goods, many of them the product of sweatshop labor. The NCL

Support for our findings comes from a most unlikely source: the field of economics, which is undergoing a behavioral revolution that challenges many of the core assumptions about rational, self-interested actors. In recent explorations of "prisoner's dilemma" games, which are designed to encourage selfish as opposed to cooperative behavior, new experimental research techniques are revealing that many subjects actually prefer to cooperate.

Similarly, participants in Ultimatum game experiments, which require two subjects to divide up a given sum of money, frequently reject the opportunity to maximize their cut, preferring to end the game with nothing rather than dividing up the money unfairly. Applying these insights to consumer behavior, Julian Rode and his colleagues found that, under carefully controlled laboratory conditions, many subjects paid more for products that were not tainted by child labor. These and other studies carried out by behavioral economists suggest that all kinds of economic actors, including ordinary consumers, can be motivated by ethical considerations alongside—and sometimes in place of—their immediate economic self-interest.

proclaimed that it was "the duty of consumers" to see that the things they bought were made under "wholesome" conditions "consistent with a respectable existence on the part of the worker."

The NCL's battle cry has been taken up today by a new generation of activists seeking to build a consumer-based movement opposed to the proliferation of sweatshops across the globe. Led by college students targeting the lucrative youth sportswear market, these groups have pressured many universities, especially in the United States, to adopt codes of conduct regarding worker rights and labor standards that all companies supplying sportswear bearing their institution's logo should meet. A national organization—the Worker Rights Consortium—investigates and publicizes noncompliance by major sportswear companies like Nike.

The student anti-sweatshop campaign has focused on a small subset of apparel—products with university logos—and targets institutional consumers (universities) that are vulnerable to student pressure. The SweatFree Communities Campaign now seeks to apply that approach to

the purchases of school boards and local governments by forming and mobilizing broad political coalitions. But can these activists legitimately claim to speak for most American consumers? If so, will these "conscientious consumers" pay a premium to induce sweatshop owners to recognize unions, increase pay, and improve working conditions to avoid being driven out of business? In short, is there a viable market for moral consumption?

the market for conscientious consumption

Four nationwide surveys have addressed these questions, and their findings are, at first glance, encouraging. A sizable majority of respondents to each survey reported that they would pay more for goods not produced by sweatshop labor. Those majorities ranged from a high of 86 percent who said they would be willing to pay $1 more on a $20 garment made under good working conditions, to a low of 61 percent who said they would be willing to pay $5 more on a $20 garment not made in a sweatshop.

Critics have questioned the reliability of such findings. As observers of survey research have long recognized, what respondents report on a survey often differs from what they actually believe, especially when one of the answers carries greater moral authority or is seen as more socially desirable. Then, too, a response is only as good as the question. In this case, the surveys posed differently worded questions about the desirability and cost premium of buying "sweat-free" goods. Some of the variation in the percentage of those responding positively is no doubt related to how much extra they were asked to pay for sweat-free products—between 5 and 25 percent, depending on the survey. Still, even if the questions posed did not vary, the results would only reflect consumer choices in a hypothetical world without real economic costs.

Recognizing these limits, we designed an experiment to see if this high level of support for buying sweat-free goods would carry over to the real world of consumer behavior, where acting on our moral convictions has real costs. Our research site was a well-known department store in a stable working-class community in southeast Michigan. We chose this store after using census data to identify nearby tracts in which the median household income was at or below the national average, targeting a population of price-conscious consumers.

Our store is located in a community of 40,000 residents within the greater Detroit area, where per capita income in 1999 was slightly below the national average. Only 7 percent of residents have a bachelor's degree or higher as compared to 25 percent of the population nationally. Our store caters to a semiskilled, unionized, blue-collar, predominantly white customer base whose limited income would presumably lead them to spend cautiously. In short, these are "middle Americans," not the affluent, highly educated, and socially liberal consumers often seen as the natural constituency of conscientious consumerism.

socks for sale

We designed this project to collect what we believe is the first empirical evidence on what ordinary consumers will actually do—rather than what they say they will do—when faced with the choice of paying more for sweat-free goods. We chose white athletic socks as our test product, both because we wanted an inexpensive item that would generate enough sales to allow us to measure consumer behavior and because socks, an undifferentiated, mass-produced item, are typical of products made in sweatshops. Between March 2002 and August 2003, we recorded consumer choices, employing two different research designs to address possible pitfalls in our approach.

In the first round of data collection, we placed identical pairs of Wigwam brand socks in two display racks next to each other in the men's and women's clothing sections of the store. The only visible difference between the two racks was that one displayed a fairly conspicuous sign, labeled "Buy GWC . . . Good Working Conditions," along with an explanation that the socks in that rack were not produced with child labor, in an unsafe environment, or under sweatshop conditions. We also placed a small "GWC" label on each package. The other rack had neither a sign nor package labels, suggesting that the socks were not made under good working conditions. (In fact, the socks in both racks were produced by union labor, but the stark visual contrast between labeled and unlabeled racks clearly suggested otherwise.) Over a period of five months, we increased the difference in price between the two racks incrementally from zero to 40 percent more for the labeled socks. We recorded the number of customers who bought socks from each rack at each price point.

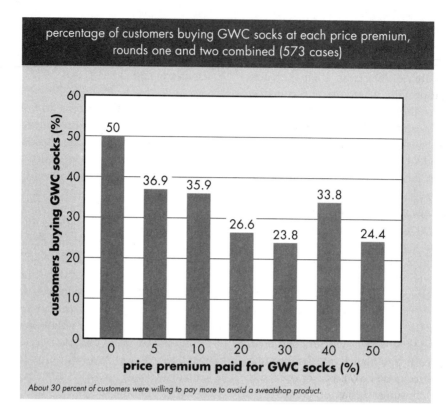

percentage of customers buying GWC socks at each price premium, rounds one and two combined (573 cases)

About 30 percent of customers were willing to pay more to avoid a sweatshop product.

Assuming that our customers noticed the GWC label and understood what it meant, the use of identical socks allowed them to choose solely on the basis of two factors: price and whether or not the product displayed a GWC label. We eliminated the appearance of any difference in quality between the two racks of socks. However, precisely because the socks were indistinguishable, some consumers may not have believed they were actually choosing between two different products, perhaps assuming that the GWC label was simply missing from one rack. Such customers were choosing only on the basis of price and not on the desirability of sweat-free production. Thus, our observations might understate the actual level of support for sweat-free products.

To address this concern, we changed the research design for the next round by using socks that were similar but not identical: white athletic socks made by Wigwam that very closely matched (in style, quality, and market price) white athletic socks made by REAC. We alternated which brand displayed the GWC label, in order to separate possible preferences for the Wigwam or REAC brand or for (minor) style differences from the desire (or lack of it) to purchase sweat-free products.

Introducing different brands in round two yielded no significant difference in consumer behavior. Combining the results from the two rounds of data collection, our graph shows the percentage of GWC sock customers as a share of all customers who bought socks from one of our racks.

As expected, GWC sales declined significantly from 50 to 37 percent as prices first diverged.

However, the decline was more modest as the price of the GWC socks continued to rise. Averaging across all trials in which there was a price difference, about 30 percent of customers were willing to pay a premium to avoid purchasing a product morally tainted by sweatshop labor.

who knew?

These findings are encouraging, but before we can call these customers "conscientious consumers," we need to look beyond their observable behavior to the perceptions and motives that guided their choice of socks. Some shoppers may not have noticed the GWC label or, if they did, may have had no idea what it meant. Still others may have based their choices in round two on the small differences in style or fabric between the two racks of socks. In short, purchasing from the GWC rack would not necessarily make one a conscientious consumer unless the decision was well informed and based at least in part on a moral preference for sweat-free products.

To get inside the heads of our customers, we began conducting brief in-store interviews. In this third round of data collection, we were not interested in the price elasticity of demand for GWC socks, so we did not vary the relative prices: the non-GWC socks always sold for $1.00, and the GWC socks sold for $1.20. A research assistant took an unobtrusive position close to our sock display and intercepted customers who had selected from one of our racks, asking permission to conduct a ten-minute interview. We designed the questions to determine whether the minimal criteria for conscientious consumption had been met: that the consumer noticed the price difference between the two racks, saw the GWC label, and understood its meaning. Most customers—regardless of which socks they chose—agreed to the interview, so we do not believe there is a problem of selection bias in who was interviewed. Conducting in-store interviews has been slow going, and the work is still in progress, but we have so far managed to conduct 45 interviews.

The interviews offer a revealing, if preliminary, glimpse into the thinking of our customers. To our surprise, only 14 (31 percent)—of our customers met all three of the criteria. Most either did not notice the GWC label or did not understand what it meant. Some failed on more than one count. Of the 14 customers who met all three criteria, 8—representing 57 percent of all adequately informed consumers—purchased the more expensive GWC socks. All of these customers said that avoiding goods made in sweatshops was important to them, and all but one characterized the GWC label as the decisive factor in choosing those socks, despite their higher price.

These results are critical for interpreting the first two rounds, in which 27 percent of customers paid more for the labeled socks at the 20 percent price differential. We initially assumed that the gap between this figure and the much higher level of conscientious consumption reported in national surveys, in which 68 percent of respondents said they would pay 20 percent more for clothes made under good working conditions, reflected the typical disjuncture between thought and action. But our interviews suggest another explanation: most customers either did not notice or did not understand the GWC label, so their choices must have been based on price alone.

Once we set aside shoppers who did not meet the criteria for conscientious consumption, the remaining customers we interviewed showed a preference for sweat-free products that was much closer to the level reported in national surveys. For shoppers who met all three preconditions, the attitude-behavior gap fell from 41 percentage points (the difference between the 68 percent in national surveys versus the 27 percent in our study) to just 11 percentage points

(68 percent in the relevant national survey versus 57 percent in our study). Put another way, we may attribute more than three quarters of the gap between the survey results and our experimental findings to customers who did not meet the criteria that serve as the baseline for all survey respondents. This suggests that the market for conscientious consumption in the real world of American shoppers is close to that reported in the national surveys.

Our finding that only a minority of the customers we interviewed met all three criteria may also partly explain why people did not buy more labeled socks when the price difference was zero. Given that most of the customers we interviewed did not qualify as conscientious consumers, the majority may simply have acted randomly at the zero price point, buying socks in roughly equal quantities from the two racks. Among those who met the criteria (31 percent in our interviews), a slight majority preferred the GWC socks. Summing the weighted percentages for these two groups, we would expect the rate of conscientious consumption at the zero price differential to be about 52 percent—very close to the 50 percent who purchased labeled socks in the first two rounds of our experiment. Although the small number of interviews does not conclusively support this interpretation, we see it as the most plausible hypothesis based on the available behavioral and interview data.

For the majority of customers who lack general knowledge of sweatshop conditions and are not accustomed to looking for GWC-type labels when they shop, meeting the criteria for conscientious consumption is clearly asking a lot. But as more information on sweatshops is made public, and with stronger and more vigorous international monitoring of overseas workplaces, credible labeling of products, and more outlets for such products, many more consumers may begin to fulfill the hope of Florence Kelly, the NCL's first general secretary, that "the power of the purchaser, which is potentially unlimited, becomes great . . . just in proportion as purchasers become organized and enlightened."

expanding the market for conscientious consumption

Our study highlights the often neglected moral dimension of economic exchange by focusing on consumers who buy on the basis of both ethical considerations and material self-interest. These conscientious consumers were willing to pay more for ordinary athletic socks made under sweat-free conditions. In choosing the socks with the "Good Working Conditions" label, they were following their hearts instead of their pocketbooks.

Focusing on a store that catered to people with modest means and education, and using a label with which the public was not familiar, our experiment offers a conservative estimate for the extent of conscientious consumption. Despite this conservative bias, we found that, on average, 30 percent of our customers bought the more expensive GWC socks. If the results of our in-store interviews are representative, the market for conscious consumption may extend to a majority of American consumers.

We cannot generalize with any confidence from our preliminary pool of 45 interviews, but if our current findings hold up as we complete more interviews, our results will provide the first behavioral confirmation for the national survey data that shows majorities of Americans willing to pay more for apparel made under good working conditions. Such support for sweat-free goods suggests that conscientious consumers could become a powerful force for improving pay and workers' rights in the apparel sector, where workers are often paid less than 10 percent of the final sales price. But this will only happen if market and regulatory institutions can be made to provide would-be conscientious consumers with accurate information on the labor conditions under which products are made. Without this information, such people cannot act on their convictions, however strong.

We do not wish to overstate the lessons to be drawn from a local study of one product. Athletic socks, like any product, occupy a particular market niche—not only with regard to consumer demand, as economists teach, but also with regard to the ability of activists to make moral claims on its behalf. Clothing, for example, is more closely tied in the public mind to sweatshops than, say, computers, breakfast cereal, or books. But again, this is where consumer education and mobilization play a central role. In the early 1960s, the United Farm Workers organized a highly publicized consumer boycott that elevated the grape from its mundane existence, known mainly as the source of either raisins or wine, into a powerful national symbol of economic justice and worker rights.

Recently, coffee beans have enjoyed a similar rise in visibility and political status as the result of a decade's work by "fair trade" activists. Last year, activists and consumers succeeded in getting two of the world's four largest coffee roasters and distributors to stock beans for which eligible coffee growers who meet "fair trade" criteria (mainly producer co-ops) are guaranteed almost three times the current international price. Starbucks now sells fair trade coffee by the bag, and Dunkin' Donuts has recently decided that all of its espresso-based coffees will come from fair trade growers. Despite the higher prices paid by roasters, outlets, and ultimately consumers, the retail value of coffee sold in the United States under the fair trade label has tripled to over $208 million in the last three years. This still represents only 2.5 percent of the $8 billion gourmet coffee market, or 1 percent of the entire $19 billion coffee market, in the United States. However, fair trade coffee is the only segment of the domestic coffee market that is growing rapidly, and its eventual share, now that retailers are finally beginning to make it more readily available, is anyone's guess.

The moral appeals on behalf of grapes, coffee, and other products clearly resonate with a large and growing segment of consumers in the United States and elsewhere. It may be possible to adapt the fair trade model's strategy of connecting conscientious consumers to the minority of producers—in apparel and other sweatshop industries around the globe—who already meet sweat-free conditions and are committed to maintaining them. If these firms flourish, their success may convince other sweatshop producers that their bottom line will not suffer if they too give up the familiar (though increasingly perilous) "low road" that they have followed so far and switch to marketing sweat-free products at higher prices. They need to be convinced, in short, that any revenue lost due to falling demand from consumers who see price as the decisive factor can be offset by increased sales to the sizable and largely untapped market of conscientious consumers who are willing to pay more for sweat-free products. In today's neoliberal environment, appealing simultaneously to the morality of consumers and to the bottom-line of employers and retailers may offer the most realistic hope for reversing the destructive "race to the bottom" that turns today's winners into tomorrow's losers.

RECOMMENDED RESOURCES

Kimberly Ann Elliott and Richard B. Freeman. *Can Labor Standards Improve Under Globalization?* (Institute for International Economics, 2003).

> An assessment of the potential of different approaches to the struggle against sweatshops, published by a Washington think tank that supports trade liberalization but recognizes the need for a "social dimension" to international economic integration.

Jill Esbenshade. *Monitoring Sweatshops: Workers, Consumers and the Global Apparel Industry* (Temple University Press, 2004).

Explores and assesses the recent proliferation of approaches to monitoring working conditions and worker rights in this industry.

Monroe Friedman. *Consumer Boycotts: Effecting Change Through the Marketplace and the Media* (Routledge, 1999).

A general overview of the history and contemporary practice of boycotts as a means of supporting various social causes.

Monica Prasad, Howard Kimeldorf, Rachel Meyer, and Ian Robinson. "Consumers of the World Unite: A Market-Based Approach to Sweatshops." *Labor Studies Journal* (Fall 2004): 57–79.

More details on the first experimental phase of this project and a discussion of its relevance for a market-based approach to sweatshops.

Robert S. J. Ross. *Slaves to Fashion: Poverty and Abuse in the New Sweatshops* (University of Michigan Press, 2004).

Analyzes the causes of the renewal of sweatshop production and what can be done to address it. Well-documented and reasoned, and written in an accessible style from an activist standpoint.

REVIEW QUESTIONS

1. Reflect upon the novel research experiment the authors conducted in a Michigan department store. Discuss the benefits and costs of this research method, paying particular attention to the stage of research in which shoppers were interviewed after selecting the socks.

2. For the most part, labor protests appear to be decreasing in rich countries like the United States and increasing in countries in the "Global South," including China. At the same time, there is a rise of organizations such as the SweatFree Communities Campaign, Fair Trade Coffee, and Working Assets in postindustrial societies. What social forces can explain these trends?

3. Activity: During the 2004 presidential elections, some organizations added a new wrinkle to "buycotting" by attempting to track the political campaign donations of major corporations and encouraging people to "vote with their wallets." Have you thought of the political leanings behind the candy bars you eat, or the sneakers you wear? Using www.buyblue.org, research the campaign contributions and environmental records of six companies from which you buy. Write a paragraph on this "hidden back story" to your purchases. Are you surprised? Will you change your buying habits?

4. Activity: What if, just as dietary information is provided on all food products, so too were the labor conditions of workers, or the environmental impact listed on all consumer goods? Design a standard label that includes what you feel are the important measures that products should list on their packaging.

part **7**

Gender and Sexualities

michael s. kimmel and rebecca f. plante

keyword: sexualities

30

spring 2007

You won't find a lot of sex in the sociological canon. Most of the founding fathers found sex theoretically discomfiting. Well into the twentieth century, sociologists left sex to the anthropologists, with their seemingly voyeuristic interests in archaic bodily taboos and practices, and to the biologists, with their claims about animals, essences, and evolutionary adaptations. If sociology's project was to chart the rationalizing trajectory of modern society, sex—what Max Weber called "the greatest irrational force of life"—was instinctual and embodied, anarchic and anachronistic, premodern, and (Weber again) "externally inaccessible to any rational endeavor."

Weber's contemporary, Sigmund Freud, sealed sex's fate in the social sciences for a generation, declaring sexual desire a primal, indeed foundational, urge, and its sublimation and redirection the basis of civilization. Discussions of sexual behavior, homosexuality, prostitution, pornography, and sexual variations were typically subsumed into the study of crime and deviance—those vestiges of irrationality, those instances of resistance.

While experts had been pronouncing upon and denouncing sexual expression for millennia, the modern social-scientific study of sex began with Alfred Kinsey's two massive studies, *Sexual Behavior and the Human Male* (1948) and *Sexual Behavior in the Human Female* (1954). Based on nearly 20,000 of the most intricate and intimate sexual histories imaginable, then or now, Kinsey's major findings rippled through American culture: the ubiquity and centrality of sexual behavior; the near-universality of masturbation among men (without deleterious effects); the apparently high incidence of homosexual acts among men, and of infidelity among both men (50 percent) and women (26 percent); and the significant presence of desire and sexual agency among women. Kinsey also found that sexual behavior varied widely, especially by social class.

In his effort to normalize sex *and* legitimate its scientific study, Kinsey mapped sexuality by eschewing moral judgment and studying only behavior, which he characterized in strictly physiological terms: the satisfaction of a biologically based urge, orgasm as a reflexive response. Kinsey's strictly behavioral approach—he counted the number of orgasms experienced in each of a variety of situations—distinguished homosexual acts from homosexual identity. This upended Freudian notions that homosexuality was a gender disorder, a problem of inversion. Nonsense, said Kinsey:

In studies of human behavior, the term *inversion* is applied to sexual situations in which males play female roles and females play male roles in sex relations. . . . [But] there are a great many males who remain as masculine, and a great many females who remain as feminine, in their attitudes and approaches in homosexual relations, as the males and females who have nothing but heterosexual relations. Inversion and Homosexuality are two distinct and not always correlated types of behavior.

Sex is both more and less than that—it is a primary mechanism by which we constitute our identities, and it. is also just another arena of social interaction (and thus becomes "sexuality" or even "sexualities": something bigger and more comprehensive than "sex").

It fell to the next generation of sex researchers, including sociologists John Gagnon and William Simon, to carve out a distinctly sociological approach to the study of sex and sexuality. In *Sexual Conduct* (1973), they proposed for the first time that sexual behavior itself was less about animal desires and more about shared social meanings, and that those meanings were the material through which we built a "self." Their intent, Gagnon later wrote, was "to bring the field of sexuality under the control of a sociological orientation, to lay a sociological claim to an aspect of social life that seemed determined by biology or psychology." Sexuality is socially constructed, built from and by cultures, eras, and institutions.

Whereas Freud had argued that there was a sexual component to all manner of nonsexual activities—he discerned libidinous motives in art, music, political movements, literature— Gagnon and Simon argued that one could find political, economic, cultural, even moral motives in sexual conduct itself. One could "do" sex for social mobility, economic gain, or spiritual transcendence. Sex could become a means to ends much larger than any particular acts—a way to solidify or destroy connections, or to express one's gender role or identity.

Second, contra Kinsey, Gagnon and Simon distinguished behavior from identity. Behavior was far less interesting than the meanings and symbols that became attached to that behavior and through which people understood and accounted for their conduct. Far from the result of blind, seemingly basic biological impulses or anarchic, romantic longings, sexual conduct was normatively organized and coherent, learned through lifelong socialization: "In any given society, at any given moment in its history, people become sexual in the same way they become everything else. Without much reflection, they pick up directions from their social environment. They acquire and assemble meanings, skills, and values from the people around them. Their critical choices are often made by going along and drifting."

Sexual behavior is, in this sense, no different from other behaviors in our lives. We learn it from the people and institutions and ideas around us, and assemble it into a meaningful narrative. There are governing rules, hierarchies structuring mobility, and standards of evaluation. Gagnon and Simon coined the phrase "sexual scripts"—the social and cultural blueprints by which we create and express what we typically experience as deeply personal and intimate.

Gagnon and Simon's insights coincided with the sexual revolution of the 1960s and 1970s, which, coupled with the gay and lesbian movement and the women's movement, generated an especially fertile new field. In particular, research expanded in four arenas: history, behaviors, identities, and inequalities. Much of this work capitalized on the concept of the social construction of sexuality, the argument that sex and sexuality are not solely functions of hard-wired, essential, animalistic urges and mandates.

Once sexuality and sexual behaviors had been uncoupled from a strictly biological and reproductive agenda, we could begin to examine their history. Historian Jonathan Ned Katz described the development of the terms *homosexual* and *heterosexual*. At the turn of the twentieth century, *heterosexual* referred to someone with a "morbid sexual interest in the opposite sex." Since "normal" sex was defined as procreative or reproductive behavior, anything else was abnormal or perverse ("morbid"). As the twentieth century progressed, *heterosexual* evolved to become the taken-for-granted and normal mode of classifying and labeling individuals. With the term *homosexual* as its polar opposite, its dramatic foil, "normal" and "abnormal" were more fully fleshed out. Behaviors attached more intimately to individuals; gradually, the nouns *heterosexual* and *homosexual* were drawn from the adjectives that described behaviors.

Such moves were hardly liberating, according to philosopher Michael Foucault. The identification of individuals and classification of behaviors is part of the discursive apparatus of nation-building in the modern era, he argued. The process of normalizing some conduct pathologizes others and subjects all behavior to the legitimate scrutiny of the state.

Before the nineteenth century, it was the confessional that provided sexual discourses. In the nineteenth century, the professions—medicine, law, education—expanded their cultural and institutional power over sex, and the production of knowledge about sex became a major instrument in its control: "One had to speak of [sex] as of a thing to be not simply condemned or tolerated but managed, inserted into systems of utility, regulated for the greater good of all, made to function according to an optimum. Sex was not something one simply judged; it was a thing one administered." Contrary to Freud, Foucault insisted that we have no true sexual selves, repressed by morality and social institutions. Instead, he said, we can only come to develop sexual selves because of these institutions and their discourses about sex. Thus sex—and sexuality—became a political object, a basic element in the "political technology of life."

Research on sexual behavior long suffered from a conceptual apparatus that bore little rela-tion to actual behaviors. A residue of nineteenth-century formulations, the research categories of sexual conduct always referred to marriage—as if all sexual activity were in some way related to that institution. Thus sexual behavior was coded as "marital" "premarital" or "extramarital," even though unmarried, heterosexual people did not think of themselves as having "premarital" sex but simply as having sex.

Much recent research has thus attempted to dislodge the taken-for-granted linkages between sexual behaviors and marriage, to locate sexual activity as it relates to other social institutions, or to disentangle behaviors from their institutional fields. Even heterosexual behavior, long the baseline of comparison, turns out to be varied and complex. In one study, interviewees "described [intercourse] as natural and normal, and as signifying intimacy, closeness, and love" but also as "easy and nonintimate."

The HIV/AIDS crisis that began in the 1980s provided a new opportunity for research into sexual practices, culminating in the National Health and Social Life Survey (NHSL Survey), carried out by the National Opinion Research Center at the University of Chicago in the early 1990s. This collaborative project was the largest and most ambitious study of American sexual behavior ever undertaken, but it was noteworthy largely because of what the researchers did not find. Americans have less sex than we imagined, much of it monogamous and within the context of legal marriage, and they enjoy it more. Fewer Americans identified as homosexual than previously believed, and fewer were unfaithful during their marriages than had been feared. The NHSL Survey had the opposite effect of the Kinsey studies. Shocked by how little sex we were having, how conventional it was, and how apparently satisfied most us were with these arrangements, the project failed to generate the sort of buzz and outrage that greeted Kinsey's reports.

HIV/AIDS increased research on all aspects of same-sex behavior. Most studies focused on men and risk-reduction, and on the effects of HIV, to the detriment of any other aspects of gay or bisexual men's sexualities. Research on lesbians and bisexual women more broadly addressed aspects of identity, politics, and choices. Cultural understandings exaggerate the differences between other-sex orientations and same-sex orientations. We often believe that the most important thing we can know about a person (after his or her sex/gender) is sexual orientation. In partial explanation for this practice's seductive appeal, Gagnon wrote:

It is a common, but false, belief that if we know that persons choose same-gender sex partners, we can successfully make inferences about the kinds of families they come from; the kinds of sex lives they lead; their tastes in clothing, art, music, interior decoration; the way they talk; the kinds of work they prefer; and their religious or leisure orientations. We do not believe we can make such inferences about persons who choose opposite-gender sex partners. Homosexuality (unlike heterosexuality) is a significant label, since it elicits a sequence of interlocked beliefs or judgments which organize our responses to ourselves and to other people.

It is through the other dimensions of identity—race, class, age, religion, and, most important, gender—that we construct our sexualities. These intersections are now the crucial starting point of studies of sexuality.

Although the last thirty years have seen many changes on the sexual landscape, discrimination persists. *Heteronormativity* refers to the prescriptions, proscriptions, and expectations of the cultural belief that heterosexuality is "normal"; heterosexuality thus becomes the standard by which all other forms of sexuality (and gender) are judged. These "boundaries and binary divides" (e.g., the hetero/homo dichotomy) characterize the terms of debate about same-sex marriage, for example, revealing the social mechanisms that organize and constrain all sexual expression.

Virtually every country today is confronting new questions about sexual equality, how sexuality should be regulated, and what "the family" will be like in the future. Ken Plummer wonders,

Who would have thought at the start of the twentieth century that by its very end we would be seriously discussing
· new forms of publicly recognized "family life";
· the growth of the new reproductive technologies, including surrogate mothers;
· the even wider use of many technologies to transform that most intimate organ, the body;
· the public discussion (and private/public practice) of an array of nonprocreative, nonpenetrative coital sexualities;
· the development of transgendered worlds;
· the emergence of all sorts of new "private problems and public troubles," including a whole gallery of new "personal types" [such as "sex addict"].

Ironically, worldwide transformations enhance greater homogeneity while also leading to greater inequalities; studies of global sex trafficking, sex tourism, Internet pornography, mail-order brides, and global sexual movements will provide rich sources of research.

Even the body, along with that steadfast, binary, biological opposition between male and female, has been blurred. Studies of transgendered individuals reveal a different embodied epistemology, and scholarship like Tracey Lee's examination of lesbian and transgendered accounts of identity foreshadows the future of research in this area—exploring the ways in which we are alike, patterned by our culture, but also different, and individual.

The future of sexuality research is the same as the future of sexualities—as social scientists we will try to understand it, and our society will attempt to name it and tame it. But sex will always be messier than our models, lying slightly outside the reach of rationality.

RECOMMENDED RESOURCES

Michel Foucault. *The History of Sexuality*. Trans. Robert Hurley (Vintage, 1990).

Against the popular thesis that sexuality in Western society has been repressed since the seventeenth century, Foucault argues that Western culture's fixation on sexuality has actually created new discourses that bring more attention to "sexuality" and "sexual identity."

John H. Gagnon and William Simon. *Sexual Conduct* (Aldine, 1973).

Connecting the structural to the individual, Gagnon and Simon develop the theory of sexual scripting: sex and sexuality are developed in the same way that *all* social performances are developed and structured, through interaction and social conventions.

Jonathan Ned Katz. *The Invention of Heterosexuality* (Plume, 1995).

Sketches the origin of *heterosexuality* (as a term and an identity), and shows how it came to be seen as normal.

Edward O. Laumann et al. *The Social Organization of Sexuality* (University of Chicago Press, 1994).

Utilizing an excellent sample of the American population, the authors describe sexual practices in the general population and examine changes in these practices.

Rebecca Plante. *Sexualities in Context: A Social Perspective* (Westview, 2006).

Provides a broad overview of how orientation, race, class, and gender affect individual sexualities.

REVIEW QUESTIONS

1. Before reading this essay, how might you have defined "sexuality"? What do you first think of when you hear this word? Why might that be?

2. Give a brief description of the perspectives of Freud, Kinsey, and Gagnon and Simon on sexuality.

3. Plante and Kimmel note the importance of Kinsey's research and the NHSL study. What are the differences in their results and their effects on the American public? How do you suppose the social context of those studies affected both the results and their impact?

4. There has been a great deal of research that demonstrates the power of words to label things in our social world, and the positive and negative consequences of such actions—both to those who do the defining and those who are defined. How does this essay help you to understand the everyday terms we use about sexuality? Do you feel that making such distinctions can, at times, be arbitrary? Why or why not?

barbara risman and pepper schwartz

after the sexual revolution: gender politics in teen dating

31

spring 2002

is the sexual revolution over? are teens returning to conservative sexual values? are we witnessing the end of sexual liberalism and a new trend toward virginity before marriage? this seems to be the consensus of the mass media, and sophisticated academic studies are substantiating these assumptions.

News of apparent decreasing sexual activity among teens, as well as possible success in abstinence programs and church- and government-based "just say no" campaigns, is widely greeted as a positive development. Americans generally regard teen sexuality as a social problem—regardless of whether it results in abortion, single teen motherhood, or sexually transmitted disease.

Signs of a new teenage conservatism are, however, at least exaggerated and, more probably, misinterpreted. Hints of increased conservatism apply only to boys, and a great deal of evidence shows that teens continue to be active sexually. Why, then, are social commentators so insistent on making the case for a teenage sexual retreat?

the case for a teenage sexual counterrevolution

Much research suggests that teens became more sexually conservative during the last decade of the twentieth century. Several studies show that a smaller proportion of youth had coitus between the ages of 15 and 17. For example, the Youth Risk Behavior Survey, designed by the Center for Disease Control (CDC) to find out which behaviors most affect student health, was conducted several times

throughout the 1990s, and every replication found a lower percentage of sexually active teens under age 18. In this nationally representative study of over 10,000 students, the percentage of high school students, ages 15 to 17, who reported they had engaged in sexual intercourse dropped from 54.1 percent in 1991 to 48.4 percent by 1997, a dramatic decrease of some 5.7 percent in a short time. Similar trends were reported in three other nationally representative surveys. While black students continue to be more sexually active than whites, the trends found in this study are similar for blacks and whites. The trend is much less pronounced for Hispanic youth (figure 1).

Accompanying these statistics is additional good news about the problems that often accompany teenage sexual activities. Not only did the percentage of teens engaging in coital sex fall, but also the serious problems that can result from irresponsible teenage sexuality declined. The teen pregnancy rate showed an impressive 14 percent reduction, lower than any time since 1975 (from a peak of 117 per 1,000 young women in 1991 to 103 in 1995). Fewer teen pregnancies mean fewer teenage mothers and fewer abortions. Reports from the Alan Guttmacher Institute show that the abortion rate decreased 31 percent from 1986 to 1996.

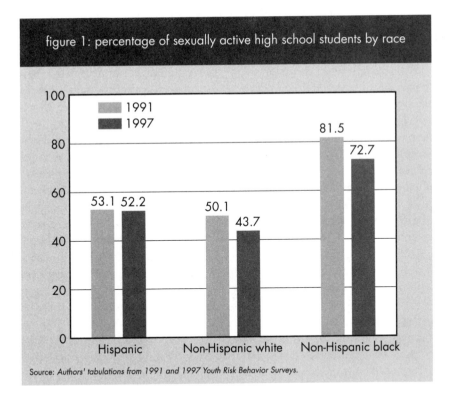

Source: *Authors' tabulations from 1991 and 1997 Youth Risk Behavior Surveys.*

The birth rate among teens rose until 1991 and fell steadily since, with a 25 percent decline between 1986 and 1996. When teens did have sex, they waited until somewhat older ages. The percentage of students in grades 9 and 10 who reported ever having had sexual intercourse was 43.7 percent in 1991, but by 1997 the percentage decreased to 40.3 percent. Even among juniors and seniors in high school, the rates of coitus fell nearly 10 percent in that time. Most research finds that the rate of sexually transmitted diseases also declined throughout the 1990s.

why the apparent declines?

These findings have many explanations, and most contradict one another. The various speculations for the decline in both sexual activity and the problems associated with it include the following: the success of abstinence education, the positive effect of comprehensive sex education, the cultural backlash against the sexual revolution, or the fear of disease (or some combination of these factors). Douglas Kirby's comprehensive analysis of the research on sex education indicates that while good studies show that comprehensive sex education delays the age of first intercourse, none indicate that abstinence-only education is similarly effective. A recent, highly publicized study suggests that abstinence pledges themselves (without actual education) deter teens from sexual activity. While this study was widely reported in the mass media, the story is much more complicated. We believe the claim is inaccurate and explain later in this article why solid scientific research can be distorted when it enters public discourse.

Some commentators have extolled newly conservative values among high school students as the explanation for less teen sex. According to this view, girls especially grew tired of the excesses of the previous decades and wanted to find safety and dignity in less sexualized relationships. Youths looked at the carnage of their parents' generation—divorce, disease, and a loss of status for women's choice to say no—and decided to reestablish their power through less, not more, sexuality. The explanation sounds possible, but little research exists to test this assertion. Fear of disease does seem to be one part of the puzzle. Considerable evidence indicates that some people have changed their sexual habits because of the perceived risk of contracting a permanent or fatal sexually transmitted disease.

Weighing these various explanations is complicated. Reports that the rates of birth, abortion, and sexually transmitted diseases fell much faster than rates of coitus convince us that young people are acting more responsibly when they are sexually active. Responsible sex, rather than postponed sex, seems to explain these improvements. For example, the Alan Guttmacher Institute calculates that less than 25 percent of the decline in pregnancy rates can be attributed to increased abstinence; they attribute the remainder of the decline to the more efficient use of birth control by sexually experienced women. Teens are primarily becoming sexually more responsible and only secondarily less sexually active. Whether such responsibility is attributable to comprehensive sex education or simply to the fear of disease, heightened by mass media reports on AIDS and other sexually transmitted diseases, remains unclear.

While credible competing explanations vie for credit when it comes to explaining the reduction of adolescent pregnancy, we still doubt the underlying premise that sexual activity is on the decline.

a closer look at the data

When we separate the data by gender, the story changes dramatically. Several rigorous studies indicate that the number of high school boys—but not girls—under 18 who remain virgins dramatically increased.

The drama of this decrease in sexual activity among high school boys was hidden in the earlier data that combined the sexes because girls' behavior did not change significantly (figure 2). And yet the story is even more complicated. Sexual trends follow the same direction for white, black, and Hispanic boys, but the picture is more complex for girls (figures 3 and 4).

The rate of sexual activity among white and Hispanic girls has remained generally stable. Black girls, however, reduced their rates of

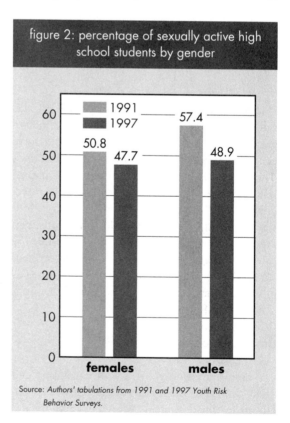

figure 2: percentage of sexually active high school students by gender

Source: Authors' tabulations from 1991 and 1997 Youth Risk Behavior Surveys.

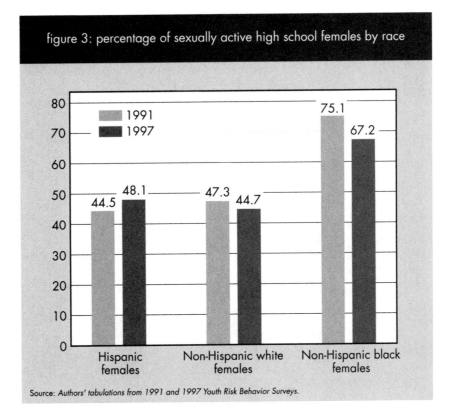

figure 3: percentage of sexually active high school females by race

Source: *Authors' tabulations from 1991 and 1997 Youth Risk Behavior Surveys.*

sexual activity, moving toward levels comparable to that of white and Hispanic girls.

So what is going on? Boys' sexual behavior is becoming more like girls' behavior. Among whites, boys are less likely than girls to be sexually active by age 17. Black and Hispanic boys are still more likely than girls to report sexual intercourse, but the gaps are closing here, too.

We can only speculate about the explanations for the complexity of these changes. We draw on several intensive interview and observational research studies to help understand the reasons for the decrease in teenage boys' sexual experience while in high school. Our best sociologically informed guess is that the cultural norms for girls' sexuality have dramatically changed. Girls are now presumed sexually active inside, but not outside, romantic relationships. Boys are therefore now much more likely to begin their sexual lives with a girlfriend.

The decline in problematic outcomes such as pregnancies is the result, we believe, of girls' increased influence in intimate relationships. In the past, boys were often introduced to sex in a furtive encounter with a girl outside their social circle, one stigmatized by her own sexual appetite or with a desperate need for any kind of approval or inclusion. These girls were often ostracized and stigmatized by both sexes and cruelly smeared as sluts. In previous decades when boys were more sexually active than girls at younger ages, a small pool of "bad" girls probably serviced many boys (otherwise, how could so many fewer girls be sexually experienced than boys?). Nowadays, with boys and girls reporting more similar rates of sexual activity (although

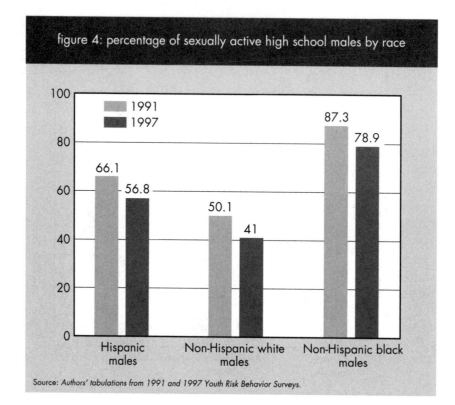

figure 4: percentage of sexually active high school males by race

1991
1997

66.1
56.8
50.1
41
87.3
78.9

100
80
60
40
20
0

Hispanic males
Non-Hispanic white males
Non-Hispanic black males

Source: Authors' tabulations from 1991 and 1997 Youth Risk Behavior Surveys.

only equal rates at the moment for whites), more boys apparently have their first sexual experiences inside a "relationship" of some sort. Adult observers may, however, have to stretch their imagination a bit to define the word *relationship* as casually as teens do, since it may mean accepting the idea of a two-week acquaintance as a relationship. Nonetheless, there seems to be good reason to suspect that the decrease in boys' activity must have something to do with girls' increasing control over the conditions of sexual intercourse.

We also speculate that girls are more likely to insist on safer sex. Dana Lear's interview study with college students at UC Berkeley found that even in that educationally elite context, it was women who responded to the threat of disease as well as pregnancy and insisted on the use of condoms, at least until the relationship gener-

ated enough trust to move toward other means of birth control. Girls' increasing ability to define sex as part of a relationship is one of the reasons for more responsible teen behavior. To the extent that boys have sexual relations with girlfriends, we would expect more condom use and less problematic outcomes of coitus.

Does this mean that the gender revolution is over, that girls are now their boyfriends' equals as sexual partners? We think not. White girls are as likely as white boys to be sexually active. But beyond that, a remnant of the sexual double standard is alive and well. In studies from London to several American college campuses to urban and rural high schools, young women still report being worried about being labeled a slut. A new definition of the word *slut*, however, has surfaced—one that demonstrates that the sexual revolution is over, even while the gender revolution has hardly been won. Girls today may be able to have sex without stigma, but only with a steady boyfriend. For girls, love justifies desire. A young woman still cannot be respected if she admits an appetite-driven sexuality. If a young woman has sexual liaisons outside of publicly acknowledged "coupledom," she is at risk of being defamed. If a girl changes boyfriends too often and too quickly, she risks being labeled a slut. This puts her one down as a power player in her relationship, because her boyfriend does not have to worry about moving on too quickly and being stigmatized for his sexual choices.

While dating relationships may continue to be somewhat inequitable, the research clearly shows that today's teenagers are sophisticated sexual actors. No evidence indicates that sex in most high schools has once again been stigmatized. In fact, survey data suggest that a variety of sexual expressions are a part of "relationships." Most boys who report coitus also report having had oral sex performed on them and having performed it themselves. Even among virgins, over one-third of the students have masturbated a member of the opposite sex to orgasm. No one really knows if oral sex is more common now or simply more openly discussed, but teens clearly often do not consider oral sex as "real" sex, nor do they understand that disease can be transmitted this way. In one study, one-third of sex educators did not even consider oral sex as real sex.

Another finding is clear. While the incidence of coitus among teenage boys under age 18 has decreased, by the end of the teen years nearly all American youth are sexually active. Nine out of ten Americans are sexually active by the time they are 20. Nearly one-half of teens who are not sexually active by age 17 have become so by their senior year or perhaps immediately after graduation. It is now the statistically atypical woman (one out of four) or man (one out of five) who is still a virgin at the end of the teen years.

Still, some changes have turned in the direction of conservatism. For example, approval of casual sex is down. It was a rare boy or girl in the 1990s who openly approved of casual sex or claimed to engage in it. But the definition of being in a relationship is a social one, and a relationship of only two weeks may count. Therefore the participants may not consider the sex that happens within it as casual sex, although it might be so defined by researchers, parents, and policy makers. Young American women no longer hold any attitudes that can be interpreted as a double standard. The majority of American women college students believe that sex with affection is acceptable for women and men, and nearly none of them support the right to casual sex for themselves or others, men or women. And yet, boys do not report being worried about being labeled as promiscuous for having too many partners or for changing partners too often. And while teenage males no longer hold any double standard for the rights of women and men to have sexual relationships with affection, they do hold a double standard in that they approve of casual sex more often for men than for women.

Teenagers are now sexual actors, if not at age 16, then by the time they are old enough to drink legally. The severing of the necessary connection between sexual activity and marriage is irrevocable. What has changed is that teens are not getting into as much trouble as they once did because of their sexual activity.

what does it all mean?

The sexual revolution is a fait accompli; no counterrevolution has taken place. Instead, the revolution was such an overwhelming success that it has revised the entire framework of how American society thinks about sex. Premarital, unmarried, and post-divorce sex are now seen as individual choices for both women and men. The revolutionary principle that divorced the right to sexual pleasure from marriage (at least for adults) is no longer controversial; it goes unchallenged by nearly everyone but the most conservative of religious fundamentalists. It is the gender revolution that is unfinished and still progressing. And it is this revolution still in the making that shows up as we see the evidence that girls are beginning to successfully assert their own right to sexuality and to negotiate more control in their heterosexual relationships.

Why are teens protecting themselves more from the unintended negative consequences of sexual activity? Our best guess is that it is related to the increasing power of girls in their sexual encounters. If we are correct in asserting that the decrease in boys' sexual activity at younger ages reflects girls' increasing negotiation power to restrict sex to relationships (however loosely defined), it is a consequence of more relational and less casual sex that aids more responsible sexual activity.

Despite decreases in abortions, teen pregnancy rates, and sexually transmitted diseases, scientists still write about teenage sexuality as if it is inherently a social problem. On even the most liberal sex education sites on the Internet (Planned Parenthood, the Sex Information and Education Council of the United States [SIECUS], and the Alan Guttmacher Institute), discussion of teenage sexuality is couched in the somber and concerned tones of what might go wrong and what has gone wrong. Yet because of the underlying presumption of nearly all the scientific literature that teen sex is necessarily bad, it is easy to underestimate how much has already been accepted about sexuality and youth in our society. The sexual revolution has changed the very way we think about this "social problem."

Note that most public concern is focused on teens in high school, not young adults or college students. Polls show that premarital sexuality is acceptable to most Americans, at least for adults. What would have been shocking during the heyday of the sexual revolution now goes unnoticed. Not long ago, Victoria's Secret ads would have been considered soft pornography, and jokes about oral sex would not have been allowed on prime-time TV. While concern with teenage sexuality continues, the public does not seem willing to desexualize the greater culture that shapes teen experiences. Rather, there seems to be some strange cultural desire, fueled by the mass media, to distort both the scientific research and the reality of teens' lives.

Every American knows that our culture is highly sexualized. We use sex to sell products to teens as well as to adults. Yet our culture is remarkably ambivalent about teens desiring sexual pleasure. Jocelyn Elders lost her position as surgeon general of the United States because she publicly advocated that masturbation be discussed, and even promoted as "safe" sex, as a

> Every American knows that our culture is highly sexualized. We use sex to sell products to teens as well as to adults. Yet our culture is remarkably ambivalent about teens desiring sexual pleasure.

A friendship totem collage made by two 15-year-old girls. (Photo by Jon Wagner)

High school prom 2000, Seattle, Washington. (Photo by Pepper Schwartz)

part of sex education. She suggested that such self-gratification might delay entry into too early or more risky sexual activities simply to satisfy sexual appetites. The reactions to her comments were outrage, loathing, and anger far above the general distaste for sex education itself. The prompt and widely publicized dismissal of Elders indicates that at least publicly, our society denies the legitimation of safe sexual expression to teens and may have difficulty accepting sexual feelings outside of a spiritual, relational, or reproductive context. The Elders incident reflects the American ambivalence toward and queasiness about the sexuality of youth. Teenage sexuality challenges both the public and the research community because teen sex is obviously not about reproduction or long-term mating behavior in kin groups—or even about love. Teen sex makes adults admit that sex may be purely about play and pleasure. Furthermore, even though today's parents lived through the sexual revolution, many are not comfortable allowing their own children the freedom they enjoyed (although they clearly cannot hinder sexual activity very effectively).

Perhaps this is why scientific studies on teen sex are often misrepresented in the media. Recently, a study of abstinence pledges was highly publicized, often with headlines such as "Abstinence Pledges Work." Yet, the headlines were hardly accurate. Indeed, Peter Bearman and Hannah Bruckner's rigorous study suggests that abstinence pledges succeed in delaying coitus only when neither too many nor too few peers pledge, so that abstinence becomes the membership badge of a social clique. When the majority of students pledge virginity or too few teens pledge to make a reasonable peer group, the pledges are ineffective. Abstinence pledges are headlined as "working" when in fact they may postpone intercourse only for 14- and 15-year-olds within an identifiable clique, and then for a total of 18 months. And when such pledges do work, they come with an unwelcome side effect: the pledgers are less likely to use condoms when their sexual activity does begin. Many in our culture are so desperate to justify the money put into abstinence programs that there is little desire to look at the downside of such programs.

The dialogue on teenage sexuality could be more useful if writers and researchers openly addressed their value presumptions about whether adolescent sexuality is developmentally appropriate or inherently pathological. Presently, the usually unstated assumption is that teenage sex is inherently a social problem. We do not believe the data support such a conclusion. Sexual exploration may in fact be part of the developmental journey of adolescence.

gay teens: what do we know?

Nearly all the survey studies on teenagers have presumed that "sex" means heterosexual sex. No trend data are available on same-sex encounters, bisexuality, or gay identity. About 10 percent of teens on some surveys report being confused about their sexual identities. We cannot tell if this simply reflects the same developmental struggles about identity that every generation of teens faces or whether the decreased stigma attached to being gay, reflected in the mass media, has encouraged more open exploration of sexual alternatives. Most gay men and many lesbians remember same-sex attractions and considering a gay identity in middle school and sometimes before. Some also remember feeling alienated from traditional masculine or feminine pursuits they were presumed to share.

Articles in the public press and some ethnographic research suggest at least more acceptance of bisexuality, and perhaps homosexuality as well, among teens, in 1995 *Newsweek* went so far as to suggest the existence of "bisexual chic," at least for girls, in some high schools in one study of fans at rock clubs, women who identified themselves as heterosexual routinely had same-sex erotic experiences with other women, without redefining their identities. Categories of gay and straight, queer or not, may be more fluid among teens today than ever before. Many students support the position that erotic attractions need not remain stable; others—both gay and straight—hold fast to their sexual identities. Solid scientific studies in the future can no longer presume that when teenagers report "having sex," all of them mean heterosexual coitus.

Whichever values one holds—that teen sex is either pathological or natural—American society cannot afford to continue to define teen sexuality as necessarily problematic. Both younger and older people no longer tie sexuality to long-term personal or institutional commitments. Teens and adults have sex before, during, and after marriage with a variety of partners over their life course. A policy that denies this reality cannot provide adequate medical and social education that promotes responsibility and safety. For most people, a sexual life begins during adolescence and is likely to include all kinds of sexual behaviors, including coitus, before people reach the legal age for drinking alcohol.

The sexual revolution has changed us. It redefined sexual activity as a right of individuals and not merely as a means for reproduction or even marital intimacy. This new view of sex is no longer a revolutionary ideal or even a liberal notion but has become a mainstream American value. Teenagers are simply living in the same culture as the rest of us. The sexual revolution is social history, the gender revolution continues, and teenagers struggle to create new norms that work for them in the twenty-first century.

RECOMMENDED RESOURCES

Alan Guttmacher Institute. Occasional Report. "Why Is Teenage Pregnancy Declining? The Roles of Abstinence, Sexual Activity, and Contraceptive Use." 1996. Online. www.agi.org.

Peter S. Bearman and Hannah Bruckner. "Promising the Future: Virginity Pledges and First Intercourse."

American Journal of Sociology 106 (2001): 859–912.

F. Scott Christopher and Susan Sprecher. "Sexuality in Marriage, Dating, and Other Relationships: A Decade Review." Journal of Marriage and the Family 62 (2000): 999–1017.

G. J. Gates and F. L. Sonenstein. "Heterosexual Genital Sexual Activity among Adolescent Males: 1988 and 1995." Family Planning Perspectives 32 (2000): 295–97, 304.

Kaiser Family Foundation. Press Release. "New KFF/YM Magazine National Survey of Teens on Dating, Intimacy, and Sexual Experiences." May 1998. Online. www.kff.org/content/archive/1373/datingrel.html.

Kaiser Family Foundation. Fact Sheet. "Sexually Transmitted Diseases in the United States." February 2000. Online.www.kff.org/content/archive/1447/std_fs.html.

Douglas Kirby. "No Easy Answers: Research Findings on Programs to Reduce Teen Pregnancy." March 1997. Washington, D.C.: National Campaign to Prevent Teen Pregnancy. Online. www.teenpregnancy.org/fmnoeasy.htm.

Dana Lear. Sex and Sexuality: Risk and Relationships in the Age of AIDS (Sage Publications, 1997).

Karin A. Martin. Puberty, Sexuality, and the Self: Girls and Boys at Adolescence (Routledge, 1996).

John Santelli, Laura Duberstein Lindberg, Joyce Abma, Clea Sucoff McNeely, and Michael Resnick. "Adolescent Sexual Behavior: Estimates and Trends from Four Nationally Representative Surveys." Family Planning Perspectives 32 (2000): 156–65.

Sharon Thompson. Going All the Way: Teenage Girls' Tales of Sex, Romance, and Pregnancy (Rill and Wang, 1995).

Deborah Tolman. "Doing Desire: Adolescent Girls' Struggles for/with Sexuality." Gender & Society 8 (1994): 324–42.

REVIEW QUESTIONS

1. What is the "best sociologically informed explanation" for why boys' sexual behavior is beginning to resemble that of girls?
2. What do you think are the social reasons for the decrease in casual sex among teens? What are the conflicting sexual expectations for adolescents?
3. Risman and Schwartz cleverly point to a difference in how adolescents and adults define "relationship." Similar definitional challenges can be made when examining how people perceive sexual activity (e.g., What is "promiscuous"? What is "sex"?). Discuss the double standards that boys and girls must face in teen dating, and whether or not the authors believe they are changing.
4. Activity: As a form of media analysis, watch a single television show that focuses on teen life and note each instance in which gender roles are reinforced or broken. Pay close attention to particular phrases, gestures, clothing, and activities. Do the differences between how men and women are treated on the show conform to or contradict the evidence presented in the article?

douglas hartmann

the sanctity of sunday football: why men love sports

32

fall 2003

the american male's obsession with sports seems to suggest that the love affair is a natural expression of masculinity. but sociologists have found that, conversely, sports teach men how to be manly, and studying sports reveals much about masculinity in contemporary america.

My father, a no-nonsense grade school principal, had little time for small talk, contemplation, or leisure—with one major exception: sports. He spent Sunday afternoons watching football games on television, passed summer evenings listening to Jack Buck announce St. Louis Cardinals baseball games, and took me to every sporting event in town. He coached all the youth sports his children played, and spent hours calculating team statistics, diagramming new plays, and crafting locker room pep talks. Though never a great athlete, his high school varsity letters were displayed in his basement work area; just about the only surefire way to drag dad out of the house after a long day at work was to play "a little catch." Sports were one of the few topics he ever joked about with other men.

My father's fascination with sports was not unique. Though women are increasingly visible throughout the sporting world, more men than women play sports, watch sports, and care about sports. Is it any wonder that corporate advertising campaigns, drinking establishments, and movements such as the Promise Keepers all use sports to appeal to men? Or that sports figures so prominently in many books and movies dealing with men and masculinity in America? Nevertheless, there is surprisingly little serious reflection about why this is the case. When

asked why so many men are so obsessed with sports, most people—regardless of their gender or their attitudes about sports—say something to the effect that men are naturally physical and competitive, and that sports simply provide an outlet for these inherently masculine traits.

To sociologists, however, men love playing, watching, and talking sports because modern, Western sports—dominated as they are by men and by values and behaviors that are traditionally regarded as masculine—provide a unique place for men to think about and develop their masculinity, to make themselves men, or at least one specific kind of man.

where boys become men

Ask sports enthusiasts why they participate in sports and you are likely to get a wide variety of answers. "Because it is fun and exciting," some respond. Others say it is because they need the exercise and want to stay physically fit. Still others talk about sports providing them a way to relax and unwind, or about the thrill of competition—these responses are especially common for that large percentage of sports lovers whose "participation" mainly takes the form of being a fan or watching sports on television. These are important parts of sports' value, but they do not really explain why men are, on average, more likely to be involved in sports than women.

For many men, the love of sports goes back to childhood. Sports provided them, as young boys and teens, with a reason to get together, to engage with other boys (and men), and in doing so to begin defining what separates boys from girls: how to act like men. Barrie Thorne's study of grammar school playgrounds illustrates the phenomenon. Thorne finds that preadolescent boys and girls use recreation on the schoolyard to divide themselves along gender lines. How they play—for example, running around or quiet games—Thorne suggests, distinguishes male and female child behavior. As they get older, kids become more aware of these distinctions and increasingly use sex-segregated athletics to discuss and act out gender differences. Gary Alan Fine, in *With the Boys,* describes how much of the learning that happens in Little League baseball involves being tough and aggressive and dealing with injuries and other setbacks; and in off-the-field conversations young ballplayers learn about sex and about what it means to be a man as opposed to a "dork," a "sissy," or a "fag."

When Michael Messner interviewed retired athletes and asked them how they initially got involved with sports, they told him it had little to do with any immediate or natural attraction to athletics and was really based upon connecting to other boys and men. "The most important thing was just being out there with the rest of the guys—being friends," said one. Sports, according to Messner, "was something 'fun' to do with fathers, older brothers, uncles and eventually with same-aged peers."

Girls start playing sports for similar reasons, and children of both genders join in other activ-

> When Michael Messner interviewed retired athletes and asked them how they initially got involved with sports, they told him it had little to do with any immediate or natural attraction to athletics and was really about connecting to other boys and men.

ities, such as choir or community se[r]? cial purposes, too. (Many boys an[d] drop out of sports at about ages 9 the sports they play become increasing[ly] petitive and require them to think of themselves primarily as athletes.) What is distinctive about the experience of boys and young men in sports, however, is that the sporting world is organized and run primarily by men, and that athletic activities require attitudes and behaviors that are typically understood to be masculine.

Of course, not all boys play sports, and boyhood and adolescent experiences in sports are not uniformly positive. A great deal of the sociological research in this area focuses on the downside of youth sports participation. Donald Sabo, for example, has written extensively about the pain and violence, both physical and psychological, experienced by many boys who compete in athletics. And Harry Edwards has long argued that over-investing in sports can divert poor and minority youth from more promising avenues of upward mobility. But, despite the harsh realities, sports remains one of the few socially approved settings in which boys and men, and fathers and sons, can express themselves and bond with each other.

sport as a masculine enterprise

Once boys and girls separate in physical play, it does not take long for gendered styles of play to emerge. Study after study confirms what most soccer moms and dads already know: boys' athletics tend to be more physical and aggressive and put more emphasis on winning, being tough in the face of adversity, and dealing with injuries and pain. Even in elementary school, Thorne finds boys take up far more of the physical space of the playground with their activities than girls, who tend to play (and talk about their play) in smaller spaces and clusters.

People debate whether there is a physiological component to these differences, but two points are clear. First, parents, coaches, and peers routinely encourage such intensity among boys in youth sports. More than a few single mothers bring their boys to the teams I coach out of concern that their sons are insufficiently tough or physical because they lack a male influence. Messner writes about how he learned— against his inclinations— to throw a ball overhand with his elbow tucked in because his father did not want him to "throw like a girl." Stories about overly competitive, physically abusive coaches may be overplayed in the American media, but in many ways they are the inevitable consequence of the emphases many parents express.

Second, the behaviors and attitudes valued in men's and boys' athletics are not just about sports, but about masculinity more generally. The inherent connection of sports to the body, physical activity and material results, the emphasis on the merit of competing and winning, the attention to rules, sportsmanship and team play, on the one hand, and gamesmanship, outcomes and risk, on the other, are not just the defining aspects of male youth sport culture, but conform to what many men (and women) believe is the essence and value of masculinity. Female reporters, homosexual athletes, and men who challenge the dominant culture of men's sports—especially in the sacred space of the locker room—quickly learn that sports are not just dominated by men but also dominated by thinking and habits understood to be masculine

Study after study confirms what most soccer moms and dads already know: boys' athletics tend to be more physical and aggressive and put more emphasis on winning, being tough in the face of adversity, and dealing with injuries and pain.

(in opposition to the more nurturing values of compromise, cooperation, sympathy, understanding, and sharing typically associated with femininity). If the military is the quintessential institution of Western masculinity, then sports is surely a close second.

The notion that sports is a masculine enterprise is closely connected with the development of modern Western sports. As historians have detailed, middle- and upper-class men used sports in the nineteenth and early twentieth centuries to present and protect their particular notions of masculinity in both schools and popular culture (the classic literary expression being *Tom Brown's School Days*, a nineteenth-century English story of boarding school boys' maturation through hard-nosed sports). The media is a critical part of perpetuating sports' masculine ethos today, because most adults participate in sports as spectators and consumers. Not only are female athletes and women's sports downplayed by most sports coverage, but the media accentuates the masculinity of male athletes. For example, Hall of Fame pitcher Nolan Ryan's media coverage, according to a study by Nick Trujillo, consistently described him in terms of the stereotypical American man: powerful, hardworking, family patriarch, a cowboy, and a symbol of heterosexual virility. Such images not only define an athlete's personal qualities but legitimate a particular vision of masculinity.

The authority of the masculine ethos is underlined by the fact that so many female athletes believe they can receive no higher compliment than to be told they "play like a man." Many feminists cringe at the irony of such sentiments. But they also realize that, while the explosion of women in sports has challenged their male dominance (2.5

million girls and young women participated in interscholastic sport in 2003, up from 300,000 in 1972—before Title IX's federal mandate for gender equality), women's sports have essentially been based upon the same single-minded, hyper-competitive masculine model. Not surprisingly, they are witnessing the emergence of the same kinds of problems—cheating, physical and emotional stress, homophobia, eating disorders—that have long plagued men's sports.

sports and maintaining masculinity

As the men Messner interviewed became more committed to being athletes, they began to construct identities and relationships that conformed to—and thus perpetuated—sport's masculine values. Athletes are so bound up with being men that when, in his initial interviews, Messner inadvertently referred to them as "ex-athletes," his interviewees responded as if he were taking away their identities, their very manhood. A professional baseball player expressed a similar sentiment when I asked how he dealt with his time on the disabled list last summer because of a serious arm injury: "I'd throw wiffle balls left-handed to my eight-year-old son—and I had to get him out! Just so I could feel like a man again."

Of course, few men participate in sports with the intensity of professional athletes. Those who cannot move up the competitive ladder can still participate in other ways—in recreational sports, in coaching, and perhaps, most of all, in attending sporting events, watching sports on television, and buying athletic gear and apparel. Indeed, it is in being a fan (derived from *fanatic*) that the male slant of sports is clearest. While women often follow sports, their interest tends to be driven by social ends, such as being with family or friends. Male spectators are far more likely to watch events by themselves, follow sports closely, and be affected by the outcomes of games and the performance of their favored teams and athletes. The basic explanation is similar to the one developed out of sports activity studies: Just as playing sports provides many boys and young men with a space to become men, watching sports serves many men as a way to reinforce, rework, and maintain their masculinity—in these cases, through vicarious identification with masculine pursuits and idealized men. Writing of his obsession with 1950s football star Frank Gifford in *A Fan's Notes*, novelist Fredrick Exley explained: "Where I could not, with syntax, give shape to my fantasies, Gifford could with his superb timing, his uncanny faking, give shape to his." "I cheered for him with inordinate enthusiasm," Exley wrote, because he helped me find "my place in the competitive world of men . . . each time I heard the roar of the crowd, it roared in my ears as much for me as for him."

It was no accident that Exley chose to write about football. With its explicit appropriation of the rhetoric and tactics of combat, the sport supplanted baseball as the most popular spectator sport in the United States in the 1970s. Football's primary ideological salience, according to Messner, "lies in its ability . . . to symbolically link men of diverse ages and socioeconomic backgrounds. . . . Interacting with other men and interacting with them in this male-dominated space . . . [is] a way to assert and confirm one's own maleness. . . ." Being with other men allows males to affirm their masculine identity. Listen to today's sports talk radio. These programs are not only sophomorically masculine, many of them serve as little men's communities unto themselves: Tiger fan Jack; Mike from Modesto; Jay the Packer's guy—even teams' announcers have unique personalities and identities, fostering the impression that this is an actual club where all the guys know each other.

The salience of sports as a medium to validate masculinity may be best illustrated when it is taken away. Journalist Susan Faludi reported on what happened when the original Cleveland Browns football team left town to become the Baltimore Ravens. The mostly working-class men who occupied the section of seats in Cleveland called the "Dawg Pound" talked about the team's departure with an overwhelming sense of loss and powerlessness. As it often is for former athletes, it was as if they'd had their manhood taken from them. In tearful media interviews, John "Big Dawg" Thompson compared the team's departure to witnessing his best friend die in the hospital.

sports as "contested terrain"

Critics of sports' heavy masculinity (most scholars doing work in this area are critics) have focused on its neglect or even exclusion of women. The way that golf outings perpetuate the privileges men enjoy in the corporate world is a frequent example. Others have gone so far as to suggest that the powerful appeal of sports for men arises because sports provide them at least symbolic superiority in a world in which men's real authority is in decline. As columnist and former professional basketball player Mariah Burton Nelson put it in the deliberately provocative title of her popular 1994 book, "The stronger women get, the more men love football."

In recent years, sociologists of sports have also begun to identify tensions within the masculine culture of athletics. Looking at Great Britain's soccer stars, for example, Garry Whannel has studied how the hedonism of the "new lad lifestyle" (as represented by players like David Beckham) rubs up against the disciplined masculinity traditionalists perceive to be necessary for international football success. Messner, for his part, has shown how "high status" men (white and from middle-class backgrounds) and "low status" men differently understood themselves as athletes. The former tended to transfer what they learned in sports about being men to pursuing success in other spheres, such as education and career. Men from lower status backgrounds saw sports as their only hope for success as a man—an accomplishment that the higher status men looked down upon as a narrow, atavistic type of masculinity. Expanding from this, some scholars have demonstrated that in popular culture the masculinity of African-American athletes is often exaggerated and linked to racial stereotypes about violence, risk, and threat. Basketball star Dennis Rodman, for example, gained notoriety by playing on his persona as a "bad" ball player. While problematic in many respects, these images of black masculinity can also provide African-American men with unique opportunities for personal advancement and broader political visibility (as I have suggested in my work on the 1968 black Olympics protest movement).

Such research has led many scholars to see sports not only as a place where mainstream masculine culture is perpetuated, but also a place where it is challenged and possibly changed. These issues have played out clearly in the debates over the implementation of Title IX legislation for women's equal access to sports. While still hotly contested (as evidenced by the recent controversy surrounding the all-male Augusta National Golf Club, as well as speculation that the legislation may be challenged in court by the Bush administration), Title IX has transformed men's relationship to sports, to women, and even to masculinity itself. Sports' most vital social function with respect to masculinity is to provide a separate space for men to discuss—often indirectly, through evaluations of favorite players or controversial incidents—what it is to be a real man. And that space is increasingly shared with women.

Some scholars envision new, more humane or even feminine sports—marked less by an emphasis on winning, record-setting, and spectatorship, and more by open participation, enjoyment, and fitness. Cross-cultural studies of sports show that these are real possibilities, that sports are not "naturally" and inherently masculine as Americans have long assumed. Sexism and homophobia, for example, have never been a real problem in Chinese sports, anthropologist Susan Brownell explains, because sports emerged there as a low-status activity that more powerful men felt no special compulsion to control or participate in. As a consequence, it is widely believed that a skilled female practitioner of kung fu should be able to defeat stronger but less-skilled men. At the same time, Brownell points out, the current proliferation of Western, Olympic-style sports in China seems to be contributing to the redefinition of gender roles there nearer the pattern of Western sports and masculinity.

playing deeply

In a famous paper on cockfighting in Bali, American anthropologist Clifford Geertz used the term "deep play" to capture the way fans make sense of such competitions as the cockfight, cricket, or American football. As passionate and articulate as they may be, these enthusiasts generally do not attempt to justify their pursuits. Instead, they downplay the significance of sports as separate from the serious concerns of real life. We can learn a great deal from such play, Geertz said, if we think about it as an "art form" which helps us figure out who people really are and what they really care about. Similarly, American men who love sports may not be able to fully articulate and understand how it is part of their being men, but their passion for sports can certainly help us understand them and their masculinity.

This peculiar, "deep play" understanding of sports makes it difficult for most men to recognize or confront the costs and consequences that may come with their sports obsessions. But in many ways isn't this true of masculine culture in general? It makes male advantages and

masculine values appear so normal and "natural" that they can hardly be questioned. Therein may lie the key to the puzzle connecting men and the seemingly innocent world of sports: they fit together so tightly, so seamlessly that they achieve their effects—learning to be a man, male bonding, male authority, and the like—without seeming to be doing anything more than tossing a ball or watching a Sunday afternoon game.

RECOMMENDED RESOURCES

Susan Birrell and Cheryl L. Cole, eds. *Women, Sport and Culture* (Human Kinetics, 1994).

> A collection of feminist critiques of sport that includes several influential contributions on men and masculinity.

Susan Brownell. *Training the Body for China: Sports in the Moral Order of the People's Republic* (University of Chicago Press, 1995).

> The chapters on sex, gender, and the body offer a fascinating cross-cultural contrast, and provide an introduction to sports in the nation that will host the 2008 Olympics.

Varda Burstyn. *The Rites of Men: Manhood, Politics and the Culture of Sport* (University of Toronto Press, 1999).

> The most comprehensive treatment of the social, cultural, and historical forces that account for the relationship between men and sports in modern society.

Gary Alan Fine. *With the Boys: Little League Baseball and Preadolescent Culture* (University of Chicago Press, 1987).

> A pioneering field study from a noted sociologist of culture.

Robin D. G. Kelley. "Playing for Keeps: Pleasure and Profit on the Postindustrial Playground." In *The House that Race Built*. ed. Wahneema Lubiano (Pantheon, 1997).

An ethnographically informed treatment of the opportunities basketball presents to inner-city African-American men produced by the country's preeminent historian of black popular culture.

Alan M. Klein. *Little Big Men: Bodybuilding Subculture and Gender Construction* (State University of New York Press, 1993).

A vivid ethnography of competitive body builders on the West Coast that draws upon Robert Connell's seminal critique of the intersection of men's bodies, identities, and sexualities in masculine culture.

Michael Messner. *Taking the Field: Women, Men, and Sports* (University of Minnesota Press, 2002).

The latest book from the leading scholar in the field. It exposes the ways in which men and women together use sports to define gender differences.

Brian Pronger. *The Arena of Masculinity: Sports, Homosexuality and the Meaning of Sex* (St. Martin's Press, 1990).

Pronger explores the problematic connections between gender and sexuality in sport, highlighting its libidinal dimensions.

REVIEW QUESTIONS

1. Before reading this article, how might you have explained why men love sports? How would you explain it now?
2. The article doesn't mention the critical issue of class. How do you think social class affects perceptions of sports and participation in it?
3. It is interesting that two of the four stars mentioned in Hartmann's article—Dennis Rodman and David Beckham—have been just as noted for playing with gender roles as they are for playing their sport. Both are known as tough competitors, but are also known to wear eyeliner, pink nail polish, and feather boas. Do you think such infusions of complexity in the tight interplay of masculinity and sports affect the spectator's perception of gender roles? How do you feel these actions are judged as compared to, for example, the stereotypes surrounding a female softball player?
4. Activity: Research the sports programs at your campus. What are the facilities like? Do you find any inequalities in resources based upon gender?

jerry a. jacobs

detours on the road to equality: women, work, and higher education   **33**

winter 2003

women are earning college degrees in increasing numbers, but entering male-dominated occupations at a decreasing pace. these two developments are linked. work barriers may be leading women to take a detour to college.

News stories about the first woman entering a field—astronaut, firefighter, professional basketball player, Ivy League university president—have largely faded, although Carly Fiorina's selection as head of Hewlett Packard was widely extolled in both the business and popular press. It is commonly assumed that the barriers that once blocked women's entry into new fields have been dismantled. But there has been less change than meets the eye. The slow but steady movement of women into formerly male-dominated occupations has tapered off, if not completely stopped, during the 1990s. Women have made greater strides, however, in their pursuit of higher education. Indeed, the second development may be the result of the roadblocks they are facing in finding employment in traditionally male fields.

layers of segregation

Despite highly visible exceptions, such as local television news anchor teams, most occupations remain skewed toward either men or women. For every news anchorwoman, there are literally thousands of women who work in traditional female settings such as at a receptionist's desk, in an elementary school classroom, or at the take-out window of a fast-food restaurant. Whether she is a white single mother in Florida or a black empty-nester in Michigan, a woman more often works next to other women than to men. Women remain crowded in certain jobs such as secretaries or administrative assistants (99 percent female), child care workers (98 percent) or registered nurses (93 percent). Among the remaining male bastions are construction trades, such as carpenters, plumbers, and electricians (3 percent female), mechanics and repairers (5 percent) and engineers (10 percent). This concentration of women and men in different jobs, occupations, and industries is what sociologists mean when they refer to the gender segregation of work.

Among the highest-status professions, law, medicine, and management have experienced a

> Despite highly visible exceptions, such as local television news anchor teams, most occupations remain skewed toward either men or women. For every news anchorwoman, there are literally thousands of women who work in traditional female settings such as at a receptionist's desk, in an elementary school classroom, or at the take-out window of a fast-food restaurant.

large influx of women. Nearly half of managers, law students, and medical students are women. But within these fields, gender disparities are unmistakable. Few female managers have reached the highest echelons of large corporations, and women middle-managers are less likely than their male counterparts to have authority over staffs and budgets. Female lawyers are more likely to be found in family law or working for the government than practicing in the more lucrative specializations at major firms. And female physicians are more likely to specialize in pediatrics or family practice than surgery or anesthesiology. Indeed, the closer you look within nominally integrated occupations, the more segregation you find. Men and women are segregated by occupation, by firms within occupation, and by jobs and specializations within firms.

> Among the highest-status professions, law, medicine, and management have experienced a large influx of women. Nearly half of managers, law students, and medical students are women. But within these fields, gender disparities are unmistakable. Few female managers have reached the highest echelons of large corporations, and women middle-managers are less likely than their male counterparts to have authority over staffs and budgets.

There are "men's jobs" and "women's jobs" at all levels of education, skills, and experience, and at each level, the women's jobs tend to be paid less. Moreover, female-dominated fields pay less even when working time, qualifications, and experience are taken into account.

One way to appreciate the income disparity is to compare the pay for male- and female-dominated occupations that have similar job qualifications. Women are 50 percent of bus drivers but only 3 percent of railroad conductors. Women are 71 percent of accountants and auditors but only 29 percent of securities and financial services sales representatives. Women are 88 percent of dressmakers but only 22 percent of upholsterers. In each of these cases, the male occupation pays more than the female one. These heavily skewed numbers suggest that, despite good intentions, many jobs are not truly open to everyone.

explaining job segregation

Why do women and men end up in different occupations? A popular view is that gender distinctions at work are as natural as boys and girls playing separately on the school playground. But sociologists tend to view gender roles as social conventions rather than natural phenomena.

People are taught to distinguish men's work from women's work, just as they are taught right from wrong. Gender stereotypes in the workplace are readily apparent, even to young children, and are often self-perpetuating. Children in elementary school report without hesitation that nurses are usually women, and firefighters,

Small group project in an education class of 60 college students, 52 of whom are female. (Photo by Jon Wagner)

engineers, and presidents are usually men. Young girls may no longer be encouraged to stay home, but now many are encouraged to work in "suitable" jobs that emphasize helping others. Ideals pressed on boys include abstract reasoning, competitive prowess in sports and business, tinkering with things, and financial success.

But persistent sex segregation at work is not the simple product of young men and women's choices. American youngsters' occupational aspirations are notoriously fickle. Occupational goals change often during the teenage years. More than half of college students change majors at least once. Even workers in their 20s and 30s continue to change occupations. For example, women engaged in emotionally demanding jobs, such as assisting children with learning disabilities, suffer from burnout, while other women working in male-dominated fields find that such jobs are not always worth the isolation and long hours. That this turnover has failed to reduce sex segregation suggests that continued pressure to pursue sex-typed work lasts well into adulthood.

For example, working in a masculine field can raise questions about a woman's femininity. Christine Williams found that female Marines feel they need to show how tough they are on the job but also how feminine they can be off the job. Men who work as nurses face some of the same issues, and respond by emphasizing the heroic aspects of nursing. Beyond the pressure of gender expectations, a web of social factors tends to press women into traditionally female occupations and hold them there in adulthood. Women have fewer acquaintances with knowledge about openings in male-dominated settings. They often lack the co-worker support necessary to succeed. They face job tasks and hours that assume a male bread-

While forecasting trends is treacherous, it seems safe to predict that the gender segregation of jobs in the year 2020 will resemble current patterns.

winner with a supportive stay-at-home wife. And their family and friends are often dubious about or hostile to a new or unconventional occupation. Some of the remaining barriers to women's economic advancement are rooted in the structure of work. For example, excessive hours in a number of demanding fields limit the opportunities of those with parental and other caregiving obligations, especially mothers. Over the last 30 years, the work week has lengthened and the pace of work has intensified for many in the labor force, accentuating the strain on women.

Historical experiences also instruct us about just how flexible these gender distinctions can be. When seats in medical school classrooms became vacant during World War II, young women rushed to fill them. Other women were recruited to fill manufacturing jobs, with the media stressing how the required skills were similar to women's domestic talents. In the 1960s young women switched rapidly from education into medicine, business, and other fields as professional schools in these fields opened their doors. These examples suggest that the gender stereotypes with which women grow up do not prevent them from seizing new opportunities as they become available.

And the things men and women say they want from their jobs are more similar than different. For example, Allison Konrad has shown that men and women overlap a great deal in the specific features of jobs they rank as important. In other words, gender segregation cannot be reduced to what men and women look for in jobs.

hitting a wall?

The early 1980s was a period of great energy and optimism both for research and policy on

hiring discrimination

A female Assistant Attorney General called the exclusive Cipriani's restaurant in New York City requesting an interview for a job on the dining room staff and was told by a manager, on tape, "We don't hire girls." In fact, this restaurant had never hired a waitress, and the Attorney General sued for hiring discrimination. In depositions, Cipriani's claimed that there were few, if any, women with experience serving in similar establishments in New York City, despite the fact that, overall, waitresses outnumber waiters by nearly four to one. To see if comparable restaurants hire women, Sara Rab and I conducted a survey of elite restaurants in New York City. We found that two-thirds of the elite restaurants in New York hired women, but the more expensive the dinner, the fewer the women servers. We found a similar pattern in Philadelphia. Servers in our sample of elite restaurants brought home an average annual salary of about $45,000, compared with less than $20,000 in less expensive establishments. Our findings are consistent with an experiment conducted on 65 Philadelphia restaurants by economist David Neumark, who directed pairs of men and women matched for their credentials to apply for jobs as servers. In high-priced restaurants, women were 35 percent less likely than men to receive an interview, and 40 percent less likely to receive a job offer. The hiring decisions of managers clearly contribute to the disparate placement and earnings of waiters and waitresses

occupational gender segregation. An entirely new dimension of social inequality appeared to be open for exploration—not an everyday event. Comparable worth—the idea of equalizing pay not only for the same work, but also for work of comparable value—seemed a realistic and even imminent possibility. Women were making notable strides, entering new occupations and receiving graduate training in professions such as law, medicine, and business. And women's entry into male fields even helped the women who remained in female fields. Fields such as nursing and teaching now face severe shortages, which stimulate higher wages for these under-valued professions.

At that time I was confident that these trends would continue, while some other analysts feared that the rate of change was so slow that it would take many decades to rectify the gender disparities at work. As it turns out, even the skeptics were too optimistic. Progress to-ward greater gender integration of occupations largely ground to a halt during the 1990s. The most widely used measure of segregation is the "index of dissimilarity," which measures the proportion of women who would have to change fields in order to be represented across types of occupations in the same proportions as men are. (Zero represents complete integration; 100 complete segregation.) This index fell from 67 in 1970 to 60 in 1980 to 56 in 1990, and then to 52 by 2000. But the modest change that occurred during the 1990s was almost all due to shifts in the size of occupations, rather than greater integration within occupations. (The more integrated occupational groups—professionals, technical workers, managers, and sales occupations—grew, while the more segregated occupational groups—clerical workers and craft workers—declined.) More mixing within occupations did not happen in the 1990s.

Stagnation is evident in several related areas as well. The gender gap in median weekly earnings has been stuck at the same level since 1993—76 percent in 2001—and segregation by gender across medical specialties actually inched upward during the 1990s.

Why has the gender integration of occupations slowed to a crawl? A longer view suggests that this stability is typical and it is the unusual changes of the 1970s and 1980s that need to be explained. For most of the century gender differentiation remained roughly constant, despite economic booms and depressions, revolutions in marriage, fertility, and divorce, and the incremental but inexorable entry of women into the labor force.

Social change often occurs in brief intervals followed by periods of renewed stagnation. The feminist movement of the late 1960s and 1970s challenged many traditional assumptions, but its force waned by the late 1980s. The idea that a woman could do anything a man could do had tremendous force, but gradually was contested by the notion that women have special values and strengths which should be better appreciated. And inevitably a backlash against ostensibly special treatment challenged affirmative action and other measures designed to broaden opportunities for women and minorities.

Gender integration occurred largely through women entering formerly male-dominated settings. Few men showed interest in breaking into the pink-collar frontier. The stigma of doing "women's work," coupled with low pay, makes many jobs performed by women unattractive to men. The puzzle, of course, is why women have not left traditional female fields in even greater numbers for the better pay, benefits, promotion opportunities, and even job flexibility found in many men's occupations. Since women continue to join the labor market in ever greater numbers and take shorter and shorter breaks from work for childbearing, one would expect that they would continue to seek out avenues toward economic self-sufficiency. Such commitments to work should keep the pressure on to open male-dominated fields. Yet, while some pressure continues, many women have sought economic independence by the alternative and time-honored route of enrolling in higher education.

degrees of difference

Women first surpassed men in obtaining bachelor's degrees in 1982, and the gap continues to widen. In 1998, the most current data available, 56 percent of bachelor's degrees went to women. Before long, college graduates will probably be roughly 60:40 women to men, or a 1.5 to 1 ratio of young women to young men. Women are even more disproportionately concentrated among associate degree recipients, and are at parity with men in garnering masters and professional degrees.

Women's domination of undergraduate education represents a remarkable turn of events. Just 40 years ago, men were earning two-thirds of college degrees, and just 20 years ago, men and women were at parity. While many expected and welcomed women's catching up to men in educational attainment, I am not aware of anyone—economist, sociologist, or educator—who predicted that women would surpass men by so much so quickly. What happened?

The surge in women's education is probably linked to gender segregation at work in several ways. First, women realize that the low wages that they face in unskilled women's jobs do not offer a living wage. In 1998, women with a high school degree working full-time, year-round brought home a median income of $22,800 a year; high school dropouts earned $16,700. Male high school graduates made $31,200 a year on average ($24,000 for high school dropouts). Young men consequently have less of a pressing need to pursue higher education. If skilled crafts and other relatively high-wage jobs open to male high school graduates were equally open to women, it is possible that fewer women would pursue higher education.

Second, by seeking specific vocational credentials, women gain some protection against hiring discrimination. If a pharmacy position requires a master's degree, women with such a diploma can expect that they will be given serious consideration. Many women returning to higher education do so to pursue particular vocational degree programs, to become nurse's aides, to get a teacher's certificate, and to update office skills. The laundry list of rationalizations for turning away women is less readily available in professional settings, especially when there is a tight market for highly specialized skills. Accordingly, sex segregation has declined more sharply for college graduates than for those with fewer educational credentials.

Finally, the educational credentials women garner are themselves segregated, which limits the financial returns they can expect. In a national survey of the college class of 1999, I

Former site of a university employment office. Increasing women's participation in male-dominated occupations may require expanded child care services as well as programs of affirmative recruitment and advancement. (Photo by Jon Wagner)

found that women college seniors expected to earn 30 percent less than their male classmates when they reached age 30, and the field of the degree they were pursuing explained the largest slice of this gap.

Women are pursuing a broader set of college programs than in the past, but here too change has slowed. About 30 percent of women would have to change fields to match their male counterparts, a difference that has been roughly constant since the mid 1980s. Biology, business, and math are among the fields that have reached a rough gender balance. Engineering and the physical sciences (astronomy, chemistry, and physics) remain male-dominated fields while psychology, education, nursing, and the romance languages are leading feminine fields of study. Girls are increasingly taking math and science in high school and testing better in those subjects, but this convergence in courses and scores has not translated into a convergence in college majors.

looking toward 2020

While forecasting trends is treacherous, it seems safe to predict that the gender segregation of jobs in the year 2020 will resemble current patterns. The major engines of gender integration have all lost steam. There are two ways in which women enter male fields: by starting their careers there or by switching later in life. The numbers taking either route have shrunk in recent years and are no longer enough to make up for the women who drop out of male-dominated careers.

As a result, it seems unrealistic to expect total gender integration. Basic changes in the way work is structured are needed, but we are in a period of political retrenchment, with bold new proposals unlikely to gain serious attention. Further reductions in occupational segregation will take another wave of political, cultural, social, and economic reforms like those initiated during the

1960s. Specific policy measures would include: vigorous enforcement of anti-discrimination laws; training programs that target highly gender-typed fields; and a broad reconsideration of the value of women's work, especially caregiving work. Restructuring of working time to make all jobs parent-friendly is needed so that responsible parents (mostly women) are not trapped in so-called mommy track positions or part-time jobs with no job security or employment benefits. Specifically, policies that reduce the length of the work week—especially for professionals and managers—could reduce work-family conflict, increase the time working parents can spend with their children, and advance gender equality at work. Reducing artificial gender barriers at work can improve economic efficiency while promoting gender equity. Recruiting more women into fields such as computer science and engineering could help to provide much needed talent in these areas, while recruiting more men to be elementary school teachers would help solve the looming national shortages we face in this area. There are many simple and effective measures that can be taken to broaden opportunities for women at work. We simply need the political will. Of course, the gender gap in voting—women were 11 percentage points more likely to vote for Gore than Bush in 2000—could return gender equality to the center of public policy discussions and put the labor force back on a course of incremental progress toward gender equality.

Most observers view the large and growing number of women in colleges and universities as yet another indication of how far women have come. But this welcome development may also have a darker side, as it reflects in part the continued obstacles women face in obtaining high-paying jobs that require no diploma. In other words, until we see more women wearing mechanic's overalls, we can expect to see more and more women marching in caps and gowns at graduation.

RECOMMENDED RESOURCES

Ann Boulis, Jerry A. Jacobs, and Jon Veloski. "Gender Segregation by Specialty During Medical School." *Academic Medicine.* 76 (2001): 565–7.

A study of gender and fields of specialization among medical students.

David A. Cotter, JoAnn M. DeFiore, Joan M. Hermsen, Breda M. Kowalewski, and Reeve Vanneman. "All Women Benefit: The Macro-Level Effect of Occupational Integration on Gender Earnings Inequality." *American Sociological Review* 62 (1997): 714–34.

An analysis of the impact of gender segregation on women's wages.

Jerry A. Jacobs. "Gender Inequality and Higher Education." *Annual Review of Sociology* 22 (1996): 153–85.

Reviews women's uneven progress in higher education.

Alison M. Konrad, J. Edgar Ritchie, Pamela Lieb, and Elizabeth Corrigall. "Sex Differences and Similarities in Job Attribute Preferences: A Meta-Analysis." *Psychological Bulletin* 126 (July 2000): 593–641.

Analyzes data on what women and men want from their jobs.

David Neumark. "Sex Discrimination in Restaurant Hiring: An Audit Study." *The Quarterly Journal of Economics* 111 (August 1996):915–41.

A case study of hiring discrimination in restaurants.

Sara Rab. "Sex Discrimination in Restaurant Hiring Practices." Master's Thesis, Department of Sociology, University of Pennsylvania, 2001.

A study of gender and elite restaurants in New York City and Philadelphia.

Irene Padavic and Barbara Reskin. *Women and Men at Work,* Second Edition (Pine Forge Press, 2002).

Broad overview of gender inequality at work.

Christine L. Williams. *Gender Differences at Work: Women and Men in Nontraditional Occupations* (University of California Press, 1989).

Case studies of female marines and male nurses.

REVIEW QUESTIONS

1. The gender gap in undergraduate degrees is striking. What is the surprising gap Jacobs identifies, and what are potential explanations for it?

2. As Jacob states, "sociologists tend to view gender roles as social conventions rather than natural phenomena." What do you remember from your childhood—from school, family, friends, or extracurricular activities—that gave you ideas about what was considered to be "men's work" and "women's work"?

3. Discuss an experience you have had in any kind of organization (e.g., school, religious organization, youth program, business, or something else). What were the different kinds of jobs within the organization? Were men or women more likely to fill each of those jobs?

4. Activity: Jacobs mentions that college students change their majors at least once. Organize a class exercise wherein some students informally ask juniors and seniors (with an even number of men and women) at your school about their changes in major, and the second group of students finds the gender composition of ten programs. From those findings, discuss as a class any differences between what kind of fields women change to and what fields men change to. Do these changes reflect traditional "masculine" and "feminine" roles in society?

verta taylor and leila j. rupp

learning from drag queens

34

summer 2006

drag queens can teach us a lot about sexual desire—especially our own.

In American society, people tend to think of males and females and heterosexuals and homosexuals as distinct and opposite categories. Drag performances challenge the biological basis of gender and the fixed nature of sexual identity. As a place where for an hour or two gay is normal and straight is other, drag shows use entertainment to educate straight people about gay, lesbian, bisexual, and transgendered lives.

Milla, one of the drag queens who performed at the 801 Cabaret, the Key West club we studied for our book *Drag Queens at the 801 Cabaret*, once proclaimed, with both exuberance and self-mockery, "We're going to be in classrooms all around the world! . . . No more George Washington, no more Albert Einstein, you'll be learning from us!" All the drag queens in the troupe laughed, but in fact, as we came to realize, they do teach their audience members complex lessons about the porous boundaries of gender and sexuality. Drag shows may be entertaining, and diverse people may flock to them to have a good time, but that does not belie the impact that a night of fun can have. The drag queens are, we think, more than entertainers. As Sushi, the house queen, insisted in a newspaper interview, "We're not just lip-synching up here, we're

> They announce from the start that they are gay men, they talk in men's voices, they make jokes about their large clitorises and "manginas" and complain that they are having "testical difficulties" when the music does not work.

changing lives by showing people what we're all about." In the process of showing people what they are all about, they bring together diverse individuals, illustrating the official Key West philosophy that we are "One Human Family." How exactly do they do that? And do people take away the lessons they teach?

These were some of the questions we explored by studying the 801 Girls, a troupe of gay men who perform as drag queens every night of the year for mixed crowds of tourists and local residents, women and men, heterosexual, gay, lesbian, bisexual, and transgender people. The performers are economically marginal men who make barely enough to support themselves in a town where property is expensive and affordable housing is in short supply, as Barbara Ehrenreich conveyed so vividly in her depiction of Key West in *Nickel and Dimed: On (Not) Getting By in America*. We interviewed in all sorts of contexts and spent time with eight drag queens to find out why they do what they do and what their performances and interactions with audience members mean to them. We spent night after night at the shows, taping their banter and the songs they lip-synch and talking to audience members. And we recruited diverse people to come back the next day and talk to us about the shows in a focus-group setting. That is how we learned that there is more to drag shows than meets the eye.

drag shows

Drag shows have a long history as central institutions in gay communities and as places where, at least in tourist towns, straight people come in contact with gay life. From the drag balls in cities such as New York and Chicago in the 1920s to the famous Finocchio's in San Francisco in the 1940s and the popularity of RuPaul and Lady Chablis in the 1990s, men dressed in women's clothing have served as a visible segment of the gay community and have also enthralled straight audiences. The 801 Girls are no exception. On a one-by-four-mile island closer to Cuba than to Miami, populated by diverse communities—Cuban, Bahamian, gay and lesbian, hippie, and increasingly Central American and Eastern European—drag queens are central to the mix. They are everywhere: on stage, on the streets, at benefits. As the local paper put it, "You know you're from Key West when . . . your Mary Kay rep is a guy in drag."

The shows at the 801 Cabaret are an institution in Key West, described by visitors as "the best show in town." Every night at quarter after ten, four or five of the girls take to the sidewalk outside the bar, hand out flyers for the show, and banter with passersby. That is how they recruit an audience. Some tourists avert their eyes or cross the street, but most are intrigued, stop to chat, and many decide to come to the show. Upstairs over a gay bar, the cabaret has small tables up front where unsuspecting tourists serve as props for the girls, a bar in the center, and mostly standing-room-only space around the bar. Gay men congregate and cruise at the back, behind the bar.

A typical show consists of 15 to 20 numbers, some performed individually and some in groups. There is a lot of interaction with the audience, which sets the show apart from similar ones performed at gay bars across the country. But in terms of the repertoire of songs, the comedy, and the dialogue, what happens at the 801 is typical of a style of drag that emerged in conjunction with the gay and lesbian movement, a style of drag that goes beyond female impersonation.

For these drag queens, although they dress in women's clothing and can be as beautiful as biological women, there is no pretending. They announce from the start that they are gay men, they talk in men's voices, they make jokes about their large clitorises and "manginas" and complain that they are having "testical difficulties" when the music does not work. Some do not even shave their legs or underarms or tuck their genitals. Inga, a statuesque blond from Sweden, would be introduced as "Inga with a pinga," and Milla, often mistaken for African American, sometimes appeared with a dildo gripped in her crotch, calling attention to the real item hidden away. Sushi occasionally pulls down her dress and bra to reveal her male chest, provoking the same kind of wild audience response a real female stripper might, even though the sight of male nipples is nothing new in a tropical town where men do not need to wear shirts walking down the street. Sushi also performs "Crazy World" from *Victor/Victoria*, a song about a world "full of crazy contradictions." Behind a sheer white curtain, she strips down to nothing but keeps her genitals tucked between her legs as she backs off stage, revealing what transgender activists would call a "gender-queer" body.

For the final number of the weekend shows, R.V. Beaumont, who perfected drag while working at Disney World and learned to do Bette Midler numbers from watching Bette Midler impersonators, used to change out of drag on stage to the Charles Aznevour ballad, "What Makes a Man a Man?," transforming himself from woman to man. And a regular feature of the Saturday night "Girlie Show" is Kylie, Sushi's best friend from high school, who does a mean California valley girl, stripping entirely to "Queen of the Night," leaving the audience with the contrast between her blond wig, makeup, high heels, and well-hung body. These are the ways they educate their audiences about the performativity of gender and the slipperiness of sexual desire.

"troubling" gender

The drag queens at the 801, at least some of them, have slipped back and forth between genders. Milla, who grew up in a working-class family in St. Petersburg, Florida, with an alcoholic and abusive father, "decided that I wanted to be a woman." She (the drag queens tend to use their drag names and female pronouns, although they also switch back and forth with some ease) got hormones from a counselor she was seeing for her adolescent drug problems by telling him that she would get them anyway from the drag queens on the street. She grew breasts and went out dressed as a woman and had "the men fall over, all over me, and with no clue, no clue." She loved it and seriously considered sex-reassignment surgery. But then "I started to love myself. I pulled away from that whole effeminate side . . . and I became a man." Milla continues to attract men and women of all sexual desires and pronounces herself "omnisexual."

Gugi, born to a Puerto Rican family in Chicago, also passed for a woman for a time. "What I've always wanted was to be a woman," Gugi said, although she added, "I don't know if it is because I wanted to be a woman or because I was attracted to men that I preferred to be a woman." She also took hormones for a time and grew breasts, but she stopped because "it wasn't the right time. . . . I did it to get away from my dad's death" and a painful breakup with a lover.

The one who is in charge of the shows and makes everything happen is Sushi, who never looks like a man even out of drag. Sushi, whose Japanese mother married an American G.I., describes herself as "some place in between" a woman and a man. She began to dress in drag in high school and for a time was a street prostitute in Los Angeles. At first, she thought that wanting to wear women's clothing meant that she wanted to be a woman, but then she came to realize that it just meant that she was a drag queen. "I know I'm a drag queen; I finally realized that I'm a gay man who puts on women's clothing and looks good." Yet she still worries that she is really a closeted transgendered person. One night we asked her the difference between being a drag queen and being transgendered and she replied, "A drag queen is someone like Kylie who has never ever thought about cutting her dick off."

What it means about the social basis of gender that men can look like beautiful women is not lost on audience members. A local straight woman described thinking of them as women during the show. A straight male tourist agreed, saying of Milla, "She was a woman." His wife agreed: "Uh-huh, she was a woman. It never even entered my mind. She was a beautiful woman." A young straight woman, at her first drag show, explained that she thought of them as both. "Back and forth, I think. Yeah, I was confused and went back about twelve times." A gay man, as if echoing what at least some of the girls might say about themselves, said, "I don't think of them as really any of it. I feel like they're their own thing. I feel like a drag queen is something completely different. . . . It's way more than being a woman and it's definitely not being a man."

As that last comment suggests, there is more going on here than just mimicking traditional female beauty. Even the girls who are the most beautiful in drag—Sushi, Milla, Inga, and Gugi—do not really look like women, because they are too tall or have muscled arms or men's waists and buttocks. They are beautiful as drag queens. And they perform alongside other girls who are old or overweight or do not shave their chests and who perform numbers that criticize traditional feminine ideals of beauty. Scabola Feces, whose very name belies any hint of impersonating beautiful women, performs "Wedding Bell Blues" in a ripped-up wedding dress, Coke-bottle glasses, and a mouthful of fake rotten buck teeth, and R.V. appears in hair curlers as a hooker or madam in such songs as "The Oldest Profession" and "When You're Good to Mama."

> Because the drag shows have the potential to arouse powerful desires that people perceive as contrary to their sexual identities, they have a real impact on people's thinking about the boundaries of heterosexuality.

Their performances force audience members to think differently about what it means to be a man, what it means to be a woman. A local gay man described "older married couples" watching R.V. perform "What Makes a Man a Man?" "with their jaws hitting the floor. Especially when the eyelashes come off and the wig and the makeup disappears like that.... And they're like, I think they're still shocked when they leave that way like, 'Oh my god, I don't believe it.' They want to believe that they're women and it's hard for them to accept that they're not." This is what feminist scholars mean when they talk of "troubling" gender, causing people to think outside the binary of male/female. The 801 girls are very good teachers.

arousing new sexual desires

The drag queens also have an impact by arousing sexual desires in audience members not congruent with their sexual identities. A central part of the show involves bringing audience members on stage to represent different sexual identity categories. The drag queens call for a straight man, a gay man, a straight woman, and a lesbian, sometimes a bisexual or transsexual. While this seems to affirm the boundaries of sexual desire, the intent of the drag queens is quite the opposite. First of all, they allow a great deal of latitude in who represents what categories, and audience members are creative, so that gay men might call out that they are lesbians and straight women might play lesbian for a night. And then, once on stage, during the time that we studied the shows, the girls arranged the couples in positions simulating sex acts, the two women as the drag queens say "bumping pussy," and the gay man on his back with the straight man crouched over his pelvis. Each participant got a shot of liquor poured into his or her mouth with a lot of teasing about fellatio.

Usually the people on stage really get into the act. One night the straight woman seemed eager to have the lesbian touch her and said she was "willing to try pussy-licking." Another time one of our research assistants volunteered as the lesbian, and a woman there with her husband came up to her and said, "I'm totally straight, but that just turned me on" and kissed her on the mouth. A young straight woman described feeling sorry for a young straight man brought up on stage. "I thought for him it had to be confusing because the drag queen that was coming on to him was, to me, the prettiest, and I kept thinking, 'God, that's a guy, that's a guy.' ... And he's probably thinking, 'God, she's hot.' Forgetting that she's a he. And I think that when she got on top of him, he was probably embarrassed because he was turned on." Sometimes audience members take the initiative. One night a very thin young woman in skimpy clothes came onstage to dance with Desiray, a new member of the troupe who became a drag queen because he fell in love with the show as a tourist. The woman stripped down to a thong and eventually grabbed Desiray to mime having anal sex with her.

For the drag queens, a central part of the show is the arousal of straight men. They love to move through the crowd and touch and fondle them. One night a straight couple got in a fight because the man got an erection when Sushi grabbed his penis. A straight woman tourist, on the other hand, loved when the girls fondled her husband. "It's like here's this man touching my husband, it's like really cool. And he's standing there letting him." She found this the "sexiest" part of the show, "there was something crackling the most. . . . The line was crossed the most at that moment. . . . And I liked it." Her husband described his own response: "I'm sitting there and there's a little bit of me saying, 'This is sexually exciting' and there's another part of me saying, 'Wait a minute, don't do this. You're not supposed to be sexually excited, this is a man." At one show, a very macho young man there with his girlfriend took one look at Sushi and confided in us, "I could do her."

And it is not just straight men who experience sexual desires outside their identities. A lesbian described feeling very attracted to Milla: "She was so sexy," and a straight woman agreed, commenting that "I was very drawn to her sexually. I felt like kissing her. And I'm not gay at all." Yet she described being attracted because Milla "was a woman. She was a beautiful woman." Another straight woman "started falling in love with" Milla and announced, "I want to make love with her." When Sushi and Milla, or Sushi and Gugi, perform the lesbian duet "Take Me or Leave Me" from *Rent*, it has

a powerful erotic impact on all sorts of audience members. More than once, during the shows, straight women started kissing their women friends. One night two Mormon women on vacation without their husbands started talking with us. By the end of the show, one confided that, if she were going to be with a woman, she would choose her friend.

As a result of these kinds of interactions and responses, many people at the shows conclude that the labels of "gay" and "straight," like "man" and "woman," just do not fit. For one gay man, "You leave them at the door." Said another, the drag queens are "challenging the whole idea of gender and so forth and they're breaking that down." A straight male tourist put it this way: "I think that one of the beauties of attending a show like this is that you do realize that you . . . shouldn't walk out and say, 'I only like men,' and you shouldn't say 'I only like women,' and it all kind of blends together a lot more so than maybe what we want to live in our normal daily lives." Because the drag shows have the potential to arouse powerful desires that people perceive as contrary to their sexual identities, they have a real impact on people's thinking about the boundaries of heterosexuality.

drag queens creating change

And this is just what the drag queens intend, as Milla's and Sushi's opening comments suggest. Kylie announces, "I intend to challenge people." Sushi explains that "I'm not just doing a number. . . . I'm trying to make more of an experience, a learning thing. . . . And I have a platform now to teach the world. . . . Even less than five minutes of talking to somebody, just that little moment I share with somebody from New Zealand or Africa or your college professor or whoever, they go back to their hometown. They remember that five-minute conversation, they realize, 'I'm not gonna call this person a fag,' you know what I mean?" Says Milla, "We are attractive to everybody. We have taken gender and thrown it out of the way, and we've crossed a bridge here. And when we are all up there, there is no gay/straight or anything."

One of the remarkable things about the drag shows is the way they bring people together across all kinds of boundaries, not just differences in gender and sexual identities. Inga described the audiences as ranging "from the worst faggot to the butchiest lesbian to the happily married couple with the kids, the honeymoon people, the people who hate gays but maybe thought it was something interesting." A gay male tourist thought the shows had a "really big mass appeal to a cross section of everyone," and in fact we have met Mormons, brides out on the town the night before their weddings, transsexuals, grandmothers and grandfathers, female strippers, bikers, and everyone in between. Although the shows express and affirm pride in gay or lesbian or bisexual or transgender identities, they also emphasize what we all have in common.

Milla, putting a negative spin on it, confessed once, "What I love the most is that all these people come to our shows—professors, doctors, lawyers, rich people—and they're as fucked up as we are." Margo, a sixty-something New Yorker who also wrote a column for the local gay newspaper, introduced the classic gay anthem "I Am What I Am" in a more positive way: "The next song I'm going to do for you will explain to everyone who, what, and why we are. We are not taxi drivers or hotel clerks or refrigerator repair people. We are drag queens and we are proud of what we do. Whether you are gay or straight, lesbian, bisexual, trisexual, transgender, asexual, or whatever in between, be proud of who you are." Sushi, too, preaches a message of pride and love. One night she raised her glass to toast to gay love and then corrected herself, "Oh no, here's to love. To love,

baby, all across the world." Another time, more vulgarly, she introduced her best friend Kylie and announced, "This is the person that . . . told me that I was special and that every single one of you is special no matter if you suck a cock or lick a pussy." Using words that typically describe same-sex sex acts to divide people into new categories, the drag queens bring together gay men and straight women, lesbians and straight men.

The audience takes in the lessons. A gay New Yorker put it this way, "The message really comes across that it doesn't matter who you are." Another gay man commented that, at the 801, "Everybody is equally fabulous." A local straight woman realtor who had seen the shows many times commented to us, "They bring a gay guy up, then a straight woman, and a straight man, and a lesbian. By the end, you just think, 'What's the difference?'" Summing up the hopes and dreams of the drag queens, a young gay man with theatrical ambitions explained that the show "signifies for me . . . that we have these differences but here we are all together within this small space. Communing, interacting, being entertained, having a good time and everything is going well. . . . and I think the idea being to make some sort of, like, utopia or this is the way it could be. Once we all leave this bar, if we can all see four different people that are different and commune together, or at least respect each other, then when we leave this bar, wouldn't the world be a little bit better place?"

The drag queens do indeed work to make the world a better place. As one of the few ways that straight people encounter gay culture—where, in fact, straight people live for an hour or two in an environment where gay people are the majority—drag shows, especially in a tourist town like Key West, have the potential to bring people together and to create new gender and sexual possibilities. Precisely because drag shows are entertaining, they attract people who might never otherwise be exposed to gay politics. As one female audience member put it, they "take something difficult and make it light." Because the shows arouse visceral emotions, even sexual desires that fall outside people's usual sexual identities, they have the potential to make a real impact. Through a complex process of separating people into gender and sexual identity categories, then blurring and playing with those boundaries, and then bringing people all together again, the drag queens at the 801 succeed, as the comments of audience members attest, in "freeing people's minds," "removing their blinders," "opening their minds," sometimes even "changing their lives." The diverse individuals who flock to the 801 come away with an experience that makes it a little less possible to think in a simple way about gender and sexuality or to ignore the experiences of gay, lesbian, bisexual, and transgendered people in American society.

RECOMMENDED RESOURCES

Patricia Gagné and Richard Tewskbury, eds. *Gendered Sexualities: Advances in Gender Research*, Volume 6 (JAI, 2002).

A collection of articles that explore the intersection of gender and sexuality.

Esther Newton. *Mother Camp: Female Impersonators in America* (University of Chicago Press, 1972).

The classic account of drag queens in the late 1960s, just before the emergence of the gay liberation movement.

Leila J. Rupp and Verta Taylor. *Drag Queens at the 801 Cabaret* (University of Chicago Press, 2003).

A full analysis of the drag queens, their shows, and their impact on audiences.

Steven P. Schacht with Lisa Underwood, eds. *The Drag Queen Anthology* (Harrington Park Press, 2004).

An interdisciplinary collection of articles about drag queens in different parts of the world.

REVIEW QUESTIONS

1. How exactly do drag queens "trouble gender"? What did you learn about drag queens from this essay that you didn't know before?

2. Write two paragraphs on how the activities that occur at the 801 Cabaret relate to those in the Hartmann essay on why men love sports. Can you make comparisons between the activities? If so, what functions does each serve in society? How do both of them challenge and reinforce gender roles? Where is there evidence of homophobia and patriarchy?

3. As one gay man talks about traditional gender roles in the essay, he says "You leave them at the door" of the 801 Cabaret. Spaces like these allow straight people to learn the variety of gender roles in a fun, contained environment. Think of four other venues for gender learning, and list the activities that occur within them.

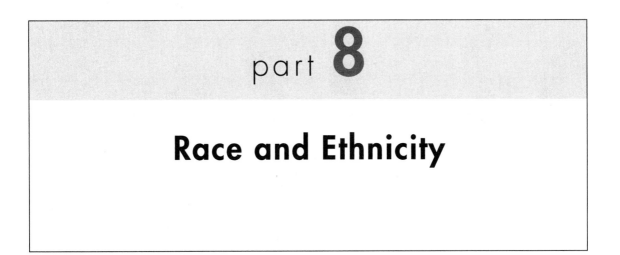

part **8**

Race and Ethnicity

ann morning

keyword: race

fall 2005

Race is part of everyday life in the United States. We're asked for our race when we fill out forms at school or work, when we visit a government agency or doctor's office. We read or hear about race in the daily news, and it comes up in informal discussions in our neighborhoods and social circles. Most of us can apply—to ourselves and the people around us—labels like white or Asian. Yet for all its familiarity, race is strangely difficult to define. When I've asked people to explain what race is, many have trouble answering.

Two uncertainties are widespread. First, there is confusion about the relationship between *race* and *ethnicity*. Are these different concepts? How often have you come across descriptions of someone's "ethnicity" that use terms like *white* and *black*? The public, the media, politicians, and scientists often use *race* and *ethnicity* interchangeably. Both terms have something to do with our ancestral origins, or "background," and we often find both linked to ideas about "culture." As historian David Hollinger points out, we often use the term *multicultural* to refer to racial diversity. In doing so, we presume that racial groups have different cultural beliefs or practices, even though the way we classify people by race has little to do with their behavior, norms, or values.

Defining race is also a challenge because we are unsure how it is related to biology. Are racial categories based on surface physical char-

acteristics? Do they reflect unobserved patterns of genetic difference? If race is a kind of biological taxonomy, we are uncertain about exactly which traits anchor it.

Clear-cut definitions of race are surprisingly elusive. *The New Oxford American Dictionary*, for example, equates *race* with *ethnic group*, and links it to a wide range of possible traits: "physical characteristics," "culture," "history," and "language." The U.S. Census Bureau is another place to look for an authoritative definition. In contrast to the dictionary definition, the federal government rejects both culture and biology as relevant to race. This is apparent in its approach to racial enumeration and how it explains its definition. The U.S. Census makes the most visible use of the official racial categories that the Office of Management and Budget (OMB) first promulgated in 1977 and revised in 1997. These standards require all federal agencies to use the following classifications in their data collection and analysis:

1. American Indian and Alaska Native
2. Asian
3. Black or African American
4. Native Hawaiian and Other Pacific Islander
5. White

The OMB deliberately refrains from naming Hispanics as a race, instead identifying them as an "ethnic group" distinguished by culture (specifically, "Spanish culture or origin, regardless of race"). The growing tendency among journalists, researchers, and the public is to treat Latinos as a *de facto* racial group distinct from whites, blacks, and others, but the government view is that cultural differences do not determine racial boundaries.

Biological differences are also declared irrelevant to the official standards. The Census Bureau maintains that its categories "do not conform to any biological, anthropological or genetic criteria." Instead, the bureau says that its classification system reflects "a social definition of race recognized in this country"—but it does not elaborate further on that "social definition." The Census Bureau and OMB see themselves as technical producers of race-based statistics largely for the purpose of enforcing civil rights laws, not as the arbiters of the meaning of race.

We may take the Census Bureau's reference to a "social definition" as a version of the social-scientific understanding of race as a "social construct." In other words, race is whatever we as a society say it is. The American Sociological Association took this view in its 2002 "Statement on the Importance of Collecting Data and Doing Social Scientific Research on Race," where it defined race as "a social invention that changes as political, economic, and historical contexts change." The association also noted that concepts of race usually involve valuations of "physical, intellectual, moral, or spiritual superiority or inferiority." Both are crucial observations about the type of idea that race is: It arises at particular moments and in particular places, and has long served to perpetuate deep social fissures. However, the constructivist position does not necessarily define the actual content of racial beliefs. Many kinds of classification schemes are socially constructed and serve as the basis for class systems. So what distinguishes racial categories from other taxonomies?

Sociologist Max Weber (1864–1920) offers a useful starting point for seeing the elements of ancestry, culture, and biology in terms of socially shaped belief. However, it is his definition of "ethnic groups"—not races—that provides the template. Like most scientists of his time, Weber felt that races stemmed from "common inherited and inheritable traits that actually derive from common descent." In his definition of *ethnicity*, however, he introduced the notion of "believed" rather than actual commonality, describing ethnic groups as "those human groups that entertain a subjective belief in their common descent because of similarities of physical type or of customs or both, or because of memories of colonization and migration; this belief must be important for the propagation of group formation; conversely, it does not matter whether or not an objective blood relationship exists." Substitute "races" for "ethnic groups," and strike "customs" but retain "physical type," and we have the basic ingredients for a comprehensive definition of race.

An emphasis on *belief* in common descent, as well as *perception* of similarity and difference, is crucial for a useful definition of race. Without them, we could not account for the traditional American "one-drop" system of racial classification, for example. According to this logic, a person with one black great-grandparent and seven white great-grandparents is a black person, because their "drop of black blood" means they have more in common with blacks than with whites. This shows how we base racial classifications on socially contingent perceptions

> The word *race*, deriving from the late-fifteenth-century Spanish designation for Jewish and Muslim origins, came freighted with Christians' belief that such people embodied an innate, permanent, and negative essence.

of sameness and difference, not on some kind of "natural" calculus.

Finally, regardless of our personal views on the biological basis of race, we must recognize that physical characteristics—Weber's "inherited and inheritable traits"—are central to the concept. As historian George Fredrickson points out, the word *race*, deriving from the late-fifteenth-century Spanish designation for Jewish and Muslim origins, came freighted with Christians' belief that such people embodied an innate, permanent, and negative essence. Although Spaniards had previously believed that infidels could become Christians through religious conversion, the suspicion that they could never truly make the transition took root after 1492, when many Jews and Muslims chose conversion over expulsion. This early notion of inherent and unchangeable difference gave rise to the understandings of race we share today. We believe, for example, that a black person can "act white" or that a white person can "act black," but that no behavior, shared ideas, or values can actually determine the race that one truly is.

With these elements in place, we can improvise on Weber to define races as *groupings of people believed to share common descent, based on perceived innate physical similarities*. This formulation addresses the relation of culture and biology to race. Culture is absent here as an explicit basis of racial membership, leaving a clear distinction between race and ethnicity. Though both refer to beliefs about shared origins, ethnicity is grounded in the discourse of cultural similarity, and race in that of biological commonality. In addition, this definition emphasizes the constructivist observation that although racial categories are ostensibly based on physical difference, they need not be so in reality. Even if we disagree about whether or not races are biological entities, we can agree that they are based on *claims* about biological commonality. As a result, this definition gives us a

shared starting point for the most contentious debate about the nature of race today, namely, whether advances in genetic and biomedical research have proven the essentialist claim that races are identifiable, biologically distinct groups that exist independently of our perceptions and preconceptions.

Sociological literature often suggests that the general acceptance by scholars of the idea of race as a "social construct" gives it the status of "conventional wisdom." Yet resurgent claims about the biological nature of race are increasingly difficult to ignore. After something of a postwar hiatus in "race science" following international condemnation of the Nazis, the question of the biological basis of race has received renewed scientific attention in recent years. In March 2005, for example, the *New York Times* published a geneticist's essay asserting that "scientists should admit that there is such a thing as race." A variety of professional scientific journals and popular science magazines have taken up the question of whether "there is such a thing as race." In December 2003, the cover of *Scientific American* inquired "Does Race Exist?" *Nature Genetics* devoted most of a November 2004 supplement to the same question. *Science*, the *New England Journal of Medicine*, *Genome Biology*, and the *International Journal of Epidemiology*, among others, have also addressed the issue. In fact, the relationship between race and human biology is far from settled in scientific circles.

The argument that race is socially constructed rests on two simultaneous claims, although we sociologists have tended to focus on just one. The constructionist idea implies that race is a product of particular historical circumstances and also that it is *not* rooted in biological difference—it only claims to be. By working harder to demonstrate the former—for example, the historical variability of racial categories, their roots in particular social institutions, their divergence from one society to the next—we have turned away from investigating why racial boundaries do not correspond to physical differences. In our teaching and writing, we have not tried to explain why race may not be rooted in biology even though Americans are accustomed to being able to see race; they see, for example, who is Asian or who is white. Yet a comprehensive constructionist account must explain why we consider only some of the many kinds of differences between geographic groupings of human beings to be racial differences. We see racial differences between Norwegians and Koreans, for example, but we do not consider the differences between Norwegians and Portuguese to be racial.

Although sociologists may be reluctant to evaluate geneticists' and medical practitioners' pronouncements on human differences, feeling that this is not our turf, the arguments made today about race and biology lend themselves to sociological analysis. As the recent *New York Times* essay demonstrated, the current claims about distinct racial genetic profiles involve assumptions about group membership that social scientists are generally accustomed to questioning. We are used to investigating problems of sample construction and potential bias, exploring how assumptions about boundary lines affect our results. If we find, for example, that African Americans and European Americans have different probabilities of having a particular gene variant, does that prove the existence of black and white "races" to which they belong? If Latinos have yet another probability of having that gene variant, have we proved that they too constitute a racial group? How about Ashkenazi Jews? Does it matter if only one in a thousand genes displays such a pattern of variation? Does it matter how many people provided the DNA samples, or how they were located? Should we be suspicious that the red/white/yellow/black racial classification that scientists and census-takers use

today is at heart the same framework that Linnaeus established in the eighteenth century without the aid of genome sequencing? In short, despite the complexity of the human genome and the tools that we now have to study it, the debate about the nature of race revolves around broader questions of logic and reasoning—which makes it that much more important to establish a comprehensive but flexible definition of race.

RECOMMENDED RESOURCES

Stephen Cornell and Douglas Hartmann. "Conceptual Confusions and Divides: Race, Ethnicity, and the Study of Immigration." In *Not Just Black and White: Historical and Contemporary Perspectives on Immigration, Race, and Ethnicity in the United States*, eds. Nancy Foner and George M. Fredrickson (Russell Sage Foundation, 2004).

> Cornell and Hartmann compare the concepts of race and ethnicity and discuss the sociological analyses that traditionally employ them.

George M. Fredrickson. *Racism: A Short History* (Princeton University Press, 2002).

> A concise and engaging history of the concept of race.

David Hollinger. *Postethnic America: Beyond Multiculturalism* (Basic Books, 1995).

> In this influential and readable essay challenging our everyday conflation of the terms race and culture, Hollinger uses the phrase "ethno-racial pentagon" to describe the current (though not official) tendency to recognize the following as races: whites, Hispanics, blacks, Asians, and American Indians.

Max Weber. *Economy and Society: An Outline of Interpretive Sociology* (University of California Press, 1978).

> In Chapter 5, "Ethnic Groups," Weber scrutinizes the concept of ethnicity as a basis for social action, yet concludes that it "dissolves if we define our

terms exactly" and is "unsuitable for a really rigorous analysis."

REVIEW QUESTIONS

1. How might you have defined race before reading this essay? How would you define it now?
2. How does the U.S. Census currently define
   race? Would you want to change in any way

how the Census Bureau defines or gathers information about race?
3. The number of children living in mixed-race
   families increased from 460,000 in 1970
   to 996,000 in 1980 to nearly 2 million in
   1990. And in 2000, 2.8 million children
   under 18 defined themselves as multiracial.
   How do these changes affect how you
   think about the evolving racial make-up of
   the United States?

herbert j. gans

race as class

fall 2005

why does the idea of race continue to exert so much influence in the united states? because the skin colors and other physical features used to define race were selected precise because they mirror the country's socioeconomic pecking order.

Humans of all colors and shapes can make babies with each other. Consequently most biologists, who define races as subspecies that cannot interbreed, argue that scientifically there can be no human races. Nonetheless, lay people still see and distinguish between races. Thus, it is worth asking again why the lay notion of race continues to exist and to exert so much influence in human affairs.

Lay persons are not biologists, nor are they sociologists, who argue these days that race is a social construction arbitrary enough to be eliminated if "society" chose to do so. The laity operates with a very different definition of race. They see that humans vary, notably in skin color, the shape of the head, nose, and lips, and quality of hair, and they choose to define the variations as individual races.

More important, the lay public uses this definition of race to decide whether strangers (the so-called other) are to be treated as superior, inferior, or equal. Race is even more useful for deciding quickly whether strangers might be threatening and thus should be excluded. Whites often consider dark-skinned strangers threatening until they prove otherwise, and none more than African Americans.

Scholars believe the color differences in human skins can be traced to climatic adaptation. They argue that the high levels of melanin in dark skin originally protected people living outside in hot, sunny climates, notably in Africa and South Asia, from skin cancer. Conversely, in cold climates, the low amount of melanin in light skins enabled the early humans to soak up vitamin D from a sun often hidden behind clouds. These color differences were reinforced by millennia of inbreeding when humans lived in small groups that were geographically and socially isolated. This inbreeding also produced variations in head and nose shapes and other facial features so that Northern Europeans look different from people from the Mediterranean area, such as Italians and, long ago, Jews. Likewise, East African faces differ from West African ones, and Chinese faces from Japanese ones. (Presumably the inbreeding and isolation also produced the DNA patterns that geneticists refer to in the latest scientific revival and redefinition of race.)

Geographic and social isolation ended long ago, however, and human population movements, intermarriage, and other occasions for mixing are eroding physical differences in bodily features. Skin color stopped being adaptive too after people found ways to protect themselves from the sun and could get their vitamin D from the grocery or vitamin store. Even so, enough color variety persists to justify America's perception of white, yellow, red, brown, and black races.

Never mind for the moment that the skin of "whites," as well as many East Asians and Latinos is actually pink; that Native Americans are not red; that most African Americans come in various shades of brown; and that really black skin is rare. Never mind either that color differences within each of these populations are as great as the differences between them, and that, as DNA testing makes quite clear, most people are of racially mixed origins even if they do not know it. But remember that this color palette was invented by whites. Nonwhite people would probably divide the range of skin colors quite differently.

Advocates of racial equality use these contradictions to fight against racism. However, the general public also has other priorities. As long as people can roughly agree about who looks "white," "yellow," or "black" and find that their notion of race works for their purposes, they ignore its inaccuracies, inconsistencies, and other deficiencies.

Note, however, that only some facial and bodily features are selected for the lay definition of race. Some, like the color of women's nipples or the shape of toes (and male navels) cannot serve because they are kept covered. Most other visible ones, like height, weight, hairlines, ear lobes, finger or hand sizes—and even skin texture—vary too randomly and frequently to be useful for categorizing and ranking people or judging strangers. After all, your own child is apt to have the same stubby fingers as a child of another skin color or, what is equally important, a child from a very different income level.

race, class, and status

In fact, the skin colors and facial features commonly used to define race are selected precisely because, when arranged hierarchically, they resemble the country's class-and-status hierarchy. Thus, whites are on top of the socio-economic pecking order as they are on top of the racial one, while variously shaded nonwhites are below them in socioeconomic position (class) and prestige (status).

The darkest people are for the most part at the bottom of the class-status hierarchy. This is no accident, and Americans have therefore always used race as a marker or indicator of both class and status. Sometimes they also use it to enforce class position, to keep some people "in their place." Indeed, these uses are a major reason for its persistence.

Of course, race functions as more than a class marker, and the correlation between race and the socioeconomic pecking order is far from statistically perfect: All races can be found at every level of that order. Still, the race-class correlation is strong enough to utilize race for the general ranking of others. It also becomes more useful for ranking dark-skinned people as white poverty declines so much that whiteness becomes equivalent to being middle or upper class.

The relation between race and class is unmistakable. For example, the 1998–2000 median household income of non-Hispanic whites was $45,500; of Hispanics (currently seen by many as a race) as well as Native Americans, $32,000; and of African Americans, $29,000. The poverty rates for these same groups were 7.8 percent among whites, 23.1 among Hispanics, 23.9 among blacks, and 25.9 among Native Americans. (Asians' median income was $52,600—which does much to explain why we see them as a model minority.)

True, race is not the only indicator used as a clue to socioeconomic status. Others exist and are useful because they can also be applied to ranking co-racials. They include language (itself a rough indicator of education), dress, and

> When the descendants of the European immigrants began to move up economically and socially, their skins apparently began to look lighter.

various kinds of taste, from given names to cultural preferences, among others.

American English has no widely known working-class dialect like the English Cockney, although "Brooklynese" is a rough equivalent, as is "black vernacular." Most blue-collar people dress differently at work from white-collar, professional, and managerial workers. Although contemporary American leisure-time dress no longer signifies the wearer's class, middle-income Americans do not usually wear Armani suits or French haute couture, and the people who do can spot the knockoffs bought by the less affluent.

Actually, the cultural differences in language, dress, and so forth that were socially most noticeable are declining. Consequently, race could become yet more useful as a status marker, since it is so easily noticed and so hard to hide or change. And in a society that likes to see itself as classless, race comes in very handy as a substitute.

the historical background

Race became a marker of class and status almost with the first settling of the United States. The country's initial holders of cultural and political power were mostly WASPs (with a smattering of Dutch and Spanish in some parts of what later became the United States). They thus automatically assumed that their kind of whiteness marked the top of the class hierarchy. The bottom was assigned to the most powerless, who at first were Native Americans and slaves. However, even before the former had been virtually eradicated or pushed to the country's edges, the skin color and related facial features of the majority of colonial America's slaves had become the markers for the lowest class in the colonies.

Although dislike and fear of the dark are as old as the hills and found all over the world, the distinction between black and white skin became important in America only with slavery and was actually established only some decades after the first importation of black slaves. Originally, slave owners justified their enslavement of black Africans by their being heathens, not by their skin color.

In fact, early Southern plantation owners could have relied on white indentured servants to pick tobacco and cotton or purchased the white slaves that were available then, including the Slavs from whom the term *slave* is derived. They also had access to enslaved Native Americans. Blacks, however, were cheaper, more plentiful, more easily controlled, and physically more able to survive the intense heat and brutal working conditions of Southern plantations.

After slavery ended, blacks became farm laborers and sharecroppers, de facto indentured servants, really, and thus they remained at the bottom of the class hierarchy. When the pace of industrialization quickened, the country needed new sources of cheap labor. Northern industrialists, unable and unwilling to recruit southern African Americans, brought in very poor European immigrants, mostly peasants. Because these people were near the bottom of the class hierarchy, they were considered nonwhite and classified into races. Irish and Italian newcomers were sometimes even described as black (Italians as "guineas"), and the eastern and southern European immigrants were deemed "swarthy."

However, because skin color is socially constructed, it can also be reconstructed. Thus, when the descendants of the European immigrants began to move up economically and socially, their skins apparently began to look lighter to the whites who had come to America before them. When enough of these descendents became visibly middle class, their skin was seen as fully white. The biological skin color of the second and third generations had not changed, but it was socially blanched or whitened. The process probably began in earnest just before the Great Depression and resumed after World War II. As the cultural and other differences of the original European immigrants disappeared, their descendants became known as white ethnics.

This pattern is now repeating itself among the peoples of the post-1965 immigration. Many of the new immigrants came with money and higher education, and descriptions of their skin color have been shaped by their class position. Unlike the poor Chinese who were imported in the nineteenth century to build the West and who were hated and feared by whites as a "yellow horde," today's affluent Asian newcomers do not seem to look yellow. In fact, they are already sometimes thought of as honorary whites, and later in the twenty-first century they may well turn into a new set of white ethnics. Poor East and Southeast Asians may not be so privileged, however, although they are too few to be called a "yellow horde."

Hispanics are today's equivalent of a "swarthy" race. However, the children and grandchildren of immigrants among them will probably undergo "whitening" as they become middle class. Poor Mexicans, particularly in the Southwest, are less likely to be whitened, however. (Recently a WASP Harvard professor came close to describing these Mexican immigrants as a brown horde.)

Meanwhile, black Hispanics from Puerto Rico, the Dominican Republic, and other Caribbean countries may continue to be perceived, treated, and mistreated as if they were African American. One result of that mistreatment is their low median household income of $35,000, which was just $1,000 more than that of non-Hispanic blacks but $4,000 below that of so-called white Hispanics.

Perhaps South Asians provide the best example of how race correlates with class and how it is affected by class position. Although the highly educated Indians and Sri Lankans who started coming to America after 1965 were often darker than African Americans, whites only noticed their economic success. They have rarely been seen as nonwhites, and are also often praised as a model minority.

Of course, even favorable color perceptions have not ended racial discrimination against newcomers, including model minorities and other affluent ones. When they become competitors for valued resources such as highly paid jobs, top schools, housing, and the like, they also become a threat to whites. California's Japanese-Americans still suffer from discrimination and prejudice four generations after their ancestors arrived here.

african-american exceptionalism

The only population whose racial features are not automatically perceived differently with upward mobility are African Americans: Those who are affluent and well educated remain as visibly black to whites as before. Although a significant number of African Americans have become middle class since the civil rights legislation of the 1960s, they still suffer from far harsher and more pervasive discrimination and segregation than nonwhite immigrants of equivalent class position. This not only keeps whites and blacks apart but prevents blacks from moving toward equality with whites. In their case, race is used both as a marker of class and, by keeping blacks "in their place," an enforcer of class position and a brake on upward mobility.

In the white South of the past, African Americans were lynched for being "uppity." Today, the enforcement of class position is less deadly but, for example, the glass ceiling for professional and managerial African Americans is set lower than for Asian Americans, and on-the-job harassment remains routine.

Why African-American upward economic mobility is either blocked or, if allowed, not followed by public blanching of skin color remains a mystery. Many explanations have been proposed for the white exceptionalism with which African Americans are treated. The most common is "racism," an almost innate prejudice against people of different skin color that takes both personal and institutional forms. But this does not tell us why such prejudice toward African Americans remains stronger than that toward other nonwhites.

A second explanation is the previously mentioned white antipathy to blackness, with an allegedly primeval fear of darkness extrapolated into a primordial fear of dark-skinned people. But according to this explanation, dark-skinned immigrants such as South Asians should be treated much like African Americans.

A better explanation might focus on "Negroid" features. African as well as Caribbean immigrants with such features—for example, West Indians and Haitians—seem to be treated somewhat better than African Americans. But this remains true only for new immigrants; their children are generally treated like African Americans.

Two additional explanations are class-related. For generations, a majority or plurality of all African Americans were poor, and about a quarter still remain so. In addition, African Americans continue to commit a proportionally greater share of the street crime, especially street drug sales—often because legitimate job opportunities are scarce. African Americans are apparently also more often arrested without cause. As one result, poor African Americans are more often considered undeserving than are other poor people, although in some parts of America, poor Hispanics, especially those who are black, are similarly stigmatized.

The second class-based explanation proposes that white exceptionalist treatment of African Americans is a continuing effect of slavery: They are still perceived as ex-slaves. Many hateful stereotypes with which today's African Americans are demonized have changed little from those used to dehumanize the slaves. (Black Hispanics seem to be equally demonized, but then they were also slaves, if not on the North American continent.) Although slavery ended officially in 1864, ever since the end of Reconstruction subtle efforts to discourage African-American upward mobility have not abated, although these efforts are today much less pervasive or effective than earlier.

Some African Americans are now millionaires, but the gap in wealth between average African Americans and whites is much greater than the gap between incomes. The African-American middle class continues to grow, but many of its members barely have a toehold in it, and some are only a few paychecks away from a return to poverty. And the African-American poor still face the most formidable obstacles to upward mobility. Close to a majority of working-age African-American men are jobless or out of the labor force. Many women, including single mothers, now work in the low-wage economy, but they must do without most of the support systems that help middle-class working mothers. Both federal and state governments have been punitive, even in recent Democratic administrations, and the Republicans have cut back nearly every antipoverty program they cannot abolish.

Daily life in a white-dominated society reminds many African Americans that they are perceived as inferiors, and these reminders are louder and more relentless for the poor, especially young men. Regularly suspected of being criminals, they must constantly prove that they are worthy of equal access to the American Dream. For generations, African Americans have watched immigrants pass them in the class hierarchy, and those who are poor must continue to compete with current immigrants for the lowest-paying jobs. If unskilled African

Americans reject such jobs or fail to act as deferentially as immigrants, they justify the white belief that they are less deserving than immigrants. Blacks' resentment of such treatment gives whites additional evidence of their unworthiness, thereby justifying another cycle of efforts to keep them from moving up in class and status.

Such practices raise the suspicion that the white political economy and white Americans may, with the help of nonwhites who are not black, use African Americans to anchor the American class structure with a permanently lower-class population. In effect, America, or those making decisions in its name, could be seeking, not necessarily consciously, to establish an undercaste that cannot move out and up. Such undercastes exist in other societies: the gypsies of Eastern Europe, India's untouchables, "indigenous people" and "aborigines" in yet other places. But these are far poorer countries than the United States.

some implications

The conventional wisdom and its accompanying morality treat racial prejudice, discrimination, and segregation as irrational social and individual evils that public policy can reduce but only changes in white behavior and values can eliminate. In fact, over the years, white prejudice as measured by attitude surveys has dramatically declined, far more dramatically than behavioral and institutional discrimination.

But what if discrimination and segregation are more than just a social evil? If they are used to keep African Americans down, then they also serve to eliminate or restrain competitors for valued or scarce resources, material and symbolic. Keeping African Americans from decent jobs and incomes as well as quality schools and housing makes more of these available to all the rest of the population. In that case, discrimination and segregation may decline significantly only if the rules of the competition change or if scarce resources, such as decent jobs, become plentiful enough to relax the competition, so that the African-American population can become as predominantly middle class as the white population. Then the stigmas, the stereotypes inherited from slavery, and the social and other arrangements that maintain segregation and discrimination could begin to lose their credibility. Perhaps "black" skin would eventually become as invisible as "yellow" skin is becoming.

the multiracial future

One trend that encourages upward mobility is the rapid increase in interracial marriage that began about a quarter century ago. As the children born to parents of different races also intermarry, more and more Americans will be multiracial, so that at some point far in the future the current quintet of skin colors will be irrelevant. About 40 percent of young Hispanics and two-thirds of young Asians now "marry out," but only about 10 percent of blacks now marry nonblacks—yet another instance of the exceptionalism that differentiates blacks.

Moreover, if race remains a class marker, new variations in skin color and in other visible bodily features will be taken to indicate class position. Thus, multiracials with "Negroid" characteristics could still find themselves disproportionately at the bottom of the class hierarchy. But what if at some point in the future everyone's skin color varied by only a few shades of brown? At that point, the dominant American classes might have to invent some new class markers.

If in some utopian future the class hierarchy disappears, people will probably stop judging differences in skin color and other features. Then lay Americans would probably agree with biologists that race does not exist. They might even insist that race does not need to exist.

RECOMMENDED RESOURCES

David Brion Davis. *Challenging the Boundaries of Slavery* (Harvard University Press, 2001).

> A historical account of the relation between race and slavery.

Joe R. Feagin and Melvin P. Sikes. *Living with Racism: The Black Middle-Class Experience* (Beacon, 1994).

> Documents continuing discrimination against middle- and upper-middle-class African Americans.

Barbara Jeanne Fields. "Slavery, Race and Ideology in the United States of America." *New Left Review* 181 (May/June 1990): 95–118.

> A provocative analysis of the relations between class and race.

Marvin Harris. "How Our Skins Got Their Color." In *Who We Are, Where We Came From, and Where We Are Going* (HarperCollins, 1989).

> An anthropologist explains the origins of different skin colors.

Jennifer Lee and Frank D. Bean. "Beyond Black and White: Remaking Race in America." *Contexts* (Summer 2003): 26–33.

> A concise analysis of changing perceptions and realities of race in America.

REVIEW QUESTIONS

1. What does Gans mean when he conceptualizes "race as class"? How does he use South Asians as perhaps "the best example" of how race correlates with class?
2. Gans writes about how commonplace assumptions obscure particular instances that might conflict with our racial stereotypes (e.g., poor whites and wealthy African Americans), and he rejects psychological and physiological explanations of racism. In the place of such explanations he offers two class-based formulations. What are they?
3. Gans offers several possible solutions to the social problem of race. Which ones do you feel are the most persuasive? Discuss and defend your position.
4. Activity: African-American feminist Bell Hooks writes about how multiple social systems intersect with each other to create multiple levels of oppression. In addition to racism, what other -ism's can you list? How do these -ism's interact with one another?

mikaila mariel lemonik arthur

race in america

37

fall 2005

	White	Hispanic	Black	Asian
Percentage of population, 2003	67.9	13.7	12.2	4.0
Median household net worth, 2000	$67,000	$6,766	$6,166	n/a
Home ownership rates, 2004	76.0	48.1	49.1	59.8
Median household income, 2000–2002	$47,194	$33,946	$29,982	$55,113
Average per capita income, 2003	$24,626	$13,492	$15,775	$24,604
April 2005 unemployment rate	4.4	6.4	10.4	4.4
Average percentage in poverty, 2001–2003	8.0	21.9	23.7	10.7
Percentage over 25 with high school diploma	83.6	52.4	72.3	80.4
Percentage white in school attended by typical student of this race, 2002	79.0	28.2	30.5	45.4
Percentage of men ever incarcerated, 2001	2.6	7.7	16.6	n/a
Percentage of murder victims, 2002–2003	49	14	49	>3
Age-adjusted death rate from AIDS, 2002	2.1	5.8	23.0	n/a
Age-adjusted death rate from cancer, 2002	195.6	128.4	242.5	n/a
Infant mortality rates, 2002	5.7	5.6	13.8	4.8
Percentage who voted, 2002	48.0	18.9	39.7	19.4
Percentage who voted for Bush, 2004	58	44	11	44

Sources may be found at www.contextsmagazine.org.

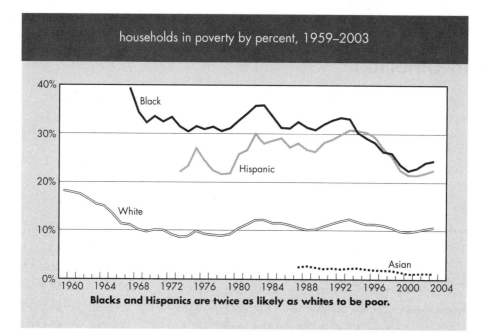

households in poverty by percent, 1959–2003

Black

Hispanic

White

Asian

Blacks and Hispanics are twice as likely as whites to be poor.

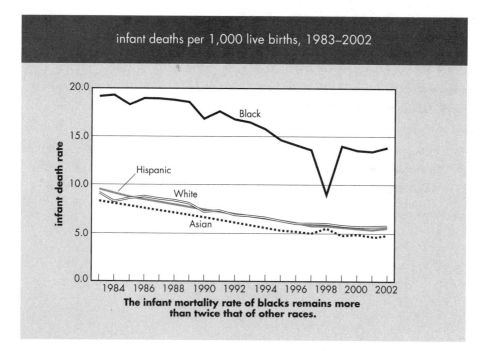

infant deaths per 1,000 live births, 1983–2002

infant death rate

Black

Hispanic

White

Asian

The infant mortality rate of blacks remains more than twice that of other races.

270   race and ethnicity

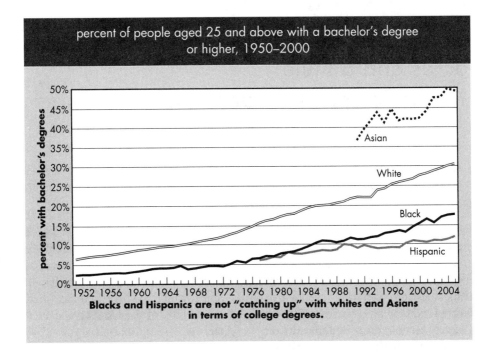

percent of people aged 25 and above with a bachelor's degree or higher, 1950–2000

Blacks and Hispanics are not "catching up" with whites and Asians in terms of college degrees.

REVIEW QUESTIONS

1. Write a paragraph on the first table. Are there any data you find surprising or provocative? Describe a research project that might be organized around two particular measures.

2. Note that while the median household income (2000–2002) of whites and blacks is less than twice as much as the average per capita income (2003), it is much more than twice as much for Hispanics and Asians. There are several possible reasons for such a finding, but what do you think is the most likely reason for this difference?

3. Why do you think blacks and Hispanics are not catching up with whites and Asians in terms of college degrees? What might this suggest about the future of racial inequality in the United States?

dalton conley

forty acres and a mule: what if america pays reparations?

38

fall 2002

in the present political climate, slavery reparations remain a remote dream of activists. but it is still worthwhile to do the math, if not for the purpose of actual payments, at least for what the numbers reveal about race and equal opportunity in america.

Marching across the Confederacy in 1865, Union soldiers seized large amounts of so-called abandoned property. The Freedmen's Bureau, the administrating agency for confiscated property, held an estimated 800,000 to 900,000 acres. Some radical Republicans on the Congressional Committee on Reconstruction hoped to use these properties to provide freed slaves with the now-legendary "40 acres and a mule" as restitution for slavery. This promise of economic self-sufficiency never came close to becoming law.

Instead, the lion's share of confiscated plantations went to white northerners who hired the former slaves to cultivate them, inaugurating the system of sharecropping that disadvantaged so many African Americans over the following century. Not only did former slaves fail to receive significant land or money as compensation for their toil; after the Civil War, Jim Crow regimes in the South and racially biased policies elsewhere led to new institutional barriers to black economic progress. Is now the time to set these accounts straight—providing African Americans with the proverbial

> Would whites who immigrated after slavery ended have to pay? Would their black counterparts be entitled to payments? And what about the descendants of blacks who lived as free individuals during the antebellum period? The free blacks who owned slaves themselves?

"40 acres and a mule" as compensation for the legacy of slavery? Politics will answer that question. However, exploring what 40 acres and a mule would be worth today sheds light on how racial differences emerged and persist in America.

contemporary debates

The issue of reparations has recently made another comeback. Armed with precedents such as payments to Japanese Americans for internment during World War II and the claims of Holocaust victims on Swiss banks for lost accounts, the most recent discourse on slavery restitution is more legalistic in tone and, as such, has been the most effective to date. For example, at least 10 cities—including Washington, D.C., and Chicago—have passed resolutions urging the federal government to take action on this issue. A new California law requires insurance companies that do business in the state to research their past to determine whether they offered policies insuring slave capital. Aetna, one of the largest insurance companies in the United States, has issued an apology for having done just that. Editorials and feature stories calling for a serious examination of the reparations possibility have cropped up with increasing frequency. Perhaps most important, a group of prominent legal scholars, litigators, and advocates, such as Harvard Law Professor Charles Ogletree and TransAfrica Corporation founder Randall Robinson, have declared their intention to bring class action suits against the government and corporations that benefited from America's "peculiar institution" (the first suit has now been filed against three companies, including Aetna). Even conservative pundits have argued for reparations as a way to end affirmative action. As Charles Krauthammer wrote in *Time* magazine, "It's time for a historic compromise: a monetary reparation to blacks for centuries of racial oppression in return for the total abolition of all programs of racial preference."

There are several important issues to sort out in this debate. Practical concerns—who would receive payments and how much they would get—blend with larger issues about race and ascription (that is, assignment to a social status by virtue of birth). Had the proverbial 40 acres and a mule been real rather than rhetorical compensation, many of these issues would not have to be addressed. Back in the mid-nineteenth century, for example, payments could have been extracted from Southern plantations, targeting most directly those who benefited from the chattel labor. Most important, payments could have been made directly to the victims of slavery rather than to their descendants. Fourteen decades later everything gets a lot more complicated.

how much?

Perhaps the simplest argument for reparations is that they are payment of back wages for slave labor. This was the underlying rationale the black power movement used in the 1970s. One researcher took slave prices during the period from 1790 to 1860 as proxies for the value of slave capital and projected that, given compound interest, the total value in 1970 was from $448 billion to $995 billion. Merely adjusted for inflation, this sum would translate to a range of $2 trillion to almost $4 trillion today (which, incidentally, was within budget surplus estimates in 2000, if paid out over six to eight years). The 1970 price happened to match the $400 billion sum that was being demanded around the same time by a prominent black separatist movement called the Republic of New Africa (RNA). The RNA also demanded sovereignty over five southern states: Alabama, Georgia, Louisiana, Mississippi, and South Carolina (which the researcher estimated to be worth $350 billion at the time).

If reparations were paid directly to the exslaves themselves, one might follow this strategy of imputing a fair wage, or splitting the profits made from the industries in which they toiled, then adding on sums for pain and suffering and lost future earnings. Even one generation later, the heirs of the slaves could be compensated as representatives of the estate.

However, this approach presents a number of difficulties six or more generations later. Using compound interest only works when we assume an unbroken chain of birth from slaves to the current African-American population, from slaveholders to today's white Americans. Would whites who immigrated after slavery ended have to pay? Would their black counterparts be entitled to payments? And what about the descendants of blacks who lived as free individuals during the antebellum period? The free blacks who owned slaves themselves? Then, of course, there is the issue of racial mixing. Would children born to a white parent and a black parent pay a reparations tax or receive a reparations payout?

is slavery a proxy for race, or race a proxy for slavery?

These questions raise the larger issue of whether being black is a good proxy for descending from slaves and, therefore, being entitled to restitution. On the one hand, Americans of all races have ancestors of various races. On the other hand, the way that race has long been classified in the United States, commonly known as the one-drop rule, suggests that African American racial identity should act as a proxy for slave ancestry since it is socially defined that way by the government. (The one-drop rule states that if either parent of a child has any black "blood" the child is classified as black.) Or, to turn this question around, we could assume that slavery stands for the sum total of oppression and discrimination that blacks have experienced in America, both before and after 1865. Are these other disadvantages not to be remedied through financial restitution as well?

One approach to the question stresses that slavery was a foundation of America's current wealth. Whether people's families arrived in 1700 or in 2000, they benefit today from businesses, such as the cotton garment industry, that profited from slave labor. Conversely, blacks in America, regardless of when their families arrived, live with the stigma and burdens that are the legacy of slavery (while gaining a disproportionately small share of its benefits).

One could persuasively argue that most black-white inequality in contemporary America is a direct result of slavery because it stripped African Americans of their ethnic honor. All other Americans are linked to a particular immigrant (or Native-American) group and therefore to a particular nation of peoples. Slavery wiped out this sense of nationhood as slaveholders purposely mixed slaves of various tribal origins. This lack of national heritage and ethnic honor places African Americans at the bottom of the racial-ethnic hierarchy in the United States. Combined with other stigmatizing aspects of slavery, this loss of ethnicity may make all black-white inequality today directly attributable to slavery, whether or not particular individual blacks or whites had ancestors in the United States before abolition. This wider interpretation of the legacy of slavery would legitimate a claim for "symbolic damages" or "group pain and suffering" in addition to back wages.

calculating reparations from the wealth gap

Given a rationale for paying reparations to twenty-first-century blacks without having to link particular individuals back to slave ancestors, we can turn to calculating the right amount. Property values offer a potentially simple procedure because they are often used as a direct measure of tort damages. For instance, if a chemical company spills its wares in my community, making my home unlivable, I am entitled to the home's full value (plus some amount for pain and suffering). Similarly, one could choose to view the wealth gap between blacks and whites as a result of slavery, both lost wages and long-term consequences.

In fact, if there were one statistic that captured the persistence of racial inequality in the United States, it would be net worth—also known as wealth, equity, or assets. (If you want to know your net worth, add up everything you own and subtract from this figure your outstanding debt.) The typical white family enjoys a net worth more than seven times greater than that of a typical nonwhite family. The wealth gap cannot be explained by annual income differences alone and is therefore distinct from current racial or class conditions. That is, while African Americans as a group earn less than whites, even when we compare black and white families that earn the same income, differences in assets remain large. For instance, among families earning under $15,000, the typical African-American family has a net worth of zero, while the typical white family holds $10,000 worth of equity. This is also true among the often-heralded new black middle class. The typical white family that earns $40,000 per year enjoys a nest egg of around $80,000. Its African-American counterpart has less than half that amount.

Why are these gaps so large, even among families with the same income levels? Some pundits—and many white Americans—believe that blacks perpetuate an oppositional culture that works to their own disadvantage. This culture, they argue, encourages spending at the cost of savings, an anti-intellectual attitude in school, and overall hostility to mainstream social institutions including the financial sector. Some theorists believe that this culture arose from slavery and oppression but has now become self-perpetuating. Others see what they often call "underclass" behavioral patterns as genetically determined. The overwhelming majority of evidence, however, refutes these claims. Several studies have shown that black and white savings rates, for example, are indistinguishable. Surveys also show that blacks value education as much as, if not more than, whites.

Rather, wealth, more than other measures of economic status, captures the long-term, multi-generational scars of prior inequality and is not easily erased by measures intended to guarantee equal opportunity. "Equity inequity" is, in part, the result of the head start that whites have enjoyed in accumulating and passing on assets. Whites not only earn more now, but they have always earned more than African Americans—a lot more—which, in turn, feeds wealth differences. Some researchers estimate that up to 80 percent of lifetime wealth results from gifts in one form or another from past generations of relatives. These gifts can range from the down payment on a first home, to a free college education, to a bequest upon the death of a parent. Over the long run, small racial differences in wealth holdings widen rapidly, especially when combined with barriers to black property accumulation (such as the "black codes" of the nineteenth century and the housing and credit discrimination of the twentieth and twenty-first centuries). Even if equal opportunity was finally here, equal wealth would take a while to achieve.

> If it is not just parental wealth that matters but also other attributes such as parental education and race itself . . . slavery would continue to find wormholes through which to wiggle its effects into the future.

If we take the broad view that all wealth inequality between blacks and whites today is directly or indirectly a result of slavery, then there might be an argument that whites should transfer 13 percent of their private wealth to blacks to close the gap. However, we may wish to distinguish between the earnings of the current generation and the legacy of past injustice (since we already have some policies in place to address current conditions, such as affirmative action). Since about half of the black-white wealth gap is attributable to current income and demographic differences, this would suggest a payment half as large. We could use another, yet more conservative approach. Using the estimate mentioned earlier that 80 percent of our wealth can be attributed in one form or another to our parents' generation, we would find that six generations after 1865, about 25 percent of the distribution of wealth today is explained by the distribution of wealth at the time of emancipation. Correcting for this much of the gap would rectify only the wealth inequalities associated directly with slavery, not with Jim Crow, sharecropping, racial violence, housing segregation, or labor, educational, and credit discrimination that has occurred since 1865.

what if, what then?

Behind each of these numbers is a theoretical assumption and a rationalization for what is essentially an irrational political process. (That includes the number implicit in the present policy: zero.) That said, numbers and logics still matter since they provide the grist for the political process. Each year, Representative John Conyers, Jr. (D-Michigan) introduces a bill to provide slavery restitution to African Americans, and every year, it goes nowhere.

What would it take to get from symbolic resolutions and theoretical calculations to a signed bill with appropriated funds? A lot. Reparations combine two policies that have been wildly unpopular in America: taxes and group preferences. In fact, property taxes—the most logical mechanism by which wealth could be redistributed—are the least popular form of taxation, even though they are generally more progressive than income or consumption taxes. Property tax revolts have occurred in political communities as diverse as Ronald Reagan's California (Proposition 13) and social-democratic Denmark. This is perhaps because private property has come to be seen as a natural right. So, if white resentment of affirmative action is strong and getting stronger, one can only imagine the backlash that would result from racially based wealth redistribution. Reparations activists, therefore, would be wise to launder the money well. That is, to the extent that reparations come from general, existing revenue sources, they would seem less like a direct transfer from individual to individual. Of course, there is a tension between the size of reparations and the ability to finance them without a direct and obviously new tax.

But what if America did overcome the political obstacles to reparations? What would be their effect? The answer, of course, depends on which plan we were to opt for and what you believe the effects of money are on life chances. For the sake of argument, let us assume we took the most radical option and completely equalized black-white wealth levels. Some research shows that when you compare blacks and whites who grew up in households with the same wealth levels, racial gaps in children's educational attainment evaporate. For example, my own study shows that when we compare African Americans and whites who come from families with the same net worth, blacks are, in fact, more likely to finish high school than their white counterparts and just as likely to complete a four-year college degree. Similarly, black-white differences in using welfare disappear when parental wealth is taken into account. However, the jury is still out on whether the black-white wealth gap accounts for other racial differences, such as health and life expectancy, test scores, occupational attainment and even wealth levels themselves.

If parental wealth levels really do determine life chances—and it is not just that parents who have wealth also are the ones who can produce good students, for instance—then we should expect racial gaps in education to close in one generation. However, if it is not just parental wealth that matters but also other attributes such as parental education and race itself, then we are back to where we started from—an unlevel playing field in which we slowly accrete greater and greater inequalities over generations. In that case, slavery would continue to find wormholes through which to wiggle its effects into the future. This second possibility argues for equalizing black-white wealth levels and keeping affirmative action policies to address the lingering, indirect consequences of being black in America.

Of course, all policies generate unintended consequences. For example, windfall payments may reduce savings rates among the recipient population. They may also cause people to opt out of jobs they do not like. If large enough, reparations may even cause a big bump in consumer spending. Perhaps the most worrisome, however, is the question of how to turn a one-time payment into a stable and growing equity base for African-American families. This is particularly an issue for the income-poor (among whom blacks are over represented), who have enormous day-to-day financial pressures that could soak up the rising tide reparations are meant to provide. As fast as progressives can think up ways to redistribute resources to underprivileged groups, the capital and credit markets are even faster at inventing ways to extract money from them. Predatory lenders target homeowners who may need cash for current expenses, draining their equity away. And check-cashing establishments are the fastest-growing sector of the banking industry. One can only imagine what kind of new financial industries would emerge if significant wealth redistribution were to occur.

That said, it is still important to try and envision what America would be like had the original promise of 40 acres and a mule been more than just words—even if a century or two late.

RECOMMENDED RESOURCES

Robert Browne. "The Economic Case for Reparations to Black America." *American Economic Review* 62 (1972): 39–46.
> A calculation of the value of slave labor.

Dalton Conley. *Being Black, Living in the Red: Race, Wealth and Social Policy in America* (University of California Press, 1999).
> An overview of the centrality of wealth to understanding racial dynamics in other arenas.

Dalton Conley. "Decomposing the Black-White Wealth Gap: The Role of Parental Resources, Inheri-

tance and Investment Dynamics." *Sociological Inquiry* 71 (Winter 2001): 39–66.
> Evidence on the persistence of the wealth gap that challenges *Being Black, Living in the Red.*

Laurence J. Kotlikoff and Lawrence H. Summers. "The Role of Intergenerational Transfers in Aggregate Capital Accumulation." *Journal of Political Economy* 89 (August 1981): 706–32.
> High-end estimate of the role of progenitors in wealth accumulation.

Paul L. Menchik and Nancy A. Jianakoplos. "Black-White Wealth Inequality: Is Inheritance the Reason?" *Economic Inquiry* 35 (April 1997): 428–42,
> A detailed analysis of the role of inheritance, narrowly construed.

Franco Modigliani. "The Role of Intergenerational Transfers and Life Cycle Saving in the Accumulation of Wealth." *Journal of Economic Perspectives* 2 (Spring 1988): 15–40.
> A more conservative accounting of the role of past wealth in explaining current wealth.

Melvin Oliver and Thomas Shapiro. *Black Wealth/White Wealth* (Routledge, 1994).
> A good summary of the history of the asset gap.

Randal Robinson. *The Debt: What America Owes to Blacks* (Dutton, 2000).
> A well-argued polemic making the case for reparations.

REVIEW QUESTIONS

1. Conley uses "net worth" to illustrate racial inequality. What is net worth? Why is it a more powerful measure of inequality than income?
2. Write a paragraph on the strongest arguments for paying reparations to blacks who came to the United States after abolition, and another paragraph on the strongest arguments for

compelling whites whose descendents arrived after abolition to pay reparations.

3. According to Conley, if we were able to level the playing field, there would be a great effect on the next generation because equality in parental wealth affects equality in education and life chances. How does he see slavery "wiggling into" future racial concerns, despite reparations? What else makes this solution a problematic one?

min zhou

are asian americans becoming "white"?   **39**

winter 2004

asian americans have been labeled a "model minority" for their high rates of achievement, and some say they are on their way to becoming "white." but these expectations can be a burden, and the predictions are surely premature. even today, many americans see asians as "forever foreign."

"I never asked to be white. I am not literally white. That is, I do not have white skin or white ancestors. I have yellow skin and yellow ancestors, hundreds of generations of them. But like so many other Asian Americans of the second generation, I find myself now the bearer of a strange new status: white, by acclamation. Thus it is that I have been described as an 'honorary white,' by other whites, and as a 'banana' by other Asians . . . to the extent that I have moved away from the periphery and toward the center of American life, I have become white inside."
—Eric Liu, The Accidental Asian (p. 34)

Are Asian Americans becoming "white"? For many public officials the answer must be yes, because they classify Asian-origin Americans with European-origin Americans for equal opportunity programs. But this classification is premature and based on false premises. Although Asian Americans as a group have attained the career and financial success equated with being white, and although many have moved next to or have even married whites, they still remain culturally distinct and suspect in a white society.

At issue is how to define *Asian American* and *white*. The term *Asian American* was coined by the late historian and activist Yuji Ichioka during the ethnic consciousness movements of the late 1960s. To adopt this identity was to reject the Western-imposed label of "Oriental." Today, "Asian American" is an umbrella category that includes both U.S. citizens and immigrants whose ancestors came from Asia, east of Iran. Although widely used in public discussions, most Asian-origin Americans are ambivalent about this label, reflecting the difficulty of being American and still keeping some ethnic identity: Is one, for example, Asian American or Japanese American?

Similarly, white is an arbitrary label having more to do with privilege than biology. In the United States, groups initially considered nonwhite, such as the Irish and Jews, have attained "white" membership by acquiring status and wealth. It is hardly surprising, then, that nonwhites would aspire to becoming "white" as a mark of and a tool for material success. However, becoming white can mean distancing oneself from "people of color" or disowning one's ethnicity. Pan-ethnic identities—Asian American, African American, Hispanic American—are one way the politically vocal in any group try to stem defections. But these group identities may restrain individual members' aspirations for personal advancement.

varieties of asian americans

Privately, few Americans of Asian ancestry would spontaneously identify themselves as

Asian, and fewer still as Asian American. They instead link their identities to specific countries of origin, such as China, Japan, Korea, the Philippines, India, or Vietnam. In a study of Vietnamese youth in San Diego, for example, 53 percent identified themselves as Vietnamese, 32 percent as Vietnamese American, and only 14 percent as Asian American. But they did not take these labels lightly; nearly 60 percent of these youth considered their chosen identity as very important to them.

Some Americans of Asian ancestry have family histories in the United States longer than many Americans of Eastern or Southern European origin. However, Asian-origin Americans became numerous only after 1970, rising from 1.4 million to 11.9 million (4 percent of the total U.S. population), in 2000. Before 1970, the Asian-origin population was largely made up of Japanese, Chinese, and Filipinos. Now, Americans of Chinese and Filipino ancestries are the largest subgroups (at 2.8 million and 2.4 million, respectively), followed by Indians, Koreans, Vietnamese, and Japanese (at more than one million). Some 20 other national-origin groups, such as Cambodians, Pakistanis, Laotians, Thai, Indonesians, and Bangladeshis, were officially counted in government statistics only after 1980; together they amounted to more than two million Americans in 2000.

The sevenfold growth of the Asian-origin population in the span of 30-odd years is primarily due to accelerated immigration following the Hart-Celler Act of 1965, which ended the national origins quota system, and the historic resettlement of Southeast Asian refugees after the Vietnam War. Currently, about 60 percent of the Asian-origin population is foreign-born (the first generation), another 28 percent are U.S.-born of foreign-born parents (the second generation), and just 12 percent were born to U.S.-born parents (the third generation and beyond).

Unlike earlier immigrants from Asia or Europe, who were mostly low-skilled laborers looking for work, today's immigrants from Asia have more varied backgrounds and come for many reasons, such as to join their families, to invest their money in the U.S. economy, to fill the demand for highly skilled labor, or to escape war, political or religious persecution, and economic hardship. For example, Chinese, Taiwanese, Indian, and Filipino Americans tend to be overrepresented among scientists, engineers, physicians, and other skilled professionals, but less-educated, low-skilled workers are more common among Vietnamese, Cambodian, Laotian, and Hmong Americans, most of whom entered the United States as refugees. While middle-class immigrants are able to start their American lives with high-paying professional careers and comfortable suburban lives, low-skilled immigrants and refugees often have to endure low-paying menial jobs and live in inner-city ghettos.

Asian Americans tend to settle in large metropolitan areas and concentrate in the West. California is home to 35 percent of all Asian Americans. But recently, other states such as Texas, Minnesota, and Wisconsin, which historically received few Asian immigrants, have become destinations for Asian American settlement. Traditional ethnic enclaves, such as Chinatown, Little Tokyo, Manilatown, Koreatown, Little Phnom Penh, and Thaitown, persist or have emerged in gateway cities, helping new arrivals to cope with cultural and linguistic difficulties. However, affluent and highly skilled immigrants tend to bypass inner-city enclaves and settle in suburbs upon arrival, belying the stereotype of the "unacculturated" immigrant. Today, more than half of the Asian-origin population is spreading out in suburbs surrounding traditional gateway cities, as well as in new urban centers of Asian settlement across the country.

Differences in national origins, timing of immigration, affluence, and settlement patterns profoundly inhibit the formation of a pan-ethnic identity. Recent arrivals are less likely than those born or raised in the United States to identify as Asian American. They are also so busy settling in that they have little time to think about being Asian or Asian American, or, for that matter, white. Their diverse origins include drastic differences in languages and dialects, religions, cuisines, and customs. Many national groups also bring to America their histories of conflict (such as the Japanese colonization of Korea and Taiwan, Japanese attacks on China, and the Chinese invasion of Vietnam).

Immigrants who are predominantly middle-class professionals, such as the Taiwanese and Indians, or predominantly small business owners, such as the Koreans, share few of the same concerns and priorities as those who are predominantly uneducated, low-skilled refugees, such as Cambodians and Hmong. Finally, Asian-origin people living in San Francisco or Los Angeles among many other Asians and self-conscious Asian Americans develop a stronger ethnic identity than those living in predominantly Latin Miami or predominantly European Minneapolis. A politician might get away with calling Asians "Oriental" in Miami but get into big trouble in San Francisco. All of these differences create obstacles to fostering a cohesive pan-Asian solidarity. As Yen Le Espiritu shows, pan-Asianism is primarily a political ideology of U.S.-born, American-educated, middle-class Asians rather than of Asian immigrants, who are conscious of their national origins and overburdened with their daily struggles for survival.

underneath the model minority: "white" or "other"

The celebrated "model minority" image of Asian Americans appeared in the mid-1960s, at the peak of the civil rights and the ethnic consciousness movements, but before the rising waves of immigration and refugee influx from Asia. Two articles in 1966—"Success Story, Japanese-American Style," by William Petersen in the *New York Times Magazine*, and "Success of One Minority Group in U.S.," by the *U.S. News & World Report* staff—marked a significant departure from how Asian immigrants and their descendants had been traditionally depicted in the media. Both articles congratulated Japanese and Chinese Americans on their persistence in overcoming extreme hardships and discrimination to achieve success, unmatched even by U.S.-born whites, with "their own almost totally unaided effort" and "no help from anyone else." (The implicit contrast to other minorities was clear.) The press attributed their winning wealth and respect in American society to hard work, family solidarity, discipline, delayed gratification, nonconfrontation, and eschewing welfare.

This "model minority" image remains largely unchanged even in the face of new and diverse waves of immigration. The 2000 U.S. Census shows that Asian Americans continue to score remarkable economic and educational achievements. Their median household income in 1999 was more than $55,000—the highest of all racial groups, including whites—and their poverty rate was under 11 percent, the lowest of all racial groups. Moreover, 44 percent of all Asian Americans over 25 years of age had at least a bachelor's degree, 18 percentage points more than any other racial group. Strikingly, young Asian Americans, including both the children of foreign-born physicians, scientists, and professionals and those of uneducated and penniless refugees, repeatedly appear as high school valedictorians and academic decathlon winners. They also enroll in the freshman classes of prestigious universities in disproportionately large numbers. In 1998, Asian Americans, just 4 percent of the nation's population, made up more than 20 percent of the undergraduates at universities such as

Berkeley, Stanford, MIT, and Cal Tech. Although some ethnic groups, such as Cambodians, Lao, and Hmong, still trail behind other East and South Asians in most indicators of achievement, they too show significant signs of upward mobility. Many in the media have dubbed Asian Americans the "new Jews." Like the second-generation Jews of the past, today's children of Asian immigrants are climbing up the ladder by way of extraordinary educational achievement.

One consequence of the model-minority stereotype is that it reinforces the myth that the United States is devoid of racism and accords equal opportunity to all, fostering the view that those who lag behind do so because of their own poor choices and inferior culture. Celebrating "model minorities" can help impede other racial minorities' demands for social justice by pitting minority groups against each other. It can also pit Asian Americans against whites. On the surface, Asian Americans seem to be on their way to becoming white, just like the offspring of earlier European immigrants. But the model-minority image implicitly casts Asian Americans as different from whites. By placing Asian Americans above whites, this image still sets them apart from other Americans, white or nonwhite, in the public mind.

There are two other less obvious effects. The model-minority stereotype holds Asian Americans to higher standards, distinguishing them from average Americans. "What's wrong with being a model minority?" a black student once asked, in a class I taught on race, "I'd rather be in the model minority than in the downtrodden minority that nobody respects." Whether people are in a model minority or a downtrodden minority, they are still judged by standards different from average Americans. Also, the model-minority stereotype places particular expectations on members of the group so labeled, channeling them to specific avenues of success,

such as science and engineering. This, in turn, makes it harder for Asian Americans to pursue careers outside these designated fields. Falling into this trap, a Chinese immigrant father gets upset when his son tells him he has changed his major from engineering to English. Disregarding his son's talent for creative writing, such a father rationalizes his concern, "You have a 90 percent chance of getting a decent job with an engineering degree, but what chance would you have of earning income as a writer?" This thinking represents more than typical parental concern; it constitutes the self-fulfilling prophecy of a stereotype.

The celebration of Asian Americans rests on the perception that their success is unexpectedly high. The truth is that unusually many of them, particularly among the Chinese, Indians, and Koreans, arrive as middle-class or upper-middle-class immigrants. This makes it easier for them and their children to succeed and regain their middle-class status in their new homeland. The financial resources that these immigrants bring also subsidize ethnic businesses and services, such as private after-school programs. These, in turn, enable even the less fortunate members of the groups to move ahead more quickly than they would have otherwise.

not so much being "white" as being american

Most Asian Americans seem to accept that "white" is mainstream, average, and normal, and they look to whites as a frame of reference for attaining higher social positions. Similarly, researchers often use non-Hispanic whites as the standard against which other groups are compared, even though there is great diversity among whites, too. Like most immigrants to the United States, Asian immigrants tend to believe in the American Dream and measure their achievements materially. As a Chinese immigrant said to me in an interview, "I hope to accomplish nothing but three things: to own a home, to be my own boss, and to send my children to the Ivy League." Those with sufficient education, job skills, and money manage to move into white middle-class suburban neighborhoods immediately upon arrival, while others work intensively to accumulate enough savings to move their families up and out of inner-city ethnic enclaves. Consequently, many children of Asian ancestry have lived their entire childhood in white communities, made friends with mostly white peers, and grown up speaking only English. In fact, Asian Americans are the most acculturated non-European group in the United States. By the second generation, most have lost fluency in their parents' native languages (see "English-Only Triumphs, But the Costs Are High," *Contexts*, Spring 2002). David Lopez finds that in Los Angeles, more than three-quarters of second-generation Asian Americans (as opposed to one-quarter of second-generation Mexicans) speak only English at home. Asian Americans also intermarry extensively with whites and with members of other minority groups. Jennifer Lee and Frank Bean find that more than one-quarter of married Asian Americans have a partner of a different racial background, and 87 percent of those marry whites; they also find that 12 percent of all Asian Americans claim a multiracial background, compared to 2 percent of whites and 4 percent of blacks.

Even though U.S.-born or U.S.-raised Asian Americans are relatively acculturated and often intermarry with whites, they may be more ambivalent about becoming white than their immigrant parents. Many only cynically agree that "white" is synonymous with "American." A Vietnamese high school student in New Orleans told me in an interview, "An American is white. You often hear people say, hey, so-and-so is dating an 'American.' You know she's dating a

white boy. If he were black, then people would say he's black." But while they recognize whites as a frame of reference, some reject the idea of becoming white themselves: "It's not so much being white as being American," commented a Korean-American student in my class on the new second generation. This aversion to becoming white is particularly common among second-generation college students who have taken ethnic studies courses, and among Asian-American community activists. However, most of the second generation continues to strive for the privileged status associated with whiteness, just like their parents. For example, most U.S.-born or U.S.-raised Chinese-American youth end up studying engineering, medicine, or law in college, believing that these areas of study guarantee a middle-class life.

Second-generation Asian Americans are also more conscious of the disadvantages associated with being nonwhite than their parents, who as immigrants tend to be optimistic about overcoming the disadvantages of this status. As a Chinese-American woman points out from her own experience, "The truth is, no matter how American you think you are or try to be, if you have almond-shaped eyes, straight black hair, and a yellow complexion, you are a foreigner by default . . . You can certainly be as good as or even better than whites, but you will never become accepted as white." This remark echoes a commonly held frustration among second-generation, U.S.-born Asians who detest being treated as immigrants or foreigners. Their experience suggests that whitening has more to do with the beliefs of white America than with the actual situation of Asian Americans. Speaking perfect English, adopting mainstream cultural values, and even intermarrying members of the dominant group may help reduce this "otherness" for particular individuals, but it has little effect on the group as a whole. New stereotypes can emerge and un-whiten Asian Americans, no matter how "successful" and "assimilated" they have become. For example, Congressman David Wu once was invited by the Asian-American employees of the U.S. Department of Energy to give a speech in celebration of Asian-American Heritage Month. Yet, he and his Asian-American staff were not allowed into the department building, even after presenting their congressional identification, and were repeatedly asked about their citizenship and country of origin. They were told that this was standard procedure for the Department of Energy and that a congressional ID card was not a reliable document. The next day, a congressman of Italian descent was allowed to enter the same building with his congressional ID, no questions asked.

The stereotype of the "honorary white" or model minority goes hand-in-hand with that of the "forever foreigner." Today, globalization and U.S.–Asia relations, combined with continually high rates of immigration, affect how Asian Americans are perceived in American society. Many historical stereotypes, such as the "yellow peril" and "Fu Manchu" still exist in contemporary American life, as revealed in such highly publicized incidents as the murder of Vincent Chin, a Chinese American mistaken for Japanese and beaten to death by a disgruntled white auto worker in the 1980s; the trial of Wen Ho Lee, a nuclear scientist suspected of spying for the Chinese government in the mid 1990s; the 1996 presidential campaign finance scandal, which implicated Asian Americans in funneling foreign contributions to the Clinton campaign; and most recently, in 2001, the Abercrombie & Fitch t-shirts that depicted Asian cartoon characters in stereotypically negative ways, with slanted eyes, thick glasses, and heavy Asian accents. Ironically, the ambivalent, conditional nature of their acceptance by whites prompts many Asian Americans to organize pan-ethnically to fight back—which consequently heightens their racial distinctiveness. So becoming white or not

is beside the point. The bottom line is: Americans of Asian ancestry still have to constantly prove that they truly are loyal Americans.

RECOMMENDED RESOURCES

John Horton. *The Politics of Diversity: Immigration, Resistance, and Change in Monterey Park, California* (Temple University Press, 1995).

> This study of a Chinese immigrant community in an affluent Los Angeles suburb explores how new immigrants confront resistance from more established Anglo, Asian-American, and Latino neighbors.

Nazli Kibria. *Becoming Asian American: Second-Generation Chinese and Korean American Identities* (Johns Hopkins University Press, 2002).

> Depicts the challenges of migration and resettlement faced by Vietnamese immigrants in inner-city Philadelphia.

Eric Liu. *The Accidental Asian* (Random House, 1998).

> A thoughtful memoir of a second-generation Chinese American.

David Lopez and Yen Espiritu. "Panethnicity in the United States: A Theoretical Framework." *Ethnic and Racial Studies* 13 (1990): 198–224.

> Examines how diverse national-origin groups organize as pan-ethnic movements.

Mia Tuan. *Forever Foreign or Honorary White? The Asian Ethnic Experience Today* (Rutgers University Press, 1999).

> Tuan's account of West Coast Asian Americans reveals the hidden and not-so-hidden injuries of race suffered by the second and third generations.

Frank Wu. *Yellow: Race in America beyond Black and White* (Basic Books, 2002).

> This insightful book explores, among other topics, the model-minority myth and issues of racial diversity.

Henry Yu. *Thinking Orientals: Migration, Contact, and Exoticism in Modern America* (Oxford University Press, 2002).

   Details how social scientists at the University of Chicago addressed the "Oriental problem" during the first half of the twentieth century.

Min Zhou and James V. Gatewood, eds. *Contemporary Asian America: A Multidisciplinary Reader* (New York University Press, 2000).

   This collection shows how contemporary immigration from Asia creates issues of identity and assimilation for both native-born and foreign-born Asian Americans.

REVIEW QUESTIONS

1. Which stereotypes does the label "honorary white" reinforce?
2. Zhou identifies factors that affect whether groups develop a pan-ethnic identity (e.g., timing of immigration). What are they? Write a paragraph on how two of them might affect the formation of a pan-ethnic identity.
3. Zhou questions the popular view that the success of Japanese and Chinese Americans is due to hard work rather than governmental assistance, thus making them "model minorities." What are the implications of this label for both Asians and other minority groups?
4. Activity: After speaking with your parents, come to class prepared to talk about your ethnic background. Break into discussion groups to address the following questions: How many generations of your family have lived in the United States? Where did most of your ancestors settle? Did they live in a very diverse community like Los Angeles or New York City or in a very homogenous one? In what ways did various members of your family assimilate into American society? Did they, for example, insist upon only speaking English in the household? Did they maintain "traditional" customs?

jennifer lee and frank d. bean, photos by kathy sloane

beyond black and white: remaking race in america

summer 2003

a new way of classifying americans by race certifies a new reality: the growing number of multiracial people and their political mobilization. the question is whether this step foretells the erasure of racial lines in america or just a redrawing of them.

Starting with the 2000 census, Americans could officially label themselves and their children as members of more than one race. Nearly 7 million Americans, 2.4 percent of the nation's population, were recorded as being multiracial. This option and these numbers signal a profound loosening of the rigid racial and ethnic boundaries that have so long divided the country. The immigration patterns behind these changes also point to potentially important re-alignments in America's color lines.

How might a black father and a white mother fill out official government documents, like U.S. Census forms, requiring them to designate the race of their child? Before 2000, such an inter-married couple had no alternative but to list their child as either black or white. Similarly, a child born to a white father and an Asian mother had to be listed as either Asian or white, but not Asian and white. Not any more. Americans can now of-ficially identify themselves and their children as black and white, or white and Asian. Indeed, re-spondents can now choose a combination of up to six different categories of races, including "Other." The 2000 Census reported one in every forty Americans was registered as belonging to two or more racial groups. Many sociologists think this ratio could soar to one in five Ameri-cans by the year 2050.

Why does this checking of additional boxes matter? For one thing, how people report them-selves racially provides information needed to implement and enforce important legislation, such as the Voting Rights Act. The Department of Justice uses the statistics to identify places where substantial minority populations exist and may be subject to disenfranchisement. For an-other, the counts document social and economic disparities among racial groups in America. Countries like France that do not collect data on race cannot verify the existence and effects of racial discrimination even when other evidence suggests such discrimination is a major problem. These data also signal the official recognition and hence the influence of groups that define themselves on the basis of common national ori-gin, skin color, or ancestry. Americans of Pacific Islander origin, for example, recently asked to be separately classified. On the other hand, critics worry that official data on race perpetuate rather than eliminate racial identities and divisions. A ballot initiative being circulated in California, for example, would largely ban the state's collec-tion of racial information.

But the new opportunity to mark more than one race is also important because it indicates that people can now officially recognize the mix-ing of racial backgrounds in American society. If

The mothers and fathers of these three children identify themselves, respectively, as Japanese and Dominican-black, Latina and African, and Mexican and Mexican.

the United States was once thought of as a black-and-white society, this is certainly no longer so. Continued immigration from Latin America and Asia, the rise in intermarriage over the past 30 years, and the formal recognition of the multiracial population are moving America far beyond black and white. Yet while America's increasing diversity implies that racial divisions may be weakening, it does not mean that race has become irrelevant. Instead, new kinds of color lines may be emerging. For now, however, the rearrangement seems to leave African Americans facing a new black-nonblack, instead of the old black-white, racial divide.

why there are more multiracial americans

The growth of the multiracial population is a result both of increasing intermarriage between whites and nonwhites and of peoples' increasing willingness to report their multiracial backgrounds. The number of racial intermarriages in the United States grew from 150,000 in 1960 to 1.6 million in 1990—a tenfold increase over three decades. It is still the exception rather than the rule for whites and blacks in this country, however. Just 6 percent of whites and 10 percent of blacks marry someone of a different race. By contrast, more than one-quarter of all native-born Asians and Latinos marry someone of a different race. (For this discussion, we will speak of Latinos as if they were a "race," although government forms count Hispanic background separately, so that people who say they are Latino can report themselves as belonging to any racial group, such as white, black, or Asian.) Even more striking is that two of every five young Latinos and two of every three young Asians born in the United States marry someone of a different race, and the majority marry whites. Asians and Latinos—many of whom are either immigrants or the children of immigrants—are three times as likely to marry whites as blacks are to marry whites.

Coinciding with the rise in intermarriage has been the growth of a new immigrant stream from Latin America and Asia. Today, immigrants and their children total more than 60 million people, approximately 22 percent of the U.S. population. The increase in immigration from non-European countries over the past 35

A multiracial mother and daughter. The mother is black and white; the girl's father is black.

years has converted the United States from a largely white and black society into one that is comprised of numerous racial and ethnic groups. This, plus increasing intermarriage, and the increasing willingness of Americans to call themselves multiracial has changed the way race is measured in America. (See sidebar, "constructing race," p. 289.)

the origin of "mark one or more races"

Since its inception in 1790, the decennial U.S. Census has determined taxation, the numbers of representatives from each state, and the boundaries of Congressional districts. And it has always counted the U.S. population by race. The way that race is measured and even the racial categories themselves, however, have changed considerably. For example, in 1850, the Census added the category "mulatto," and in 1890, it added the categories "quadroon" and "octoroon" in an effort to more precisely measure the representation of black mixtures in the population. ("Mulatto" refers to people of mixed black and white "blood," "quadroon" to people with one-fourth black blood, and "octoroon" to those with one-eighth black blood.) However, "quadroon" and "octoroon" were promptly removed in 1900 because they caused countless statistical inaccuracies. The Census Board determined that the "mulatto" category provided clearer data on the U.S. population with mixed blood, but eventually dropped this category in 1930. By that time, the law of the country, with the census following suit, had adopted the "one-drop rule" of hypodescent (by which all persons with any trace of black ancestry were labeled racially

> If the United States was once thought of as a black-and-white society, this is certainly no longer so. Continued immigration from Latin America and Asia, the rise in intermarriage over the past 30 years, and the formal recognition of the multiracial population are moving America far beyond black and white.

black) as an appropriate criterion by which to attempt to measure race. Importantly, census enumerators classified the people they interviewed by race.

In the 1960s, racial categories came under scrutiny once again, and the Civil Rights Movement prompted one of the most significant changes in the political context and purpose of racial categorization. The argument spread that Americans should be able to mark their own race to identify themselves and their children rather than leaving this to enumerators. Some politicians and experts asserted that the racial categories should more accurately reflect America's diversity and lobbied for new categories, distinguishing among categories of whites, and substituting the term "ethnic" in place of "race." Changes in the 1970 Census reflected some of these currents, with self-identification replacing enumerator identification in order to satisfy public sentiments. By the mid 1970s, groups wanting to be recognized as racial minorities organized advisory committees to seek official statistical representation so that they could participate in federal programs designed to assist racial "minorities." These advisory committees lobbied for the adoption of five racial categories—white, black, Asian, Native American, and other—by the Census and all federal agencies. In 1980, the Census categories changed yet again, this time including the category of Hispanic origin separately from race, and modifying one of the racial categories to Asian-Pacific Islander.

During the early 1990s, new advocacy groups arose with a different agenda. These groups criticized the government standards for not accurately reflecting the diversity in the country

constructing race

Social scientists generally agree that race is not a biological category, but a social and cultural construction, meaning that racial distinctions have not existed since time immemorial, are not rooted in biology and are not fixed. Rather, they have changed and been reinterpreted throughout our nation's history. For instance, when the Irish, Italians, and Jews first arrived in the United States in the nineteenth century. Anglo Americans considered them racially distinct and inferior. They were not considered white. However, they successfully achieved "whiteness" by deliberately and forcefully distinguishing themselves from African Americans. Today, few would contest the claim that the Irish, Italians, and Jews are white.

Race and racial boundaries have changed for other groups as well. For example. Asian ethnic groups like the Chinese in Mississippi have changed their racial status from almost black to almost white. Sociologist James Loewen details how the Chinese there achieved near-white status by becoming as economically successful as whites, copying their cultural and social practices, and distancing themselves from African Americans and Chinese Mississippians who married African Americans.

As historian Gary Gerstle explains, whiteness as a category "has survived by stretching its boundaries to include Americans—the Irish, eastern and southern Europeans—who had been deemed nonwhite. Contemporary evidence suggests that the boundaries are again being stretched as Latinos and Asians pursue whiteness much as the Irish, Italians, and Poles did before them." Given the change in racial boundaries over time, it is likely that the boundaries may continue to stretch to include newer groups. For instance, some sociologists argue that Asians are the next in line to become white. Whether or not they do, we should understand that race is a cultural product that has changed over time, rather than a fixed, primordial category rooted in biology.

brought about by increases in immigration and interracial marriage. In particular, advocates from groups such as the Association for Multi-Ethnic Americans (AMEA) and Project RACE (Reclassify All Children Equally) lobbied the Census Bureau to adopt a "multiracial" category. Advocates argued that it was an affront to force them or their children into a single racial category. Furthermore, they argued that forced mono-racial identification was inaccurate because it denies the existence of interracial marriages, and is ultimately discriminatory. A year later in 1994, the Office of Management and Budget (OMB), which managed this issue, ac-knowledged that the racial categories were of decreasing value and considered an alternate strategy: allowing respondents to identify with as many races as they wished. While the spokespeople for the multiracial movement were not entirely satisfied with this option, they conceded that it was an improvement over forced mono-racial identification.

Not everyone favored adding a multiracial category or allowing Americans to mark more than one race. Civil rights groups—and in particular, black civil rights groups such as the NAACP—strongly objected. They feared that those who would otherwise be counted as black or Hispanic would now choose to identify as multiracial, and, depending on how such persons were counted, diminish their official counts. This, in turn, could undermine enforcement of the Voting Rights Act and potentially reduce the size and effectiveness of government programs aimed at helping minorities.

On October 30, 1997, the Census Bureau announced its final decision that all persons would have the option to identify with two or more races, starting with the 2000 Census and extending to all federal data systems by the year 2003. The racial options on the 2000 Census included "White," "Black," "Asian," "Native Hawaiian or Other PacificIslander," "American Indian and Alaska Native," and "Other." While "Latino" or "Hispanic" was not a racial category on the 2000 Census, OMB mandated two distinct questions: one on race and a second asking whether a person is "Spanish/Hispanic/Latino." Because those who classify themselves as "Spanish/Hispanic/ Latino" can be of any race, the Census asks both questions in order to identify the Latino population in the United States.

The Census Bureau's decision to allow Americans to "mark one or more races" is a landmark change in the way the U.S. government collects data on race. Perhaps even more importantly, it gives official status and recognition to individuals who see themselves or their children as having mixed racial heritage—an acknowledgement that speaks volumes about how far the country has come since the days when the "one-drop rule" enjoyed legal legitimacy. Moreover, such changes may mean that old racial divides are beginning to fade. Multiracial

Interracial marriage was illegal in 16 states as recently as 1967, but today, about 13 percent of American marriages involve persons of different races. If we go back even further to 1880, the rates of intermarriage among Asians and Latinos in this country were close to zero, but now, more than a quarter of all native-born Asians and Latinos marry someone of a different racial background, mostly whites.

reporting, however, has not been equally distributed across all racial and ethnic groups. Rather, those who choose to mark two or more races are distinctive.

who are the multiracials?

As we noted, in 2000, 6.8 million people, or 2.4 percent of the population, were reported as multiracial. While these figures may not appear large, a recent National Academy of Science study estimated that the multiracial population could rise to 21 percent by the year 2050 because of rising intermarriage, when as many as 35 percent of Asians and 45 percent of Hispanics could claim a multiracial background. Of the multiracial population in 2000, 93 percent reported two races, 6 percent reported three races, and 1 percent reported four or more races.

As table 1 illustrates, the groups with high percentages of multiracial persons include "Native Hawaiian or Other Pacific Islander," "American Indian and Alaska Native," "Other," and "Asian." The categories with the lowest proportion of persons who claim a multiracial background are "White" and "Black."

The proportion of blacks who identify as multiracial is quite small, accounting for just 4.2 percent of the total black population. These figures stand in sharp contrast to those among American Indian/Alaska Natives and Native Hawaiian or other Pacific Islanders who have the highest percentage of multiracials as a proportion of their populations at 36.4 and 44.8 percent, respectively. The particular combinations are of interest. Among those identified as black,

	racial identification (millions)	multiracial identification (millions)	percent multiracial
table 1: multiracial identification by race: people recorded as one race who are also recorded as one or more other races.			
White	216.5	5.1	2.3%
Black	36.2	1.5	4.2
Asian	11.7	1.4	12.4
Other	18.4	3.0	16.4
American Indian and Alaska Native	3.9	1.4	36.4
Native Hawaiian or other Pacific Islander	0.7	0.3	44.8

Source: U.S. Census 2000

Asian, or Latino, 2 percent, 7 percent, and 5 percent, respectively, also claim a white identity. Among Asians, the Asian-white multiracial combination is about three and a half times more likely to occur, and among Latinos, the Latino-white combination is more than two and a half times more likely to occur, as the black-white combination occurs among blacks. Why this is so is particularly perplexing when we consider that the Census Bureau has estimated that at least three-quarters of black Americans have some white ancestry and thus could claim a multiracial identity on this basis alone.

The tendency of black Americans not to report multiracial identifications undoubtedly owes in part to the legacy of slavery, lasting discrimination, and both the legal and de facto invocation of the "one-drop rule." For no other racial or ethnic group in the United States does the one-drop rule limit identity choices and options. Recent sociological studies find that about 50 percent of American Indian-white and Asian-white intermarried couples report a white racial

identity for their children. In a study of multiracial Hispanic students, we found that 44 percent chose a Hispanic identity. Without the imposition of the "one-drop rule" that historically imposed a black racial identity on multiracial black Americans, multiracial Asians, Latinos, and American Indians appear to have much more leeway to choose among different racial options.

In addition, because a significant proportion of Latinos and Asians in the United States are either immigrants or the children of immigrants, their understanding of race, racial boundaries, and the black-white color divide is shaped by a different set of circumstances than those of African Americans. Most importantly, Latinos' and Asians' experiences are not rooted in the same legacy of slavery with its systematic and persistent patterns of legal and institutional discrimination and inequality through which the tenacious black-white divide was formed and cemented. For these reasons, racial and ethnic boundaries appear more fluid for the newest immigrants than for native-born blacks, providing multiracial Asians and Latinos more racial options than their black counterparts.

remaking race and redrawing the color line

What do current trends and patterns in immigration, intermarriage, and multiracial identification tell us about the remaking of race in America? It appears that increases in intermarriage and the growth of the multiracial population reflect a blending of races and the shifting of color lines. Because interracial marriage and multiracial identification indicate a reduction in social distance and racial prejudice, these phenomena provide evidence of loosening racial boundaries. At first glance, these patterns offer an optimistic portrait of the weakening of color lines. For instance, interracial marriage was illegal in 16 states as recently as 1967, but today, about 13 percent of American marriages involve persons of different races. If we go back even further to 1880, the rates of intermarriage among Asians and Latinos in this country were close to zero, but now, more than a quarter of all native-born Asians and Latinos marry someone of a different racial background, mostly whites.

Yet, upon closer examination, we find that patterns of intermarriage and multiracial identification are not similar across all groups. Not only are Latinos and Asians more likely to intermarry than blacks, they are also more likely to report a multiracial identification. These different rates suggest that while racial boundaries may be fading, they are not disappearing at the same pace for all groups.

What is crucial here is how we interpret the intermarriage and multiracial identification rates for Latinos and Asians. If we consider Latinos and Asians as discriminated-against racial minorities, closer to blacks than whites in their social disadvantages, then their high levels of multiracial identification suggest that racial border lines might be fading for all nonwhite groups. Latinos and Asians look more, however, like immigrant groups whose disadvantages derive from their not having had time to join the economic mainstream, but who soon will. Their high levels of intermarriage and multiracial reporting therefore signal an experience and trajectory different from that of blacks. Their situations do not necessarily indicate that similar assimilation can be expected among blacks.

Based on the patterns of intermarriage and multiracial identification noted above, the color line appears less rigid for Latinos and Asians than blacks. Asians and Latinos have high rates of intermarriage and multiracial reporting because they were not and are not treated as blacks have been. While the color line may also be shifting for blacks, this shift is occurring more slowly, leaving Asians and Latinos socially nearer to whites. Much of America's racial history has revolved around who was white and who was not; the next phase may revolve instead around who is black and who is not.

The emergence of a black-nonblack divide in a context where diversity is increasing and other racial and ethnic boundaries are diminishing represents a good news–bad news outcome for America. That a white-nonwhite color line does not seem to be enduring is the good news. But that newer nonwhite immigrant groups appear to be jumping ahead of African Americans in a hierarchy still divided by race is the bad news. Based on immigration, intermarriage, and multiracial identification, it appears that Latinos and Asians are closer to whites than to blacks, and consequently may be participants in a new color line that continues to disadvantage blacks.

As a final matter, one might ask: What does all of this imply for the future of measuring race in the census? Critics of racial labels argue that if racial and ethnic boundaries are loosening, we

A multiracial girl with her Latina mother and black father.

should abandon the use of racial categories in the census altogether and learn to get along without them in our policy making. They argue that if racial labels could be eliminated, racial discrimination itself would be eradicated. However, in the United States today, because the practice of discrimination based on physical characteristics such as skin color continues to persist, at least for African Americans, eradicating racial labels would simply put us in a position where we know less about the disadvantages experienced by blacks and can do less about it.

RECOMMENDED RESOURCES

Frank D. Bean and Gillian Stevens. *America's Newcomers and the Dynamics of Diversity* (Russell Sage Foundation, 2003).

> Explores the significance of immigration for America, including its implications for loosening racial and ethnic boundaries.

F. James Davis. *Who is Black? One Nation's Definition* (Pennsylvania State University Press, 1991).

> Details the history of the "one-drop rule" in the United States.

Gary Gerstle. "Liberty, Coercion, and the Making of Americans." In *The Handbook of International Migration*, eds. Charles Hirschman, Philip Kasinitz, and Josh DeWind (Russell Sage Foundation, 1991).

> A history of racial categories and how they have changed.

James Loewen. *The Mississippi Chinese: Between Black and White* (Harvard University Press, 1971).

> Shows how Chinese immigrants changed their racial classification from almost black to almost white.

Melissa Nobles. *Shades of Citizenship: Race and the Census in Modern Politics* (Stanford University Press, 2000).

> A history of racial categories in the Census in the United States.

Joel Perlmann and Mary C. Waters, eds. *The New Race Question: How the Census Counts Multiracial Individuals* (Russell Sage, 2002).

> Examines the history of racial enumeration, the likely effects of the Census change in the race question, and possible policy implications for the future.

Zhenchao Qian. "Breaking the Racial Barriers: Variations in Interracial Marriage Between 1980 and 1990." *Demography* 34 (1997): 263–76.

> Illustrates the growing trends in interracial marriage.

Mary C Waters. "Multiple Ethnicities and Identity in the United States." In *We Are a People: Narrative and Multiplicity in Constructing Identity*, eds. Paul Spikard and W. Jeffrey Burroughs. (Temple University Press, 2000).

Examines the different ways interracial couples identify their children.

REVIEW QUESTIONS

1. Explain how race is "socially constructed"?
2. Prior to the 2000 Census, African-American leaders encouraged parents of mixed-race children to categorize them as "Black." The essay mentions that the NAACP was unhappy with the idea of a new multiracial category. What explains this? Was the NAACP's view justified?
3. Why do you think Latinos and Asians are more likely to intermarry than Blacks?
4. As the article indicates, some people would like to abolish race categories altogether, as in France. What would be the benefits and disadvantages of such a move, and for whom? Overall, is this a good idea?

part **9**

Religion

mark chaves, photos by dianne hagaman

abiding faith

41

summer 2002

contrary to the popular impression that americans have become more secular, in some ways they are as religious as ever. but organized religion occupies less of americans' time, and exerts less influence on society as a whole than in the past.

God is dead—or God is taking over. Depending on the headlines of the day, soothsayers pronounce the end of religion or the ascendancy of religious extremists. What is really going on?

Taking stock of religion is almost as old as religion itself. Tracking religious trends is difficult, however, when religion means so many different things. Should we look at belief in the supernatural? Frequency of formal religious worship? The role of faith in major life decisions? The power of individual religious movements? These different dimensions of religion can change in different ways. Whether religion is declining or not depends on the definition of religion and what signifies a decline.

Perhaps the most basic manifestation of religious observance is piety: individual belief and participation in formal religious worship. Recent research on trends in American piety supports neither simple secularization nor staunch religious resilience in the face of modern life. Instead, Americans seem to believe as much but practice less.

religious belief

Conventional Judeo-Christian religious belief remains very high in the United States, and little evidence suggests it has declined in recent decades. Gallup polls and other surveys show that more than 90 percent of Americans believe in a

higher power, and more than 60 percent are certain that God exists. Approximately 80 percent believe in miracles and in life after death, 70 percent believe in heaven, and 60 percent believe in hell. Far fewer Americans—from two in three in 1963 to one in three today—believe the Bible is the literal Word of God. The number who say the Bible is either the inerrant or the inspired Word of God is still impressively high, however—four of every five.

Religious faith in the United States is more broad than deep, and it has been for as long as it has been tracked. Of Americans who say the Bible is either the actual or the inspired Word of God, only half can name the first book in the Bible and only one-third can say who preached the Sermon on the Mount. More than 90 percent believe in a higher power, but only one-third say they rely more on that power than on themselves in overcoming adversity. People who claim to be born-again or evangelical Christians are no less likely than others to believe in ideas foreign to traditional Christianity, such as reincarnation (20 percent of all Americans), channeling (17 percent), or astrology (26 percent), and they are no less likely to have visited a fortune teller (16 percent).

Despite the superficiality of belief among many, the percentage of Americans expressing religious faith is still remarkably high. How should we understand this persistent religious belief? High levels of religious belief in the

United States seem to show that, contrary to widespread expectations of many scholars, industrialization, urbanization, bureaucratization, advances in science and other developments associated with modern life do not automatically undermine religious belief. In part this is because modernization does not immunize people against the human experiences that inspire religious sentiment. As anthropologist Mary Douglas points out, scientific advances do not make us less likely to feel awe and wonder when we ponder the universe and its workings. For example, our feelings of deference to physicians, owing to their experience and somewhat mysterious scientific knowledge, may not be so different from the way other people feel about traditional healers—even if the outcomes of treatment are indeed different. Likewise, bureaucracy does not demystify our world—on the contrary, it may make us feel more helpless and confused in the face of powers beyond our control. When confronted with large and complex bureaucracies, modern people may not feel any more in control of the world around them than a South Pacific Islander confronted with the prospect of deep-sea fishing for shark. Modern people still turn to religion in part because certain experiences—anthropologist Clifford Geertz emphasizes bafflement, pain, and moral dilemmas—remain part of the human condition.

> Conventional Judeo-Christian religious belief remains very high in the United States, and little evidence suggests it has declined in recent decades.

That condition cannot, however, completely explain the persistence of religious belief. It is clearly possible to respond in nonreligious ways to these universal human experiences, and many people do, suggesting that religiosity is a feature of some responses to these experiences, not an automatic consequence of the experiences themselves. From this perspective, attempting to explain religion's persistence by the persistence of bafflement, pain, and moral paradox sidesteps a key question: Why do so many people continue to respond to these experiences by turning to religion?

Another, more sociological explanation of the persistence of religious belief emphasizes the fact that religion—like language and ethnicity—is one of the main ways of delineating group boundaries and collective identities. As long as who we are and how we differ from others remains a salient organizing principle for social movements and institutions, religion can be expected to thrive. Indeed, this identity-marking aspect of religion may also explain why religious belief often seems more broad than deep. If affirming that the Bible is the inerrant Word of God serves in part to identify oneself as part of the community of Bible-believing Christians, it is not so important to know in much detail what the Bible actually says.

Mass broadcast from Rome is received at a church in Seattle, Washington. Televised images of Pope John Paul II are projected on screens beside the altar.

The modern world is not inherently inhospitable to religious belief, and many kinds of belief have not declined at all over the past several decades. Certain aspects of modernity, however, do seem to reduce levels of religious observance. In a recent study of 65 countries, Ronald Inglehart and Wayne Baker find that people in industrialized and wealthy nations are typically less religious than others. That said, among advanced industrial democracies the United States still stands out for its relatively high level of religious belief. When asked to rate the importance of God in their lives on a scale of 1 to 10, 50 percent of Americans say "10," far higher than the 28 percent in Canada, 26 percent in Spain, 21 percent in Australia, 16 percent in Great Britain and Germany, and 10 percent in France. Among advanced industrial democracies, only Ireland, at 40 percent, approaches the U.S. level of religious conviction.

religious participation

Cross-national comparisons also show that Americans participate in organized religion more often than do people in other affluent nations. In the United States, 55 percent of those who are asked say they attend religious services at least once a month, compared with 40 percent in Canada, 38 percent in Spain, 25 percent in Australia, Great Britain, and West Germany, and 17 percent in France.

The trends over time, however, are murkier. Roger Finke and Rodney Stark have argued that religious participation has increased over the course of American history. This claim is based mainly on increasing rates of church membership. In 1789 only 10 percent of Americans belonged to churches, with church membership rising to 22 percent in 1890 and reaching 50 to 60 percent in the 1950s. Today, about two-thirds of Americans say they are members of a church or a synagogue. These rising figures

should not, however, be taken at face value, because churches have become less exclusive clubs than they were earlier in our history. Fewer people attend religious services today than claim formal membership in religious congregations, but the opposite was true in earlier times. The long-term trend in religious participation is difficult to discern.

Although we have much more evidence about recent trends in religious participation, it still is difficult to say definitively whether religious-service attendance—the main way Americans participate collectively in religion—has declined or remained stable in recent decades. The available evidence is conflicting. Surveys using the traditional approach of asking people directly about their attendance mainly show stability over time, confirming the consensus that attendance has not declined much.

New evidence, however, points toward decline. Drawing on time-use records, which ask individuals to report everything they do on a given day, Stanley Presser and Linda Stinson find that weekly religious-service attendance has declined over the past 30 years from about 40 percent in 1965 to about 25 percent in 1994. Sandra Hofferth and John Sandberg also find a decline in church attendance reported in children's time-use diaries. Time-use studies mitigate the over-reporting of religious-service attendance that occurs when people are asked directly whether or not they attend. Also, these time-use studies find the same lower attendance rates found by researchers who count the number of people who actually show up at church rather than take them at their word when they say they attend.

Additional evidence of declining activity comes from political scientist Robert Putnam's book on civic engagement in the United States, *Bowling Alone*. Combining survey data from five different sources, Putnam finds some decline in religious participation. Perhaps more important,

Monthly women's Bible study group.

because of the context they provide, are Putnam's findings about a range of civic and voluntary association activities that are closely related to religious participation. Virtually every type of civic engagement declined in the last third of the twentieth century: voting, attending political, public, and club meetings, serving as officer or committee member in local clubs and organizations, belonging to national organizations, belonging to unions, playing sports and working on community projects. If religious participation has indeed remained constant, it would be virtually the only type of civic engagement that has not declined in recent decades. Nor did the events of September 11, 2001, alter attendance patterns. If there was a spike in religious service attendance immediately following September 11, it was short-lived.

Overall, the following picture emerges from recent research: Since the 1960s, Americans have engaged less frequently in religious activities, but they have continued to believe just as much in the supernatural and to be just as interested in spirituality. This pattern characterizes many other countries around the world as well. Inglehart and Baker's data suggest that American trends are similar to those in other advanced industrialized societies: declining religious activities, stability in religious belief and increasing interest in the meaning and purpose of life.

Important differences among subgroups remain nonetheless. Blacks are more religiously active than whites, and women are more active than men. There is little reason to think, however, that the recent declines in participation vary among subgroups.

New forms of religious participation are not replacing attendance at weekend worship services. When churchgoers are asked what day they attended a service, only 3 percent mention a day other than Sunday. Perhaps more telling, when those who say they did not attend a religious service in the past week are asked if they participated in some other type of religious event or meeting, such as a prayer or Bible study group, only 2 percent say yes (although 21 percent of nonattendees say they watched religious television or listened to religious radio). The vast majority of religious activity in the United States takes place at weekend religious services. If other forms of religious activity have increased, they have not displaced traditional weekend attendance.

Overall, the current knowledge of individual piety in the United States does not conform to expectations that modernity is fundamentally hostile to religion. Many conventional religious beliefs remain popular, showing no sign of decline. That said, research on individual piety neither points to stability on every dimension nor implies that social changes associated with modernity leave religious belief and practice unimpaired. The evidence supports neither a simple version of secularization nor a wholesale rejection of secularization. Moreover, focusing on levels of religious piety diverts attention from what may be more important: the social significance of religion.

religious piety in context

Focusing exclusively on levels of religious belief and practice overlooks something crucial about religion's social significance. Consider, for example, the difference between two charismatic worship services, complete with speaking in tongues, one occurring outside a village in colonial central Africa early in the twentieth century and the other occurring in an urban Pentecostal church on a Sunday morning in the contemporary United States. In the first case, described by anthropologist Karen Fields, charismatic religion—simply by encouraging baptism and speaking in tongues—challenged the traditional religious authority on which colonial rule was based; the American service plays no such political role. Similarly, consider the difference between two "new age" religious groups, both of which encourage certain kinds of physical exercise to achieve spiritual peace and growth, with one group meeting in a YMCA somewhere in New York City and the other meeting in a park somewhere in Beijing. In the two examples, the same religious action takes on dramatically different meanings that can lead to very different consequences depending on the institutional and political context. In some times and places, speaking in tongues or seeking health by stretching one's limbs shakes social institutions and provokes hostile reactions. In other times and places, such displays shake nothing but the bodies of the faithful, provoking little hostility or, indeed, any other reaction. The social significance of religious piety—its capacity to mean something beyond itself—depends on the context in which it occurs.

From this perspective, we can wonder how high levels of belief and practice are relevant to understanding the social importance of religion. Where people are interested in the spiritual and the supernatural, both traditional religions and new religious movements try to capture that interest. Some successfully bring people into the fold, energize members' beliefs and activities and build impressive organizations. But even a wildly successful religious movement does not

Interfaith Prayer Service for Peace, University of Washington, Seattle

expand religion's dominion if its success is limited to influencing how people spend an hour or two a week of their leisure time in a society where such activity only occasionally reverberates beyond the walls of the church. Increases in charismatic religion in the United States, for example, may be interesting to chart, but when religious institutions do not generally shape other important social institutions, like government or the market, such increases lack the consequences they have where speaking in tongues challenges a village leader's authority. The same can be said of ebbs and flows of any religious style.

Of course, when many people are religiously active, religion can have more social influence. A society like the United States, with more than 300,000 religious congregations, presents opportunities for political mobilization that do not exist in societies where religion is a less prominent part of society. Witness the Civil Rights Movement, the Religious Right, and other causes that mix religion and politics. Nonetheless, religion in the United States, as in most other advanced societies, is organizationally separate from (even if occasionally overlapping) government, the economy, and other parts of civil society. This limits a religion's capacity to change the world, even if it converts millions.

The social significance of religious belief and participation depends on the institutional settings in which they occur. This is why the religious movements of our day with the greatest potential for increasing religion's influence are not those that simply seek new converts or spur belief and practice, no matter how successful they may be. The movements with the greatest such potential are those that seek to expand religion's authority or influence in other domains. In some parts of the contemporary world, this has meant religious leaders seeking and sometimes achieving the power to veto legislation, dictate university curricula, exclude girls from schooling and women from working in certain jobs, and determine the kinds of art or literature offered to the public. In the United States, the most significant contemporary movement to expand religious influence probably is the effort to shape school curricula concerning evolution and creationism. Wherever they occur, when such movements succeed they change the meaning and significance of religious piety. Efforts like these reflect and shape the abiding role of religion in a society in ways that go beyond the percentages of people who believe in God, pray, or attend religious services.

RECOMMENDED RESOURCES

Mark Chaves. "Secularization as Declining Religious Authority." *Social Forces* 72 (1994): 749–74.

George Gallup, Jr. and D. Michael Lindsay. *Surveying the Religious Landscape* (Morehouse Publishing, 1999).

Sandra L. Hofferth and John F. Sandberg. "Children at the Millennium: Where Have We Come From, Where Are We Going?" In *Advances in Life Course Research*, eds. T. Owens and S. Hofferth. (Elsevier Science, 2001). Also available at www.ethno.isr.umich.edu/06papers/html.

Ronald Inglehart and Wayne E. Baker. "Modernization, Cultural Change, and the Persistence of Traditional Values." *American Sociological Review* 65 (2000): 19–51.

Stanley Presser and Linda Stinson. "Data Collection Mode and Social Desirability Bias in Self-Reported Religious Attendance." *American Sociological Review* 63 (1998): 134–45.

Robert Putnam. "Religious Participation." In *Bowling Alone: The Collapse and Revival of American Community* (Simon and Schuster, 2000).

REVIEW QUESTIONS

1. Might church membership or church attendance be problematic measures of religiosity? How else might we measure religiosity?
2. The essay notes that industrialization, urbanization, and bureaucratization "do not automatically undermine religious belief." How might one or more of these processes actually encourage religiosity?
3. Sociologist Emile Durkheim wrote that "we do not find religion without a church." Thinking about the relationship between ideas and practices, what do you think he was referring to? How does this statement relate to the essay?
4. The essay includes an image of a congregation in song. In this photo, there is a projected image on a screen. Perhaps this service is being televised. In what ways do you think technology may be changing American religiosity?

charles kurzman

bin laden and other
thoroughly modern muslims

42

winter 2002

osama bin laden may have operated from a cave in one of the least-developed countries in the world, but his radical islamic movement is thoroughly modern. in many ways, radical islamists are a mirror image of islamic liberals, whose peaceful struggle to establish democracy is actually more popular.

As the United States wages war on terrorism, media coverage has portrayed the radical Islamism exemplified by Osama bin Laden as medieval, reactionary, and eager to return the Islamic world to its seventh-century roots.

In one sense this is accurate: Islamists, like almost all Muslims, regard the early years of Islam as a golden era, and they aspire to model their behavior after the Prophet Muhammad and his early followers, much as Christians idealize the example of Jesus.

Islamists seek to regain the righteousness of the early years of Islam and implement the rule of *shari'a* (see sidebar on page 309 for a description of *shari'a* and other Islamic terms), either by using the state to enforce it as the law of the land or by convincing Muslims to abide by these norms of their own accord. Litmus-test issues for Islamists, as for traditional Muslims, include modest dress for women—ranging from headscarves to full veils—abstention from alcohol and other intoxicants, and public performance of prayers. However, Islamists have no

> Islamists envision overturning tradition in politics, social relations, and religious practices. They are hostile to monarchies, such as the Saudi dynasty in Arabia; they favor egalitarian meritocracy, as opposed to inherited social hierarchies; and they wish to abolish longstanding religious practices such as the honoring of relics and tombs.

wish to throw away electricity and other technological inventions. Most have graduated from modern schools, share modern values such as human equality and rule of law, and organize themselves along modern lines, using modern technologies and—some of them—the latest methods of warfare.

Indeed, radical Islamists have much in common with Islamic liberalism, another important movement in the Islamic world. Both Islamic liberals and radical Islamists seek to modernize society and politics, recasting tradition in modern molds. Both Islamist movements maintain that there are multiple ways of being modern, and that modernity is not limited to Western culture. Islamists may ally themselves on occasion with traditionalist Islamic movements, and they may share certain symbols of piety, but they are quite distinct in sociological terms. Traditionalists such as the Taliban of Afghanistan, by contrast with Islamists such as bin Laden's Al Qaeda network, draw on less educated sectors of society, believe in mystical and personal authority, and are skeptical of modern organizational forms. For this reason, traditionalist movements are finding it increasingly difficult to survive in a competitive religious environment and occupy only isolated pockets of Muslim society. Modern movements have taken over the rest.

the islamists' roots in secular education

Start with bin Laden himself. Though he issued *fatwas* (religious judgments) as though he were a seminary-educated Islamic scholar, his training was in civil engineering. Similarly, many other Islamist leaders have university rather than seminary backgrounds: Hasan Turabi of the Sudan is a lawyer trained in Khartoum, London, and Paris; Necmettin Erbakan of Turkey studied mechanical engineering in West Germany; Hasan al-Banna of Egypt, who founded the first mass Islamist group, the Muslim Brotherhood, in the 1920s, was a teacher educated and employed in secular schools.

Ironically, the West, generally the underminer of tradition, now supports traditional elites in the Islamic world. Bin Laden and other Islamists make repeated use of the Irony: America, supposed proponent of democracy and rights, clings to a regime [in Saudi Arabia] that detests these modern concepts.

These leaders railed against seminary-trained scholars, the *'ulama*, for being obscurantist and politically inactive. Bin Laden lambasted the *'ulama* of Saudi Arabia as playing "the most ominous of roles. Regardless of whether they did so intentionally or unintentionally, the harm that resulted from their efforts is no different from the role of the most ardent enemies of the nation." Even Islamist leaders with traditional seminary educations—such as Abu'l-'Ala Maudoodi of Pakistan, Ruhollah Khomeini of Iran, 'Abd al-Hamid Kishk of Egypt—frequently railed against their alma maters for similar reasons. Seminaries were considered so backward in Islamist eyes that for decades Maudoodi hid the fact that he had a seminary degree.

Not only the Islamist leaders but also the rank and file emerge disproportionately from secular universities. The classic study on this subject was performed in the late 1970s by Saad Eddin Ibrahim, the Egyptian sociologist who was recently jailed for his pro-democracy activities. Of the 34 imprisoned Islamist activists whom he interviewed, 29 had some college education. In a follow-up study in the 1990s, Ibrahim found the Islamist movement had added poorer and less educated members, but as political scientist Carrie Wickham has discovered through interviews with Islamists in Cairo, Islamist recruitment efforts are still geared toward university graduates in Egypt. Outside of Egypt, too, bin Laden's 1996 open letter identified "high school and university students" and the "hundreds of thousands of unemployed graduates" as prime targets for mobilization. The 19 alleged hijackers of September 11, 2001 included a city planner, a physical education instructor, a business student, a teacher, and two engineers; even the Saudi "muscle" among them were largely middle-class youths educated in state-run high schools.

Contrast this with the Taliban. Afghanistan's school system was virtually demolished in two decades of civil war, so the Islamists' usual constituency of educated young men was unavailable. Taliban leader Mullah Muhammad Omar had no advanced education. Other top officials had seminary backgrounds as well; according to reports, many were educated at the Haqqani seminary near Peshawar, Pakistan, and three of six members of the Taliban ruling council studied at the same seminary in Karachi. The foot soldiers were drawn largely from students at Haqqani and other refugee seminaries in Pakistan—hence the name *Taliban*, which means seminary students or seekers. (The singular is *talib*, so references to a single American Taliban are grammatically incorrect.) This force was created in large part by the Pakistani intelligence ministry, which is staffed at its higher ranks by well-educated Muslims from secular universities; it made an alliance with Al Qaeda, which also appears to draw on the highly educated. But these connections should not obscure the fact that the Taliban had an entirely different social base. According to an Egyptian Islamist, top officials of Al Qaeda considered their Afghan hosts to be "simple people" who lacked the "ability to grasp contemporary reality, politics and management."

Indeed, the rise of Islamist movements in the twentieth century is closely associated with the sidelining of the seminary educational system. Beginning in Ottoman Turkey and Egypt in the early nineteenth century and ending in the 1950s with the Arab emirates of the Persian Gulf, states—colonial or local—have founded their own schools to operate in competition with the seminaries. At first these were small elite schools, designed to produce government officials. In the past two generations, however, state-run school systems have expanded to include significantly larger sectors of the population. In one sample of 22 Muslim-majority countries, 70 percent of adults had no formal education in 1960; by 1990, this figure had been reduced to 44 percent. In 1960, only four of these countries had more than 1 percent of the adult population with some higher education; in 1990, only four of these countries had less than 1 percent with some higher education. Seminaries have grown,

In the short run, the war on terrorism has not generated the massive negative reaction among Muslims that some observers expected. Yet there is evidence to suggest that Islamism is gaining in popularity.

too, in some countries; but even where seminarians control the state, as in the Islamic Republic of Iran, these schools remain marginal to the nation's educational system.

The growth of secular education has led expanding numbers of Muslims to approach religious questions without the skills—or blinders, depending on one's perspective—inculcated in the seminaries. College graduates have turned to the sacred texts and analyzed them in a sort of do-it-yourself theology, developing liberal interpretations in addition to radical ones. In Pakistan, for example, a study group of educated Muslim women met and produced a feminist interpretation, "For Ourselves: Women Reading the Koran" (1997). In North America, a gay convert to Islam produced a Web site called Queer Jihad that espoused tolerance for homosexuality. In Syria, a soil engineer named Muhammad Shahrour decided that traditional scholarship on the Koran was unscientific and that he had a better approach, one that happened to support liberal political positions. According to booksellers interviewed by anthropologist Dale Eickelman, Shahrour's tomes are bestsellers in the Arab world, even where they are banned.

In addition, governments have waded into the religious field throughout the Islamic world. In each country, the state has established its own official religious authorities, which may be pitted against every other state's religious authorities. Many states produce their own schoolbooks to teach Islamic values in the public schools. In Turkish textbooks, these values include secular government; in Saudi textbooks, these values include monarchy; in Palestine National Authority textbooks, according to a review by political scientist Nathan J. Brown, these values include the defense of the Palestinian homeland (though they do not, as often charged, include the destruction of Israel).

The result is a tremendous diversity of Islamic opinion and a corresponding diversity of Islamic authority. There is no universally recognized arbiter to resolve Islamic debates. For most of Islamic history, at least a symbolic arbiter existed: the caliph (*khalifa*), that is, the successor to the Prophet. Caliphs could never impose interpretive uniformity on all Muslims, although some were more inclined than others to try. But since the Turkish Republic abolished the Ottoman caliphate in 1924, even this symbol of authority is gone. Any college graduate in a cave can claim to speak for Islam.

modern goals, modern methods

Just as the social roots of Islamism are modern, so too are many of its goals. Do not be misled by the language of hostility toward the West. Islamist political platforms share significant planks with Western modernity. Islamists envision overturning tradition in politics, social relations, and religious practices. They are hostile to monarchies, such as the Saudi dynasty in Arabia; they favor egalitarian meritocracy, as opposed to inherited social hierarchies; they wish to abolish long-standing religious practices such as the honoring of relics and tombs.

Bin Laden, for example, combined traditional grievances such as injustice, corruption, oppression, and self-defense with contemporary demands such as economic development, human rights, and national self-determination. "People are fully occupied with day-to-day survival; everybody talks about the deterioration of the economy, inflation, ever-increasing debts and jails full of prisoners," bin Laden wrote in 1996. "They complain that the value of the [Saudi] *riyal* is greatly and continuously

deteriorating against most of the major currencies."

These mundane concerns do not mean that Islamist states look just like Western states, but they are not entirely different, either. The Islamic Republic of Iran, for example, has tried to forge its own path since it replaced the Pahlavi, monarchy in 1979. Yet within its first year it copied global norms by writing a new constitution, ratifying it through a referendum with full adult suffrage, holding parliamentary and presidential elections, establishing a cabinet system, and occupying itself with myriad other tasks that the modern world expects of a state, from infrastructure expansion to narcotics interdiction. The 1986 Iranian census conducted by the Islamic Republic was scarcely different from the 1976 census conducted by the monarchy. Similarly in Pakistan and the Sudan, where Islamic laws were introduced in the 1980s, there were changes, but there were also massive continuities. The modern state remained.

Contrast this continuity with the traditionalist Taliban. While most well-educated Islamists disdain relics as verging on idol worship, Taliban leader Mullah Muhammad Omar literally wrapped himself in the cloak of the Prophet—a cherished relic in Qandahar—one April day in 1996. While successful Islamist movements have ensconced themselves in the offices of their predecessors, Omar remained in his home province. The Taliban government reproduced a few of the usual ministries—foreign affairs, for example—but did not bother with most. The Taliban preferred informal and personal administration to the rule-bound bureaucracies favored by modern states.

Western bias tends to lump Khomeini's Iran and the Taliban's Afghanistan in the same category, and indeed both claimed to be building an Islamic state. However, one is a modern state and the other was not. Perhaps the most vivid distinction involved gender. While the Taliban barred girls from attending school, the Islamic Republic of Iran more than doubled girls' education from prerevolutionary levels. While the Taliban barred women from working at most jobs, Iranian women entered the labor force in unprecedented numbers, as television anchors, parliamentary deputies, government typists, and sales clerks—even while dressed in headscarves and long coats. Iranian leaders were as outspoken as Western feminists in condemning Taliban policies on gender and other subjects and felt the Taliban were giving Islam a bad name.

The Taliban reintroduced tradition; Khomeini and other Islamists reinvented it. This process is entirely consistent with the "invention of tradition" identified by historians Eric Hobsbawm and Terence Ranger. The Victorians in England, for example, developed anthems, symbols, and a mythical lineage that they then projected backward in time, pretending that these were the outgrowth of an ancient tradition. Similarly, the Islamists' ideals of early Islamic society are contemporary constructions. The Islamists wish to return to God's law and the sacred practices of the first Muslims, but they downplay early Islamic practices such as slavery that are at odds with their modern values. In place of the clear social hierarchies in early Islam based on tribe, lineage, and seniority, Islamists emphasize human equality. In place of personal regimes, Islamists insist on codified law. In place of submission to authority, Islamists speak the language of individual rights. These modern values set Islamists apart from their precursors in earlier periods, such as Ibn Taymiyya in the fourteenth century and Muhammad Ibn 'Abd al-Wahhab and Shah Wali-Allah in the eighteenth century.

Not all Islamist demands are consonant with modern norms, of course. Islamists are openly hostile to certain elements of modernity in its Western forms, such as dating, decriminalized drug use and separation of church and state. Moreover, certain high-profile Islamist goals such as corporal punishment, legalized polygyny, automatic male custody in divorce, restrictive garb for women, bans on heresy and apostasy, and judicial authority keyed to sacred texts are unpalatable to modern Western sensibilities. Yet even these demands are framed in the familiar modern idiom of rediscovering authenticity. The goal is to "Islamicize modernity," in the phrase of Moroccan Islamist leader Abdessalam Yassine: to forge an alternative modernity that combines basic elements of modernity with selected elements of Islamic heritage.

Ironically, the West, generally the underminer of tradition, now supports traditional elites in the Islamic world. The British and French installed monarchies in much of the Middle East after World War I. More recently, Western military might forced a republic to disgorge a monarchy—albeit a liberalized one—when Kuwait was liberated in 1991. Since that time, U.S. troops have been stationed in Saudi Arabia to defend an absolute monarchy. Bin Laden and other Islamists make repeated use of the irony: America, supposed proponent of democracy and rights, clings to a regime that detests these modern concepts.

Not just in ideology but also in practice, bin Laden and other radical Islamists mirror Western trends. They term their mobilization *jihad*, or sacred struggle, although many Muslims point out that the Prophet called struggle against others the "lesser jihad," with the internal struggle to lead a good life being the "greater jihad." Regardless of the ancient terminology, Al Qaeda and other Islamist groups operate globally like transnational corporations, with affiliates and subsidiaries, strategic partners, commodity chains, standardized training, off-shore financing, and other features associated with contemporary global capital. Indeed, insiders often referred to Al Qaeda as the "company."

Documents discovered by the *New York Times* in Afghan training camps after Al Qaeda's departure show a bureaucratic organization with administrative lines of authority and an insistence on budgeting. Islamists use the latest high-tech skills, not just airplane piloting and transponder deactivation, as the world learned tragically on September 11, 2001, but also satellite phones, faxes, wired money orders, and the like. Mullah Muhammad Omar was so suspicious of modern technology that he refused to be photographed; bin Laden, by contrast, distributed videotapes of himself to the world's media.

Like other covert networks, such as mafiosi and narcotraffickers, Islamists organize themselves through informal personal ties. Political scientist Quintan Wiktorowicz was able to document this phenomenon among radical Islamists in Jordan, who allowed him to attend their illegal meetings. These activists are harassed by the security forces, frequently arrested, and barred from regular employment. In this repressive context their main avenue for collective action is to draw on friendship networks, people whom they trust to maintain the secrecy that their illegal activities require.

Some Islamists also benefit from "front" organizations that gain legitimacy and launder money. Indeed, some of these organizations do tremendous good works, such as supporting medical clinics in poor neighborhoods in Egypt, offering earthquake relief in Turkey and mobilizing women into micro-enterprises in Yemen. Surprisingly, however, many of these welfare organizations are quite unsuccessful in mobilizing political support among the poor. Political scientist Janine Clark, who has conducted extensive fieldwork among these organizations in the Arab world, found that the beneficiaries of Islamic charity often receive such a pittance of financial aid that they are forced to seek benefits from other charities as well—state-run, missionary-run, secular, or otherwise—and have no particular loyalty to the Islamists.

Like other political movements, Islamists are divided as to how to achieve their goals. Some prefer a hearts-and-minds strategy, "calling" Muslims to increased piety. "There is no compulsion in religion," they argue, quoting the Koran, so conquering the state without preparing the populace is both morally impermissible and strategically foolhardy. Others argue that state conquest cannot be delayed. Oppression, foreign and domestic, operates through the state and can only be addressed at that level. But state-oriented Islamists are themselves divided: some seek to take power democratically, while others pursue putsches and terrorism. This division reveals one of the least-known aspects of the Islamist movement: for all their notoriety, Islamists remain unpopular among Muslims.

the radical minority

A minority of Muslims support Islamist organizations, and not just because they are illegal in many countries. There are only a handful of reputable surveys on the subject, but they show consistently that most Muslims oppose Islamists and their goals. Surveys in 1988 found that 46 and 20 percent of respondents in Kuwait and Egypt, respectively, favored Islamist goals in religion and politics. A 1986 survey in the West Bank and Gaza found 26 percent calling for a state based on *shari'a*, and polls in the same regions showed support for Hamas and other Islamist groups dropping from 23 percent in 1994 to 13 to 18 percent in 1996–97. A 1999 survey in Turkey found 21 percent favoring implementation of *shari'a*, consistent with other surveys in the mid-1990s. In a Gallup poll of nine Muslim societies at the end of 2001, only 15 percent of respondents said they considered the September 11 attacks to be morally justifiable.

When free or partially free elections are held, Islamists rarely fare well. Islamist candidates

Islam is the faith of roughly one billion Muslims, centered historically and symbolically on the cities of Mecca and Medina in the Arabian Peninsula, where the word of God was revealed to Muhammad ibn 'Abdullah from 610 until the Prophet's death in 632. This revelation, called the Koran, is the ultimate source of authority for Muslim piety. Yet the Koran is a difficult text: 114 chapters in poetic classical Arabic, each word layered with multiple meanings. It is not arranged in chronological order, and the context in which each verse was revealed can only be determined through familiarity with dozens of volumes of eyewitness testimony, called *hadith*, which were handed down orally for generations. Since the ninth century A.D., Muslim scholars, or *'ulama*, have developed elaborate historiographical methods to distinguish legitimate from spurious *hadith*. *Hadith* testimony is also the basis for knowledge of the activities and sayings of the Prophet and his Companions, known as the *sunna*, which Muslims take as a model for righteous comportment. Together, the Koran and the *sunna* are often referred to as *shari'a*, or Islamic law, although only a small portion of the revelation and *hadith* testimony refer specifically to matters of state.

Demographically, the center of the Islamic world is well to the east of the Middle East. Only one-fifth of Muslims are Arab, and the largest populations of Muslims live in Indonesia, India, Pakistan, and Bangladesh. Muslims have lived in the Americas since the seventeenth century, when many were brought as slaves from West Africa. However, the recent growth in Muslim population is due to immigration from the Middle East and South Asia, which has expanded greatly since the 1960s, and conversion, primarily among African Americans. Tom W. Smith recently estimated the number of Muslims in the United States as 1.9 to 2.8 million.

and parties have won less than 10 percent of the vote in Bangladesh, Egypt, Pakistan, and Tajikistan. They have won less than 25 percent of the vote in Egypt, Malaysia, Sudan, Tunisia, Turkey, and Yemen. Their best showings have been in Kuwait, where they won 40 percent of seats in 1999, and Jordan, where moderate Islamists won 43 percent of seats in 1989 before dropping to 20 percent in the next election. Virtually the only majority vote that Islamists have ever received was in Algeria in 1991, when the Islamic Salvation Front dominated the first stage of parliamentary elections, winning 81 percent of the seats; it was about to win the second stage of voting when the military annulled the elections and declared martial law.

In the few elections where Islamists fared relatively well, success followed from promises to abide by democratic norms. The Algerian Islamist leader 'Abbasi Madani, who earned a doctorate in education from the University of London, developed a Muslim Democrat position analogous to the Christian Democrat parties of Europe: culturally conservative but committed to democracy. "Pluralism is a guarantee of cultural wealth, and diversity is needed for development. We are Muslims, but we are not Islam itself," Madani said while campaigning. "We do not monopolize religion. Democracy as we understand it means pluralism, choice and freedom." These sentiments may have been insincere, but we will never know.

A secular military regime barred Madani from office before he could develop a track record, just as secular military officials in Turkey removed Necmettin Erbakan as prime minister in 1997, after less than a year in office. Islamists now cite Algeria and Turkey while debating whether it is naive to think that they will ever be allowed to play by the same rules as other parties.

Still, when given a choice between liberal and radical Islamists, Muslim voters prefer the liberal. In Indonesia, Abdurrahman Wahid's liberal party received 17 percent of the vote in 1999, and Amien Rais's semi-liberal party received 7 percent, compared with 11 percent for the more radical United Development Party. In Kuwait, more than twice as many candidates associated with the moderate Islamic Constitutional Movement were elected in 1996 and 1999 than candidates associated with the more hard-line Islamic Popular Movement. Most dramatically, in Iran, for years the role model for Islamists, the liberal reform movement swept a series of elections as soon as it was allowed to run against hard-liners: the presidency in 1997, city councils in 1998, parliament in 1999, and the presidency again in 2001. The reformists must still contend with other branches of government that the constitution sets aside as unelected. However, President Muhammad Khatami and his allies, all former radicals themselves, serve as high-profile defectors from the Islamist cause.

Islamists thus face a dilemma that is common to other radical movements of the past century: whether to water down their message to attract popular support or maintain a pure vision and mobilize a relatively small cadre. Like leftist splinter groups that rejected democratic socialism, bin Laden and his ilk have opted for the second path. Like radical leftists, radical Islamists fare best when the liberals are forcibly removed from the scene: by repressive regimes, as in Pahlavi-era Iran, contemporary Saudi Arabia,

and elsewhere; or by the Islamists themselves, as in the Algeria, Chechnya, and Kashmir assassination campaigns, among others.

Sadly, the U.S.-led war on terrorism may inadvertently benefit the Islamists. This is the great debate among scholars of Islamic studies in the months since September 2001. Do the United States and its allies appear hypocritical in supporting autocrats in Muslim-majority countries while claiming to defend human rights and democracy? Will Muslims perceive the war on terrorism as evidence of Western hostility toward Islam? Will military action stoke Islamist radicalism or extinguish it?

In the short run, the war on terrorism has not generated the massive negative reaction among Muslims that some observers expected. Yet there is evidence to suggest that Islamism is gaining in popularity. Gallup polls of nine Muslim societies at the end of 2001 found that a majority considered the United States and the West to be hostile to Islam and Muslims. Since the beginning of 2002, Israel's military operations in Palestinian territories, with Western acquiescence, may have further radicalized Muslim attitudes.

Longer-term approaches to the war on terrorism also face ambivalences. The modernization of Muslim societies, promoted by the United States and its allies as a buffer against traditionalism, may wind up fueling Islamism. Modern schools produce Islamists as well as liberals; modern businesses fund Islamist as well as other causes; modern communications can broadcast Islamist as well as other messages. Western culture, we are learning, is not the only form that modernity may assume.

RECOMMENDED RESOURCES

Khaled Abou El Fadl. *Rebellion and Violence in Islamic Law* (Cambridge University Press, 2001).

A thorough critique of Islamists' misuse of sacred sources as justification for terrorism.

Dale F. Eickelman and James Piscatori. *Muslim Politics* (Princeton University Press, 1996).

A valuable globe-trotting overview of variation in contemporary Muslim politics.

Carl W. Ernst. *Following Muhammad: An Introduction to Islam in the Contemporary World* (Shambala, 2002).

A sensitive and insightful introduction to historical and contemporary developments in Islam.

Charles Kurzman, ed. *Liberal Islam: A Source-Book* (Oxford University Press, 1998).

An anthology of 32 influential writings, mostly late twentieth century, by Muslims favoring democracy, multireligious coexistence, women's rights, and other liberal themes.

Charles Kurzman, ed. *Modernist Islam: A Source-Book, 1840–1940* (Oxford University Press, 2002)

An anthology of 52 influential writings by Muslims in the nineteenth and early twentieth centuries favoring constitutionalism, nationalism, science, women's rights, and other modern values.

Bruce Lawrence. *Shattering the Myth: Islam Beyond Violence* (Princeton University Press, 1998).

A highly readable examination of key issues in contemporary Islamic debates.

Paul Lubeck. "The Islamic Revival: Antinomies of Islamic Movements Under Globalization." In *Global Social Movements*, eds. Robin Cohen and Shirin M. Rai (Athlone Press, 2000).

A provocative analysis linking economic globalization with global Islamic activism.

Carrie Wickham. *Mobilizing Islam: Religion, Activism and Political Change in Egypt* (Columbia University Press, 2002).

The definitive work on Islamists in Egypt, documenting the methods through which secular university students are drawn to Islamist activism.

Quintan Wiktorowicz. *The Management of Islamic Activism: Salafis, the Muslim Brotherhood, and State Power in Jordan* (State University of New York Press, 2001).

A path-breaking study of radical Islamist groups in Jordan, based on extensive interviews with activists in illegal cells.

REVIEW QUESTIONS

1. What are the key differences between radical Islam and liberal Islam? Are there similar divisions in other religions?
2. Kurzman notes that modernity challenges Islam in various ways. How? Does the modern world also raise challenges for Christianity, Judaism, and other religious traditions?
3. There are many views about how an Islamic government should be organized and how it should educate its youth. What are the similarities and differences between the Islamic governments in Iran and Afghanistan? Why is education, in particular, such a crucial issue in the Muslim world?

wendy cadge and courtney bender

yoga and rebirth in america: asian religions are here to stay

43

winter 2004

new movies, store names, and organizations herald a growing interest among americans in asian religions. beyond the fads, sociologists are finding that these eastern faiths, along with their practitioners and centers, play an increasingly important role in american spiritual life.

Every Saturday at a Thai Buddhist temple in the suburbs of Philadelphia, a Thai-born monk teaches a group of mostly European Americans how to meditate. Every Sunday, first-generation Thai immigrants gather in the same hall to chant, meditate, hear the Buddha's teachings, and donate money to the monks. Outside the temple walls, Americans meet Asian religions such as Buddhism, Hinduism, Sikhism, Jainism, Shinto, Taoism, and Confucianism when they watch movies such as *Little Buddha* and *Seven Years in Tibet* or read *The Tao of Pooh*, *Zen and the Art of Falling in Love*, and *Yoga for Dummies*. They attend yoga classes and visit meditation centers in record numbers, wash with karma soaps, and eat nirvana chocolates. Although much of Americans' fascination with Asian spirituality seems like a fad that will soon fade, their involvement with these religions also can be serious and sustainable.

Research clearly demonstrates that there is more to Americans' recent interest in Asian religions than Madison Avenue's discoveries of mystical energy fields and reincarnation. While inclusion of Asian religions in advertising campaigns and store names is often superficial, national surveys and detailed sociological research

show that Asian religions are a growing component of the American religious landscape. Asian religions are no longer practiced only by Asian immigrants and their families or European-American counterculturalists like the Hare Krishnas. According to a 2003 national survey designed by Robert Wuthnow, 30 percent of adult Americans (63 million people) say that they are at least somewhat familiar with Buddhist teachings and 22 percent (45 million people) claim to be similarly familiar with Hindu teachings. More than half of the people surveyed (55 percent) said they had personal contact with a Buddhist and 50 percent had personal contact with a Hindu. Of course, some Americans have more encounters with Asian religions than others. People who are young, more educated, or live on the West Coast are more likely to have contact with Buddhists, for example.

Sociologists have also studied the growing number of organizations and sites in which Asian religions are learned and practiced across the country. These settings include temples and ashrams (Hindu retreats) as well as alternative health clinics and yoga studios. While it is difficult to track the exact number of such centers nationally, there are now thousands of them ranging from small storefront halls to multimillion-dollar buildings. New, too, are many specialized magazines and books such as *Tricycle: The Buddhist Review* and *Hinduism Today* that have emerged in response to Americans' interest in Asian religions. The Berkeley, California–based *Yoga Journal*, founded in 1975, boasted 300,000 subscribers and nearly one million monthly readers in 2002—a 300 percent increase from just three years earlier. The number of books published about Buddhism in English also more than tripled between 1965 and 2000.

The recent burgeoning of Americans' fascination with Asian religions is rooted in increasing immigration, widening global networks, and changes in American religious and health care institutions. But the fascination dates back at least two centuries.

romantic and real origins

Before 1965, the Asian population in the United States was relatively small and concentrated in the West. American immigration laws at the turn of the twentieth century restricted and later prohibited most Asian immigration. As a result, few nineteenth- and early twentieth-century Americans learned about Asian religions first-hand. Instead, they relied on stories told by traveling Asian religious teachers and printed sources such as missionary reports. Consequently, non–Asian Americans curious about Buddhism, Hinduism, and other Asian religions often romanticized them and practiced them according to American and European visions (leading, for example, to the occult-oriented Theosophy and to the spiritualist Transcendentalist movement associated with Ralph Waldo Emerson). Texts and itinerant teachers continued to be the primary sources for Americans to learn about Asian religions through the mid-twentieth century. These overly idealized and often incomplete or incorrect interpretations nevertheless forcefully shaped American countercultural and alternative lifestyle movements, from the Beat writers to the International Society for Krishna Consciousness (better known as the Hare Krishnas). Such homegrown interpretations continue to play a significant role in the ways that non–Asian Americans view and understand Asian religions.

Prior to 1965, Americans interested in Asian religions paid little attention to the existing religious communities and organizations built by Chinese, Japanese, Indian, and other Asian immigrants who had largely come to the United States as laborers and endured discrimination. Rarely noticed by native-born Americans, Asian immigrants have been practicing their religions ever since their arrival. In 1906, for example, the U.S. Census counted 62 Chinese temples and 141 shrines. The visibility of Asian religions and the number of their organizations expanded vastly after changes in U.S. immigration laws in 1965 ended country-of-origin quotas. Between 1960 and 2000, the number of Asians in America increased tenfold to nearly 12 million people, or 4 percent of the American population. They have built Buddhist, Hindu, and Christian religious centers across the country where they gather for worship and support. Major cities like San Francisco, New York, and Chicago remain popular homes for Asian religious organizations, but they have been joined in recent years by large cities like Houston, which has several Hindu and Buddhist temples, and smaller cities like Lowell, Massachusetts, which is home to several Cambodian Buddhist temples. Across the country, these religious centers increasingly provide the organizational base from which immigrants and their children claim recognition as equal partners in a multireligious America—for example, by lobbying to lead the opening prayers in Congress and by pursuing government funds earmarked for faith-based social service organizations.

translating the teachings

Asians and non–Asians alike, inside and outside of formal organizations, practice and teach Asian religions. Thai Buddhist temples, for example, increased from fewer than five in 1975 to more than 80 in 2000, and Buddhist centers teaching meditation more than doubled between 1987 and 1997. Thais, Laotians, Cambodians, and other Asian and non–Asian Americans attend Thai temples, about one-third of which have programs in English specifically for non–Asian Americans. Paul Numrich has described these immigrant Theravada Buddhist temples with programs in English as "parallel congregations." Asians and non–Asian Americans gather at separate times for separate rituals and practices, but under the guidance of the same monks. At a few temples, Asians and non–Asians are even beginning to gather side-by-side to hear simultaneous translations of the teachings in Thai and English. This mixing of Asians and non–Asian Americans also takes place at some Sri Lankan and Burmese Buddhist temples as well as at centers associated with the International Society for Krishna Consciousness.

Many Americans also participate in religious practices that developed within Asian religious traditions but are taught or practiced in other kinds of organizations. For example, Americans no longer only practice yoga in free-standing yoga studios or ashrams, and yoga has lost much of its connection with alternative or countercultural lifestyles. Now taught in American fitness and health organizations, often as a "stress management" technique, this religious practice is translated into a viable therapy for certain health problems. A growing number of managed care and health insurance plans even pay for yoga classes. Sociologists have not yet enumerated where yoga is taught and by whom, but our informal observations find it in public and private elementary schools, fitness clubs, retirement centers, and corporate offices.

Although secular organizations teach yoga, many, if not most, yoga teachers train at explicitly Hindu or devotional yoga centers. One of us, Bender, found that many of the yoga teachers she interviewed in a large northeastern city teach in various locations and tailor their descriptions of yoga and its benefits accordingly. Although most try to tell their students, as one put it, that there is "more to yoga than breathing," teachers consider the setting when deciding whether to include chanting, meditation, or reading from classic yoga texts such as Patanjali's Yoga Sutras. The option to teach yoga and other disciplines as both fitness and as devotional practice makes Asian religions available to a more varied American audience than ever before. But it also shows how practices considered religious by teachers may not be considered so by students. This is one way, also, that those practices are becoming less traditional as they spread to different parts of American society. Recent controversies in the national yoga community about the "authenticity" of new forms of yoga that downplay meditation (including "hot" or Bikram yoga and "power" yoga) point to the currently unsettled meaning of these practices. T'ai-chi, qigong, and various forms of meditation with roots in Asian traditions are undergoing similar transformations from religious to secular devotions as they are introduced to the national mainstream as part of Americans' quest for health and fitness.

explaining the growth

Asian religions have spread largely because of new immigrants, global connections, and changes in American churches and health care. Not only has the number of Asians in the United States grown exponentially since 1965, it has done so especially in America's urban cultural centers. Moreover, the newcomers are also more likely to be middle-class professionals than earlier generations of immigrants, giving them more influence on other Americans. The Wuthnow study found that of the 50 percent of Americans who have had contact with a Buddhist, the majority report that this contact occurred at their workplace, while conducting personal business dealings, or while shopping, implying that Buddhist practitioners (both Asians and non–Asian Americans) are well integrated into the American mainstream. The growing number of second- and third-generation Asian Americans in some regions of the United States have also led schools to note and teach their religious holidays in the classroom. Non–Asian-American children also learn about these traditions in the homes of their Asian-American friends. Some of this increased awareness of Asian religions develops directly from interfaith dialogues, like the Catholic-Buddhist dialogue in Los Angeles, which includes Buddhist teachers and monks, Hindu priests, and other Asian religious leaders who typically have not previously mixed with representatives of Western religions.

Expanding global travel and communications have allowed Americans to supplement their reading about Asian religions with in-person instruction here and abroad. Asian-born teachers often visit the United States, like the Dalai Lama whose public teachings and writings have been central to the spread of Tibetan Buddhism in America. Numerous American-born instructors like early Theravada Buddhist teachers Jack Kornfield and Joseph Goldstein have spent time in Asia and have returned there to continue to study over the years. Lay practitioners, some of whom are affluent, also travel with relative ease between Asia and the United States to attend retreats, hear teachings, and visit sacred religious sites. For example, followers of Sai Baba, an Indian holy man with tens of millions of devotees, gather regularly at his ashram outside of Bangalore to catch a glimpse of him in Sai darshan (sacred viewing).

Many Asian immigrants also regularly return to Asia for particular life-cycle rituals, often developing and maintaining ties between their religious leaders in the United States and their home countries in the process. These new Asian immigrants, as well as American-born non–Asian practitioners, continue to facilitate the movement of Asian religions between Asia and the United States.

Finally, several ongoing changes in medical practices and institutions in the United States have propelled the spread of Asian religions in America. Alternative and complementary health and medicine, for example, is becoming increasingly established and integrated into traditional Western-style medicine. A 1997 survey published in the *Journal of the American Medical Association*, for example, reported that Americans made 629 million visits to complementary and alternative medicine providers, paying $27 billion in out-of-pocket expenses. In addition, federal funds now support studies of whether these traditions work and the creation of university-based complementary health research and treatment centers at UCLA, Columbia, Harvard, and other prominent institutions—all of which give new legitimacy to these practices and their practitioners. Many complementary and alternative techniques, however, stem from Asian religious healing traditions, including acupuncture, traditional Chinese medicine and Ayurvedic medicine (an Indian healing system), and meditation techniques, *rather than a faith tradition*. The increased popularity and acceptance of alternative medicine nonetheless introduces Americans to Eastern ideas of spirituality and health, even if taught by acupuncturists and Ayurvedic healers.

Reorganization and reorientation of Western religions in America has also facilitated the emergence and popularity of Asian religions. The decline of many mainline Protestant churches and the continued religious curiosity of the baby boom generation led many spiritual seekers to Asian religions in the 1960s and many of them

Theravada Buddhism, the branch of Buddhism traditionally practiced in Southeast Asia, officially arrived in the United States in 1966 when its first permanent organization was started in Washington, D.C. Since then, temples and meditation centers have opened across the country and the number of people involved in them has grown exponentially. Today there are more than 80 such Thai Buddhist temples scattered across 29 states. Approximately 375 monks, born and trained in Thailand, live at these temples and lead the daily activities. In addition to hosting classes, festivals, and other gatherings, more than half of the temples support local community activities like cultural centers, interfaith organizations, and prison ministries.

One of the authors, Wendy Cadge, studied Wat Mongkoltempunee, a Thai Buddhist temple in the suburbs of Philadelphia, and the Insight Meditation Center, an organization started and attended primarily by non–Asian converts in Cambridge, Massachusetts. She found that Asian and non–Asian Buddhists at these two centers share basic ideas about the Buddha and his core teachings, but have adapted those teachings in many different ways. At Wat Mongkoltempunee, for example, regular activities include chanting, meditating, listening to talks by the monks, and the exchange of material goods and spiritual teachings between lay people and the monks. By donating to the temple, many lay people believe they will be reborn in a better life. Ideas about rebirth are largely absent from the Cambridge Insight Meditation Center where non–Asian lay teachers (not monks) see Buddhism as rooted in meditation and focus on ways that practitioners can bring that meditation and mindfulness into their daily lives.

Despite these differences, however, the two centers are adapting the Theravada Buddhist tradition to the United States in some common ways. Both centers teach that the Buddha told people to "come and see" and emphasize flexibility in their teachings and practices. Both centers are loosely bounded, rather than strictly hierarchical, organizations based largely on practices rather than beliefs. And questions about Buddhist identities are deemphasized at each organization.

continue to experiment with Asian religions today. Some liberal Protestant and Jewish denominations have also opened up to learning about non-Western religions through book groups, guest speakers, yoga, or meditation teachings that take place in their buildings. In Cambridge, Massachusetts, for example, members of a congregational church can attend a Wednesday evening laity-led meditation in the main sanctuary. The evening begins with readings from the Psalms, then proceeds to an hour-long meditation based explicitly on Buddhist techniques, and ends with Communion. Anecdotal evidence from Christian and Jewish congregations suggests that congregations in urban areas that draw from more affluent populations are particularly likely to host such programs. One conservative Jewish congregation in San Francisco hired a rabbi who had previously headed the local Zen center, thereby exemplifying the local catch phrase, "Bu-Jews." Some Christian and Jewish leaders have also become more open to using Asian beliefs in their own teachings. For instance, one ongoing interfaith dialogue between Catholic, Buddhist, and Hindu nuns and monks, institutionalized in the group "Monastics in Dialogue," has published books with titles like Benedict's Dharma, explicitly linking the Benedictine monastic tradition to Buddhism. The increased openness of liberal Christian and Jewish leaders and organizations, coupled with the increased prevalence of Asian religious practices outside of formal Asian organizations, is a central reason that Asian spirituality has become so popular in recent years.

higher stages?

The shape, content, and practice of Asian religions in America has changed dramatically, particularly in the wake of post-1965 immigration. Some of this interest, like that displayed in advertising campaigns, is likely a fad that will soon yield to the next fashion. Beneath the fad, however, hundreds of organizations have emerged around Asian religions in America and millions of people have been exposed to Asian religious teachings and practices. All of this influence has and will likely continue to significantly shape American life.

RECOMMENDED RESOURCES

Courtney Bender. "Yoga in Contexts." Unpublished manuscript, Department of Religion, Columbia University, 2003.

> Drawing on interviews with teachers in a large northeastern city, Bender examines how social class influences teaching styles and practices.

Wendy Cadge. Heartwood: The First Generation of Theravada Buddhism in America (University of Chicago Press, 2004).

> Reports Cadge's research on two Theravada Buddhist communities.

Diana L. Eck. A New Religious America (HarperCollins, 2001).

> A useful overview of how non-Western religions are practiced in different American contexts.

Paul D. Numrich. Old Wisdom in the New World: Americanization in Two Immigrant Theravada Buddhist Temples (University of Tennessee Press, 1996).

> A comprehensive study of how Asians and native-born white Americans are involved in a Sri Lankan temple in Los Angeles and a Thai temple in Chicago.

Sita Reddy. "Asian Medicine in America: The Ayurvedic Case." Annals of the American Academy of Political and Social Science 583 (2002): 97–121.

> An overview of the history and transformation of Ayurveda, the classical South Asian medical tradition, in America.

Thomas Tweed. The American Encounter with Buddhism: 1844–1912: Victorian Culture and the Limits of Dissent (Indiana University Press, 1992).

> A history of Buddhism's popularity in nineteenth-century America.

Thomas Tweed and Stephen Prothero. Asian Religions in America: A Documentary History (Oxford University Press, 1999).

> These selections demonstrate the breadth and depth of the American encounter with Asian religions from 1784 to the present.

Robert Wuthnow and Wendy Cadge. "Buddhists and Buddhism in the United States: Accounting for Americans' Receptivity." Unpublished paper, Center for the Study of Religion, Princeton University, 2003.

> Examines the influence of Buddhists on Americans.

REVIEW QUESTIONS

1. What do Cadge and Bender believe are the main reasons for the recent fascination in the West with Asian religions?

2. Discuss how Asian religion has been incorporated into U.S. society, and how this has affected both religion and society. For example, consider the framing of yoga and acupuncture as techniques for "stress management." Since we do not view these "alternative and complementary techniques" holistically, what has been lost in translation?

3. Compare this essay with the two previous essays. How does the rise of Eastern religious practices fit into American religiosity more generally? How do tradition and authenticity in Asian religions come into contact and conflict with modernity?

w. bradford wilcox

religion and the domestication of men

44

fall 2006

should we worry that evangelical protestantism turns men into abusive and insensitive patriarchs in the home? not exactly.

A wife should "submit herself graciously" to her husband's leadership, and a husband should "provide for, protect, and lead his family." So proclaimed the Southern Baptist Convention—the nation's largest evangelical Protestant denomination—in 1998. Statements like this, and religious support for gender traditionalism and antifeminist public policies more generally, indicate how conservative religious institutions have helped to stall the gender revolution of the last half century. The crucial role that Phyllis Schlafly's Eagle Forum played in defeating the ERA in the 1970s is but one example.

Beneath the politics, we know less about how religious institutions influence individual men. Journalists, academics, and feminists have been skeptical—to say the least—about the influence of religion on American family men. Journalists Steve and Cokie Roberts responded to the 1998 Southern Baptist statement, for instance, by writing that such thinking "can clearly lead to abuse, both physical and emotional." Similarly, sociologists Julia McQuillan and Myra Marx Ferree have argued that evangelical Protestantism is an influential force "pushing men toward authoritarian and stereotypical forms of masculinity and attempting to renew patriarchal relations."

Academics, journalists, and feminists raise an important question: Are religious institutions, especially conservative ones such as evangelical Protestantism or Mormonism, a force for patriarchy?

Critics have yet to examine how religious institutions, particularly conservative ones, have also become deeply concerned about the family revolution of the last half century. Increases in divorce, nonmarital childbearing, and premarital sex in the society at large and in their own ranks have disturbed many conservative churches, organizations, and leaders. Partly as a consequence of this revolution, and partly because feminism has raised women's expectations of men in the society at large and within conservative churches, conservative religious institutions have turned their focus on men with the aim of encouraging them to devote more time, attention, and emotional energy to their families. They hope to strengthen families that seem increasingly vulnerable to fragmentation.

Does religion domesticate men in ways that make them more engaged and attentive husbands and fathers? To answer this question, I focus not only on white middle-class families, but also on the urban poor, who have borne the brunt of our nation's retreat from marriage.

a force for patriarchy?

So how do religious institutions affect men who are married with children? In my book, *Soft Patriarchs and New Men: How Christianity Shapes Fathers and Husbands*, I find some evidence that religion is a force for patriarchy.

When it comes to work and family life, evangelical Protestantism (theologically conservative churches such as the Southern Baptist Church, Assemblies of God, the Presbyterian Church of America, and nondenominational evangelical churches) fosters gender inequality. Evangelical Protestant family men are more likely to endorse traditional gender attitudes than are other men. For instance, I found that 58 percent of churchgoing, evangelical men who are married with children believe that it is "much better for everyone if the man earns the main living and the woman takes care of the home and family," compared to only 44 percent of churchgoing, mainline Protestant men and 37 percent of unaffiliated men. (Mainline Protestantism encompasses the Episcopal Church, Presbyterian Church [USA], the Lutheran Church [ELCA], and the United Methodist Church.)

These attitudes, reinforced by church-based activities and social networks, matter. Evangelical Protestant husbands do an hour less housework per week than other American husbands; not surprisingly, the division of household labor is less equal in evangelical homes than in other American homes. Sociologists Jennifer Glass and Jerry Jacobs have shown that women raised in evangelical Protestant families are more likely to focus on motherhood than work: they marry earlier, bear children earlier, and work less than other women in the United States. So it is true that evangelical Protestantism—but not mainline Protestantism, Reform Judaism, and Roman Catholicism—appears to steer men (and women) toward gender inequality.

Evangelical Protestantism also steers fathers in a patriarchal direction when it comes to discipline. Drawing in part on their belief in original sin and on biblical passages that seem to promote a strict approach to discipline—"He who spares the rod hates his son, but he who loves him is careful to discipline him" (*Proverbs* 13:24)—evangelical Protestant leaders, such as Focus on

the Family President James Dobson, stress the divine authority of parents and the need for parents to take a firm hand with their children. As Dobson writes, "If a little child is taught to disrespect the authority of his parents, systematically from the tender years of childhood—to mock their leadership, to 'sass' them and disobey their instructions, to exercise extreme self-will from the earliest moments of awareness—then it is most unlikely that this same child will turn his face up to God, about twenty years later, and say humbly, 'Here I am Lord; send me!' "

Many evangelical fathers take these views to heart. They are more likely to value obedience in their children. They are also more likely to spank their children when they do not get that obedience. Specifically, evangelical fathers are significantly more likely to use corporal punishment on their children than Catholic, Jewish, and unaffiliated fathers. In important respects, evangelical Protestantism appears to be a force for patriarchal authority and gender relations.

turning the hearts of men toward their families

But this is not the whole story about religion and men in the United States. Because they are worried about the social and religious consequences of divorce and nonmarital childbearing, and because they view the vocations of marriage and parenthood in a transcendent light, churches and family ministries have devoted countless radio broadcasts, books, and sermons to the task of encouraging Americans to make their marriages and children a top priority.

Conservative religious groups, such as Promise Keepers and the Southern Baptist Convention, have been particularly attentive to the family failures of men. Recognizing that men are often the weak link in families—because they fail to focus emotionally and practically on their wives and children, and because they are often absent, physically or financially—evangelical Protestant churches and ministries have generally taken the lead in the religious world in calling on men to put their families first. Drawing also on a therapeutic emphasis that entered evangelical Protestantism in the 1970s, evangelical elites urge men to be emotionally and practically engaged with their wives and children.

For instance, one popular book among evangelicals, *If Only He Knew: What No Woman Can Resist*, by therapist Gary Smalley, chides husbands for their insensitivity toward their wives. He lists 122 ways in which husbands are insufficiently attuned emotionally to their wives—from "not inviting her out on special romantic dates from time to time" to "being easily distracted when she is trying to talk"—and exhorts men to comfort, to listen, to praise, and to communicate with their wives. Likewise, popular Christian pastor Charles Swindoll urges men to model God's love to their children in the following way: "Your boy must be very aware that *you love him*. . . . When is the last time you took him in your arms and held him close so no one else could hear, and whispered to him how happy you are to have him as your son?"

Mainline Protestant, Catholic, and Reform Jewish congregations also encourage men to invest in their families, although they do it more in the context of encouraging both men and women to honor the Golden Rule by treating their spouses and especially their children with care and consideration. As sociologist Penny Edgell reports in her new book, *Religion and Family in a Changing Society*, moderate-to-liberal congregations in these traditions criticize lives centered around careers or materialism and stress the importance of putting family life first.

This emphasis on family seems to be bearing fruit. I found that men who are religious—especially evangelical fathers and husbands—are more involved and affectionate with their children and wives than are unaffiliated family

men. As fathers, religious men spend more time in one-on-one activities like reading to their children, hug and praise their kids more often, and keep tabs on the children more than unaffiliated fathers do. For instance, churchgoing fathers spend 2.9 hours per week with their children in youth activities such as soccer, Boy Scouts, and religious youth groups, and churchgoing evangelical fathers spend 3.2 hours per week on these activities, compared to 1.6 hours for unaffiliated fathers.

As husbands, religious men are more affectionate and understanding with their wives, and they spend more time socializing with them, compared to husbands who are not regular churchgoers. I also found—contrary to the expectations of critics—that churchgoing, evangelical married men have the lowest rates of reported domestic violence of any major religious or secular group in the United States. (On the other hand, evangelical married men who do not attend church regularly have the highest rates of domestic violence.) Not surprisingly, wives of religious men report higher levels of marital happiness than wives of men who are not religious.

Religious family men—especially more conservative ones—combine elements of the new and the old in their approach to family life. They are more likely to have unequal marriages and to take a strict approach to discipline; but they are also more emotionally and practically engaged than the average secular or nominally religious family man. In a word, their approach to family life can be described as neotraditional.

faith and marriage in the city

In their recent book, *Promises I Can Keep: Why Poor Women Put Motherhood Before Marriage* (and in their *Contexts* article, Spring 2005), Kathy Edin and Maria Kefalas argue that one important reason that poor women in urban America put motherhood before marriage is that they do not have ready access to a pool of "decent," marriageable men. They claim that most of the men whom these women encounter are unemployed or underemployed in the legal economy, are in and out of jail, are unfaithful, are violent, or cannot leave drugs and alcohol alone.

It is certainly true that many young urban men do not seem to be promising candidates for marriage. But my current research on religion and marriage in America's cities suggests that religious institutions play an important and understudied role in keeping marriage alive in poor and especially working-class urban communities—including African-American communities—where marriage is often comparatively fragile. They do so in part by supplying churchgoing women with churchgoing men who are responsible, faithful, and employed.

Marriage persists in American cities partly because the three largest religious traditions—Black Protestantism, Roman Catholicism, and evangelical Protestantism—depict marriage as a sacred institution that is the best context in which to have sex, raise children, and enjoy divine favor for an intimate relationship. As Wallace Charles Smith, pastor of Shiloh Baptist in Washington, D.C., has written, "God's revelation clearly points to male-female monogamous relationships as the gift by God to humankind for the purposes of procreation and nurturing. Even for people of African descent, this concept of monogamy must be at the heart of even the extended family structure."

In my ethnographic research in the Bronx and Harlem, I have found that many pastors and priests touch on the joys and challenges of married life, encouraging spouses to be kind and forgiving to one another; more conservative clergy also encourage their members to avoid nonmarital sex and, if they are cohabiting, to consider marriage. Married church members—especially married men—are usually given prominent roles as deacons, ushers, and Bible-study leaders. Marriage is depicted as the ideal in these churches, even when many, sometimes most, of the congregants are unmarried.

But churches do more than idealize marriage. They also encourage their members—male and female—to live "decent" lives. Decent or righteous living is exalted from the pulpit as divinely ordained, and it is reinforced by fellow believers who model decent behavior and sanction members who betray the church's code of decency. At a minimum, decency encompasses hard work, sexual fidelity, the Golden Rule, avoiding drug use and excessive drinking, and responsible parenting.

For instance, earlier this year at the Abyssinian Church in Harlem, Rev. Calvin Butts III delivered a sermon entitled, "The Recovery of Righteousness": "So, Beloved, I am suggesting to you that there is no greater need before us today than the recovery of plain old-fashioned righteousness. . . . who among us would . . . eschew drunkenness, idleness, and immorality? Who would dare to stand in the face of the onslaught of the culture of sin that has enveloped our nation and say, 'I refuse to succumb. I will not yield to the temptation. I will stand like a tree planted by the water. I will not move.'?"

By lifting up the ideal of marriage, and especially by encouraging their members to live decent lives, urban churches encourage marriage and help their members to have higher-quality relationships. The effects of church attendance are particularly strong among urban men. Using

> Men who are religious—especially evangelical fathers and husbands—are more involved and affectionate with their children and wives than are unaffiliated family men.

data from the Fragile Families and Child Well-being Study, demographer Nicholas Wolfinger and I found that urban couples are 40 percent more likely to bear a child in wedlock if the mother attends church on a regular basis (several times a month or more) and 95 percent more likely if the father also regularly attends church. The man's attendance is also a better predictor than the woman's of whether urban parents will marry after a nonmarital birth.

Wolfinger and I also found that couples with children in urban America report higher levels of marital happiness and supportive behavior (affection, compromise, and encouragement) from their partners when the father, but not necessarily the mother, regularly attends church. In other words, his church attendance seems to matter for the quality of both men's and women's marriages in urban America. We also find that male church attendance improves the quality of relationships among unmarried couples.

Why is his attendance so important? Because decent men are in relatively short supply in many urban communities, especially among African Americans, churches play a crucial role in enabling urban women to locate good men and in encouraging men to remain or become decent. (Many of the urban, churchgoing men I spoke with have overcome previous problems with the law, substance abuse, or sexual promiscuity.) Although these men are by no means perfect, they are regularly encouraged by their pastors and fellow congregants to avoid the siren calls of the street, to give God glory through righteous living, and to treat their wives and children with love and respect. Besides being more supportive than other husbands, churchgoing, urban fathers are also more likely to be employed full-time and to be clean and sober. As a result, urban women are more likely to marry, and be happy in their marriages, if they find a decent, churchgoing husband.

Religion also plays an important role in reducing the wide gap between white and black marriage rates. My research suggests that church attendance is as important in promoting marriage among African Americans as it is among other racial and ethnic groups in the United States. Indeed, were it not for higher-than-average levels of church attendance among African Americans, the racial gap in marriage rates between African Americans and whites in urban America would be even larger than it already is.

Let me be clear: religion is no magic bullet for strengthening family life in urban America. Slightly more than one-third of urban mothers attend church regularly, compared to about one-fifth of urban fathers. Most urban adults—especially men—are not exposed to the family message and focus, and the code of decency, found in churches. Even couples who attend church regularly experience nonmarital pregnancies, infidelity, and the larger forces of poverty, discrimination, unemployment that can throw their relationships and lives into a downward spiral. Thus, academics, religious leaders, and especially policy makers should not view religious institutions as a panacea for nonmarital childbearing, family instability, and relationship problems in urban America.

religion in men's lives

The United States has witnessed two distinct but related revolutions in the last half-century: a gender revolution marked by increased equality in the opportunities, rewards, and responsibilities that men and women face, and a family revolution marked by the weakening of marriage as the central institution for organizing sex, childbearing, childrearing, and adult life more generally. The gender revolution has not completely triumphed, in part because men have not taken up an equal share of housework and child care. My research and that of others suggests another reason: religious institutions—particularly more conservative ones like the Southern Baptist Convention—often lend ideological and practical support to traditional gender attitudes and family behaviors; thus, feminist, academic, and journalistic critics are rightly concerned about how some religious institutions reinforce gender inequality.

But critics miss how religious institutions—especially more conservative ones—also encourage men to put their families first. Most of the institutions that men encounter in their daily lives—work, popular culture, and sports, for instance—do not push men to invest in family life. But religious institutions—especially traditional ones worried about the well-being of the family in the modern world—do encourage men to focus on their families. They provide men with messages, rituals, and activities that help them to see their roles as husbands and fathers as meaningful and important, and to improve their performance of these roles.

Churchgoing family men in the United States are more involved and affectionate fathers and husbands, compared to their peers who are secular or just nominally religious. Their wives report greater marital happiness, and are therefore less likely to divorce them. At least in urban America, these men also appear more likely to engage in "decent" behavior—for example, holding regular jobs and avoiding drug and alcohol abuse—than their less religious peers.

This neotraditional approach to family life, combining a progressive insistence on men's active engagement in family life with a traditional insistence on some degree of gender complementarity in family life, has not received much scholarly attention. But if we seek to understand family pluralism and family change in the United States in all of its complexity, we must keep these neotraditional men and their families in our sociological imagination.

RECOMMENDED RESOURCES

John P. Bartkowski. *Remaking the Godly Marriage: Gender Negotiation in Evangelical Families* (Rutgers University Press, 2001).

> Evangelical Protestant couples draw selectively on both essentialist and feminist gender ideals in negotiating married life.

Penny Edgell. *Religion and Family in a Changing Society* (Princeton University Press, 2005).

> Men, more than women, attend church to socialize their children, and—as a consequence—are more likely than women to be attracted to churches that cater to traditional families.

Sally Gallagher. *Evangelical Identity and Gendered Family Life* (Rutgers University Press, 2003).

> The conventional critique of evangelical Protestant gender politics does not capture the ambiguities and heterogeneity of gender beliefs and behaviors in this subculture.

Jennifer Glass and Jerry Jacobs. "Childhood Religious Conservatism and Adult Attainment among Black and White Women." *Social Forces* (2005) 84: 555–79.

> Evangelical Protestantism puts many women on a trajectory toward early motherhood and marriage, and away from full-time employment.

W. Bradford Wilcox. *Soft Patriarchs, New Men: How Christianity Shapes Fathers and Husbands* (University of Chicago Press, 2004).

> The religious rituals, social networks, and ideas associated with evangelical Protestantism.

REVIEW QUESTIONS

1. Wilcox suggests that evangelical Protestantism fosters gender inequality. How so? Provide an example of the statistical evidence that Wilcox offers to support this assertion.

2. In poor and especially working-class urban communities, how do religious institutions play an important role in keeping marriage alive?
3. Why have conservative religious groups like Promise Keepers and the Southern Baptist Convention paid particular attention to the family failures of men as opposed to women? If one compares churchgoing fathers with un-affiliated dads, do these efforts seem to be successful?

part **10**

Medicine and Health

david mechanic

targeting hmos: stalemate in the u.s. health care debate

spring 2004

americans love to hate health maintenance organizations (hmos). but popular opinion of managed care is based more on myth than performance. more important, americans fail to realize the inevitable clash between what they want and what they are willing to pay for.

In the 1997 film *As Good As It Gets*, actress Helen Hunt curses HMOs for neglecting her asthmatic son. Newspapers reported that audiences around the country applauded, a scene I witnessed in my local theater. Managed care has become something Americans love to hate.

This emotion fuels popular perceptions of a growing crisis in health care. Recent Kaiser Health polls find that health care ranks among the important problems that the public wishes government to address, third only to the economy and national security. Our health care system is indeed troubled: medical costs and insurance premiums are rising; growing numbers of people lack adequate health insurance or have none at all; lapses in the quality of medical care lead to avoidable injuries and deaths; and the cost of Medicare and Medicaid are expected to skyrocket as seniors begin to receive prescription drug benefits, baby boomers retire, and new, more expensive technologies and procedures become available. These problems fuel the competing proposals of presidential hopeful John Kerry and incumbent George W. Bush on how to handle the growing crisis in health care. Most agree that reforms of our health care system are essential, but there is no consensus on solutions. Given rising costs, some system for

rationing scarce resources is required if access to medical care is not to depend exclusively on ability to pay out of pocket. As much as the public dislikes managed care, there is no escaping the need for such management.

the american difference

Why is America in such a quandary over health care? Other developed countries provide universal health insurance and still spend much less on health care than the United States. None of these countries has a trouble-free medical system, but many national health insurance systems—including those in Canada, France, and Germany—are reasonably efficient and achieve results comparable to ours at a lower cost. Scholars have identified several reasons for America's unusual approach to health care. Consider the following three factors.

First, people with insurance expect wide choices in doctors, services, and treatments. Technological advances in medicine make many new treatments possible, but these come with a high price tag. Insured patients have neither the economic incentive nor the expertise to make considered choices about the value for money of different medical services. If expensive treatments are not rationed, medical insurance leads inevitably to quickly rising costs.

Second, our society resists paying the additional taxes that would be necessary to provide health care to all Americans. European systems of national health insurance are motivated by social solidarity, the notion that the entire society has an obligation to ensure that basic needs such as health care are covered for all. Although Americans in social surveys generally endorse the same idea, they balk at increasing taxes to achieve this goal.

Universal health insurance would require not only tax hikes, but also government regulation to ration expenditures of limited resources. Health care rationing remains unacceptable to the public. Americans tend to distrust government and regulatory activities, placing more confidence in private enterprise and marketplace competition to allocate health care than do people in many other countries. In reality, the government subsidizes three-fifths of our nation's health care expenditures through Medicare and Medicaid, tax subsidies, and other programs. Still, we maintain an illusion of a private system of health care, in part by administering the biggest government health care programs through a network of private middlemen. Administering both public and private health insurance through scattered private firms requires massive paperwork and administrative expense. Some experts estimate that 30 cents of every dollar spent on health care go to pay for administration, contributing to the United States' high medical costs.

This huge administrative apparatus creates a third barrier to reform of our health care system. The medical industry's administrative bulk helps sustain the livelihoods and profits of many powerful interests. These insurers and administrators, as well as the actual providers of health care who benefit economically from our decentralized system, all wish to perpetuate it.

the failure of clinton care and the rise of managed care

In 1993, President Clinton's administration tried to create a system of universal health care in the United States. Theda Skocpol explains the failure of this initiative as follows: Clinton's proposal promised benefits for average Americans, but also required tight new regulations to push employers, doctors, hospitals, and insurance companies to control costs. This plan to save money by substituting government regulation for more spending on health care alarmed the groups that are economically dependent on this $1.5 trillion-per-year industry. And more privileged Americans who already had adequate medical coverage feared that Clinton's health care plan might make their health care more costly and cumbersome.

After Congress defeated the Clinton plan, employers faced rising medical insurance expenses. Cost pressures had been building since the mid-1960s, when the introduction of Medicare and Medicaid increased demand for services, the rising costs of which spread into private insurance. In the ensuing decades, health care costs grew faster than the rest of the economy. By 2001, we were spending an average of $5,035 per person annually on health care. Health care costs are projected to grow to 18.4 percent of our gross national product (GNP) in the next 10 years, an estimate of $3.4 trillion ($10,709 per person). Inflation in charges and wider access to medical care explain rising costs in part. Technological advances in medicine, many of which make treatment more effective and convenient, also pushed costs upward. However, other modern nations have adopted similar improvements, but most have arranged to control the rate of growth.

The United States, with its commitment to free markets, only halfheartedly tried to control the widening use and excessive price of medical services, as commonly done in other countries. Enthusiasts of market economics thought competition would control health care costs, but in reality health care providers rarely compete for consumers directly. Employers are the primary providers of health insurance in America. As costs rose, companies increasingly switched from providing plans that reimbursed direct fees paid to doctors to health maintenance organizations and other managed care as a way to constrain use and costs.

Initially, the large managed care plans could bargain down costs. They work by encouraging or requiring consumers to get their health care from a limited set of doctors, hospitals, or clinics. Providers who do not like what a managed care plan is willing to pay for their services lose the steady business it provides them. Managed care organizations also employ other strategies to ration health care use. Some require patients to visit a "gatekeeper" doctor before visiting expensive specialists. Some make patients get permission before undergoing certain nonemergency procedures, and they review and restrict lengthy hospital stays or expensive treatments. Yet another strategy is to implement special programs for managing the health care of especially costly patients. These approaches for a time kept costs in line with the growth of the overall economy.

the backlash against managed care

Health professionals, the media and much of the public reacted with Helen Hunt–like hostility to such restrictions, forcing management companies to contain costs less vigorously. Hospitals and other health care organizations also entered into mergers and partnerships to increase their bargaining power with managed care plans. The result is what some call "managed care lite," a retreat from aggressive cost controls that has contributed to a dramatic rise in health insurance premiums. The 2003 Annual Employer Health Benefits Survey reported that private health insurance premiums grew almost 14 percent in 2003, the third year in a row of double-digit increases. Companies often pass these rising costs on to workers by increasing their co-pays for care or taking more money out of their paychecks for premiums. Between 2001 and 2003, payments by employees for family insurance coverage grew from $1,619 to $2,412. The total cost of health insurance for a family policy now averages more than $9,000 a year. While employers still pay most of this total, the cost of insurance ultimately comes out of employees' pockets in the form of lower wages. Experts foresee further increases in the share of health care costs borne by employees.

Analyzing the backlash against managed care shows how myth often trumps reality in public opinion and in the political process. Managed health plans did make significant errors and were sometimes insensitive in how they handled criticism and complaints. Nevertheless, this alone cannot explain the backlash as reflected in television, the movies, the press, and in the responses of politicians. Our health care system has always generated a certain amount of error, misjudgment, insensitivity, and even fraud. Typically, when such incidents have come to light, they have been seen as aberrant events involving misbehavior by individual professionals, clinics, or hospitals. But with the consolidation of medical activities under massive managed care plans, individual mistakes or misdeeds appeared to be instances of greater institutional iniquity. Managed care plans came to compete with tobacco companies for the lowest standing in public opinion. Politicians, from President Clinton to local legislators, saw this as a no-lose issue and introduced hundreds of legislative proposals to regulate the industry. Although "managed care" is a vague term and poorly understood policy, it plays an important symbolic role in public political debates.

the myths and realities of managed care

Americans' collective outrage against managed care is not primarily based on personal experiences or systematically gathered evidence. Many patients who encounter strict "gatekeeping" strategies dislike this restriction on their freedom, but most studies find satisfaction with all plans to be reasonably high. In a review of recent research, Robert Miller and Harold Luft found that HMO enrollees are more dissatisfied with the interpersonal aspects of care and perceive lower quality of care than those in fee-for-service plans—but they are more satisfied with costs, prevention, and the appropriate use of tests. Ironically, objective studies document little difference in quality between the two systems. Nevertheless, anecdotes of people being denied the treatment they need alarmed patients. They began to worry that if they became seriously ill, their health plans might prioritize profits over care.

Doctors and hospitals also felt threatened by managed care and helped supply the media with horror stories. They lobbied for "any provider" legislation to require managed care organizations to include any doctor or facility in their plan. Doctors particularly resented what they perceived as business executives telling them how to make medical decisions, undermining the independence that the profession had built up for over a century. Highly paid medical specialists had to choose between taking lower payments or risk being replaced by less expensive practitioners. Hospitals were unhappy because an oversupply of hospital beds in many localities forced them to accept reimbursements that did not cover the cost of providing care. These professionals and institutions had a major stake in convincing the public that managed care reduces quality and threatens health.

Most of us find these claims credible. We are used to a system that allows us to seek care when and where we want, and to have most of the tab picked up by insurance companies. We have learned to expect whatever treatment we think we need, to choose whatever doctor we like, and to have our doctors' medical judgment go unchallenged. We dislike having to make a phone call or go through our primary care physician to get permission for specialized care, practices that have long been routine in other national health systems. We also resent being told it is time to leave the hospital when our doctor recommends a few more days. These kinds of strategies for reducing costs feel intrusive and offensive. Insensitive policies pursued by some managed care organizations, such as the insistence that mothers leave the hospital only 24 hours after a normal birth, even if it makes sense medically, feed public alarm and generate negative publicity about "drive-through deliveries" and similar indignities.

There are interesting anomalies in this picture. Studies show that the public does not trust managed care plans to put patient health before corporate profit, but these studies also find that up to half of people mistakenly report whether they themselves are in a managed care plan. This confusion is understandable because the term "managed care" itself is now widely used to label many kinds of organizational arrangements. Also, managed care plans differ a great deal in the extent to which they limit consumers' choice of doctors or regulate the use of various medical services.

Much of the debate about managed care has focused on HMOs, the most controlling form of managed care. Sociological and economic studies show that HMOs have their pros and cons in terms of the quality, cost, and access to health care they provide. Any fair evaluation of the evidence finds much more variability within each type of health plan—including old-fashioned fee-for-service—than between types. Advocates cite only those studies that support their point of view, but the evidence suggests no large differences in access or quality between care that is managed and care that is not.

three misconceptions about managed care

A number of myths influence professional and public conceptions of managed care. Their persistence serves the interests of groups who oppose health plans' efforts to constrain expenditures. For example, people believe that managed care forces doctors to work faster, resulting in shorter visits with each patient. Another misconception is that health plans "gag" doctors, prohibiting them from telling patients about treatment options. A third myth is that managed care makes it difficult for patients to get in-patient hospital care when they or their doctors feel they need it. Yet professionals themselves often disagree on how much time is necessary for a visit or whether a patient needs to be hospitalized. One physician's assertion of authority for these decisions does not necessarily make her or his decision wise.

My colleagues and I have studied how much time doctors spent with patients in visits over a 10-year period during the rise of managed care plans. We used two national data sources that measure visit time differently: a large national annual survey of Americans, carried out by the National Center for Health Statistics, that asks about their doctor visits; and an annual survey of physicians conducted by the American Medical Association. Both surveys show that the duration of the average visit to the doctor modestly increased over time. This is true for both fee-for-service and HMO visits, for primary and specialty care, for new and continuing patients, for serious and less serious illnesses, and for young and old patients. Similar studies by other researchers using different time periods and varying classifications of patients have yielded consistent findings.

Similarly, fears about "gag rules" are exaggerated. Managed care plans have occasionally intimidated physicians in one context or another. The important question, however, is how often this happens and what effect it has on patient care. Media attention to one or two instances of gagging brought a response from the President and prominent legislators. They formed a variety of committees to examine the issue and passed laws and regulations restricting the practice. Studies, however, found that contract clauses gagging physicians were uncommon and not really a problem. The General Accounting Office, a nonpartisan research arm of Congress, and patient advocates who studied gag rules came to the same conclusion independently.

The question of whether managed care plans make it difficult for patients to get the hospital care they need is more complicated. Standards for hospital admission vary, the evidence is often uncertain, and reasonable people disagree on the subject. Mistakes in judgment inevitably occur both in fee-for-service and in managed care among the millions of admission decisions made every year. Moreover, experts agree that many admissions are unneeded and can sometimes be dangerous to the patient—some 50,000 to 100,000 people die each year due to medical error, most in hospitals. Studies of administrative records as well as interviews with physicians indicate managed care plans rarely prevent physicians from admitting their patients to hospitals. Managed care programs do, however, reduce the average length of time patients spend in the hospital. It is difficult to say exactly how many days of hospital care a patient really needs, although the trend for decades has been toward less hospital time and fewer days of pure bed rest. In some cases, spending too many days in bed is debilitating and makes for longer recovery times. The accusation that patients are being discharged "sicker and quicker" was first leveled when health insurance plans began paying hospitals a fixed fee for a certain procedure rather than paying more for each day a patient spent in the facility. The same accusation has reemerged with the advent of managed care. Yet, researchers have had difficulty documenting the claim that shorter stays in the hospital hurt patients. The overall quality of medical treatment seems to be what counts, not simply what happens in the hospital.

The backlash has eroded but not eliminated managed care. Most plans have retreated to more modest management strategies, such as eliminating gatekeepers to specialty care and dropping reviews of hospital admissions. Many HMOs now pay for patients' visits to doctors outside of their plan's networks, albeit with higher patient co-payments. At the same time, hospitals and physician groups are partnering and merging to gain greater leverage over health insurance organizations.

the future of health care

Many people applaud the victory over managed care. The truth is, however, that if managed care disappeared, we would have to reinvent it. There is no other way to both extend care and control costs. Many managed care strategies persist and even dominate some settings. For example, most states require people with Medicaid to enroll in managed care plans. Some Medicaid programs are applying managed care to disabled people, who have the most complicated and extensive medical needs. President Bush's administration would like to provide incentives for Medicare enrollees to join HMOs, although many large plans have abandoned the Medicare market and seniors are reluctant to change doctors. Managed care organizations now coordinate most of the treatment for substance abuse and mental health disorders. This approach has significantly reduced costs, but mental health professionals dislike managed care, in part be-

cause it substantially reduces the payments they receive, and mental health advocates dislike the limitations it places on patients' choices. The evidence on how managed care affects the quality of treatment for mental disorders and substance abuse is mixed and uncertain, and results vary among state programs. Managed care has also moved into the area of prescription drugs. Pharmacy Benefit Managers (PBMs) steer patients toward cheaper or (in theory) more effective drugs by restricting lists of approved medication or charging different co-payments for various classes of treatments. Some popular and expensive drugs have become "over-the-counter" and are now available without a prescription, which means that patients must now pay out-of-pocket for the same medications their plans used to cover.

More broadly, however, managed care is in retreat. The nation has returned to a dispirited discussion about how to heal its health care system. A few advances have been made. Although many children lost Medicaid coverage with welfare reform, the Children's Health Insurance Program (CHIP) has, in many states, reduced the uninsured child population. Some states have developed prescription drug programs for their most needy senior citizens. However, the national recession, the federal budget deficit, and budgetary problems in most states are bringing cutbacks in Medicaid and many other safety-net programs.

As the 2004 election approaches, each of the presidential hopefuls has a proposed solution to the growing crisis in health care. President Bush recommends redesigning Medicare, the controversial extension of prescription drug coverage to the elderly through the private sector, and providing tax credits so more people can purchase insurance. He proposes modest additional tax credits so 4 million more people can purchase health insurance privately. Senator Kerry proposes an $895 billion program over 10 years that would cover 27 million uninsured within a

President Clinton's health care plan was a complex proposal introduced in 1992–93 to bring about universal health insurance for all Americans. The proposal combined managed competition and managed care with considerable new regulation.

HMOs include a variety of organizations that are prepaid to care for enrollees. They vary from highly structured group practices, such as the Kaiser Permanente medical groups, to associations of independent practitioners and networks of doctors. Many of these physicians provide care to both prepaid and fee-for-service patients and work in their own offices.

Medicare is a national health insurance plan covering persons aged 65 and older, people with disabilities who meet eligibility criteria, and people with end-stage renal disease. It is paid for by a tax on earnings for all workers, enrollee premiums, and funds from general revenues.

Medicaid is a federal-state matching program that provides care to low-income people. Its main constituents are poor mothers and their children, people with disabilities, and low-income senior citizens. Although the federal government establishes minimal standards, eligibility and scope of coverage varies among states.

Preferred Provider Organizations (PPOs) are a form of managed care in which the insurance plan negotiates with specific doctors and health facilities to have their enrollees treated at reduced fees. Patients who use providers affiliated with the PPO have lower out-of-pocket costs.

mixed public-private program, using employer and individual tax credits and public program expansions. Former Democratic candidate John Edwards proposed a similar but more modest $590 billion program that would cover an additional 22 million uninsured, and begin expansions with an individual mandate for universal coverage of children under age 21.

Whoever wins the 2004 election will have difficulty honoring their campaign promises. They will face challenges with rising medical costs, covering the large uninsured population, and maintaining the public safety net. Reform will be further complicated by sluggish economic performance, the ongoing costs of Iraqi reconstruction, the political risks of rescinding recent tax cuts, and Americans' general unwillingness to pay higher taxes. Comprehensive government coverage of health care is probably not on the horizon.

Nonetheless, any viable health care system in the future will require rationing of health care. Addressing this openly seems like political suicide to public officials. The health debate, like much else in federal policy, has a strong ideological component. Conflicting ideas about the virtues of government versus the private market, individual and social responsibility, and the appropriateness of for-profit or nonprofit enterprise in health care all complicate the debate. These ideological conflicts transcend evidence and experience, blinding us to the successes of other advanced nations that provide health care more rationally and equitably.

Many members of the public, health care professionals, and even some members of Congress see a centralized national health insurance system, such as the Canadian model or extension of Medicare, as the best way to establish universal health care in America. But advocates of such an approach remain a minority and face enormously powerful opposition. It seems safe to predict that, in the foreseeable future, we will muddle along and retain our exceptional status in the world. Reform, if it comes, is most likely to come a little at a time. The largest myth of all is that health care in America is the best in the world.

RECOMMENDED RESOURCES

Institute of Medicine. *Crossing the Quality Chasm: A New Health System for the 21st Century* (National Academy Press, 2001).

This influential report proposes a design for improving the quality of health care.

David Mechanic. "The Managed Care Backlash: Perceptions and Rhetoric in Health Care Policy and the Potential for Health Care Reform." *Milbank Quarterly 79* (2001): 35–54.

This paper provides an in-depth analysis of what triggered the managed-care backlash.

David Mechanic, Donna D. McAlpine, and Marsha Rosenthal. "Are Patients' Office Visits with Physicians Getting Shorter?" *New England Journal of Medicine* 344 (2001): 198–204.

This study documents the enormous gap between the rhetoric and reality of doctor visits during the era of managed care growth.

Theda Skocpol. *Boomerang: Health Care Reform and the Turn Against Government.* (Norton, 1997).

Skocpol provides an insightful analysis of the defeat of the Clinton health care plan, with lessons for the future.

Paul Starr. The *Social Transformation of American Medicine* (Basic Books, 1982).

This Pulitzer Prize–winning volume explains how medicine developed its professional dominance in the twentieth century.

REVIEW QUESTIONS

1. What is the main thesis of Mechanic's essay? What is he attempting to disprove?
2. What are the three main barriers to reform of the U.S. health care system?
3. A number of myths have shaped beliefs about managed health care. What are the myths presented by the author, and how does he disprove them? Can you think of any other myths?

lisa f. berkman

the health divide

46

fall 2004

the united states is one of the world's wealthiest nations, yet the health of average americans lags behind that of citizens in other developed countries. the huge amounts we spend on health care are not buying our population good health. the reason is a widening gap between the health of rich and poor americans.

The United States spends more on health care than any other nation in the world, both in absolute dollars and as a proportion of the national economy. Yet it ranks in the bottom half of industrialized countries in life expectancy. Overall, Americans' health is worse than that of people in Japan, Sweden, and France, as well as less affluent countries like Spain, Italy, and Cyprus. While the richest and best-educated Americans are as healthy as their counterparts in other rich nations, poor and less-educated Americans have a life expectancy comparable to adults in many Third World countries. A recent study found that African-American men in Harlem were less likely to live to age 65 than were men in Bangladesh. The vast sums we spend on health care do not buy most Americans good health.

Americans' health has improved considerably over the past century. But the health gap between rich and poor persists and may have even increased over the past two decades. The gap encompasses men and women, blacks and whites, recent immigrants and those who have been here for many generations. Improving the health of the worst-off Americans remains a major challenge. Meeting that challenge depends on understanding the causes of poor health in people who are socially and economically disadvantaged and on our ability to do something about those causes.

understanding americans' ill health

One possible explanation for why the United States lags so noticeably behind other developed countries in health is that many Americans lack access to quality medical care. Some researchers believe that if all Americans received top-notch treatment, the United States would rank near the top in citizens' health. But the evidence does not support this hope. While good health care for all Americans should remain a high priority for many reasons, studies in Great Britain have found that better access to care does not necessarily reduce health disparities between the rich and poor. By the 1980s, British citizens had 30 years of experience with free and universal access through the National Health Service. But according to Mel Bartley, during the 1980s the gap in death rates between rich and poor had actually increased—in step with rising economic inequality.

Over a longer period, 1930 to 1990, the death rate for middle-aged British men with the lowest levels of education and income dropped from about 1,300 to about 900 deaths per 100,000 people, but among men with the most money and schooling death rates dropped much faster, from 920 to 310. Thus, the death rate of British men at the bottom of the social scale went from being 50 percent higher than that of men at the top to 300 percent higher. The experience of the

United Kingdom suggests that improving access alone is unlikely to solve the problem. It also suggests that we should look more closely at the link between economic inequalities and health. In particular, the large health differences among groups in the United States may explain our low international ranking. For example, consider the proportion of infants who die each year. In the 1990s, about 11 of every 1,000 infants born in the United States died before the age of one, an unusually high rate. But this number masks enormous variability. White women with at least some college education lost fewer than 6 infants per 1,000 born, compared to 9 infant deaths per 1,000 births to white women who had not finished high school. Black women confront even higher infant mortality rates. Black mothers who had attended college lost 14 per 1,000 infants, while black women with less than a high school education lost 20. This compounded risk is sometimes referred to as the double jeopardy of poor black women, among whom infant mortality rates are four times higher than the best-off white women.

Even with all the neonatal technology in the United States, it ranks 25th in infant mortality among 38 developed countries. Neonatal intensive care units now regularly save small, low birth weight infants who years earlier would have died. Yet American infant mortality rates remain similar to those in the Czech Republic, Greece, Portugal, Belgium, and Cuba. Why? In the United States, less-affluent mothers are more likely to smoke, and are less likely to get prenatal care, have health insurance, or vaccinate their children. Poor American women have limited resources for housing, nutrition, and transportation. Frequently, their jobs provide no sick leave. All of these factors contribute to poor health for their infants.

American children born today can expect to live eight years longer than children born in the 1950s. But, again, aggregate statistics conceal substantial differences across socioeconomic groups. For example, the life expectancy of 45-year-old Americans, an excellent indicator of adult health, rises steadily as family income rises. This is true for men, women, and people in all racial and ethnic groups. Thus, in the 1980s, 45-year-old black and white men in families earning at least $25,000 could expect to live about seven years longer than white and black men in families earning less than $10,000. Income made less difference for black and white women—four and three years, respectively—but it mattered nonetheless.

To show this connection between social standing and health, Figure 1 displays death rates from different causes—chronic diseases, injuries, and communicable diseases—for men and women, according to the level of education they attained (more education typically brings better jobs and more wealth). In all cases, as education increases, death rates drop. We see that not only do the least-educated Americans experience the worst health, but also that there is a gradient of risk—each increase in education brings better health. The same pattern holds for diabetes, homicide, suicide, and Americans' ratings of their own health.

Not every cause of death follows this pattern. For instance, lung cancer rates among older women actually increase as education rises. This is in part because affluent women started smoking in the 1950s and 60s, before less well-to-do women did, and now, decades later, they are suffering the deadly consequences. However, over the past 20 years smoking rates have remained steady for less-educated men and women while they have fallen among the better educated. Today, smoking is highest among high school dropouts. In addition, men and women with at least some college education are less likely to drink heavily and to lead sedentary lifestyles than the less educated, while poorer women are more likely to be overweight. Thus, the connec-

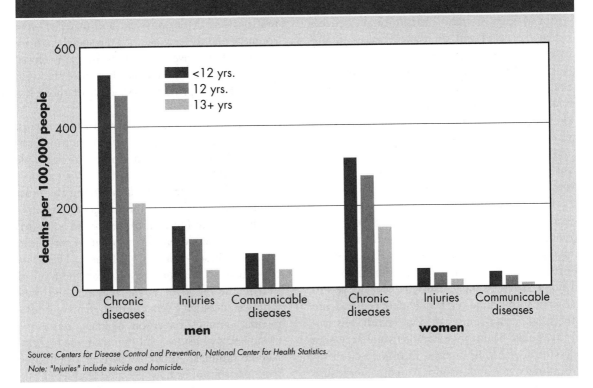

deaths per 100,000 people

600

400

200

0

<12 yrs.
12 yrs.
13+ yrs

Chronic
diseases

Injuries

Communicable
diseases

men

Chronic
diseases

Injuries

Communicable
diseases

women

Source: *Centers for Disease Control and Prevention, National Center for Health Statistics.*

Note: *"Injuries" include suicide and homicide.*

tion between disease and social standing changes over time depending upon the underlying causes of those diseases and who is vulnerable. In general though, the economically better-off have significantly better odds of experiencing a long life relatively free of disability, disease, or risk of death by violence.

understanding health inequality

Some researchers argue that it is not being poor that makes people sick, but being sick that makes people poor. Sickly children have trouble learning and doing well in school, and adults who are sick miss work and lose income. While part of the connection between poverty and ill health is undoubtedly due to the debilitating effects of ill-

ness, most studies suggest that this can only partly explain the relationship between illness and income. Studies that follow children or working adults over a number of years find that where people are on the social and economic ladder affects their health in several ways. The accumulation of disadvantage over decades significantly impairs health. Also, people are particularly vulnerable to the effects of poverty and disadvantage in certain periods of life, notably early childhood. Disadvantaged people become less healthy than others both because of their living conditions and their social circumstances, such as their relationships and jobs. These situations affect people's health biologically—through exposure to toxins, increases in blood pressure, and suppressed immune responses—and psychologically—through reduced self-confidence, greater depression, and turning to potentially self-destructive behavior like smoking and drinking.

Social scientists have often distinguished between the distal and proximate causes of diseases, or to use less jargon, upstream conditions (such as people's work) and downstream conditions (such as their blood pressure). The great majority of recent health campaigns in the United States have targeted the downstream or physical conditions rather than the economic and social sources of disease (neighborhood environment, work settings, or poverty). The national institutes that fund health research, such as the National Institutes of Health and the Centers for Disease Control, spend the bulk of their funds to study the biological and behavioral risk factors for disease. Only recently have new efforts emerged in many countries, including the United States, to understand and attack the upstream social conditions that underlie and are the fundamental causes of poor health. Historically, public health interventions were very successful in reducing disease. Efforts to clean up drinking water and air and to reduce exposure to toxins in the workplace substantially improved Americans' health by changing collective conditions rather than individual behavior. For example, once scientists discovered the problem of contaminated water in the nineteenth century, officials did not simply ask people to boil their household water before drinking it. Instead, they built facilities to clean the water in each city before piping it into peoples' homes. Often, asking individuals to change their behavior is less effective than changing their environment.

Today, many public health experts contend that if we were to emphasize altering the broader, environmental conditions that lead to poor health, we would increase our chances of reducing social inequalities in health. Our historical experience suggests that environmental interventions that do not rely heavily on the actions of individuals—especially people with the fewest resources and options—are most likely to succeed. Consider two additional examples. The first deals with the physical and material environment and the second with the social environment. In both cases, the health divide is closed by maintaining the excellent health of the well-to-do while improving the health of those less well-off.

Material deprivation and exposure to toxins. Inequality manifests itself in the conditions under which people live and work; poorer people are less able to avoid harmful environments. Take lead exposure, which is among the most dangerous and yet common threats to cognitive development and health. In the United States today, young children most often absorb lead from lead-based paint in old houses. There is a clear, inverse relationship between the level of lead in the blood of young children and their family's income. Even children from middle-income families have, on average, twice the blood levels of lead as children from the highest-income families. About 12 percent of children from poor families have elevated lead levels and poor black children have rates of more than 20 percent. Researchers in the environmental justice movement also have documented the proximity of hazardous waste sites to neighborhoods of minorities and those with concentrated poverty. Studies of air pollution show that such neighborhoods have less healthy air than wealthier neighborhoods.

Poor people and ethnic minorities face greater risks of toxic poisoning and injuries at work, too. For example, agricultural work, which is done almost exclusively by Hispanic and migrant workers, accounts for 13 percent of U.S. workplace fatalities even though just 3 percent of the workforce labors in such occupations. Pesticide toxicity alone causes more than 300,000 cases of illness and 100,000 deaths annually among farm workers.

Social deprivation and stress. The social conditions of work, not just the physical conditions, pose a greater health risk for those in low-ranking as opposed to high-ranking occupations. In his study of British civil servants, Michael Marmot found that workers in lower occupational grades had less control at work, received less support, and faced greater demands than workers above them in the system. Civil servants with less control and more demands at work were also more likely than others to get sick and die. Job stress explained a large part of the link between occupational grade and poor health. Having little control over one's work—for example, not being able to take time off for personal calls and errands or not being able to manage the work pace—is a particularly important health risk. Studies of city bus drivers show how highly stressed they are as they make their rounds on a schedule that is virtually impossible to maintain. After weeks on the job, many experience increases in blood pressure, gain weight, and often become hypertensive and diabetic—results both of hard hours at work and lack of control over their circumstances.

The nature of work in the United States has changed over the past decades such that job insecurity, instability, shift-work and reduced investment in training has placed increasing stress on employees, especially those with less education and fewer opportunities to move up the job ladder. The percentage of workers who are satisfied with their jobs has dropped over the past 10 years. As one worker interviewed by Studs Terkel said, "Most of us, like the assembly line worker, have jobs that are too small for our spirit. Jobs are not big enough for people." In a recent *New York Times* editorial, Adam Cohen suggests that work today is even less likely than 30 years ago to provide meaning and a sense of accomplishment for workers. It is this social experience that translates into poor health. In addition, jobs that strain the balance between work and home by not providing adequate family and sick leave may undermine the health of entire families, not only of the employees. Imagine the stress that a young single mother working in a small business that does not allow sick leave faces when she comes to work knowing that her young child is ill. She might experience increases in blood pressure, changes in the way her body metabolizes food, changes in immune response as she worries about losing her pay or even her job if she leaves work to care for her child—or similar responses if she stays at work and worries. The long shifts that many parents work before returning to family responsibilities take a toll, especially on those with few social and economic resources. The day-to-day difficulties of juggling an insecure and inflexible job with the demands of family life is physiologically hard on many Americans.

People who are socially isolated run notably high risks for early death, according to research in the United States, the United Kingdom, and throughout Europe. In the first study I conducted on this topic, my colleagues and I suspected that one of the reasons that poor economic conditions resulted in poor health was that they disrupted the key social relationships that people depend on practically and emotionally. We found, in a sample of almost 7,000 adults in Alameda County, California, that men and women who were economically disadvantaged were more likely than others to be isolated—to lack intimate connections such as a spouse, close friends, or relatives, and ties to their communities such as club or church memberships. For example, both black and white women with less than a high school education were more likely to be single mothers than their better-educated counterparts. As part of the study, these people were followed over many years. Those who were socially isolated were much more likely to die prematurely. Many studies that track people for decades find the same outcome: people who report few close ties and community memberships are two to three times more likely to die early than those with extensive social bonds.

That poor people tend to be more isolated than others is one reason that their risks are elevated. It is true that working-class families tend to have closely knit social networks, heavily composed of kin. However, these ties may not substitute for connections that help people find jobs, get loans and obtain other practical help (see "Social Networks: The Value of Variety," *Contexts*, Winter 2003). As William Julius Wilson points out, African Americans living in poor, racially and economically segregated neighborhoods often lack access to the kinds of connections and relationships that would help them get better jobs and maintain strong families. Thus, economic inequality, especially poverty, impairs health by making it more difficult to find and maintain the kinds of social relationships that are essential to well-being.

The job stress, economic insecurity, and isolation common among the less affluent affect their health indirectly, through lack of resources, inadequate information, and harmful habits. The same social circumstances also directly affect people's physiology. When people are confronted with long-term, chronically stressful circumstances—like fearing a job layoff or being short of money at the end of the month—their bodies experience a stress reaction often called the "fight or flight" response. While adaptive in the short term, over the long run this response exhausts the body and takes a toll on many of its systems. Elevations in blood pressure, blood sugar, and other such metabolic changes increase the risk of diabetes, cardiovascular disease, and strokes. These same stress responses can also reduce immune system functions, leading to a greater risk of infectious diseases and cancer. People pay a biological price for the heightened and continued vigilance required of them in stressful social situations.

People also encounter very different social and physical circumstances in their homes, neighborhoods, schools, and workplaces. These circumstances influence their health and well-being over a lifetime, leading to more frequent sickness and earlier deaths. It is not simply that poverty leads to poor health, but each step up the economic ladder, from the bottom to the top rung, brings with it improved health and lower risks.

It is this inequality in health, derived from inequalities in economic situations, that accounts for the disappointing place of the United States in the international health rankings. If we could reduce the "health divide" between rich and poor either by improving the health of the most disadvantaged or by reducing the extent of economic disadvantage, we could remedy this national failure.

San Francisco city buses stuck in mid-day traffic. The stress on bus drivers of trying to meet unrealistic schedules—and on other workers who have little control over their work—increase their risk of being overweight, and of having high blood pressure, hypertension, and diabetes.

what are the policy options?

There are two general approaches to reducing inequalities in health. The first involves the use of progressive taxation, economic safety nets, or other redistributive policies to reduce economic inequality. This approach stems from the notion that inequality needs to be attacked directly. In the United States, both private and public policies—negotiated wage rates and the minimum wage, for example—affect this goal. The second approach tries to block the downstream paths by which economic inequality creates health inequality. Cleaning up the environmental dangers, improving working conditions, re-balancing work and family responsibilities, increasing access to health care, and improving nutrition are some ways to block the conversion of inequality into poor health. In the current political climate, the second approach may be the more viable alternative. However, both are worthy of more serious consideration.

These two options are not mutually exclusive and may be pursued simultaneously. Promoting healthful public and private policies at all levels requires collective effort. Most Americans are comfortable with the notion of living in a society with economic inequality. However, they are less comfortable with inequalities of death and with America's dismal ranking on health. Therein may lie some leverage.

This work is supported by the Russell Sage Foundation and Robert Wood Johnson Scholars in Health and Society Program.

RECOMMENDED RESOURCES

Donald Acheson. *Independent Inquiry into Inequalities in Health Report* (The Stationery Office, 1998).

Summarizes a governmental inquiry into health inequality in the United Kingdom.

Mel Bartley. *Health Inequality: An Introduction to Theories, Concepts and Methods* (Blackwell Publishing, 2004).

Bartley provides an introduction to assessing health inequality, especially from the American perspective, directed at both social scientists and journalists.

Lisa F. Berkman and Thomas A. Glass. "Social Integration, Networks and Health." In *Social Epidemiology*, eds. Lisa F. Berkman and Ichiro Kawachi (Oxford University Press, 2000).

Reviews the work on social networks and health.

Howard Frumkin. "Minority Workers and Communities." *Occupational Medicine: State of the Art Reviews* 14(1999): 495–517.

This excellent study details the working conditions of minority workers in the United States.

Bruce G. Link and Jo C. Phelan. "Social Conditions Are Fundamental Causes of Disease." *Journal of Health and Social Behavior*, Special Issue (1995): 80–94.

The authors review the connection between social and economic disadvantage, social networks, and health.

Michael G. Marmot. "Health Inequalities Among British Civil Servants: The Whitehall Study." *Lancet* 337 (1991): 1387–93.

This is an excellent paper on the longstanding Whitehall Study of Inequality in Health.

United States Department of Health and Human Services. *Health, United States, 1998 with Socioeconomic Status and Health Chart Book* (United States Department of Health and Human Services, 1998).

This government publication displays health statistics drawn from national surveys.

William Julius Wilson. *The Truly Disadvantaged* (University of Chicago Press, 1987).

A classic work on the influence of residential segregation in the United States.

REVIEW QUESTIONS

1. What does Berkman describe as the "double risk" for black mothers?
2. How would you explain our health care system to someone who lived outside the United States? Compare our system with those of other industrialized countries. Why do you think we have kept our current health care system despite our high spending and low rankings on life expectancy and infant mortality?
3. Identify the specific factors Berkman discusses to break down health care inequality. Can you think of any she did not include?
4. Health care seems to be constantly debated. Using your school's library, find an article on the 1993–1994 Universal Health Care debate. Can you find anything in the article that is supported by the research of Berkman or Mechanic? Is there anything that is refuted by Berkman and Mechanic's research?

allan v. horwitz and jerome c. wakefield

the epidemic in mental illness: clinical fact or survey artifact?

47

winter 2006

do half of all americans suffer from mental disorders at some point in their lives? or do surveys misdiagnose the distress that is a normal part of every life?

According to large, community-based research studies that the media report with great fanfare, alarming numbers of Americans suffer from mental disorders. The most frequently cited study, the National Comorbidity Survey, claims that half the population suffers from a mental illness at some point. Moreover, these same studies show that few people diagnosed as mentally ill seek professional treatment.

Policy discussions, scientific studies, media reports, advocacy documents, and pharmaceutical advertisements routinely cite such figures to show that mental disorder is a public health problem of vast proportions, that few sufferers receive appropriate professional treatment, that untreated disorders incur huge economic costs, and that more people need to take medication or seek psychotherapy to overcome their suffering. Awareness of large numbers of untreated, mentally ill people in the community has reshaped mental health policy, justifying efforts to address this "unmet need for treatment"—for example, by training general practitioners or public school personnel to screen for and treat mental disorders.

Despite their rhetorical value, the high rates are a fiction; the studies establish no such thing. In fact, the extraordinarily high rates of untreated mental disorder reported by community studies are largely a product of survey methodologies that inherently overstate the number of people

with a mental disorder. The inflated rates stem from standard questions about symptoms with no context provided that might distinguish the normal distress experienced in life from genuinely pathological conditions that indicate an underlying mental illness. Both get classified as signs of disorders. Moreover, because people experiencing normal reactions to stressful events are less likely than the truly disordered to seek medical attention, such questions are bound to inflate estimates of the rate of untreated disorders.

We use depression to illustrate such exaggeration. However, our argument applies equally well to estimates of other presumed mental illness such as sexual dysfunctions, anxiety disorders, or drug and alcohol abuse. Some history will help to frame the problem.

origins of symptom-based diagnosis

All major surveys in psychiatric epidemiology, the field that assesses the patterns of mental illness in a population, attempt to translate as exactly as possible into survey questions the diagnostic criteria published in various editions of the American Psychiatric Association's *Diagnostic and Statistical Manual of Mental Disorders* (DSM). Often called the "Bible of psychiatry" because of its authoritative status and almost universal use by clinicians, researchers, and medical insurers, the *DSM* provides official diagnostic definitions for all mental disorders.

Since its third edition, published in 1980, the *DSM* has attempted to provide precise, reliable, easily applied criteria for diagnosing each mental disorder. This approach was a response to a variety of criticisms of psychiatry common at the time, many of which hinged on the unreliability of psychiatric diagnosis. That is, different clinicians were likely to diagnose the same individual in different ways. Two problems led to this embarrassing result. First, members of different theoretical schools often conceived of and defined disorders differently, on the basis of their own theoretical concepts, whether psychodynamic, biological, or behavioral. Second, earlier definitions were generally vague and referred to fuzzily defined internal processes. To increase reliability, the third edition of the *DSM* (*DSM-III*) addressed both problems by stating diagnostic criteria strictly in terms of observable or reportable symptoms. Theoretical concepts were left out of diagnosis, which became "theory neutral." The new definitions used only symptoms that clinicians could precisely describe and reliably ascertain.

The *DSM-III* approach of defining disorders by presenting lists of symptoms is still used in the current edition published in 2000. For example, the definition of depressive disorder requires that five of the following nine symptoms be present during a two-week period: depressed mood, lack of pleasure or interest in usual activities, change in appetite or weight, insomnia or excessive sleep, psychomotor agitation or retardation (slowing down), fatigue or loss of energy, feeling worthless or inappropriately guilty, lack of concentration or indecisiveness, and recurrent thoughts of death, suicide, or a suicide attempt. Cases of normal bereavement after the death of a loved one are exempted from diagnosis, but only if the grief involves no severe symptoms and lasts no more than two months.

using standardized questions in community surveys

Epidemiologists study rates and patterns of disease in order to find clues about causes and determine possible treatments. They eagerly embraced the *DSM*'s symptom-based approach to diagnosis. Because researchers generally accepted the *DSM* criteria as authoritative, psychiatric epidemiologists could use them without having to do elaborate studies of their own to establish their validity. Moreover, the approach seemed to resolve a series of problems that plagued contemporary community studies of mental disorder.

Early studies in psychiatric epidemiology had simply surveyed various treatment settings and relied on the diagnoses contained in medical charts to determine rates of mental disorder. But it soon became apparent that the number of treated patients did not reliably indicate the degree of mental disorder in a community for a variety of reasons, such as lack of access to appropriate treatment, people's reluctance to seek professional help because of stigma or cost, and variations in diagnostic practices. Community studies of mental disorders try to get around these problems by attempting to determine directly how many people in the community have various mental disorders, regardless of whether they have undergone treatment. This requires interviewing many normal as well as disordered people.

In contrast to respondents in treatment studies, most of the people in community studies have never been diagnosed with mental disorders. Thus, to establish rates of disorders in the overall population, community surveys must collect thousands of cases. This poses formidable challenges. For one thing, psychiatric or other professional interviewers are expensive. For another, unless questions are carefully standardized, there is a danger of unreliability in the way the interviews are conducted. Additionally, valid

CATEGORY #4		YES (1)	NO (5)
D9. Have you ever had 2 weeks or more when nearly every night you had trouble falling asleep?	(#6)		Go to D11
D10. Have you ever had 2 weeks or more when nearly every night it took you at least 2 hours to fall asleep?	(#7)		
D11. Have you ever had 2 weeks or more when nearly every night you had trouble staying asleep?	(#8)		Go to D13
D12. Did you ever have 2 weeks or more when nearly every night you lay awake more than one hour?	(#9)		
D13. Have you ever had 2 weeks or more when nearly every morning you woke up too early?	(#10)		Go to D15
D14. Have you ever had 2 weeks or more when nearly every morning you would wake up at least 2 hours before you wanted to?	(#11)		
D15. Have you ever had 2 weeks or longer when nearly every day you were sleeping too much?	(#12)		

D15a. INTERVIEWER: IF ANY YES RESPONSE IN D9–D15, CHECK "SADNESS" CATEGORY #4 BOX ON REFERENCE CARD.

Examples of screening questions for depression from the National Comorbidity Study.

analysis of qualitative data such as psychiatric interviews is extremely difficult.

The *DSM*'s symptom-based diagnostic criteria offered a solution to these problems. Epidemiologists conducting community studies simply translated the *DSM*'s symptoms into closed-format questions about symptoms experienced by respondents. This yielded a questionnaire that nonprofessionals could be trained to administer, allowing cost-effective collection of data from large numbers of people. Computer programs using the *DSM* criteria could determine if a disorder was present.

Accurate estimates of prevalence require that different interviewers ask these questions in exactly the same way. As one study notes, "The interviewer reads specific questions and follows positive responses with additional prescribed questions. Each step in the sequence of identifying a psychiatric symptom is fully specified and does not depend upon the judgment of the interviewers." Without such standardization, even minor variations in wording or in the interviewer's probes or instructions can lead to different results. The resulting standardized interview format excluded any discussion of the reported symptoms and their context. The rigid approach of structured interviews improves the consistency of symptom assessment across interviewers and research sites and thus the reliability of diagnostic decisions. Note, however, that the decision to use decontextualized, symptom-based measures in community studies assumes an uncritical acceptance of the *DSM*'s symptom-based criteria and is based largely on considerations of practicality and cost, not on independent tests that prove the accuracy of such methods in identifying disorders in the community.

are survey-based diagnoses equivalent to clinical diagnoses?

The diagnoses of particular disorders in surveys, however reliable they may be, provide poor measures of mental illness in community populations. The core assumption in community studies is that tightly structured questions allow researchers to obtain diagnoses that are comparable to those of a psychiatrist, since the questions match the *DSM*'s symptom criteria. This assumption rests in turn on the assumption that those criteria are valid for identifying disorders. However, those diagnosed as having mental disorders in community populations differ in two fundamental ways from those who seek mental health treatment.

First, people seeking help are highly self-selected and use all sorts of contextual information to decide for themselves if their feelings exceed ordinary and temporary responses to stressful events. David Karp, for example, found that depressed people sought help from psychiatrists only after they attributed their symptoms to internal psychological problems and not to stressful situations:

[O]nce it becomes undeniable that something is really wrong, that one's difficulties are too extreme to be pushed aside as either temporary or reasonable, efforts begin in earnest to solve the problem. Now choices to relieve pain are made with a conscious and urgent deliberation. The shift in thinking often occurs when the presumed cause of pain is removed, but the difficulty persists. Tenure is received, you finally get out of an oppressive home environment, a destructive relationship is finally ended, and so on, but the depression persists. Such events destroy theories about the immediate situational sources of depression and force the unwelcome interpretation that the problem might be permanent and have an internal locus. One has to consider that it might be a problem of the self rather than the situation.

People who enter treatment thus have already decided that their problems go beyond normal reactions.

Second, clinicians as well as patients make contextual judgments of symptoms when they diagnose mental illness in treated populations. Psychiatrists have long recognized that symptoms such as depressed mood, loss of interest in usual activities, insomnia, loss of appetite, inability to concentrate, and so on might naturally occur in response to major losses, humiliations, or threats to one's meaning system, such as having a marriage unravel, losing one's job or pension, or failing a test that has serious implications for one's career.

Such reactions, even when quite intense, are part of normal human nature. Applying the *DSM*'s symptom-based criteria literally, with no professional judgment, would result in classifying such normal reactions as disordered. Clinical diagnosis has a built-in backup system for catching such potential misdiagnoses: the clinician takes a psychiatric history in an interview that includes questions about context. The clinician is free to deviate from the literal *DSM* criteria in arriving at a diagnostic judgment and is responsible for doing so when the criteria erroneously classify a normal reaction as disordered. How often clinicians actually use this corrective option is unknown, but at least it exists in principle.

Thus, in treated populations, contextual judgments by both patients and clinicians precede clinical diagnosis. In contrast, the diagnostic process in community studies, which involves neither self-evaluation by respondents nor clinical judgment, ignores the context in which symptoms develop. Survey interviewers are forbidden to judge the validity of responses or to discuss the intent of questions, and they neither exercise clinical discretion nor use flexible probes about responses. Even if the respondent seems to misunderstand a question, the interviewer is instructed to repeat the question verbatim. The absence of interviewer probes can produce seriously misleading results. For example, when asked, "Have you ever had a period of two weeks or more when you had trouble sleeping," a person might recall a time when ongoing construction across the street interrupted her sleep. In such a case, she can disregard the literal meaning of the question, self-censor her response, and not report the "symptom." Or she can give an answer that is literally true, with the result that her troubled sleep will be counted as a potential symptom of a mental illness. The lack of clinical judgment based on exploring context can easily inflate reported rates of pathological conditions.

the prevalence of depression

The most widely cited estimates of the prevalence of depression in the United States in the scientific, policy, and popular literatures stem from the National Comorbidity Survey (NCS) conducted in the early 1990s, with a 10-year follow-up, and from a similar study, the Epidemiologic Catchment Area (ECA) study undertaken in the early 1980s. The NCS uses two steps to obtain diagnoses of depression based on *DSM* criteria. First, respondents must answer yes to at least one of the following stem questions at the beginning of the interview: (1) "In your lifetime, have you ever had two weeks or more when nearly every day you felt sad, blue, or depressed?"; (2) "Have you ever had two weeks or more when nearly every day you felt down in the dumps, low, or gloomy?"; (3) "Have there ever been two weeks or more when you lost interest in most things like work, hobbies, or things you usually liked to do?" and (4) "Have you ever had two weeks or more during which you felt sad, blue, depressed or where you lost all interest and pleasure in things that you usually cared about or enjoyed?" Since these questions are so broad and do not allow for reference to the circumstances in which the moods arose, it is no surprise that 56 percent of the population replies yes to at least one of them. Later in the interview, these respondents are asked questions about symptoms derived from the *DSM* criteria for Major Depressive Disorder. To be diagnosed with depression, community members must report having depressed mood or inability to feel pleasure along with four additional symptoms, such as loss of appetite, difficulty sleeping, fatigue, or inability to concentrate on ordinary activities.

The NCS estimates that about 5 percent of subjects have a current (30-day) episode of major depression, about 10 percent had this condition in the past year, about 17 percent at some point in their lives, and about 24 percent report enough symptoms for a lifetime diagnosis of either depression or dysthymia, a related disorder. It

> Community studies, rather than uncovering high rates of depressive disorders, simply show that the natural results of acute or chronic stressful experiences could be distressing enough to fit the *DSM* definition of a disorder.

also finds that relatively few people diagnosed with these conditions have sought professional help: only about a third of those with survey-identified Major Depressive Disorders had sought professional treatment, and far fewer sought any kind of help from mental health professionals.

Are the many cases of Major Depressive Disorder uncovered in such community studies equivalent to treated clinical cases? In contrast to clinical settings, where the judgments of both lay persons and clinicians distinguish ordinary sadness from depressive disorders, symptom-based diagnoses in community studies consider everyone who reports enough symptoms as having the mental disorder of depression. A respondent might recall symptoms such as depressed mood or insomnia that lasted longer than two weeks after the breakup of a romantic relationship, during a loved one's serious illness, or the unexpected loss of a job. Although these symptoms might have dissipated as soon as a new relationship developed, the loved one recovered, or another job was found, this person would be counted among the many millions who suffer from the presumed disorder of depression each year. For example, in the ECA study the most commonly reported symptoms are "trouble falling asleep, staying asleep, or waking up early" (33.7 percent); being "tired out all the time" (22.8 percent); and "thought a lot about death" (22.6 percent). College students during exam periods, people who must work overtime, who are worried about an important upcoming event, or who take the survey soon after the death of a famous person would all naturally experience such symptoms.

Symptoms that neither respondents nor clinicians would see as requiring treatment may nevertheless qualify as signs of disorder in community surveys. Moreover, the duration criteria only require that the symptom last for a two-week period, so that many transient and self-correcting symptoms are counted as disordered.

In other cases, reported symptoms could be normal responses to long-standing conditions of poverty, oppression, or injustice. Diagnostically oriented community studies, rather than uncovering high rates of depressive disorders, simply show that the natural results of acute or chronic stressful experiences could be distressing enough to fit the *DSM* definition of a disorder.

why are the high rates perpetuated?

The exaggerated rates of mental disorder in community surveys do not mean that untreated psychiatric disorders are not a significant problem. Nor do they mean that people who experience normal distress may not sometimes benefit from drugs or psychological treatments. It does, however, contribute to a pervasive medicalization of many problems that we might view more constructively as expectable results of social circumstances.

Community surveys could more adequately separate normal responses to stressful situations from mental disorders by including questions about the context in which symptoms develop and persist. Interviewers could ask, for example, if symptoms of depression emerged during periods of intense stress and disappeared as soon as these crises were over. Clinical interviews often include such probes, which are also compatible with basic principles of survey methodology; psychiatrists have always recognized the need for such considerations. The decision not to include contextual criteria in community surveys may involve not only the efficiency and practicality of decontextualized, standardized methods but also resistance to change by groups that benefit from the reported high rates of mental illnesses.

During the 1960s the National Institute of Mental Health (NIMH) promoted an expansive agenda of community mental health and sponsored projects that attempted to alleviate poverty, combat juvenile delinquency, and promote social change, but political changes in the 1970s forced the NIMH to change its focus from social and economic problems to specific diseases. This was more politically palatable than addressing controversial social problems. In addition, the rise of the biological paradigm in psychiatry naturally shifted emphasis from the social circumstances that can produce mental illness toward internal sources. The NIMH funded the epidemiological studies in the 1980s and 1990s in an effort to show that presumed disease conditions were widespread yet untreated. The resulting belief in high prevalence rates, which became the focus of well-known and widely disseminated documents such as the Surgeon General's Report on Mental Health, insulated the agency from political pressures, expanded its mandate, enhanced the importance of the problem it addressed, and protected its budget. Political support is more likely for an agency devoted to preventing and curing widespread disease than for one that confronts controversial social problems.

Pharmaceutical companies have also capitalized on these survey findings, which create a broader market for their products. Their ads focus on symptoms such as sadness, loneliness, exhaustion, and anxiety that are common among normal people. These ads also routinely feature the alleged numbers of people who suffer from particular mental disorders, sending the message that potential consumers are not unique but share their problems with millions of others. The explosive growth in sales of antidepressants shows the effectiveness of this appeal.

Family advocacy groups such as the National Alliance for the Mentally Ill embrace claims about the prevalence of mental disorders, which allow them to equate the millions of people that community surveys identify with the far smaller number of people with truly serious mental disorders. This presumably reduces the social distance between the mentally disordered and others, and lowers the stigma of mental illness,

potentially aiding efforts to obtain more funding for treatment.

These groups promote high prevalence rates in the belief that if they can convince politicians that mental illnesses are widespread, they can gain more funding for mental health services. But their efforts to get more treatment for currently untreated cases are just as likely to shift resources from people who truly need professional mental health services to those who might be distressed but are not disordered. Moreover, such high rates may make the problem of mental illness seem so overwhelming and potentially costly that it will not be addressed. Erasing the distinction between normal and disordered conditions and calling both mental disorders may harm the truly disabled.

RECOMMENDED RESOURCES

Allan V. Horwitz. *Creating Mental Illness* (University of Chicago Press, 2002).

> Describes how and why the general pathologies of psychoanalysis changed into the specific mental disorders of the DSM-III in 1980.

Lee Robins and Darrell Regier. *Psychiatric Disorders in America: The Epidemiological Catchment Area Study* (The Free Press, 1991).

> The best compilation of conventional views regarding psychiatric epidemiology.

U.S. Department of Health and Human Services. *Mental Health: A Report of the Surgeon General* (National Institute of Mental Health, 1999).

> A government report shows how epidemiological findings are used for the purposes of public policy.

Jerome C. Wakefield. "The Measurement of Mental Disorder." In *A Handbook for the Study of Mental Health: Social Contexts, Theories, and Systems,* eds. Allan V. Horwitz and Teresa L. Scheid (Cambridge University Press, 1999).

This chapter indicates how symptom-based diagnostic categories inflate estimates of the amount of mental disorder in epidemiological studies.

REVIEW QUESTIONS

1. Before reading this essay, how might you have defined "mental illness"? How do psychiatrists define mental illness?
2. How did the *DSM-III* mark a shift in the way psychiatrists diagnose mental illness? What are the potential problems of this diagnostic procedure?
3. What does this essay say about the importance of contextualizing information? What are the pitfalls of the type of decontextualization evident in the community studies mentioned in the article? Can you think of two additional social measures that would be grossly misrepresented or misinterpreted if taken out of context? What would they obscure?
4. Whenever myths are perpetuated, it is worthwhile to ponder which social groups benefit and lose the most from them. Which groups benefit and lose the most from the myths associated with mental illness?

john h. evans

a brave new world? how genetic technology could change us

spring 2003

48

forthcoming genetic technologies will allow people to design their children. although these tools are unlikely to produce a society of castes like the alphas and epsilons in aldous huxley's novel brave new world, they may already be changing our understanding of what it means to be human.

"These," he waved his hand, "are the incuba-tors." . . . [T]he fertilized ova went back to the in-cubators, where the Alphas and the Betas remained until definitely bottled; while the Gam-mas, Deltas and Epsilons were brought out again, after only thirty-six hours, to undergo Bokanovsky's Process . . . But one of the students was fool enough to ask where the advantage lay. "My good boy!" . . . "Can't you see? Can't you see?" He raised a hand; his expression was solemn. "Bokanovsky's Process is one of the major instruments of social stability!" (Huxley, Brave New World, 1932, pp. 3–6)

Brave New World, Aldous Huxley's dystopian novel, depicts a society in which babies are grown in jars, each genetically designed for a particular purpose and social rank. Now that the technology is at hand, what kinds of realistic scenarios might we forecast, 70 years after Huxley's fearful vision? We already have in vitro fertilization, which seems akin to Huxley's first step, growing babies in jars. Will the rest of his scenario soon follow?

Probably not. Our increasingly precise gene-tic technologies will allow us to design children, but they are unlikely to sharpen the class dis-tinctions we already have. What the technolo-gies are likely to do, instead, is to accelerate an

ongoing trend toward seeing people as biologi-cal machines rather than as social beings. Be-cause the undesirable consequences will be side effects of technologies that promise to eliminate genetic disease and enhance our lives, the ques-tion of whether or how we want to limit them remains open and pressing. It is best that we know what we are getting ourselves into.

Huxley's novel yields at least two readings, each corresponding to a different claim about the social effects of genetic technology. The first and more common reading is that *Brave New World* forecasts a society with rigid class distinc-tions where no one can move up or down be-cause genes determine position. In the second reading, the novel describes a world in which people are no longer fully human because they no longer struggle, love, or suffer. Today's gene-tic technologies may, in the second sense, be teaching us a new, more biological, view of what makes us human. They may even bring cultural changes as deep as Copernicus's discovery that we are not at the center of the universe and Dar-win's that we are but another species of animal.

from coercion to counseling

In *Brave New World*, the Alphas, at the top of the hierarchy, and Epsilons, at the bottom, are born that way and cannot change their status. Huxley wrote the bleak novel in reaction to the eugenicists of the nineteenth and early twentieth centuries who wanted to "improve" the human species by encouraging the reproduction of the "best" people and discouraging the reproduction of "inferior" people. Later revelations of Nazi practices based upon this logic discredited the idea of coercive eugenics. However, the eugenic idea did not die. Post-Nazi eugenicists, such as Hermann Muller and, ironically, Aldous Huxley's brother Julian, wanted people at risk of producing "inferior" genetic offspring voluntarily to refrain from having children.

The first technology of these new eugenicists was genetic counseling, which advised potential parents of the risks of having children with genetic diseases based upon the genetic histories of their families. After the invention and widespread use of amniocentesis in the late 1960s, doctors could examine fetuses directly for a few genetic conditions, instead of just providing parents with the odds that their children could be affected. The Supreme Court's 1973 decision to legalize abortion, *Roe v. Wade*, meant that pregnant women could decide for themselves whether to abort fetuses identified as having genetic disorders, without having to get permission from doctors. This was a novel idea—that, to a certain extent, people could determine the qualities they desired in their offspring. Eugenics became an individual affair, with any collective eugenic effects being uncoordinated—not controlled by government,

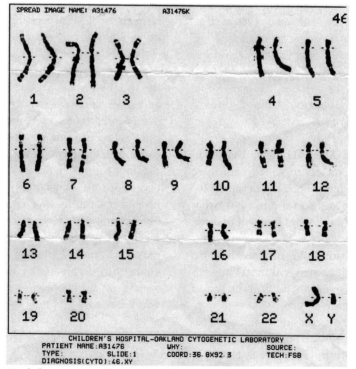

Fetal chromosome chart prepared for genetic counseling of prospective parents.

nor by the norms of the medical profession or eugenicists, but by the desires of pregnant women themselves. The end result was a free market in genetic diagnoses, in which physicians and parents began to decide which children to bring or *not* to bring into the world.

Although originally amniocentesis could only identify gross chromosomal errors like Down's Syndrome, its diagnostic capabilities increased rapidly. Additionally, new technologies such as chorionic villi sampling, maternal blood tests, and diagnostic ultrasounds, which developed in the 1980s and 1990s, allow for diagnosis earlier in pregnancy with often less invasive techniques. If a woman is undergoing more complicated fertility treatments like in vitro fertilization, the resulting fertilized egg can also be screened before being inserted into her uterus. Many observers expect that these techniques will continue to become less invasive and identify even more genetic traits, thus further encouraging their use.

Yet all of these techniques only eliminate fetuses or fertilized eggs that have a particular genetic trait. A more precise form of eugenics would select genetic traits that could not naturally result from joining the genes of the parents. Germline human genetic engineering, which adds and deletes selected genes from sperm, eggs, or embryos, would allow parents to choose the desired genetic traits of their children. Another technique, reproductive cloning—which, like germline engineering, has thus far only been attempted with animals—would allow parents to make a genetic copy of an adult that had genetic traits they desired.

from consumer choice to class hierarchy?

A key Huxleyian worry in our public debates is that powerful interests will use governmental authority to produce humans for particular tasks, such as Rambo-like soldiers and worker drones, resulting in a rigid class hierarchy. But the chances that governments—at least, democratic ones—will push eugenics on parents are low. It would buck the trend toward individual decision making in reproduction; public opinion would be solidly opposed; and, more important, there is no identifiable interest group to push such a program. Both the pro-choice and anti-abortion movements that dominate American public discourse about reproduction would be hostile to state-mandated eugenics. Therefore, a more rigid class society would have to come about through free-market choices, by the general social forces that determine the decisions individual parents make about what kinds of children they want.

Only the positive engineering of certain genetic traits could lead to a rigid class hierarchy. All of the current technology is simply screening—eliminating eggs, zygotes, or fetuses that are within the parents' normal genetic range, allowing parents to have children who are not any worse off than they are. Class divisions based upon genetics would require the technical ability to insert superior qualities into children beyond what the two parents could have produced.

Even if technologically feasible, it is not at all clear what sorts of qualities would produce class advantages. Movies, television, and the print media depict the public as worried about the rich being able to engineer six-foot-tall beautiful children. Yet even this level of perfection in genetic engineering or cloning will not necessarily widen class differences. Most of these envisioned eugenic changes will not allow the "designer child" to dominate others. Instead, creating a designer child would simply display parents' wealth in the same way that a 16-year-old with a Ferrari displays his parents' wealth now. For a child whose parents can buy such genetic technology, the marginal increase in power obtained from looking like the ideal of beauty pales in comparison to the economic power his or her family already has. A wealthy family could instead produce a daughter "the old fashioned way" and give her the money they would have paid genetic engineers to make her look like a supermodel. She could then spend the money on more traditional and probably more effective ways of maintaining status, such as increased investment in education or owning property. In other words, there is nothing inherent to the genetic change that would give the children of the wealthy more advantages than they already have.

The first use of genetic engineering will not be for looks, but for health. Parents would presumably pay to ensure that their children do not have genetic diseases such as sickle-cell anemia or susceptibility to mental illness. Again, this would not be a fundamental change, given that the children of the well-off already have greater access to prenatal, baby, and childhood health care. Nor would engineering physical power or prowess lead to a more rigid class hierarchy. A Michael Jordan clone would presumably have a promising professional basketball career, if one makes the dubious assumption that basketball skills are primarily genetic. But if only 400 couples cloned Jordan, the NBA rosters would be full. The 401st Jordan clone would be at no particular advantage, making this sort of scenario an unlikely source of inequality. Strength and athletic prowess are not the main source of class distinctions in our society anyway.

The only engineering that could increase an offspring's social power over others—in the countries where people will be able to afford this technology—is in "intelligence," perhaps by increasing thought processing speed or memory. Yet the genetic basis of this one critical trait is almost completely unknown, which should comfort those concerned about the Alpha-Epsilon threat of genetic technology. Unlike genetic traits such as sickle-cell anemia, which is the result of a well-described error in one gene on the genome, "intelligence" is a multifaceted genetic effect that we cannot even agree how to define, let alone

enhance. If cloning were to become available, people who are perceived as more intelligent could be cloned without understanding the exact underlying genetic causation of "intelligence." Even then, however, engineering intelligence would still be limited to the normal range currently found in humans.

changing what it means to be human

An alternative reading of *Brave New World* is that its residents do not mind the sort of rigid class society that would violate today's ideals, because they are no longer what we consider to be human. What makes them human has been bred or conditioned out of them.

Some definitions of "human" locate the quality in an aspect of our consciousness or linguistic ability. Another tradition, rooted in the ideas of German philosopher Immanuel Kant, argues that it is freedom that makes us human—to restrict our freedom is to dehumanize. The dominant theological argument in the West is that since humans are "made in the image of God," we are fully human when we are in relationship with God. Theologians and sociologists share the belief that human-ness requires relationships with other humans. Huxley clearly had at least the Kantian version in mind while writing, because the characters in the novel had lost their freedom to strive, love, have families or, most obviously, to choose the occupation they desired.

Proponents of these positions do agree on their enemy: a biological definition of the human, one that sees people as nothing more special than a series of interconnected biological devices. To be human in this definition is to be a particular form of biochemical machine that exists to propagate its genes to the next generation. At its most specific, advocates of this view have created "the gene myth"—the idea that we are our genes.

How could the new technologies change our understanding of humanity? One way would be for people to be exposed continuously to the claim that we are biological, rather than theological, philosophical, psychological, or social beings. Sociologists have worried about exactly this development. Howard Kaye argues:

In both aim and impact, the end of [the genetic science] revolution is a fundamental transformation in how we conceive of ourselves as human beings and how we understand the nature and purpose of human life rightly lived. . . . [W]e are in the process of redefining ourselves as biological, rather than cultural and moral beings. Bombarded with white-coated claims that "Genes-R-Us," grateful for the absolution which such claims offer for our shortcomings and sins, and attracted to the promise of using efficient, technological means to fulfill our aspirations, rather than notoriously unreliable moral or political ones, the idea that we are essentially self-replicating machines, built by the evolutionary process, designed for survival and reproduction, and run by our genes continues to gain.

How does this "bombardment" of claims happen? Consider the recent debate about human cloning. The media endlessly repeated one morally justified use of cloning—to "bring back" a child who had died. The *New York Times* in 1997 wrote that the public should consider "the case of a couple whose baby was dying and who wanted, literally, to replace the child." The idea that a clone would "be" the dead child assumes, and simultaneously teaches the public, a fundamentally biological view of what a human is. The cloning debate is simply the most recent example of this "bombardment." Dorothy Nelkin and M. Susan Lindee, in their study of popular conceptions of DNA, show that depictions of human behavior as ultimately driven by biology are everywhere—in television, movies, comic books, newspapers, and, of course, in the statements of genetic scientists themselves. For example, a 1993 prime-time movie called *Tainted Blood* depicts a 17-year-old boy who killed his parents and himself. It turns out that he was adopted, and his birth mother had been a murderer. He had "inherited the gene for violence."

Whether or not the biological view of the human is "true" is not at issue here. As W. I. Thomas and D. S. Thomas wrote many decades ago, if people "define situations as real, they are real in their consequences." For instance, few upper-middle-class Americans know someone on welfare, but they have an image of people on welfare from the media. Media images are potentially even more powerful shapers of our reality when they concern something like the essence of human nature that is impossible to see or experience any other way.

If discussion of the new technologies impels us to think of ourselves as biological machines, then we may end up treating each other accordingly. In a Thomas-like reference to the power of definition, bioethicist Leon Kass quipped, "if we come to think about ourselves like pork bellies, pork bellies we will become." One consequence of seeing ourselves this way would be an increasing reliance upon genetic relationships rather than social relationships. For example, men who fathered a child during a one-night stand are gaining parental rights, though they have had no further connection to mother or child. This development suggests that genetic bonds are already being privileged over social ones. Or, more strongly, if we begin to think of our children mainly as our genetic progeny, we would no longer protect our children because we love them, but because we have an interest in propagating our own genes through them. Sociologists studying organ transplantation argue that a biological view of the human could encourage us to think of our organs as interchangeable parts, which would decrease the public's resistance to poor people selling their kidneys on the open market. Finally, and more subtly, we would come to think of others in terms of their usefulness for the human gene pool. If this occurs, we will have traveled full circle—from the early eugenicists' concern for "species uplift," through an emphasis on individual freedom to produce "the optimal child," and back to the idea that people's value to the species should determine whether they survive. A strictly biological notion of the human would be a radical, and many would say distressing, shift in human self-understanding.

Ironically, the new genetic technologies need not alter a single person to alter our view of the person. All humans—whether genetically changed or not—would be assigned the new human identity. While the creation of a rigid class society through actual genetic manipulations must await great breakthroughs in genetic knowledge, the subtle change in our notions of what it means to be human seems to be occurring now. Before we dismiss the notion that a simple idea can change society, remember that historians consider Copernicus's argument that the earth revolves around the sun—an equally unobservable phenomenon to the average person—to have permanently altered Western society.

should something be done?

A technology to alter intelligence might not be available for many years, but that does not mean the risks of creating a rigid class society inherent in this technology should be ignored. Instead, those concerned should lay the groundwork for opposing it now, because the wealthy—precisely those who could use the technology to exacerbate class differences—could monopolize it should it become available.

These techniques would surely not be covered by insurance, so they will be available only to the affluent. The wealthy tend to have fewer children—one study found that poorer people had double the fertility rate of richer people. With fewer children, the wealthy focus more of their resources on each child. The wealthy also already show, by their heavy investment in educational advantages such as private schools and tutoring, that they seek every edge for their children. And according to surveys, it is the most educated—typically also the wealthier—who have the fewest qualms about the reproductive technologies that would be required to engineer intelligence.

Furthermore, we could not expect Americans to resist on moral principle a genetically engineered expansion of class distinctions. We already tolerate vast differences in educational opportunity and seem relatively unconcerned that toxins or poor nutrition impede some children's intellectual development. Indeed, one could imagine that an intelligence-expanding technology, even if available to only a few, would be celebrated as a way to produce great scientists and artists. The one American ideal that argues against the genetic engineering of intelligence is the Horatio Alger dream of upward mobility. The idea that poor people can, through luck and pluck, pull themselves up by their bootstraps is still endorsed by rich and poor alike. But allowing the well-off to engineer more intelligent children would permanently enshrine them as an overclass in a society that continues to reward such cognitive skills. It is here—on the thin ground of belief in equal opportunity—that the threat of solidifying class divisions through eugenics might be politically resisted.

This relatively benign assessment about the inequality implications of genetic technologies presumes the continuation of liberal democracy and the emphasis on the rights of the individual. While intelligence-enhancing technology could rigidify inequalities, and ought to be guarded against, there is time yet to build a wall around "improvements to intelligence." However, that wall already may have been breached in regard to the other serious threat of genetic technology—the subversion of our sense of what it means to be human.

Whether or not these dangers should compel us to halt genetic technologies is a complicated question because they are the potential side effects of trying to do good. That is, the motivation for human genetic engineering is to relieve us of disease and otherwise improve our lives. In my own research on the public debates about genetic engineering, I found that proponents of this technology were sincere in their desire to relieve human suffering through genetic technology; for a variety of reasons they simply discounted the more abstract worries.

It is difficult to oppose these goods in the name of an esoteric danger, tricky to define or document, that the technology will alter our conception of ourselves. What is probably most important is that if we march into the Brave New World we do so with our eyes open.

RECOMMENDED RESOURCES

Troy Duster. *Backdoor to Eugenics* (Routledge, 1990).

> Explains how genetic technologies can lead to a reinstatement of genetic explanations for social problems.

John H. Evans. *Playing God? Human Genetic Engineering and the Rationalization of Public Bioethical Debate* (University of Chicago Press, 2002).

> Shows how our public debates on genetic (and other) issues have become less substantive over time.

Aldous Huxley. *Brave New World* (Harper & Row, 1998 [1932]).

> A dystopian novel about a highly controlled society. Written in reaction to the eugenic ideas circulating at the time.

Howard Kaye. *The Social Meaning of Modern Biology: From Social Darwinism to Sociobiology* (Transaction Publishers, 1997 [1986]).

> Kaye claims that modern biology is promoting a particular view of the human behind a patina of scientific "facts."

Howard Kaye. "Anxiety and Genetic Manipulation: A Sociological View." *Perspectives in Biology and Medicine* 41 (1998): 483–90.

> Kaye applies his argument that modern biology is promoting a particular view of the human to the current debate over cloning and other recent technologies.

Dorothy Nelkin and M. Susan Lindee. *The DNA Mystique: The Gene as a Cultural Icon* (W.H. Freeman Co., 1995).

> A study of popular conceptions of "the gene" and "genetic effects."

Barbara Katz Rothman. *Genetic Maps and Human Imaginations* (W. W. Norton, 1998).

> Discusses the view of the human promoted by genetic science and defends a more social definition of humanity.

REVIEW QUESTIONS

1. What are some of the positive and negative consequences of genetic technologies? What are the consequences for class divisions?
2. While Evans notes that we are far from locating an "IQ gene," we can certainly guess the consequences of altering someone's skin color or gender. Would it be wise to change someone's genes with the goal of making their life easier or more productive in some way?
3. While cloning whole humans to "bring someone back" seems a bit fantastic, there are some who believe that we ought to be cloning

for "spare parts." (Imagine if you had kidney failure, for example, and had a choice between taking one from a family member or a clone.) Do you think cloning for spare body parts is a good idea?

4. Write two paragraphs on what it means to be "human." Consider the "human-ness" of clones, fetuses, and people who are severely mentally impaired (aka "brain dead"). What do you think is necessary to count as a human?

part 11

Crime and Deviance

allan v. horwitz

keyword: normality

(forthcoming in *contexts*; not previously published)

49

Sociologists typically study phenomena that stand out from the commonplace. They pay more attention to crime than conformity, homosexuality than heterosexuality, blackness than whiteness, or holidays than regular days. What is conventional, usual, and expectable is usually taken for granted and more rarely studied. Normality has not received much sociological attention. Despite its general neglect, normality has an extraordinarily powerful effect on how people behave. Most people want to be normal, and they act so as to accomplish this. A few people might rebel against the normal, but even this group uses a conception of the normal as a guide. So, what is normal?

One dilemma in the study of normality is that in most cases no formal body of rules indicates what conditions are normal—unlike, for example, the study of disease, which relies on the presence or absence of symptoms, or of crime, which can be defined in relation to a body of laws. This lack of standards for defining normality has led many common definitions to rely on statistical distributions. In the statistical tradition, the normal is whatever trait most people in a group display. Tests of intelligence provide the model for this conception of normality. These tests measure intelligence by relating the number of correct answers given by one person to the number that other people answer correctly. For example, the average or normal IQ is set, by definition, at 100. What is normal, then, is whatever the average or

typical behavior is. Conversely, subnormal people are those who test at the bottom of the statistical curve, while the supernormal are those at the top of the curve. The IQ score of any particular person is only meaningful in comparison to the scores of others who take the test.

An unusual characteristic of the statistical conception of normality is that normality is *not* a characteristic of individuals; it is a quality of the distribution of a trait within a particular group. As with measures of intelligence, it is impossible to know if any given individual is normal or not without also knowing about that same trait in other people. Indeed, when normality is viewed as an average, we often find that no individual could possibly be normal. For example, a statistically normal woman in the United States has 2.09 children, which no individual could have. Statistical normality is a property of groups, not individuals.

If statistical normality is a property of groups, then it will differ from group to group. In societies where the average person dies at age 65, someone who lives to 80 might be statistically abnormal. In the contemporary United States, however, an 80-year lifetime falls within the range of a normal life span. And someone whose scores on a personality test in Japan indicate that they are outgoing, gregarious, and friendly might be judged as shy, introverted, and hostile in the United States, despite giving exactly the same answers. When statistics establish normality, a person may be defined as normal or abnormal depending on the personality characteristics of the relevant reference group.

The sociologist Emile Durkheim gave an unusual twist to the statistical conception of normality. He postulated that the needs of specific social groups, rather than statistical forces, generate distributions of normality. Because all groups need to construct definitions of what normal behavior is, they single out behavior at the tails of statistical distributions as "deviant" in order to insure that behavior within the tails is normal. He used the example of a "society of saints" to illustrate how all groups develop statistical definitions of normality that in turn become valued standards. These groups—such as members of monasteries or convents—develop norms of appropriate behavior so that a certain proportion of members is defined as deviant. Actions such as not closing ones eyes while praying that would be unremarkable in other settings are subject to punishment in societies of saints. Because all social groups develop standards of what is normal behavior, Durkheim believed that rates of nonconformity would be roughly equal in all groups, regardless of whether these groups were composed of what we generally regard as saints or of sinners.

Durkheim's contribution was to show how the statistical fact of normality in any group often comes to be equated with what is valued behavior. That is, statistically normal behavior often becomes a norm, or ideal standard, of behavior so that frequent behaviors are seen as desirable behaviors. People often want to be normal and strive to achieve normality, so that statistical conceptions are transformed from group averages into traits that people seek to emulate. Conversely, all groups use these standards of normality to define deviant behavior as behavior that falls outside of statistical norms.

Several problems arise with statistical conceptions of normality. One is that purely statistical views can often make abnormal phenomena appear to be normal. During World War II, for instance, up to 70 percent of soldiers who were exposed to extended periods of continuous combat developed mental illnesses. Similarly, more adolescents report having some symptoms of mental illness than report having none. In such contexts, people who are psychologically healthy are statistically abnormal. Viewing abnormal phenomenon as if they were normal is one anomaly of a statistical perspective.

Another anomaly of the statistical view is that the connection between normality and social values can be arbitrary. Consider the citizens of Nazi Germany during the 1930s and 1940s. A majority of them supported policies of genocide, racialism, and aggressive military conquest. Yet, many people object to claims that such horrific beliefs, however common they might have been in this context, should ever be considered normal.

Another difficulty with the statistical conception lies in how to handle people who differ from normality in positive rather than negative ways. Geniuses, athletic stars, and exceptionally talented people receive very different social responses than the intellectually deficient, the clumsy, or the incompetent, so that a purely statistical view does not conform to commonsense practices, which sharply distinguish positive from negative deviations from normality.

A final limitation of the statistical conception is that when we consider increasing numbers of independently distributed traits, it becomes less and less likely that anyone can ever be normal. For example, one prominent theory assumes that personality is divided into five major dimensions, each independent of the others. People who are within two standard deviations of the mean, or two-thirds of the population, are considered normal on each trait. Using this standard, however, only a minority of people (40 percent) would be normal on any two traits, and only 13 percent would be normal on all five traits. Someone who fits a profile that contains multiple dimensions of normality can be a very extraordinary person!

Because of these problems, few sociologists use statistical conceptions to define normality. They are more likely to view normality as some sort of ideal or social norm instead of as a purely statistical distribution. The second major way of viewing normality, the normative approach, drops the statistical aspect of normality and treats what is normal entirely as conformity to a standard or ideal, regardless of how many people actually display the relevant trait.

The normative approach defines what is normal by assuming that normality stems from conforming to some ideal or standard. Normality, in this view, is not just a statistical state but some valued characteristic. In contrast to statistical conceptions of normality, normative conceptions imply that everyone or no one in any particular group can be normal. Another difference from the statistical conception is that when we consider normality to be a valued state, we can determine whether or not a person is normal by measuring the qualities of that person without knowing anything about the distribution of the trait in question among other members of the group.

Consider the use of a body mass index (BMI) to calculate what normal weight is. The BMI is found by taking a person's weight and dividing it by the square of that person's height. For example, someone who weighs 175 pounds and is 5 feet 8 inches tall would have a BMI of 26.6 ($175/68^2$). Current guidelines state that people with BMIs less than 18.5 are underweight, those between 18.5 and 24.9 are normal weight, those between 25 and 29.9 are overweight, and those whose BMI is more than 30 are obese. Using these guidelines, which use valued goals such as living longer and having fewer diseases associated with obesity to define ideal weight, far more Americans are overweight than have normal weight. Most people (an estimated 60 percent) are overweight, with BMIs over 25. Indeed, it is theoretically possible that nobody would be of normal weight. In contrast, statistical conceptions of normality require that most people would have to be of normal weight.

Another view of normality as conformity to an ideal standard sees these standards as relative to particular groups rather than as universal. An individual is normal or not with reference to some culturally grounded standard that defines what is conventional in that particular group. Different groups have different ranges of expected behaviors, so that a trait that is normal in one culture might be deviant in another and vice versa. The military, for example, might strive to recruit soldiers who will conform to standards of discipline, subordinate themselves to group demands, and display obedience to authority. Universities, in contrast, might value qualities of autonomy, self-motivation, and independence. What is normal in one setting would not be valued in another.

The normative view of normality overcomes many of the problems of the statistical view, but it suffers from deficiencies of its own. One is that those who view normality as a standard that applies to everyone, such as seemingly scientific measurements of weight and height, use universal criteria that apply across all groups. Yet, as the influential French philosopher Michel Foucault emphasized, these views often depend on the values of those who hold them, and more powerful groups can impose their standards on less powerful people in the name of the general value of normality. Alternatively, conceptions of normality that apply only to particular groups are culturally relative. What is considered normal varies from culture to culture, so that we have no universal standards by which to judge normality.

A third definition of normality stems from

evolutionary theory. In this view, promoted by philosopher Jerome Wakefield and evolutionary psychiatrist Randolph Nesse, among others, normality is defined by whatever characteristics humans were designed by natural selection to have. Just as normal dogs chase cats, and normal birds fly to warm climates in the winter, normal humans are naturally designed to have certain traits. For example, nature has designed our eyes to allow us to see and our ears to allow us to hear; thus, people who cannot see or hear are abnormal.

Most evolutionary perspectives regard normal human emotions and behaviors as products of the interaction between people and their environments: Norms are defined in relationship to particular contexts. For example, it is not normal for people to always be sad or happy without regard to the situations they are in. Normal humans would respond with despair in environments marked by widespread impoverishment, violence, and turmoil; a happy person in such circumstances would not be normal. Conversely, someone who is consistently sad even in favorable environments would be abnormal. No trait is normal or pathological in itself but only acquires the quality of normality (or deviance) with regard to the environment in which it arises.

Evolutionary conceptions differ from statistical conceptions of normality because universal standards of natural functioning, rather than the statistical distribution of a trait, are used to judge the normality of any behavior. These conceptions differ from views of normality as conformity to an ideal because criteria of normality are not supposed to be evaluative; rather, they stem from how humans are biologically designed to function in certain ways in certain environments. In addition, evolutionary views diverge from conceptions of normality as statistical and as conformity to a standard because they presume that criteria for normality are universal aspects of human nature rather than culturally relative.

Like the other two conceptions of normality, the evolutionary view also has been criticized. According to critics, the so-called value-free standards of biological functioning derived from nature are actually social values that one group imposes on others. For example, some deaf people claim that we should not consider the ability to hear as a natural property because deafness can have a positive value. Even such normal-seeming traits as the ability to hear, therefore, can become subjects of debate between different social groups.

Little agreement exists among sociologists about what normal behavior is. Nevertheless, normality—however we view it—is a critical aspect of everyday social life. Conceptions of normality are used to sort people into jobs, screen out supposedly abnormal people from valued social roles, define what deviance is, and set norms by which people judge valued behaviors. People use views of normality to orient their own behavior and conform to what they think are the expectations of others. Institutions such as corporations, the military, or professional athletic teams often use personality tests in attempts to insure that potential recruits are normal. Legal systems use standards of normality when bringing people to trial and allowing defenses against charges of criminal behavior. Advocacy groups claim that we should regard their members as normal members of society. Doctors classify many conditions, such as levels of cholesterol, blood pressure, or body mass, as "within normal limits" or not. Advice columnists, not to mention professional therapists, constantly handle questions about whether someone is normal or not. Despite the various views of normality that sociologists and others hold, conceptions of normality are clearly important aspects of social life.

RECOMMENDED RESOURCES

Michel Foucault. *Discipline and Punish: The Birth of the Prison* (Vintage, 1979).

A central work of a prominent critic of universal conceptions of normality.

Stephen J. Gould. *The Mismeasure of Man* (W. W. Norton, 1996).

Considers the history, uses, and misuses of intelligence testing and related statistical views of normality.

Randolph N. Nesse. "Is Depression an Adaptation?" *Archives of General Psychiatry 57* (2000): 14–20.

An evolutionary psychiatrist indicates the positive value of some depressive conditions.

Jerome C. Wakefield. "The Concept of Mental Disorder: On the Boundary between Biological Facts and Social Values." *American Psychologist 47* (1992): 373–88.

Shows how biological views of normal functioning and social views about harmful behavior are both necessary components of adequate definitions of normality.

Michael Warner. *The Trouble with Normal: Sex, Politics, and the Ethics of Queer Life* (Harvard University Press, 2000).

Questions why normality should be viewed as a positive characteristic.

REVIEW QUESTIONS

1. How might you have defined "normal" before reading this essay? What thoughts or feelings does the word provoke? Are these all positive?
2. Actions that deviate from the norm might serve the greater good of society. List up to five examples of this possibility, and write a sentence for each that explains your thinking.
3. What are some possible repercussions of an individual adopting an evolutionary model of normality? Ponder a government enacting a new law or policy based on this model.
4. Activity: Read a horoscope, advice column, and a wedding announcement in your local newspaper, and describe how it reinforces one of the three kinds of normality discussed by Horwitz.

richard rosenfeld

crime decline in context

50

spring 2002

skyrocketing violent crime rates obsessed americans for decades. crime rates have now been dropping for 10 years what has happened, and how can we learn from it?

After rising to a peak in the early 1990s, crime rates in the United States have been falling for almost a decade. The turnaround was sudden, unexpected, and years later remains something of a puzzle. Some observers attribute most of the drop to tougher sentences and rising rates of imprisonment. Others believe more vigilant policing of loitering, public drunkenness, and other so-called quality-of-life offenses is responsible. Still others point to shrinking drug markets or the booming economy of the 1990s. No strong consensus exists regarding the sources of the crime drop.

Even if we cannot say with certainty what is responsible for the crime decline of the 1990s, it is possible to rule out some of the usual causes and identify some of the real factors in the crime drop. But the first step in unraveling the mystery of the crime decline is to determine whether it happened at all.

real crime decline?

Several years after the rate of crime began declining, most Americans continued to rank crime among the nation's most serious public problems and to believe that crime rates were still going up. A relatively small percentage of Americans have direct experience with serious crime. The primary source of public information about crime is the mass media. Given the constant media drumbeat of murder and mayhem,

it is not surprising that people would be unaware or skeptical of claims that crime rates were dropping. But they were and still are.

The crime decline is real, not an artifact of changes in the rate at which crimes are reported to or recorded by the police. It is significant, long, and deep enough to qualify as a trend and not just a short-run statistical anomaly. It is pervasive, cutting across major offense categories and population groups. Finally, it is time-limited. Crime rates cannot be negative, so the rate of decline curve should slow in the coming years. And it is possible, of course, that crime rates will increase, as they did in the 1980s. Predicting the future is always hazardous, but the best guesses about the next decade will be based on an informed assessment of the recent past.

documenting the decline

A "crime rate" is the number of offenses of a specified type divided by the population of some jurisdiction. By taking population size into account, crime rates can be compared across places and times with different populations. The nation has two "official" crime rates. One consists of offenses known to the police. These are compiled in the FBI's Uniform Crime Reports (UCR). The other is based on reports by victims to the Justice Department's annual National Crime Victimization Survey (NCVS). Both of the crime indicators include information on serious violent and property offenses, such as assault, rape, robbery, burglary, and auto theft. The UCR also records homicides which, of course, are not counted in victim surveys. Both the FBI report and the Justice Department survey are limited to so-called street crimes and omit serious white-collar, corporate, and governmental offenses (e.g., price-fixing, violations of workplace safety rules, pollution, corruption, antitrust violations and false advertising). National indicators for such "suite" crimes do not exist, so no one knows whether they have been rising or falling.

The FBI statistics indicate that street crime has substantially decreased over the past decade. In 1991 the FBI counted 24,700 criminal homicides in the United States, or 9.8 homicides for every 100,000 Americans. By the end of 1999, the number of homicides had dropped to 15,500, and the rate fell to 5.7 per 100,000, a 42 percent decline. The nation's robbery rate also fell by about 40 percent and the burglary rate dropped by one-third during the 1990s. The decreases were less steep, but still appreciable, for rape and aggravated assault (assaults involving serious injury or the use of a weapon), both of which declined by about 20 percent. There is some reason to believe that the declines in nonlethal violence are even sharper than those reported in the FBI report because victims became bolder about reporting such incidents to the police and the police recorded more of them. However, the drop registered in the FBI report and police statistics is mirrored in Justice Department survey results that are unaffected by patterns in reporting and recording.

So the declines in crime are real, but are they meaningful? The simple answer is yes. By the year 2000, homicide and burglary rates were lower than at any time since the mid-1960s. Victimization rates have fallen for youth, adults, blacks, whites, males, and females, in large cities and rural areas, in every region of the country. But the timing and magnitude of these changes differ across population groups, and those differences offer important clues regarding the causes of the crime decline.

> So the declines in crime are real, but are they meaningful? The simple answer is yes. By the year 2000, homicide and burglary rates were lower than at any time since the mid-1960s. Victimization rates have fallen for youth, adults, blacks, whites, males, and females, in large cities and rural areas, in every region of the country. But the timing and magnitude of these changes differ across population groups, and those differences offer important clues regarding the causes of the crime decline.

Consider the difference in the timing of the decrease in youth and adult homicide victims. The victimization rates for people over the age of 24 have fallen more or less continuously since 1980. On the other hand, youth homicide followed a more cyclical pattern, falling during the early 1980s, rising from the mid-1980s to a peak in 1993 and then falling again since then. The increase in youth homicide during the 1980s and early 1990s was so dramatic that it gave rise to concerns about a national youth violence "epidemic." The victimization rate for 14- to 17-year-olds nearly tripled, and that for 18- to 24-year-olds almost doubled between 1984 and 1993. The fall from the 1993 peak in youth homicide has been equally pronounced (figure 1). The trends in the rates at which teenagers and young adults committed homicide were almost identical to the victimization trends.

I focus on criminal homicide in this discussion because more accurate and detailed information about the characteristics of victims and offenders exists for homicide than for other crimes and because it is the most serious. However, the same

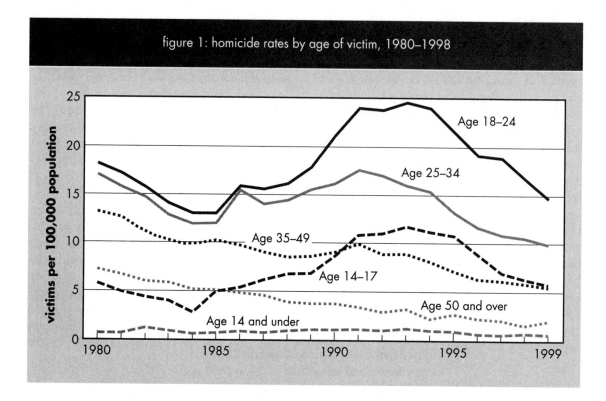

figure 1: homicide rates by age of victim, 1980–1998

basic patterns also characterize serious nonlethal criminal violence.

A credible explanation of the homicide decline, then, must explain why the time trends were different for adult and youth homicides, the first dropping steadily since 1980, the second fluctuating. Another notable pattern in the homicide drop involves the differing time trends for offenses committed with and without firearms. Roughly two-thirds of homicides in the United States are committed with a gun. Both the increase in youth homicide during the 1980s and early 1990s and the decrease over the last several years are restricted largely to the firearm category. Youth homicides involving other weapons or no weapons exhibit a gradual downward shift over the past 20 years, and adult homicide rates have decreased in both the firearm and nonfirearm categories. The "action," then, in the national homi-

cide rate for the last two decades is a consequence of rising and falling rates of youths killing and being killed with guns. A sufficient explanation of recent homicide trends cannot ignore the prominent role of guns in the cycle of youth violence.

The cycling up and down in youth firearm violence occurred earliest and was most pronounced in the largest cities and among young African-American males. The same changes happened in smaller cities and among white teenagers and young adults, but happened a year or two later and the fluctuations were smaller. (Persons of "other races" constitute only 2 to 3 percent of the nation's homicide victims.) A sufficient explanation of the recent homicide trends should accommodate these race, sex, and city-size differences as well.

An explanation of the crime drop should account for why the trends differ for youth and adults and why they are most evident in firearm homicides, in the large cities and among young black men. Serious explanations should account for both the rise and the decline in crime rates since the 1980s. And the best explanation will connect those recent changes to longer-term trends and to the social conditions that make the United States the murder capital of the industrial world, the crime decline notwithstanding.

drug markets and the spread of firearms

No single explanation of the crime decline has been proposed that meets all of these conditions. One of the more promising, however, attributes the increase in youth homicide rates beginning in the mid-1980s to the diffusion of violence in and around urban crack markets. The high demand for crack led drug dealers to recruit young inner-city males as sellers and arm them to fend off attacks from rival dealers and protect themselves from street robbers. A classic arms race resulted as other young people acquired guns in an increasingly threatening urban environment. The diffusion of firearms fueled escalating rates of youth homicide, with the sharpest increases occurring in the largest cities where the crack epidemic began. The increases in youth homicide, in turn, drove up the total homicide rate.

If this explanation of the increase also applies to the homicide decline, the turning point and drop in youth homicide should have been preceded by corresponding changes in the urban crack markets. That is exactly what happened. The crack epidemic crested around 1990 and the drug markets began to shrink, the process occurring first in the largest cities. The firearm-diffusion hypothesis squares with most of the basic facts underlying the crime decline. It accounts for why the drop occurred in the larger cities before the smaller ones, why it has been concentrated among young African Americans and why it has involved firearms. (Drug dealers do not use fists, sticks, or knives to settle disputes.) Most important, it highlights the changes among adolescents and young adults, and thereby situates the crime decline of the 1990s in the context of earlier increases.

what about adults?

The firearm-diffusion story does not explain everything we want to know about the crime decline. It is silent on the long-term decrease in homicide among adults. What little we know about that decline suggests it is driven in part by a marked decrease in "intimate partner" homicides—killings involving husbands, wives, boyfriends, and girlfriends—and in part by the explosive increase in incarceration since 1980. But neither of these factors explains the adult homicide decline in its entirety, and the reduction in intimate partner homicide itself requires explanation.

Recent research suggests that plummeting marriage rates and the growth of hot lines, shelters, legal advocacy, and other domestic violence prevention resources have contributed to the drop in intimate partner killings. One study found the greatest declines in intimate partner homicides over the last 25 years occurred in those cities with the largest drops in marriage rates, the largest increases in divorce rates, and the most rapid growth in shelters and legal advocacy programs for domestic violence victims. Interestingly, the largest homicide drops occurred in the rate at which women kill their husbands or boyfriends and not, as might be expected, in the rate at which women are killed by their male partners. Researchers speculate that domestic violence programs, by offering women a nonviolent means of escaping abusive relationships, make it less likely they will have to kill their way out. However, because prevention programs are designed to assist women, their growth should have little effect on male behavior. Although interesting, such speculations remain just that. In general, criminologists know even less about the causes of the 20-year adult homicide drop than about the youth homicide epidemic.

criminal justice, the economy, and firearms policy

Even allowing for some lag between shrinking drug markets and falling rates of youth firearm violence, the crime decline is far longer and deeper than can be explained by the waning of the crack epidemic alone. It seems certain that other factors are at work, and there is no lack of alternative explanations, some of which are truly inspired. For example, economists Steven Levitt and John Donahue have proposed that the drop in youth violence during the 1990s is due in large part to the legalization of abortion in the 1970s. Their logic is that the increase in abortions, especially among poor women, led to fewer births of unwanted children who, had they been born, would have contributed more than their share of criminal violence as teenagers in the 1990s. Although Levitt and Donahue offer some intriguing evidence for their thesis, proving the counterfactual—that is, demonstrating that something would have happened (more crime) had something else not happened (legal abortions)—is inherently difficult. And even if they are correct about how the increase of abortion might have led to the contraction of youth crime, their argument is silent on the long-term decline in adult crime, as well as on the abrupt increase in youth crime during the 1980s. Finally, who is to say how many children, once born, remain "unwanted"?

The "more abortions, less crime" thesis is, not surprisingly, controversial. It is also quite new, and replication studies by other researchers have not yet appeared. Several other explanations for the crime drop have received greater research attention. Four are particularly prominent in both scholarly and policy circles: better policing, growing imprisonment, the booming economy, and firearms policies.

policing Some analysts believe that smart and tough policing is behind the crime drop. That is the reason former Mayor Rudolph Giuliani and former police commissioner William Bratton gave for the dramatic drop in New York City's homicide rate during the 1990s. However, homicide rates also have decreased sharply in cities that did not noticeably alter their policing policies, such as Los Angeles, or that instituted very different changes from those in New York, such as San Diego. Aggressive policing against minor offenses may have contributed to the crime decline in New York and elsewhere but, as Orlando Patterson and Christopher Winship have pointed out, at the price of heightened police-citizen tension and violence.

prison expansion The other criminal justice response that has been touted as responsible for the crime drop is the massive expansion in incarceration. The prison population has quadrupled since 1980 and now numbers more than 1.3 million inmates. It would be surprising if incarceration growth of that magnitude had no effect on the crime rate. But little agreement exists on the size of that effect. Also, whatever crime suppression effects incarceration may have must be reckoned against possible crime increases resulting from the diminished economic prospects of ex-prisoners and the disruptions in the local community when so many men are away in prison.

Prison expansion has been accompanied by a growth in the number of sentenced offenders subject to the death penalty and a dramatic rise in executions since the revival of capital punishment in the United States in the 1970s. By the end of 1999, more than 3,500 inmates were on death row, and nearly 600 had been executed. However, whatever the merits of the death penalty, less violent crime does not appear to be one of them. No credible evidence supports the use of capital punishment to reduce homicide or other forms of criminal violence.

the economy One benign alternative to expanded imprisonment is expanded employment. There seems little doubt that the record drops in unemployment rates, including those for minority teenagers, during the economic boom of the 1990s contributed in some way to the crime decline over the same period. But in what way? The relationship between employment and crime is far from simple and is the subject of ongoing debate among social scientists. Do crime rates fall during periods of economic growth because more people are working or because working people are making more money? And if people are earning more and buying more, that creates more opportunities for theft and the violence that sometimes accompanies it. Moreover, a drop in the unemployment rate or an increase in wages may reduce crime only when illegitimate opportunities for making money, such as drug dealing, are disappearing. If that is true, it is the combination of rising legitimate and falling illegitimate opportunities that has made criminal activity a less attractive alternative to legal work for many low-income youth.

A sizable fraction of teenagers, inner-city teenagers in particular, switch back and forth from low-end jobs in the legitimate and illegitimate labor markets, depending on shifts in prevailing opportunities. During periods of stagnation in the legitimate labor market and growth in illegitimate opportunities, such as the 1980s crack epidemic, we should observe increases in youth crime and violence. Likewise, we should observe drops in teenagers' criminal involvement when their legitimate opportunities are expanding and their illegitimate opportunities are shrinking, as during the economic boom and crack market crash of the 1990s. Both observations fit the temporal pattern of serious youth violence over the past two decades.

firearms policy Given the significant role of guns in serious criminal violence, it is not surprising that the crime decline has been linked to changes in firearm regulations. Some analysts believe that granting persons permission to carry firearms in public deters violent crime by making offenders wary of armed victims. Others favor background checks and waiting periods, such as those required by the 1994 Brady Act, as a way to reduce criminal misuse of handguns. Some people think, in the words of one pro-gun enthusiast, that more guns lead to less crime, while others believe that fewer guns, or fewer guns in the "wrong" hands, will reduce serious criminal violence. Evidence regarding the effectiveness of either policy is mixed. Some firearm initiatives, such as the popular gun buyback programs that have sprung up over the past decade, clearly do not reduce levels of firearm violence. More promising strategies include longer prison sentences for using a gun in a crime and police "gun patrols" in which seizures of illegal guns are focused in high-risk areas. However, we do not know how much of the crime decline can be attributed to either of these factors.

the big picture

What is the significance of these various partial accounts of the 1990s crime decline? First, none of them is a complete explanation for the crime drop. That is not just because researchers lack sufficient evidence; more important is that major social phenomena, such as serious crime, are rarely driven by a single factor. A comprehensive explanation of the crime decline will have to encompass multiple, interacting factors. Second, we cannot create a comprehensive explanation simply by adding together the various causal factors highlighted in these partial accounts, because we lack a theory that tells us just how it is that law enforcement, imprisonment, economic expansion, drug markets, and firearm diffusion—not to mention abortion—combine to reduce crime in the context of long-term trends. We badly need such an account if we are to anticipate and prepare for, much less forestall, the next increase.

Although such a theory has not yet been produced, productive first steps have been taken. Gary LaFree argues that changes in crime rates reflect the rise and fall of institutional legitimacy in a society. The basic function of institutions such as the family, economy, and political system is to regulate social behavior in the service of basic human needs. When institutions function properly, they enjoy high levels of legitimacy. People believe in the institutions, play by the rules, and crime rates decline. At other times, people question whether institutions are getting the job done—for example, when divorce and unemployment rates rise. Institutions lose people's allegiance and the capacity to control people's behavior, and crime rates go up. LaFree has applied his theory to the dramatic rise in crime rates that occurred during the late 1960s and in the 1970s, a period of significant social upheaval, political scandal, and institutional challenge. Crime rates stabilized in the 1980s, in part, LaFree suggests, because some of the changes that had wrenched the family and economy slowed or reversed (divorce rates stopped climbing, the economy began to grow), and also because policy makers responded to the increase in crime by expanding other institutions, such as the social welfare and criminal justice systems. Those expansions helped to head off further crime increases.

When LaFree published his argument, the crime decline of the 1990s had just begun, yet if the theory of institutional legitimacy is correct, crime rates will fall when the economy is booming, consumer confidence (an indicator of economic "legitimacy") is climbing, and prisons are expanding—all trademark characteristics of the roaring nineties. These changes evidently were sufficient to offset the effects of the Clinton scandals on political legitimacy and to permit a substantial downsizing of the welfare rolls.

Legitimacy theory, however, is both too broad and too narrow to fully explain the crime decline and the longer trend of which it is a part. It is too broad because it tells us little about the youth violence epidemic of the 1980s and the social conditions in the cities that nourish drug markets and high levels of firearm violence. And it is too narrow because it does not explain why, even during periods of strong institutional legitimacy such as the 1950s, rates of criminal violence in the United States remain higher than those in most other developed nations (figure 2).

The sharp increase in youth homicide rates in the late 1980s, as noted earlier, was brought about by the firearm violence emanating in and around the inner-city crack markets. But why were the crack markets so heavily concentrated in already distressed urban areas, and why were they so violent? The insights of a number of sociologists shed light on these issues. Crack sellers were attracted to those neighborhoods where residents were least able to keep them out. William Julius Wilson describes such areas as being subject to multiple "dislocations" in the form of chronically high levels of joblessness, family disruption and extreme social isolation. Their residents are often unable to engage in the kind of cooperative and supervisory activities that Robert Sampson and his colleagues term "collective efficacy." Collective efficacy enables communities to

> The basic function of institutions such as the family, economy, and political system is to regulate social behavior in the service of basic human needs. When institutions function properly, they enjoy high levels of legitimacy. People believe in the institutions, play by the rules, and crime rates decline.

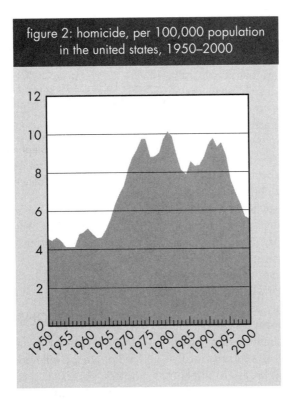

figure 2: homicide, per 100,000 population in the united states, 1950–2000

contain street crime and resist the predations of drug dealers—in fact, it very much defines what we mean by the word *community*. Along with isolation from mainstream patterns of conduct, alienation from formal institutions of justice, and diminished personal security comes the development of an alternative "code of the street" that, according to Elijah Anderson, encourages violent responses, particularly among young men, to perceived slights, insults, and disrespect.

Prolonged joblessness and reduced collective efficacy explain why illicit drug markets emerge when and where they do; isolation, alienation, and the code of the street explain why they are so violent. These ideas help to fill in the gaps in LaFree's theory, but they do not contradict its basic premise that crime rates increase with the loss of institutional legitimacy. On the contrary, it is hard to imagine a better illustration of that premise than the barren institutional landscape typical of so many high-crime inner-city neighborhoods.

how long will it last?

If the ideas of Wilson, Sampson, Anderson, and others help to narrow the focus of the legitimacy theory on the isolated ghetto poverty areas of the inner cities, we should remember that even at its low points, criminal violence in the United States remains very extensive by international standards. The U.S. homicide rate in particular—even the white homicide rate alone—is higher than that of every other developed nation. Some analysts have, reasonably enough, tied the high level of lethal violence to the limited regulation and widespread possession of firearms in the United States. Certainly firearms are deadly implements, but still we must ask why they are so unrestricted and plentiful in comparison with other nations, and more basically, why they are so often used to kill people.

An influential theory proposes that people use violence as a means of "self-help" when they lack lawful means of resolving conflicts or protecting themselves. Abused women's use of violence when they lack alternative ways to protect themselves from abusive partners is one example. Now consider the role of gun violence in illicit drug markets. Unable to use the police and courts for resolving disputes with suppliers, competitors, and customers, dealers use violence to enforce discipline, secure territory and supplies, collect debts, and protect against theft. Once guns enter the picture, the violence that begins as an enforcement code in drug markets can quickly diffuse throughout a community as people seek to protect themselves by any means necessary.

As the demand for crack diminished, so did the markets that supplied the drug and generated the violence, and the crime drop began. Multiple factors caused the crime decline of the 1990s, as well as the increase that preceded it. These factors tend to be cyclical. While cycles in the demand for particular drugs, in economic conditions, and in police aggressiveness in going after guns can reduce crime, those reductions are cyclically limited. Lasting and deeper reductions in crime will require correspondingly major reductions in the chronic economic insecurity, social isolation, and alienation found in our nation's most violent communities. The current decline in crime offers opportunities for social change that are not available when people are too afraid to participate in their communities. But time is running out.

RECOMMENDED RESOURCES

Elijah Anderson. *Code of the Street: Decency, Violence, and the Moral Life of the Inner City* (W.W. Norton, 1999).

Alfred Blumstein and Joel Wallman, eds. *The Crime Drop in America* (Cambridge University Press, 2000).

Gary LaFree. *Losing Legitimacy. Street Crime and the Decline of Social Institutions in America* (Westview, 1998).

Robert J. Sampson, Stephen W. Raudenbush, and Felton Earls. "Neighborhoods and Violent Crime: A Multilevel Study of Collective Efficacy." *Science* 277 (1997): 918–24.

William Julius Wilson. *When Work Disappears: The World of the New Urban Poor* (Alfred A. Knopf, 1996).

REVIEW QUESTIONS

1. Why are there two different crime rates? What are the differences that result in the two rates?
2. Identify the major factors that explain the drop in crime during the 1990s. While these factors undoubtedly interact with one another, which would you guess explains the greatest amount of the decrease? Explain your position.
3. As mentioned in the essay, particular types of crime are not discussed because of the way that crime rates are reported. Write two paragraphs on how these omissions might affect public opinion. Why do some types of crime evade our awareness? How do you think this might affect public perceptions of the race, class, and age of criminals?
4. William Julius Wilson describes "dislocations" and Robert Sampson mentions "collective efficacy" when discussing how the social characteristics of particular areas may facilitate crime. What do these concepts refer to? Are they related to the major facts that explain the drop in crime during the 1990s?

bruce western and becky pettit

beyond crime and punishment: prisons and inequality

fall 2002

changes in government policy on crime and punishment have put many poor minority men behind bars, more than their arrest rates would indicate. the growth of the penal system has also obscured the extent of economic inequality and sowed the seeds for greater inequality in the future.

ven during the economic boom of the 1990s, more young black men who had dropped out of school were in prison than on the job. Despite rapid growth in employment throughout the economy, released prisoners in the 1990s earned little and were often unemployed. In these two ways—high imprisonment rates among disadvantaged men and poor economic prospects for ex-inmates—the penal system affects inequality in the American society.

Inequality is disguised because data on employment often do not include the mostly poor men who are locked away behind bars. When we count prisoners among the unemployed, we find that racial inequality in employment and earnings is much greater than when we ignore them. Taking prisoners into account substantially alters our understanding of how young black men are faring, dramatically so when we focus on young black men with little education. In addition, the penal system fuels inequality by reducing the wages and employment prospects of released prisoners. The low-wage, unstable employment they experience when they return to society deepens the divisions of race and class.

For most of the twentieth century, imprisonment policies had little effect on social inequality. Prison was reserved for the most violent or incorrigible offenders, and the inmate population was consequently small. This began to change in the early 1970s when stricter law enforcement enlarged the prison population. While incarceration once used to flag dangerousness or persistent deviance, by 2000 it had become a common event for poor minority males.

the expansion of the penal system

Between 1920 and 1970, about one-tenth of one percent of Americans were confined in prisons. The prison population increased sixfold in the three decades after 1970. By June 2000, about 1.3 million people were held in state and federal prisons, and 620,000 inmates were in local jails. This translates into a total incarceration rate of seven-tenths of one percent of the U.S. population. The current incarceration rate is five times the historical average of the 1925–70 period and six to eight times the incarceration rates in Western Europe. With the important exception of homicide, however, American levels of crime are similar to those in Western Europe.

These numbers mask the concentration of imprisonment among young black men with little schooling. Although there are no official statistics, we've calculated the proportion of penal inmates among black and white men at different ages and levels of education by combining data from labor force and correctional surveys. In-carceration rates doubled among working-age men between 1980 and 1999 but increased threefold for high school dropouts in their twenties. By 1999, fewer than one percent of working-age white men were behind bars, compared to 7.5 percent of working-age black men (figure 1). Figures for young black unskilled men are especially striking: 41 percent of all black male high school dropouts aged 22–30 were in prison or jail at midyear in 1999.

Although 9 out of 10 inmates are male (92 percent), women represent the fastest-growing segment of the inmate population. During the recent penal expansion, the female inmate population has grown more than 60 percent faster than the male inmate population. African-American women have experienced the greatest increase in criminal justice supervision.

Racial disparities in incarceration are even more stark when one counts the men who have ever been incarcerated rather than just those in prison on a given day. In 1989, about 2 percent of white men in their early thirties had ever been

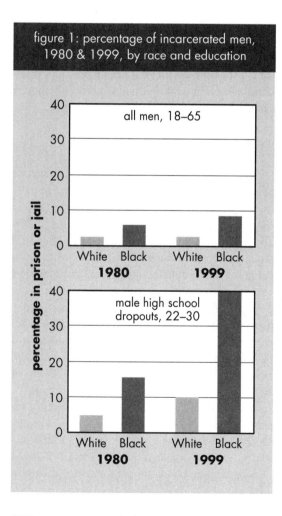

figure 1: percentage of incarcerated men, 1980 & 1999, by race and education

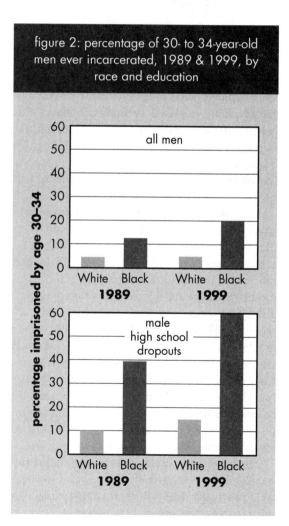

figure 2: percentage of 30- to 34-year-old men ever incarcerated, 1989 & 1999, by race and education

to prison compared to 13 percent of black men of the same age (figure 2). Ten years later, these rates had increased by 50 percent. The risks of going to prison are about three times higher for high school dropouts. At the end of the 1990s, 14 percent of white and 59 percent of black male high school dropouts in their early thirties had prison records.

The high rate of imprisonment among black men is often explained by differences in patterns of arrest and criminal behavior. Blacks are eight times more likely to be incarcerated than whites. With the important exception of drug offenses, blacks are over represented among prison inmates due to race differences in crime and arrest statistics. In 1991, for instance, black men accounted for 55 percent of all homicide arrests and 47 percent of homicide offenders in prison. Drug offenses aside, about three-quarters of the racial disparity in imprisonment can be linked to racial differences in arrests and in criminal offending as reported in surveys of crime victims. Although age and educational differences in incarceration have not been studied as closely as race, crime rates are also known to be high among young, poorly educated men. In short, young, black, male high school dropouts are over represented in prison mainly because they commit a disproportionate number of crimes (or, at least, street crimes) and are arrested for them. But that is not the whole story.

The explosion of the penal population after 1970 does not reflect increasing crime rates. The prison population has grown steadily every year since 1974, but crime rates have fluctuated up and down with no clear trend. For example 13.4 million crimes were reported to the police in 1980. In that year 182,000 people were admitted to state and federal prisons. In 1998, 12.4 million crimes were reported, and 615,000 people were sent to prison. Crime had gone down (see "Crime Decline in Context," *Contexts*, Spring 2002), but the number of people going to prison had tripled.

To explain the prison boom, we need to look beyond trends in crime. The exceptional pattern of incarceration among drug offenders provides an important clue. Drug offenders account for a rapidly increasing share of the prison population and the surge in drug-related imprisonment coincides with shifts in drug policy. Beginning in the 1970s, state and federal governments increased criminal penalties and intensified law enforcement in an attempt to reduce the supply, distribution, and use of illegal narcotics. Drug arrests escalated sharply throughout the 1980s and 1990s, and drug offenders were widely sentenced to mandatory prison terms. While the total state prison population grew at about 8 percent annually between 1980 and 1996, the population of drug offenders in state prisons grew twice as quickly.

The war on drugs was just one part of a broad trend in criminal justice policy that also toughened punishment for violent and repeat offenders. For example, between 1980 and 1996, the average time served in state prison for murder increased from 5 to more than 10 years. Habitual offender provisions, such as California's three-strikes law, mandated long sentences for second and third felony convictions. Rates of parole revocation have also increased, contributing to more than a third of all prison admissions by the late 1990s.

Why did the punitive turn in criminal justice policy affect young male dropouts so dramatically? Consider two explanations. First, as we have seen, socially marginal men are the most likely to commit crimes and be arrested for them, so simply lowering the threshold for

> To explain the prison boom, we need to look beyond trends in crime. The exceptional pattern of incarceration among drug offenders provides an important clue.

imprisonment—jailing offenders who in an earlier era would have just been reprimanded—will have the biggest impact on this group. Second, some legal scholars claim that policy was redrawn in a way that disproportionately affected young minority males with little schooling. Michael Tonry makes this argument in a prominent indictment of recent anti-drug policy. Street sweeps of drug dealers, mass arrests in inner cities and harsh penalties for crack cocaine were all important elements of the war on drugs. These measures spotlighted drug use among disadvantaged minorities but neglected the trade and consumption of illicit drugs in the suburbs by middle-class whites. From this perspective the drug war did not simply lower the threshold for imprisonment, it also targeted poor minority men.

> The penal system not only conceals inequality, it confers stigma on ex-prisoners and reduces their readiness for the job market. Consequently, ex-convicts often live at the margins of the labor market, precariously employed in low-wage jobs.

Although the relative merits of these two explanations have not yet been closely studied, it is clear that going to prison is now extremely common for young black men and pervasive among young black men who have dropped out of school. Imprisonment adds to the baggage carried by poorly educated and minority men, making it harder for them to catch up economically and further widening the economic gap between these men and the rest of society.

incarceration conceals inequality

Regardless of its precise causes, the effects of high incarceration rates on inequality are now substantial. Although the 1990s was a period of economic prosperity, improved job opportunities for many young black men were strongly outweighed by this factor. The stalled economic progress of black youth is invisible in conventional labor force statistics because prison and jail inmates are excluded from standard counts of joblessness.

Employment rates that count the penal population among the jobless paint a bleak picture of trends for unskilled black men in the 1990s. Standard labor force data show that nearly two-thirds of young black male high school dropouts had jobs in 1980 compared to just half in 1999 (figure 3). When inmates are counted in the population, however, the decline in employment is even more dramatic. In 1980 55 percent of all young black dropouts had jobs. By the end of the 1990s fewer than 30 percent had jobs, despite historically low unemployment in the labor market as a whole. Incarceration now accounts for most of the joblessness among young black dropouts, and its rapid growth drove down employment rates during the 1990s economic boom.

Because black men are overrepresented in prison and jail, incarceration also affects estimates of racial inequality. A simple measure of inequality is the ratio of white to black employment rates. In 1999, standard labor force data (which do not count convicts) show that young white dropouts were about one and a half times more likely to hold a job than their black counterparts. Once prison and jail inmates are counted among the jobless, the employment rate for young white dropouts is about two and a half times larger than for blacks. If we relied just on the usual labor force surveys, we would underestimate employment inequality for this marginal group by 50 percent.

Isolating many of the disadvantaged in prisons and jails also masks inequality in wages. When low earners go to prison and are no longer counted in the wage statistics, it appears that the average wage of workers has increased. This

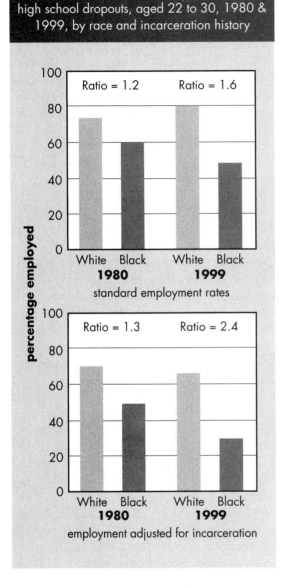

figure 3: employment percentages of male high school dropouts, aged 22 to 30, 1980 & 1999, by race and incarceration history

Ratio = 1.2   Ratio = 1.6

White Black   White Black
1980   **1999**

standard employment rates

Ratio = 1.3   Ratio = 2.4

White Black   White Black
1980   **1999**

employment adjusted for incarceration

percentage employed

The penal system not only conceals inequality, it confers stigma on ex-prisoners and reduces their readiness for the job market. Consequently, ex-convicts often live at the margins of the labor market, precariously employed in low-wage jobs. Ethnographic research paints a vivid picture. For example, in Mercer Sullivan's *Getting Paid*, delinquent youth in New York City cycled through many jobs, each held for just weeks or months at a time. One subject, after entering an ex-offender employment program at age 20, briefly held a factory job, but "he was fired for being absent and then went through three different jobs in the next four months: he tried delivering groceries, being a messenger, and doing maintenance in a nursing home." His experience was typical of Sullivan's subjects.

James Austin and John Irwin's interviews with current and former inmates in *It's About Time* reveal some of the difficulties ex-convicts have finding jobs. Released prisoners may have to disclose their criminal history or risk its discovery in a background check, or jobs may require special licenses or membership unavailable to most ex-convicts. Both may serve as substantial obstacles to employment. For example, a 38-year-old ex-convict living in the San Francisco Bay Area recalls, "I was supposed to get this light industrial job. They kept putting obstacles in front of me and I talked my way over them every time, till she brought up my being on parole and then she went sour on me. If they catch me lying on the application about being in prison or being on parole, they will [report a violation] and give me four months [in prison]." He also was unable to get a job in dry cleaning because he lacked certification: "I had dry-cleaning training a long time ago, but this time I wasn't in long enough to go through the program. It takes several years. You have to have the paper to get a job. I could jump in and clean

seeming rise in average wages doesn't represent a real improvement in living standards, however. We estimate that the wage gap between young black and white men would be 20 percent wider if all those not working, including those in prison and jail, were counted.

anything—silks, wools—remove any spot, use all the chemicals, but I don't got any paper. They won't let you start without the paper."

Statistical studies have tried to estimate the toll incarceration takes on earnings after release. Ideally, to measure the effect of prison time, we would compare the pay of groups who were the same in all respects except for their prison records. However, criminal offenders are unusual in ways that are hard to observe. They may be more impulsive or aggressive, and these sorts of characteristics aren't consistently measured by our usual surveys. Thus different studies yield different estimates.

With these caveats in mind, statistical studies suggest that serving time in prison, by itself and with other characteristics of workers accounted for, reduces wages by between 10 and 30 percent. However, this is a simplified picture of how imprisonment affects job opportunities. Research also shows that incarceration affects the growth—and not just the level—of wages. While pay usually increases as men get older, this is not so true for ex-convicts. This suggests that men with prison records find it hard to get jobs with career ladders or seniority pay. Instead, they are more likely to work in day labor or other casual jobs.

Because young black men with little education are imprisoned in such large numbers, the economic effects of incarceration on individual ex-convicts can add up to large economic disadvantages for minority communities. Neighborhoods with many people going to prison develop bad reputations that smear even the law abiding. In *When Work Disappears*, William Julius Wilson reports on interviews with Chicago employers which show how the stigma of criminality can attach to entire minority communities. Considering job candidates from the West Side, one employer observed, "Our black management people [would] say 'No, stay away from that area. That's a bad area . . .' And then it came

out, too, that sooner or later we did terminate everybody from that area for stealing . . . [or] drinking." National statistics also show how imprisonment widens the inequality between groups. Estimates for 1998 show that the reduced earnings of ex-convicts contribute about 10 percent to the wage gap between black and white men. About 10 percent of the pay gap between all male college graduates and all high school dropouts is due to the reduced wages that inmates earn after they are released.

the price of safety

The inequalities produced by the penal system are new. The state and federal governments have never imprisoned so many people, and this increase is the result not of more crime but of new policies toward crime. This expansion of imprisonment represents a more massive intrusion of government into the lives of the poor than any employment or welfare program. Young black men's sustained contact with official authority now sets them apart from mainstream America in a novel way.

The inegalitarian effects of criminal justice policy may be justified by gains in public safety. We have in this article treated the penal population primarily as disadvantaged and not as dangerous people, but a large proportion of prisoners are violent offenders. Many commit crimes again and again. Criminals may be poor men, but they also perpetrate crime in poor neighborhoods. From this viewpoint, the proliferation of prisons represents a massive investment in the public safety of disadvantaged urban areas.

But can enduring public safety be achieved by policies that deepen social inequality? A great deal of research indicates that effective crime control depends on reducing economic divisions, not increasing them. There is a strong link between criminal behavior and economic disadvantage. To the extent that prison undermines economic opportunities, the penal boom may be doing little to discourage crime in communities where most men have prison records. If high incarceration rates add to the stigma of residence in high-crime neighborhoods, the economic penalties of imprisonment may affect ex-convicts and law-abiding citizens alike. The criminal justice system is now a newly significant part of a uniquely American system of social inequality. Under these conditions, the punitive trend in criminal justice policy may be even tougher on the poor than it is on crime.

RECOMMENDED RESOURCES

Alfred Blumstein and Allen J. Beck. "Population Growth in U.S. Prisons, 1980-1996." In *Crime and Justice: Prisons*, vol. 26, eds. Michael Tonry and Joan Petersilia (University of Chicago Press, 1999).

Mercer L. Sullivan. *"Getting Paid": Youth Crime and Work in the Inner City* (Cornell University Press, 1989).

Michael Tonry. *Malign Neglect: Race, Crime, and Punishment in America* (Oxford University Press, 1996).

Bruce Western, Jeffrey R. Kling, and David F. Weiman. "The Labor Market Consequences of Incarceration." *Crime and Delinquency* 47 (July 2001): 410–27.

Bruce Western and Becky Pettit. "Incarceration and Racial Inequality in Men's Employment." *Industrial and Labor Relations Review* 54 (October 2000): 3–16.

William Julius Wilson. *When Work Disappears: The World of the New Urban Poor* (Knopf, 1996).

REVIEW QUESTIONS

1. What do Western and Pettit mean when they state that incarceration rates "mask" other measures of inequality?
2. The authors offer two explanations for how the increasingly punitive criminal justice system has affected young male dropouts. Compare these explanations, with particular attention to the differences between the groups at risk.
3. This article ends with an important question: Should we insure short-term public safety by supporting inequalities that will assuredly bring about longer-term social ills? What do you think will be the unintended consequences of prioritizing short-term public safety?
4. Activity: Many police departments give detailed statistics online by precinct (or neighborhood or district). Find the police department Web site for two locations (e.g., your hometown and where you are going to school), and do a search for "crime statistics" for each. Compare the results. What sorts of statistics are provided (e.g., different types of crimes, changes over time)? Are you statistically safer in one of the two locations?

erich goode

legalize it? a bulletin from the war on drugs   **52**

summer 2004

discontent over the efficacy and costs of america's war on drugs has led to calls for drug legalization. but this course, too, has its pitfalls. the wisest policy may be to "do less harm."

The explosion of crack cocaine use in the mid-1980s set off a fierce debate in the United States. In the midst of calls to crack down on drug users and suppliers, a formerly politically unpalatable proposal emerged: drug legalization. Advocates argue that enforcing the drug laws has fattened the wallets of drug gangs, increased drug-related violence, corrupted law enforcement, dissuaded drug abusers from seeking medical help, and in the end failed to deter drug use. It is time, these critics claim, to legalize illicit drugs, stop arresting drug users, and focus entirely on treatment.

It is true that the "war" approach to controlling drug abuse and its side effects has failed. But the hope that simply legalizing drugs will work is also unrealistic. The optimal strategy is a program focused largely—and pragmatically—on reducing the damage that both drug abuse and the war on drugs inflict on users and society at large.

Legalization proposals vary across a wide spectrum. Some plans call for regulating all psychoactive substances in the same way we currently regulate alcohol. The alcohol model would legalize the possession of any and all drugs, but the government would control how they can be sold. Others endorse dispensing certain substances by prescription to the drug-dependent. The most radical proposals call for no state control whatsoever. This laissez-faire model of full decriminalization is endorsed by libertarians. Other decriminalization approaches are limited to certain drugs—usually marijuana—in small quantities, and to possession, not sale or distribution. Advocates of these various models agree that law enforcement should not and cannot solve the problem of drug abuse. They argue that the current system causes harm, which some form of legalization would alleviate, and that drug use would not skyrocket under legalization.

"Harm reduction"—more a strategy for evaluating policies and their consequences than a specific proposal—is often confused with legalization. Harm reductionists are pragmatic rather than programmatic. They weigh costs and benefits, focus more on the health of the community than on individual rights, tend to be cautious or even pessimistic about some legalization models and argue that policy should be set on a drug-by-drug basis. According to this approach, the goal of drug policy is to reduce death, disease, predatory crime, and other costs, not to attain some idealized outcome.

legalize it?

Would any form of drug legalization work better than the war on drugs? In what specific ways might legalization succeed or fail? While most of what is written on drug laws has been polemical, serious researchers have studied the possible consequences of changes to the law.

Most focus on the practical effects of various policy proposals, leaving the moral issues to philosophers, politicians, and pundits. One strategy is to look at the history of drug regulation.

drug policy and drug use, past and present

Journalist Edward Brecher described nineteenth-century America as "a dope fiend's paradise." For much of the 1800s, few jurisdictions controlled psychoactive substances. During the first half of the century, children were permitted to purchase and drink alcohol, politicians and the military distributed liquor, and work in rural planting fields and urban workshops was usually accompanied by more than one pull at the jug. Tax records indicate that in 1830, per-capita alcohol consumption was more than three times what it is today. As for narcotics, the problem of addiction has hardly improved from the days when these substances were legal. During the nineteenth century, under a laissez-faire policy, there were at least as many narcotic addicts as there are today. Historians estimate that at the end of the nineteenth century there were at least 300,000 opiate addicts, most of whom started using drugs to treat medical problems. That amounts to about 3.7 addicts per 1,000 people. Today, about 1 million people are addicted to heroin, which is approximately 3.55 per 1,000 people.

But a comparison between then and now should take into consideration more than numbers alone. Under a more or less laissez-faire nineteenth-century legal system, few addicts committed crimes to pay for their habit, the criminal-addict subculture was small and violent gangs did not distribute drugs. Today, our laws prohibit and penalize the possession and distribution of nearly all psychoactive substances for recreational purposes—and some for any reason. Each year, we arrest 1.5 million people for drug offenses, and between 300,000 and 400,000 drug offenders reside in state and federal prisons, more than the number of violent offenders. Today, about one-third of state prison inmates and half of federal inmates are serving time for drug crimes. There are more than 15 times as many people in state prisons for drug crimes now than there were in 1980, and the proportion of all state prisoners who are drug offenders has quadrupled. Likewise, federal prisons house four times more drug offenders now than in 1980, and the proportion of all federal prisoners who are drug offenders has doubled. Comparatively, the United States incarcerates more drug offenders (150 per 100,000 people) than the European Union does for all crimes put together (fewer than 100 per 100,000). It seems the social costs of drug use are higher than ever.

Perhaps the fear of arrest and imprisonment discourages potential users from taking up the joint, pipe, or needle. Supporters of prohibition consider Reagan's war on drugs a success, because use—especially among adolescents and young adults, which had shot up during the permissive 1960s and 70s—declined significantly and spectacularly during the 1980s. (Ironically, the crack epidemic hit precisely when casual, recreational drug use declined.) Yet, beginning in the early 1990s, rates of recreational drug use increased again among young people. (After 2000, they declined a bit.) Another blow to advocates of a law enforcement approach is that today American schoolchildren are more than twice as likely to use marijuana—and almost four times as likely to use other illicit drugs—as are their European peers. Also, Reagan's drug war failed to curb supply. During his presidency, the purity of the two most dangerous illicit drugs—heroin and cocaine—increased, while their price declined. Methamphetamine, a powerful and once-popular stimulant commonly referred to as "speed," also made a strong comeback. Moreover, "club" drugs such as Ecstasy, GHB, and Rohypnol, which were not on anyone's radar screen a decade ago, are now widespread.

For these reasons, critics of the current system believe that drug prohibition has been a failure. Legalizers believe that enforcement of drug laws has untoward social side-effects. They argue that the prohibitions more than the drugs are responsible for the crime, violence, and medical pathology. And they think the solution to the substance abuse problem is legalization. Under close scrutiny, however, the evidence does not always back up their claims.

lessons from alcohol prohibition

Critics of the drug laws often point to national prohibition of alcohol in the United States as evidence that banning illicit substances does not work. Actually, Prohibition (1920–33) offers a complex lesson. Evidence on cirrhosis of the liver and hospital admissions for alcohol-related dementia indicates that alcohol consumption almost certainly declined during Prohibition—mainly among the heaviest drinkers. (Interestingly, these measures of heavy alcohol consump-

This store in Albany, California, is licensed to sell alcohol and tobacco, but not marijuana or hashish, even though most drug deaths in the United States result from tobacco (440,000 per year) and alcohol consumption (150,000).

tion began to decline before both state and federal prohibitions were imposed.) Tax records indicate that American adults drank an average of two gallons of absolute alcohol per year before Prohibition. During 1934, the first full year after Prohibition was repealed, this figure came to just under one gallon, suggesting that the experience of Prohibition deterred drinking even after it became legal again. The first lesson we learn from Prohibition is that criminalization can work—at least partially—to discourage use.

Deterrence aside, Prohibition proved a costly mistake. It enriched and empowered organized crime, increased murders, generated disrespect for the law, encouraged corruption among government officials, deprived the government of tax revenue and drove people to drink toxic "bootleg" substitutes. The second lesson of Prohibition is that outlawing illicit substances may generate damaging unanticipated consequences.

The fact is, most Americans did not regard alcohol consumption as a sin. When state referenda were held, voters chose to repeal rather than continue Prohibition by 15 million to 4 million votes. Alcohol was a part of the lives of many Americans—something that is untrue today of heroin, cocaine, or speed. Hence, Prohibition offers a third lesson: behavior that is in the mainstream of American culture probably cannot be successfully prohibited. But behavior that runs against the grain may be an altogether different matter.

the lesson of marijuana decriminalization

Possessing small amounts of marijuana has been decriminalized—or, to use a term coined by Robert MacCoun and Peter Reuter, "depenalized"—in 12 states. This means that, if apprehended with pot, users cannot be arrested, will not serve jail or prison time, and will have no criminal record. Instead, they may have their stash confiscated and be required to pay a small fine. (Marijuana possession in any quantity—approved scientific research excepted—remains illegal according to federal law.) Surveys as recent as an October 2002 Time/CNN poll show that 7 out of 10 Americans favor assessing fines over jail time.

Most policy analysts believe—based on systematic before-and-after comparisons—that removing criminal penalties on small-quantity possession did not open a floodgate of marijuana use in the depenalized states. Year-by-year changes in use in the decriminalized states basically follow the same up-and-down patterns as the nation as a whole. Also, many law enforcement officials feel that decriminalization has saved the states money at relatively little risk to public health.

The Netherlands provides another case study of the consequences of legalizing marijuana. There, anyone beyond the age of 18 can walk into one of roughly 800 "coffee shops" and purchase up to five grams of marijuana or hashish, a bit less than a quarter of an ounce. No "hard" drugs may be sold in these shops, selling to minors is illegal, and blatant advertising is not permitted. Studies of marijuana use in the Netherlands do not provide clear-cut evidence either for or against legalization. On the one hand, use among Dutch youth increased rather dramatically after legalization. In 1984, only 15 percent of 18- to-20-year-olds had ever used marijuana; by 1996, 44 percent had. Similarly, the percentage of youth who had used the drug in the previous month more than doubled from 8 to 18 percent during that period. This evidence seems to support the prohibitionists' argument.

On the other hand, usage rates have increased only modestly during the past decade and appear to be leveling off. According to surveys, rates of Dutch high schoolers using cannabis, although lower than in Ireland, the United Kingdom, and France, are among the highest in Europe. Yet, they are still consider-

ably below the rates for high school students in the United States, where most states continue to criminalize marijuana. Clearly, the *de facto* legalization of cannabis in the Netherlands has not brought about a torrent of marijuana and hashish consumption, and most Dutch citizens and officials favor the current laws. In short, the experiences of the Netherlands and the United States suggest that decriminalization would not produce significantly higher levels of marijuana use. It is entirely possible that, uniquely for marijuana, nearly everyone who wants to use the drug already does so.

the economics of drug use

Legalizers typically argue that we need not worry about decriminalization making drugs cheaper and thus more enticing, because the relationship between the price of drugs and demand for them is weak or nonexistent. Economists, however, find that cost significantly influences demand for drugs. Elasticity—the variation in demand for goods as prices rise and fall—differs considerably from drug to drug. Demand for heroin drops only 0.2 to 0.3 percent for every 1 percent increase in price, but the demand for marijuana drops roughly 1 percent for every 1 percent increase in price. Cigarettes (a 0.4 percent decrease) and alcohol (a 0.7 percent decrease) fall somewhere in between.

Prohibition hugely increases the price of illicit drugs and therefore should discourage use. (Decriminalization retains penalties on distribution, sale, and large-quantity possession. Hence, even in the decriminalized states, marijuana remains fairly expensive.) Legalization would lower prices, which would probably reduce the property crimes committed by addicts (their habits would be cheaper), but it would almost certainly increase rates of use. Prohibitionists predict that tens of millions of Americans would take up cocaine or heroin. This worst-case scenario is almost certainly wildly off the mark. Use would increase the most not among current nonusers, but among the heaviest current users. Studies indicate that if these drugs were cheaper and less difficult to acquire, addicts would use them in much greater volume.

When drugs are legal, the government can use taxes to raise prices and discourage use. Current state and federal taxes on legal drugs—alcohol and tobacco—are far too low, at less than 50 cents per drink and 1 dollar per pack of cigarettes, to significantly deter drinking and smoking. Not included in that dollar is the price markup charged by cigarette companies to pay off the $200 billion that they have agreed to pay the states in a legal settlement; in effect, this is taxation by another means. Since most drug-related deaths stem from alcohol (85,000 per year, according to the Centers for Disease Control) and tobacco (440,000 per year), increasing alcohol and cigarette taxes could save lives. Whether through prohibition or taxes, policies that raise costs are a powerful way to depress demand.

Of course, financial cost is not the only way in which prohibition might reduce use. Criminalization imposes other types of costs: the extra time and effort required to get drugs and the risk of incarceration. Proponents of "absolute deterrence" believe that enforcing drug laws yet more firmly can drastically reduce or eliminate illegal drug use by locking up users and dealers and scaring off would-be violators. From that perspective, the war on drugs has been a failure, because it has been insufficiently aggressive. But "stamping out" drug use is a fool's errand. "Stamping out"—or even drastically reducing—drug use is an unrealistic standard by which to judge the effectiveness of the drug laws. No one expects laws penalizing robbery, rape, or murder to "stamp out" those crimes.

"Relative deterrence"—a more moderate position—argues that, while prohibition cannot

eliminate it, drug use would be more common in the absence of law enforcement. Imagine if any adult could freely purchase currently illegal drugs in licensed shops or markets, out of a catalogue, or over the Internet. Drug use would surely increase. And it would rise significantly under almost any of the more radical forms of proposed legalization. Would such increased drug use be bad? It depends on the drug, and for some drugs, it depends on how the drug is used and who uses it. Apparently, for alcohol, a drink or two a day can actually stimulate good health. But for tobacco, any use is harmful, and the greater the use, the greater the harm. The story is a bit more complicated with heroin and cocaine. The way they are used today is harmful, and while legalization would eliminate some features of that harm, others would remain. Hence, higher levels of use would inevitably mean higher levels of harm.

On the other hand, the more similar a system of "legalization" is to the current system of prohibition, the more the black market would step in to provide an alternative supply of illegal drugs as it does today.

harm reduction

Today, critics of the war on drugs are less likely to advocate legalization, and more likely to endorse some form of "harm reduction." There is a vast middle ground between strict criminal punishment and outright legalization. That territory should be explored, harm reductionists argue, to reduce deaths, disease, financial cost, and crime. Find out what programs work to reduce harm, they urge, and adopt them. These advocates believe that better results will be achieved by being experimental, pragmatic, and empirical.

The United States currently spends three times more money on law enforcement than on treatment and prevention. Harm reduction strategists suggest that we reverse the priority of these expenditures. They also advocate eliminating programs for drug eradication and crop substitution in source countries. Evidence gathered by the RAND Corporation indicates that these programs do not work. In addition, they are financially and politically costly. Tax dollars would be far better spent on more effective ways to combat addiction, such as treatment programs.

Needle exchange programs are another effective approach to reducing harm. They appear to lower rates of HIV transmission. Between 1988 and 1993, HIV rates decreased by 6 percent in major cities with needle exchange programs, and increased by 6 percent in cities without them. Critics of needle exchange have been unable to explain this phenomenon. These programs have been adopted nearly everywhere in the Western world. Yet they reach only 10 percent of intravenous drug users in the United States. In spite of favorable evaluations of the policy by expert panels—including the General Accounting Office and the Institute of Medicine of the National Academy of Sciences—and in spite of positive findings from the dozens of studies done to evaluate these programs, the federal government staunchly opposes needle exchange programs as "encouraging drug abuse." From a harm reduction perspective, such objections are counter-productive because the programs can help control a deadly epidemic.

Researchers have also conducted hundreds of studies of drug treatment. Overwhelmingly, these studies show that treatment works. Drug addicts and abusers who spend time in treatment programs—and the more time spent, the more this is true—tend to reduce their levels of drug abuse, commit less predatory crime, and live longer, healthier lives, than those who do not. Methadone maintenance has been studied particularly carefully. It cuts crime and saves lives. Equating the administration of methadone to heroin addicts with giving vodka to an alcoholic, as some critics do, is semantic hocus-pocus, harm reductionists argue. Even with cheating, enrollees significantly reduce their drug use and its by-products, such as crime.

As with all policy research, the causal arrows are not always easy to draw, but most analysts are convinced from controlled studies that, over the long run, treatment is considerably more cost-effective than incarceration. Although failure rates are high, treatment programs reduce the total volume of illicit drug use and criminal behavior by roughly one-third to one-half. And a majority of drug abusers significantly reduce or abandon their use of illicit substances after a second, third, fourth, or fifth attempt at treatment—roughly comparable to the repeated failures following treatment for smoking.

Experimental programs that administer injected methadone are under way in the United Kingdom. Oral morphine is being tried in Austria, Australia, Switzerland, and the Netherlands. In Germany, programs involving the use of codeine have been tried. Switzerland and the Netherlands have inaugurated injected heroin maintenance programs. Do they work? At this writing, we do not have definitive answers. But, if the goal is reducing harm and not simply drug use, American authorities should also be exploring such avenues.

a choice

The outright legalization of hard drugs is both politically impossible and potentially dangerous for our society. Debating drug legalization is at present little more than cocktail party chatter, what legal scholars Franklin Zimring and Gordon Hawkins refer to as a "sideshow." Public opinion polls show that fewer than 5 percent of

Americans support the legalization of hard drugs. The prospects for harm reduction strategies look somewhat better. While these strategies face formidable political obstacles in the United States, they can be adopted pragmatically, one step at a time, in individual locales or jurisdictions. Such programs are being instituted in Western Europe. They should be studied and, if they work, emulated.

Yet even after the facts are in, moral issues cannot be circumvented. Decisions about public policy ultimately rest on morality and ideology, because all programs result in a "mixed bag" of results, some good, some less desirable. How do we weigh the outcomes? Debate over which mixed bag is the least bad can never be resolved on strictly scientific grounds.

Many concerned citizens oppose any program that appears to condone drug use, even if it saves lives, while many proponents of legalization or decriminalization—especially free market libertarians—favor fully decriminalizing drugs, even if that results in higher rates of drug-related fatalities. Still, the sanctity of human life is a rhetorical "ace in the hole" for harm reduction proponents. It is time, they argue, to begin taking steps to save lives.

RECOMMENDED RESOURCES

Erich Goode. *Between Politics and Reason: The Drug Legalization Debate* (St. Martin's Press, 1997).

This book provides an overview of the effect of prohibition and the likely effect of drug legalization.

Erich Goode. *Drugs in American Society*, 6th ed. (McGraw-Hill, 2004).

This study provides background detail on drug use in the United States.

James A. Inciardi. ed. *The Drug Legalization Debate*, 2nd ed. (Sage, 1999).

This is a book of essays, pro and con, on the question of legalization.

Robert J. MacCoun and Peter Reuter. *Drug War Heresies: Learning from other Vices, Times, and Places* (Cambridge University Press, 2001).

This is an informative, well-reasoned volume on the consequences of drug policy.

Ethan Nadelmann. "The Case for Legalization." *The Public Interest* 92 (Summer 1988): 3–31; and "Commonsense Drug Policy." *Foreign Affairs* 77 (January/February 1998): 111–26.

These two articles reflect how a prominent spokesperson for drug legalization has shifted to a more moderate position of harm reduction.

Project Cork. "Cork Bibliography: Harm Reduction." Online. http://www.projectcork.org/bibliographies/data/Bibliography-HarmReduction.html.

A 128-citation bibliography of empirical studies on harm reduction published between January 2002 and September 2003.

Franklin E. Zimring and Gordon Hawkins. *The Search for Rational Drug Control* (Cambridge University Press, 1992).

This is an excellent general framework for understanding the foundations and implications of drug control policy.

REVIEW QUESTIONS

1. What evidence does Goode provide in his essay to explain how "deviant drug use" is "socially constructed"? How does the case of alcohol support this contention?

2. Consider the current culture of American society as regards *legal* drugs. How do you feel Americans use prescription drugs? What about caffeine? Nicotine? Aspirin? Write a paragraph on how the prominence of legal

drug use in our society may or may not reinforce illicit drug use.

3. Goode's essay makes little mention of race, yet this is obviously a key factor in the "war on drugs." Convictions for possessing crack cocaine, for example, which is commonly used by Latino and African-American addicts, tend to result in longer jail sentences than convictions for powder cocaine, which is more commonly used by white addicts. Is the war on drugs, like the surge in incarceration discussed in the previous reading, really a type of war on black and Latino men? Why?

4. Do you think U.S. drug policy makes sense? Does Goode's essay make you more inclined to support the decriminalization of drugs? Why or why not?

richard b. felson

is violence against women about women or about violence?

53

spring 2006

when men are violent to women, is it a form of sexist oppression? or are they simply brutes? and are there political reasons to view them one way or the other?

uppose a group of men murdered millions of women. Before doing so they shaved their heads, stripped them, and sometimes beat and sexually assaulted them. Would this be an appalling example of sexism? Not necessarily. The Nazis committed these deeds, but they killed millions of men as well. If we ignore their violence against men and look only at that against women, their behavior appears to reflect sexism. Perhaps this same kind of selective focus affects our understanding of violence against women today. Are the offenders sexist or just violent men? Are women victimized because of their gender, or because they make up half the population?

Most sociologists who study violence against women study it separately from violence against men, and they interpret it as a form of sexism. They argue that misogynist men assault women in order to maintain their dominance. They believe that misogynist societies tolerate violence against women, leading offenders to think they can get away with it. They get away with it because victims usually do not report the incidents to the police; when they do, they get blamed, and the offender gets off. The result is an epidemic of violence against women, most of it

> The women who kill their husbands are not usually sweet and innocent. We found that they are just as likely to have criminal records as women who kill in other circumstances.

hidden. This approach, which I call a "gender perspective," is conventional wisdom among sociologists and much of the general public.

Some researchers are beginning to challenge the gender perspective. They take what I call a "violence perspective," arguing that we should rely on theories of violence and crime, not theories of sexism, to explain violence against women. I take this perspective in my book, *Violence and Gender Reexamined*, and my research articles support it. From this point of view, sexism plays at most a trivial role in rape and in physical assault on wives. Typically, men who commit these crimes commit other crimes as well, and their backgrounds and attitudes toward women are similar to those of other criminals. They are versatile "bad guys"— selfish, not sexist. When they assault women, they do so "behind closed doors" because we stigmatize the behavior—a man should not hit a woman. Traditional values inhibit violence against women rather than encouraging it.

Both sides in this debate would agree about some basic facts regarding gender and violence. They would agree that the typical violent incident involves two men: men are much more likely to commit violent crime than women, and men are much more likely to be the victims. They would also agree that when the victim is a woman, the offender is more likely to be an intimate partner or a family member than when the victim is a man. Finally, they would agree that those who commit sexual assault are almost always men, while their victims are mostly women.

On other issues the two sides disagree. They disagree about whether wives are as likely to hit their husbands as husbands are to hit their wives; they disagree about the motivation of offenders; and they disagree about whether men who assault women get off easily because society tolerates violence against women. I discuss these issues in turn.

frequency of partner violence

In the 1970s, Murray Straus and Suzanne Steinmetz created an uproar with survey evidence that wives and husbands hit each other with equal frequency. They faced a protest and even a bomb threat. Straus and Steinmetz acknowledged that husbands are more likely to injure their wives than the reverse; a woman may slap her husband, but a husband is more likely to do serious damage. This point got lost in the battle that followed.

More recent surveys of violent behavior have found the same patterns among both spouses and dating couples. Both women and men use physical force at the same rates. But crime surveys find that women are more likely to be victims because these surveys include more serious forms of violence.

Once the distinction between minor and serious violence is made, the acrimonious debate over frequency becomes unnecessary. The term "battered husbands," despite its media appeal, is a gross exaggeration. We need shelters for women not men. Nevertheless, the finding of gender parity in the overall frequency of spousal violence has important implications. It leads us to wonder why men, who are eight times more likely to commit violence than women, are no more likely than women to hit their spouses. They are bigger and stronger, so there is less risk. What stops them? The violence perspective suggests that violent men are less likely to assault their partners because of the chivalry norm. Even Richard "The Iceman" Kuklinski, who killed more than 200 people during his lifetime, had a chivalrous tendency. He said that hitting his wife was his only regret.

Even if we agree that wives and husbands hit each other with equal frequency but unequal effect, a bone of contention remains. R. P. and R. E. Dobash, taking a gender perspective, argue that frequency counts are misleading because wives use violence mainly to defend themselves. However, John Archer's analysis of a large number of surveys shows that wives are actually more likely to initiate violence than husbands in domestic assaults. It is still possible, however, that when the violence escalates, women start using violence in self-defense.

Homicide research does show that women are more likely to kill in self-defense than men, but police investigators attribute only 10 percent of homicides committed by wives to self-defense; women kill their husbands for a variety of reasons. In addition, the women who kill their husbands are not usually sweet and innocent. We found that they are just as likely to have criminal records as women who kill in other circumstances. They are no more likely to be motivated by self-defense than other female killers. In general, the evidence suggests that the greater tendency for wives to kill in self-defense reflects the fact that women are generally less violent than men. Most violent wives do not have innocent motives or suffer from "battered wife syndrome"; they kill their husbands for the same diverse reasons that husbands kill their wives.

domineering husbands?

A gender perspective implies that men use violence against their wives to maintain their dominance. However, the accompanying table suggests that husbands are no more controlling than wives, and are perhaps less so. The table is based on a survey that asked more than 10,000 men and women about their spouse's behavior. It shows, for example, that men are more likely to prevent their wives from working outside the home, but women are more likely to insist on knowing who their husbands are with at all times. Overall, the women are slightly more bossy. However, relatively few husbands or wives engage in any of these domineering behaviors.

Even though husbands are no more domineering than wives, perhaps those who are tend to use violence to get their way, while domineering women use other methods. We found some supporting evidence, but only in troubled marriages. Apparently, in troubled marriages men are more likely to use violence to get their way. However, our findings suggest that the difference has to do with method, not motive. From the violence perspective, size, not sexism, explains their behavior.

My colleague, Mike Johnson, has suggested a compromise position, arguing that sexism and a desire for dominance motivate only those husbands who commit the most serious violence. These "intimate terrorists" commit violence that is more injurious, frequent, and unilateral than the "common couple violence" typically committed by both husbands and wives. However, our research suggests that controlling husbands are not particularly likely to commit serious violence. They have many techniques at their disposal. Some women are certainly terrorized by their husbands, but those husbands may be nasty brutes, not domineering sexists.

Perhaps there is some other compromise. Perhaps sexism is one of several things that lead to violence against women. Whatever the case, assertions about the effect of sexism should be based on scientific evidence, not political compromise. At this point, sexism remains an untested hypothesis.

---

the control behavior of american husbands and wives

Does their current spouse...	Husbands	Wives
Prevent them from knowing about or having access to family income even when they ask?	2.1%	1.7%
Prevent them from working outside the home?	1.6%*	1.0%
Insist on knowing who they are with at all times?	7.1%*	9.6%
Insist on changing residences even when they don't want or need to?	1.0%*	2.0%
Try to limit their contact with family and friends?	3.2%	3.8%

* Asterisks indicate a statistically significant difference between husbands and wives (N = 10,067).
Source: National Violence Against Women Survey.

rape frequency

An even more heated debate concerns the frequency of rape. One prominent survey carried out by Mary Koss asked American college students about their sexual experiences since age 14. It found that about 9 percent of college women reported that they had engaged in sexual intercourse "because a man threatened or used some degree of physical force (twisting your arm, holding you down, etc.) to make you." But only 27 percent of the women with this experience thought of these incidents as rape. Scholars with a gender perspective think that these victims buy into "rape myths," blaming themselves or thinking that the term *rape* applies only when the offenders are strangers. Those with a violence perspective suggest that many of these encounters are ambiguous. They note that many of the women attribute these incidents to misunderstandings. In addition, Charlene Muehlenhard finds that three out of four college women report that they had, at least at times, engaged in "token resistance": they said no when they meant yes or maybe. The line between coercion and consent is apparently ambiguous. Because we do not yet know exactly what happens in these incidents, it is impossible to determine the frequency of rape.

Men use a variety of techniques to influence women to have sex, and some of them use force. Young men have sex on their minds, not the domination of women.

---

rape motives

Gender scholars have suggested that rape is used as a form of male domination and control. In the most influential book ever written on rape, Susan Brownmiller argued that rape is used to keep women "in their place" and dependent on their husbands for protection. Anthropologists have found a few tribal societies that use rape to deter women from violating certain rules. For example, the Mehinaku, a Brazilian Indian tribe, use the threat of group rape to prevent women from observing certain male ritual objects. Because of their intense fear, the women stay away from the objects and, according to the anthropologist who studied them, a group rape had not occurred for 40 years (and perhaps had never occurred).

Whether rape is a form of social control in modern societies is disputed. Evidence shows that women's fear of rape leads them to curb their activities more often than men do. Yet the fact that the fear of rape constrains women's activities does not necessarily mean that the goal of rape is social control, much less that offenders are acting in some way as society's agents. Unlike the Mehinaku, modern societies have severe penalties for rape.

Gender scholars reject sexual motivation for rape, although some recent treatments acknowledge a sexual element. Gender scholars ask why men would use force when other sexual outlets are available. They claim that what the rapist wants instead is to dominate the victim. Studies based on interviews with incarcerated rapists are inconclusive. Nicholas Groth claimed that 65 percent of the 133 rapists he interviewed had a power motive, but others have interpreted his data as implying sexual motivation. Diana Scully reported that some of the rapists she interviewed said they enjoyed the power they had over the victims, but she did no counting.

Other scholars argue that rape is usually sexually motivated. They point to Eugene Kanin's evidence that date rapes typically occur during consensual sexual activity when the man is sexually aroused. He wants intercourse, but she does not want to go that far. Kanin has also found that rapists tend to have high sexual aspirations. They masturbate frequently and spend a lot of time searching for consensual sexual partners. Finally, when rapists are interviewed, they express a preference for attractive victims, and they overwhelmingly choose young women. Only 1.5 percent of rape victims in the United States are over 50.

Young women might be at greater risk than older women because they go out more often. But we found that the average victim of rape committed in conjunction with robbery was seven years younger than the average robbery victim. This suggests that rapists prefer young women, as does the fact that rapes in war zones usually target young women.

The idea that rape is typically sexually motivated is consistent with the feminist argument that men often treat women as sex objects. Much evidence suggests that men often think of women, or at least attractive women, in sexual terms, and that some use underhanded means to influence them to have sexual relations. They seem to think that "all is fair in love and war." The evidence is clear that men are much more likely than women to be indiscriminate and casual in their attitudes toward sexual relations, and that their interest in sex is greater. Evolutionary psychologists argue that the sex difference is biological. Whether biological or learned, sex differences in sexuality lead to conflict between the sexes, according to a violence perspective. Men use a variety of techniques to influence women to have sex, and some of them use force. Young men have sex on their minds, not the domination of women. On a Saturday night they aspire to find a sexual partner, not a woman to boss around.

sexism and violence against women

Another way to look at motivation is to determine whether men who assault women also have negative attitudes toward women. We need to be clear about whether negative attitudes refer to hatred of women or traditional attitudes about gender roles. While hatred of women goes along with violence toward women, some evidence indicates that traditional men are less likely to assault women. One laboratory study showed that traditional men were less likely to hit women with pillow clubs than were men with more liberal attitudes toward gender roles.

In addition, men who assault their wives and commit rape have attitudes toward women that are similar to those of other male offenders. They tend to commit a variety of crimes, rather than specializing in violence against women. This versatility suggests that men who assault women are criminals, not sexists. Some of them certainly hit their wives but no one else; perhaps they are the domineering sexists. On the other hand, marital conflicts can be intense, so we should not be surprised that husbands who are drunk or have bad tempers sometimes become violent.

Violence against women may be more frequent in societies where women have lower status. Peggy Sanday found this to be true in her study of tribal societies, but no one has found it so in larger, more complex societies. For modern societies, rates of violence against women tend to be high when rates of violence against men are high. Violence is violence. But everywhere, men are much more likely to be victims than are women.

do men get away with it?

A gender approach implies that men assault women because "they can." Are these offenders more likely to evade the law than other offenders, as the gender perspective suggests? The evidence suggests not. Physical assaults against wives are more likely to be reported to the police than assaults against husbands, even when the offenses are of equal severity. Husbands and wives who engage in minor forms of violence are less likely to be reported than offenders who commit minor violence against strangers, probably because of privacy concerns.

The evidence on sexual assault is more mixed. We have found that sexual assaults are less likely than physical assaults to be reported to the police, particularly if the offender is an acquaintance. However, the criminal justice system does not treat sexual assaults more leniently than physical assaults. Arrest and conviction are just as likely, and the sentences are more severe. No one has examined whether rape victims are assigned more blame than victims of physical assault and other crimes. However, experimental evidence shows that observers assign just as much blame to male victims of rape as to female victims. But they assign the overwhelming amount to offenders—they just think victims can make mistakes.

Scholars who take a gender perspective claim that only women who conform to gender roles are protected from harm. Those who take a violence perspective think it is important to make gender comparisons. For example, a man who dresses like a woman is stigmatized more than a woman who dresses like a man. In general, the evidence on sentencing by the criminal justice system suggests that we respond more harshly to deviant men than deviant women. The tendency to respond more harshly to female promiscuity than male promiscuity—the double standard—appears to be an exception.

science versus social activism

These controversies in part reflect the policy concerns of social scientists who are also social activists. From a scientific perspective, it is important to be accurate and to use the most general principles possible to understand human behavior. From the social activist's point of view, it is important to emphasize the frequency and seriousness of violence against women in order to build political support and raise money for social programs. Exaggerating the frequency of social problems is standard practice among activists. So is emphasizing dramatic cases, even though most cases are not so serious. It is useful, for example, to claim high frequencies of "wife beating," and to describe victims as "battered wives" or "survivors," even though most violence against women does not involve beatings and is not life-threatening. The media also focus on the worst cases, since they grab attention. Perhaps without these strategies we would not have shelters for battered wives and rape crisis centers—both of them good things. An examination of gender differences in victimization is less conducive to social action on behalf of women.

Social activism and science are clearly at cross purposes when it comes to their perspectives on motive. Those who take a gender perspective worry that judges and jurors might blame victims and treat rapists more leniently if they thought rape was sexually motivated. They believe that the offender might excuse his behavior by saying he was overcome with desire or she somehow enticed him. Alas, no one knows whether beliefs about the offender's motive have these effects. Judges and juries might be just as punitive when they believe rapists are sexually motivated. Moreover, we must understand the offender's real motives if we are to provide effective counseling and treatment.

I am not arguing that we should ignore gender in our response to violence. It may make more sense to arrest and punish violent husbands than violent wives, even when they commit the same offense. Differences in size and strength make violent men more dangerous than violent women. Women are more vulnerable, particularly when they are living with violent men. Equivalent responses to the violence of husbands and wives may not provide women with the protection they need. Of course, if justice is our only goal, then we should ignore gender in the criminal justice system and treat everyone equally. However, equal treatment ignores gender differences in dangerousness and in the need for protection. Special efforts to protect women may be justified.

Ambivalence about special protection for women is not new. After the sinking of the *Titanic*, one women's group built a monument to honor the men who gave up their lives so that the female passengers might be saved. Other women's groups complained about what they saw as an outdated concept of chivalry. Special protections for women are controversial now (as they were then) because of the image of dependence they imply. The vulnerability of women justifies treating violence against women more seriously than violence against men, even when statistical evidence does not.

RECOMMENDED RESOURCES

R. E. Dobash and R. P. Dobash. *Rethinking Violence against Women* (Sage, 1998).

A radical feminist approach.

Richard B. Felson. "Blame Analysis: Accounting for the Behavior of Protected Groups." *American Sociologist* 22 (1991): 5–23.

A discussion of the role of ideology in sociology.

Richard B. Felson. *Violence and Gender Reexamined* (American Psychological Association, 2002).

Extensive presentation of the violence perspective.

Mary P. Koss. *No Safe Haven: Male Violence against Women at Home, at Work, and in the Community* (American Psychological Association, 1994).

A moderate feminist approach by a psychologist.

Murray A. Straus. "The Controversy Over Domestic Violence by Women: A Methodological, Theoretical, and Sociology of Science Analysis." In *Violence in Intimate Relationships*, eds. Ximena B. Arriaga and Stuart Oskamp (Sage, 1999).

A major participant in the domestic-violence controversy presents his side.

REVIEW QUESTIONS

1. According to Felson, how is the "violence perspective" similar to, but also distinct from, the "gender perspective"?

2. Consider the research on violence between husbands and wives (and between intimate partners more generally): Do men hit their wives more often than women hit their husbands? Do men hit more violently than women? Why do husbands hit wives? Do women more often hit men to hurt, to provoke, or to defend themselves? How many husbands kill their wives? How many wives kill their husbands? How often do wives kill in self-defense? Overall, do you think the evidence tends to support the "violence perspective," as Felson believes, or the "gender perspective," or perhaps elements of both?

3. How might feminists respond to this essay? What findings or interpretations might they question? Are there "feminist" questions that Felson hasn't asked? Does Felson have convincing responses to feminists?

4. At the end of the essay, Felson suggests that social science and social activism are at "cross purposes" when it comes to domestic or intimate violence. Do you agree? Do the violence and gender perspectives lead to different kinds of activism? Do you think one or the other perspective lends itself to better or more effective public policies or programs?

part **12**

Politics

steven lukes

keyword: power

(summer 2007)

54

The word *power* lies at the center of a semantic field that includes *authority, influence, coercion, force, violence, manipulation, strength,* and so on. We use these terms all the time in everyday talk and generally know what we mean, and yet scholars endlessly debate their definition. Such contests matter because how we think about power can have momentous consequences. For example, voters may choose among candidates on the basis of which one they see as "stronger," and what counts as "strong" will derive from what they think it means to be "powerful."

At its most general, *power* simply means the capacity to bring about outcomes. It is important from the outset to avoid two fallacies. The first is the "exercise fallacy": this occurs when we equate power with its exercise, as when we define power as winning, as achieving success in decision making, or as prevailing over others. The desire to make the concept of power "operational" can lead to this fallacy, but power is a dispositional concept: it names a potentiality that may never be actualized (just as a brittle window may never break).

The second fallacy is the "vehicle fallacy," which occurs when we equate power with the means or resources of power. Sociologists sometimes identify power with wealth or status, and military analysts sometimes measure it in terms of military forces and weaponry. But as the United States discovered in Vietnam and postwar Iraq, having the means of power is not the same as being powerful.

In social and political contexts, we typically attribute power to agents when we hold them responsible for bringing about significant outcomes. This can be straightforward when both agent and outcome are specified (as in the president's power to veto Congressional bills). But we often want to know how to locate power (who has it? who can exercise it, and who has exercised it? who has more, and who less?). We also want to assess its impact (who is affected, and in what ways?). Such inquiries involve attributing causal responsibility to the supposedly powerful when they exercise their power, and also moral, political, legal, or historical responsibility that identifies them as accountable in some way for the consequences of their power. They also involve attributing significance to those consequences by seeing them as affecting people's interests, whether positively or negatively. (Entirely trivial consequences would not suggest powerfulness.) And such inquiries must involve a mechanism—a causal process that links the powerful with the outcomes they can bring about.

Controversy already attaches to attributing responsibility (holding agents accountable) and significance (judging where people's interests lie). How are we to disentangle the responsibility of agents in complex situations? Who, for example, was responsible for the bungled response to Hurricane Katrina (and in what sense of *responsible*—moral, political, legal)? And how do we assess which interests weigh more than others (since, if I can affect your central or basic interests, my power, in relation to you, is greater than if I can affect you only superficially). Thus multimedia magnates have more power than celebrities, and a judge who can sentence people to life or death has greater power than a judge who cannot.

But that is only the beginning of the complexities of this topic. How are agents to be understood—as autonomous centers of choice or as enacting predetermined scripts and roles? (This is sometimes called the "structure/agency" problem.) Must those who are powerful be individuals, or can they be collectives (groups? classes? organizations? states?) and, if so, under what conditions? And if their power is to be effective, must those with power exercise it intentionally? Does power, as Bertrand Russell and many others thought and continue to think, involve, when actualized, "the production of intended effects," or can it operate in routine and unconsidered ways, without being willed by the powerful? And must I act, by positively intervening in the world, in order to actualize my power? Can my power consist in abstaining from acting? C. Wright Mills in *The Power Elite* wanted to call "the men of power" to account for the decisions they did not make. And can my power consist in not having to act, because others favor or advance my interests without my having to lift a finger?

These few complexities (there are more) are enough to show that ways of viewing power range from the very narrow to the very broad. In the narrowest, individualist, intentional, and active view, the powerful are individuals who, when they choose, can intentionally advance their interests by positive actions: for instance by winning in decision-making situations—say a governing coalition on a city council. In the broadest view, the powerful can be individuals or collectivities whose interests may be advanced by acting or not acting—whether they intend such consequences or not—as when members of privileged classes may be unaware of others' deference to and acceptance of limited horizons that may sustain their privileges. In the former view, an elite's power is limited to its capacity to achieve coordinated policy goals; in the latter view, its power (and what count as its interests) will extend wider and deeper. As stated above, these differing views of power matter: if we view power narrowly, we will see less of it about than if we view it broadly.

So far we have considered power, in its most general sense, as the capacity to advance one's interests and affect the interests of others, whether negatively or positively. It is important to stress this last point, for it is often mistakenly assumed that, by definition, the power of the powerful affects others' interests adversely. But power can be empowering, even transformative, increasing others' resources, capabilities, and effectiveness. Examples are nurturing relationships such as apprenticeship, teaching, parenting, and therapy. Consider Plato's account of a domineering Socrates in the *agora* creating fertile confusion in his young interlocutors so that they might achieve self-knowledge. Other examples are command-obedience relations that are indispensable to valued, cooperative activities, such as those in armies, orchestras, and sports.

The likely reason for this mistake is that power is commonly understood, in both everyday and academic usage, in a more restrictive sense, to refer to asymmetrical relations in which to have power is to have power *over* another or others. This widespread understanding of power incorporates the ideas of subordination, dependency, and control. Spinoza called it *potestas*, to capture the idea of someone being *in the power of* another and thus prevented from living "as his own nature and judgment dictate." Yet, as the previous paragraph indicates, there are countless examples of such asymmetrical power being "positive," or beneficent. Perhaps the widespread tendency to see asymmetric power, or power over others, as negative (ignoring such cases) derives from a liberal-inspired aversion to dependency relations and a Marxist-inspired vision of the social order as inherently conflictual.

The common understanding of power relations, then, is in terms of *domination*, and the remainder of this essay focuses on this more restrictive understanding. How are we to understand power as domination: the power of some over others that has a negative effect on the interests of those subject to it? What is sometimes called "the power debate" among Anglo-American political scientists has hinged on this question—a debate begun by Robert Dahl, who, in 1958, criticized what he called "the ruling elite model" (as advanced by Floyd Hunter and C. Wright Mills). In part that debate was over the question, considered above, of whether to conceptualize power narrowly or broadly. But more was at stake.

Dahl's objection was to the lack of empirical evidence for a ruling elite or ruling class, so he proposed a method for studying power that defined interests as preferences, as revealed in political participation, and measured power by quantifying the extent to which the preferences of a group regularly prevail over those of other likely groups in key decisions in the presence of observable conflict. This conception of power was, plainly, the narrow individualist, intentional, and active view. Dahl and his colleagues concluded, on the basis of this view of power, that U.S. cities and, indeed, U.S. politics nationally were "pluralistic" because different actors prevailed over different key issues, and thus that the elite model was thereby refuted.

Their view was criticized by political scientists Peter Bachrach and Morton Baratz for ignoring a "second face" of power, namely, the power to shape political agendas: the power to keep potential issues from becoming actual by determining which are to be the key political issues, preventing existing grievances from entering the political arena and contributing to the "mobilization of bias" in various ways (such as co-opting potential opponents and manipulating voting rules), through what they called "non–decision making." Their view remained, however, intentional and active: non–decision making remained deliberate and had to consist in suppressing observable, albeit covert, grievances. In their account, observable (though not necessarily overt) conflict of interests as preferences was still assumed to exist between the preferences of the putative elite and the grievances of the excluded.

In 1974 I in turn criticized this view by proposing a third dimension of power (incorporating insights from the Marxist tradition, notably one interpretation of Gramsci's idea of "hegemony"). This three-dimensional view, while embracing both the first and second views, proposed that power can also consist in the securing of consent to dominant power relations through the shaping of desires and beliefs. To the extent that this occurs, observable (even covert) conflict can disappear from view, and the processes and mechanisms involved need no longer be intentional and active, though they must still be specifiable if we are to attribute power. On this account, power in its third dimension is not inimical to the preferences or the grievances of those subject to it. Because it helps to shape the former and suppress the latter, we can characterize it as working against their "real interests."

This inflammatory suggestion prompted severe criticisms on the ground that it was both presumptuous and patronizing. One reply to such criticism is that any view of power that cannot allow for this possibility fails to account for what we can all recognize to be both a possibility and, indeed, a widespread actuality, however uncomfortable we may feel in justifying that recognition.

Another criticism, advanced at length by James Scott in his book *Domination and the Arts of Resistance: Hidden Transcripts*, is that power's third dimension—securing the consent of willing subjects to their domination—is nonexistent or very rare. In Scott's account, the victims of domination are in a state of constant rebellion and dissemble in order to survive. His book gives a compelling account of the tactics and strategies of ingenious, ever-watchful slaves, peasants, and untouchables. But while convincing as ethnography in highly coercive settings, this does not, as Scott claims, offer an interpretation of quiescence that provides "a critique of hegemony and false consciousness." It fails to show that there is not also widespread consent and resignation in both premodern and modern societies that are best explained by viewing them as both expressing and resulting from relations of hegemonic power.

The three-dimensional view of power, which I have described as "radical," suggests the paradoxical conclusion that power, as it shapes desires and beliefs in the absence of observable conflict, may be at its most effective when least observable, thereby posing a considerable challenge to empirical social science. One major contemporary writer on power who has carried this thought to its ultra-radical extreme is Michel Foucault, whose writings on power also focus on the shaping of desires and beliefs. Foucault also perceived power's positive or empowering effects, and warned against seeing power as inherently repressive. He explored what he called "the micro-physics of power": the manifold ways in which, in capillary fashion, what sociologists call "socialization practices" have been conducted by employers, administrative authorities, social workers, parents, teachers, medical personnel, and experts of all kinds. Some of those he has inspired have explored subtle forms of the securing of willing compliance, which enlist people into wider patterns of normative control, in which they often act as their own overseers, while believing themselves—sometimes falsely—to be free of power, making their own choices, assessing arguments rationally, and coming to their own conclusions.

Yet for Foucault, at his most rhetorical, there is no liberation from power: it "is ubiquitous, and there can be no personalities formed independently of its effects"; it imposes "regimes of truth"; it produces "docile bodies." Indeed, the West has produced "men's subjection: their constitution as subjects in both senses of the word." These extravagant and influential claims (some of which he later withdrew) have subversive implications for the way we are to think about freedom and reason: that we are all "subjected subjects," "constituted" by power; that the modern individual is the "effect" of power; that since rationality is "penetrated" by power, power cannot be based on rational consent; and so on. To follow Foucault down this path, seeing power as existing "everywhere" and as "constituting" its subjects, is to abandon social science and the project of studying power empirically.

Two broad conclusions follow. The first is that our use of the terms *power, powerful,* and *powerless* are interest-driven and that we have several distinct interests in locating and assessing the impact of the power of agents in social and political life. (I assume that we attribute power to agents, however conceived, but that too is contestable: some want to attribute power to the structures within which agents act.) One of our interests is to identify the extent to which agents are able to advance their interests and/or the interests of others. Another is to identify the extent to which they are able to harm others' interests. A third is to identify the extent to which an agent or agents can induce and reproduce the subordination, dependency, or control of others in ways that may or may not involve their willing consent.

The second conclusion is that there is no neutral, canonical, uncontestable way of conceiving power that is free of controversial political implications. (This is due in part to the links between power, responsibility, and interests. To attribute responsibility and to identify where agents' interests lie is inherently controversial.) Power can be conceived narrowly or broadly and as incorporating one or more dimensions, yielding different pictures of how power is configured.

RECOMMENDED READINGS

Robert A. Dahl. "A Critique of the Ruling Elite Model." *American Political Science Review* 52 (1958): 463–69.

> Compellingly criticizes both Mills's view and his substantive conclusions, advocating a behavioral approach and pointing to pluralist conclusions elaborated in the later works of Dahl and his colleagues.

Michel Foucault. *Power*, ed. J. D. Faubion. Vol. 3 of *Essential Works of Foucault, 1954–1984* (New Press, 2000).

> A collection of shorter pieces relating to power, including Foucault's more rhetorical and extreme statements.

Steven Lukes. *Power: A Radical View*, 2nd ed. (Palgrave Macmillan, 2000).

> Surveys recent major debates about power and defends the idea of "third-dimensional power" against its critics.

C. Wright Mills. *The Power Elite* (Oxford University Press, 2000 [1956]).

> A modern classic, which deploys a view of power that is broad but methodologically inadequate.

James C. Scott. *Domination and the Arts of Resistance: Hidden Transcript* (Yale University Press, 1990).

> A fascinating survey of material from highly coercive societies that criticizes hegemony and false consciousness.

Dennis Wrong. *Power: Its Forms, Bases and Uses* (1979; repr., Transaction Publishers, 1995).

> A magisterial survey of debates about power.

REVIEW QUESTIONS

1. How might you have defined "power" before reading this essay? How would you define it now?
2. Describe the differences between the "exercise fallacy" and the "vehicle fallacy."
3. Does a small minority of the American people have power over the majority? How does the minority employ this power? Why does the majority go along?
4. Can you think of an example (real or hypothetical) of how a less powerful group was able to use the mechanisms of a more powerful group to make a change? What was the outcome in your example? How do you feel your example fits (or does not fit) with the views of power presented in this essay? Which perspective best explains your example?

daniel chirot and jennifer edwards

making sense of the senseless: understanding genocide   **55**

spring 2003

all genocides are horrific, but not all genocides are the same. they can arise from cold-blooded calculations, realistic fears instincts for revenge, or ideologies of purification. understanding—and perhaps forestalling—genocide requires clear distinctions

Skeletal bodies clutching barbed-wire fences, the expressionless faces of the recently tortured and starved—the pictures that emerged from Yugoslavia in the 1990s were frighteningly reminiscent of Nazi concentration camps. In 1994, the images of thousands of bloated bodies filling the rivers of Rwanda, of men and women pleading not to be abandoned, and of their hacked up corpses a day later conjured images of the Rape of Nanking (1937–38). There, the Japanese army systematically tortured, raped, and killed 300,000 Chinese in six weeks. In Rwanda, 800,000 were killed while the world watched on satellite television.

The inevitable comparisons of these recent atrocities to those of the past, most notably the Holocaust, are highly controversial. Classifying an event as a genocide can be used to legitimate the claims of survivors or as justification for reprisals against perpetrators. Therefore, several questions about genocide should be considered:

· How successful does an attempted "cleansing" of a group need to be to warrant classification as genocide?
· Does a certain number or percentage of a population need to be killed?
· Does the intent of the perpetrators make any difference?
· Should the term *genocide* be reserved for the murder and expulsion of religious or ethnic minority groups or can political dissidents or enemies in war be victims of genocide?

Although burdened with issues of morality and politics, these questions are critical to understanding why (and when) genocides occur. The usual, narrow definition delimits genocide as a rare event produced by religious or racial ideologues. As such, we often overlook important similarities between the infamous large-scale attempts at extermination and the lesser-known, less successful, and smaller-scale mass murders. When we expand our definition, however, we discover that there are several important distinctions in the types of motivation and justifications political leaders give when committing genocidal acts. These differences can help us to better understand and anticipate genocide.

> We define genocide as politically motivated mass murder. Importantly, this definition encompasses variations in murder, from "first degree," or intentional and premeditated killing, to negligent or reckless "manslaughter."

defining genocide

Scholars vary widely in how they define and, thus, explain genocide—a term coined only in 1944 in response to the Holocaust. For some, genocide lies at the end of a continuum of violence. It may be a by-product or the culmination of a violent civil war or even of a state's attempt to control a recalcitrant population. It is a step beyond massacres, mass murder, or the violence of war.

For others, genocide is a distinct and rare event unlike other episodes of mass violence. The United Nations originally defined it as an attempt to destroy "in whole or in part, a national, ethnic, racial or religious group." If genocide is distinct from other types of violence, it requires its own unique explanation. This has led many to view genocide, like its name, as a peculiarly modern phenomenon. Zygmunt Bauman, for example, sees genocide as the product of large governmental bureaucracies combined with pseudo-scientific ideas and utopian visions of modern totalitarian states, such as Nazi Germany and Soviet Russia.

If genocide is defined too narrowly, as something that exists only on the scale of the Holocaust, Rwanda, or the killing of almost 1 million Armenians in 1915 by the Ottoman Empire, then it is rare and hard to explain. Defined too broadly, however, it can devolve into a purely political label to even cover what some call "cultural genocide," which includes voluntary assimilation. To better understand them, genocidal acts should be defined more simply, in a way that sidesteps the political disputes raised by claims that certain groups have been subjected to genocide. We define genocide as politically motivated mass murder. Importantly, this definition encompasses variations in murder, from "first degree," or intentional and premeditated killing, to negligent or reckless "manslaughter."

Genocides are politically motivated mass murders perpetrated by elites or agents of the government that kill a substantial portion of a targeted population, combatants and non-combatants alike, regardless of their age or gender. Both mass murders that were planned ahead of time, as in the Holocaust, Rwanda, or Armenia, and those that were the by-product of mass expulsions, such as the Cherokees' eviction from the southeast to Oklahoma in 1838, are included. Genocidal events may be on a large scale, or on a smaller scale, when only one particular community is targeted and most of its population is killed.

Because the model cases have been interpreted as ethnic—the Holocaust, Rwanda, and Yugoslavia—that is how most people think of genocide, as the effort by one ethnic group to wipe out another. But genocides have also included the attempted destruction of peoples because of their religion, ideology, economic class, or merely because of the region in which they lived. Ethnicity and nationalism have been the major issues in twentieth century cases, but class and region played a major role in the mass political murders perpetrated by Stalin and the Khmer Rouge, and religion has been critical in cases such as the slaughter of several thousand Muslims by Hindu activists in Gujarat, India, in 2002, and the killing of hundreds of thousands of Muslims and Hindus during the partitioning of Pakistan and India in 1947. The best way to begin making sense of such events is to distinguish types of genocide according to the motivations of the political elites who order and condone them. In the end, genocides are not, as so many would like to believe, the products of sick minds or diseased societies. With such distinctions, we can begin to predict the likelihood of genocide by studying the pronouncements of political elites, the circumstances in which they come to power, and their ideological commitments.

the varieties of genocide

We identify four basic types of genocide based on the rationale and objectives of the perpetrators. Any particular case can fall into more than one type—perpetrators can have more than one motive—but these distinctions help us interpret past cases and weigh the likelihood of future ones.

convenience

Sometimes it is simply expedient to kill all of an enemy population. Julius Caesar did not hesitate to exterminate recalcitrant tribes in Gaul, though he much preferred to have them cooperate. William the Conqueror wanted Anglo-Saxon peasants alive after his conquest of England to work for him and his lords, and he was willing to co-opt Anglo-Saxon lords if they submitted. But when Yorkshire continued to resist, he killed most of its population, burning villages and crops. This eliminated what could have become the focus of a more widespread uprising.

Strong resistance is not necessary to provoke genocidal killings or expulsions. The Cherokee in the southeastern United States worked hard to adapt themselves to white rule, but their lands were coveted, especially once gold was discovered there. In 1838–39 they were expelled to Oklahoma, despite a Supreme Court ruling that the seizure of their lands was illegal. Historical demographer Russell Thornton estimates that because of this forced ethnic cleansing, about 20 percent of the 16,000 expelled Cherokees died of hunger, privation, and disease on the "Trail of Tears," and perhaps up to 50 percent died, if deaths from disease immediately after resettlement are counted. This was genocide purely for the sake of greed and convenience.

Killing large numbers of civilians as part of a calculated strategy in war may also be genocidal, even if the ultimate aim is only to force a surrender. While different than the deliberate extermination of a whole people, it still comes under the definition we are using—the mass killing of noncombatants. Some of Genghis Khan's mass murders in the thirteenth century were similar to the American strategy of dropping nuclear weapons on Japan: surrender or face complete annihilation.

revenge

Genocidal acts are rarely based entirely on simple, cold, unemotional calculations. Caesar claimed it was to preserve his "prestige" that he ordered the extermination of the Eburons, whose king he felt had betrayed a prior treaty. Genghis Khan was equally outraged by the treachery of the city of Herat when he ordered its several hundred thousand inhabitants slaughtered. Herat had previously surrendered, but then revolted against his rule. The fire bombings of civilian cities by the Americans and British during World War II (the most notorious case was Dresden, in 1945, where there were no obvious military or industrial targets) were meant to end the war, but also carried a strong element of vengefulness.

The desire for revenge, however, can go much further and provoke genocidal slaughters that have no conceivable military purpose. In 1904 the Herero in the German colony of Southwest Africa (today's Namibia) revolted and defeated a small German army. The infuriated Kaiser Wilhelm II sent a large force to this essentially worthless territory (before the event, the Germans were trying to get rid of it by selling it to the British) and explicitly ordered that the Herero be exterminated. They were shot, herded into the desert to starve, or put into concentration camps where they died. Of 80,000 Herero, at least 60,000 perished. Militarily, this was entirely unnecessary, but the commanding German general had ordered that not even women or children were to be spared.

The Rape of Nanking in 1937–38 was also a matter of revenge. Though the intent was to avenge the stiff resistance of the defending Chinese army, the victims were the civilians of Nanking. The Japanese army, obsessed with "honor," felt humiliated by the "inferiors," much as the Germans had in Southwest Africa. They salvaged their wounded pride by genocidal retribution, even though the Japanese warrior code demanded that noncombatants be treated better than enemy soldiers.

Despite the horror of these examples, from the viewpoint of the perpetrators, these mass murders were in some way retributive justice and, in that sense, "rational." The Japanese and German military believed, as had Caesar, that to forego revenge would incite further acts of resistance and convince the world that their armies were weak.

> Genocidal acts are rarely based entirely on simple, cold, unemotional calculations. Caesar claimed it was to preserve his "prestige" that he ordered the extermination of the Eburons, whose king he felt had betrayed a prior treaty.

fear

The examples so far were genocidal acts carried out against weak enemies and inflicted on mostly helpless populations. There are, however, many genocidal episodes that result from fear—whether real or imagined. Fear can quickly escalate and provoke mass murder by a group, clan, tribe, or nation that feels it must save itself from destruction by another. Deadly ethnic riots, for example, are usually instigated by leaders who invoke such fears.

In Yugoslavia, political elites bent on creating strong, separate Croatian and Serbian states manipulated fear of other ethnic groups. There had been ethnic tensions before World War II, mass killings in a complex civil war, and growing economic competition and insecurity in the 1970s and 1980s. But when ethnic entrepreneurs stirred up memories of past killings and strategically linked them to contemporary murders, they set off the genocidal wars and ethnic cleansings of the 1990s. The historical memories behind the fears were largely fabricated, and as Anthony Oberschall has shown, before this critical turn the various ethnic groups had gotten along well. Unfortunately, the new waves of killings and counter-killings reinforced these dubious historical memories and made them increasingly real.

Stalin's war against the Kulaks (prosperous peasants), 8 million of whom died, was based on an explicit fear that a rural middle class would obstruct socialism. It hardly mattered that there was no distinct Kulak class, only some peasants who had done relatively well. Kulaks, just average peasants in good farming areas who were unhappy about giving up their produce for nothing, were starved, killed, or deported to camps where they died of privation and overwork.

Sometimes, of course, fears are grounded in reality. When the Ottoman Empire unleashed its genocide against the Armenians in 1915, it was desperately struggling to survive as an ally of Germany in World War I. Some Armenian nationalists were collaborating with the Empire's enemy Russia and sought to establish an Armenian state in a large part of Anatolia. The Ottoman authorities believed that if they did not rid themselves of this menace they would themselves face destruction. They used mass expulsion and extermination as "defensive" tactics. When the Hutu regime in Rwanda committed genocide in 1994, it was in response to a serious (and ultimately successful) invasion of Rwanda by Tutsi refugees, aided by Uganda, who aimed to overthrow the existing power structure. In both cases, the genocides were preceded by years of mistrust, killings, and increasing fear.

Even realistic fears do not justify genocides that wipe out mostly innocent bystanders. But we have to take into account both how fear motivates political elites and also how those elites deliberately manipulate fear among their followers. Had Western leaders followed the political maneuvering and statements of leading political figures in Rwanda in 1993, they would not have been taken by surprise at what happened. Gérard Prunier, a French expert on Africa, claims that Western governments did know what was happening, but deliberately chose to downplay this information because they believed their electorates would be unwilling to bear the costs of intervention.

purification

There is a special, more insidious fear that also motivates genocide: the fear of pollution. It is the most difficult to explain because it depends on deep cultural beliefs that portray a group as a moral danger that demands extermination. Notorious among ideologues of pollution in the twentieth century are Hitler and Stalin, although they were not the first.

The Catholic-Protestant Wars in sixteenth-century France killed some 750,000 people and gave us the term *massacre*. Though they were the result of a complex mixture of economic, political, and dynastic causes, there was a genuinely theological component to these wars. The urge to purify Catholicism of the stain of heresy was at the heart of the worst killing. Catholic mobs repeatedly felt it necessary not only to kill Protestants, but also to burn their possessions and mutilate their bodies in order to purify the land. The genital mutilation of men and cutting open of pregnant Protestant women was part of this ritual of purification.

The Bible contains many genocidal episodes, and whether these actually happened or not, the mere fact that they are found in a holy text indicates that God may demand such extreme purification. For example, the Lord commanded Joshua's men to kill "both men and women, young and old, oxen, sheep, and asses, with the edge of the sword" after the fall of Jericho. Subsequently, one of the main causes given for Israel's downfall was its failure to exterminate all of the Canaanites.

> The Bible contains many genocidal episodes, and whether these actually happened or not, the mere fact that they are found in a holy text indicates that God may demand such extreme purification.

The major totalitarian ideologues of the twentieth century had their own utopian views of the world that called for the cleansing of polluting elements. For Adolf Hitler, utopia would result from the triumph of a healthy, racially pure Aryan nation. All of civilization's ills were ascribed to racial mixing and weakness. This is why Jews, the ultimate carriers of racial pollution, had to be exterminated, along with gypsies, homosexuals, the mentally retarded, and eventually, Slavs. As historian Christopher Browning has explained, the bitter scholary disputes of the 1970s and 1980s about whether or not Hitler's ideology, or structural conditions and political contingencies were responsible for the Holocaust is resolved by the fact that without Hitler's vision of a racially pure utopia the Holocaust would have been inconceivable.

In one of the major genocides of recent times, 500,000–1 million suspected Communists were killed in Indonesia in 1965–1966. In East Java, where some of the worst episodes occurred, this was the culmination of a long class war in the countryside. Not only were whole families massacred, but torture and mutilation, much of it of a sexual nature, were also common. The military wanted to be rid of Communists for political reasons, but the killings also arose from the murderous frenzy stirred by fear of religious pollution. Muslim activists carried out most of the killing, destroying infidels to restore the natural order.

Similarly, the Cambodian Communists' destruction of one-quarter of their population was committed in pursuit of a classless, racially pure Khmer utopia. Non-Khmers, especially Vietnamese, were the first to be killed; those influenced by Western or Vietnamese ways followed. Here also the killers sought to wipe out a polluting influence they feared.

looking ahead

Mass political murder follows its own "logic," and we can only understand it if we follow the logic. Genocides are not specifically modern, but when they are controlled by modern states they tend to be more thorough and bloodier than premodern genocides. There will be more genocides in the future unless we learn to recognize their symptoms and are prepared to intervene.

Understanding the different sources of genocide gives us one tool. Sociology contributes by distinguishing among the causes that lead to genocidal acts. Today, public opinion can restrain genocides of convenience, such as the deaths of the Cherokees; such acts are no longer acceptable. We can foresee how the demands of war in a place like Chechnya might lead to genocidal acts by the Russians trying to keep control of that strategic province. But seemingly irrational fears can still lead to genocidal policies. Leaders who deliberately stoke a sense of fear and a thirst for revenge greatly increase the likelihood that their followers will extract terrible retributions. When it comes to the ideologies of purification, however, all we can do is to recognize these and warn the world. The religious absolutists, the ethnic and nationalist chauvinists, and the utopian ideologues, who are all prepared to eliminate whole classes of people to create a perfect world are all unlikely to change their opinions because of their genocidal implications—Osama bin Laden is only the most recent example of these. Understanding the distinctions among the various motivations for genocide—however disturbing—is an important first step toward preventing them.

RECOMMENDED RESOURCES

Zygmunt Bauman. *Modernity and the Holocaust* (Cornell University Press, 1989).

A clear, if controversial, sociological explanation of the thesis that modernity is responsible for genocide.

Christopher R. Browning. *The Path to Genocide* (Cambridge University Press, 1992).

These essays by Browning, a leading Holocaust historian, lay out a balanced and thorough explanation of how the mass murders in World War II Germany came about.

Danie Chirot. *Modern Tyrants* (Princeton University Press, 1996).

Explains how twentieth-century tyrants have come to power, and why they caused so many millions of deaths.

Donald L. Horowitz. *The Deadly Ethnic Riot* (University of California Press, 2001).

A political scientist shows under what conditions ethnic tensions have led to murderous violence throughout the world.

Norman M. Naimark. *The Fires of Hatred: Ethnic Cleansing in 20th Century Europe* (Harvard University Press, 2001).

A historian's account of five major cases, it offers a disconcerting view of vicious ethnic nationalism.

Anthony Oberschall. "From Ethnic Cooperation to Violence and War in Yugoslavia." In D. Chirot and M. E. P. Seligman, eds., *Ethnopolitical Warfare*

Causes, Consequences, and Possible Solutions (American Psychological Association Press, 2001).

Oberschall's field work in the former Yugoslavia is a superb study of how this multiethnic society fell apart.

Gérard Prunier. *The Rwanda Crisis: History of a Genocide* (Columbia University Press, 1997).

The best explanation of the 1994 Rwanda genocide, told by one of France's foremost scholars of Africa.

REVIEW QUESTIONS

1. How is genocide both similar to and different from ethnic cleansing?

2. Identify and describe the four kinds of genocide outlined in this essay.

3. Even the Bible offers examples of genocide, yet the modern world has made such atrocities both easier and more difficult. Write two paragraphs explaining how this is so. Refer to specific developments and institutional structures in your answer.

4. The authors mention that 800,000 people were killed in Rwanda "while the world watched on satellite television." Yet there has been much criticism of the media's silence on the slaughter of Rwandan Tutsis and moderate Hutus. What do you think explains the lack of media attention in the United States to Rwanda and the Darfur region of Sudan?

paul burstein

is congress really for sale?

56

summer 2003

many americans lament the way special interests sway politicians with campaign contributions and lobbying, procuring privileged treatment even when the public is opposed. research shows, however, that contributions and lobbying determine public policy much less than most people think. when major issues arise, party, ideology, and public opinion matter much more.

obbyists Are the Loudest in Health Care Debate," read the *New York Times* headline in August 1994. President Clinton's proposal for health care reform had provoked hundreds of interest groups into spending well over $100 million to influence the congressional response. Opposition was intense; political action committees (PACs) were reported to be spending over $2 million a month to modify the plan or kill it outright. And they got what they wanted; by the end of September Bill and Hillary Clinton's health plan was dead.

The fight over health care was unusually intense but otherwise typical, according to journalists' conventional wisdom about American politics: interest groups get what they want, regardless of the public's needs. Paul Krugman informed his readers in the *New York Times* last year, for example, that there would be no anti-pollution legislation under the Bush administration because "the big polluters get what they paid for in campaign contributions." Frank Rich, also in the *Times*, claimed that the Clinton administration did Enron's bidding on a power-plant project after getting $100,000 in Enron contributions. And Molly Ivins, writing from Texas, stated that CSX (formerly headed by Bush's new Treasury Secretary John Snow) got $164 million in federal tax rebates in return for the "investment" of a "mere $5.9 million in campaign contributions." The result, William Raspberry wrote

in the *Washington Post,* is the "increased influence of moneyed interests while the ordinary voter seems to dwindle to insignificance."

Most Americans agree with this view. Three out of five people polled for the American National Election Studies said in 2000 that "the government is pretty much run by a few big interests looking out for themselves" rather than for the benefit of all the people, and almost as many agreed that public officials don't care much about what "people like me" think. Early in 2002, a Gallup poll showed that two-thirds of the public believe that no matter how campaign finance laws are reformed, "special interests will always find a way to maintain their power in Washington." Public cynicism about the federal government has become so pervasive that many observers fear the public is withdrawing from politics, leading to a self-fulfilling prophecy in which the public's retreat opens the way to even more special interest power.

Does anyone dissent from this view? Yes—many academic experts on American politics do, particularly those in political science and economics. For decades, a pattern of research has emerged that has surprised them as much as anyone else: A major study shows that campaign contributions or lobbying have little influence on policy. The findings are met with disbelief. Researchers refine their theories and methods, anticipating that more sophisticated studies—looking at more aspects of the policy process—will show that campaign contributions and lobbying have a powerful effect. Contrary to expectations, the new studies find that money and the efforts of special interest groups have little influence, and the cycle repeats.

One recent review (by political scientist Stephen Ansolabehere and his colleagues), found that on most issues studied PAC contributions have no effect on legislation. A review April Linton and I conducted considered the effect not only of PAC contributions, but of other ways of influencing policy as well—lobbying, demonstrating, union organizing—and found that they have no effect at all at least half the time. When groups do have an effect, it is typically slight. Even business lobbying and campaign contributions typically have little impact.

How can campaign contributions and lobbying have little or no effect on policy? Here it is important to be precise about what the issue is. Even though stories in the mass media highlight how much money is spent to influence policy makers, that is not what concerns the public most. The crucial questions are: Do campaign contributions and lobbying get legislators to act differently than they would have in the absence of contributions and lobbying? Do contributions and lobbying influence enough legislators to tip the balance on important votes? And, most critically, do contributions and lobbying enable interest groups to get what they want over the opposition of the public?

It turns out that the effect of campaign contributions and lobbying is limited for several reasons: Campaign contributions are not really that large; most lobbyists cannot even get to see members of Congress, much less influence them; members of Congress are more strongly affected by their parties, ideology, and constituents than by interest groups; and when some are influenced by campaign contributions or lobbying, the number is often too small to determine the outcome of key votes. The effect of campaign contributions and lobbying is overestimated because people tend to remember the egregious but atypical cases of apparent influence, ignore other influences on members of Congress, and don't consider how the sheer complexity of modern politics affects policy change.

Do campaign contributions and lobbying get legislators to act differently than they would have in the absence of contributions and lobbying? Do contributions and lobbying influence enough legislators to tip the balance on important votes? And, most critically, do contributions and lobbying enable interest groups to get what they want over the opposition of the public?

campaign contributors

In most accounts, interest groups have two ways to influence politicians: contributing to their campaigns and lobbying.

Campaign contributions are often seen as especially powerful, bordering on legalized bribery. We are told constantly that American political campaigns are awash in money. Every campaign costs more than the previous one, and the total amount spent on campaigns for Congress and the presidency—$3 billion in the 1999–2000 election cycle—seems astronomical. How can such huge sums not turn into tremendous interest group influence?

A closer look at the money—how much there is, where it comes from, and where it goes—provides some context. First, it may be argued that $3 billion isn't really all that much money, when Democrats' and Republicans' efforts to win "market share" are compared to other industries. All the money spent to influence candidates and campaigns amounted to less per year than the combined amount that corporations spent to influence our choice of soft drinks (Coca-Cola

Corporation's advertising budget is $1.6 billion per year), phone companies (AT&T—$750 million) or computers (IBM—$650 million). In addition, only one-third of the total—about $1 billion—came from interest groups. 380 million dollars of this amount came directly, in the form of "soft money," from corporations, unions, and other groups. An additional $600 million came from PACs. The rest came from individuals' contributions directly to parties and candidates, and from government funds.

Most PACs contribute very little to campaigns. During the 2000 campaign, approximately 4,500 PACs were registered with the Federal Election Commission. Of these, one-third spent no money at all on the campaign. Of those that did, the average contribution to each candidate they aided was $1,700—approximately $1,400 from corporations, $1,700 from trade associations and membership groups, and $2,200 from labor unions. These amounts are not trivial, but considering that the average House candidate spent about $700,000 in 2000, and the average Senate candidate $5.7 million, it is difficult to see particular groups winning tremendous influence over most members of Congress through their campaign contributions. (Contributions from individuals aren't very large, either. Ansolabehere et al. estimate that the average political contribution from an individual was $115 in 2000, while a study of top executives showed them contributing—as individuals rather than through PACs—an average of $4,500.)

Of course, campaign contributions are only one way to influence officeholders. Lobbying—attempts to persuade politicians how to vote—is important to consider as well.

lobbying

What interest groups don't get through campaign contributions, they must get by lobbying, says the conventional wisdom. Indeed, there's an army of lobbyists around Capitol Hill—more than 20,000 registered in 2002.

The sheer number of lobbyists shows why it is believed that campaign contributions go simply to win access. No member of Congress and his or her entire staff could possibly see more than a tiny fraction of all the lobbyists over the course of a year, even if they stopped spending any time meeting ordinary constituents, visiting their districts, taking part in hearings, and casting hundreds of votes.

It is also important to remember that many organizations that lobbyists represent are organizations of ordinary people, not the business organizations frequently cited in critiques of the system. Members of Congress hear not only from the National Association of Manufacturers, but also from organizations representing teachers, college students, minorities, crime victims, truck drivers, and parochial schools—organizations that, taken together, represent a substantial proportion of the American people. Thus, when Congress is affected by interest groups, the groups may very well represent labor (unions sometimes affect congressional action on taxes), the elderly (who have influenced policy on pensions), or ordinary citizens concerned about guns (both the National Rifle Association and its opponent, Handgun Control, have at times influenced members of Congress).

It still may be said that it is not the typical lobbyist who distorts the political process, it is the well-connected lobbyist representing powerful groups with guaranteed access to members of Congress. Surely, there is something to this point of view. But when trying to determine whether access leads to influence, it is essential to return to the key questions: Do interest groups get members of Congress to act differently than they would otherwise? Do they get many members of Congress to do so? And do they win policies in opposition to what a majority of the public wants?

To answer these questions, it is necessary to ask how legislators would act in the absence of contributions and lobbying. What other factors influence their actions? Research consistently shows three factors to be especially important: ideology, party affiliation and public opinion.

ideology and parties

Every year, the *Congressional Quarterly,* journalists' and academics' primary source of information about Congress, lists what it calls "key votes"—votes that, in the editors' opinion, determined the outcome on the most important and controversial issues Congress addressed. For 2002, it listed 11 votes in the House and 13 in the Senate. Some were on issues that most people wouldn't think are subject to interest group influence in a conventional sense, including the use of force against Iraq, establishment of an independent commission on 9/11, and some homeland security measures. Votes on these issues were probably determined by factors other than special interest actions. On most votes, though, interest groups had a strong interest in the outcome: pharmaceutical manufacturers and the American Association of Retired Persons (AARP) in votes on a Medicare prescription drug benefit; energy companies and environmental groups in votes on oil and gas drilling in the Arctic National Wildlife Refuge; agribusiness and small farmer groups in votes on farm subsidies, etc. What was most striking about many of the key votes was how often they were almost entirely along party lines. In the House vote on prescription drug benefits, 16 representatives crossed party lines, out of 427 voting. In the Senate vote on farm subsidies, 11 of 97. On drilling in the Arctic National Wildlife Refuge, 13 of 99. Divisions were similar on defense spending, welfare reform, total government spending, campaign finance reform and the estate tax.

Why the differences between parties? One might argue that campaign contributions and lobbying led Republicans to vote one way and Democrats the other—that, for example, Republicans vote for Arctic drilling because of campaign contributions from the oil industry, and Democrats vote against it because of contributions from environmentalists. But if that were true, the energy companies could have outbid environmental groups and gotten what they wanted when the Democrats were in power. The party balance matters because the Republican party is ideologically committed to the needs of the oil industry, and the Democratic party to the environmental movement. Party and ideology matter far more than campaign contributions and lobbying.

But what about those who vote against their party, for example the eight Republicans who opposed drilling and the five Democrats who favored it? Campaign contributions and lobbying surely matter sometimes, but often those who vote against their parties are voting in line with their own longstanding, well-known views and with the views dominant in their regions. Among the five Democrats who favored drilling, three were rated by the League of Conservation voters as having voting records in 2002 (and for years before) very much like Republicans and very much in line with attitudes in their region, while three of the Republicans who defected consistently voted with Democrats on environmental issues, in line with the more liberal stance of the New Englanders they represent.

Also consider the Clinton health care plan. Among those who got the most in campaign contributions from health and insurance industries were Edward Kennedy and Newt Gingrich. Yet nothing could have turned Kennedy, a staunch Democrat, against health care reform, or dissuaded Gingrich from using opposition to the plan as the basis for the Republicans' ultimately successful fight for Congress in the 1994 election. These are not isolated examples. Though it is very difficult to separate the effect of party affiliation from ideology (because ideology influences choice of party and vice versa), there is little question that party and ideology together have far more effect on congressional action than interest groups do, even on issues usually seen as greatly influenced by interest groups, such as taxes on corporate profits and capital gains. Even when political scientists very carefully estimate how many legislators are affected by interest groups, they usually find the number too small to determine the result.

Political scientist John R. Wright's work provides a particularly interesting illustration. Wright gauged interest group influence on congressional voting on tobacco. He began his research soon after an article in the *Journal of the American Medical Association (JAMA)* claimed that congressional opposition to tobacco control was clearly due to tobacco-industry PAC contributions to members of Congress. Wright was dubious, however, because the *JAMA* article hadn't considered how voting might have been affected by members' political ideology. When he took ideology into account (using ratings by Americans for Democratic Action), it turned out that campaign contributions may have had some effect, but not as much as ideology and, most importantly, not enough to affect the outcome of the vote. Tobacco industry contributions went mostly to conservatives and Republicans who were already predisposed to vote against regulations of any kind.

The power of interest groups to get legislators to change their votes in the face of personal ideology and party commitments is real but very limited. But what is arguably the most important question remains: Do interest groups get what they want against the opposition of the public?

public opinion and policy

According to the *New York Times,* the fate of the Clinton health care plan was a stark example of special interest lobbying "overwhelming the decision-making process." The process, in this case, is the democratic process. The claim is that interest groups won out over the public.

It is easy to see why people believe this. When Clinton's task force began developing plans for health care reform, 71 percent of the public said they approved of what they heard or read about it. When the plan was announced in September 1993, 59 percent of the public supported it. Yet it lost. What explanation could there be but interest group influence?

The explanation, many analysts have come to believe, is public opinion itself. In 1992, even before Clinton took office, health policy analyst Robert Blendon and his colleagues published an article in the *JAMA* describing public opinion on health care. They showed that the public was interested in health care reform, but was concerned about costs, coverage, the extent of government control and other issues. Presented with competing plans during the Clinton administration, the public turned out to be opposed to increasing income taxes to pay for universal coverage, and were much more interested in improving their own care than in providing care for the uninsured. Given a choice among possible plans, no single one was favored by a majority. By the time the plan was defeated, it had the support of only 43 percent

> When Clinton's task force began developing plans for health care reform, 71 percent of the public said they approved of what they heard or read about it. When the plan was announced in September 1993, 59 percent of the public supported it. Yet it lost. What explanation could there be but interest group influence?

of Americans. As Theda Skocpol has written, only "steadfast majority public support" could have gotten Congress to act, but such support "was gone by the time the Democratic congressional leaders finally got bills to the floor of the House and Senate."

Some observers have objected that although Congress acted in line with public opinion, public opinion itself had been influenced by interest groups pouring vast sums of money into media campaigns against the plan. This raises an interesting point. If interest groups devote great effort to changing public opinion, perhaps that is because they see public opinion as the prime mover behind policy change. In fact, as political scientist Ken Kollman has recently shown, that is how interest groups often see the political process. Interest groups of all types (labor, business, public interest, etc.) expend considerable resources on what he calls "outside lobbying"—attempts to mobilize citizens outside the policy making community to pressure public officials. Naturally, interest groups would like to alter public opinion, but that is usually difficult. As a practical matter, what they try to do most often is take advantage of public opinion—to mobilize the public when it already favors their views.

It makes sense for interest groups to take public opinion seriously, because systematic studies comparing the effect of public opinion to that of lobbying and campaign contributions find consistently that public opinion matters more. For example, political scientist Mark A. Smith analyzed congressional action on over 2,300 issues on which the U.S. Chamber of Commerce took a stand between 1953 and 1996. He found that although business lobbying and PAC contributions

> One reason most people think lobbying and campaign contributions are crucial is because reporters say they are; and reporters think they are important because of the striking cases they can't help but notice.

had some effect on policy—it would be amazing if they had none—public opinion swayed Congress far more. Similarly, I found that interest group activity influenced employment discrimination legislation (which corporations were not enthusiastic about) far less than did public opinion. Similar results have been found for welfare policies and hate crime laws. Social scientists find it difficult practically to separate the effects of interest groups from that of public opinion, but the weight of the evidence to date clearly emphasizes the role of public opinion.

what about common sense?

In the face of findings that campaign contributions and lobbying have little effect on policy, and that party, ideology, and public opinion have far more, we still confront a key problem: the conclusions seem utterly contrary to everyone's experience and common sense. Is it possible to reconcile the conventional wisdom with what research shows?

The conventional wisdom may be mistaken for three reasons: people are especially likely to remember egregious examples of interest group power; it is difficult to sort out the multiple influences on policy change; and people often mistake their own policy preferences for those of the majority.

One reason most people think lobbying and campaign contributions are crucial is because reporters say they are; and reporters think they are important because of the striking cases they can't help but notice. But a focus on striking cases can be misleading. Discussions of interest group power return again and again to gun control, an issue on which a majority of the public, which favors gun control, is frustrated by the apparent power of the National Rifle Association. But the gun issue is an exception. Much less often do people systematically consider the role of interest groups on issues that matter more to most people but win less attention. Until very recently, the public was terribly afraid of crime and demanded government action; government at all levels responded by toughening laws, building prisons, and spending more money on police. The public always wants economic growth, and every administration works to bring it about. The quality of education rose in the public's list of concerns during the 1990s, and both state governments and Congress responded with reforms intended to improve K-12 education. Any fair assessment of the power of interest groups would have to take into account all these issues, not only blatant cases of interest group influence.

Common sense tells us that campaign contributions and lobbying matter because the influence seems so obvious—as with the Clinton health care example, we see that lobbyists were active and that they got what they wanted, so it seems only natural to conclude that Congress acted as it did because of special interest influence. But frequently, as with Wright's tobacco regulation example, it turns out that it is not really contributions or lobbying that matter most, but rather party, ideology or public opinion.

Finally, it sometimes seems obvious that interest groups control events because particular decisions seem so awful that there can be no other explanation—the decisions must have been opposed by a majority of the public. In fact, though, individuals are often mistaken about the majority's preference. What's more, on most of the hundreds of issues contemporary governments address, most people have no opinion at all. Most citizens neither know nor care about even some of the issues on which "key votes" occurred (such as competition in the telecommunications industry, fast-track trade procedures, farm subsidies or

accounting standards). And the proportion that has meaningful opinions about the hundreds of other issues voted on by Congress every year (such as extension of copyright protection, tariffs on steel, federal funding of social science research, etc.) is small. The harsh truth is not that interest groups persistently win out over public opinion, but that on a wide range of issues, the public has no opinion. Many observers who view the results of decisions with dismay incorrectly assume that the general public shares their dismay—or would, if they only paid attention.

RECOMMENDED RESOURCES

Stephen Ansolabehere, John de Figueiredo, and James M. Snyder Jr. "Why Is There So Little Money in U.S. Politics?" *Journal of Economic Perspectives* 17 (2003): 105–130.

> An analysis of how much money is given to political campaigns, the influence of campaign contributions on members of Congress and a discussion of why people contribute to campaigns.

Paul Burstein and April Linton. "The Impact of Political Parties, Interest Groups, and Social Movement Organizations on Public Policy." *Social Forces* 81 (December 2002): 380–408.

> An overview of how strongly policy is affected by the party balance, interest groups, and social movement organizations.

Mark A. Smith. *American Business and Political Power* (University of Chicago Press, 2000).

> Smith analyzes how well bills supported by the U.S. Chamber of Commerce do in Congress, comparing the influence of business to that of public opinion.

John R. Wright. "Tobacco Industry PACs and the Nation's Health." In *The Interest Group Connection*, eds. Paul S. Herrnson, Ronald Shaiko, and Clyde Wilcox (Chatham House Publishers, 1997).

Wright shows that the apparent impact of tobacco industry PACs on Congress has been greatly exaggerated.

REVIEW QUESTIONS

1. Prior to reading this essay, would you have said that politicians are for sale? Has Burstein convinced you otherwise?
2. Burstein claims that campaign contributions, contrary to popular opinion, are an ineffective way to change a politician's point of view. Why? What *is* the best avenue for maximum impact? Does this essay make you think differently about the importance of public opinion? Why or why not?
3. What are the three reasons with which the author concludes to explain why the conventional wisdom on this issue is questionable?
4. While Burstein recognizes that lobbyists may potentially affect policy, what about the various ties politicians may have with corporations and/or wealthy businesspeople prior to taking public office? Write a paragraph on the potential effects of such ties.

david s. meyer

how social movements matter

fall 2003

social movement activists, such as those who protested the iraq war, often become discouraged when their immediate goals are not attained. but research shows that such movements can have deep and long-lasting consequences for politics, society, and the activists themselves.

In January 2003, tens if not hundreds of thousands of people assembled in Washington, D.C. to try to stop the impending invasion of Iraq. It did not look good for the demonstrators. Months earlier, Congress authorized President Bush to use force to disarm Iraq, and Bush repeatedly said that he would not let the lack of international support influence his decision about when—or whether—to use military force. Opposition to military action grew in the intervening months; the Washington demonstration coincided with sister events in San Francisco, Portland, Tampa, Tokyo, Paris, Cairo, and Moscow. Protests, albeit smaller and less frequent, continued after the war began. Did any of them change anything? Could they have? How? And how would we know if they did?

Such questions are not specific to this latest peace mobilization, but are endemic to protest movements more generally. Social movements are organized challenges to authorities that use a broad range of tactics, both inside and outside of conventional politics, in an effort to promote social and political change. Opponents of the Iraq War wrote letters to elected officials and editors of newspapers, called talk radio shows and contributed money to antiwar

groups. Many also invited arrest by civil disobedience; some protesters, for example, blocked entrances to government offices and military bases. A group of 50 "Unreasonable Women of West Marin" lay naked on a northern California beach, spelling out "Peace" with their bodies for a photographer flying overhead. Besides using diverse methods of protest, opponents of the war also held diverse political views. Some opposed all war, some opposed all U.S. military intervention, while others were skeptical only about this particular military intervention. This is a familiar social movement story: broad coalitions stage social movements, and differences within a movement coalition are often nearly as broad as those between the movement and the authorities it challenges.

Political activists and their targets act as if social movements matter, and sociologists have been trying, for the better part of at least four decades, to figure out why, when, and how. It is too easy—and not very helpful—to paint activists as heroes or, alternatively, as cranks. It is similarly too easy to credit them for social change or, alternatively, to dismiss their efforts by saying that changes, such as advances in civil rights or environmental protections, would

> Social movements crest and wane, often failing to attain their immediate goals, but they can lastingly change political debates, governmental institutions, and the wider culture.

have happened anyway. What we have learned is that social movements are less a departure from conventional institutional politics than an extension of them—a "politics by other means." In the end, we find that movements crest and wane, often failing to attain their immediate goals, but they can lastingly change political debates, governmental institutions and the wider culture.

It is often difficult to tell whether activism makes a difference because the forces that propel people to mobilize are often the same forces responsible for social change. For example, it is difficult to decide whether the feminist movement opened new opportunities to women or whether economic changes fostered both the jobs and feminism. Also, authorities challenged by movements deny that activism influenced their decisions. What politicians want to admit that their judgments can be affected by "mobs"? Why risk encouraging protesters in the future? Finally, movements virtually never achieve all that their partisans demand, and so activists are quick to question their own influence. As a result, proving that movements influence politics and policy involves difficult detective work.

But research shows that social movements can affect government policy as well as how it is made. And movement influence extends further. Activism often profoundly changes the activists, and through them, the organizations in which they participate, as well as the broader culture. The ways that movements make a difference are complex, veiled, and take far longer to manifest themselves than the news cycle that covers a single demonstration, or even a whole protest campaign.

when movements emerge

Activists protest when they think it might help them achieve their goals—goals they might not accomplish otherwise. Organizers successfully mobilize movements when they convince people that the issue at hand is urgent, that positive outcomes are possible and that their efforts could make a difference. In the case of the war on Iraq, for example, President Bush set the agenda for a broad range of activists by explicitly committing the country to military intervention. More conventional politics—elections, campaign contributions, and letter-writing—had already played out and it became clear that none of these activities were sufficient, in and of themselves, to stop the war. In addition, the President's failure to build broad international or domestic support led activists to believe that direct pressure might prevent war. The rapid worldwide growth of the movement itself encouraged activism, assuring participants that they were part of something larger than themselves, something that might matter. In effect, President Bush's actions encouraged anti-war activism to spread beyond a small group of perpetual peace activists to a broader public.

With peace movements, it is clear that threat of war helps organizers mobilize people. Threats generally help political opposition grow beyond conventional politics. Movements against nuclear armaments, for example, emerge strongly when governments announce they are building more weapons. Similarly, environmental movements expand when government policies toward forests, pesticides, or toxic wastes become visibly negligent. In the case of abortion politics, each side has kept the other mobilized for more than 30 years by periodically threatening to take control of the issue. In each of these cases, those who lose in traditional political contests such as elections or lobbying campaigns often take to the streets.

Other sorts of movements grow when the promise of success arises. American civil rights activists, for example, were able to mobilize most broadly when they saw signals that substantial change was possible. Rosa Parks knew about Jackie Robinson and *Brown v. Board of Education*—as well as Gandhian civil disobedience—before deciding not to move to the back of the bus in Montgomery, Alabama. Government responsiveness to earlier activism—such as President Truman's desegregation of the armed forces and calling for an anti-lynching law—though limited, fitful, and often strategic, for a time encouraged others in their efforts. And the success of African-American activists encouraged other ethnic groups, as well as women, to pursue social change through movement politics.

As social movements grow, they incorporate more groups with a broader range of goals and more diverse tactics. Absent a focus like an imminent war, activists inside and political figures outside compete with one another to define movement goals and objectives. Political authorities often respond with policy concessions designed to diminish the breadth and depth of a movement. While such tactics can divide a movement, they are also one way of measuring a movement's success.

how movements matter: public policy

By uniting, however loosely, a broad range of groups and individuals, and taking action, social movements can influence public policy, at least by bringing attention to their issues. Newspaper stories about a demonstration pique political, journalistic, and public interest in the demonstrators' concerns. By bringing scrutiny to a contested policy, activists can promote alternative thinking. By displaying a large and engaged constituency, social movements provide political support for leaders sympathetic to their concerns. Large demonstrations show that there are passionate citizens who might also donate money, work in campaigns, and vote for candidates who will speak for them. Citizen mobilization against abortion, taxes, and immigration, for example, has encouraged ambitious politicians to

cater to those constituencies. In these ways, social movement activism spurs and supports more conventional political action.

Activism outside of government can also strengthen advocates of minority positions within government. Social movements—just like presidential administrations and congressional majorities—are coalitions. Anti-war activists in the streets may have strengthened the bargaining position of the more internationalist factions in the Bush administration, most notably Colin Powell, and led, at least temporarily, to diplomatic action in the United Nations. Mobilized opposition also, for a time, seemed to embolden Congressional critics, and encouraged lesser-known candidates for the Democratic presidential nomination to vocally oppose the war.

Social movements, by the popularity of their arguments, or more frequently, the strength of their support, can convince authorities to reexamine and possibly change their policy preferences. Movements can demand a litmus test for their support. Thus, George H. W. Bush, seeking the Republican nomination for president in 1980, revised his prior support for abortion rights. A few years later, Jesse Jackson likewise reconsidered his opposition to abortion. Movements raised the profile of the issue, forcing politicians not only to address their concerns, but to accede to their demands.

Although movement activists promote specific policies—a nuclear freeze, an equal rights amendment, an end to legal abortion, or, more recently, a cap on malpractice awards—their demands are usually so absolute that they do not translate well into policy. (Placards and bumper stickers offer little space for nuanced debate.) Indeed, the clearest message that activists can generally send is absolute rejection: no to nuclear weapons, abortion, pesticides, or taxes. These admonitions rarely become policy, but by promoting their programs in stark moral terms, activists place the onus on others to offer alternative policies that are, depending on one's perspective, more moderate or complex. At the same time, politicians often use such alternatives to capture, or at least defuse, social movements. The anti-nuclear weapons movement of the late 1950s and early 1960s did not end the arms race or all nuclear testing. It did, however, lead to the Limited Test Ban Treaty, which ended atmospheric testing. First Eisenhower, then Kennedy, offered arms control proposals and talks with the Soviet Union, at least in part as a response to the movement. This peace movement established the framework for arms control in superpower relations, which subsequently spread to the entire international community.

In these ways, activists shape events—even if they do not necessarily get credit for their efforts or achieve everything they want. The movement against the Vietnam War, for instance, generated a great deal of attention which, in turn, changed the conduct of that war and much else in domestic politics. President Johnson chose bombing targets with attention to minimizing political opposition; President Nixon, elected at least partly as a result of the backlash against the antiwar movement nonetheless tailored his military strategy to respond to some of its concerns. In later years, he suggested that the anti-war movement made it unthinkable for him to threaten nuclear escalation in Vietnam—even as a bluff. In addition, the movement helped end the draft, institutionalizing all-volunteer armed forces. And, according to Colin Powell, the Vietnam dissenters provoked a new military approach for the United States, one that emphasized the use of overwhelming force to minimize American casualties. Thus, the military execution of the 1991 Persian Gulf war was influenced by an anti-war movement that peaked more than three decades earlier. This is significant, if not the effect most anti-war activists envisioned.

political institutions

Social movements can alter not only the substance of policy, but also how policy is made. It is not uncommon for governments to create new institutions, such as departments and agencies, in response to activists' demands. For example, President Kennedy responded to the nuclear freeze movement by establishing the Arms Control and Disarmament Agency, which became a permanent voice and venue in the federal bureaucracy for arms control. A glance at any organizational chart of federal offices turns up numerous departments, boards, and commissions that trace their origins to popular mobilization. These include the Department of Labor, the Department of Housing and Urban Development, the National Labor Relations Board, the Environmental Protection Agency, the National Council on Disability, the Consumer Product Safety Commission and the Equal Employment Opportunity Commission. Although these offices do not always support activist goals, their very existence represents a permanent institutional concern and a venue for making demands. If, as environmentalists argue, the current Environmental Protection Agency is often more interested in facilitating exploitation of the environment than in preventing it, this does not negate the fact that the environmental movement established a set of procedures through which environmental concerns can be addressed.

Government responses to movement demands also include ensuring that diverse voices are heard in decision making. In local zoning decisions, for example, environmental impact statements are now a routine part of getting a permit for construction. Congress passed legislation establishing this requirement in 1970 in response to the growing environmental movement. Indeed, movement groups, including Greenpeace and the Sierra Club, negotiated directly with congressional sponsors. Similarly, juries and judges now routinely hear victim impact statements before pronouncing sentences in criminal cases, the product of the victims' rights movement. Both public and private organizations have created new departments to manage and, perhaps more importantly, document personnel practices, such as hiring and firing, to avoid being sued for discrimination on the basis of gender, ethnicity, or disability. Workshops on diversity, tolerance, and sexual harassment are commonplace in American universities and corporations, a change over just two decades that would have been impossible to imagine without the activism of the 1960s and 1970s. In such now well-established bureaucratic routines, we can see how social movements change practices, and through them, beliefs.

Social movements also spawn dedicated organizations that generally survive long after a movement's moment has passed. The environmental movement, for example, firmly established a "big ten" group of national organizations, such as the Wildlife Defense Fund, which survives primarily by raising money from self-defined environmentalists. It cultivates donors by monitoring and publicizing government actions and environmental conditions, lobbying elected officials and administrators, and occasionally mobilizing supporters to do something more than mail in their annual membership renewals. Here, too, the seemingly permanent establishment of "movement organizations" in Washington, D.C. and in state capitals across the United States has—even if these groups often lose—fundamentally changed policy making. Salaried officers of the organizations routinely screen high-level appointees to the judiciary and government bureaucracy and testify before legislatures. Mindful of this process, policy makers seek to preempt their arguments by modifying policy—or at least their rhetoric.

political activists

Social movements also change the people who participate in them, educating as well as mobilizing activists, and thereby promoting ongoing awareness and action that extends beyond the boundaries of one movement or campaign. Those who turn out at anti-war demonstrations today have often cut their activist teeth mobilizing against globalization, on behalf of labor, for animal rights or against welfare reform. By politicizing communities, connecting people, and promoting personal loyalties, social movements build the infrastructure not only of subsequent movements, but of a democratic society more generally.

Importantly, these consequences are often indirect and difficult to document. When hundreds of thousands of activists march to the Supreme Court to demonstrate their support for legal abortion, their efforts might persuade a justice. More likely, the march signals commitment and passion to other activists and inspires them to return home and advocate for abortion rights in their communities across the country, thereby affecting the shape of politics and culture more broadly.

The 2003 anti–Iraq War movement mobilized faster, with better organizational ties in the United States and transnationally, than, for example, the movement against the 1991 Persian Gulf War. But how are we to assess its influence? Many activists no doubt see their efforts as having been wasted, or at least as unsuccessful. Moreover, supporters of the war point to the rapid seizure of Baghdad and ouster of Saddam Hussein's regime as evidence of the peace movement's naïveté. But a movement's legacy extends through a range of outcomes beyond a government's decision of the moment. It includes consequences for process, institutional practices, organizations, and individuals. This anti-war movement changed the rhetoric and international politics of the United States' preparation for war, leading to a detour through the United Nations that delayed the start of war. The activists who marched in Washington, San Francisco, and Los Angeles may retreat for a while, but they are likely to be engaged in politics more intensively in the future. This may not be much consolation to people who marched to stop a war, but it is true. To paraphrase a famous scholar: activists make history, but they do not make it just as they please. In fighting one political battle, they shape the conditions of the next one.

RECOMMENDED RESOURCES

William M. Arkin. "The Dividends of Delay." *Los Angeles Times*, February 23, 2003.

> Details the influence of the peace movement on U.S. military strategy in the Iraq War.

Marco Giugni, Doug McAdam, and Charles Tilly. *How Social Movements Matter* (University of Minnesota Press, 1999).

> This collection employs diverse approaches in examining the outcomes of social movements across a range of cases.

Rebecca Klatch. *A Generation Divided: The New Left, The New Right, and the 1960s* (University of California Press, 1999).

> Traces individual life stories of activists on both ends of the political spectrum during a turbulent period and beyond.

Doug McAdam and Yang Su. "The War at Home: Antiwar Protests and Congressional Voting, 1965 to 1973." *American Sociological Review* 67 (2002): 696–721.

> Antiwar protests set an agenda for Congress, forcing resolutions about the war, but could not influence the outcomes of those votes.

David S. Meyer. "Protest Cycles and Political Process: American Peace Movements in the Nuclear Age." *Political Research Quarterly* 46 (1993): 451–79.

> Details how government responses to peace movements affect policy and subsequent political mobilization.

David S. Meyer, Nancy Whittier, and Belinda Robnett, eds. *Social Movements: Identity, Culture, and the State* (Oxford University Press, 2002).

> A collection that addresses the link between protesters and context across different settings and times.

Thomas Rochon. *Culture Moves: Ideas, Activism, and Changing Values* (Princeton University Press, 1998).

> Looks at social movements as a primary way to promote new ideas and alter culture.

Sidney Tarrow. *Power in Movement* (Cambridge University Press, [1994] 1998).

> A broad and comprehensive review of scholarship on movements, synthesized in a useful framework.

REVIEW QUESTIONS

1. Why does Meyer find it difficult to gauge the effects of social movements?
2. Meyer shows that social movements have left their imprint on our government's bureaucratic structure. Try to match as many social movements as you can think of with particular government agencies.
3. Social movements often have quite unintended effects on government policy. The essay, for example, quotes Colin Powell's suggestion that the anti-war movements of the 1960s and '70s were a strong force behind new forms of warfare in the 1991 Persian Gulf War, in which there were limited American casualties. Prepare for class discussion by selecting a current social movement and hypothesizing its intended and unintended consequences.

charlotte ryan and william a. gamson

the art of reframing political debates

winter 2006

activists cannot build political power simply by framing their message in ways that resonate with broader cultural values. to succeed, framing strategies must be integrated with broader movement-building efforts.

"What is power? Power is the ability to say what the issues are and who the good guys and bad guys are. That is power."
—Conservative pundit Kevin Phillips

Social movements in the United States have long recognized "framing" as a critical component of political success. A frame is a thought organizer, highlighting certain events and facts as important and rendering others invisible. Politicians and movement organizations have scurried to framing workshops and hired consultants who promise to help identify a winning message. In the current political climate, demoralized social movements and activists find this promise appealing.

After two decades of conducting framing workshops at the Media/Movement Research and Action Project (MRAP), which we codirect, we have concluded that framing is necessary but not sufficient. Framing is valuable for focusing a dialogue with targeted constituencies. It is not external packaging intended to attract news media and bystanders; rather, it involves a strategic dialogue intended to shape a particular group into a coherent movement. A movement-building strategy needs to ground itself in an analysis of existing power relations and to position supporters and allies to best

> Framing is valuable for focusing a dialogue with targeted constituencies. It is not external packaging intended to attract news media and bystanders.

advantage. Used strategically, framing permeates the work of building a movement: acquiring resources, developing infrastructure and leadership, analyzing power, and planning strategy. The following success story illustrates this approach.

October 2003: The setting was unusual for a press conference—a pristine, cape-style house surrounded by a white picket fence. The mailbox in front read A. Victim. The car in the driveway had a Rhode Island license plate, VICTIM. The crowd in front of the makeshift podium included film crews, photographers, and reporters from every major news outlet in Rhode Island.

The young woman at the podium wore a t-shirt and carried a coffee mug, both reading, "I'm being abused." Her mouth was taped shut. As the crowd grew silent, she pulled off the tape and began to speak. "Domestic violence is never this obvious. This could be any neighborhood, any community. But as victims, we don't wear signs to let you know we're being abused." After a pause, she continued, "Look around you to your left and right. We are everywhere, in all walks of life." At that, the cameras swiveled around to capture a sea of faces in the audience. Scattered throughout the crowd were other survivors of domestic violence, each with her mouth taped shut. That evening and the following day, the press carried the words and images.

The press conference was the beginning of a campaign by the Rhode Island Coalition Against Domestic Violence (RICADV) in collaboration with its survivor task force, Sisters Overcoming Abusive Relations (SOAR). The campaign was part of a continuing effort to reframe how domestic violence is understood—as a widespread problem requiring social, not individual, solutions. Follow-ups to the press conference included events at schools and churches, soccer tournaments, and softball games involving police, firefighters, and college teams, dances, fashion shows, health fairs, self-defense classes, marches, and candlelight vigils, culminating in a Halloween party and open house sponsored by SOAR.

The campaign was a new chapter in a multi-year effort not only to reframe public understanding of domestic violence but to translate into practice this call for social, not private, responses. RICADV promoted a seven-point plan to close gaps in the safety net of domestic violence services and, along with SOAR and other allies, shepherded the plan through the Rhode Island legislature.

As recently as the mid-1990s, when RICADV began working with MRAP on using the media for social change, the media coverage and public understanding of domestic violence issues was very different. The Rhode Island media, like the media in general, framed domestic violence issues as private tragedies. A typical story told of a decent man who had lost control, cracking under life's burdens: "A model employee whose life fell apart," read one *Providence Journal* headline (March 22, 1999). Or neighbors say that they could never imagine their friendly neighbor shooting his wife and child before turning the gun on himself: "They seemed nice, you know. They always seemed to get along as far as I could see" (*Providence Journal,* April 29, 1996). The

media coverage of domestic violence a decade later reflects a successful effort to reframe the political debate.

why framing matters

Like a picture frame, an issue frame marks off some part of the world. Like a building frame, it holds things together. It provides coherence to an array of symbols, images, and arguments, linking them through an underlying organizing idea that suggests what is essential—what consequences and values are at stake. We do not see the frame directly, but infer its presence by its characteristic expressions and language. Each frame gives the advantage to certain ways of talking and thinking, while it places others "out of the picture."

Sociologists, cognitive psychologists, political scientists, and communications scholars have been writing about and doing frame analysis for the past 30 years. With the help of popular books such as psychologist George Lakoff's *Don't Think of an Elephant!,* the idea that defining the terms of a debate can determine the outcome of that debate has spread from social science and is rapidly becoming part of popular wisdom.

a few things we know about frames

· Facts take on their meaning by being embedded in frames, which render them relevant and significant or irrelevant and trivial. The contest is lost at the outset if we allow our adversaries to define what facts are relevant. To be conscious of framing strategy is not manipulative. It is a necessary part of giving coherent meaning to what is happening in the world, and one can either do it unconsciously or with deliberation and conscious thought.

The idea dies hard that the truth would set us free if only the media did a better job of presenting the facts or people did a better job of paying attention. Some progressives threw up their hands in dismay and frustration when polls showed that most Bush voters in 2004 believed there was a connection between Al Qaeda and Saddam Hussein. The "fact" was clear that no connection had been found. If these voters did not know this, it was because either the news media had failed in their responsibility to inform them, or they were too lazy and inattentive to take it in.

But suppose one frames the world as a dangerous place in which the forces of evil—a hydra-headed monster labeled "terrorism"—confront the forces of good. This frame depicts Saddam Hussein and Al Qaeda as two heads of the same monster. In this frame, whether or not agents actually met or engaged in other forms of communication is nit-picking and irrelevant.

· People carry around multiple frames in their heads. We have more than one way of framing an issue or an event. A specific frame may be much more easily triggered and habitually used, but others are also part of our cultural heritage and can be triggered and used as well, given the appropriate cues. For example, regarding the issue of same-sex marriage, witness the vulnerability of the Defense of Marriage frame. What it defends is an idea—in the minds of its advocates, a sacred idea. The idea is that a man and a woman vow commitment to each other until death parts them and devote themselves to the raising of a new generation.

Same-sex couples can and do enter into relationships that, except for their gender, fit the sacred idea very well—they are committed to each other for life and to raising a new generation. Part of the ambivalence that many traditionalists feel about the issue comes from their uneasy knowledge that same-sex couples may honor this idea as much or more than do opposite-sex couples. In the alternative frame, the focus of the issue is not on gender, but on the question Why should two people who are committed for life be denied legal recognition of their commitment, with all of the attendant rights and responsibilities, just because they are of the same sex?

One important reframing strategy involves making the issue less abstract and more personal. Sociologist Jeffrey Langstraat describes the use of this strategy in the debate in the Massachusetts State House. A generally conservative legislator, who somewhat unexpectedly found himself supporting same-sex marriage, called it "putting a face on the issue." He pointed to a well-liked and respected fellow legislator involved in a long-term, same-sex relationship. "How can we say to her," he asked his colleagues, "that her love and commitment [are] less worthy than ours?"

· Successful reframing involves the ability to enter into the worldview of our adversaries. A good rule of thumb is that we should be able to describe a frame that we disagree with so that an advocate would say, "Yes, this is what I believe." Not long ago, a reporter at a rare George Bush press conference asked the president why he keeps talking about a connection between Saddam Hussein and Al Qaeda when no facts support it. When the president responded, "The reason why I keep talking about there being a connection is because there is a connection," he was not lying or being obtuse and stupid, he was relying on an unstated frame. Frames are typically implicit, and although Bush did not explicitly invoke the metaphor of the hydra-headed monster or the axis of evil, we can reasonably infer that he had something like this in mind—the forces of evil are gathering, and only America can stop them.

· All frames contain implicit or explicit appeals to moral principles. While many analysts of conflicts among frames emphasize how frames diagnose causes and offer prognoses about consequences, Lakoff usefully focuses on the moral values they invoke. Rather than classifying frames into those that emphasize causes and consequences and those that emphasize moral values, however, it is even more useful to think of all frames as having diagnostic, prognostic, and moral components.

why framing is not all that matters

Too much emphasis on the message can draw our attention away from the carriers of frames and the complicated and uneven playing fields on which they compete. Successful challenges to official or dominant frames frequently come from social movements and the advocacy groups they spawn. Although they compete on a field in which inequalities in power and resources play a major role in determining outcomes, some movements have succeeded dramatically against long odds in reframing the terms of political debate. To succeed, framing strategies must be integrated with broader movement-building efforts. This means building and sustaining the carriers of these frames in various ways—for example, by helping them figure out how to gain access where it is blocked or how to enable groups with similar goals to collaborate more effectively.

Too narrow a focus on the message, with a corresponding lack of attention to movement-building, reduces framing strategy to a matter of pitching metaphors for electoral campaigns and policy debates, looking for the right hot-button language to trigger a one-shot response. Adapted from social marketing, this model ignores the carriers and the playing field, focusing only on the content of the message. In isolation from constituency-building, criticism of the media, and democratic media reform, framing can become simply a more sophisticated but still un-

grounded variation on the idea that "the truth will set you free." The problem with the social-marketing model is not that it doesn't work—in the short run, it may—but that it doesn't help those engaged in reframing political debates to sustain collective efforts over time and in the face of formidable obstacles.

Political conservatives did not build political power merely by polishing their message in ways that resonate effectively with broader cultural values. They also built infrastructure and relationships with journalists and used their abundant resources to amplify the message and repeat it many times. Duane Oldfield shows how the Christian Right built media capacity and cultivated relationships with key political actors in the Republican Party, greatly expanding the carriers of their message beyond the original movement network. Wealthy conservatives donated large amounts of money to conservative think tanks that not only fine-tuned this message but also created an extended network of relationships with journalists and public officials.

participatory communication

The Rhode Island Coalition Against Domestic Violence did not succeed because it found a better way to frame its message but because it found a better model than social marketing to guide its work. Call it the participatory communication model. The social marketing model treats its audience as individuals whose citizenship involves voting and perhaps conveying their personal opinions to key decision makers. The alternative model treats citizens as collective actors—groups of people who interact, who are capable of building long-term relationships with journalists and of carrying out collaborative, sustained reframing efforts that may involve intense conflict.

Widely used in the Global South, this alternative approach—inspired by Paulo Freire—argues that without communications capacity, those directly affected by inequalities of power cannot exercise "the right and power to intervene in the social order and change it through political praxis." The first step is to map the power relations that shape structural inequalities in a given social and historical context. This strategic analysis informs the next phase, in which communities directly affected by structural inequalities cooperate to bring about change. This is empowerment through collective action. Finally, participatory communication models include a third, recurring step—reflection.

By encouraging reflection about framing practices, participatory communicators foster ongoing dialogues that build new generations of leaders and extend relational networks. "Everyone is a communicator," says RICADV, and all collective action embodies frames. SOAR's staging of the bit of street theater described at the beginning of this article did not come out of the blue. SOAR was part of the Rhode Island Coalition, which had been building communication infrastructure during a decade of collaboration with MRAP.

MRAP and RICADV began working together in 1996, but to begin our story there would be historically inaccurate. RICADV explains to all new members that they "stand on the shoulders" of the women who founded the domestic violence movement in the 1970s. The Rhode Island Coalition against Domestic Violence began in 1979 and, until 1991, operated roughly on a feminist consensus model. At this point an organizational expansion began that resulted in the hiring of new staff in 1995. The framing successes we describe, therefore, grew out of one of the more successful initiatives of the U.S. women's movement. Groups working to end domestic violence during the last three decades can claim significant progress, including the establishment of research, preventive education, support systems, and the training of public safety, social service, and health care providers.

History matters. In this case, the efforts on which RICADV built had already established many critical movement-building components:

· Activists had established a social movement organization committed to a mission of social change—to end domestic violence in the state of Rhode Island.
· They had established a statewide service network with local chapters in each region of the state.
· They had created a statewide policy organization to integrate the horizontal network into focused political action at the state and national legislative levels.
· They had obtained government funding for part of RICADV's education and service work, protecting the organization against fluctuation in other revenue sources such as fund-raisers, corporate sponsors, donations, and grants.
· On the grassroots level, RICADV had supported the growth of an organization that encouraged victims of domestic violence to redefine themselves as survivors capable of using their experience to help others.
· Finally, they had created a physical infrastructure—an office, staff, computerized mailing lists, internal communication tools such as newsletters, and institutionalized mechanisms for community outreach. The most prominent of these was Domestic Violence Awareness Month in October, during which stories about domestic violence are commonly shared.

In short, RICADV's framing successes were made possible by the generous donations of people who had formed a social movement that encouraged internal discussion, decision making, strategic planning, focused collective action, resource accumulation, coalition-building, reflection, and realignment. The conscious use of framing as a strategic tool for integrating its worldview into action ensured that the organization could consistently "talk politics" in all its endeavors.

By the mid-1990s, the organization had made great strides on the national framing front regarding the public portrayal of domestic violence. In the wake of several high-profile domestic violence cases, made-for-TV movies, and star-studded benefits, domestic violence was positioned as an effective wedge issue that cut across hardening Right-Left divisions. The Family Violence Prevention Fund headed a national public education effort, working hard through the 1990s to frame domestic violence as a public as opposed to a private matter. High visibility had gained recognition of the issue, but much work remained to be done on the grassroots level and in legislative circles.

changing media frames and routines

When MRAP and RICADV began to collaborate in 1996, we had a running start. Already, RICADV routinely attracted proactive coverage, particularly during Domestic Violence Awareness Month. But all was not rosy. RICADV and other state coalitions across the nation had discovered that, despite media willingness to cover domestic violence awareness events, reporters covering actual incidents of domestic violence ignored the movement's framing of domestic violence as a social problem. Their stories reverted to sensationalized individual framings such as "tragic love goes awry."

In part, such stories represented the institutionalized crime beat tradition that tended to ignore deeper underlying issues. Crime stories about domestic violence routinely suggested that victims were at least partially responsible for their fate. At other times, coverage would focus on the perpetrator's motive, while the victim would disappear. News beats created split coverage: a reporter might sympathetically cover an event sponsored by a domestic violence coalition and yet write a crime story that ignored the movement's framing of domestic violence as social. All these effects were intensified if the victims were poor or working-class women and/or women of color.

> Crime stories about domestic violence routinely suggested that victims were at least partially responsible for their fate. At other times, coverage would focus on the perpetrator's motive, while the victim would disappear

At the beginning of our joint effort, RICADV routinely experienced this split-screen coverage: in covering coalition events, the media routinely reported that domestic violence was everyone's business and that help was available. On the front page and in the evening news, however, these coverage patterns isolated the victim, implying complicity on her part (more than 90 percent of victims in this study were female):

- She was a masochistic partner in a pathological relationship.
- She provoked her batterer.
- She failed to take responsibility for leaving.

Such stories undermined efforts to change policy and consciousness. They portrayed isolated victims struggling for protection while obscuring the social roots of domestic violence.

To address these and other framing issues systematically, RICADV Executive Director Deborah DeBare urged her board to hire a full-time communication coordinator in the spring of 1996. They chose Karen Jeffreys, a seasoned community organizer, who took a movement-building approach to communications. Jeffreys had previously drawn our MRAP group into framing projects on housing and welfare rights.

With MRAP support, she began an effort to make RICADV an indispensable source for news and background information about domestic violence in the Rhode Island media market. Gaining media standing was not an end in itself but a means to promote the reframing of domestic violence as a social problem requiring social solutions. By 2000, RICADV had published a handbook for journalists summarizing recommendations from survivors, reporters, advocates, and MRAP participants. Local journalists actively sought and used it, and it has been widely circulated to similar groups in other states.

To help implement the participatory communications model, Jeffreys worked out an internal process called a "media caucus" to ensure widespread participation in media work. Participants discussed how to respond to inquiries from reporters and how to plan events to carry the message. The media caucus conducted role-playing sessions, in which some participants would take the part of reporters, sometimes hardball ones, to give each other practice and training in being a spokesperson on the issue. RICADV encouraged the development and autonomy of SOAR, a sister organization of women who had personally experienced domestic violence. They worked to ensure that the voices of abused women were heard.

The press conference in 2003 was the culmination of years of work with reporters that succeeded in making the conference a "must attend" event for journalists. They had not only learned to trust RICADV and the information it provided but perceived it as an important player. RICADV and SOAR jointly planned the press conference, choosing the setting, talking about what clothes to wear, and planning the order in which people would speak. Without Karen Jeffreys' knowledge, but to her subsequent delight, the two spokespersons from SOAR, Rosa DeCastillo and Jacqueline Kelley, had caucused again and added visual effects, including the tape over the mouths. The planning

and support gave the SOAR women the courage and the skills to innovate and helped make the press conference an effective launching pad for the campaign that followed.

conclusion

Framing matters, but it is not the only thing that matters. There is a danger in "quick fix" politics—the sexy frame as the magic bullet. Framing work is critical, but framing work itself must be framed in the context of movement-building. If those who aim to reframe political debates are to compete successfully against the carriers of official frames, who have lots of resources and organization behind them, they must recognize power inequalities and find ways to challenge them. This requires them to recognize citizens as potential collective actors, not just individual ones.

The participatory communication model appeals to people's sense of agency, encouraging them to develop the capacity for collective action in framing contests. You cannot transform people who feel individually powerless into a group with a sense of collective power by pushing hot buttons. Indeed, you cannot transform people at all. People transform themselves through the work of building a movement—through reflection, critique, dialogue, and the development of relationships and infrastructure that constitute a major reframing effort.

In the spirit of the communication model that we are advocating, it is only fitting to give our RICADV partners the last words. The collaborative process inside the organization allows them to finish each other's sentences:

Alice: Each concerned group is a small stream. RICADV's job is to make the small streams come together, to involve the whole community and make social change for the whole state. And that's our mission—to end domestic violence in Rhode Island. But to do this, all RICADV's work—lobbying, policy, services, public relations—had to come together. We were moving . . . (pause)

Karen: . . . moving a mountain. As organizers, we think strategically. Organizers think of social justice, and social justice is always about changing systems. So we were trained to read situations differently, to see gaps in institutional layers and links. We saw the potential of . . . (pause)

Alice: . . . of social justice, of making that change. Whereas a traditional publicist thinks, "Let's get publicity for our organization's work," as organizers, we saw systems and movements. We were definitely going to move the domestic violence issue to another place!

Karen: It's our instinct to . . . (pause)

Alice: . . . to get the community involved and fix this. We saw a whole movement.

RECOMMENDED RESOURCES

David Croteau, William Hoynes, and Charlotte Ryan, eds. *Rhyming Hope and History: Activist, Academics, and Social Movements* (University of Minnesota Press, 2005).

Essays on the joys and frustrations involved in collaborations between academics and activists.

George Lakoff. *Don't Think of an Elephant! Know Your Values and Frame the Debate* (Chelsea Green Publishing, 2004).

Popularizes many of the most important insights of frame analysis, but implicitly adopts a social-marketing model that ignores movement-building and power inequalities.

Duane M. Oldfield. *The Right and the Righteous: The Christian Right Confronts the Republican Party* (Rowman and Littlefield, 1996).

Describes the methodical movement-building process that helped the Christian Right succeed in its reframing effort.

Rhode Island Coalition Against Domestic Violence (RICADV). *Domestic Violence: A Handbook for Journalists* (www.ricadv.org, 2000).

Succinct and practical lessons for journalists on the reporting of domestic violence.

Charlotte Ryan, Michael Anastario, and Karen Jeffreys. "Start Small, Build Big: Negotiating Opportunities in Media Markets." *Mobilization* 10 (2005): 111–28.

Detailed discussion of how the RICADV built its media capacity and systematic data on how this changed the framing of domestic violence in the Rhode Island media market.

REVIEW QUESTIONS

1. What is a "frame"? How do frames affect one's perception of everyday life?
2. Write two paragraphs on "participatory communication." What are the three steps to this approach? How are these activities "alternative"? Reflect on why these actions are widely used in the "Global South," but less so in the United States.
3. Since we hold many frames in our heads at any given time, what happens when they conflict? (For example, consider the American belief in privacy, on the one hand, and the post-9/11 concern with security, on the other.) How might some frames blend together, while others create dissonance? What factors do you think play a key role in this process?
4. Activity: Think of some concrete examples of framing (e.g., "tax relief" and the "death tax"). As a class, compile a list of frames on the blackboard. Now break into groups and try to think of ways to "re-frame" the issues at hand. What seems to make particular ways of framing an issue especially powerful or persuasive?

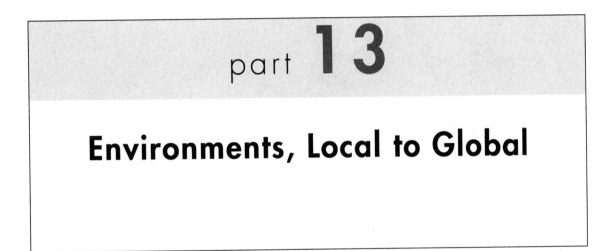

part **13**

Environments, Local to Global

john logan

life and death in the city: neighborhoods in context

spring 2003

59

neighborhoods differ greatly in security and attractiveness. it is generally believed that responsibility for the state of a community lies with its residents. but new research illustrates how external forces shape the fates of neighborhoods and their residents.

Everyone who has searched for a home knows that there are "good" neighborhoods and "bad" neighborhoods. Those differences occur neither by accident nor by design of their residents. The housing market and discrimination sort people into different neighborhoods, which in turn shape residents' lives—and deaths. Bluntly put, some neighborhoods are likely to kill you.

According to the research tradition developed decades ago by sociologists at the University of Chicago, as neighborhoods age they naturally attract poorer and more troubled residents. These bad neighbors make bad neighborhoods. Another, more modern way of thinking about neighborhoods, however, suggests that this is far from a natural process. Public policies often accelerate a neighborhood's downward spiral, and areas with sufficient political clout protect themselves at the expense of poorer neighborhoods. Understanding this evolution in thinking about bad neighborhoods is critical to dealing with their problems.

what makes a neighborhood bad?

Sociologists for over a century have been compiling reams of statistics from censuses, school districts, health authorities, and police departments that distinguish "good" from "bad" neighborhoods—bad usually meaning disorderly and unsafe. Throughout, both scholars and the public have focused on one question: what's wrong with bad neighborhoods? We will see that this is the wrong question. Social reformers at the turn of the last century (like the well-known photographer of New York City, Jacob Riis) thought that the problem with bad neighborhoods was the environment, specifically the densely packed tenements. Researchers at the University of Chicago in the 1920s broadened that interpretation to argue that certain areas of the city simply could not sustain wholesome family and neighborhood relations.

A report on juvenile delinquency in poor neighborhoods of New York City, prepared in the 1930s by researchers for the city's Housing Authority, illustrates this point of view and its implications for policy. "The same conditions which make slums," the authors wrote, "are often present in delinquent careers. Bad housing, low income levels or poverty itself, the weakened grip of regulatory institutions like the family, objectionable groupings, unwholesome or inadequate recreational outlets are but some [of these]." Scholars emphasized the way that "slum" neighborhoods undermined social relations: "Cultural levels and living standards are lower. There is neither neighborhood solidarity in the community sense, nor that strongly organized group opinion which frequently acts like a brake upon individual misbehavior. Attitudes, either of apathy or indifference, toward acceptable modes of behavior and individual delinquencies are common."

The solution for these authors was to eliminate the slums. Outside the ghetto, they argued, poor immigrants and minority families will shed ghetto behavior, making "slum clearance as effective an aid for crime control, as machine guns are for an infantry attack." This way of thinking infuses policies aimed at the inner city today. Massive public housing projects in some cities are being demolished. In Chicago, an experiment in public housing, the Gautreaux program, reverses decades of policy. Instead of concentrating the poor in housing projects, it moves residents into outer city and suburban neighborhoods, calling it "moving to opportunity." Such policies assume that to depopulate the ghetto, gentrify it, or blow it up is an effective solution to the problems concentrated in it.

This tradition of thought dominates current understandings of neighborhood disparities in crime and public health. But there is a better way to think about them.

what makes some neighborhoods unsafe?

Both earlier scholars and modern ones focus on the quality of social life in neighborhoods to explain variations in crime among them. This sociological approach has its roots in work begun at the University of Chicago by Clifford Shaw in the 1920s and later continued by his collaborator and student Henry McKay. Their thesis was that juvenile delinquency occurred where there was physical deterioration and weak community ties. Regardless of who lives in a particular locality, they argued, some neighborhoods consistently lacked the institutions needed to control the behavior of local youth, such as trust among neighbors, intact families and recreational activities for children. "Traditions of delinquency" are passed on by neighborhood youth, families do not work well, residents are poor, and the result is gangs. Some more recent scholars add on the problem of rapid urban change, noting that the northern neighborhoods that received waves of African-American migrants in the 1950s also experienced the highest rates of increase in delinquency.

An illustration of the neighborhood differences in crime that propelled Shaw and McKay's theories is presented in figure 1. It depicts rates of juvenile delinquency by census tracts in Chicago in 1917–23. The areas that are more darkly shaded are those with higher rates of serious crimes. The densest cluster of delinquent tracts is to the west of the downtown Loop, including a mélange of neighborhoods, some largely African American at that time, and others of East European and Italian immigrants. To the south of the Loop is the well-known Black Belt, the area of high African-American in-migration, which also had high rates of delinquency. Finally, at the southern edge of the city—an industrial blue-collar district close to the steel mills—is another concentration of delinquents, variously African American or East European tracts. This geography of crime encouraged sociologists to think of it as the product of the neighborhoods themselves.

Current researchers seek to show that aspects of community "disorganization" really do stimulate crime. Robert Sampson used census data to show that the higher the proportion of divorced adults and the higher the proportion of households headed by a single woman in a neighborhood, the higher the proportion of residents who have been victims of crime.

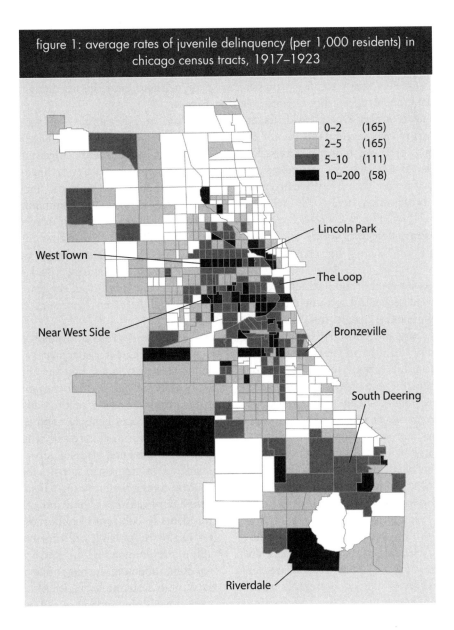

figure 1: average rates of juvenile delinquency (per 1,000 residents) in chicago census tracts, 1917–1923

☐ 0–2	(165)
▨ 2–5	(165)
▨ 5–10	(111)
■ 10–200	(58)

Lincoln Park

West Town

The Loop

Near West Side

Bronzeville

South Deering

Riverdale

Family disruption, he believes, decreases a community's control over youths tempted to misbehave. For example, overburdened single mothers have little energy to watch out for their own teenagers, much less their neighbors' kids. Sampson has also studied local communities' ability to control their environments more directly, using surveys to ask residents about their ability to supervise teen peer groups, the strength of friendships in the neighborhood, and their participation in local organizations. He found that the more supervision, friendship, and participation in a neighborhood, the lower its crime rate.

Sampson's most recent research in Chicago combines videotapes of street activity, new surveys, census data, and official crime reports. He finds that crime is higher where residents are both unattached to one another and do not expect neighbors to keep watch on the streets. The social arrangements within the neighborhood and the kinds of people who live there are what makes a neighborhood unsafe.

what makes some neighborhoods unhealthy?

Concern over neighborhood differences in disease has even deeper roots than studies of crime and delinquency, and it, too, has led to looking inside the neighborhoods to explain their problems. Health officials have long pointed to variations among localities in mortality, infant deaths, and infectious disease to press for public policies such as water and sewer improvements, tenement law reform, and quarantine and vaccination programs. For example, U.S. Army Surgeon John Billings compiled information from death certificates of New York City and Brooklyn residents for the years 1884–1890. He found large differences in death rates among neighborhoods, which he attributed especially to physical features of the neighborhood itself. He showed that death rates were typically greatest for low-lying areas located on previously swampy or filled land, notably below 50th Street in Manhattan.

Four decades after Billings' study, the spatial disparities that he noted remained strong. The highest disease rates were found in immigrant lower Manhattan, in black Harlem and the working-class Italian neighborhoods near it, in the South Bronx and in older sections of Brooklyn. Most districts with the lowest levels

of disease were in areas that had been outside the city boundaries in 1890—the relatively undeveloped sections of South Brooklyn, Queens, Staten Island, and the northern reaches of the Bronx.

What are the sources of these disparities? The medical model of disease naturally led Billings to focus on the physical environment within the neighborhood. Sociologists today give more attention to social factors. One key hypothesis is that rapid community change creates stress in people which in turn lowers their resistance. There are many potential sources of chronic stress in disadvantaged neighborhoods: poor housing, few stores, a lack of health services and transportation, the threat of crime, a noxious physical environment, crowding, and noise.

While these stressors promote disease, other community characteristics make residents more vulnerable to stresses. Like criminologists, public health analysts point to variations in the extent to which residents talk to one another, agree on what is proper behavior, and lean on one another to conform. Where this tends not to happen, environmental stress is more likely to lead residents to aggression, risky behaviors, unhealthy coping patterns, such as smoking and alcohol or drug abuse, and individual isolation. Residents in cohesive neighborhoods foster better health by passing on information, encouraging preventative habits such as the use of condoms, and admonishing unhealthy ones such as smoking. Strong local ties also contribute to mental health by improving self-esteem and mutual respect.

Evidence is mounting that neighborhood social conditions do affect disease. Thomas LaVeist, for example, has shown that black infant mortality rates are higher in cities with higher levels of racial residential segregation (and conversely, white infant mortality rates are lower in those cities). Felecia LeClere and her colleagues found that adult men of whatever race ran a 10 percent greater chance of dying over a five-year period if they lived in a neighborhood that was more than about 3 percent black—even taking into account differences in age, income and the like. We do not yet have solid explanations for these patterns. Nonetheless, these studies illustrate that the current approach to understanding why some neighborhoods "go bad" is to look for sources of poor health in the neighborhood itself.

looking beyond the neighborhood

The most sophisticated research on neighborhood inequalities, as illustrated in criminology and medical sociology, is strongly focused on what is wrong with bad neighborhoods. But sociology teaches us to look farther, to look at the contexts of situations. Where should we look instead of within the neighborhoods to explain their conditions? I suggest that we try to answer two questions about the links between places and the world around them:

Partially abandoned buildings and cheap hotels characterize this area of Oakland, California. A few blocks away a similar area has been gentrified through public and private investments.

First, what happened to these places to create their conditions? All places have a history; currently troubled neighborhoods in Chicago and New York are much the same ones as those identified in the early maps. (The South Bronx, for example, had its problems long before it became a famous ghetto in the 1960s.) What forces protect the best neighborhoods over generations and leave others vulnerable to deterioration?

Second, how and why do certain kinds of people come to live in places with such problems? Think of the delinquency and infectious disease maps as maps of the distribution of victims. Then the question to be answered is who, by virtue of where they live, is most exposed to these hazards? Who lives in an unsafe area or an unhealthy neighborhood, and why? Most observers ask why the crimes were committed or why the disease spread in particular places. It is an entirely different question to ask who is most successful in avoiding such areas altogether.

The traditional analysis posited that people were allocated to neighborhoods mainly by the market (their ability to pay versus the costs of housing in different places). Where people lived was, in this sense, natural and expected. Of course, poor people would be concentrated in certain neighborhoods. We could say more broadly, those who have least choice are most likely to live in the high-crime or high-disease district. But lacking choice is not only a matter of lacking money; because of discrimination, racial minorities, immigrants, non-English speakers, and people in unusual households also have less choice than others. In my own study of Cleveland, for example, I found that African Americans on average live in neighborhoods with violent crime rates four times higher than the neighborhoods whites live in. Even after adjusting this comparison for differences in age, household, income, and education, African Americans still have twice the exposure of whites to violent crime. Affluent blacks face higher risks than do lower-income whites.

If we focus on the places, rather than the people, we could ask—the first question I posed—why some neighborhoods have more resources, why these neighborhoods are protected over time, and why some even improve their relative standing compared to others. Conversely, why are other neighborhoods in a downward spiral?

Here again there is a standard view: The urban mosaic reflects the natural evolution of individual communities. As a neighborhood ages, its housing becomes less fashionable and more expensive to maintain, affluent residents begin to leave, homes are broken up into multiple family dwellings to accommodate more people at low rents, and the new residents are poorer than the old. It's just how the economy works.

Developments in urban theory in the past 25 years provide another view. New thinking emphasizes instead how "un-natural" processes, such as the exercise of political power and public protest, alter the operations of the housing market. Neighborhoods are targeted for preservation or change according to the interests of politically influential real estate and business organizations. Neither the opening up of new areas nor the gentrification or decline of old areas is accomplished without government action. From this point of view, the concentrations of crime and disease are created by decisions that are mainly taken outside the neighborhood itself.

In the 1930s and 1940s, for example, the federal government contributed to racial segregation by its explicit policy against insuring home loans in racially mixed neighborhoods and its implicit policy of allowing housing authorities to locate public housing projects in minority areas (and to exclude minorities from public housing in white neighborhoods). The same government subsidies that encouraged the flight of middle class residents and industrial jobs to the suburbs—highway construction, home mortgage deductions, investment tax credits—equally undercut the inner city. It was taken for granted at the time that Robert Moses, the grand builder of New York's transportation infrastructure, would weave his Northern State Parkway around the borders of private estates on Long Island, but sink the Cross-Bronx Expressway right through the heart of working-class Tremont. Ameliorative public policy, at its best, simply puts health clinics and more police in the most troubled neighborhoods.

Market forces exacerbate the problems of particular neighborhoods. An increase in crime or disease or any hazard makes a neighborhood less desirable. People who can leave do and people who can avoid the neighborhood do. Eventually only those with the least choice live there, and it becomes a minority neighborhood of concentrated poverty, with high proportions of female-headed households and other types of residents with limited options. There is evidence that such social problems determine the residents, rather than the other way around. So, for example, areas of high crime tend to become more African American as whites leave. What many typically interpret as an effect of changing social composition may also be its cause.

the wider problem

Neighborhood inequality seems to be a permanent feature of modern cities. It matters, because even in the era of cyberspace, most of us are affected by the risks in the places where we live. It matters more widely because the public as a whole pays a price when crime or disease is concentrated anywhere.

The old Chicago School tradition deserves great credit for paying attention to the question of why there are systematic and persistent differences among neighborhoods. They took us beyond studying delinquency only in terms of adolescents' personalities, social class, and family backgrounds, or studying disease in terms of genetic predispositions and individual risk behavior. They showed us that places, as social contexts, matter.

But we have to reexamine some of the assumptions in the Chicago School approach. Its key question, "What is wrong with bad neighborhoods?" is the obvious one only if we are willing to assume that impersonal market processes put people in their places and then the characteristics of those people determine the destinies of neighborhoods. These are erroneous assumptions.

Some people are unnaturally squeezed into risky places. The misdirection of state power contributes to the unequal fortunes of disparate neighborhoods. As long as our only question is what's wrong with bad neighborhoods, and we do not ask how those neighborhoods came to be and how people came to live there, we will not know what to do about them.

RECOMMENDED RESOURCES

Douglas Anderton, Andy B. Anderson, J. M. Oakes, and M. Fraser. "Environmental Equity: The Demographics of Dumping." *Demography* 31 (1994): 221–40.

> The environmental justice movement asks why some neighborhoods are made unsafe by outsiders.

Bruce Link and Jo Phelan. "Social Conditions as Fundamental Causes of Disease." *Journal of Health and Social Behavior* (1995): 80–94.

> An innovative essay on the social origins of poor health.

John R. Logan and Harvey Molotch. *Urban Fortunes: The Political Economy of Place* (University of California Press, 1987).

> An overview of the political processes of neighborhood development and spatial inequality.

John R. Logan and Brian Stults. "Racial Differences in Exposure to Crime: The City and Suburbs of Cleveland in 1990." *Criminology* 37 (1999): 251–76.

> Explains how the color line continues to expose minorities to higher crime, regardless of their socioeconomic position.

Douglas S. Massey and Nancy A. Denton. *American Apartheid: Segregation and the Making of the Underclass* (Harvard University Press, 1993).

> The classic work on how segregation creates and reinforces inner city poverty.

Robert Sampson and Stephen Raudenbush. "Systematic Social Observation of Public Spaces: A New Look at Disorder in Urban Neighborhoods." *American Journal of Sociology* 105 (1999): 603–51.

> A multi-method approach looking at neighborhood social problems from within.

Clifford Shaw and Henry McKay. *Juvenile Delinquency and Urban Areas,* revised ed. (University of Chicago Press, 1969).

> The classic study of what's wrong with high-crime neighborhoods.

REVIEW QUESTIONS

1. What is the Gautreaux program in Chicago and how is it a departure from previous policy?
2. What is the relationship between the "quality of life" in neighborhoods and their crime rates (as suggested by the work of Clifford Shaw and Henry McKay)?
3. Logan refers to studies that used census data to understand variations in crime rates between

neighborhoods and the demographic characteristics of their residents. Why is census data a valuable resource in this case? Can you think of ways in which the use of census data in social research might lead to questionable findings?

4. To explain the conditions in a neighborhood, Logan suggests we must answer two questions. What are these questions, and how do they differ from the approach of most studies of neighborhood inequalities?

peggy levitt

salsa and ketchup: transnational migrants straddle two worlds

60

spring 2004

transnational immigration will continue to increase during the twenty-first century. though newcomers strive to assimilate, they often retain strong ties to their native land. living across borders poses challenges for both the country immigrants come from and the new nation they adopt.

The suburb, with its expensive homes with neatly trimmed lawns and sport-utility-vehicles, seems like any other well-to-do American community. But the mailboxes reveal a difference: almost all are labeled "Patel" or "Bhagat." Over the past two decades, these families moved from the small towns and villages of Gujarat State on the west coast of India, first to rental apartments in northeastern Massachusetts and then to their own homes in subdivisions outside Boston. Casual observers watching these suburban dwellers work, attend school, and build religious congregations might conclude that yet another wave of immigrants is successfully pursuing the American dream. A closer look, however, reveals that they are pursuing Gujarati dreams as well. They send money back to India to open businesses or improve family homes and farms. They work closely with religious leaders to establish Hindu communities in the United States, and also to strengthen religious life in their homeland. Indian politicians at the state and national level court these emigrants' contributions to India's political and economic development.

The Gujarati experience illustrates a growing trend among immigrants to the United States and Europe. In the twenty-first century, many people will belong to two societies at the same time. Researchers call those who maintain strong, regular ties to their homelands and who organize aspects of their lives across national borders "transnational migrants." They assimilate into the country that receives them, while sustaining strong ties to their homeland. Assimilation and transnational relations are not mutually exclusive; they happen simultaneously and influence each other. More and more, people earn their living, raise their family, participate in religious communities, and express their political views across national borders.

Social scientists have long been interested in how newcomers become American. Most used to argue that to move up the ladder, immigrants would have to abandon their unique customs, language, and values. Even when it became acceptable to retain some ethnic customs, most researchers still assumed that connections to homelands would eventually wither. To be Italian American or Irish American would ultimately have much more to do with the immigrant experience in America than with what was happening back in Italy or Ireland. Social scientists increasingly recognize that the host-country experiences of some migrants remain strongly influenced by continuing ties to their country of origin and its fate.

These transnational lives raise fundamental issues about twenty-first-century society. What are the rights and responsibilities of people who belong to two nations? Both home- and host-country governments must decide whether and how they will represent and protect migrants and what they can demand from them in return. They may have to revise their understandings of "class" or "race" because these terms mean such different things in each country. For example, expectations about how women should balance work and family vary considerably in Latin America and in the United States. Both home- and host-country social programs may have to be reformulated, taking into account new challenges and new opportunities that arise when migrants keep one foot in each of two worlds.

two cases: dominicans and gujaratis in boston

My research among the Dominican Republic and Gujarati immigrants who have moved to Massachusetts over the past three decades illustrates the changes that result in their origin and host communities. Migration to Boston from the Dominican village of Miraflores began in the late 1960s. By the early 1990s, nearly two-thirds of the 550 households in Miraflores had relatives in the Boston area, most around the neighborhood of Jamaica Plain, a few minutes from downtown. Migration has transformed Miraflores into a transnational village. Community members, wherever they are, maintain such strong ties to each other that the life of this community occurs almost simultaneously in two places. When someone is ill, cheating on their spouse, or finally granted a visa, the news spreads as fast on the streets of Jamaica Plain, Boston, as it does in Miraflores, Dominican Republic.

Residents of Miraflores began to migrate because it became too hard to make a living at farming. As more and more people left the fields of the Dominican Republic for the factories of Boston, Miraflores suffered economically. But as more and more families began to receive money from relatives in the United States (often called "remittances"), their standard of living improved. Most households can now afford the food, clothing, and medicine for which previous generations struggled. Their homes are filled with the TVs, VCRs, and other appliances their migrant relatives bring them. Many have been able to renovate their houses, install indoor plumbing, even afford air conditioning. With money donated in Boston and labor donated in Miraflores, the community built an aqueduct and baseball stadium, and renovated the local school and health clinic. In short, most families live better since migration began, but they depend on money earned in the United States to do so.

Many of the Miraflorenos in Boston live near and work with one another, often at factories and office-cleaning companies where Spanish is the predominant language. They live in a small neighborhood, nestled within the broader Dominican and Latino communities. They participate in the PTA and in the neighborhood organizations of Boston, but feel a greater commitment toward community development in Miraflores. They are starting to pay attention to elections in the United States, but it is still Dominican politics that inspires their greatest passion. When they take stock of their life's accomplishments, it is the Dominican yardstick that matters most.

The transnational character of Miraflorenos' lives is reinforced by connections between the Dominican Republic and the United States. The Catholic Church in Boston and the Church on the island cooperate because each feels responsible for migrant care. All three principal Dominican political parties campaign in the United States because migrants make large contributions and also influence how relatives back home vote. No one can run for president in the Dominican Republic, most Miraflorenos agree, if he or she does not campaign in New York. Conversely, mayoral and gubernatorial candidates in the northeastern United States now make obligatory pilgrimages to Santo Domingo. Since remittances are one of the most important sources of foreign currency, the Dominican government instituted policies to encourage migrants' long-term participation without residence. For example, under the administration of President Leonel Fernandez (1996–2000), the government set aside a certain number of apartments for Dominican emigrants in every new construction project it supported. When they come back to visit, those of Dominican origin, regardless of their passport, go through the customs line for Dominican nationals at the airport and are not required to pay a tourist entry fee.

religious ties

The people from Miraflores illustrate one way migrants balance transnational ties and assimilation, with most of their effort focused on their homeland. The Udah Bhagats, a subcaste from Gujarat State, make a different set of choices. They are more fully integrated into certain parts of American life, and their homeland ties tend to be religious and cultural rather than political. Like Gujaratis in general, the Udah Bhagats have a long history of transnational migration. Some left their homes over a century ago to work as traders throughout East Africa. Many of those who were forced out of Africa in the 1960s by local nationalist movements moved on to the United Kingdom and the United States instead of moving back to India. Nearly 600 families now live in the greater Boston region.

The Udah Bhagats are more socially and economically diverse than the Miraflorenos. Some migrants came from small villages where it is still possible to make a good living by farming. Other families, who had moved to Gujarati towns a generation ago, owned or were employed by small businesses there. Still others, from the city

of Baroda, worked in engineering and finance before migrating. About half of the Udah Bhagats now in Massachusetts work in factories or warehouses, while the other half work as engineers, computer programmers, or at the small grocery stores they have purchased. Udah Bhagats in Boston also send remittances home, but for special occasions or when a particular need arises, and the recipients do not depend on them. Some still own a share in the family farm or have invested in Gujarati businesses, like one man who is a partner in a computer school. Electronics, clothing, and appliances from the United States line the shelves of homes in India, but the residents have not adopted Western lifestyles as much as the Miraflorenos. The Gujarati state government has launched several initiatives to stimulate investment by "Non-Resident Gujaratis," but these are not central to state economic development policy.

In the United States, both professional and blue-collar Gujaratis work alongside native-born Americans; it is their family and religious life that is still tied to India. Some Bhagat families have purchased houses next door to each other. In an American version of the Gujarati extended family household, women still spend long hours preparing food and sending it across the street to friends and relatives. Families gather in one home to do puja, or prayers, in the evenings. Other families live in mixed neighborhoods, but they too spend much of their free time with other Gujaratis. Almost everyone still speaks Gujarati at home. While they are deeply grateful for the economic opportunities that America offers, they firmly reject certain American values and want to hold fast to Indian culture.

As a result, Udah Bhagats spend evenings and weekends at weddings and holiday celebrations, prayer meetings, study sessions, doing charitable work, or trying to recruit new members. Bhagat families conduct these activities within religious organizations that now operate across borders. Rituals, as well as charitable obligations, have been redefined so they can be fulfilled in the United States but directly supervised by leaders back in India. For example, the Devotional Associates of Yogeshwar or the Swadhyaya movement requires followers back in Gujarat to dedicate time each month to collective farming and fishing activities; their earnings are then donated to the poor. An example of such charitable work in Boston is families meeting on weekends to assemble circuit boards on subcontract for a computer company. For the Udah Bhagats, religious life not only reaffirms their homeland ties but also erects clear barriers against aspects of American life they want to avoid. Not all Indians are pleased that Hindu migrants are so religious in America. While some view the faithful as important guardians of the religious flame, others claim that emigrants abroad are the principal underwriters of the recent wave of Hindu nationalism plaguing India, including the Hindu-Muslim riots that took place in Ahmedabad in 2002.

the rise of transnational migration

Not all migrants are transnational migrants, and not all who take part in transnational practices do so all the time. Studies by Alejandro Portes and his colleagues reveal that fewer than 10 percent of the Dominican, Salvadoran, and Colombian migrants they surveyed regularly participated in transnational economic and political activities. But most migrants do have occasional transnational contacts. At some stages in their lives, they are more focused on their country of origin, and at other times more committed to their host nation. Similarly, they climb two different social ladders. Their social status may improve in one country and decline in the other.

Transnational migration is not new. In the early 1900s, some European immigrants also returned to live in their home countries or stayed in America while being active in economic and political affairs at home. But improvements in telecommunications and travel make it cheaper and easier to remain in touch than ever before. Some migrants stay connected to their homelands daily through e-mail or phone calls. They keep their fingers on the pulse of everyday life and weigh in on family affairs in a much more direct way than their earlier counterparts. Instead of threatening the disobedient grandchild with the age-old refrain, "wait until your father comes home," the grandmother says, "wait until we call your mother in Boston."

The U.S. economy welcomes highly educated, professional workers from abroad, but in contrast to the early twentieth cetury, is less hospitable to low-skilled industrial workers or those not proficient in English. Because of poverty in their country of origin and insecurity in the United States, living across borders has become a financial necessity for many less-skilled migrant workers. At the same time, many highly skilled, professional migrants choose to live transnational lives; they have the money and know-how to take advantage of economic and political opportunities in both settings. These days, America tolerates and even celebrates ethnic diversity—indeed, for some people, remaining "ethnic" is part of being a true American, which also makes long-term participation in the homeland and putting down roots in the United States easier.

Nations of origin are also increasingly supportive of long-distance citizenship, especially countries that depend on the remittances and political clout of migrants. Immigrants are no longer forced to choose between their old and new countries as they had to in the past. Economic self-sufficiency remains elusive for small, nonindustrialized countries and renders them dependent on foreign currency, much of it generated by migrants. Some national governments actually factor emigrant remittances into their macro-economic policies and use them to prove credit-worthiness. Others, such as the Philippines, actively promote their citizens as good workers to countries around the world. Transnational migrants become a key export and their country of origin's main connection to the world economy. By footing the bill for school and road construction back home, transnational migrants meet goals that weak home governments cannot. The increasingly interdependent global economy requires developing nations to tie themselves more closely to trade partners. Emigrant communities are also potential ambassadors who can foster closer political and economic relations.

the american dream goes transnational

Although few immigrants are regularly active in two nations, their efforts, combined with those of immigrants who participate occasionally, add up. They can transform the economy, culture, and everyday life of whole regions in their countries of origin. They transform notions about gender relations, democracy, and what governments should and should not do. For instance, many young women in Miraflores, Dominican Republic, no longer want to marry men who have not migrated because they want husbands who will share the housework and take care of the children as the men who have been to the United States do. Other community members argue that Dominican politicians should be held accountable just like Bill Clinton was when he was censured for his questionable real estate dealings and extramarital affairs.

Transnational migration is therefore not just about the people who move. Those who stay behind are also changed. The American-born children of migrants are also shaped by ideas, people, goods, and practices from outside—in their case, from the country of origin—that they may identify with during particular periods in their lives. Although the second generation will

not be involved with their ancestral homes in the same ways and with the same intensity as their parents, even those who express little interest in their roots know how to activate these connections if and when they decide to do so. Some children of Gujaratis go back to India to find marriage partners and many second-generation Pakistanis begin to study Islam when they have children. Children of Miraflorenos born in the United States participate actively in fundraising efforts for Miraflores. Even Dominican political parties have established chapters of second-generation supporters in the United States.

Transnational migrants like the Miraflorenos and the Udah Bhagats in Boston challenge both the host and the origin nations' understanding of citizenship, democracy, and economic development. When individuals belong to two countries, even informally, are they protected by two sets of rights and subject to two sets of responsibilities? Which states are ultimately responsible for which aspects of their lives? The Paraguayan government recently tried to intercede on behalf of a dual national sentenced to death in the United States, arguing that capital punishment is illegal in Paraguay. The Mexican government recently issued a special consular ID card to all Mexican emigrants, including those living without formal authorization in the United States. More than 100 cities, 900 police departments, 100 financial institutions, and 13 states accept the cards as proof of identity for obtaining a drivers' license or opening a bank account. These examples illustrate the ways in which countries of origin assume partial responsibility for emigrants and act on their behalf.

Transnational migration also raises questions about how the United States and other host nations should address immigrant poverty. For example, should transnationals qualify for housing assistance in the United States at the same time that they are building houses back home? What about those who cannot fully support themselves here because they continue to support families in their homelands? Transnational migration also challenges policies of the nations of origin. For example, should social-welfare and community-development programs discriminate between those who are supported by remittances from the United States and those who have no such outside support? Ideally, social programs in the two nations should address issues of common concern in coordination with one another.

There are also larger concerns about the tension between transnational ties and local loyalties. Some outside observers worry when they see both home-country and U.S. flags at a political rally. They fear that immigrants' involvement in homeland politics means that they are less loyal to the United States. Assimilation and transnational connections, however, do not have to conflict. The challenge is to find ways to use the resources and skills that migrants acquire in one context to address issues in the other. For example, Portes and his colleagues find that transnational entrepreneurs are more likely to be U.S. citizens, suggesting that becoming full members of their new land helped them run successful businesses in their countries of origin. Similarly, some Latino activists use the same organizations to promote participation in American politics that they use to mobilize people around homeland issues. Some of the associations created to promote Dominican businesses in New York also played a major role in securing the approval of dual citizenship on the island.

These are difficult issues and some of our old solutions no longer work. Community development efforts directed only at Boston will be inadequate if they do not take into account that Miraflores encompasses Boston and the island, and that significant energy and resources are still directed toward Miraflores. Education and health outcomes will suffer if policymakers do not consider the many users who circulate in and out of two medical and school systems. As belonging to two places becomes increasingly common, we need approaches to social issues that not only recognize, but also take advantage of, these transnational connections.

RECOMMENDED RESOURCES

Luis Guarnizo, Alejandro Portes, and William Haller. "Assimilation and Transnationalism: Determinants of Transnational Political Action among Contemporary Migrants." *American Journal of Sociology* 108 (2003): 1211–48.

> The authors report on a survey of the political activism among Salvadoran, Colombian, and Dominican transnational migrants.

Peggy Levitt. *The Transnational Villagers* (University of California Press, 2001).

> A study of the social, political, and religious life of a transnational community conducted in Boston and in the Dominican Republic.

Peggy Levitt, Josh DeWind, and Steven Vertovec, eds. Special Volume on Transnational Migration. *International Migration Review* 37 (2003).

> A synthesis of research to date on transnational migration, including articles by European and U.S. scholars.

Alejandro Portes, William Haller, and Luis Guarnizo. "Transnational Entrepreneurs: The Emergence and Determinants of an Alternative Form of Immigrant Economic Adaptation." *American Sociological Review* 67 (2002): 278–98.

> Summarizes results from a survey of transnational economic activity by Dominican, Salvadoran, and Colombian migrants.

Glick Schiller and Georges Fouron. *Georges Woke Up Laughing: Long Distance Nationalism and the Search for Home* (Duke University Press, 2001).

> This study of Haitian transnational migration emphasizes its effects on citizenship and national sovereignty.

Michael Peter Smith and Luis Gurnizo, eds. *Transnationalism from Below: Comparative Urban and Community Research*. Vol. 6. (Transaction Publishers, 1998).

The editors introduce the field and present articles on selected topics.

REVIEW QUESTIONS

1. Identify and define the key terms used in this essay. For example, what are "remittances"? What is "transnational migration"?

2. Of the two groups Levitt mentions, one appears to have their "salsa and ketchup" a little more mixed. Which one do you think best fits this description? Which measures support your answer?

3. The essay details important differences between the transnational migrants of a century ago and today. What are these differences?

4. The notion of America as a "melting pot" is pervasive. Canadians, on the other hand, tend to describe their diversity as a cultural "mosaic." What metaphor would you use to describe the cultural phenomenon described in this essay, and why?

saskia sassen

the u.s. at a time of global conflict: challenges we face beyond war

spring 2005

61

When it comes to sources of instability in today's world, most attention has gone to the wars in Iraq and Afghanistan. But I want to argue that there are deep structures that feed conflict and instability beyond the self-evident contributions of war. Here I discuss two of these deep structures: the growing hyper-indebtedness of an increasing number of countries in the global south and the accumulation of contradictions in global immigration. Both of these make clear the growing interdependence between the global south and north and how there is no complete escape from disastrous conditions no matter how far away; and, further, that we in the global north are not innocent bystanders to those disastrous conditions—we often contribute to them.

Part of the challenge is to recognize the interconnectedness of forms of violence not recognized as being connected or, for that matter, as being forms of violence. For instance, the debt trap in the global south is far more significant than many in the global north recognize. The focus tends to be on the size of these debts, and these are indeed a small fraction of the overall global capital market, estimated in 2003 at about 200 trillion dollars (the value of traded derivatives, the leading financial instrument in the global capital market).

There are at least two utilitarian reasons why rich countries should worry. One is that since these debts do not simply concern a firm, but a country's government, they have the ability to produce significant disruptions of basic systems in global south countries already on fragile ground. Eventually these disruptions will entrap rich countries: (1) directly via the explosion in illegal trafficking in people, in drugs, in arms; (2) indirectly via the reemergence of diseases we had thought were under control, a result of the further devastation of our increasingly fragile ecosystem. Secondly, the debt trap is entangling more and more countries and now has reached middle-income countries, those with the best hopes for genuine development.

Socioeconomic devastation is increasingly a breeding ground for extreme responses, including illegal trafficking in people and successful recruitment of young people for terrorist activity, both random and organized. For example, consider the militarized gangs that emerged in the aftermath of the Bosnian conflict: These young men had no jobs and no hope, so the most exciting option was continuing warfare, facilitated by a vast supply of arms. In the global south, the growth of poverty and inequality and the disablement of governments by indebtedness, which left them less able to put resources into development, are all part of the broader landscape within which rage and hopelessness thrive. If history is any indication, only a minuscule number will resort to terrorism, even as rage and hopelessness may engulf billions. Yet the growth of debt and unemployment, the decline of traditional economic sectors, and the growth of incapacitated governments are all feeding multiple forms of extreme reactions, including, for example, an exploding illegal trade in people, largely directed to the rich countries.

There are now about 50 countries recognized as hyper-indebted and unable to redress the situation. It is no longer a matter of loan repayment but a fundamental structural condition that will require innovations in order to get these countries going. One consequence is that the debt cycle for poor countries has changed, and debt relief is not enough to address the situation. One of the few ways out, perhaps the only one, is for the governments of the rich countries to take a far more active and innovative role.

It is always difficult to accept the failure of an effort that mobilized enormous institutional and financial resources. The IMF and World Bank adjustment programs in the 1980s and 1990s did not get most of these countries out of debt and on the path to development. We now know that what has been done thus far about government debt in the global south will not solve the problem. Even full cancellation of their debt would not necessarily put these countries onto a sustainable development path. Even had the "Jubilee 2000" campaign to cancel all existing debt of poor countries succeeded, it would not necessarily have solved the basic structural trap. There is enough evidence now to suggest that a new structural condition has evolved from the combined effect of massive transformations in the global capital market and the so-called economic "liberalization" related to globalization. Middle-income countries

are also susceptible—as demonstrated by the financial crises of 1997 (South Korea, Thailand) and 1998 (Russia), and Argentina's 2001 default on approximately $141 billion, the largest sovereign default in history.

The bundle of new policies imposed on states to accommodate new conditions associated with globalization includes the opening up of economies to foreign firms, the elimination of multiple state subsidies, and financial deregulation. It is now clear that in most of the countries involved, whether Mexico and South Korea or the United States and the United Kingdom, these conditions have created enormous costs for certain sectors of the economy and of the population. In the poor countries these costs have been overwhelming. They are today trapped in a syndrome of growing debt, with the "obligation" to use state revenue for debt servicing rather than development. The actual structure of these debts, their servicing, and how they fit into debtor countries' economies, suggests that most of these countries will not be able to pay their debts in full under current conditions. According to some estimates, from 1982 to 1998 indebted countries paid four times their original debts, and at the same time their debt stocks went up by four times. Debt service ratios to GNP in many poor countries exceed sustainable limits. Many of these countries pay over half their government revenues toward debt service, or 20 to 25 percent of their export earnings. Africa's debt service payments reached $5 billion in 1998, which means that for every dollar in aid, African countries paid $1.40 in debt service. Most of the debt is to private lenders.

Immigration is at the intersection of a number of key dynamics that have gained strength over the last decade and, in some cases, after

> Even full cancellation of the debt would not necessarily put these countries onto a sustainable development path.

9/11. Among the most prominent are the conditions likely to function as inducements for emigration and trafficking in people, much of it directed to the global north. A second set of conditions is the population decline forecast for much of the global north. A third is the increasingly restrictive regulation of immigration in the global north, to which we must now add new restrictions after 9/11. A fourth is the shift in the trade-off between the protection of civil liberties and control over immigrant populations, which after 9/11 shifted toward the latter.

What I want to extricate from this bundle of issues is the existence of some serious tensions among these different conditions. The expected "demographic deficit" in the global north and illegal trafficking for the sex industry illustrate some of these tensions.

Even as the rich countries try harder to keep would-be immigrants and refugees out, they face a growing population decline and rapidly aging populations. According to a major study by the Austrian Institute of Demography, at the end of the current century and under current fertility and immigration patterns, the population of Western Europe will have shrunk by 75 million, and almost 50 percent of the population will be more than 60 years old—a first in its history. The estimate for the United States is 34 million fewer people; already today, population growth is disproportionately fed by immigration and by immigrant fertility. Europe, perhaps more than the United States with its relatively larger intake of immigrants, faces some difficult decisions. Where will rich countries get the new workers needed to support the growing elderly population and to do jobs considered unattractive by the native-born, particularly in a context of rising educational attainment? The number of these jobs is not declining, even if the incidence of some of them is; one sector that is likely to add jobs is home and institutional care

for the growing numbers of old people. The export of older people and of economic activities is one option now being considered. But there is a limit to how many old people and low-wage jobs an economy can export and a society can tolerate. Immigration is expected to be part of the solution.

Trafficking in workers for both licit and illegal work (for instance, unauthorized sex work) illuminates a number of intersections between the problems described in the first part of this essay and some of the tensions in the immigration regime discussed above. Trafficking in migrants is a profitable business. According to a UN report, criminal organizations in the 1990s generated an estimated $3.5 billion per year in profits from trafficking in migrants (excluding most of the women trafficked for the sex industry). The entry of organized crime is a recent development in migrant trafficking; in the past it was mostly petty criminals who engaged in such trafficking. The Central Intelligence Agency reports that organized crime groups are creating intercontinental strategic alliances through networks of co-ethnics throughout several countries; this facilitates transport, local contact and distribution, provision of false documents, and so on. The United Nations estimates that 4 million women were trafficked for the sex industry in 1998, producing a profit of $7 billion for criminal groups.

Some of the features of immigration policy and enforcement may well make women who are victims of trafficking even more vulnerable and give them little recourse under the law. If they are undocumented, which they are likely to be, they are not treated as victims of abuse but as violators of the law insofar as they have violated entry, residence, and work laws. Further, tighter border control raises the profitability of trafficking.

The growing debt of governments in the global south and the accumulation of contradictions in the immigration regime call for specific and distinct governance mechanisms, even though they are connected in some ways. Each captures a broad range of intersections between governments, supranational institutions, and markets. Examining them is a way of dissecting the nature of the challenge and identifying specific governance deficits. Both will require innovations in our conceptions of governance. Both show us that as the world becomes more interconnected, we will need more multilateralism and internationalism. But these will have to consist of multiple and often highly specialized cross-border governance regimes. Simply relying on overarching institutions will not do.

REVIEW QUESTIONS

1. Sassen expresses concern over the high (and rising) levels of debt incurred by numerous countries in the global south. What are two practical reasons why rich countries should worry about this "debt trap"?
2. According to Sassen, what is the relationship between global debt and immigration?
3. How have the IMF and World Bank adjustment programs affected the ability of poor countries to shape their local policies and future?
4. How might immigration policy potentially affect women who are victims of trafficking?

john e. farley and gregory d. squires

fences and neighbors: segregation in twenty-first-century america

62

winter 2005

after more than three decades of fair housing laws, residential segregation is declining, but it remains pervasive. it undermines minority families' search for good jobs, quality schools, health care, and financial success. however, new organizing efforts, tools, and tactics offer hope for greater progress.

"Do the kids in the neighborhood play hockey or basketball?"

—*anonymous home insurance agent, 2000*

America became less racially segregated during the last three decades of the twentieth century, according to the 2000 Census. Yet, despite this progress, despite the Fair Housing Act, signed 35 years ago, and despite popular impressions to the contrary, racial minorities still routinely encounter discrimination in their efforts to rent, buy, finance, or insure a home. The U.S. Department of Housing and Urban Development (HUD) estimates that more than 2 million incidents of unlawful discrimination occur each year. Research indicates that blacks and Hispanics encounter discrimination in one out of every five contacts with a real estate or rental agent. African Americans, in particular, continue to live in segregated neighborhoods in exceptionally high numbers.

What is new is that fair-housing and community-development groups are successfully using antidiscrimination laws to mount a movement for fair and equal access to housing. Discrimination is less common than just ten years ago; minorities are moving into the suburbs, and overall levels of segregation have gone down. Yet resistance to fair housing and racial

integration persists and occurs today in forms that are more subtle and harder to detect. Still, emerging coalitions using new tools are shattering many traditional barriers to equal opportunity in urban housing markets.

segregation: declining but not disappearing

Although segregation has declined in recent years, it persists at high levels, and for some minority groups it has actually increased. Social scientists use a variety of measures to indicate how segregated two groups are from each other. The most widely used measure is the index of dissimilarity (labeled D in figure 1 on page 459), which varies from 0 for a perfectly integrated city to 100 for total segregation. (See sidebar for a definition of *segregation* and more detail about the index of dissimilarity.) Values of D in the 60s or higher generally represent high levels of segregation.

Although African Americans have long been and continue to be the most segregated group, they are notably more likely to live in integrated neighborhoods than they were a generation ago. For the past three decades, the average level of segregation between African Americans and whites has been falling, declining by about

Segregation refers to the residential separation of racial and ethnic groups in different neighborhoods within metropolitan areas. When a metropolitan area is highly segregated, people tend to live in neighborhoods with others of their own group, away from different groups. The index of dissimilarity (D), a measure of segregation between any two groups, ranges from 0 for perfect integration to 100 for total segregation. For segregation between whites and blacks (imagining, for the sake of the example, that these were the only two groups), a D of 0 indicates that the racial composition of each neighborhood in that metropolitan area is the same as that of the entire area. If the metropolitan area was 70 percent white and 30 percent black, each neighborhood would reflect those percentages. A D of 100 would indicate that every neighborhood in the metropolitan area was either 100 percent white or 100 percent black. In real metropolitan areas, D always falls somewhere between those extremes. For example, the Chicago metropolitan area is 58 percent non-Hispanic white and 19 percent non-Hispanic black. Chicago's D was 80.8 in 2000. This means that 81 percent of the white or black population would have to move to another census tract in order to have a D of 0, or complete integration. On the other hand, in 2000 the Raleigh-Durham, North Carolina, metropolitan area, which is 67 percent non-Hispanic white and 23 percent non-Hispanic black had a D of 46:2—a little more than half that of Chicago.

ten points on the D scale between 1970 and 1980 and another ten between 1980 and 2000. But these figures overstate the extent to which blacks have been integrated into white or racially mixed neighborhoods. Part of the statistical trend simply has to do with how the census counts "metropolitan areas." Between 1970 and 2000, many small—and typically integrated—areas "graduated" into the metropolitan category, which helped to bring down the national statistics on segregation. More significantly, segregation has declined most rapidly in the southern and western parts of the United States, but cities in these areas, especially the West, also tend to have fewer African Americans. At the same time, in large northern areas with many African-American residents, integration has progressed slowly. For example, metropolitan areas like New York, Chicago, Detroit, Milwaukee, Newark, and Gary all had segregation scores in

the 80s as late as 2000. Where African Americans are concentrated most heavily, segregation scores have declined the least. As figure 1 shows, in places with the highest proportions of black population, segregation decreased least between 1980 and 2000. Desegregation has been slowest precisely in the places African Americans are most likely to live. There, racial isolation can be extreme. For example, in the Chicago, Detroit, and Cleveland metropolitan areas, most African Americans live in census tracts (roughly, neighborhoods) where more than 90 percent of the residents are black and fewer than 6 percent are white.

Other minority groups, notably Hispanics and Asian Americans, generally live in less segregated neighborhoods. Segregation scores for Hispanics have generally been in the low 50s over the past three decades, and for Asian Americans and Pacific Islanders, scores have been in the low 40s.

Native Americans who live in urban areas also are not very segregated from whites (scores in the 30s), but two-thirds of the Native Americans who live in rural areas (about 40 percent of their total population) live on segregated reservations. Although no other minority group faces the extreme segregation in housing that African Americans do, other groups face segregation of varying levels and have not seen a significant downward trend.

causes of continuing segregation

Popular explanations for segregation point to income differences and to people's preferences for living among their "own kind." These are, at best, limited explanations. Black-white segregation clearly cannot be explained by differences in income, education, or employment alone. Researchers have found that white and black households at all levels of income, education, and occupational status are nearly as segregated as are whites and blacks overall. However, this is not the case for other minority groups. Hispanics with higher incomes live in more integrated communities than Hispanics with lower incomes. Middle-class Asian Americans are more suburbanized and less segregated than middle-class African Americans. For example, as Chinese Americans became more upwardly mobile, they moved away from the Chinatowns where so many had once lived. But middle-class blacks, who have made similar gains in income and prestige, find it much more difficult to buy homes in integrated neighborhoods. For example, in 2000 in the New York metropolitan area, African Americans with incomes averaging above $60,000 lived in neighborhoods that were about 57 percent black and less than 15 percent non-Hispanic white—a difference of only about 6 percentage points from the average for low-income blacks.

Preferences, especially those of whites, provide some explanation for these patterns. Several surveys have asked whites, African Americans, and in some cases Hispanics and Asian Americans about their preferences concerning the racial mix of their neighborhoods. A common technique is to show survey respondents cards displaying sketches of houses that are colored-in to represent neighborhoods of varying degrees of integration. Interviewers then ask the respondents how willing they would be to live in the different sorts of neighborhoods. These surveys show, quite consistently, that the first choice of most African Americans is a neighborhood with about an equal mix of black and white households. The first choice of whites, on the other hand, is a neighborhood with a large white majority. Among all racial and ethnic groups, African Americans are the most disfavored "other" with regard to preferences for neighborhood racial and ethnic composition. Survey research also shows that whites are more hesitant to move into hypothetical neighborhoods with large African-American populations, even if those communities are described as having good schools, low crime rates, and other amenities. However, they are much less hesitant about moving into areas with significant Latino, Asian, or other minority populations.

Why whites prefer homogeneous neighborhoods is the subject of some debate. According to some research, many whites automatically assume that neighborhoods with many blacks have poor schools, much crime, and few stores; these whites are not necessarily responding to the presence of blacks per se. Black neighborhoods are simply assumed to be "bad neighborhoods" and are avoided as a result. Other research indicates that "poor schools" and "crime" are sometimes code words for racial prejudice and excuses that whites use to avoid African Americans.

These preferences promote segregation. Recent research in several cities, including Atlanta, Detroit, and Los Angeles, shows that whites

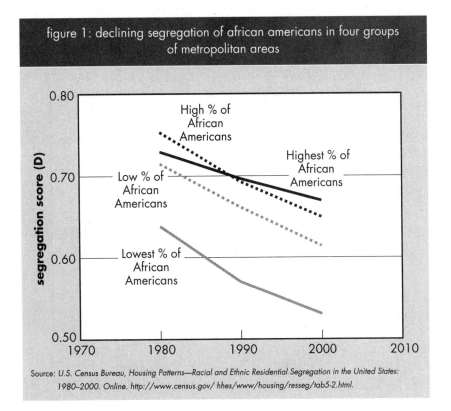

Source: U.S. Census Bureau, Housing Patterns—Racial and Ethnic Residential Segregation in the United States: 1980–2000. Online. http://www.census.gov/ hhes/www/housing/resseg/tab5-2.html.

who prefer predominantly white neighborhoods tend to live in such neighborhoods, clearly implying that if white preferences would change, integration would increase. Such attitudes also imply tolerance, if not encouragement, of discriminatory practices on the part of real estate agents, mortgage lenders, property insurers, and other providers of housing services.

housing discrimination: how common is it today?

When the insurance agent quoted at the beginning of this article was asked by one of his supervisors whether the kids in the neighborhood played hockey or basketball, he was not denying a home insurance policy to a particular black family because of race. However, he was trying to learn about the racial composition of

the neighborhood in order to help market his policies. The mental map he was drawing is just as effective in discriminating as the maps commonly used in the past that literally had red lines marking neighborhoods—typically minority or poor—considered ineligible for home insurance or mortgage loans.

Researchers with HUD, the Urban Institute, and dozens of nonprofit fair housing organizations have long used "paired testing" to measure the pervasiveness of housing discrimination—and more recently in mortgage lending and home insurance. In a paired test, two people visit or contact a real estate, rental, home-finance, or insurance office. Testers provide agents with identical housing preferences and relevant financial data (income, savings, credit history). The only difference between the testers is their race or ethnicity. The testers make identical applications

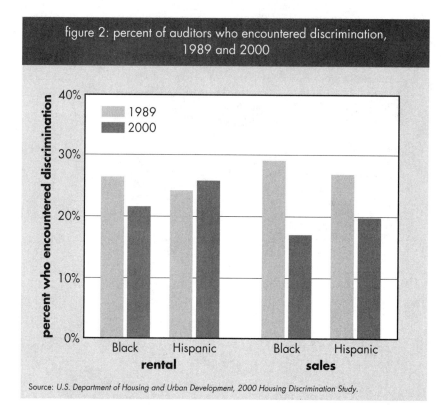

figure 2: percent of auditors who encountered discrimination, 1989 and 2000

Source: U.S. Department of Housing and Urban Development, 2000 Housing Discrimination Study.

and report back on the responses they get. (Similar studies have exposed discrimination in employment; see "Is Job Discrimination Dead?" *Contexts*, Summer 2002.) Discrimination can take several forms: having to wait longer than whites for a meeting; being told about fewer units or otherwise being given less information; being steered to neighborhoods where residents are disproportionately of the applicant's race or ethnicity; facing higher deposit or down-payment requirements and other costs; or simply being told that a unit, loan, or policy is not available, when it is available to the white tester.

In 1989 and 2000, HUD and the Urban Institute, a research organization, conducted nationwide paired testing of discrimination in housing. They found generally less discrimination against African Americans and Hispanics in 2000 than in 1989, except for Hispanic renters (see figure 2). Nevertheless, discrimination still occurred during 17 to 26 percent of the occasions when African Americans and Hispanics visited a rental office or real-estate agent. (The researchers found similar levels of discrimination against Asians and Native Americans in 2000; these groups were not studied in 1989.)

In 2000, subtler forms of discrimination, such as invidious comments by real estate agents, remained widespread. Even when whites and nonwhites were shown houses in the same areas, agents often steered white homeseekers to segregated neighborhoods with remarks such as "Black people do live around here, but it has not gotten bad yet"; "That area is full of Hispanics and blacks that don't know how to keep clean"; or "(This area) is very mixed. You probably wouldn't like it because of the income you and your husband make. I don't want to sound prejudiced."

Given the potential sanctions available under current law, including six- and seven-figure compensatory and punitive damage awards for victims, it seems surprising that an agent would choose to make such comments. However, research shows that most Americans are unfamiliar with fair housing rules, and even those who are familiar and believe they have experienced racial discrimination rarely take legal action because they do not believe anything would come of it. Most real estate professionals do comply with fair housing laws, but those who work in small neighborhoods and rely on word of mouth to get clients often fear losing business if they allow minorities into a neighborhood where local residents would not welcome them. In a 2004 study of a St. Louis suburb, a rental agent pointed out that there were no "dark" people in the neighborhood to a white tester. She said that she had had to lie to a black home-seeker and say that a unit was unavailable because she would have been "run out of" the suburb had she rented to a black family.

Discrimination does not end with the housing search. Case studies of mortgage lending and property insurance practices have also revealed discriminatory treatment against minorities. White borrowers are offered more choice in loan products, higher loan amounts, and more advice than minority borrowers. The Boston Federal Reserve Bank found that even among equally qualified borrowers in its region applications from African Americans were 60 percent more likely to be rejected than those submitted by whites. Other paired-testing studies from around the country conclude that whites are more likely to be offered home insurance policies, offered lower prices and more coverage, and given more assistance than African Americans or Hispanics.

the continuing costs of segregation

Beyond constricting their freedom of choice, segregation deprives minority families of access to quality schools, jobs, health care, public services, and private amenities such as restaurants, theaters, and quality retail stores. Residential segregation also undercuts families' efforts to accumulate wealth through the appreciation of real estate values by restricting their ability both to purchase their own homes and to sell their homes to the largest and wealthiest group in the population, non-Hispanic whites. Just 46 percent of African Americans owned their own homes in 2000, compared to 72 percent of non-Hispanic whites. In addition, recent research found that the average value of single-family homes in predominantly white neighborhoods in the 100 largest metropolitan areas with significant minority populations was $196,000 compared to $184,000 in integrated communities and $104,000 in predominantly minority communities. As a result of the differing home values and appreciation, the typical white homeowner has $58,000 in home equity compared to $18,000 for the typical black homeowner. Segregation has broader effects on the quality of neighborhoods to which minorities can gain access. In 2000, the average white household with an income above $60,000 had neighbors in that same income bracket. But black and Hispanic households with incomes above $60,000 had neighbors with an average income of under $50,000. In effect, they lived in poorer neighborhoods, and this gap has widened since 1990.

Segregation restricts access to jobs and to quality schools by concentrating African Americans and Hispanics in central cities, when job growth and better schools are found in the suburbs. Amy Stuart Wells and Robert Crain found, for example, that black children living in St. Louis who attend schools in the suburbs are more likely to graduate and to go on to college

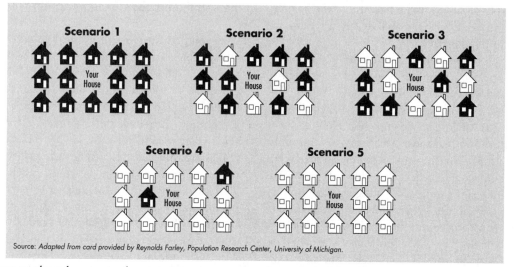

Source: Adapted from card provided by Reynolds Farley, Population Research Center, University of Michigan.

In surveys about housing preferences, interviewers often show respondents this card, which represents the racial composition of five different neighborhoods. Card provided by Reynolds Farley, Population Research Center, University of Michigan.

than those attending city schools. Yet only busing makes it possible for these students to attend suburban schools, and America has largely turned away from this remedy to segregation. According to research by Gary Orfield at the Harvard Civil Rights Project, our nation's schools are as segregated today as they were 35 years ago. Most job growth also occurs in suburban areas, and difficulty in finding and commuting to those jobs contributes to high unemployment rates among African Americans and Latinos.

The risks of illness and injury from infectious diseases and environmental hazards are also greater in minority neighborhoods, while resources to deal with them are less available than in mostly white areas. For example, in Bethesda, Maryland, a wealthy and predominantly white suburb of Washington, D.C., there is one pediatrician for every 400 residents compared to one for every 3,700 residents in Washington's predominantly minority and poor southeast neighborhoods. As John Logan has argued, "The housing market and discrimination sort people

into different neighborhoods, which in turn shape residents' lives—and deaths. Bluntly put, some neighborhoods are likely to kill you." (See "Life and Death in the City," *Contexts,* Spring 2003.)

Finally, segregation helps perpetuate prejudice, stereotypes, and racial tension. Several recent studies show that neighborhood-level contact between whites and African Americans reduces prejudice and increases acceptance of diversity. Yet with today's levels of housing segregation, few whites and blacks get the opportunity for such contact. More diverse communities generally exhibit greater tolerance and a richer lifestyle—culturally and economically—for all residents.

a growing movement

In 1968, the U.S. Supreme Court ruled that racial discrimination in housing was illegal, characterizing it as "a relic of slavery." In the same year, Congress passed the Fair Housing Act, providing specific penalties for housing discrimination along with mechanisms for addressing individual complaints of discrimination. These legal developments laid the groundwork for a growing social movement against segregation that has brought limited but real gains. Members of the National Fair Housing Alliance, a consortium of 80 nonprofit fair housing organizations in 30 cities and the District of Columbia, have secured more than $190 million for victims of housing discrimination since 1990 by using the Federal Fair Housing Act and equivalent state and local laws. In addition, they have negotiated legal settlements that have transformed the marketing and underwriting activities of the nation's largest property insurance companies, including State Farm, Allstate, Nationwide, American Family, and Liberty Mutual. The key investigative technique members of the alliance have used to secure these victories is paired testing.

Community reinvestment groups have secured more than $1.7 trillion in new mortgage and small business loans for traditionally underserved low- and moderate-income neighborhoods and minority markets since the passage of the Community Reinvestment Act (CRA). The CRA was passed in order to prevent lenders from refusing to make loans, or making loans more difficult to get, in older urban communities, neighborhoods where racial minorities are often concentrated. Under the CRA, third parties (usually community-based organizations) can formally challenge lender applications or requests by lenders to make changes in their business operations. Regulators who are authorized to approve lender applications have, in some cases, required the lender to respond to the concerns raised by the challenging party prior to approving the request. In some cases, just the threat of making such challenges has provided leverage for community organizations in their efforts to negotiate reinvestment agreements with lenders. Community groups have used this process to generate billions of new dollars for lending in

low-income and minority markets. Sometimes, in anticipation of such a challenge, lenders negotiate a reinvestment program in advance. For example, shortly after Bank One and JP Morgan Chase announced their intent to merge in 2004, the lenders entered into an agreement with the Chicago Reinvestment Alliance, a coalition of Chicago-area neighborhood organizations. The banks agreed to invest an average of $80 million in community development loans for each of the next six years. Research by the Joint Center for Housing Studies at Harvard University indicates that mortgage loans became far more accessible in low-income and minority neighborhoods during the 1990s and that the CRA directly contributed to this outcome.

Many housing researchers and fair-housing advocates have criticized fair-housing enforcement authorities for relying too heavily on individual complaints and lawsuits to attack what are deeper structural problems. Currently, most testing and enforcement occurs when individuals lodge a complaint against a business rather than as a strategic effort to target large companies that regularly practice discrimination. Reinvestment agreements recently negotiated by community groups and lenders illustrate one more systemic approach. More testing aimed at detecting what are referred to as "patterns and practices" of discrimination by large developers and rental management companies would also be helpful. Such an undertaking, however, would require more resources, which are currently unavailable. Despite the limits of current enforcement efforts, most observers credit these efforts with helping to reduce segregation and discrimination.

Resistance to fair housing and integration efforts persists. For example, lenders and their trade associations continually attempt to weaken the CRA and related fair-housing rules. Yet fair-housing and community-reinvestment groups like the National Fair Housing Alliance and the National Community Reinvestment Coalition have successfully blocked most such efforts in Congress and among bank regulators. As more groups refine their ability to employ legal tools like the CRA and to litigate complex cases under the jurisdiction of the Fair Housing Act, we can expect further progress. The struggle for fair housing is a difficult one, but with the available tools, the progress we have made since 1970 toward becoming a more integrated society should continue.

RECOMMENDED RESOURCES

John Iceland and Daniel H. Weinberg, with Erika Steinmetz. "Racial and Ethnic Residential Segregation in the United States: 1980–2000." *Census 2000 Special Reports,* 2002. Online. http://www.census .gov/hhes/www/housing/resseg/front_toc.html.

Summarizes housing segregation in the year 2000 and trends in segregation since 1980.

Keith R. Ihlanfeldt and Benjamin Scafidi. "Whites' Neighborhood Preferences and Neighborhood Racial Composition in the United States: Evidence from the Multi-City Study of Urban Inequality." *Housing Studies* 19 (2004): 325–59.

The authors demonstrate whites' preference for predominantly white neighborhoods and how that promotes segregation in three metropolitan areas.

John R. Logan, Brian J. Stults, and Reynolds Farley. "Segregation of Minorities in the Metropolis: Two Decades of Change." *Demography* 41 (2004): 1–22.

Reviews patterns of desegregation since 1980. One critical finding is that black-white segregation

did not decline more in areas where income gaps were reduced than in other areas.

Douglas S. Massey and Nancy Denton. *American Apartheid: Segregation and the Making of the Underclass* (Harvard University Press, 1993).

The most thorough and comprehensive account of racial housing segregation in the United States.

Margery Austin Turner, Stephen L. Ross, George C. Galster, and John Yinger. *Discrimination in Metropolitan Housing Markets: National Results from Phase I HDS 2000. Final Report* (U.S. Department of Housing and Urban Development, 2002). Online. http://www.huduser.org/Publications/pdf/Phase 1_Report.pdf.

Presents findings from the most recent national study of discrimination in the sale and rental of housing.

REVIEW QUESTIONS

1. What is residential segregation? How do sociologists measure it?
2. In which areas of the United States did segregation decrease the least between 1980 and 2000?
3. According to survey results, how do African-American and white preferences about the racial mix in their neighborhoods differ? How might this difference relate to the persistence of residential segregation?
4. In what ways might housing-related discrimination continue after the search for housing? How does residential segregation affect access to jobs and quality schools?

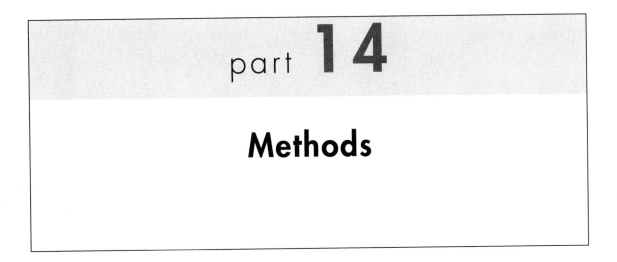

part **14**

Methods

steven shapin

keyword: science

summer 2006

63

We prize the referents of some words in our culture so highly that they have scarcely any stable reference. Take, for instance, reality, reason, and truth. And take the word that speaks most authoritatively in the name of reality, reason, and truth: science. Even "intelligent design" and "creation science" represent themselves as forms of science, not as nonscience or antiscience. Advocates of "intelligent design" want it taught in science classrooms. The problem today is not antiscience, but a contest for the winner of the designation "science." Public figures worry about "public ignorance of science"; we hear few complaints about "public ignorance of the novels of George Eliot" or "public ignorance of sociological theory." Our esteem for science is enormous. Moreover, the instability of the reference of science flows partly from the ways in which the word folds together description and prescription. We generally consider it good to be scientific and to speak in the name of science, and that is why so many claim the title: domestic science, nutrition science, sexual science, management science.

But in one sense fewer things are scientific today than ever before. In the early modern period, the Latin *scientia* just meant "knowledge," usually in the sense of an organized body of knowledge, acquired through a course of study. Francis Bacon's *De augmentis scientiarum* (translated in the seventeenth century as *The Advancement of Learning*) catalogued "the division of the sciences," which were taken to include history, philosophy, the principles of morals, and theology (traditionally "the queen of the sciences"). When, in 1660, the members of the newly founded Royal Society of London wanted to indicate their lack of concern with things like civil history, politics, and dogmatic theology, they described their business not as "science" but as "the improvement of natural knowledge." During the course of the nineteenth and especially the twentieth centuries, the term science came overwhelmingly to signify practices that involved observation and experiment, thus jettisoning history and philosophy and leaving the "social sciences" as a courtesy title, with limited credibility in the general culture or among natural scientists "proper." Some social scientists argued that social science and natural science could be and ought to be identical in their methods and in their relationships to their objects of study. But others reckoned that the human sciences should reject the methods and goals of the natural sciences. So, for instance, some claimed that the human sciences—unlike the natural sciences—were inescapably interpretative: human behavior was meaningful, that of molecules was not, and the task of the human scientist was to make out of meaningful behavior a particular kind of meaning. The human scientist, but not the natural scientist, was said to be caught in a loop of self-reference.

Linguistically, this more restrictive sense of science is an artifact of how English usage has developed and changed in recent centuries. Into the twentieth century, and up to the present, the French plural *les sciences* had a greater tendency to acknowledge procedural and conceptual similarities between, say, geology and sociology, as did the Russian singular *nauka* (with its Slavic cognates) and the German *Wissenschaft* (with its Scandinavian and Dutch cognates). Vernacular English once employed science in its original, inclusive, Latin sense (as in the skeptical proverb "Much science, much sorrow"), but by the nineteenth century, science did not usually need the qualifying "natural" to summon up the idea of organized, methodical research into the things, phenomena, and capacities belonging to nature as opposed to culture. So, by 1959, the chemist-turned-novelist C. P. Snow could complain about the divorce between "the two cultures," which he blandly distinguished as "science" and "literary studies," while conceding in an aside that the "social sciences" might constitute a third culture.

We still do not fully understand how this shift in reference of the word "science" occurred. Influential seventeenth century English experimentalists aimed to rigorously separate bodies of knowledge capable of generating certainty from those whose conclusions were at best probable or at worst conjectural, arbitrary, or ideologically colored. Insofar as the natural sciences were based on legitimate fact, with disciplined means for moving from fact to judiciously framed causal account, they could produce a just degree of certainty. By contrast, intellectual practices based on speculation or metaphysical dictate and buffeted by human passion and interest were unlikely to yield consensual certainty. The early Royal Society of London protected the quality of its natural knowledge by policing the boundary between it and potentially divisive "affairs of church and state." Certainty in natural knowledge thus rested on a publicly advertised, methodical separation between knowledge of things and knowledge of morals, between "is" and "ought." It was difficult to keep human passions and interests at bay when the objects of inquiry had to do with the human condition, and so the prerequisite for scientific certainty was a degree of moral inconsequentiality. A quality of certainty was, therefore, one means by which the prized designation of "science" might be exclusively attached to methodically proper inquiries into nature. Such an imperative and its boundaries were embraced in seventeenth-century England with greater enthusiasm than in France, where Descartes promised that the outcome of his philosophical method would include a demonstratively certain science of morals.

The so-called naturalistic fallacy—originally formulated in the eighteenth century by David Hume and most clearly articulated by the early-twentieth-century philosopher G. E. Moore—identified the impossibility of moving logically from an "is-statement" to an "ought-statement," that is, from scientific description to moral prescription. If that argument was accepted, then the distinct domains proper to science and to morality could also be accepted and boundaries agreed upon. The authority of science should be properly circumscribed within the spheres of description and explanation. By the middle of the twentieth century, scientists generally agreed that the authority of science did not extend to the spheres of morality and politics. As the physicist Edward Teller said in 1950, in relation to some scientists' sense of their "social responsibility," "The scientist is not responsible for the laws of nature. It is his job to find out how these laws operate. It is the scientist's job to find the ways in which these laws can serve the human will. However, it is not the scientist's job to determine whether a hydrogen bomb should be constructed, whether it should be used, or how it should be used."

Another distinction, increasingly important through the nineteenth century, concerned the relative ability of different intellectual practices to predict and control their objects. Bacon's dream was to enlist methodically reformed natural knowledge in the expansion of man's, and the state's, dominion, but the argument for the material utility of theoretical science was not widely credited until the nineteenth century, and was not decisively secured until Hiroshima experienced the power that theoretical physicists could unleash. As the ultimate patron of organized inquiry, the state was to fund intellectual practices that could demonstrably enhance its power and increase its wealth. Despite wide skepticism, by the mid-nineteenth century most Western states had accepted their role as paymasters for a range of natural sciences, including certain strands of cartography, geology, astronomy, botany, zoology, physiology, chemistry, and physics.

The emergent human sciences made utilitarian claims as well, promising governments certain, causal knowledge of the springs of human action: knowledge that lay people lacked and that those who had it could use not only to understand but to manipulate human conduct and belief, just as if human beings were molecules. Here the promise of certainty guaranteed by methods of research—on the model of the natural sciences—suggested the ability of the human sciences to predict and control. Such attempts did not fail utterly. Many modern governmental and commercial practices powerfully, if imperfectly, predict and manage human conduct through embedded forms of social-science-in-action. Consider, for example, projections of retail expenditures, traffic engineering, the design of kitchen appliances, and the arrangement of goods on supermarket shelves.

Moreover, the human sciences have the tremendous capacity, occasionally and uncontrollably, to realize their concepts, to see them enter the popular imagination, and thus become a part of the world that expertise seeks to describe and explain. Consider the careers of such concepts as "charisma," "penis envy," "being in denial," and "the grieving process." Each of these phrases has jumped from the domains of expert human science to vernacular usage, and, as they have done so, they provide resources for self-understanding, for the practical explanation, justification, or criticism of human behavior. That is a legitimate sense in which human science can be—in certain circumstances—more powerful than natural science: physics, chemistry, and biology may, through technology, rearrange the furniture of the natural world, and so produce powerful material effects, while the human sciences can, every now and then, bring new ways of being into the world. But the human sciences have never managed to establish their unique expertise as sources of knowledge in their domains, nor have they won the argument that effective prediction and control derive uniquely from theoretical, academic expertise. Much "social-science-in-action" does not trace back very clearly to the doings of academic disciplines: advertising, product design, and corporate management often develop "in-house" forms of human science appropriate to their practical tasks. The academic human sciences therefore have an imperfect hold on their objects of inquiry and their findings. The flow of cash from government and industry to the different modes of academic inquiry is a vulgar, but surprisingly reliable, index of what is now officially accounted a science and what is not.

The "official" reference of "science" promises some definitional stability and coherence. Suppose one just says that science is what is done in the departments of a science faculty; that it is what the U.S. National Science Foundation and the science bits of the Research Councils U.K. fund; that it is what we find in the pages of *Science* magazine; and what is taught in science classrooms. This "institutional" or "sociological" sensibility suggests that "we" moderns live in a scientific culture, while it acknowledges that many of that culture's inhabitants have little idea of what scientists do and know.

Because the "official" or "sociological" definition of science sets aside its prescriptive aspect, few intellectuals have been content to leave matters there. Efforts to distinguish science from lesser forms of culture and to make science available as a pattern to emulate have traditionally involved specifying its supposedly unique conceptual content and, especially, its uniquely effective method. Some scientists have asserted the noncommonsensical nature of scientific concepts (Lewis Wolpert), while others have insisted that "[s]cience is nothing but trained and organized common sense" (T. H. Huxley) and that "[t]he whole of science is nothing more than a refinement of everyday thinking" (Albert Einstein). Some philosophers and sociologists have identified the unique "normative ethos" of science, stressing the value scientists place on criticism and skepticism (Robert K. Merton), but others have emphasized how scientific training fruitfully narrows perception and how their favored models and theories constrain scientists' judgments (Thomas Kuhn).

For all the confidence with which various versions of "the scientific method" have been propounded in the past, we have never reached consensus about what that method is. Each account of the scientific method has its philosophical champions—inductivism, deductivism, hypothetico-deductivism, falsificationism, and so on—while eminent scientists intermittently suggest that "[t]here is no such thing as The Scientific Method" (immunologist Peter Medawar) and that we ought not to listen to scientists when they pronounce on methodology (Einstein): "If you want to find out anything from the theoretical physicists about the methods they use, I advise you to stick closely to one principle: don't listen to their words, fix your attention on their deeds." Encyclopedia definitions of science commonly specify that science is the quest for the most general laws or for principles of the greatest scope, universality, or abstraction, even as increasing numbers of scientists are apparently engaged in the search for quite particular knowledge—figuring out when Mount St. Helens is likely to erupt again or hunting for the gene or genes that regulate human appetite.

Talk about "the scientific method" is predicated upon some version of the "unity" of science. In the early twentieth century, many philosophers embraced a moral mission to formalize the bases of that unity, but, since Kuhn's *The Structure of Scientific Revolutions* (1962), a variety of "disunity" theories have flourished that suggest a more relaxed and naturalistic mood. Disunity theorists doubt that any methodical procedures are held in common by invertebrate zoology, seismology, microbial genetics, or any of the varieties of particle physics, which are *not* to be found in nonscientific forms of culture. How can the human sciences coherently either embrace or reject "the natural science model" when the natural sciences themselves display such conceptual and methodological heterogeneity? Yet, for all the localized academic fashion of naturalism and pluralism about the nature of science, the outraged reactions to these tendencies that surfaced in the "Science Wars" of the past decade testify to the enduring power of the idea of science as integral, special, even sacred in its integrity. To dispute the coherent and distinct identity of science is to challenge its unique and coherent value as a normative resource, and that is one reason why the idea of a unitary science persists in the absence of any substantial consensus about what such a thing might be.

RECOMMENDED RESOURCES

Zygmunt Bauman. *Legislators and Interpreters: On Modernity, Post-Modernity and Intellectuals* (Polity Press, 1987).

Debates about the nature of human science.

John Dupré. *The Disorder of Things: Metaphysical Foundations of the Disunity of Science* (Harvard University Press, 1993).

Modern philosophical skepticism about the unity of science.

Stephen Jay Gould. "Nonoverlapping Magisteria— Evolution versus Creationism." *Natural History* 106 (March 1997): 16–25.

On the distinct domains of science and religion.

Simon Schaffer. "What Is Science?" In *Science in the Twentieth Century*, eds. John Krige and Dominique Pestre (Harwood Academic, 1997).

An overview of the question.

Steven Shapin. "How to Be Antiscientific." In *The One Culture? A Conversation about Science*, eds. Jay A. Labinger and Harry Collins (University of Chicago Press, 2001).

For scientists' varying specifications of what science is.

REVIEW QUESTIONS

1. How might you have defined "science" and "scientific" before reading this essay? How would you define these terms now?
2. How does the rift between the natural sciences and the human sciences affect sociology?
3. Sociologist Zygmunt Bauman posits that scholars can be "legislators" as well as "interpreters." How does this distinction relate to Shapin's essay? Do you think sociologists should heed Marx's pronouncement that "philosophers have only interpreted the world, in various ways; the point, however, is to change it"? What exactly should be the sociologist's role in society?

howard schuman

sense and nonsense about surveys

summer 2002

understanding surveys is critical to being an informed citizen, but popular media often report surveys without any guidance on how to interpret and evaluate the results. some basic guidelines can promote more sophisticated readings of survey results and help teach when to trust the polls.

Surveys draw on two human propensities that have served us well from ancient times. One is to gather information by asking questions. The first use of language around 100,000 years ago may have been to utter commands such as "Come here!" or "Wait!" Questions must have followed soon after: "Why?" or "What for?" From that point, it would have been only a short step to the use of interrogatives to learn where a fellow hominid had seen potential food, a dangerous animal, or something else of importance. Asking questions continues to be an effective way of acquiring information of all kinds, assuming of course that the person answering is able and willing to respond accurately.

The other inclination, learning about one's environment by examining a small part of it, is the sampling aspect of surveys. A taste of something may or may not point to appetizing food. A first inquiry to a stranger, a first glance around a room, a first date—each is a sample of sorts, often used to decide whether it is wise to proceed further. As with questions, however, one must always be aware of the possibility that the sample may not prove adequate to the task.

> The percentage of people who refuse to take part in a survey is particularly important. In some federal surveys, the percentage is small, within the range of 5 to 10 percent. For even the best non-government surveys, the refusal rate can reach 25 percent or more, and it can be far larger in the case of poorly executed surveys.

sampling: how gallup achieved fame

Only within the past century—and especially in the 1930s and 1940s—were major improvements made in the sampling process that allowed the modern survey to develop and flourish. A crucial change involved recognition that the value of a sample comes not simply from its size but also from the way it is obtained. Every serious pursuit likes to have a morality tale that supports its basic beliefs: witness Eve and the apple in the Bible or Newton and his apple in legends about scientific discovery. Representative sampling has a marvelous morality tale also, with the additional advantage of its being true.

The story concerns the infamous *Literary Digest* poll prediction—based on 10 million questionnaires sent out and more than two million received back—that Roosevelt would lose decisively in the 1936 presidential election. At the same time, George Gallup, using many fewer cases but a much better method, made the more accurate prediction that FDR would win. Gallup used quotas in choosing respondents in order to represent different economic strata, whereas the *Literary*

Digest had worked mainly from telephone and automobile ownership lists, which in 1936 were biased toward wealthy people apt to be opposed to Roosevelt. (There were other sources of bias as well.) As a result, the *Literary Digest* poll disappeared from the scene, and Gallup was on his way to becoming a household name.

Yet despite their intuitive grasp of the importance of representing the electorate accurately, Gallup and other commercial pollsters did not use the probability sampling methods that were being developed in the same decades and that are fundamental to social science surveys today. Probability sampling in its simplest form calls for each person in the population to have an equal chance of being selected. It can also be used in more complex applications where the chances are deliberately made to be unequal, for example, when oversampling a minority group in order to study it more closely; however, the chances of being selected must still be known so that they can later be equalized when considering the entire population.

intuitions and counterintuitions about sample size

Probability sampling theory reveals a crucial but counterintuitive point about sample size: the size of a sample needed to accurately estimate a value for a population depends very little on the size of the population. For example, almost the same size sample is needed to estimate, with a given degree of precision, the proportion of left-handed people in the United States as is needed to make the same estimate for, say, Peoria, Illinois. In both cases a reasonably accurate estimate can be obtained with a sample size of around 1,000. (More cases are needed when extraordinary precision is called for, for example, in calculating unemployment rates, where even a tenth of a percent change may be regarded as important.)

The link between population size and sample size cuts both ways. Although huge samples are not needed for huge populations like those of the United States or China, a handful of cases is not sufficient simply because one's interest is limited to Peoria. This implication is often missed by those trying to save time and money when sampling a small community.

Moreover, all of these statements depend on restricting your interest to overall population values. If you are concerned about, say, left-handedness among African Americans, then African Americans become your population, and you need much the same sample size as for Peoria or the United States.

who is missing?

A good sample depends on more than probability sampling theory. Surveys vary greatly in their quality of implementation, and this variation is not captured by the "margin of error" plus/minus percentage figures that accompany most media reports of polls. Such percentages reflect the size of the final sample, but they do not reveal the sampling method or the extent to which the targeted individuals or households were actually included in the final sample. These details are at least as important as the sample size.

When targeted members of a population are not interviewed or do not respond to particular questions, the omissions are a serious problem if they are numerous and if those missed differ from those who are interviewed on the matters being studied. The latter difference can seldom be known with great confidence, so it is usually desirable to keep omissions to a minimum. For example, sampling from telephone directories is undesirable because it leaves out those with unlisted telephones, as well as those with no telephones at all. Many survey reports are based on such poor sampling procedures that they may not deserve to be taken seriously. This is especially true of reports based on "focus groups," which offer lots of human interest but are subject to vast amounts of error. Internet surveys also cannot represent the general population adequately at present, though this is an area where some serious attempts are being made to compensate for the inherent difficulties.

The percentage of people who refuse to take part in a survey is particularly important. In some federal surveys, the percentage is small, within the range of 5 to 10 percent. For even the best nongovernment surveys, the refusal rate can reach 25 percent or more, and it can be far larger in the case of poorly executed surveys. Refusals have risen substantially from earlier days, becoming a major cause for concern among serious survey practitioners. Fortunately, in recent years research has shown that moderate amounts of nonresponse in an otherwise careful survey seem in most cases not to have a major effect on results. Indeed, even the *Literary Digest*, with its abysmal sampling and massive nonresponse rate, did well predicting elections before the dramatic realignment of the electorate in 1936. The problem is that one can never be certain as to the effects of refusals and other forms of nonresponse, so obtaining a high response rate remains an important goal.

questions about questions

Since survey questions resemble the questions we ask in ordinary social interaction, they may seem less problematic than the counterintuitive and technical aspects of sampling. Yet survey results are every bit as dependent on the form, wording, and context of the questions asked as they are on the sample of people who answer them.

No classic morality tale like the *Literary Digest* fiasco highlights the question-answer process, but an example from the early days of surveys illustrates both the potential challenges of question writing and the practical solutions.

In 1940 Donald Rugg asked two slightly different questions to equivalent national samples about the general issue of freedom of speech:

· Do you think the United States should forbid public speeches against democracy?
· Do you think the United States should allow public speeches against democracy?

Taken literally, forbidding something and not allowing something have the same effect, but clearly the public did not view the questions as identical. Whereas 75 percent of the public would not allow such speeches, only 54 percent would forbid them, a difference of 21 percentage points. This finding was replicated several times in later years, not only in the United States but also (with appropriate translations) in Germany and the Netherlands. Such "survey-based experiments" call for administering different versions of a question to random subsamples of a larger sample. If the results between the subsamples differ by more than can be easily ex-plained by chance, we infer that the difference is due to the variation in wording.

In addition, answers to survey questions always depend on the form in which a question is asked. If the interviewer presents a limited set of alternatives, most respondents will choose one, rather than offering a different alternative of their own. In one survey-based experiment, for example, we asked a national sample of Americans to name the most important problem facing the country. Then we asked a comparable sample a parallel question that provided a list of four problems from which to choose the most important; this list included none of the four problems mentioned most often by the first sample but instead provided four problems that had been mentioned by fewer than 3 percent of the earlier respondents. The list question also invited respondents to substitute a different problem if they wished (see table 1). Despite the invitation, the majority of respondents (60 percent) chose one of the rare problems offered, reflecting their reluctance to go outside the frame of reference provided by the question. The form of a question provides the "rules of the game" for respondents, and this must always be kept in mind when interpreting results.

Other difficulties occur with survey questions when issues are discussed quite generally, as though there is a single way of framing them and just two sides to the debate. For example, what is called "the abortion issue" really consists of different issues: the reasons for an abortion, the trimester involved, and so forth. In a recent General Social Survey, nearly 80 percent of the national sample supported legal abortion in the case of "a serious defect in the baby," but only 44 percent supported it "if the family has a low income and cannot afford any more children." Often what is thought to be a conflict in findings between two surveys is actually a difference in the aspects of the general issue that they queried. In still other cases an inconsistency

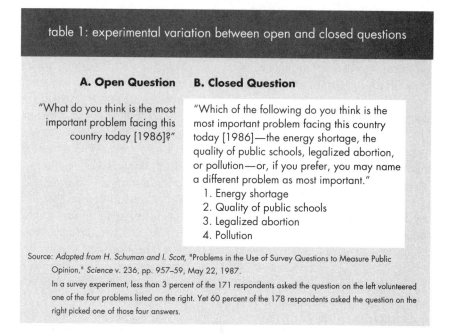

table 1: experimental variation between open and closed questions

A. Open Question

"What do you think is the most important problem facing this country today [1986]?"

B. Closed Question

"Which of the following do you think is the most important problem facing this country today [1986]—the energy shortage, the quality of public schools, legalized abortion, or pollution—or, if you prefer, you may name a different problem as most important."
1. Energy shortage
2. Quality of public schools
3. Legalized abortion
4. Pollution

Source: *Adapted from H. Schuman and I. Scott,* "Problems in the Use of Survey Questions to Measure Public Opinion," *Science* v. 236, pp. 957–59, May 22, 1987.

In a survey experiment, less than 3 percent of the 171 respondents asked the question on the left volunteered one of the four problems listed on the right. Yet 60 percent of the 178 respondents asked the question on the right picked one of those four answers.

reflects a type of illogical wish fulfillment in the public itself, as when majorities favor both a decrease in taxes and an increase in government services if the questions are asked separately.

solutions to the question wording problem

All these and still other difficulties (including the order in which questions are asked) suggest that responses to single survey questions on complex issues should be viewed with considerable skepticism. What to do then, other than to reject all survey data as unusable for serious purposes? One answer can be found from the replications of the forbid/allow experiment above: Although there was a 21 percentage points difference based on question wording in 1940 and a slightly larger difference (24 percentage points) when the experiment was repeated some 35 years later, both the forbid and the allow wordings registered similar declines in Americans' intolerance of speeches against democracy

(see figure 1). No matter which question was used—as long as it was the same one at both times—the conclusion about the increase in civil libertarian sentiments was the same.

More generally, what has been called the "principle of form-resistant correlations" holds in most cases: if question wording (and meaning) is kept constant, differences over time, differences across educational levels, and most other careful comparisons are not seriously affected by specific question wording. Indeed, the distinction between results for single questions and results based on comparisons or associations holds even for simple factual inquiries. Consider, for example, a study of the number of rooms in American houses. No God-given rule states what to include when counting the rooms in a house (bathrooms? basements? hallways?); hence the average number reported for a particular place and time should not be treated as an absolute truth. What we can do, however, is try to apply the same definitions over time, across social divisions, even across nations. That way, we gain confidence in

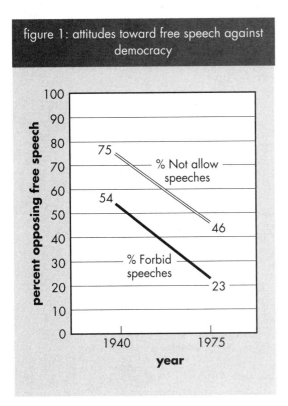

figure 1: attitudes toward free speech against democracy

[chart showing "percent opposing free speech" on y-axis from 0 to 100, and "year" on x-axis from 1940 to 1975. Upper line "% Not allow speeches" from 75 to 46. Lower line "% Forbid speeches" from 54 to 23.]

vided by any single question. A further safeguard is to carry out frequent experiments like that on the forbid/allow wordings. By varying the form, wording, and context of questions, researchers can gain insight into both the questions and the relevant issues. Sometimes variations turn out to make no difference, and that is also useful to learn. For example, I once expected support for legalized abortion to increase when a question substituted *end pregnancy* for the word *abortion* in the phrasing. Yet no difference was found. Today, more and more researchers include survey-based experiments as part of their investigations, and readers should look for these sorts of safeguards when evaluating survey results.

the need for comparisons

To interpret surveys accurately, it's important to use a framework of comparative data in evaluating the results. For example, teachers know that course evaluations can be interpreted best against the backdrop of evaluations from other similar courses: a 75 percent rating of lectures as "excellent" takes on a quite different meaning depending on whether the average for other lecture courses is 50 percent or 90 percent. Such comparisons are fundamental for all survey results, yet they are easily overlooked when one feels the urge to speak definitively about public reactions to a unique event.

Comparative analysis over time, along with survey-based experiments, can also help us understand responses to questions about socially sensitive subjects. Experiments have shown that expressions of racial attitudes can change substantially for both black and white Americans depending on the interviewer's race. White respondents, for instance, are more likely to support racial intermarriage when speaking to a black than to a white interviewer. Such self-censoring mirrors variations in cross-race conversations outside of surveys, reflecting not a

the comparisons we make—who has more rooms than who, for example.

We still face the task of interpreting the meaning of questions and of associations among questions, but that is true in all types of research. Even an index constructed from a large number of questions on the basis of a sophisticated statistical calculation called factor analysis inevitably requires the investigator to interpret what it is that he or she has measured. There is no escaping this theoretical challenge, fundamental to all research, whether using surveys or other methods such as field observations.

Survey researchers should also ask several different questions about any important issue. In addition to combining questions to increase reliability, the different answers can be synthesized rather than depending on the angle of vision pro-

A2. We are interested in how people are getting along financially these days. Would you say that you (and your family living there) are *better off* or *worse off* financially than you were *a year ago*?

| 1. BETTER NOW | 3. SAME | 5. WORSE | 8. DON'T KNOW |

A3. Now looking ahead—do you think that *a year from now* you (and your family living there) will be *better off* financially, or *worse off*, or just about the same as now?

| 1. WILL BE BETTER OFF | 3. SAME | 5. WILL BE WORSE OFF | 8. DON'T KNOW |

A4. Now turning to business conditions in the country as a whole—do you think that during the next 12 months we'll have *good* times financially, or *bad* times, or what?

| 1. GOOD TIMES | 2. GOOD WITH QUALIFICATIONS | 3. PRO-CON |

| 4. BAD WITH QUALIFICATIONS | 5. BAD TIMES | 8. DON'T KNOW |

A8. Looking ahead, which would you say is more likely—that in the country as a whole we'll have continuous good times *during the next 5 years* or so, or that we will have periods of widespread *unemployment* or depression, or what?

_____

_____

A18. About the big things people buy for their homes—such as furniture, a refrigerator, stove, television, and things like that. Generally speaking, do you think that now is a good or a bad time for people to buy major household items?

| 1. GOOD | 3.PRO-CON | 5. BAD | 8. DON'T KNOW |

Section of interview form used in the Surveys of Consumers conducted by the Survey Research Center, University of Michigan. Courtesy of Survey Research Center, University of Michigan.

methodological artifact of surveys but rather a fact of life about race relations in America. Still, if we consider time trends, with the race of interviewer kept constant, we can also see that white responses supporting intermarriage have clearly increased over the past half century (see table 2), that actual intermarriage rates have also risen (though from a much lower level) over recent years, and that the public visibility of cross-race marriage and dating has also increased. It would be foolish to assume that the survey data on racial attitudes reflect actions in any literal sense, but they do capture important *trends* in both norms and behavior.

Surveys remain our best tool for learning about large populations. One remarkable advan-

table 2: percent of white americans approving or disapproving of racial intermarriage, 1958–1997		

"Do you approve or disapprove of marriage between blacks and whites?"

Year	Approve	Disapprove
1958	4	96
1978	34	66
1997	67	33

Source: Gallup Poll

tage surveys have over some other methods is the ability to identify their own limitations, as illustrated by the development of both probability theory in sampling and experiments in questioning. In the end, however, with surveys as with all research methods, there is no substitute for both care and intelligence in the way evidence is gathered and interpreted. What we learn about society is always mediated by the instruments we use, including our own eyes and ears. As Isaac Newton wrote long ago, error is not in the art but in the artificers.

RECOMMENDED RESOURCES

Philip E. Converse. "The Nature of Belief Systems in Mass Publics." In *Ideology and Discontent*, ed. D. E. Apter (The Free Press, 1964).

A profound and skeptical exploration of the nature of public attitudes.

Robert M. Groves. *Survey Errors and Survey Costs* (Wiley, 1989).

A sophisticated consideration of the sources of error in surveys.

Graham Kalton. *Introduction to Survey Sampling* (Sage Publications [Quantitative Applications in the Social Sciences], 1983).

A brief and lucid introduction to sampling.

Benjamin I. Page and Robert Y. Shapiro. *The Rational Public: Fifty Years of Trends in Americans' Policy Preferences* (University of Chicago Press, 1992).

In part, a persuasive reply to Converse's skepticism.

Howard Schuman and Stanley Presser. *Questions and Answers in Attitude Surveys: Experiments on Question Form, Wording, and Context* (Academic Press, 1981) (Reprint edition with new preface, Sage Publications, 1996).

Several experiments discussed in the present article are drawn from this volume.

Samuel A. Stouffer. *Communism, Conformity, and Civil Liberties*, with introduction by James A. Davis (Doubleday, 1955; Transaction Publishers, 1992).

Stouffer's keen awareness of both the possibilities and the limitations of survey data is reflected in this classic investigation. Also relevant to today's political climate.

Seymour Sudman, Norman M. Bradburn, and Norbert Schwarz. *Thinking About Answers: The Application of Cognitive Process to Survey Methodology* (Jossey-Bass, 1996).

A clear discussion of survey questioning by three well-known researchers.

Roger Tourangeau, Lance J. Rips, and Kenneth Rasinski. *The Psychology of Survey Response* (Cambridge University Press, 2000).

A comprehensive account of response effects, drawing especially on ideas from cognitive psychology.

REVIEW QUESTIONS

1. Schuman suggests that telephone directories do not provide one with an

adequate listing of possible survey respondents. Why? Is there another reason, one that might be in your pocket or purse?

2. Table 1 offers a good example of how a respondent can be asked an open or closed question. What are the advantages and disadvantages of both? Try constructing two questions, one open and one closed, on the same topic, selected from an earlier essay.

3. In the final section of his essay, Schuman describes how many researchers now try to use multiple methodologies (e.g., participant observation, survey data, longitudinal studies, case studies). Write a paragraph reflecting on what you think the benefits would be to such an approach.

michael j. lovaglia

from summer camps to glass ceilings: the power of experiments

65

fall 2003

social science experiments on a few individuals from similar backgrounds can give rise to strategies for coping with social problems, ranging from intergroup conflict to women's inequality in the workplace. how does research on such narrow groups contribute to broad social understanding and insight?

A man in torn clothes sprawls across an urban sidewalk. He moans softly. Pedestrians hurry by with no more than a worried glance. No one stops to help. Someone watching from afar might wonder at such uncaring behavior; surely some conscientious person would stop. Moreover, these pedestrians are all young adults wearing clerical garb, seminarians studying for the ministry. They are hurrying to the church to deliver sermons on the Good Samaritan. Why did they not stop? Researchers who staged this test found that seminary students did not stop because they worried about being late. Their personal obligation to keeping an appointment outweighed their general commitment to helping others.

Experiments such as this one startle us into new ways of understanding people. Although we tend to explain why people do what they do—or, in this case, not do—as an expression of personal character, experiments show that the context of events determines behavior to a significant extent. Experimental studies carry great weight in the social sciences, gaining acceptance in prestigious journals and, in a high-profile example, last year's Nobel Prize in Economics. Some experiment results also get exposure in popular media, generating prime-time news coverage and Hollywood films.

Many people who hear about these experiments—and some social scientists, too—wonder how experiments achieve their power to convince, especially when their results often defy common sense. Experiments usually feature contrived conditions and record the behavior of at most a few hundred participants, many of whom are college students. Yet the results can tell us a lot about society.

the robbers cave experiment and summer camp movies

A sociological experiment in the 1950s demonstrated the effectiveness of a now common strategy in which competing corporations form joint ventures that would appear to prevent one firm from gaining advantage over the other (much like the United States and Russia cooperating on the space station). In 1954, Muzafer Sherif, an early proponent of social science experiments, set up a summer camp near Robbers Cave State Park in Oklahoma to test theories about group conflict and how to avoid it. He believed that individuals develop a group identity when they work together toward a common goal. Groups become more cohesive and rigid when faced with competition from another group. This competition creates frustration, triggering hostility and conflict between the groups. Sherif thought a solution to the conflict might be found in the same process by which groups form: working toward a common goal. If hostile groups have to work together, then members might learn to see each other as part of a combined larger group, which would reduce their conflict.

A group of 22 boys—all white, middle-class and close to their 12th birthdays—came to the Robbers Cave summer camp. Sherif and his colleagues divided them into two teams, the Eagles and the Rattlers. Each team completed projects requiring the cooperation of members, such as building a diving platform at a swimming hole. In the second phase of camp activities, the two teams competed against each other in various contests. The results are familiar. Rivalry between teams generated hostility and even a little mayhem (exaggerated in subsequent summer camp movies), and threatened to spin out of control. Hostility emerged during the first contest— a baseball game. Boys in each group cursed members of the opposing group and called them names. At dinner, Eagles refused to eat with Rattlers. Later, the Eagles tore down the Rattlers' flag and burned it. The Rattlers retaliated by vandalizing the Eagles' cabin. A food fight erupted in the mess hall.

The experiment showed that hostility between groups develops spontaneously when individuals within a group work together and then compete as a team against another group. The final phase of the experiment showed how to reduce conflict. On a hot summer day, researchers disabled the water supply and asked volunteers to find the problem. Boys from both groups stepped forward, located the problem, and worked together to solve it. Afterward, they all shared the water in a friendly manner. Finding water was important enough that it neutralized the groups' mutual antipathy, fostering cooperation and the beginning of trust.

An overarching cooperative task that requires the contributions of both groups for success reduced intergroup conflict. This principle is widely applied today, in contexts as distant as international relations, even though the experiment had nothing directly to do with such serious settings.

describing the world or testing theories

The logic of social experiments differs from that of other social research. Survey researchers, for example, try to describe a population of people by selecting a large, representative sample and then asking questions to determine respondents' attitudes and other characteristics. In contrast, experiments test theories rather than describe a population. That is, they test for evidence of a specific social process in a small sample of people, chosen to be as similar as possible. If a theory predicts a particular result under certain conditions, experimenters then set up only those conditions. In this way, researchers can tell whether the predicted differences in behavior are produced by the conditions of the experiment instead of by individual differences among the participants.

Psychologist Philip Zimbardo's prison experiment at Stanford University is another famous example. He tested the theory that the brutal behavior of guards in prison camps (such as those in Nazi Germany) was a result of their being guards, rather than a result of their being individuals psychologically prone to act brutally. Zimbardo predicted that normal, mentally healthy, American men would become brutal or be brutalized simply because they became either prison guards or prisoners.

In the early 1970s, Zimbardo created a "prison" in the basement of the psychology building at Stanford. He selected only male Stanford undergraduates to participate, ruling out those with any prior psychological problems. He

The hallmarks of good experimental research:

· A comparison between two groups as similar as possible but for one theoretically important difference (for example, undergraduate women assigned by coin flip to be team leaders or followers).
· Controlled conditions that allow the experiment to be repeated by other researchers.
· Follow-up studies that confirm the initial results and rule out competing explanations.
· A theory supported by experimental results that makes valid predictions in other contexts, spawning new research that reinforces the theory.

Pitfalls to avoid:

· Experimental results in one context cannot be simply exported to other contexts or cultures; they can support theories, which may then be used to make predictions for findings in other contexts.
· Ethical problems must be carefully considered. What effect might the research have on the lives of experiment participants?

then randomly assigned the participants to be either prisoners or prison guards. The procedure is like flipping a coin. Heads and the participant becomes a guard, tails and he gets arrested. Random assignment helped to ensure that the two groups in the experiment—guards and prisoners—would be similar in other ways. Within a day of the prisoners' arrival, guards began acting brutally and prisoners showed signs of anxiety. Conditions rapidly deteriorated until the experiment had to be stopped. (Because social experiments directly change people's lives, extraordinary care must be taken to avoid causing harm. Some social experiments have the potential to be as dangerous as a clinical trial testing a new drug. Today, universities' Institutional Review Boards review proposed social experiments as stringently as they do medical and other scientific studies on people.)

The Stanford prison experiment helped shift thinking away from blaming German culture for the Holocaust and toward the social condi-

tions that promote brutal behavior. The study received much media attention and was made into a popular German movie, *Das Experiment*. Ironically, the film version concluded that the solution to brutality is for individuals to take personal responsibility for their actions. But a solution that follows more consistently from the study itself is to construct social situations that discourage brutality. (See "Making Sense of the Senseless: Understanding Genocide," page 406.)

Why was this experiment so influential? It said nothing directly about German behavior during the Holocaust. Rather, it tested a theoretical prediction that a coercive setting can induce brutal behavior. A good experiment subtly shifts the burden of scientific proof, challenging other researchers to show whether a social process demonstrated in the experiment operates differently in a complex, naturally occurring setting. Simple experiments are convincing in part because they demonstrate a difference in the behavior of people in contrasting situations. Simplicity helps build agreement; most people observing the results of the Stanford and Robbers Cave experiments would interpret their meanings similarly. Controlled conditions also allow other researchers to repeat the experiments to see if the same results occur, perhaps using slightly different procedures. Good experiments can in these ways extend theories and produce new knowledge.

Of course, no single study, theory, or method, no matter how good, establishes a scientific fact. Instead, science synthesizes different kinds of research from a variety of researchers to reach its conclusions. An experiment such as Zimbardo's Stanford prison makes a simple yet forceful statement that builds on earlier and inspires later research pointing to a conclusion. Eventually, we better understand the social processes underlying a problem and can attempt a practical intervention. Experiments also can be used to directly assess the effectiveness of alternative social policies.

arresting domestic violence: experimenting with social policy

In 1981, police in Minneapolis changed the way they responded to reports of domestic violence. Before 1981, police officers had the discretion to arrest the person who committed the assault, order him (or her) to leave the home for a short period or provide on-site counseling. Advocates expressed concern that police were treating episodes of domestic violence too leniently, thereby failing to deter future assaults. Lawrence Sherman and Richard Berk designed an experiment to test whether making an arrest in a domestic violence case deterred future assaults better than the other two options of separating the couple and counseling.

The experiment had important implications for public policy, but it also addressed a long-standing dispute between two theoretical traditions in criminology. Deterrence theory holds that punishment discourages future criminal behavior. This school of thought maintains that suspects who are arrested will be less likely to commit another assault than those who are separated or counseled. A second theoretical tradition, known as labeling theory, suggests that when individuals are arrested, they become stigmatized as criminals by both society and in their own eyes. Their new self-image as a criminal then increases the likelihood of subsequent criminal behavior. (Labeling theory is the reason that names of juvenile offenders are kept out of the media except for serious offenses.) If labeling theory is valid, then those arrested for domestic violence actually would be more likely to commit another assault.

During the Sherman-Berk experiment, whenever Minneapolis police officers responded to a domestic violence call, they determined which procedure—arrest, separation, or counseling—to follow by random assignment. Researchers tracked the behavior of suspects in the study for six months following the domestic violence incident. Results showed a deterrent effect for arrest and no evidence for labeling theory. That is, suspects who had been arrested were slightly less likely to commit another assault during the subsequent six months than were those who had been separated or counseled.

Although the deterrence effect of arrest was small, the experiment had a large effect on public policy. Arrest in domestic violence cases became the preferred procedure in many police departments and 15 states passed mandatory arrest laws. Meanwhile, debate over implications for social theory continued. During the next decade, other researchers repeated the experiment in several other police jurisdictions. The new results were more complicated. Arrest deterred suspects who were employed, perhaps because arrest is more serious for those who have a lot to lose. For unemployed suspects, arrest had the opposite effect, as predicted by labeling theory. They were more likely to commit a subsequent assault than the unemployed men who had been separated or counseled. The theoretical advance was exciting, but it left policy implications unresolved. In practice, police officers are still uncertain whether making an arrest will be beneficial in a domestic violence case. More systematic research could better equip police and judges to make such critical, sometimes life-and-death decisions.

We may need a system that produces public policies in a way similar to the system of clinical trials that produces new medical drugs. None of the alternatives available to the police in the Minneapolis experiment was new. But we do not have an organized system to formulate new policies, test them, and then compare them to alternative policies in controlled experiments. Such a system is worth considering. It might lead to more effective public policy the way that our system of developing new drugs has led to more effective medicine.

why do some groups score low on standardized tests?

Low intelligence seems the obvious explanation for low scores on a mental ability test. But what if something besides intelligence determines test scores? In the 1990s, psychologist Claude Steele's experiments yielded the startling discovery that scores on standardized tests depend not only on students' ability to answer, but also on what they expect the consequences of their test scores to be. Students who are stereotyped as having low ability may underperform when they are apprehensive about getting a low score.

Steele and his colleagues conducted a simple experiment. They gave a difficult standardized test—like the college SAT but harder—to a group of Stanford students. Instructions for taking the test varied. Some students, selected at random, were told the test results could be used to compare their performance to that of other students. Some students were told the test was only to familiarize them with similar tests they would encounter at the university. When students were told the tests were just for familiarization, black students scored about the same as white students of similar academic attainment. But when students thought they were going to be compared, black students scored lower than did comparable white students—as is common on standardized tests.

My colleagues and I conducted subsequent experiments showing that Steele's theory was not limited to particular racial groups, but applied to any stigmatized group. We randomly assigned white university undergraduates to be treated as an advantaged "majority" or disadvantaged "minority," by telling some students that their left- or right-handedness made it unlikely that they would be able to contribute to a group project, and also that other group members might resent their inability to contribute. Then, we gave the students a standard test of mental ability, explaining that the results of the test would be used to assign them to group positions such as "supervisor," "analyst," or "menial" in the group project. We found that students' test scores were substantially lower if they were treated as a disadvantaged "minority" for as little as 20 minutes.

The line of research begun by Claude Steele now includes many studies by different researchers. They show that when black and white students take the same standardized test, different expectations for the consequences of the test—not differences in mental ability—determine whether white students have an advantage. That is, while the best mental ability tests do a fair job of determining differences in cognitive skills among otherwise similar individuals, differences in test scores between racial and ethnic groups are created by social conditions rather than by the groups' mental abilities.

Applied programs based on this research show promise for increasing the academic performance of disadvantaged students. One surprising detail is that the performances of the best black students suffer the most. The threat of fulfilling a negative stereotype is felt most keenly by black students with the potential to excel; it is they who worry most about the potential backlash from their competition with white students. This may explain why remedial programs to improve academic performance of weaker students have not closed the gap between blacks and whites generally. Honors programs that encourage black students to undertake accelerated studies may have more effect, because promising black students have more academic ability than their grades and test scores suggest. Claude Steele helped develop a successful program to improve the performance of incoming minority students at the University of Michigan that emphasizes high academic standards, affirming students' ability to achieve those standards, and building trust that successful minority students can be accepted in the academic community.

how can women attain status equal to men at work?

Social experiments can also suggest strategies individuals can use to improve their lives. Status Characteristics Theory explains how individuals attain influence in work groups: people who are expected to contribute more to the group gain more influence in the group and receive greater rewards from the group. That is, expected contributions often count more than actual contributions. Individuals expected to perform well are more often followed by the group and rewarded accordingly. For example, a woman

may make a brilliant suggestion that guarantees a successful project, but her suggestion may be ignored until a respected male coworker endorses it. He then gets the credit.

Research using the theory confirms that people expect men to contribute more to group success than women and that men do have more influence in decision making. Men get more credit for the group's successes and less blame for the group's failures. And when group members are evaluated, men get higher performance ratings and bigger rewards. To achieve the same level of rewards, women must work harder and contribute more than men. Status Characteristics Theory can also explain the familiar strategies women have used to break through to positions of influence in the workplace. Traditionally, they have out-competed men, following a masculine model that includes demonstrating competence through hard work and aggressive, even ruthless, competition. Successful women sometimes feel that they have sacrificed too much of themselves by following "male" strategies.

In the early 1980s, Cecilia Ridgeway conducted experiments using this theory that produced remarkable results for professional women struggling for career advancement under a glass ceiling. Ridgeway realized that people value not only the ability of a person to contribute, but also whether that person is motivated by a desire to help the group; they would not expect a person who is competent but selfish to contribute much of value. Ridgeway proposed that, because of gender stereotypes, however, people expect that even selfishly motivated men will contribute to the group, but expect contributions from women only when women demonstrate that they care about the group.

Ridgeway conducted an experiment to test this theory. Four team members worked together to reach a decision. One of the team members—secretly collaborating with the experimenters—made comments that were either group-motivated

the hawthorne experiment

In the late 1920s and early 1930s, a Western Electric Company assembly plant near Chicago was the site of a series of studies aimed at developing scientifically based strategies for increasing worker productivity.

One experiment led to a concept called the "Hawthorne Effect." The researchers took a small group of female workers away from their peers, and placed them in a separate room so the experimenters could study the effect of changes in lighting, work procedures, and break times on their productivity. It came as no surprise that improved lighting increased the workers' productivity, at least at first. But when the experimenters lowered the lighting to earlier levels, productivity continued to increase. Similar results after changing other aspects of the workers' environment led researchers to a conclusion that has since become known as the Hawthorne Effect: Workers increased their efforts because they were getting attention from the researchers, and because they bonded together as members of a prestigious "special" group.

Though legendary in its implications, the experiment has been criticized for design flaws and for confounding key variables, for example, two members of the study group were replaced mid-experiment with two new workers selected for their industriousness and cooperativeness. Simultaneous investigations by other sociologists revealed that workers who bonded strongly could unite to suppress work effort as well as speed it up.

Despite such shortcomings, reports of the Hawthorne experiment were used with enthusiasm by advocates of the human relations approach to workplace management. They felt that the results of the experiment challenged the scientific management perspectives that had shaped the Hawthorne studies in the first place. As a concept, the Hawthorne Effect—which posits that many interventions work, whatever they are, simply because people respond to being studied—also has been applied to a range of situations, such as student achievement in experimental schools, community organizing, and military campaigns. Such applications confirm the power of relatively small experiments to stimulate thinking about issues of great importance, both for sociologists and for the larger public.

("It is important that we cooperate") or self-motivated ("I want to win points for myself"). As predicted, in the self-motivated condition, male collaborators had more influence over the groups' decisions than female collaborators. In the group-motivated conditions, however, women collaborators' influence increased while the men's stayed at about the same high level as when they appeared selfish. Put another way, group-motivated women had as much influence as equally competent men regardless of the males' motivations.

The results suggest a strategy to succeed at work that women could use as an alternative to the competitive male one. Demonstrated competence is primary. Assertiveness also helps, but the focus on ruthless competition may be unnecessary for women's success. Instead, emphasizing a concern for other group members and the importance of working together to accomplish group goals can help competent women achieve recognition for their contributions. Future research in actual workplaces will help refine an effective strategy.

from summer camps to glass ceilings: the power of experiments   487

from theory to practice

The power of experiments flows from their use to test general theories. Sherif's Robbers Cave experiment tested a theory that explains how cooperation forms within groups and competition develops between them. Ridgeway tested her theory that influence in groups flows from the expectations people have about the ability and motivation of group members to contribute to group success.

Alone, a social experiment only demonstrates some phenomenon in one restricted context. But when experiments test theories, and their results lead to more tests in wider contexts, as well as other research with other methods, then we gain knowledge capable of transforming society. The experiments described have inspired lines of research with the potential to increase cooperation among competing organizations, decrease domestic violence, reduce the racial gap in academic success, and remove the glass ceiling limiting women in business. They successfully made the leap from small groups to helping us understand society at large.

RECOMMENDED RESOURCES

American Sociological Review. "Employment, Marriage, and the Deterrent Effect of Arrest for Domestic Violence: Replications and Re-Analyses," 57 (1992): 679–708.

> Three research articles analyze followup studies to the original Sherman and Berk experiment on police responses to domestic violence.

Joseph Berger and Morris Zelditch, Jr., eds. *Status, Rewards and Influence* (Jossey-Bass, 1985).

> An overview of research on status processes in task groups.

Bernard P. Cohen. *Developing Sociological Knowledge: Theory and Method* (Nelson Hall, 1989).

> A classic text that describes social science as a reciprocal process in which research tests theory and theory develops through the interpretation of research.

Michael J. Lovaglia. *Knowing People: The Personal Use of Social Psychology* (McGraw-Hill, 2000).

> An accessible overview of social psychological research useful for individuals in their personal lives.

Michael J. Lovaglia, Jeffery W. Lucas, Jeffrey A. Houser, Shane R. Thye, and Barry Markovsky. "Status Processes and Mental Ability Test Scores." *American Journal of Sociology* 104 (1998): 195–228.

> A research article demonstrating the adverse effect of a negative stereotype on the standardized test scores of white students.

Cecilia Ridgeway. "Status in Groups: The Importance of Motivation." *American Sociological Review* 47 (1982): 76–88.

> An important research article that suggests a way for women to achieve equal status in the workplace.

Muzafer Sherif, O. J. Harvey, B. Jack White, William R. Hood, and Carolyn W. Sherif. *The Robbers Cave Experiment: Intergroup Conflict and Cooperation* (Wesleyan University Press, [1961] 1988).

> The classic study on the origins of conflict between groups and a method for bringing together competing groups.

Claude M. Steele. "Thin Ice: 'Stereotype Threat' and Black College Students." *Atlantic Monthly.* August, 1999.

> An accessible overview of research and applied programs for reducing the disadvantage of black college students.

REVIEW QUESTIONS

1. In what ways might experiments on only a few individuals potentially contribute to sociological knowledge?

2. Muzafer Sherif conducted an experiment with 22 boys at a summer camp, separated into two groups, "Eagles" and "Rattlers." Explain why hostility developed between the two groups and the circumstances in which intergroup hostility could be reduced.
3. Describe the Hawthorne study, and explain what the "Hawthorne Effect" is. On what methodological grounds has this experiment been criticized?
4. The author mentions the ethical challenges posed by social-science experiments. If some experiments can offer a richer understanding of intergroup conflict and help explain surprisingly brutal behavior, why should Institutional Review Boards (IRBs) be involved in the research process?

patricia a. adler and peter adler

the promise and pitfalls of going into the field

66

spring 2003

firsthand reports from the field comprise some of the most valuable work in the social sciences. but findings are often controversial. understanding how fieldwork is carried out can help readers assess ethnographic research.

Barbara Ehrenreich, a white, divorced Ph.D. in her 50s, spent a year working low-wage jobs as a waitress in Florida, a housecleaner in Maine, and a Wal-Mart sales clerk in Minnesota. Her detailed ethnography, the best-selling *Nickel and Dimed,* reveals how physically demanding and personally demeaning these jobs are, and how workers are trapped in them. Ehrenreich's book has received wide critical acclaim, a typical book review in the *Minneapolis Star Tribune* calling it "piercing social criticism backed by first-rate reporting."

Some ethnographies are, however, more controversial. William Foote Whyte, then a young, Protestant graduate student at Harvard, wrote a classic ethnography of Italian-American youth in the early 1940s, *Street Corner Society,* describing the "corner boys" who hung around the neighborhood and participated in illegal activities. He described them as a "gang." Yet Marianne Boelen, an Italian immigrant to America who years later revisited his setting and re-interviewed his subjects, asserted that Whyte had made methodological and substantive errors in his work. These boys were not a gang, she claimed, but rather followed a typical Italian pattern: women occupied indoor space and men claimed the outdoors. He might have realized this had he paid greater attention to gender. His

errors also resulted, she alleged, from relying too closely on one key informant, "Doc," whose role he exaggerated.

That two important ethnographies can produce such different reactions, from critical acclaim to academic controversy, raises several questions about ethnographic methods. How can readers know if researchers have gotten the evidence and its interpretation right? What kinds of stories should we believe? We need to be able to assess the validity and value of ethnographic work, just as we do with other methods. Herbert Gans, in *The Urban Villagers,* notes that "every social research method is a mixture of art and science," but that participant observation is the best empirical research method available because it allows us to study, firsthand, what people do, think, and believe, in their own groups. While all methods may be subject to problems such as shaping findings to fit preconceptions, Gans continues, "ethnography is most successful when it becomes an all encompassing 14- to 16-hours a day experience, with at least a year's full-time fieldwork, and a good deal of additional time to analyze and think about the data."

Ethnography, as we defined it when we edited the *Journal of Contemporary Ethnography,* includes observing social activities as an outsider,

Philippe Bourgois during his study of a homeless encampment in San Francisco, 1994. (Photo courtesy of Philippe Bourgois)

observing while participating in the activities, and conducting intensive interviews. Considered the most accessible to readers of all the social scientific methods, ethnography draws on the language and perspective of everyday members of society, and is often written like investigative journalism. A successful ethnography captures readers' fancies, bringing them closer to the lives of others, and, like a good movie or book, offers insight into people's ordinary worlds. Literally translated as a "portrait of the people," ethnography describes and analyzes the beliefs, motivations, and rationales of a people in a particular setting or subculture. It makes the familiar distant and the distant familiar.

Although ethnography resembles journalism, it differs by requiring the systematic, long-term gathering of data and by engaging general theories of human behavior rather than simply reporting the news. Ethnography resembles literature as well, but differs in focusing on social trends and patterns rather than character development. Finally, ethnography differs from commonsense interpretations by drawing on meticulous field research rather than popular stereotypes. But as the controversy around Whyte's classic ethnography teaches us, it is not always obvious which ethnographic reports are sufficiently systematic, sufficiently accurate or sufficiently useful.

the ethnographic genre

Ethnography can be divided into three crucial stages: data gathering, data analysis, and data presentation. One might be an exemplary field researcher, able to fit into myriad social settings and to elicit the insiders' view from a variety of people, but this is not enough. Ethnographers need to step back as well, to take a detached look at people's worlds so they can analyze underlying patterns of behavior. These careful observations and astute interpretations must be backed up by prose that brings readers into people's complex lives. We will see how exemplary researchers optimize the rewards of fieldwork while avoiding its pitfalls.

data gathering

Good ethnography takes time. The strength of ethnographers' data depends on the quality and depth of the relationships they forge and the rapport and trust they establish with the people they study. Superficial relationships yield superficial insights. Researchers sometimes spend up to several years in the field, as we did in our studies of drug dealers and smugglers in *Wheeling and Dealing* and elite college athletes in *Backboards & Blackboards*.

Ethnographers, in having to gain people's trust, require highly developed social skills. They must be able to get along with all sorts of people, from powerful managers to weak employees. For instance, in an outstanding ethnography of the homeless, *Down on Their Luck*, Leon Anderson and David Snow spent parts of two years under bridges, in Salvation Army shelters and plasma centers, at the city hospital and police department, and on the streets of

notable ethnographies

Ethnography's vitality and breadth is shown by the number of awards given to books employing this approach in the past decade. Some recent titles have garnered special attention:

Anderson, Elijah. *Code of the Street*. New York: Norton, 1999. An examination of inner-city black America, this book describes the complex code of rules governing violence in urban areas.

Bourgois, Philippe. *In Search of Respect*. New York: Cambridge University Press, 1995. A provocative account of crack dealing in Spanish Harlem.

Casper, Monica. *The Making of the Unborn Patient*. New Brunswick, NJ: Rutgers University Press, 1998. Discusses controversies in biomedical experimentation by looking at doctors who perform surgeries on unborn babies.

Duneier, Mitchell. *Sidewalk*. New York: Farrar, Straus, and Giroux, 1999. An ethnography of poor black men who make their living selling magazines and secondhand goods on the streets of Greenwich Village.

Fine, Gary Alan. *Morel Tales*. Cambridge, MA: Harvard University Press, 1998. An insider's look at the subculture of mushroom collectors.

Hondagneu-Sotelo, Pierrette, *Domestica*. Berkeley: University of California Press, 2001. An excellent portrayal of the new immigrant women in Los Angeles who serve as housecleaners, nannies, and domestics.

Karp, David. *Speaking of Sadness*. New York: Oxford University Press, 1996. Using autobiographical and participant observation data, this book examines the lives of people who live with depression.

Miller, Jody. *One of the Guys*. New York: Oxford University Press, 2001. Drawing on comparative research in two Midwestern cities, this book looks at the underlying causes and meanings of female gang membership.

Mitchell, Richard. *Dancing at Armageddon: Survivalism and Chaos in Modern Times*. Chicago: University of Chicago Press, 2002. A rare look at a secretive group, survivalists, who inhabit the backwoods of America and prepare themselves for civilization's collapse.

Sanders, Clinton. *Understanding Dogs*. Philadelphia: Temple University Press, 1999. Explores the everyday experiences of living with canine companions.

Snow, David, and Leon Anderson. *Down on Their Luck*. Berkeley: University of California Press, 1993. Provides one of the most trenchant accounts of the problems involved with living on the streets of America today.

Austin, Texas (see "Street People," page 153). Ethnography also requires intimacy and commitment. For example, in studying drug traffickers, our long-term relationships with central figures were often tested by crises or suspicions of betrayal, and loyalty was expected on both sides during the six years of explicit research and for many years afterwards.

According to current thinking, ethnographers should get as near to the people they are studying as possible. Even studying one's self (auto-ethnography), as Carolyn Ellis did in *Final Negotiations*, where she documented the changing emotions she and her partner experienced as he was dying of emphysema, or as Carol Rambo Ronai did in her writings on incest, has become acceptable. Some ethnographers combine the intimacy of autobiography with the more general approach of talking to others who have gone through similar traumas or events. Best illustrated by David Karp in *Speaking of Sadness*, a study of manic-depressives, the author recounts his own bouts with depression as well as data gleaned from numerous observations and interviews with self-help groups for this illness. Karp's own experiences helped him gain participants' trust and gave him a deeper understanding of the emotional complexity of mood fluctuation. In evaluating ethnography, then, readers should pay attention to not only the length of time researchers spent in the field (a year or two tends to be the minimum depending upon the locale and topic of study), but also the depth of involvement they established with their subjects.

Sometimes problems arise when researchers are either too close or similar to their subjects or too distant or different from them. Researchers who are too close may "go native," uncritically accepting their subjects' perspectives. Researchers too distant may fail to penetrate beyond the fronts people design for public presentation. For example, Richard Mitchell, in *Dancing at Armageddon*, a study of survivalists, became involved with people whose behaviors evoked some repugnance. To forge the necessary rapport, he had to overcome his initial feelings of alienation, to spend time getting to know participants, and to establish friendship and trust on other planes. Readers who suspect ethnographers may have such problems should look for frank and personal methodological discussions that specifically address how they encountered and dealt with these issues.

Good ethnography is systematic, rigorous, and scientific. One of the chief criticisms leveled at ethnography is that it is anecdotal, careless, and casual, depending too much on researchers' subjectivity. Poor ethnography may result when researchers are biased by their own opinions or history, or when they carry their preconceived attitudes, either personal or professional, into the field and cannot transcend them. Derek Freeman aimed this charge against Margaret Mead, claiming that in *Coming of Age in Samoa* she uncritically accepted the assertions of a few adolescent girls about their uninhibited sexuality to support her mentor's views that nurture trumped nature. Bias may also result from researchers' poor location or sponsorship in the field, where their access to the group is somehow impeded. And researchers can generate problems when they fail to gather multiple perspectives or prefer their own beliefs to the beliefs of others. (Recently, some "postmodern" ethnographers have concluded that the process is so idiosyncratic that there should be no claims to describe the world, only to describe researchers' reactions to the world.)

To overcome these problems, ethnographers should include the voices of a full spectrum of participants, not just the ones they can easily reach. Generally, it is easier for researchers to "study down," looking at the downtrodden, the powerless, and the underclass, who, unlike the powerful, do not have the ability to insulate themselves. Researchers may also more easily gather data from people like themselves, overlooking members of dissimilar groups. Part of Boelen's allegation against Whyte was that his perspective was skewed toward "Doc," his key informant, a man much like himself. Good ethnography gains the perspectives of all involved, so that the ultimate portrait is rounded and thorough. In Jack Douglas and Paul Rasmussen's study, *The Nude Beach*, the voices of the nudists, other beachgoers, residents, and police are all heard, providing this sort of completeness. An ethnography that only privileges some voices and perspectives to the exclusion of others may not be as representative.

An array of methodological tactics may help to generate the multiple perspectives required. Ethnographers may combine direct observation, participation, interviewing, and casual conversation to triangulate their findings. For instance, in researching drug traffickers, we cross-checked our observations against our own common sense and general knowledge of the scene, against a variety of reliable, independent sources, and against hard evidence such as newspaper and magazine reports, arrest records, and material possessions. Similarly, Judith Rollins, in her study of domestics and their employers, *Between Women*, worked as a domestic for ten employers. In studying human-canine relationships for *Understanding Dogs*, Clinton Sanders not only drew on his own love of dogs and experiences as a dog owner, but also participated in the training of guide dogs and their owners, a "puppy kindergarten," observations of dogs and their owners in public settings, participant observation at a veterinary hospital for 14 months, and formal interviews with dog owners, veterinarians, and trainers.

To help readers assess what role the researchers' personal views played in their reports, an ethnographic report should include methodological reflections. Researchers use these "confessional tales" to explain problems, and then describe the ways they overcame them. Alan Peshkin confessed the problems he faced studying Bethany, a Christian fundamentalist community and school, for *God's Choice*: "I discovered, so to speak, that being Jewish would be the personal fact bearing most on my research . . . They taught their children never to be close friends, marry, or to go into business with someone like me. What they were expected to do with someone like me was to proselytize . . . To repeat, Bethany gored me." Yet, Peshkin was able to surmount his role as "odd man out" and to forge close research ties by living in the community for 18 months, attending all regular church and school activities, dressing and speaking as a member, and interviewing a significant portion of the school's teachers, students, and parents.

Ethical concerns are often raised about ethnography, since researchers interact so closely with their subjects and could potentially deceive or harm them. A maelstrom of controversy surrounded Laud Humphreys' *Tearoom Trade*, a study of impersonal homosexual encounters in public restrooms, partly because he was covert, observing without telling the men he watched that he was a researcher. Humphreys rejoined that he caused no harm to his subjects, and would not have been able to conduct the research under the strictures of "informed consent," rules that require the permission of those studied. New "Institutional Review Board" regulations at universities now require researchers to relinquish their data to the authorities, often raising conflicts between their loyalty to the people they studied and to the government. When faced with this dilemma, Rik Scarce went to jail for six months rather than turn over his field notes on environmental activists in the state of Washington to the police. Not everyone will take such drastic steps, though, and recent guidelines have been designed to safeguard subjects from their researchers by making sure people know that what they say cannot be protected.

Some feminist and "activist" ethnographers believe researchers improve their ethical stance by eschewing the traditional "value neutral" position and openly aligning themselves with their subjects, "making the personal political" and working for social change. Others seek an ethical stance in "taking their findings back to the field," showing their writings to subjects and asking for feedback. At the same time, however, some ethnographers believe this leads researchers to censor themselves from writing things their subjects might interpret as too critical, pushing them toward "going native" in the field.

Perhaps most importantly, good ethnography conveys what it is like to "walk in the shoes" of the people being studied. No other method lets researchers adequately study hidden, secretive, and sensitive groups, since deviants, criminals, and others with something to hide are unlikely to talk to strangers. Jeffrey Ferrell's work on illegal graffiti artists and Jeffrey Sluka's investigation of violent political combatants in Ireland, for example, provide insightful ethnographic research into subterranean worlds. Readers should understand people's joys, feel their frustrations and sorrows, and know their problematic, complex, and contradictory worlds. For instance, Karp's *Speaking of Sadness* delves deeply into the poignant fears and frustrations experienced by people who suffer from depression. One person Karp interviewed described the way depression stole away who she was and replaced her life with a black hole: "Depression is an insidious vacuum that crawls into your brain and pushes your mind out of the way. It is the complete absence of rational thought. It is freezing cold, with a dangerous, horrifying, terrifying fog wafting through whatever is left of your mind." In *Sidewalk*, Mitchell Duneier explains some of the practical problems that Greenwich Village African-American street vendors encounter in doing what we all take for granted: going to the bathroom. In the words of one of his informants: "I gotta get me a paper cup and I'm gonna be all right. . . . Now everybody out here gets a cup. You can't go to the bathroom in the stores and restaurants, because they don't want you in there if you ain't got no money to spend. So how you gonna piss? You gotta get a cup." Thus, we learn about not only the vernacular of the men themselves, but also the everyday turmoil that they encounter.

data analysis

Ethnographers begin forming their analyses early in their fieldwork, testing and refining them over time. Researchers usually remain near, or connected to their settings throughout the time they write up their data, to fill in holes they discover and to check their interpretations against their informants'. Yet their observations about the specifics of a particular time and place must be joined by more far-reaching, general analyses. They want, for example, to speak about not just a poor neighborhood, but poor neighborhoods in general. One test of how well ethnographers have succeeded in capturing more general patterns comes when people in comparable settings recognize the descriptions they read. For instance, in our college athlete study, we were frequently satisfied when we gave lectures at universities and athletes in the audience came up afterwards to say that we "got it right."

Good ethnography generates, modifies, extends, or challenges existing understandings of social life. For instance, Pierrette Hondagneu-Sotelo's study of immigrant domestic workers in Los Angeles, *Doméstica*, is powerful because it shows that American husbands' failures to share household duties and the influx of immigrant workers have combined to create a pattern in which housekeepers work in affluence but live in poverty.

data presentation

Ethnographers must write clearly and actively, avoiding jargon, highly technical terms, or obscure phrases. Ethnography also should "give voice" to participants, enabling readers to get a sense of how people converse and what language they use. In *Code of the Streets*, Elijah Anderson uses a voice from the neighborhood to explain why low-income African-American girls in vulnerable situations may become pregnant early: "I done see where four girls grow up under their mama . . . Mama working three to eleven o'clock at night . . . Can't nobody else tell 'em what to do. Hey, all of 'em pregnant by age sixteen. They can get they own baby, they get they own [welfare] check, they get they own apartment. They wanna get away from Mama."

What anthropologist Clifford Geertz called "thick description" is another hallmark of ethnography. Good ethnographies vividly present participants' stories, using colorful words, adjectives, or other literary devices to highlight the vibrancy of group culture. With sounds and action, Philippe Bourgois brings readers into the midst of the scene in this excerpt from *In Search of Respect*, his ethnography of Puerto Rican crack dealers in East Harlem: "But then when we stepped out of the room, she turns to me and whispers [snarling], 'You motherfucker.' She like turns on me again. And then I went [burying his head in his hands], 'Oh, my God.' And I got mad [making exaggerated whole-body wrestling motions], and I grabbed her by the neck, and I threw her to the sofa. [pounding fist to palm] BOOM . . . and I WHAAAAM, POOM [pounding again], smacked her in the face with all my might." Even when the subject matter is disturbing, it should be easy, not hard, to read this type of social science.

Successful ethnography elicits the "uh-huh" effect in readers, presenting subjects' everyday behavior in ways that people can recognize. Lyn Lofland, an observer of public places, succinctly summarized behavior that we all do, but rarely acknowledge. She described how people get ready to enter a public space: they "check for readiness" (clothes, grooming, mirror glances), "take a personal reading" (pause, scan the area, check the layout), and "reach a position" (find a secure location or niche). These sorts of rich and resonating descriptions serve to authenticate ethnographic presentations.

the contributions of ethnography

In making the familiar distant, researchers find new ways of looking at what we think we know and bringing the unknown to light. Weak ethnography runs the risk of rediscovering the obvious. Poorly presented ethnography may stop at subjects' understandings of their worlds, or may analyze these in mundane, trivial or superficial ways. Gary Alan Fine's work is notable for introducing readers to the nuances of unusual subcultures, such as mushroom collecting, or taking familiar worlds, such as the Little League, and providing a framework for a much broader understanding of children's culture.

Good ethnography may also be socially influential. It may speak to social policy and public awareness as well as to scholarly knowledge and theoretical understanding. For example, Arlie Hochschild brought recognition to contemporary working women—who still do most of the housework and child care—with her research on *The Second Shift*. What seemed to be individuals' personal problems, she showed, emerged from social changes affecting many families. In the 1990s, government agencies implemented programs to distribute condoms, clean needles, and bleach after ethnographies of the drug world exposed the HIV dangers in the practices of street people. Whether or how ethnographic findings are used depends on the administration in power and the tenor of the times, however. The traditionally liberal leanings of sociologists have made their suggestions more appealing to Democratic politicians. Others believe, however, that ethnography should take theory-building, not political activism, as its goal. As famed ethnographer Erving Goffman put it: "I can only suggest that he who would combat false consciousness and awaken people to their true interests has much to do, because the sleep is very deep. And I do not intend to provide a lullaby, but merely to sneak in and watch the people snore."

Ethnography has the power to incite, infuriate, enthrall, and excite. Ethnographers need to be careful in their representation of others, scrupulous in how they relate to informants in order to obtain data, and true to their own integrity in not violating others' privacy. However, their stories are vital, allowing readers insight into worlds to which they will never be privy or to ones that they would otherwise never understand. The great ethnographies endure for decades because the evidence is accessible, the messages remain critical, and the stories of people's complex worlds continue to be fresh and insightful.

RECOMMENDED RESOURCES

Paul Atkinson, Amanda Coffey, Sara Delamont, John Lofland, and Lyn Lofland. *Handbook of Ethnography* (Sage, 2001).

A useful resource on the history of ethnography, its current disciplinary borders, substantive foci, and methodological advances.

Norman K. Denzin and Yvonna Lincoln. *Handbook of Qualitative Research*, 2nd ed. (Sage, 2000).

A definitive source on controversies, nuances, and new directions for all qualitative research, but particularly focused on ethnography.

http://www.soc.sbs.ohio-state.edu/rdh/welist.htm.

A comprehensive website that lists workplace ethnographies.

This inventory of articles and books includes ethnographic research on organizations, cutting across a wide variety of disciplines.

John Lofland and Lyn Lofland. *Analyzing Social Settings*, 3rd ed. (Wadsworth, 1995).

First published in 1971, this is the longest standing primer on doing ethnography, covering data gathering, data analysis, and data presentation.

REVIEW QUESTIONS

1. Define "ethnography." How does it differ from journalism?

2. One of the most challenging aspects of ethnography is also one of its main benefits: The close, personal contact with respondents and the rich, meaningful tales that intimacy provides may come into conflict with a felt need for "objectivity." Write two paragraphs on the challenge of being both "participant" and "observer." How do the costs and benefits of this approach resonate with your own notions of sociology and science?

3. From class readings and your own understanding of sociological research, discuss what you think the role of theory should be in ethnography. Should one keep theory out of the process of data collection and analysis? Is this possible? Should theory be established at the outset, as something to be proved or disproved? Should it be "built" from the "ground up"?

4. Activity: Pick a social setting. Write two paragraphs describing the character of the place, the people one finds there, and the activities that take place within it. Try to evoke the "feel" of this setting as much as possible for the reader. Now write a third paragraph attempting to generalize from your description to a broader social issue raised somewhere within this *Reader* (e.g., power, racism, sexuality, inequality).

robert s. weiss

in their own words: making the most of qualitative interviews

67

fall 2004

successfully conducting in-depth interviews requires much more than being a good listener. researchers must choose interview subjects carefully, push for concrete details, and pore over reams of transcripts to develop their stories. but the result can be a rich and compelling understanding of people's lives.

In the 1840s, British sociologist-journalist Henry Mayhew sought to learn about the lives of London's seamstresses—how they did their work and managed to survive on so little income. He found his answers by asking the women themselves and his interviews made vivid the dismal conditions of their lives. One young woman, after describing how little she was paid for long hours of work, said: "I was single. . . . I had a child, and he used to cry for food. So, as I could not get a living for him myself by my needle, I went into the streets and made out a living that way." The novels of Charles Dickens captured readers' sympathies, but they were only fiction. Mayhew presented the experiences of real people.

Such "qualitative interviews" are now so common that it is easy to forget how radical Henry Mayhew's procedure—which assumes that ordinary people can provide valid accounts of their own lives—was in his day. Indeed, qualitative interviewing was considered by many researchers so simple that it required no special techniques; listening attentively and respectfully was enough. More recently, practitioners have recognized that training is needed to make the most of interviewing and to avoid its pitfalls.

Studies based on in-depth interviews illuminate the social world. They describe the survival struggles of families on welfare, the ups and downs of physicists' careers and the tendency of two-job couples to assign homemaking to the wives. They reveal the emotional and social implications of organizational charts, from prisons to medical schools. Diane Vaughan's interview study of the bureaucratic processes that led to the disastrous 1986 *Challenger* launch has become an important reference for institutions—medical schools as well as NASA—trying to reduce catastrophic errors.

The type of interview used in these studies is often called "qualitative" to distinguish it from an interview done for a survey. Qualitative interviews ask about the details of what happened: what was done and said, what the respondent thought and felt. The aim is to come as close as possible to capturing in full the processes that led to an event or experience. The researchers' report will likely be a densely detailed description of what happened, but it may also provide a basis for a theory of why it happened. In contrast, surveys ask well-crafted questions that elicit brief answers. The answers are then added up and expressed as numbers or percentages. Surveys are quantitative; they report the distribution of people's actions or opinions in tables or statistics (see "Sense and Nonsense about Surveys," page 472). In-depth interviews yield descriptions of experiences, processes, and events.

More than any other technique social scientists use, in-depth interviewing can shed light on events that would otherwise remain unknown because they happened in the past or out of public sight. In-depth interviews can provide vivid descriptions of personal experience—for example, what it feels like to succeed or to fail at an undertaking, or the emotional consequences of a new child or a death in the family. They are the best source of information about people's thoughts and feelings and the motives and emotions that lead them to act as they do.

but can we trust what we are told?

For her study of religiously inspired terrorism, national security expert Jessica Stern interviewed leaders of terrorist groups. They seemed entirely truthful when they told her about their commitment to producing a better world, but when she asked about the sources of their funds, they exaggerated the importance of small gifts and minimized contributions from wealthy donors. Most of those who were widely known to have received funds from governments simply lied. The adequacy and accuracy of interview data depends on what respondents are willing to report.

Lies or evasions such as these are not the only way interview findings can be compromised. Even respondents who want to be accurate may distort. Memory of an event is never simply a replay of a mental videotape. It is a reconstruction, an integration of fragments of stored knowledge, perceptions, and emotions. From these elements people build a coherent story, perhaps accompanied by visualized scenes of the event. The account and its accompanying images may be close to what happened, but inevitably there will be omissions, distortions, and additions.

Psychologist Elizabeth Loftus and her students have repeatedly demonstrated that memory is vulnerable to false associations. In one study, they showed subjects who lived in the Disneyland area advertisements in which Bugs Bunny appeared as a member of the Disneyland staff. Actually, Bugs Bunny has never entered Disneyland; he is a Warner Brothers property. But nearly a quarter of the subjects who read the false advertisements later reported meeting Bugs Bunny at Disneyland. They seemed to have put together memories of an actual visit to Disneyland with awareness of a link between Disneyland and Bugs Bunny, forgetting that the awareness stemmed from the advertisements. How can sociologists depend on data that are so fallible? And how can readers assess the trustworthiness of their reports?

To begin with, things are not so bad; it is easy to exaggerate the unreliability of interview data. Loftus and her students found that when her subjects reported a false memory, they tended to be less confident than when they reported something that had actually happened. Other indicators of the trustworthiness of a report include the density of detail the respondent provides, the apparent vividness of recall, and the extent to which the respondent's description makes sense in the context of his or her life.

Reports based mainly on interviews are often strengthened by the inclusion of other kinds of information. Jessica Stern, in her report on terrorism, provided a context for her interviews by describing the settings in which the interviews were held: homes, hotel rooms, restaurants, house trailers, and isolated terrorist camps. She also described the dress, manner, and facial features of the terror group members she interviewed and her own reactions of sympathy, repugnance, and fear. In her *Challenger* report, Diane Vaughan relied on interviews to explain what could not be understood from NASA's internal memos, but she reported the memos as well. Often a survey can strengthen arguments based primarily on qualitative interviews, by showing how one person's story or opinion fits into larger patterns.

The interviewer's direct observations can also help readers judge whether skepticism is appropriate. Did a respondent seem to be straightforward or evasive? The interviewer's observations of settings can corroborate what respondents say, as when a view of spacious grounds supports a respondent's claim that an organization is successful, but it can also contradict their claims, as when someone professing asceticism is interviewed in an opulent setting.

doing it right

The cooperation of the respondent is of paramount importance to the success of an interview. While full cooperation cannot always be achieved, cooperation is likely to be maximized by an interviewer who is respectful and friendly, yet task-focused. In my own research, I bring two copies of consent forms describing the study to my interviewees, both copies bearing my signature. After briefly explaining the study, I give both forms to the respondent, ask him or her to read one and, if comfortable with it, to sign one of the copies and keep the other. I usually have a tape recorder and ask if it is all right to turn it on. My aim is to establish that the respondent and I are coworkers in producing information the study requires.

A good research partnership is more important to the quality of the interview than the phrasing of specific questions. If the respondent and I get along well, he or she will accept that the detailed accounts I request are important for the study and will tolerate any fumbling or uncertainty in my questions.

In qualitative interviewing, questions are usually formulated during the interview rather than written out beforehand. There are no magic phrasings which will reliably elicit illuminating responses. However, there are several principles that are helpful. Concrete observations are almost always more useful than a respondent's generalizations. It is hard to guess from generalizations what underlying events the respondent is drawing on, or even whether the generalizations are based on specific events at all. So if a respondent says, "We got along fine," the interviewer should ask something like, "When you say that, what are you thinking of?" or "Can you tell me the last time that happened?" or "Can you think of a time that really showed that happening?" It can sometimes help for an interviewer to add, "The more concrete you can be, the better."

Respondents can provide fuller and more accurate reports if they are asked about events that happened recently. To know about the respondent's use of time, it makes sense to ask about yesterday; to learn about an event that occurs frequently, it makes sense to ask about the last time it happened. Should the respondent object that yesterday or the most recent event was not typical, it is then possible to ask what made it unusual, and then to ask for a description of an earlier day or event that was more nearly typical.

When a respondent is describing an important sequence of events, the interviewer might mentally check that the description contains adequate detail. In a study of work stress in an organization, a respondent might say, "I knew I was in trouble so I looked up this vice president and asked him for help." The interviewer might then have the respondent fill in what happened between when he recognized that he had a problem and when he asked for help from a particular executive. So, the interviewer might ask, "Could you start with when you realized you were in trouble and walk me through what happened next? How did the thought of going to the vice president come to you and what happened then?"

Although qualitative interviews are sometimes called conversational, they are not. Imagine a conversation in which a retiree, asked by a

The following excerpts are from a study of retirement. The first part illustrates the sort of specific interview material a researcher might obtain. It is drawn from one of about a dozen interviews that address "puttering." The second part illustrates how such data are integrated into a general report.

Excerpts

Interviewer: What are your days like?

Respondent: Very quiet and uneventful.

Interviewer: Like yesterday, what, how did yesterday work? Maybe start in the morning.

Respondent: Well, I, I got up, had some breakfast I went out, ah, went out for about three or four hours and did a little bit of window shopping, a little Christmas shopping. I got back around noontime or so. Ah, I had lunch, watched the news . . . then just puttered around the house. Then I usually go to bed around 9 or 10 o'clock. Last night it was 10 o'clock. I had supper and watched television for a while and then I usually go to bed. But, like I said, very unexciting, very uneventful.

Interviewer: If you wanted to describe a really boring hour and get across what it felt like and what was going on. . . .

Respondent: Well I don't have a problem with that. I, ah, I can sit down and do absolutely nothing for an hour. And it doesn't bother me. I enjoy a chance to relax and not have the pressure of having to do something.

Report

Puttering is a relaxed way of moving through a day, engaging in activities as they attract one's attention, undertaking nothing that demands energy and concentration. The dishes need doing, so why not do them now? It's nice out, and a bit of gardening might be enjoyable. It's noontime, time for a sandwich and the news on television. Later, magazines need to be picked up and a room straightened. There is time for a bit of reading. E-mail may be checked, or an hour taken to organize the attic. Nothing has special urgency.

Retirees seem not to be bored by puttering. There is always something to fill time with, and the puttering is regularly interrupted by an activity to attend to, a hobby to pursue, a walk, or a bit of shopping or coffee with a friend. Mr. Oldsten was among the many respondents who liked taking it easy. He had been the purchasing director for a high-tech company, a job that was frequently stressful. His wife was still employed and so he spent most of the day alone.

Yesterday, I got up, had some breakfast, I went out for about three or four hours and did a little bit of window shopping. I got back around noontime or so. I had lunch, watched the news, then just puttered around the house. I had supper and watched television for a while. I usually go to bed around 9 or 10 o'clock, last night it was 10 o'clock. Very unexciting, very uneventful. I can sit down and do absolutely nothing for an hour. And it doesn't bother me. I enjoy a chance to relax and not have the pressure of having to do something.

friend whether he had gone back to the office to see the people he had worked with, had replied, "People who come back after they've retired, the people who're there are nice, but there's nothing to talk about." The friend would hardly press the retiree for details he had not volunteered by asking, "Is there a specific time you're thinking of? Can you walk me through what happened?" But those are the questions an interviewer would ask.

shaping the study

Good interviews are windows into people's lives. Researchers can often edit the transcripts to cut out the questions and rearrange respondents' answers into engrossing first-person stories. Anthropologist Oscar Lewis, in his book *Children of Sanchez*, painted a compelling portrait of the lives of people in an impoverished Mexican family by presenting edited transcripts of qualitative interviews with the family's father and his four adult children. Journalist Studs Terkel has used excerpts from qualitative interviews as the entire content of books such as *Working*, in which his respondents discuss their jobs.

Both Lewis and Terkel focused on the stories of particular individuals, but many social scientists want to generalize about people's experiences and so want the breadth of information that multiple cases can provide. They want to be able to report not only about one particular retiree's experience, but about the experience of a population of retirees. That requires a sample of cases that includes the full range of important differences in the population. For example, an investigator studying the experience of retiring would want to talk with retirees from a range of occupations, both men and women, the married and unmarried, and people who liked their work and those who hated it.

Sometimes the topic makes it difficult to obtain a good sample. For example, in a study of active drug users an investigator may be restricted to a small group within which he or she finds acceptance. Investigators in such situations must make do, but they must also be aware of the limitations of their sample. They may learn how their respondents are distinct, but in any case, generalizations from unsystematic "convenience samples" have to be treated with caution.

Several factors must be taken into account when determining how many people should be interviewed. The more varied the population, the larger the sample needs to be to cover an adequate range. A study of retired executives requires a broader sample than one of retired bankers. Also important is the extent to which the investigator wants more than one respondent from the same category—for example, how many retired bankers? Redundancy can compensate for omissions and distortions, and can also uncover important variations among people who are apparently similar.

If there seem to be between a half dozen and a dozen important types of respondents, and if the investigator would like five instances of each variation, a sample size of between 30 and 60 is a rough ideal. The larger the sample, the more confidence the investigator will have that there is adequate range and enough redundancy to make other important, perhaps unsuspected, differences apparent.

Most investigators find that the amount of data produced by qualitative interviewing sets an upper limit on the number of respondents. One and a half hours of interviewing can produce 40 single-spaced pages of typescript. A study with 80 respondents might come close to filling a file drawer. Follow-up interviews with each respondent can double the volume. In my experience, 100 respondents are the most that can be dealt with comfortably, and so large a sample will almost surely provide enough material to yield an adequate basis for trustworthy generalization.

what to do with the data

Analyzing interview data can be daunting. There is likely to be a great deal of it, and no obvious place to start. Researchers may read through a few transcripts and feel excited by what is there, yet wonder how they can ever extract the essential message of those few transcripts, let alone the entire set. But there are fairly systematic ways of proceeding.

Just as in solving a jigsaw puzzle, the analysis of qualitative interview material requires sorting and integrating. For a study on retirement, one might begin by separating out the materials that deal with the decision to retire, with retirement parties, with the immediate reaction to being retired and so on. Within each of the sorted sets of materials, the investigator will identify "meaning units"—passages that deal with the same issue. A respondent's description of being urged to retire by a boss can be a single meaning unit, whether it was a brief comment or a full story. The investigator then summarizes all the mean-

These audio tapes and written transcripts provide a durable record of in-depth interviews with teachers from two different schools about recent school reforms. The transcripts were subsequently coded and imported into a computer database so that passages from different interviewees addressing the same issue could be compared systematically.

ing units dealing with an issue. That summary, perhaps augmented by interpretations or explanations, constitutes a report on the particular sector. The final study is then produced by integrating all of the sector reports into a single coherent story.

Before computers, researchers made marginal notes on interview transcripts, cut out passages with scissors, and sorted the resulting slips of paper into physical file folders. Computers have changed all this into virtual cutting and sorting. Some investigators use one of several computer programs designed specifically to assist in analyzing interview materials.

Investigators sometimes want to do more than use responses to narrate a subject, they want to explain what they have found. Developing an explanatory theory is a task that inevitably challenges the investigator's knowledge, insight, and creativity. But researchers have the ability to return to their interview transcripts to assess the validity of their conclusions in light of everything they were told.

rooting out bias

In recent years, social scientists who do qualitative interview studies have questioned some of the assumptions that underlie this method. Two lines of critique have been especially important. The feminist critique focuses primarily on the relationship of interviewer and respondent, while the constructivist approach is more concerned with interpretation of interview materials.

The feminist critique arose from the experiences female investigators had while interviewing other women. The researchers were struck by the difference between their relationships with respondents and the sort of relationships that had been taken for granted in earlier studies. Previously, rapport was recognized as important, but respondents were largely related to only as providers of data, people whose words would be taken down, analyzed, and interpreted. Feminist scholars feel that this approach dehumanizes respondents and requires researchers to deny any identification with the interviewees. They feel it is essential to acknowledge their kinship with respondents. After all, the researchers were themselves insiders in their respondents' worlds: they too have families and family problems, work to which they are committed and priorities to juggle. It is more in keeping with this reality to replace inquiring with sharing.

Feminist investigators, among whom Ann Oakley has been a leading figure, also dislike the idea that after extracting information from respondents, they have nothing further to do with them. They want to acknowledge that interviewing establishes a relationship and that gaining access to someone's private life brings with it responsibilities. They feel it important to be of help to those respondents who are doing badly or, at the least, to accurately represent their plight. They also dislike the idea of owning the data drawn from respondents' lives. Some discuss their reports with their respondents and modify statements with which respondents disagree.

Constructivist investigators, such as Kathy Charmaz, were worried by investigators' insufficiently reflective leap from the reports of respondents to more general conclusions. They recognize that interpretations are not implicit in the data, but rather are influenced by the ideas and concerns that investigators bring to the data. In their view, investigators should acknowledge explicitly that their conclusions do not capture reality in the way that one might capture a butterfly. Instead, investigators shape respondents' reports in many possible ways. For example, a respondent's description of a problem with a boss may be classified as an instance of organizational friction rather than as a cause of work stress.

The constructivist perspective recasts the question of how close to reality an investigator can really get by talking to people. It argues that there is no single clear-cut reality to be located by means of interviews. Rather, what an investigator makes of interview information depends on his or her preconceptions and concerns. The interviews themselves may provide a basis for a number of interpretations, each of them consistent with the interview information.

The feminist and constructivist critiques draw attention to problems of ethics and interpretation that are implicit in the conduct of qualitative interview studies. When judging the credibility of a report these issues should be considered alongside other possible challenges, such as respondent credibility and the potential for investigator bias.

Perhaps the major threat to the validity of qualitative interviewing studies, more than distortions during the interview, is investigator bias. An investigator who is determined, consciously or unconsciously, to have a particular theme emerge from his or her study can choose respondents whose interviews are likely to produce that picture, encourage the respondents to give answers consistent with it, and write a report that neglects whatever might disconfirm it. Only a small minority of qualitative interview studies are significantly biased and these can usually be recognized easily.

reading interview studies

How can a reader evaluate a qualitative interview study? A good place to begin is with the sample. If the study was of people in a similar situation, did the sample have adequate range and redundancy? Did the interviews take place in a setting that encouraged respondents to provide full and accurate reports? If an event was witnessed by a number of people, are all relevant perspectives represented? And did the interview guide cover the full range of relevant issues? (Reports will often include an "interview guide," a list of the topics covered in the interviews, in an appendix.)

The trustworthiness of the data interpretation also can be judged by how closely it seems to be linked to the interviews, whether it appears to take all the interviews into consideration and the extent to which key points are buttressed by convincing quotations. Also worth considering is the investigator's use of supporting data from quantitative studies or from interviewers' observations. Finally, the investigator's conclusions could be matched against the conclusions of other studies and evaluated for their consistency with everything else the reader knows.

More than 150 years after Mayhew's groundbreaking work, qualitative interviewing is and will remain a fundamental method of social science. Even if other sources of information exist in archives or are accessible to observation, only qualitative interviewing can provide firsthand access to the experience of others. An oft-repeated joke describes a drunk searching for a lost wallet under a streetlight. "Did you drop it here?" someone asks. "Nope," he replies. "Dropped it in the alley. But the light's better here." Qualitative interviewing is looking in the dark alley, whatever might be the problems of doing so. If we want to learn from the experiences of other people, we must ask them to inform us. Although we are much more knowledgeable about how to conduct an interview than was Mayhew, and more aware of the difficulties that can arise as we try to achieve understanding from the information we obtain, fundamentally our approach remains the same.

RECOMMENDED RESOURCES

Kathy Charmaz. "Grounded Theory: Objectivist and Constructivist Methods." In *Handbook of Qualitative Research*, eds. Norman Denzin and Yvonna Lincoln (Sage Publications, 2000).

This is both a brief exposition of how to do a qualitative study and a discussion of constructivist ideas.

Joseph C. Hermanowicz. *The Stars Are Not Enough: Scientists—Their Passions and Professions* (University of Chicago Press, 1998).

Describes the interplay of ambition, career, and self-appraisal among physicists.

Arlie Russell Hochschild, with Anne Machung. *The Second Shift: Working Parents and the Revolution at Home* (Viking, 1989).

Describes the unequal distribution of familial responsibilities in two-job families.

Oscar Lewis. *The Children of Sanchez, Autobiography of a Mexican Family* (Random House, 1961).

In this classic study, Lewis recounts the life stories of a Mexican worker and his children.

Ann Oakley. "Interviewing Women: A Contradiction in Terms." In *The American Tradition in Qualitative Research* Vol. III, eds. Norman Denzin and Yvonna S. Lincoln (Sage Publications, 2001).

An influential feminist critique of traditional approaches to interviewing.

Jessica Stern. *Terror in the Name of God: Why Religious Militants Kill* (HarperCollins, 2003).

Uncovers the aims, strategies, and motives of terrorists who believe they are doing God's work.

Diane Vaughan. *The Challenger Launch Decision: Risky Technology, Culture, and Deviance at NASA* (University of Chicago Press, 1996).

Describes the rational decision making that led to the tragically mistaken Challenger launch.

Robert S. Weiss. *Learning from Strangers: The Art and Method of Qualitative Interview Studies* (Free Press, 1994).

A text on qualitative interview methods.

REVIEW QUESTIONS

1. What are some reasons for being careful about trusting interviewees? How can such problems be minimized?
2. Why is cooperation important in qualitative interviews?
3. What are the feminist and "constructivist" critiques of qualitative interviews? How do these critiques recast the relationship between interviewer and respondent?
4. Activity: Develop a 15-question interview to administer to one of your classmates. Prepare both closed and open questions (see the Schuman article on surveys, page 472), and be ready to improvise during the interview session. Afterwards, drawing on the "From Interview to Report" sidebar, prepare your own report of the interview. Which questions elicited the most interesting or unexpected answers, and why?

editors

Jeff Goodwin edited *Contexts* magazine with James Jasper from 2005 to 2007. He is the author of *No Other Way Out: States and Revolutionary Movements, 1945–1991* (2001) and coeditor (with Jasper) of *The Social Movements Reader* (2003) and *Rethinking Social Movements* (2004). He teaches sociology at New York University.

James M. Jasper teaches at the Graduate Center of the City University of New York. His most recent book is *Getting Your Way: Strategic Dilemmas in Real Life* (2006), which presents a sociological alternative to game theory that incorporates culture and emotions. For more information, or to leave suggestions and comments about the reader, visit his website: www.jamesjasper.org.

contributors

Patricia A. Adler is professor of sociology at the University of Colorado, Boulder. She is the coauthor (with Peter Adler) of *Wheeling and Dealing* (1993), *Peer Power* (1998), and *Paradise Laborers* (2004).

Peter Adler is professor of sociology at the University of Denver.

Leon Anderson is professor of sociology at Ohio University. Anderson is currently researching the regulation of the international blood products industry and the social organization of sport skydiving.

Mikaila Mariel Lemonik Arthur recently completed her Ph.D. at New York University. Her dissertation explores the creation of women's and ethnic studies programs at U.S. colleges and universities.

Jack Barbalet is an Australian sociologist currently working in England. In addition to the sociology of emotions, his interests include political and economic sociology and the sociology of science.

Frank D. Bean is professor of sociology and director of the Center for Research on Immigration, Population and Public Policy at the University of California, Irvine. His most recent book, coauthored with Gillian Stevens, is *Amer-*

ica's Newcomers and the Dynamics of Diversity (2003).

Courtney Bender is assistant professor of religion and sociology at Columbia University. She is the author of *Heaven's Kitchen: Living Religion at God's Love We Deliver* (2003).

Mitch Berbrier is associate professor and chair of sociology at the University of Alabama, Huntsville. He has authored several articles, including "Assimilationism and Pluralism as Cultural Tools," *Sociological Forum* (2004).

Lisa F. Berkman is Thomas D. Cabot Professor of Public Policy at the Harvard School of Public Health. She coedited *Social Epidemiology* (2000), the first systematic report on the social determinants of health.

Fred Block is a professor of sociology at the University of California, Davis, and a senior fellow with the Longview Institute, a progressive think tank.

Paul Burstein is professor of sociology at the University of Washington, Seattle. His research focuses on policy change in democratic countries, analyzing how issues get on the public agenda, how problems are defined, and how policy proposals are developed.

Wendy Cadge teaches sociology at Bowdoin College. She is the author of *Heartwood: the First Generation of Theravada Buddhism in America* (2003).

Mark Chaves is professor of sociology at the University of Arizona. He is the author of *Ordaining Women: Culture and Conflict in Religious Organizations* (1997) and *Congregations in America* (2004).

Andrew J. Cherlin is Griswold Professor of Public Policy in the department of sociology at Johns Hopkins University. He has written widely about American family life.

Daniel Chirot is professor of sociology and international studies at the University of Washington, Seattle. He is the author of *Modern Tyrants* (1994), *How Societies Change* (1994), and (with Clark McCauley) *Why Not Kill Them All? The Logic and Prevention of Mass Political Murder* (2006).

Lee Clarke, a sociologist at Rutgers University, writes about organizations, culture, and disasters. His most recent book is *Worst Cases: Terror and Catastrophe in the Popular Imagination* (2006).

Dan Clawson teaches sociology at the University of Massachusetts, Amherst. With Naomi Gerstel and Robert Zussman, he coedited *Families at Work: Expanding the Bounds* (2002).

Patricia Hill Collins is professor of sociology at the University of Maryland, College Park, and professor emeritus of African American studies at the University of Cincinnati.

Dalton Conley is University Professor of the Social Sciences and chair of sociology at New York University. He has written or edited several books and many articles on racial inequalities and the measurement of class and social status.

Gerald F. Davis is Wilbur K. Pierpont Professor of Management and Organizations at the Ross School of Business, University of Michigan. His research examines the influence of politics and social networks on corporate governance.

Kathryn Edin is professor of sociology at the University of Pennsylvania. She is coauthor (with Maria Kefalas) of *Promises I Can Keep: Why Poor Women Put Motherhood before Marriage* (2005).

Jennifer Edwards is a Ph.D. student in the department of sociology at the University of Washington, Seattle. Her work focuses on the causes and consequences of ethnic violence in Southeast Asia.

Bonnie Erickson is professor of sociology at the University of Toronto. She studies social networks, culture, inequality, work, and gender.

John H. Evans teaches sociology at the University of California, San Diego. He is the author of *Playing God? Human Genetic Engineering and the Rationalization of Public Bioethical Debate* (2002).

George Farkas is professor of sociology, demography, and education at Pennsylvania State University. His research focuses on schooling inequality and how it can be reduced. His tutoring project, Reading One-to-One, inspired President Clinton's America Reads program.

John E. Farley has written four books, including *Majority-Minority Relations*, 5th ed. (2005). He recently retired after teaching sociology for twenty-eight years at Southern Illinois University, Edwardsville.

Richard B. Felson is Professor of Crime, Law, and Justice and Sociology at Pennsylvania State University. His current research concerns the role of alcohol in different types of assaults, race differences in violence, and the relationship between academic performance and delinquency.

Frank F. Furstenberg Jr. is Zellerbach Family Professor of Sociology at the University of Pennsylvania. His current research focuses on the family in disadvantaged urban neighborhoods, adolescent sexual behavior and children's well-being.

Jay Gabler is currently a Ph.D. candidate in sociology at Harvard University. His research concerns the production and reception of culture and the social/organizational construction of childhood.

Joshua Gamson teaches sociology at the University of San Francisco. He is the author of *Claims to Fame: Celebrity in Contemporary America* (1994), *Freaks Talk Back: Tabloid Talk Shows and Sexual Nonconformity* (1998), and *The Fabulous Sylvester: The Legend, the Music, the Seventies in San Francisco* (2005).

William A. Gamson is professor of sociology and codirects the Media Research and Action Project (MRAP), Boston College. He is currently working on a game simulating the effects of globalization and political action.

Herbert J. Gans is the author of many books, including *Making Sense of America* (1999), which reports some of his work on race and ethnicity.

Kathleen Gerson teaches sociology at New York University. She is author (with Jerry A. Jacobs) of *The Time Divide* (2004) and *No Man's Land: Men's Changing Commitments to Family and Work* (1993).

Naomi Gerstel teaches at the University of Massachusetts, Amherst. Her current research examines gender and racial differences in care given to relatives and friends as well as the processes shaping work hours and schedules.

Erich Goode is emeritus professor of sociology at the State University of New York, Stony Brook. He is the author of ten books, mainly on drug use and deviance.

Joseph R. Gusfield helped inspire the "cultural turn" in sociology through books such as *Symbolic Crusade* (1986), *The Culture of Public Problems* (1980), and *Contested Meanings* (1996).

Dianne Hagaman is an artist and photographer who lives and works in San Francisco. She is the author of *How I Learned Not to Be a Photojournalist* (1996).

Douglas Hartmann teaches sociology at the University of Minnesota. His first book, *Race, Culture and the Revolt of the Black Athlete* (2003), was about the 1968 African-American Olympic protest movement.

Cedric Herring is professor of sociology at the University of Illinois, Chicago (UIC). He is former president of the Association of Black Sociologists and Founding Director of the Institute for Research on Race and Public Policy at UIC.

Allan V. Horwitz teaches sociology at Rutgers University. For the past thirty years, he has studied various social aspects of mental disorders and normality.

Robert Max Jackson is professor of sociology at New York University. He recently completed five years as editor of *Sociological Forum*.

Jerry A. Jacobs is Merriam Term Professor of Sociology at the University of Pennsylvania. He is coauthor (with Kathleen Gerson) of *The Time Divide* (2004).

Jason Kaufman played last-string doubles on his high school tennis team. He is currently John L. Loeb Associate Professor of the Social Sciences at Harvard University.

Maria Kefalas is an ethnographer who writes about social class, community, and culture. She teaches at Saint Joseph's University in Philadelphia.

Sheela Kennedy is a Ph.D. candidate in sociology and demography at the University of Pennsylvania. She is completing her dissertation on the relationship between education and recent shifts in U.S. and European family formation patterns.

Howard Kimeldorf has written extensively on the history of the American labor movement, including *Battling for American Labor* (1999). He is a professor of sociology at the University of Michigan, Ann Arbor.

Michael S. Kimmel is a sociologist at the State University of New York, Stony Brook. He is the author of a number of books on men and masculinity, including *Against the Tide: Pro-Feminist Men in the United States, 1776–1990* (1992), and *Manhood in America: A Cultural History* (1996).

Anna C. Korteweg is assistant professor of sociology at the University of Toronto. She researches gender, welfare, and immigrant integration policies in North America and Europe.

Charles Kurzman teaches sociology and Islamic studies at the University of North Carolina, Chapel Hill. He has edited two anthologies of Islamic thought, *Liberal Islam* (1998) and *Modernist Islam, 1840–1940* (2002), and has written *The Unthinkable Revolution in Iran* (2004).

Pearl Latteier is a Ph.D. candidate in communication arts at the University of Wisconsin, Madison. She is working on a dissertation about Hollywood social problem films.

Jennifer Lee is a sociologist at the University of California, Irvine. She is author of *Civility in the City: Blacks, Jews, and Koreans in Urban America* (2002) and coedited (with Min Zhou) *Asian American Youth: Culture, Identity, and Ethnicity* (2006).

Peggy Levitt teaches sociology at Wellesley College and is a research fellow at the Hauser Center for Nonprofit Organizations at Harvard University. She is the author of *The Transnational Villagers* (2001) and coeditor (with Mary Waters) of *The Changing Face of Home: The Transnational Lives of the Second Generation* (2003).

John Logan is professor of sociology at Brown University. His books include *Urban Fortunes: The Political Economy of Place* (1987), *Beyond the City Limits: Urban Policy and Economic Restructuring in Comparative Perspective* (1990), and *The New Chinese City: Globalization and Market Reform* (2002).

Michael J. Lovaglia is chair of the department of sociology at the University of Iowa. His interest include social psychology, especially power and status processes, the reciprocal effects of evolution and physiology on social behavior, social factors that affect academic performance, theory construction, and the sociology of science.

Steven Lukes is professor of sociology at New York University. The second edition of his book, *Power: A Radical View*, was published in 2004.

Vonnie C. McLoyd is professor of psychology and a research scientist at the Center for Developmental Science, University of North Carolina, Chapel Hill. She is interested in the effects of economic disadvantage, work-related transitions, and parents' jobs on family life.

Tey Meadows is a lawyer and a doctoral candidate at New York University.

David Mechanic is the René Dubos Professor of Behavioral Sciences at Rutgers University. He is also director of Rutgers' Institute for Health, Health Care Policy and Aging Research, an interdisciplinary collaboration that addresses difficult challenges in health and health care.

David S. Meyer is professor of sociology and political science at the University of California, Irvine. His most recent book is *The Politics of Protest: Social Movements in America* (2006).

Rachel Meyer is a doctoral student at the University of Michigan, Ann Arbor. She is writing a dissertation on forms of collective action in the American labor movement.

Ann Morning teaches sociology at New York University. She writes about the uses of racial classification in demography, public policy, biology, education, and everyday life.

Richard A. Petersen is emeritus professor of sociology at Vanderbilt University. Author of

Creating Country Music: Fabricating Authenticity and the Production of Culture (1997), he continues his work on status displays and is currently researching the importance of local and virtual music scenes in fostering the development of music genres.

Becky Pettit is a sociologist at the Center for Studies in Demography and Ecology, University of Washington. Her research focuses on the relationship between demographic processes and inequality.

Rebecca F. Plante teaches sociology at Ithaca College. She is coeditor (with Michael S. Kimmel) of the anthology *Sexualities: Identities, Behaviors, and Society* (2004) and has written on sexuality and gender for scholarly journals and the popular press.

Alejandro Portes is professor of sociology at Princeton University, and faculty associate of the Woodrow Wilson School of Public Affairs. He is the author of more than 200 articles and chapters on national development, international migration, Latin American and Caribbean urbanization, and economic sociology.

Monica Prasad teaches sociology at Northwestern University. Her book, *The Politics of Free Markets* (2006), was recently published by the University of Chicago Press.

Zhenchao Qian has published on topics related to union formation, mate selection, interracial cohabitation and marriage, and racial identification of biracial children. He is a professor at Ohio State University.

Mark R. Rank is the Hadley Professor of Social Welfare in the George Warren Brown School of Social Work at Washington University, St. Louis. His most recent book is *One Nation,*

Underprivileged: Why American Poverty Affects Us All (2004).

Barbara Risman is the author of *Gender Vertigo: American Families in Transition* (1998) and nearly two dozen articles. She is professor of sociology at the University of Illinois at Chicago.

Ian Robinson, codirector of the Institute of Labor and Industrial Relations' Labor and Global Change Program, has written widely on globalization and labor issues.

Richard Rosenfeld is professor and chair of the department of criminology and criminal justice, University of Missouri, St. Louis. He is coauthor with Steven F. Messner of *Crime and the American Dream,* 3rd ed. (2001) and has published widely on the social sources of criminal violence.

Rubén G. Rumbaut is professor of sociology at the University of California, Irvine, and codirector of the Center for Research on Immigration, Population and Public Policy. His most recent book (with Marta Tienda et al.) is *Multiple Origins, Uncertain Destinies: Hispanics and the American Future* (2006).

Leila J. Rupp teaches at the University of California, Santa Barbara. She coauthored (with Verta Taylor) *Drag Queens at the 801 Cabaret* (2003).

Charlotte Ryan is professor of sociology at the University of Massachusetts, Lowell, and codirects the Media Research and Action Project at Boston College. She is working (with William Gamson) on a pamphlet, "Strategic Framing for Activists."

Saskia Sassen, the Ralph Lewis Professor of Sociology at the University of Chicago and Centennial Visiting Professor at the London School of Economics, is the author of *Denationalization: Territory, Authority and Rights in a Global Digital Age* (2006).

Howard Schuman is emeritus professor of sociology and research scientist in the Institute for Social Research (ISR) at the University of Michigan. He has served as director of the university's Detroit Area Study and of the ISR's Survey Research Center.

Pepper Schwartz is professor of sociology at the University of Washington, Seattle. She is past president of the Society for the Scientific Study of Sexuality and coauthor of *Ten Talks Parents Must Have With Children about Sex and Character* (Hyperion, 2001).

Richard Settersten Jr. is professor of sociology at Case Western Reserve University. His research addresses how the life course is conditioned by time, age, and social contexts. He is the author of *Lives in Time and Place: The Problems and Promises of Developmental Science* (1999).

Stephen Shapin is Franklin L. Ford Professor of the History of Science at Harvard. His works include *Leviathan and the Air-Pump: Hobbes, Boyle, and the Experimental Life* (1985), and *The Scientific Revolution* (1996).

Kathy Sloane is a professional freelance photographer who has documented the cultural and ethnic diversity of California for more than two decades. Her photographs have been exhibited in San Francisco, Los Angeles, New York, and Eastern Europe.

David A. Snow is professor of sociology at the University of California, Irvine. He has written widely on social movements, identity, and homelessness, and is currently involved in an interdisciplinary, comparative study of homelessness and marginality in four global cities (Los Angeles, Paris, São Paulo, and Tokyo).

Gregory D. Squires has worked or consulted for several government agencies and nonprofit fair housing organizations including HUD, the Federal Reserve Board, and the Woodstock Institute.

Judith Stacey teaches in the department of social and cultural analysis and the department of sociology at New York University. She authored *Brave New Families: Stories of Domestic Upheaval in Late Twentieth-Century America*, 2nd ed. (1998).

Karen Sternheimer is the author of *Kids These Days: Facts and Fictions About Today's Youth* (2006) and *It's Not the Media: The Truth About Pop Culture's Influence on Children* (2003). She teaches in the sociology department at the University of Southern California.

Richard Swedberg is an economic sociologist at Cornell University. He is coeditor, with Victor Nee, of *The Economic Sociology of Capitalism* (2005).

Verta Taylor is professor of sociology at the University of California, Santa Barbara. She coauthored (with Leila Rupp) *Drag Queens at the 801 Cabaret* (2003).

Jerome C. Wakefield was trained in philosophy and clinical social work and writes on the conceptual foundations of the mental health professions. He is University Professor and professor in the school of social work at New York University.

Robert S. Weiss is a senior fellow in the Gerontology Institute and emeritus professor of sociology at the University of Massachusetts, Boston, and a lecturer in sociology in the department of psychiatry at Harvard Medical School. He is the author of *Marital Separation* (1975), *Learning from Strangers* (1995), and *Staying the Course* (1990).

Barry Wellman is a sociologist at the University of Toronto, where he directs the NetLab at the Centre for Urban and Community Studies. Wellman studies social, communication, information, and computer networks.

Bruce Western teaches sociology at Princeton University. In addition to his work on the growth of the U.S. penal system, he is conducting research on labor unions in the United States and Europe.

W. Bradford Wilcox is currently writing a book on religion, sex, and marriage among African Americans and Latinos in urban America. He teaches sociology at the University of Virginia and is a member of the James Madison Society at Princeton University.

Kerry Woodward is a Ph.D. candidate at the University of California, Berkeley. Her dissertation examines the implementation of welfare reform at two California welfare offices.

Min Zhou is professor of sociology and founding chair of the Asian American Studies Interdepartmental Degree Program at UCLA. Her areas of research include immigration and immigrant adaptation, children of immigrants, ethnic and racial relations, and ethnic entrepreneurship.

Robert Zussman teaches at the University of Massachusetts, Amherst. He is the author of *Intensive Care: Medical Ethics and the Medical Profession* (1992).